DRUGS LAW AND LEGAL PRACTICE IN SOUTHEAST ASIA

Drugs Law and Legal Practice in Southeast Asia investigates criminal law and practice relevant to drugs regulation in three Southeast Asian jurisdictions: Indonesia, Singapore and Vietnam.

These jurisdictions represent the spectrum of approaches to drugs regulation in Southeast Asia, highlighting differences in practice between civil and common law countries, and between liberal and authoritarian states.

This book offers the first major English language empirical investigation and comparative analysis of regulations, jurisprudence, court procedure, and practices relating to drugs law enforcement in these three states.

Drugs Law and Legal Practice in Southeast Asia

Indonesia, Singapore and Vietnam

Tim Lindsey and Pip Nicholson

·HART·
PUBLISHING
OXFORD AND PORTLAND, OREGON
2016

Published in the United Kingdom by Hart Publishing Ltd
Kemp House, Chawley Park, Cumnor Hill,
Oxford, OX2 9PH, UK
E-mail: mail@hartpub.co.uk
Website: http://www.hartpub.co.uk

Published in North America (US and Canada) by
Hart Publishing
c/o International Specialized Book Services
920 NE 58th Avenue, Suite 300
Portland, OR 97213-3786
USA
Tel: +1 503 287 3093 or toll-free: (1) 800 944 6190
Fax: +1 503 280 8832
E-mail: orders@isbs.com
Website: http://www.isbs.com

Hart Publishing is an imprint of Bloomsbury Publishing plc.

British Library Cataloguing in Publication Data
Data Available

Library of Congress Cataloging-in-Publication Data

Names: Lindsey, Timothy, 1962– author. | Nicholson, Penelope, author.

Title: Drugs law and legal practice in Southeast Asia : Indonesia, Singapore and Vietnam / Tim Lindsey and Pip Nicholson.

Description: Oxford ; Portland, Oregon : Hart Publishing, 2016. | Includes bibliographical references and index.

Identifiers: LCCN 2016008649 (print) | LCCN 2016009290 (ebook) | ISBN 9781782258315 (hardback : alk. paper) | ISBN 9781782258322 (Epub)

Subjects: LCSH: Narcotic laws—Indonesia. | Narcotic laws—Singapore. | Narcotic laws—Vietnam. | Drugs of abuse—Law and legislation—Indonesia—Criminal provisions. | Drugs of abuse—Law and legislation—Singapore—Criminal provisions. | Drugs of abuse—Law and legislation—Vietnam—Criminal provisions. | Criminal procedure—Indonesia. | Criminal procedure—Singapore. | Criminal procedure—Vietnam.

Classification: LCC KNC691.L56 2016 (print) | LCC KNC691 (ebook) | DDC 345.59/0277—dc23

LC record available at http://lccn.loc.gov/2016008649

ISBN: 978-1-78225-831-5

Typeset by Compuscript Ltd, Shannon
Printed and bound in Great Britain by
TJ International Ltd, Padstow, Cornwall

Front cover illustration:

Geoff Todd, 'Portrait of Emmanuel. Kerobokan Gaol. Bali', 2008. 91 cms × 122 cms, acrylic on canvas, private collection. Reproduced by permission of the artist.

This book is dedicated to the courageous pro bono lawyers who defend men and women on death row around the world.

Acknowledgements

We could not have written this book without the support of the Australian Research Council. Its funding from 2010 to 2015 of our Discovery Project, 'Drugs, Law and Criminal Procedure in Southeast Asia: A Comparative Analysis', enabled the demanding trilingual documentary research and extensive fieldwork across Vietnam, Singapore and Indonesia on which the book is based. We are grateful to the University of Melbourne Ethics Committee for its approval of our research Ethics Application No 1136801, which allowed interviews to be conducted in these three countries.

This volume's title page lists two authors but the production of this book was, to a great extent, the result of an energetic and talented team of researchers who worked closely with us. This team's membership changed as the project progressed but it included, in particular, Sarah Rennie, Tim Mann, Phạm Lan Phương and Trish Prentice. These talented young scholars each made a huge contribution to research and drafting. Without their help this project could not have been brought to completion.

Other researchers who also made important contributions include Mary Kozlovski, Sienna Merope-Synge, Đỗ Hải Hà, Katerina Stevenson, Nguyễn Vũ Thu Trang, Hồ Thụy Ngọc Trâm, Võ Hoàng Đức Long, Đinh Ngân Hà, Andrew Conley, Bryn Davies, Nicholas Parsons, Heidi Edwards, Rheny Pulungan, Samantha Wimala and Rifqi Assegaf. Nguyễn Hưng Quang and Nguyễn Thị Phương Hoa provided valuable advice on Vietnam as well. Helen Pausacker helped too, both as a researcher and by finalising formatting and referencing with her usual exceptional attention to detail, patience, and unflagging enthusiasm. Our heartfelt thanks go to all of you!

We are grateful also to Bill Asquith, our editor at Hart, for his strong support for this book, and the prominent Australian artist, Geoff Todd, for his great generosity in allowing us to use his dramatic portrait of Emmanuel, a drugs offender on death row in Indonesia, on the cover.

This list of thanks would be incomplete without mentioning the dedicated staff of the Asian Law Centre and the Centre for Indonesian Law, Islam and Society—in particular, the Manager of these Centres, Kathryn Taylor and, in recent years, Tessa Shaw, Vicky Aikman and Ade Suharto. They provided us with a supportive and enthusiastic institutional base over the life of this project. Finally, we express our gratitude to our Dean, Professor Carolyn Evans, for her strong commitment to the study of Southeast Asian legal systems in the Melbourne Law School.

It remains only to state that, despite the great contributions made to this project by many able people over many years, errors and shortcomings in this volume remain entirely our own responsibility.

Tim Lindsey and Pip Nicholson
Melbourne, September 2015

Contents

Acronyms

Acronym/Abbreviation	English
ACCORD	ASEAN-China Cooperative Operations in Response to Dangerous Drugs
ADHD	attention deficit hyperactivity disorder
AIDS	acquired immune deficiency syndrome
AIFOCOM	ASEAN Inter-Parliamentary Assembly Fact Finding Committee
AIPA	ASEAN Inter-Parliamentary Assembly
APG	Asia/Pacific Group on Money Laundering
ASEAN	Association of Southeast Asian Nations
ASEANAPOL	ASEAN Chiefs of Police
ATS	amphetamine type stimulants
BAKIN (Badan Koordinasi Intelijen Negara)	National Intelligence Co-ordination Agency
Bappenas (Badan Perencanaan Nasional)	National Development Planning Agency
BNN (Badan Narkotika Nasional)	National Narcotics Agency
BPOM (Badan Pengawas Obat dan Makanan)	Food and Drug Monitoring Agency
CCTV	closed-circuit television
CDSC	Corruption, Drug Trafficking and Other Serious Crimes
CNB	Central Narcotics Bureau
CPV	Communist Party of Vietnam
DPR (Dewan Perwakilan Rakyat)	People's Representative Assembly, House of Representatives, the national legislature
GMS	Greater Mekong Subregion
GRULAC	Group of Latin America and Caribbean Countries
HAM (*hak asasi manusia*)	human rights
HIV	human immunodeficiency virus

Acronym/Abbreviation	English
HONLEA	Heads of National Drug Law Enforcement Agencies
INCB	International Narcotics Control Board
IPWL (Institusi Penerima Wajib Lapor)	Compulsory Reporting Institutions
JASPOC	Joint ASEAN Senior Police Officers Course
Komnas HAM (Komisi Nasional Hak Asasi Manusia)	National Commission on Human Rights
KPK (Komisi Pemberantasan Korupsi)	Corruption Eradication Commission
KUHAP (Kitab Undang-undang Hukum Acara Pidana)	Criminal Procedure Code
KUHP (Kitab Undang-undang Hukum Pidana)	Criminal Code
LBH	Legal Aid Foundation
LPSK (Lembaga Perlindungan Saksi dan Korban)	Witness and Victim Protection Agency
LSD	lysergic acid diethylamide, a psychedelic drug
MDA	methylenedioxyamphetamine or 3,4-methylenedioxy-amphetamine, a psychoactive drug similar to ecstasy
MDA	Misuse of Drugs Act (Singapore)
MDMA	3,4-methylenedioxy-methamphetamine, ecstasy
OBH (Organisasi Bantuan Hukum)	Legal Aid Providers
P4GN (*Pencegahan dan Pemberantasan Penyalahgunaan dan Peredaran Gelap Narkoba*)	Prevention and Elimination of Illicit Narcotics Trafficking and Abuse
PAP	People's Action Party (Singapore)
PCP	phencyclidine, a dissociative drug sometimes called angel dust
PK (*peninjauan kembali*)	reconsideration
PMK	a precursor to MDMA

Acronym/Abbreviation	English
PP	Public Prosecutor
PPATK (Pusat Pelaporan dan Analisis Transaksi Keuangan)	Financial Transaction Reports and Analysis Centre
Prolegnas (*Program Legislasi Nasional*)	National Legislation Programme, a list of priority bills for deliberation in the national legislature
puskesmas (*pusat sesehatan masyarakat*)	community health centre
RUU (*rancangan undang-undang*)	draft law or bill
SCORE	Singapore Corporation of Rehabilitative Enterprises
SPC	Supreme People's Court
SRVN	Socialist Republic of Vietnam
UNCND	United Nations Commission on Narcotic Drugs
UNDCP	United Nations International Drug Control Programme
UNDND	United Nations Division of Narcotic Drugs
UNDP	United Nations Development Programme
UNFDAC	United Nations Fund for Drug Abuse Control
UNGASS	United Nations General Assembly Special Session
UNIDCP	United Nations International Drug Control Programme
UNODC	United Nations Office on Drugs and Crime
UU (*undang-undang*)	law or statute

Table of Parliamentary Speeches and Debates

Singapore

Chua Sian Chin 'Second Reading Speech by Mr Chua Sian Chin, Minister for Health and Home Affairs', vol 32, col 416 (16 February 1973).

Chua Sian Chin, Minister for Home Affairs and Education, *Singapore Parliamentary Debates, Official Report* vol 34, col 1380 (20 November 1975).

Ho Peng Kee, 'Second Reading Speech of the Penal Code (Amendment) Bill, by Senior Minister of State A/P Ho Peng Kee' (22 October 2007): 26–27.

Ho Peng Kee, 'Singapore Parliamentary Debates, Hansard Reports, 'Budget' (Minister of State for Law Associate Professor Ho Peng Kee)' (27 February 2008).

Iswaran, S, 'Second Reading of the Criminal Law (Temporary Provisions) (Amendment) Bill: Response Speech by Mr S Iswaran, Minister in Prime Minister's Office and Second Minister for Home Affairs and Trade & Industry' (11 November 2013).

Lien, NMP Laurence, Parliamentary speech (12 November 2012).

Lim, Sylvia 'Speech on Misuse of Drugs Amendment Bill—MP Sylvia Lim' (12 November 2012).

'Second Reading of the Misuse of Drugs (Amendment) Bill', *Singapore Parliamentary Debates, Official Report* vol 34 at col 1379ff (20 November 1975).

'Second Reading of the Misuse of Drugs (Amendment) Bill', *Singapore Parliamentary Debates, Official Report* vol 89 (12 November 2012).

Shanmugam, K, 'Second Reading Speech by Law Minister K Shanmugam on the Criminal Procedure Code Bill' (18 May 2010).

Singapore Parliamentary Debates, Official Report (20 November 1975) vol 34.

Singapore Parliamentary Debates, Official Report (20 November 1975) vol 34 at cols 1379–1381.

Singapore. Ministry of Home Affairs, 'Second Reading Speech for the Misuse of Drugs (Amendment) Bill 2006, Ministry of Home Affairs' (21 June 2007).

Teo Chee Hean, 'Enhancing Our Drug Control Framework and Review of the Death Penalty', Teo Chee Hean, Deputy Prime Minister and Minister for Home Affairs, *Singapore Parliamentary Debates, Official Report*, vol 89 (9 July 2012).

Teo Chee Hean, 'Second Reading on the Misuse of Drugs (Amendment) Bill—Speech by Mr Teo Chee Hean, Deputy Prime Minister For Home Affairs' (12 November 2012).

Teo Chee Hean, 'Response Speech by Mr Teo Chee Hean, Deputy Prime Minister and Minister for Home Affairs on the Misuse of Drugs (Amendment) Bill' (14 November 2012).

Wong Kan Seng 'Bill No 40/2005, Second Reading Speech, Mr Wong Kan Seng', vol 80, col 2095 (16 January 2006).

Wong Kan Seng 'Singapore Parliamentary Debates, Mr Wong Kan Seng', Official Record, col 45 (1 June 1998).

Wong Kan Seng 'Second Reading Speech by Minister for Home Affairs Mr Wong Kan Seng: Drug Trafficking (Confiscation Of Benefits) (Amendment) Bill' (6 July 1999).

Zulkifli, Masagos 'Second Reading Speech of the Senior Minister of State for Home Affairs, Mr Masagos Zulkifli BMM' (14 November 2012).

Table of Cases

European Court of Human Rights

Indonesia—Cases

Indonesia—District Court Cases

Indonesia—High Court Cases

Indonesia—Supreme Court Cases

Indonesia—Constitutional Court Cases

Singapore—Cases

Vietnam—Cases

Table of Legislation

International Protocols, Conventions etc

Australia—Legislation

European Union—Legislation

Indonesia—Legislation

Indonesia—Laws [Undang-Undang]

Indonesia—Presidential Regulations [Peraturan Presiden]

Indonesia—Government Regulations [Peraturan Pemerintah]

Indonesia—Ministerial Regulations [Peraturan Menteri]

Indonesia—Supreme Court Regulations [Peraturan Mahkamah Agung]

Vietnam—Legislation

Vietnam—Policy

Vietnam—Legislation and Implementing Documents

1

Introduction: Drugs Law and Practice in Indonesia, Singapore and Vietnam

This book offers an account of criminal law and practice relevant to drugs regulation in three Southeast Asian jurisdictions: Indonesia, Singapore and Vietnam. The core of the book comprises three country studies based on extensive fieldwork, each offering original analysis of criminal law and procedure in drugs regulation in three very different Southeast Asian states. We approach each country by examining, in turn, investigation, trial, and sentencing. The last category also includes the death penalty, as well as the different mechanisms available for pardon and clemency. In short, we frame our analysis to reflect how a defendant prosecuted for drugs offences is treated in each jurisdiction, in a loosely sequential order.

Although their legal systems are very different, the three countries selected for investigation share a commitment to the current international drugs law regime. This is based on three major United Nations (UN) conventions to which each is a signatory: the UN Single Convention on Narcotic Drugs, 1961 (as amended by the Protocol of 1972); the UN Convention on Psychotropic Substances, 1971; and the UN Convention against the Illicit Traffic in Narcotic Drugs and Psychotropic Substances, 1988. The next chapter offers a brief overview of these conventions and the international system for regulation of drugs they establish. An indicative summary of the extent to which Indonesia, Singapore and Vietnam have met their obligations under the Conventions in their domestic laws appears in an appendix at the end of the book.

These three jurisdictions were selected because each has experienced controversy over its approach to drugs-related crime in recent years. They also represent different approaches to drug regulation, even though each is seen as adopting a hard line against drug offenders. A comparison of their legal regimes for drugs offences also highlights key differences in practice between civil and common law countries, as well as between liberal and authoritarian states.

The legal systems of Indonesia, Singapore and Vietnam are, in fact, fundamentally different. Indonesia has a plural civil law system that combines limited elements of Islamic legal tradition and *adat* (traditional customary law) within an overarching European civil law structure inherited from Dutch colonialism. Drugs are regulated within the civil law system, which is still strongly influenced by colonial legal culture but has followed its own trajectory since independence. *Reformasi* (Reformation) refers to the sweeping democratisation implemented after Soeharto's authoritarian rule collapsed in 1998. It triggered major efforts to reform the legal system, including the introduction of formal judicial independence. Many of the changes delivered by *Reformasi* are ambitious and potentially transformative. Their implementation, however, remains incomplete and this is particularly obvious in the judicial system.

Singapore, a tiny former British colony that has become a major East Asian commercial hub, has a sophisticated common law system. This is embedded within a one-party state that has been led by the People's Action Party (PAP) since independence in 1965. While Singapore adopted the British judicial model, its legal system also developed its own characteristics, many of which reflect the overwhelming political and social dominance of PAP and, in particular, its conservative social policies and tough 'law and order' approach.

Vietnam, by contrast, has a socialist legal system, in which the Communist Party of Vietnam is paramount. Little or no legal shadow remains from the French colonial period. This is particularly true in the north of the country, which has been socialist since 1945. The Vietnamese legal system has undergone widespread and fundamental reform since 1987. This has targeted both doctrine and institutions. Despite this, the Vietnamese system of criminal law remains largely influenced by communist ideology, led by the single-party state. In this, Vietnam is radically different to Indonesia and Singapore, which have long been regional bastions of opposition to socialism and still regard communism as inherently subversive.

Despite their differences, legal institutions in the three states selected for study in this book share a common vulnerability to government influence, albeit for different reasons. In Indonesia, legal institutions, while greatly reformed since Soeharto's fall, are still subject to pressure from political elites, as well as outright corruption. Bribery of police, prosecutors and judges continues to pervert many investigations and trials, with the justice system often dismissed by Indonesians as the *mafia peradilan* or 'judicial mafia'. In recent years, however, Indonesia has also become a site of creative litigation, as counsel and activists test the limits of law and the new democratic system through still-emerging and troubled institutions like the Constitutional Court.[1]

While Singapore's criminal law is practised in open court, complete with due process and procedural safeguards, substantial unreviewable power is retained by law enforcement authorities. In particular, decisions whether to prosecute, and for what crimes, are made largely beyond the public gaze. This is also true of decisions about whether a defendant has provided sufficient assistance to the authorities to escape the death penalty that is otherwise mandatory for most drug offences. As in Indonesia, litigation is used in Singapore to test the limits of the law in relation to constitutional guarantees, such as, for example, the right to counsel. Defence lawyers also regularly test the PAP's position that the rights of the criminal defendants are always to be qualified by the interests of society in punishing criminal activity, although they do so with limited success.[2]

As mentioned, Vietnam's legal system differs significantly from those of Indonesia and Singapore. Its socialist roots remain strong, particularly in the field of criminal

[1] pp 49, 64, 65, 87–8, 94 and 135.
[2] See, for example, pp 142–4, 152–7, 163–4 and 179–81.

law, and this manifests in the way trials are conducted and how legal institutions relate to each other and their Party leadership. Courts are not independent, although they are now more transparently managed than before 1987. In that year, a program of wholesale economic reform was triggered by the introduction of the *đổi mới* (renovation) policy. This opened the country to international and global influence in the name of diversifying the economy and enabling foreign investment. While the initial focus was on laws and legal institutions that would enable investment, Vietnam's integration with global and regional regulatory systems has led to substantial reforms to its Constitution, the Penal Code 1999, the Criminal Procedure Code 2003, and a range of other drug-related laws.

These changes aim, among other things, to balance international approaches to drugs regulation, criminal procedure and human rights against Vietnamese Party-led authoritarian principles. A right to counsel and a presumption of innocence were, for example, constitutionally embedded as recently as 2013. They began to have effect from 2014. Attitudes to the death penalty are also changing, moving towards a less harsh position. There is, however, a real tension created by the fact that the Party-state continues to invoke the socialist ideology that privileges it, while at the same time expanding personal rights in the Constitution. This expansion is more aspirational than a matter of practice, not least because Vietnam does not have a constitutional court. As in Indonesia, there are also widespread accusations of corruption directed at police, investigating authorities and courts. Some suggest, however, that drugs cases are among those least affected by corruption because of the social opprobrium drug offences attract.

I. LOCATING DIFFERENCES AND SIMILARITIES

In summary, Indonesia, Singapore and Vietnam, have markedly different legal systems and, as a result, divergent criminal laws and practice. These differences are most apparent in criminal procedure and approaches to the death penalty, in both policy and practice. We now offer a brief overview of the ways in which these three jurisdictions regulate and practice drug-related law. We begin with substantive offences and then move to investigations, trials, sentencing, and, finally, the death penalty. All the issues raised below are covered in more detail in the individual country studies that follow. Our aim here is simply to demonstrate the diversity of approaches in the three countries, rather than offer a detailed comparative analysis of the three systems.

Applicable Law

All three countries have criminalised the cultivation and trafficking of narcotics, as is required by the international conventions to which they are signatories. In Indonesia and Singapore, drug use is also an offence, although Vietnam recently de-criminalised it. All provide rehabilitation for drug addicts, both voluntary and compulsory, although the extent to which this is actually implemented varies.

Sentencing is harsh in all jurisdictions, with the death penalty firmly within the sentencing range. Generally speaking, the death penalty can currently apply for transporting in excess of 600 grams of heroin or cocaine across borders or within Vietnam,[3] while in Singapore trafficking 15 grams attracts the death penalty.[4] In Indonesia, the amount that triggers the possibility of a capital sentence is, in the case of plants, 1 kilogram or five plants, or 5 grams of non-plant substances.[5]

While all three states claim to be 'tough on drugs', Singapore is the only jurisdiction that retains a mandatory death sentence for some drugs offences, and is seen as the most punitive in practice. Being a foreigner has, however, been held by the Indonesian courts to be an aggravating circumstance and our research suggests that a foreign drug offender convicted of drugs offences in that country faces a higher likelihood of receiving the death penalty than a local convicted of the same crime. This is not the case in Singapore or Vietnam, where foreigners are, in fact, much less commonly executed.

Investigations

Despite increasing oversight of law enforcement agencies and their compliance with the law, police and investigators in Indonesia and Vietnam still enjoy a great deal of discretion, which sometimes involves entrapment and corruption. In Singapore, the prosecution has 'potent' powers of interrogation,[6] with no video or tape recording of witness interrogation required. These are not compulsory in Indonesia or Vietnam either.

The right to counsel exists in the Constitutions of all three states but in each its implementation is weak. In Indonesia, the right to counsel is seldom a reality during the investigation phase. Many detainees are unaware of the right to counsel, and there are reports from some who seek to exercise it of being threatened by police.[7] Outside major cities in Vietnam, the assistance of counsel during the investigation phase is inconsistently facilitated and often routinely blocked, partly or in full.[8] Counsel also report real difficulties in obtaining timely approval of the certificate of defence needed to access or represent clients. In both countries, the court must appoint counsel if the defendant faces the death penalty but the quality of court-appointed counsel varies greatly. In Singapore, the court has held that there is, in fact, no right to be informed of the constitutional right to counsel[9] and so access to representation during the investigation phase is limited. In any case, other judicial

[3] pp 259–60.
[4] pp 60–63.
[5] This applies to producing, importing, exporting and dealing in both Category I (heroin, cocaine, marijuana, ecstasy, amphetamines and methamphetamines, etc) and II (morphine, codeine, etc) drugs, and causing death through their provision. See pp 60–63.
[6] See *Muhammad bin Kadar v Public Prosecutor (PP)* [2011] 3 SLR 1205 at [57]–[60]. See also pp 177–78.
[7] pp 83–90.
[8] pp 293, 241–42.
[9] pp 179–81.

decisions suggest that counsel does not need to be made available to the defendant if that would risk 'obstructing' the state's investigation of cases, something surely inevitable in most instances.[10]

Counsel in Indonesia and Singapore have acknowledged status and rights in trials but in Vietnam they are deemed subordinate to both judges and the procuracy.[11] This severely compromises the capacity of counsel to take advantage of the recent developments in Vietnamese criminal law and procedure on behalf of their clients. Although fundamental reforms have introduced adversarial elements in Vietnamese criminal trials, the safeguards necessary to make them a standard feature are not yet in place.

All three jurisdictions provide for a presumption of innocence, although they also apply the internationally common presumption of ownership where a defendant is found with drugs, something that can significantly qualify the presumption. In the case of Vietnam, the presumption of innocence has, in any case, only existed constitutionally since 2014 and it is not yet clear how it will work in practice.[12] In Vietnam, defendants are still obliged to make a statement, so there is no right to silence.[13] In Indonesia, while the presumption of innocence exists, it can be problematic in narcotics trials.[14] Some argue there is an implicit right to silence arising from a Criminal Procedure Code provision that states that the defendant does not bear the burden of proof but not all accept that this is so.[15] In Singapore, there is no constitutional right to silence, and jurisprudence in drugs cases states that an adverse inference may be drawn where defendant withholds information that might have assisted him or her.[16]

Trials

As mentioned, Indonesia and Vietnam both have inquisitorial legal systems ultimately derived from European models, including the Soviet Union in the case of Vietnam. A panel of judges (Indonesia) or a judge and two people's assessors (Vietnam) decide the case on the basis of the evidence before it, which is presented by a prosecutorial agency. In both countries, the courts seek 'the truth' and there is no system of stare decisis or precedent, at least not in the way it is understood in common law countries.

The Vietnamese procuracy is a Soviet-style institution introduced in the 1960s to oversee the observance of laws by all government agencies.[17] While its supervisory

[10] pp 180–81.
[11] pp 252–53, 298.
[12] pp 236–38, 298.
[13] p 238.
[14] pp 70, 88.
[15] p 88.
[16] pp 177–78.
[17] p 201.

power has been reduced, the procuracy retains the power to supervise investigations and trials, including a now controversial power to review the work of courts. The Vietnamese courts meet with the procuracy (and usually separately with counsel) before the case to determine key issues and how to proceed. They also consult with more senior judges about particular cases.[18] In addition, the courts remain susceptible to leadership (or manipulation) by the political leadership of the day, both central and local. As a result, criminal trials in Vietnam are not usually marked by substantive legal contests.

In Indonesia, there is a long-standing and much analysed law-practice gap, which often reflects the difficulties the courts have in understanding and properly implementing the formal independence granted them after 1998.[19] More particularly, the courts remain vulnerable to manipulation and informal approaches by a range of actors, including police, prosecutors, parties and the political leadership of the day, whether local or centrally based. Trials in Indonesia are more adversarial than their Vietnamese counterparts but are moderated by both their civil law roots and the impact of politics, personalities and patronage. Further problems are created by the brevity and poor quality of many written decisions. This often creates real uncertainty about how laws are interpreted and applied, and serious and persistent problems of inconsistency in sentencing.[20]

Singapore has an adversarial common law system that allows each party to lead and contest evidence. A system of precedent applies and there are established and firmly enforced rules of evidence derived from British common law practice. While trials are conducted within an explicitly anti-drug context that enables procedural and doctrinal constraints on defendants' rights, the trials themselves are relatively open and transparent.

Appeals

As a common law system, Singapore has a system of appeals to the next highest court in the hierarchy. These must be brought within 15 days and can be made against conviction, sentence or any order of the court,[21] except where the accused

[18] p 200.

[19] For just a few of many examples of this literature, see Daniel Lev, 'Between State and Society: Professional Lawyers and Reform in Indonesia' in Daniel Lev and Ruth McVey (eds), *Making Indonesia* (Ithaca, Cornell University Press, 1996); Sebastiaan Pompe *The Indonesian Supreme Court: Fifty Years of Judicial Development* (Leiden, Leiden University Press, 1996); Simon Butt, 'Surat Sakti: The Decline of the Authority of Judicial Decisions in Indonesia' in Tim Lindsey (ed), *Indonesia: Law and Society* (Sydney, Federation Press, 2008) 346–62; David Linnan, 'Commercial Law Enforcement in Indonesia: The Manulife Case' in Tim Lindsey (ed), *Indonesia: Law and Society* (Sydney, Federation Press, 2008) 596–619; Daniel Fitzpatrick, 'Culture, Ideology and Human Rights: The Case of Indonesia's Code of Criminal Procedure' in Tim Lindsey (ed), *Indonesia: Law and Society* (Sydney, Federation Press, 2008) 499–514; and Simon Butt and Tim Lindsey, 'Judicial Mafia: The Courts and Illegality in Indonesia' in Edward Aspinall and Gerry van Klinken (eds), *The State and Illegality in Indonesia* (Leiden, KITLV Press, 2011) 189–216.

[20] pp 119–34.

[21] pp 188–89.

has pleaded guilty, in which case only an appeal against sentence is allowed. The District and Magistrates Courts are able to submit a reference on a point of law for advice to the High Court of Singapore. These processes are open and transparent, particularly when compared with the appeal and review mechanisms operating in Indonesia and, in particular, Vietnam.

In Indonesia, there are three levels of appeal possible. First, the defendant and prosecution can appeal any first instance (that is, District Court) criminal decision, except decisions in expedited procedures. There are also restrictions on the prosecution's ability to challenge decisions of not guilty but appeals against acquittals are, in fact, often heard.[22] All appeals from the District Courts are heard in the provincial level High Courts and must be lodged within seven days. From the High Court, appeal lies by cassation to the Supreme Court but solely on issues of law.[23] Applications must be lodged within fourteen days, and both appeal and cassation time limits are rigidly enforced. Although not strictly an appeal, the Criminal Procedure Code also allows for 'reconsideration' (*peninjauan kembali*, PK) by the Supreme Court of almost any decision of any court (including its own) that has acquired 'binding legal force', that is, in respect of which no further appeal or cassation is possible. Requests for reconsideration are lodged with the court of first instance, and there is no time limit applicable. The Supreme Court refuses to hear more than one reconsideration application in any case, despite a recent Constitutional Court decision holding that the number of reconsiderations may not be limited.[24]

Generally speaking, criminal appeal, cassation and reconsideration decisions in Indonesia are notable for brevity and lack of detail in their reasoning. They are also often criticised for inconsistency and lack of predictability. In part, this reflects lack of basic curial skills in a newly-independent judiciary still struggling to emerge from more than three decades of repression and deliberate neglect under the Soeharto. It is also, however, the result of the continued influence of the so-called 'judicial mafia'. As mentioned, this term is understood in Indonesia as a reference to systems of institutionalised corruption within the legal sector, which have proved very resilient.[25]

Vietnam also has three mechanisms by which a decision can be taken to a higher court: appeal, cassational review and the reopening of the case. Time limits apply, as do constraints on who can bring a particular type of application. Generally, the convicted person, his or her counsel or the procuracy may bring an appeal within 15 days to a higher court.[26] A policy decision is currently awaited as to the implications for this process of the introduction in 2014 of a new level of court, the High Court, which takes its place between the current Supreme and Provincial Courts.

[22] pp 85–87.
[23] p 93.
[24] pp 87–88.
[25] pp 49–50, 100, 135.
[26] pp 266–68.

In the meantime, appeals must be brought to the next highest court in the hierarchy. Cassational review (essentially where there has been an error of law) is sought by the branch of procuracy at the next level up from that at which the trial was held.[27] Neither counsel nor a person convicted may seek cassational review. It is also not possible to seek cassational review of a case heard on appeal by the highest court, that is, where the Judicial Council of the Supreme Peoples Court has heard the case. Proposed reforms to the Criminal Procedure Code that are currently being debated include, however, a complex mechanism whereby cassational review from this body may eventually be possible. There is no time limit on cassational reviews and they are not limited in number although, again, they may only be initiated by the procuracy. Finally, an application can be made to reopen a case on the basis of new evidence.[28] While this application can only be made by the procuracy, anyone may request it to do so. There is no time limit on an application to reopen.

This trio of review options creates obviously difficulties for convicted persons and their counsel. The procuracy's monopoly on applications for cassation and reopening vests substantial discretionary decision-making in its hands, which is rarely exercised transparently. There is great scope for pressure to be brought to bear on the procuracy by influential figures linked to it and by local governments—and, of course, for outright corruption as well.

Death Penalty and the State: Indonesia, Singapore and Vietnam

Johnson and Zimring have recently argued that it is time to closely analyse the prospects for the 'export' to Asia of abolitionism.[29] Put another way, they ask whether what they see as a gradual global trend toward abolition of the death penalty is likely to be replicated in Asia. As this book shows, Indonesia, Singapore and Vietnam all retain the death penalty for drug trafficking and the courts in each country sentence certain traffickers to death, some of whom are eventually executed. The three governments also share a 'tough on drugs' rhetoric, with drugs cast as a serious social evil. There are, however, vocal critics of the death penalty both within and outside the political leadership in each country. These commonalities, however, obscure very different death penalty practices.

In none of these jurisdictions is the death penalty mandatory in all cases. In each, there is provision for minors to avoid the death penalty and, in the case of Vietnam, for pregnant women as well. In Indonesia and Vietnam, capital punishment is discretionary, although in Vietnam detailed court guidance effectively dictates that the death penalty currently applies where certain amounts of drugs are involved

[27] p 268.
[28] pp 270–71.
[29] David T Johnson and Franklin E Zimring, *The Next Frontier: National Development, Political Change and the Death Penalty in Asia* (New York, Oxford University Press, 2009).

and there are no extenuating circumstances.[30] Until 2012, the death penalty was mandatory in Singapore where a person was convicted of trafficking drugs in particular quantities.[31] There is now a judicial discretion to avoid capital punishment where two specific conditions are met. First, the defendant must he held, on the balance of probabilities, to be courier; and, second, the Central Narcotics Bureau must certify to the court that the defendant provided information to it enabling the disruption of drug trafficking.[32]

Each country has a different mode of execution and they execute at different rates. In Indonesia, numbers fluctuate, with execution policy influenced by domestic politics, including electoral cycles.[33] President Susilo Bambang Yudhoyono imposed an unofficial moratorium from late 2008 until 2013 but executions by firing squad resumed with his approval in 2014. At the end of that year, he was succeeded by President Joko 'Jokowi' Widodo, who, as at the time of writing (mid-2015), had presided over the execution of 14 people, mostly foreigners, despite strong international criticism.[34] A long delay of between 10 and 20 years before execution is not uncommon in Indonesia.

In Singapore, execution is by hanging and broadly speaking follows an established procedure and a time line that allows two years between sentencing and execution. These apply regardless of whether a foreign or local is being punished.[35] In Singapore, numbers executed have altered dramatically in the last twenty years. Between 1991 and 2004, this small nation state reportedly executed more than 400 prisoners.[36] It is suggested the current number of executions is now markedly lower, with only four executions in the five years from 2007 to 2012.[37]

In Vietnam, sentencing to death has been common for trafficking offences involving more than 600 grams of heroin or cocaine. Since 2013, death is by lethal injection but the timing of executions appears to be uncertain—and perhaps vulnerable to manipulation. Time on death row varies, with Pascoe suggesting a range of between five months to four years.[38] Estimates suggest around 60 executions take place in Vietnam every year. These estimates vary substantially, however, and their reliability has been further compromised by a suspension of executions from mid-July to late 2013, because of a lack of a key ingredient needed for

[30] pp 259–62, 300.

[31] pp 164–68.

[32] pp 183, 190–92.

[33] Simon Rogers and Mona Chalabi, 'Death Penalty Statistics, Country by Country' *The Guardian* (London, 13 December 2013), www.theguardian.com/news/datablog/2011/mar/29/death-penalty-countries-world#data. Data for years 2007–12 suggest 11 executions over five years.

[34] pp 106–07.

[35] p 192. See also Daniel Pascoe, 'Clemency in Southeast Asian Death Penalty Cases', (2014) Centre for Indonesian Law, Islam and Society Policy Paper No 4; Asian Law Centre Briefing Paper No 1 (CILIS and ALC, Melbourne Law School, the University of Melbourne).

[36] pp 190–92.

[37] See also Rogers and Chalabi, 'Death Penalty Statistics, Country by Country', which provides a link to Amnesty International's data at: https://docs.google.com/spreadsheet/ccc?key=0AonYZs4MzlZbdGJiUzRwTVhlM25DWDlPdjBmNURjOUE&hl=en#gid=0.

[38] Daniel Pascoe, 'Explaining Death Penalty Clemency in the Socialist Republic of Vietnam' (12 September 2015), see papers.ssrn.com/sol3/papers.cfm?abstract_id=2659417.

lethal injections.[39] Many foreigners, particularly Westerners, escape execution in Vietnam.[40]

The three countries also have different mechanisms for, and attitudes to, clemency. In Indonesia, Constitution and statute provide that clemency must be sought from the President and it has recently become clear that his decision is not capable of review by a court. Applications have historically been successful in 24 to 33 per cent of cases, although clemency is now very rarely granted where the death penalty is imposed for trafficking.[41] President Widodo has reportedly so far refused all applications for clemency made by drugs offenders.

In Singapore, the Constitution says that clemency can be sought from the President, acting on the advice of the Cabinet.[42] Clemency rates generally are the lowest here in Southeast Asia[43] and, again, clemency is very unlikely in drug trafficking cases.

In Vietnam, the President holds the discretion to award clemency,[44] with the clemency rate suggested to be between 6 and 23 per cent.[45] Foreigners facing execution may hope for clemency in the form of commutation to a life sentence if they are from countries that enjoy good relations with the Vietnamese government and engage in high-level police co-operation, and their country of origin does not usually apply the death penalty.[46] There is no transparency about the clemency process and grants of clemency to foreigners are not reported in the Vietnamese press. Local convicts may also apply for clemency but it has not been possible to track the results of such applications with any confidence. Some are apparently successful judging by a comparison of the available death penalty sentencing rates with execution rates, although these figures are not reliable.

Pascoe has identified three key legal and political factors that influence the proportion of cases in which clemency is granted.[47] The first is that where there is discretion allowing lenient treatment at earlier stages in the proceeding there is less prospect of clemency. Second, Pascoe argues that the extent to which clemency enhances or detracts from political power is also relevant. In cases where the political leader is not elected, and where the granting of clemency can either 'demonstrate

[39] p 276. Johnson and Zimring, *The Next Frontier*, compared with Hai Thanh Luong 'The Application of Death Penalty for Drug-Related Crimes in Vietnam: Law, Policy, and Practice' (2014) 17(1) *Thailand Journal of Law and Policy*, www.thailawforum.com/articles/Vietnam-death-penalty.html. See also Rogers and Chalabi (n 32), for a link to Amnesty International data. The data for 2007–12 suggests 58 executions over five years, including two years when no executions were possible.

[40] Daniel Pascoe, 'Explaining Death Penalty Clemency'.

[41] Daniel Pascoe 'Clemency in Southeast Asian Death Penalty', 5.

[42] See pp 192, 198.

[43] Pascoe (n 35) 5.

[44] pp 285–88.

[45] Pascoe (n 35) 5.

[46] pp 288–90.

[47] Pascoe (n 35) 6.

benevolence' or act 'as a demonstration of power of life and death so as to gain authority over domestic constituents', it is more likely to be granted.[48] Likewise, where the prisoner is a foreign national, the decision to grant clemency is often seen as contributing to 'greater international legitimacy' for unelected leaders.[49] Pascoe notes that where a state promotes a 'rule of law' approach to criminal justice, and concurrently places great emphasis on 'law and order', clemency may be less likely to be exercised as doing so is seen as a 'political liability.[50] He gives Singapore as an example of the latter approach. The third factor relevant to assessing the incidence of clemency is time spent on death row.[51]

The three states covered in the book are not abolitionist, even if abolitionism is used simply to refer to a trajectory that could possibly culminate in the removal of the death penalty as a sentencing option. Indonesia's approach to execution appears subject to the political leadership of the day and there has, in fact, been a significant increase in executions year-on-year over the last two decades. It is thus no longer even reductionist.

There is an argument, however, that Vietnam is reductionist. It has steadily reduced the incidence of the death penalty and is expected to do so further in late 2015.[52] If the number of executions is used as the indicator, Singapore is also reductionist. In Singapore, violent crimes like murder seem likely, however, to continue to attract capital punishment, and this is true also of crimes against the state in Vietnam. Vietnam's move to execution by lethal injection and current debates about adopting an approach that allows the imposition of a suspended death penalty subject to good behaviour suggest it may be the most innovative of the three Southeast Asian nations considered here, at least so far as reductionism is concerned (although Indonesia is now considering a similar proposal). There is considerable irony in the fact that the state ordinarily characterised as the most authoritarian of the three seems to be the one most willing to make changes to its death penalty laws and practices.

Other Drug-related Sentencing

Each of the three states investigated in this book has a range of non-custodial sentencing options available for drug offences, although most of those convicted of trafficking are jailed. Conditions in jails vary substantially. Singapore has reportedly some of the cleanest and most efficient jails regionally, if not globally.[53] They contrast markedly with the harsh conditions in Vietnamese jails where inmates are expected

[48] Pascoe (n 35) 9.
[49] Pascoe (n 35) 9–11.
[50] Pascoe (n 35) 12.
[51] Pascoe (n 35) 13–16.
[52] p 273.
[53] Peter Lloyd, *Inside Story: From ABC Foreign Correspondent to Singapore Prisoner #12988* (Sydney, Allen & Unwin, 2010). Lloyd was jailed for four months in Singapore for drug offences in 2008.

to have funds available to them from relatives to buy food and water, although basic supplies exist.[54] It is reported that foreigners have better jail experiences than locals with access to 'airier rooms' possible, and even television.[55] Indonesian jails show similar patterns to those in Vietnam but are also notable for the extent to which they allow media and public access.[56]

In each jurisdiction, courts may also order detention in drug rehabilitation facilities. In Indonesia, the requirement is for medical and social rehabilitation, and detention for these purposes can be substituted for jail time, at least since reforms introduced in 2009.[57] That said, jail time remains more common, and only limited advantage is taken of the legislated alternatives, as the traditional punitive approach continues to dominate.

In Vietnam, addicts can access detoxification centres on either a mandatory or voluntary basis. Conditions are reportedly basic, if not exploitative.[58] In addition to state-run detoxification centres, the Vietnamese Party-state calls on community and family to take responsibility for those addicted to drugs. They are expected to either support a program of voluntary detoxification or report addicts to the police.

Singapore appears to have the most coercive and extensive rehabilitation regimes. Those arrested for drug use can be compulsorily detained in a rehabilitation centre managed by the Singapore Prison Service.[59] There have been recent changes to the system of compulsory detention for young drug users to enable them to retain links to community, including at work or school, and avoid exposure to hardened drug users.[60] There is an extensive program of post-release monitoring and supervision to minimise relapse into drug use.

In short, each country has adopted rehabilitation as a possible response to drug addiction, alongside the established highly punitive approach to sentencing drug offenders, particularly those found guilty of trafficking. Singapore's extensive investment in detox and rehabilitation reflects the greater resources it has committed. It also illustrates the capacity of the PAP to design and implement a focussed anti-drugs agenda. This is made possible, at least in part, by the nation's small population, unitary government, and history of assertive and intrusive law and order policies. In Indonesia and Vietnam, by contrast, the country studies demonstrate common challenges for uniform implementation of reforms, complicated by much larger populations, strong provincial and local governments, highly discretionary decision-making, and long-established patterns of institutionalised corruption.

[54] p 266.
[55] Interviewee 8, 4 June 2012.
[56] See, for example: SBS TV, 'Condemned to Die', SBS Dateline (17 July 2011), www.youtube.com/watch?v=fXjpQkPfnaY. See also Foreign Prisoner Support Service, 'Exclusive Look inside Kerobokan Prison' (2012), www.foreignprisoners.com/prison-indonesia03.html.
[57] pp 113–17.
[58] p 212.
[59] pp 194–95.
[60] p 194.

II. MAPPING THE LITERATURE

This book responds to a significant lack of comparative analysis of drugs-focused criminal law and practice in Southeast Asia, although the extent of material available does vary between the three countries selected for study. In Singapore, for example, there is a range of texts examining drugs law and criminal practice, many of which are written by, or for, practising lawyers. These often compare Singapore's criminal law with that of Malaysia, a country of which Singapore was once, briefly, a part (from 1963 to 1965).[61] This literature is relatively long-standing, with analysis of criminal law in Singapore dating from at least the 1970s.[62]

This rich body of work is not, however, replicated for either Indonesia or Vietnam. Unlike Singapore, neither of these countries experienced a long period of British rule, and there is a severe dearth of detailed English-language analysis of the applicable criminal and procedural law in drugs cases, or the ways in which these cases are litigated. In Indonesia and Vietnam, legal commentary on drugs law and the death penalty, like criminal law and procedure generally, is predominantly in the local language and often significantly limited in scope and quality.

Criminologists focusing on drugs regulation as a health and law and order issue have recently begun to explore trends in Southeast Asia.[63] In the main, their publications are edited papers or reports by international organisations gathering insights about drugs regulation and drug use across the region.[64] These are growing in

[61] See, for example, Chan Wing Cheong, Stanley Yeo and Michael Hor, *Criminal Law for the 21st Century: A Model Code for Singapore* (Singapore, Academy Publishing, 2013); Judges of the Subordinate Courts of Singapore, *Practitioners' Library: Sentencing Practice in the Subordinate Courts* (Singapore, LexisNexis, 2013); Rafiah Salim and Cheong May Fong, *Evidence in Malaysia and Singapore: Cases, Materials, and Commentary*, 3rd edn (Malaysia, LexisNexis, 2013); Yock Lin Tan and S Chandra Mohan, *Criminal Procedure in Singapore and Malaysia* (Singapore, LexisNexis, 2012); Jennifer Marie (ed in chief) and Mohamed Faizal Mohamed Abdul Kadir (general eds), *The Criminal Procedure Code of Singapore: Annotations and Commentary* (Singapore, Academy Publishing, 2012); Keng Siong Kow, *Sentencing Principles in Singapore* (Singapore, Academy Publishing, 2009); Stanley Yeo, *Criminal Defences in Malaysia and Singapore* (Singapore, LexisNexis, 2005); Daljit Sen Adel, *Law of Dangerous Drugs: Cases and Commentaries* (Petaling Jaya, International Law Book Services, 2001); Chan Wing Cheong and Andrew Phang, *The Development of Criminal Law and Criminal Justice in Singapore* (Singapore, National University of Singapore, 2001); and Kheng Lian Koh, Christopher MV Clarkson and Neil A Morgan, *Criminal Law in Singapore and Malaysia: Text and Materials* (Singapore, Malayan Law Journal, 1989).

[62] Examples include Molly Cheang, *Criminal Law of Malaysia and Singapore: Principles of Liability* (Kuala Lumpur, Professional Law Books Publishers, 1990); William Clifford, 'Some Characteristics of the Application of the Criminal Justice System in Japan and Singapore', Selected Issues in Criminal Justice, (1985) HEUNI Publication Series No 4 (Helsinki Institute for Crime Prevention and Control affiliated with the United Nations); and EA Pereira, 'Exercise of Prosecutorial Discretion in the Administration of Criminal Justice in Singapore', (1982) UNAFEI Resource Material Series No 22 (Tokyo, UNAFEI). This review does not include materials published before 1980.

[63] Liu Jianhong, Bill Hebenton and Susyan Jou, *Handbook of Asian Criminology* (New York, Springer, 2013); M Emdad Ul Haq, *Drugs in South Asia* (London, Macmillan, 2000).

[64] See Fifa Rahman and Nick Crofts (eds) *Drug Law Reform in East and Southeast Asia* (Lanham, Lexington Books, 2013). See also UNODC (United Nations Office on Drugs and Crime), *World Drug Report 2014*, (Vienna, United Nations, June 2014) 48, www.unodc.org/documents/wdr2014/World_Drug_Report_2014_web.pdf.

number, in part provoked by increasing international focus on trade in drugs as a global phenomenon. There is also a robust critique of the 'war on drugs' that has provoked a search for new modes of regulation.[65] While informative on the development of drugs-focussed policy, these publications do not pay much attention to criminal law and practice and largely eschew sentencing issues, particularly as regards the death penalty.

Scholars of international law have also turned their attention to the need for global responses to drug trafficking.[66] This body of research includes work on the regulation of precursors and how to sustain supply of pharmaceutical drugs.[67] It does not, however, usually deal with substantive criminal law or sentencing issues in domestic jurisdictions as does this book.

This book also contributes to the literature on the death penalty.[68] As noted below, there is a real need for detailed studies of the death penalty in Asia, particularly regarding the positions regional states take on the abolition debate.[69] China has attracted much English language commentary about the death penalty but there has been comparatively less written about Southeast Asia.[70] While there is now detailed work emerging on clemency practice in Southeast Asia,[71] most publications on the

[65] Howard Rahtz, *Drugs, Crime, and Violence from Trafficking to Treatment* (Lanham, Hamilton Books, 2012).

[66] See, for example, David R Bewley-Taylor, *International Drug Control: Consensus Fractured* (Cambridge/New York, Cambridge University Press, 2012); Neil Boister, *Drugs, International Regulation, and Criminal Liability* (New York, Oxford University Press, 2013); Neil Boister, *An Introduction to Transnational Criminal Law* (Oxford, Oxford University Press, 2012); Hamid Ghodse, *International Drug Control into the 21st Century* (Aldershot, Ashgate, 2008); Gregory Lee, *Global Drug Enforcement: Practical Investigative Techniques* (Boca Raton, CRC Press, 2004); and Neil Boister, *Penal Aspects of the UN Drug Conventions* (The Hague/London, Kluwer Law International, 2001).

[67] Examples include Pierre-Louis Lexotre, *International Cooperation, Convergence and Harmonization of Pharmaceutical Regulations: A Global Perspective* (Oxford, Elsevier, 2014); Sally Shorthose (ed), *Guide to EU Pharmaceutical Regulatory Law* (The Hague, Kluwer, 2013); Leon Shargel and Isadore Kanfer (eds), *Generic Drug Product Development: International Regulatory Requirements for Bioequivalence* (New York, Informa Healthcare, 2010); and DC Jayasuria, *Regulation of Pharmaceuticals in Developing Countries: Legal Issues and Approaches* (Geneva, WHO Publications Center, 1985).

[68] See, in particular, Roger Hood and Carolyn Hoyle, *The Death Penalty: A Worldwide Perspective*, 5th edn (Oxford, Oxford University Press, 2015); Roger Hood and Surya Deva (eds), *Confronting Capital Punishment in Asia: Human Rights, Politics and Public Opinion* (Oxford, Oxford University Press, 2013); and Roger Hood, *The Death Penalty in Malaysia: Public Opinion on the Mandatory Death Penalty* (London, The Death Penalty Project, 2013), http://portfolio.cpl.co.uk/DPP/Malaysia-report/2/. See also Cornell Law School, 'Death Penalty Worldwide' (2015), www.deathpenaltyworldwide.org/index.cfm.

[69] Johnson and Zimring (n 29).

[70] Work on China includes Susan Trevaskes, 'China's Death Penalty: The Supreme People's Court, the Suspended Death Sentence and the Politics of Penal Reform' (2013) 53 *British Journal of Criminology* 482–99; Susan Trevaskes, 'Suspending Death in Chinese Capital Cases: The Road to Reform' in Roger Hood and Surya Deva (eds), *Confronting Capital Punishment in Asia: Human Rights, Politics and Public Opinion* (Oxford, Oxford University Press, 2013) 221; Susan Trevaskes (2015) 'Lenient Death Sentencing and the "Cash for Clemency" Debate' 73(1) *The China Journal* 38; Michelle Miao, 'Examining China's Responses to the Global Campaign against the Death Penalty' in Roger Hood and Surya Deva (eds), *Confronting Capital Punishment in Asia: Human Rights, Politics and Public Opinion* (Oxford, Oxford University Press, 2013) 46; and Hong Lu and Terance D Miethe, *China's Death Penalty: History, Law, and Contemporary Practices* (New York, Routledge, 2007) 66.

[71] Pascoe (n 35). Pascoe also has a forthcoming book on clemency in the region. See also Pascoe (n 37).

death penalty in that region usually focus on single jurisdictions.[72] They also only rarely consider the death penalty specifically in the context of narcotic crimes, despite the fact that a series of executions of drugs offenders in Southeast Asia have led to major international controversies over the last two decades.[73] This book, therefore, also scrutinises the administration of the death penalty in Indonesia, Singapore and Vietnam to contribute to the discussion about abolition and offer insights into death penalty practice in each jurisdiction.

Drug trafficking relies, in part at least, on mules and couriers to convey illegal narcotics across borders. Consequently, nationals foreign to the jurisdiction in which they find themselves facing prosecution are common defendants in drugs cases in all three countries. They face a range of problems, including as regards legal representation and, in some cases, politicisation of their cases and discriminatory treatment. This book has, therefore, also taken as part of its focus the treatment of those foreign to the prosecuting jurisdiction. Many practitioners who are also foreign to these jurisdictions generously give a great deal of their time and energy to assist their clients to navigate the criminal justice systems of Indonesia, Singapore or Vietnam. We hope this book may be of some use to them in the future, and, of course, to the consular officials and local lawyers with whom they work.

This brief review demonstrates that there is a gap when it comes to nuanced analyses of comparative criminal law and practice relating to drugs in Southeast Asia. This is despite the fact that there is a concerted effort emerging globally, including in Asian jurisdictions, to escalate criminal law reform generally and drugs law reform in particular. As suggested at the outset, although there are shared features of drugs law across the three jurisdictions, the actual practice of criminal law varies greatly between them. The nature of investigation and trial, the likelihood of conviction, and the standard sentences imposed for similar crimes differ so markedly that it is not possible to say that there is a standard Southeast Asian model—at least not one shared by Indonesia, Singapore and Vietnam. Instead, to understand how a defendant will fare in a drugs case in any one of these three countries, it is absolutely essential to have a detailed understanding of the specific laws applied in that country and recent decisions in comparable drugs cases in that jurisdiction. This book seeks to provide that information, at least in an introductory form, to students, English-speaking practitioners, and others interested in developments in this under-studied area of public law.

[72] See, for example, Daniel Pascoe, 'Three Coming Legal Challenges to Indonesia's Death Penalty Regime' (2015) II(2) *Indonesian Journal of International & Comparative Law* 256; Tsan Hang Tey, 'Death Penalty Singapore-Style: Clinical and Carefree' (2010) 39 *Common Law World Review* 315; and David T Johnson, 'The Jolly Hangman, the Jailed Journalist, and the Decline of Singapore's Death Penalty' (2013) 8 *Asian Criminology* 41.

[73] The exceptions here are Colman Lynch, 'Indonesia's Use of Capital Punishment for Drug-Trafficking Crimes: Legal Obligations, Extralegal Factors, and the Bali Nine Case' (2009) 40 *Columbia Human Rights Law Review* 523; and Yingyos Leechaianan and Dennis R Longmire, 'The Use of the Death Penalty for Drug Trafficking in the United States, Singapore, Malaysia, Indonesia and Thailand: A Comparative Legal Analysis' (2013) 2 *Laws* 115.

2

International and Regional Frameworks for Drugs Control

The country studies in this book show that the drugs law regimes of Indonesia, Singapore and Vietnam are different in many ways. The legislation of the three countries follows very different models and their courts have procedures that sometimes have very little in common. The outcomes of drugs prosecutions also often vary dramatically, as is shown later in this book. The three countries do, however, share a commitment to the current international drugs law regime. This is based around the three major United Nations conventions to which each is a signatory. They are also participants in regional organisations designed to facilitate co-operation between Southeast Asian states to prevent the illicit use of drugs.

This chapter offers an overview of the three major conventions, including their origins and key features. It closes with a short summary of institutions relevant to regional co-operation on drugs in Southeast Asia.

I. INTERNATIONAL FRAMEWORK

International co-operation on the regulation and control of narcotic drugs began in the early twentieth century with the establishment of the International Opium Commission in Shanghai in 1909.[1] Its recommendations led to the Hague Opium Convention, which was signed by Germany, the United States, China, France, the United Kingdom, Italy, Japan, the Netherlands, Persia, Portugal, Russia and Siam.[2] In 1919, this convention was incorporated into the post-war Treaty of Versailles and became the foundation of a series of international treaties that were introduced over the rest of the century. The resulting international regime for the control of narcotics gradually regulated an increasingly wide range of drugs in an increasingly restrictive fashion, although this took some decades to achieve.[3]

[1] Hamid Ghodse (ed), *International Drug Control into the 21st Century* (Hampshire, Ashgate, 2008), 19; David F Musto, *The American Disease: Origins of Narcotic Control*, 3rd edn (New York, Oxford University Press, 1999) 30–38.

[2] The Hague Opium Convention, 23 January 1912.

[3] M Cherif Bassiouni, 'Critical Reflections on International and National Control of Drugs' (1990) 18 *Denver Journal of International Law and Policy* 311, 313.

At first, international attention focused on opium. This was chiefly because Western states wanted to prevent the spread of opium addiction to the United States and Western Europe from China,[4] where its use had been aggressively promoted by Western colonial powers in the nineteenth century to tip the balance of trade in their favour.[5]

The Opium Convention and successor treaties negotiated in the 1930s were, however, more regulatory than prohibitive in nature.[6] The 1912 Opium Convention provided, for example, that:

> The contracting Powers shall use their best endeavours to control, or to cause to be controlled, all persons manufacturing, importing, selling, distributing, and exporting morphine, cocaine, and their respective salts, as well as the buildings in which these persons carry such an industry or trade.

The revised International Opium Convention, signed in Geneva on 19 February 1925 came into force in 1928. It established a statistical control body, the Permanent Central Opium Board, as an agency of the League of Nations but it was not empowered to enforce prohibition. This reflects the fact that before the Opium Convention was signed most domestic regimes made no provision for the control of narcotic drugs. These were not only often freely available for consumption and sale but had, in fact, formed an important part of the economic foundations of Western colonisation in the nineteenth century.

This approach to drugs began to change as addiction involving a wider range of drugs became recognised as a problem in the West. The multilateral treaties signed in the decades that followed the Opium Convention, therefore, imposed greater obligations on signatories. These were produced under the auspices of the League of Nations and required member countries to adopt appropriate enforcement strategies in their own domestic legal system, and co-operate with international drug control agencies and other parties to the treaties.[7] Over time, the treaties gradually became more repressive and came to encompass a range of naturally-derived drugs in addition to opium, such as various types of *cannabis sativa* (marijuana, hashish, quat, and Indian hemp).[8]

The next significant treaty, the Convention for Limiting the Manufacture and Regulating the Distribution of Narcotic Drugs was introduced in 1931, and created a new technical organ, the Drug Supervisory Body.[9] Its aim was to restrict

[4] David F Musto, *The American Disease: Origins of Narcotic Control*, 3rd edn (New York, Oxford University Press, 1999) 5–6.

[5] Timothy Brook and Bob Tadashi Wakabayashi (2000) 'Introduction: Opium's History in China', in Timothy Brook and Bob Tadashi Wakabayashi (eds), *Opium Regimes: China, Britain and Japan, 1839–1952* (Berkeley, University of California Press, 2000) 6–7.

[6] Martin Jelsma (2011) 'The Development of International Drug Control: Lessons Learned and Strategic Challenges for the Future' (2011) Global Commission on Drug Policies Working Paper prepared for the First Meeting of the Commission, Geneva, 24–25 January, www.globalcommissionondrugs.org/wp-content/themes/gcdp_v1/pdf/Global_Com_Martin_Jelsma.pdf, 2.

[7] Ghodse, *International Drug Control* 19.

[8] Bassiouni, 'Critical Reflections' 313.

[9] Bertil Arne Renborg, *International Drug Control: A Study of International Administration by and through the League of Nations* (Washington, DC, Carnegie Endowment for International Peace, Division of International Law, 1947).

world manufacture of drugs to the amount actually needed for medical and scientific purposes. This was followed in 1936 by the Convention for the Suppression of the Illicit Traffic in Dangerous Drugs, which called for severe punishment of illicit traffickers in narcotics and extradition for drug offences.[10]

Over the course of the twentieth century, the United States became increasingly concerned to outlaw the production and non-medical use of drugs, and, between the World Wars, the production and non-medical use of alcohol. Its views were at first not shared by colonial powers such as France, Great Britain, Portugal and the Netherlands. Most of these operated large drug monopolies in their overseas possessions but lost them as their colonies became independent in the wake of World War II.[11] Only after the establishment of the United Nations in 1945 was the United States able to use its newly hegemonic position to attract the international political support necessary to prohibit narcotics drugs globally.

By the 1970s, the United States had been able to establish an international norm that led to broad acceptance of the punitive policies associated with its so-called 'war on drugs'.[12] This was largely achieved through a series of new conventions established under the United Nations system, which we now describe. All are currently in force.

The 1961 Single Convention on Narcotic Drugs (Single Convention)[13]

This convention replaced previous existing international conventions on drugs. For that reason its adoption is widely regarded as a milestone in the history of international drug control. The United Nations Economic and Social Council initiated it by authorising the Commission on Narcotic Drugs to work on codification of a new convention. The Commission prepared a draft with help from various governments and a range of international and intergovernmental bodies. The Single Convention was adopted and opened for signature by the Conference on 30 March 1961. It came into force on 13 December 1964.[14]

The Single Convention's objectives are to codify existing multilateral conventions on drugs; simplify international control mechanisms; extend control systems to the cultivation of certain other natural products (in addition to opium and poppy straw) that produce narcotic effects; and adopt appropriate measures for the treatment and rehabilitation of drug addicts.[15] The Single Convention does not contain the general prohibition of drug production that some member states demanded, particularly with regard to cannabis. Instead, it recognises that narcotic drugs are extremely

[10] Renborg, *International Drug Control*.
[11] Jelsma, 'The Development of International Drug Control' 2.
[12] Jelsma (n 6) 3.
[13] Single Convention on Narcotic Drugs, 1961 (opened for signature 25 March 1961, entered into force 13 December 1964) 520 UNTS 280 (Single Convention).
[14] Syamal Kumar Chatterjee, *Legal Aspects of International Drug Control* (The Hague, Nijhoff, 1981) 343.
[15] Chatterjee, *Legal Aspects* 343–44.

important for medical purposes and, therefore, seeks to restrict their use to medical and scientific purposes.[16] It provides that production of any controlled substance can be carried out but only under certain conditions and only for medical or scientific purposes.[17]

More specifically, the Single Convention imposes controls on opium poppy, coca bush and cannabis plant, and their products. Members are obliged to 'limit the production, manufacture, export, import, distribution, stocks of, trade in and use and possession of the controlled drugs'.[18] State parties are also required to adopt measures that will ensure offences under the convention are punishable, including cultivation of drugs and their production, manufacture, extraction, preparation, possession, offering, offering for sale, distribution, purchase, sale, delivery on any terms whatsoever, brokerage, dispatch, dispatch in transit, transport, importation, and exportation.[19]

Each of the offences in the Convention is deemed to be included as an extraditable offence in any extradition treaty existing between the parties.[20] If there is no extradition treaty between two state parties and one of the states receives a request for extradition from another party, it may consider the Convention a legal basis for extradition.[21]

At present, the Single Convention controls 118 narcotic drugs, which are listed in the schedules to the convention. They cover natural products such as opium and its derivatives (including morphine, codeine and heroin), cannabis, cocaine, etc, as well as synthetic narcotic drugs such as fentanyl and its analogues, methadone and pethidine. The measures of control that the convention prescribes vary in strictness for different groups of drugs or preparations of drugs. Article 2 of the convention specifies certain provisions that apply variously to the drugs in the four schedules annexed to the convention and refers to relevant provisions contained in other articles of the convention. The schedules are arranged according to the dependence potential, abuse liability and therapeutic usefulness of the drugs included in them. They range from the most to the least restricted drugs in this order: Schedule IV, I, II, and III. There is significant overlap between Schedules I and IV, as we now explain:[22]

Schedule I: This covers substances that are highly addictive and liable to abuse, or are convertible into drugs that are similarly addictive and liable to abuse. They include cannabis and cannabis resin (and extracts and tinctures), narcotic raw materials (coca

[16] United Nations International Narcotics Control Board, 'Training Material 1961 Single Convention on Narcotic Drugs—Part I: The International Control System for Narcotic Drugs' (2005) www.incb.org/documents/Narcotic-Drugs/Training-Materials/English/NAR_1_English.pdf.

[17] UNODC (United Nations Office on Drugs and Crime), 'World Drug Report 2008' (Vienna, United Nations, 2008) 61.

[18] Ghodse (n 1) 20.

[19] Single Convention, Art 36.

[20] Single Convention, Art 36(2)(b)(i).

[21] Single Convention, Art 36(2)(b)(ii).

[22] A Lande, *Commentary on the Protocol Amending the Single Convention on Narcotic Drugs, 1961* (New York, United Nations, 1973). See also United Nations International Narcotics Control Board, 'Training Material'.

leaf, concentrate of poppy straw, opium), the stronger opiate analgesics (morphine, oxycodone), drugs of the ecgonine-cocaine group and a large number of synthetic drugs (fentanyl and its analogues, methadone).

Schedule II: This deals with substances that are less addictive and liable to abuse than those in Schedule I, such as codeine and its derivatives.

Schedule III: This includes preparations containing narcotic drugs that are intended for legitimate medical use and are compounded in such a way that the preparation is unlikely to be abused and the base drug cannot be easily extracted.

Schedule IV: This selects certain drugs listed in Schedule I that are considered particularly harmful in terms of their addictive properties and abuse potential (in other words, all drugs in Schedule IV also appear in Schedule I). Substances in Schedule IV are supposed to be rarely used in medical practice and may be subjected to special control measures by countries.

The schedules were designed to impose significantly stricter regulation than predecessor treaties. Cannabis, for example, was added to the list of internationally-controlled drugs for the first time, and the text of the treaty regulates the cannabis plant, the opium poppy, the coca bush, poppy straw and cannabis leaves.[23] Prior to this, misuse of the cannabis plant was seen as a purely domestic problem in many parts of the world. The Single Convention, however, outlawed all non-medical use of narcotic drugs anywhere in the world, including opium smoking, opium eating, consumption of cannabis (hashish, marijuana) and the chewing of coca leaves.[24]

Limitation of Cultivation

Poppy straw, coca bush, coca leaves and cannabis

The convention reflects the view that to be able to supress illicit traffic, limitations on cultivation are necessary. It provides that whenever:

> the prevailing conditions in the country or a territory of a Party render the prohibition of the cultivation of the opium poppy, the coca bush or the cannabis plant the most suitable measure, in its opinion, for protecting the public health and welfare and preventing the diversion of drugs into the illicit traffic, the Party concerned shall prohibit cultivation.[25]

The convention authorises some exceptions to this. Contracting parties are allowed to cultivate: opium poppies but only for purposes other than the production of opium;[26] coca leaves but only for the preparation of a flavouring agent;[27] and cannabis plants for horticultural and industrial purposes (fibre and seed) purposes.[28]

[23] Single Convention, Arts 24–28.
[24] UNODC, 'The Plenipotentiary Conference for the Adoption of a Single Convention on Narcotic Drugs' (1962) 1 *Bulletin on Narcotics*, www.unodc.org/unodc/en/data-and-analysis/bulletin/bulletin_1962-01-01_1_page007.html.
[25] Single Convention, Art 22.
[26] Single Convention, Art 25.
[27] Single Convention, Art 27.
[28] Single Convention, Art 28.

Opium

Opium is dealt with in two categories: medicinal opium[29] and opium (the coagulated juice of the opium poppy).[30] A party intending to produce opium or increase its production must take into account the global need for it, which will be determined by the International Narcotics Control Board.[31] Limitations also apply to the import and export of opium, which is only permitted for medical purposes.[32] A government agency for the production of opium must be established by any contracting party whose domestic laws permit the cultivation of the opium poppy.[33] All cultivators of the opium poppy in the contracting state party must report their total cultivation yield to that agency.[34]

Control of Trade and Traffic in Narcotic Drugs

The trade in narcotic drugs cannot be abolished entirely because, as mentioned, they are important for medical and scientific purposes. A regular supply for those purposes is not just desirable but essential. Tight control of their manufacture is, however, seen as equally essential. The Single Convention, therefore, creates a comprehensive international control regime to prevent drugs being sold and distributed illegally.[35] This is based on the requirement in Article 4 that contracting parties take such legislative and administrative measures as may be necessary:

> a) to give effect to and carry out the provisions of this Convention within their own territories;
> b) to co-operate with other States in the execution of the provisions of this Convention; and
> c) subject to the provisions of this Convention, to limit exclusively to medical and scientific purposes the production, manufacture, export, import, distribution of, trade in, use and possession of drugs.[36]

Article 30 deals specifically with drug trade and distribution, stating that 'Parties shall require that the trade in and distribution of drugs be under licence except where such trade or distribution is carried out by a State enterprise'. In addition, the parties must control individuals and enterprises carrying on, or engaged in, the trade in, or distribution of, drugs and also to control, under licence, the establishments and premises in which such trade or distribution may occur.[37] These include medical practitioners, dentists, veterinary surgeons and scientists using drugs in their experiments.

[29] Single Convention, Art 1(o).
[30] Single Convention, Art 1(p).
[31] Single Convention, Art 24(1).
[32] Single Convention, Art 24(4)–(5).
[33] Single Convention, Art 23(1).
[34] Single Convention, Art 23(2)(d).
[35] Chatterjee (n 14) 424.
[36] Single Convention, Art 4.
[37] Single Convention, Art 30(1)(b).

The convention also imposes specific rules to control the importation and exportation of controlled drugs. More particularly, it provides that contracting parties conducting export with other countries must have knowledge of the laws and regulations of those countries and, in particular, about the amount of drugs that may be imported into them.[38] International trade under the Single Convention is regulated by licence, which limits the number of importers and exporters and enables governments to monitor the flow of drugs across their borders.[39]

The assumption underpinning the regime these provisions create is that it will lead to the suppression of illicit trade and traffic in drugs. There are, however, gaps in the regulatory framework. For example, the convention prohibits transportation of a consignment of drugs from one country to another unless a copy of the export authorisation for the consignment is produced to the competent authorities.[40] In practice, drug traffickers can often get by with false export authorisations, as proper inspections conducted by competent personnel are rare in many countries. Further, although co-operation between contracting parties and competent international organisations, is strongly encouraged,[41] a lack of adequate and effective policing systems and co-ordination between various related agencies will obviously undermine it.

Penal Provisions

The Single Convention does not just establish a regulatory system for drug control. It also ensures there are penal sanctions to give it teeth by requiring contracting parties to impose sanctions for any breach of the regime it establishes. They must ensure that any acts of cultivation, production, manufacture, extraction, sale, distribution, importation and exportation of drugs contrary to the provisions of the Single Convention are punishable offences when committed intentionally. They must also ensure that such offences result in adequate punishment, such as imprisonment.[42] These requirements have some limitations. In particular, the penal provisions are subject to any limitations arising by reason of the constitution of a Contracting Party.[43]

Extradition is another source of difficulties. The 1972 Protocol, which amended the Convention, states:

> If a Party which makes extradition conditional on the existence of a treaty receives a request for extradition from another Party with which it has no extradition treaty, it may at its option consider this Convention as the legal basis for extradition in respect of the offences enumerated in paragraphs 1 and 2 a) ii) of this article. Extradition shall be subject to the other conditions provided by the law of the requested Party.[44]

[38] Single Convention, Art 31(1).
[39] Chatterjee (n 14) 428–29.
[40] Single Convention, Art 31.
[41] Single Convention, Art 35(c).
[42] Single Convention, Art 36(1).
[43] Single Convention, Art 36(2).
[44] Single Convention, Art 36(2)(b)(ii).

The last sentence in this clause has the effect that a requested party is only required to implement this provision to the extent compatible with its existing laws.[45] Given that extradition of criminal suspects has traditionally been a source of difficulties—and sometimes political tensions—between countries, this provision is a significant limitation on the effectiveness of the Single Convention.[46] It is a reminder that, in the end, the implementation of its penal provisions depends heavily on the attitudes of contracting parties towards drugs crimes and, in particular, the extent of co-operation between them in dealing with drug trafficking.[47]

The convention also provides that only those criminal activities committed intentionally may be punished.[48] As a consequence, criminal acts resulting from negligence are not punishable offences.[49]

Finally, the use of the words 'adequate punishments' in the convention reflects a somewhat ambiguous approach to sentencing offenders.[50] It provides that the punishment may be imprisonment or other penalties involving deprivation of liberty. Different countries, however, often have different views about the seriousness of the same offence. As a consequence, the severity of punishments varies enormously between contracting parties.[51] To give just one regional example, the variety of approaches to sentencing in Southeast Asia is made clear through the case studies of Indonesia, Singapore and Vietnam that appear later in this book. Their divergent approaches complicate extradition and other forms of bilateral co-operation with countries in and beyond Southeast Asia, particularly as regards the application of the death penalty to drugs offences.

The 1972 Protocol Amending the Single Convention[52]

The 1972 Protocol Amending the Single Convention on Narcotic Drugs made several further changes to the 1961 Single Convention. It strengthens prohibitions on the production, control, traffic and use of narcotics by imposing punishments that mostly involve imprisonment.[53] It also, however, invites member states to consider control policies such as 'treatment, education, after-care, rehabilitation and social reintegration'.[54]

The Protocol added a 'Limitation of Production of Opium', which allowed the International Narcotics Control Board to deduct from a nation's opium production quota the amounts it determines have been produced within that nation and illicitly

[45] Single Convention, Art 36(3).
[46] Chatterjee (n 14) 445.
[47] Chatterjee (n 14) 439.
[48] Single Convention, Art 36.
[49] Single Convention, Art 36(2)(a)(ii).
[50] Single Convention, Art 36(1).
[51] Chatterjee (n 14) 439. See also pp 60–63, 95–100, 103–07, 164–68, 189–93, 258–66, 272–90.
[52] Protocol Amending the Single Convention on Narcotic Drugs (opened for signature 25 March 1972, entered into force 8 August 1975) 976 UNTS 3 (1972 Protocol).
[53] Ghodse (n 1) 20.
[54] Single Convention, Art 36.

trafficked.[55] This could happen as a result of failure to control either illicit production or conversion of licit to illicit purposes. It allows the Board to punish a country that does not control its illicit opium traffic by imposing an economic sanction on its medicinal opium industry. Unfortunately, this provision is obviously ineffective for nations that are not opium exporters.

Finally, the Protocol adds a provision stating that a party prohibiting cultivation of the opium poppy or the cannabis plant shall take appropriate measures to seize any illicitly cultivated plants and destroy them, except for small quantities required by the party for scientific and research purposes.[56] This amendment is intended to make nations enforce their national laws against cultivation of illicit drugs.

The 1971 Convention on Psychotropic Substances[57]

Around the same time the 1961 Single Convention was being amended, many contracting parties developed the view that chemical and pharmaceutical drugs should also be controlled.[58] The 1971 Convention on Psychotropic Substances is a separate instrument but applies the same principles as the 1961 Convention, extending them to 'cover drugs such as central nervous stimulants, sedative hypnotics and hallucinogens'.[59]

The international community at the time was divided between countries that produced and consumed natural drugs and those that produced and consumed chemical and pharmaceutical drugs. Most producers of natural drugs were third world developing countries, while the consumers of these types of drugs were mostly industrialised Western countries. Conversely, the producers of chemical drugs were principally the industrialised western countries, while the consumers tended to be the Third World developing countries. This dichotomy largely persists today,[60] and has led to imbalances in the international regimes for the regulation of natural and chemical drugs. The Western countries were keen to enforce strong controls over the cultivation, production, and distribution of natural drugs but were unwilling to impose similar controls over their own chemical and pharmaceutical industries.[61] This resulted in a much stronger system of controls being adopted in the 1972 Protocol amending the 1961 Single Convention than in the 1971 Convention on Psychotropic Substances. The imbalance between these two systems of control has not been resolved.[62]

On the basis of a draft drawn up by the Commission on Narcotic Drugs in close collaboration with the World Health Organisation, a plenipotentiary conference

[55] Single Convention, Art 21.
[56] Single Convention, Art 22.
[57] Convention on Psychotropic Substances (opened for signature 21 February 1971, entered into force 16 August 1976) 1019 UNTS 175 (1971 Convention).
[58] Bassiouni (n 3) 314.
[59] Ghodse (n 1) 21.
[60] Bassiouni (n 3) 313.
[61] Bassiouni (n 3) 313.
[62] Bassiouni (n 3) 313.

for the adoption of a protocol on psychotropic substances met in Vienna in 1971, with 71 states represented. On 21 February 1971, it adopted the convention and opened it for signature. It has been in force since 1976, and its objectives, as stated in the Preamble, are to bring psychotropic substances and many of their preparations under international control, and reduce the incidence of abuse of those substances, and their illicit trafficking.

The 1971 Convention mimics the scope of the Single Convention.[63] Under the 1971 Convention, the contracting parties are required to maintain records in respect of substances in the following schedules.

Schedule I: Dangerous drugs creating a serious risk to public health, the therapeutic value of which is doubtful or nil, including synthetic hallucinogenics (LSD 25, DMT) and tetrahydrocannabinol (THC).

Schedule II: Stimulants of the amphetamine type, of limited therapeutic value, as well as some analgesics such as phencyclidine, which are of no therapeutic value to humans.

Schedule III: Barbiturate products with fast or average effects that have been the object of serious abuse, even though useful therapeutically.

Schedule IV: Hypnotics, tranquilisers (benzodiazepine) and analgesics that engender an appreciable dependence but are mainly used in therapy.[64]

Means of Control

The contracting parties are required to ensure that the manufacture of, trade in, and distribution of, substances listed in Schedules II, III and IV are carried out under licence or other similar control measure.[65] The parties must also control all duly authorised persons and enterprises carrying on, or engaged in, the manufacture of, trade in, or distribution of, psychotropic substances.[66] The phrase 'duly authorised persons and enterprises' refers to those persons and enterprises (including their premises) given licences by their governments (other than medical practitioners and scientists).[67]

The convention establishes elaborate provisions for the maintenance of records of the various psychotropic substances. These differ according to the schedule in which the substance appears.[68] Records in relation to Schedule I substances consist of details of the quantities manufactured and details of the quantity, date, supplier

[63] 1971 Convention, Art 2. See also the Single Convention, Art 3.

[64] 1971 Convention, Art 2. See also KM Buitenweg, 'Report Including a Proposal for a Recommendation of the European Parliament to the Council on the Reform of the Conventions on Drugs' European Parliament, Committee On Citizens' Freedoms and Rights, Justice and Home Affairs (24 March 2003), www.europarl.europa.eu/sides/getDoc.do?pubRef=-//EP//TEXT+REPORT+A5-2003-0085+0+DOC+XML+V0//EN.

[65] 1971 Convention, Art 8(1).

[66] 1971 Convention, Art 8(2).

[67] 1971 Convention, Art 8(2)(b–c).

[68] 1971 Convention, Art 11.

and recipient for each acquisition and disposal.[69] Contracting parties must ensure that retail distributors, institutions for hospitalisation and care, and scientific institutions keep records for each acquisition and disposal of a Schedule II drug, including details of the quantity, date, supplier and recipient.[70] The contracting parties must also require that manufacturers, exporters and importers keep records of the details of the quantities of Schedule IV drugs manufactured, exported and imported.[71]

The 1971 Convention also imposes a duty on the contracting parties to provide the Secretary-General of the United Nations with information on important changes in their laws and regulations concerning psychotropic substances, as well as significant developments in the abuse of, and the illicit traffic in, psychotropic substances within their territories.[72]

Penal Provisions

The convention sets out penal provisions that may be imposed when contracting parties breach their obligations under the convention.[73] More specifically, it states that:

> subject to its constitutional limitations, each Party shall treat as a punishable offence, when committed intentionally, any action contrary to a law or regulation adopted in pursuance of its obligations under this Convention, and shall ensure that serious offences shall be liable to adequate punishment, particularly by imprisonment or other penalty of deprivation of liberty.[74]

This provision is equivalent to Article 36(1) of the Single Convention and, again, the implementation of these provisions is hindered by the phrase 'subject to its constitutional limitations'. As a consequence, drug offences can be punished differently in different contracting party jurisdictions. Further, the 1971 Convention provides that if a series of related offences are committed in different countries, each should be treated as a distinct offence, and consequently punished according to the law of the country in which it was committed.[75]

On the punishment of offenders, the 1971 Convention states that national courts are allowed to assume jurisdiction to try drug offenders,[76] whether they are nationals or foreigners, so long as the offence was committed within their territory, and there is no extradition treaty between the offender's country of citizenship and the country in which he or she was found.[77]

[69] 1971 Convention, Art 11(2).
[70] 1971 Convention, Art 11(3).
[71] 1971 Convention, Art 11(5).
[72] 1971 Convention, Art 16.
[73] 1971 Convention, Art 22.
[74] 1971 Convention, Art 22(1).
[75] 1971 Convention, Art 22(2).
[76] 1971 Convention, Art 22(2)(a).
[77] 1971 Convention, Art 22(2)(a)(iv).

The Single Convention's general statement on rehabilitative punishment is also echoed in the 1971 Convention, which provides that:

> when abusers of psychotropic substances have committed such offences, the Parties may provide, either as an alternative to conviction or punishment or in addition to punishment, that such abusers undergo measures of treatment, education, after-care, rehabilitation and social reintegration.[78]

The implementation of this provision will obviously depend upon the availability of an effective system of treatment, education and after-care etc in the country concerned and, again, this varies hugely between jurisdictions.[79]

The 1988 Convention Against Illicit Traffic[80]

This convention was created to deal with the growth of international trafficking in illegal substances in the 1970s and 1980s, because the previous conventions only dealt with the issue in a limited fashion.[81]

In 1988, a United Nations conference in Vienna attended by 106 nations adopted the new convention, which was immediately ratified by 43 nations and entered into force on 11 November 1990. It covers both narcotic and psychotropic substances and serves mostly to provide additional legal mechanisms for the implementation of the 1961 and 1971 Conventions.[82] It acknowledges in its Preamble that recognition and prohibition alone were not solving international drug problems. It, therefore, contains provisions for tighter control of the processes surrounding the sale, transportation and consumption of narcotics and psychotropic substances, and promotes co-operation among the contracting parties.[83]

Two tables of substances used in the illicit manufacture of narcotic drugs or psychotropic substances are attached to the 1988 Convention. Contracting parties are required to impose controls on their manufacture and shipment.[84] In essence, this convention imposes the same controls on the chemicals used to manufacture illicit drugs as are imposed on natural materials like opium and cocaine.[85] The substances controlled by the convention include ephedrine, ergometrine, ergotamine, lysergic acid, 1-phenyl-2-proanone, pseudoephedrine, acetic anhydride, acetone, anthranilic acid, ethyl ether, phenyl acetic acid, and piperidine.

78 1971 Convention, Art 22(1)(b). See also Single Convention, Art 36.

79 Chatterjee (n 14) 485.

80 United Nations Convention against Illicit Traffic in Narcotic Drugs and Psychotropic Substances (opened for signature 20 December 1988, entered into force 11 November 1990) 1582 UNTS 95 (1988 Convention).

81 David R Bewley-Taylor and Cindy S Fazey with Tim Boekhout van Solinge, 'The Mechanics and Dynamics of the UN System for International Drug Control' (London, Forward Thinking on Drugs Initiative, 2003), www.forward-thinking-on-drugs.org/docs/Bewley-Taylor-full-report.pdf, 3.

82 Ghodse (n 1) 21.

83 1988 Convention, Art 2(1).

84 1988 Convention, Art 12.

85 1988 Convention, Art 12.

Penal Provisions

The 1988 Convention requires each party to establish the following as criminal offences under its domestic law, when committed intentionally: production, manufacture, extraction, preparation, offering, offering for sale, distribution, sale, delivery on any terms whatsoever, brokerage, dispatch, dispatch in transit, transport, importation or exportation of any narcotic drug or any psychotropic substance contrary to the provisions of the 1961 Convention, the 1961 Convention (as amended) or the 1971 Convention.[86]

The Convention may also require contracting parties to make the possession, purchase or cultivation of narcotic drugs or psychotropic substances for personal consumption contrary to the provisions of the 1961 Convention (as amended) a criminal offence.[87]

Previous drug control treaties had targeted drug manufacturers and traffickers, rather than users. Responding to the international tensions described above, the 1988 Convention was an attempt to reach a political balance between consumer and producer countries. Consequently, the duty to suppress illicit supply to suppress the demand for drugs was no longer just a duty of producing countries (the developing countries of Asia and South America). It was now also imposed on consumer countries (the industrialised countries of Europe and North America). The criminalisation of personal possession is, however, once again limited by the qualification that it must be 'subject to its constitutional principles and the basic concepts of [the state party's] legal system'.[88] This is problematic because, as mentioned, approaches to criminalisation of drug use vary greatly from country to country.

A notable provision of the 1988 Convention is the requirement to establish as a domestic offence the laundering of proceeds from drug-related offences. Although the term 'laundering' is not used in the convention, the activity that constitutes it is carefully described:

(i) The conversion or transfer of property, knowing that such property is derived from any offence or offences established in accordance with [Art 3(1)(a)], or from an act of participation in such offence or offences, for the purpose of concealing or disguising the illicit origin of the property or of assisting any person who is involved in the commission of such an offence or offences to evade the legal consequences of his actions.

(ii) The concealment or disguise of the true nature, source, location, disposition, movement, rights with respect to, or ownership of property, knowing that such property is derived from an offence or offences established in accordance with [Art 3(1)(a)] of this paragraph or from an act of participation in such an offence or offences.[89]

States' Obligations

As mentioned, the major obligations of the parties to the 1988 Convention include making the production, sale, and transport of narcotic and psychotropic substances,

[86] 1988 Convention, Art 3(1)(a)(i).
[87] 1988 Convention, Art 3(2).
[88] 1988 Convention, Art 3(2).
[89] 1988 Convention, Art 3(1)(b)(i–ii).

as well as the laundering of proceeds from drug-related activities, domestic criminal offences. It also, however, imposes other obligations, which include:

Extradition: This forms a central part of the treaty obligations.[90] Again, however, it is restricted by the addition of the usual domestic law safeguard clauses.[91]

Confiscation of assets: Parties are required to adopt measures to confiscate assets or proceeds derived from drugs production or trafficking, including those converted, intermingled, or laundered.[92] This also applies to materials and equipment employed by traffickers and producers. A party may not decline to act on this provision on the grounds of bank secrecy and parties must co-operate internationally in these efforts.

Mutual legal assistance: Parties must engage in the widest possible mutual assistance relating to investigations, prosecutions, and other legal actions, such as taking evidence or statements from persons, executing searches and seizures, providing information and evidentiary items and providing originals or certified copies of relevant documents and records, including bank, financial, corporate or business records.[93]

Controlled delivery: This allows a consignment of banned goods to pass out of, through, or into, the territory of a party under supervision, so as to identify and apprehend traffickers.[94]

Precursors: Parties are obliged to implement measures to monitor, label, and share information on legal chemical substances used in the manufacture of illegal drugs, such as common industrial solvents.[95] This obligation falls primarily on industrialised states, because they are the typical source of such precursors.[96]

Equipment control: Equipment commonly used in drug production is also covered, including glassware, tableting machines, and mixing tanks, and parties are obliged to control the movement of such equipment.[97]

International Agencies for Drugs Control

Under the current international system, the following international agencies have been established to control drugs. They are designed only as administrative support, funding or monitoring agencies, and lack effective enforcement powers.[98]

[90] 1988 Convention, Art 6(2).
[91] 1988 Convention, Art 6(5) and (9).
[92] 1988 Convention, Art 5.
[93] 1988 Convention, Art 7(2).
[94] 1988 Convention, Art 11.
[95] 1988 Convention, Art 12.
[96] 1988 Convention, Art 12; DW Sproule and Paul St-Denis (1989) 'The UN Drug Trafficking Convention: An Ambitious Step' 27 *Canadian Yearbook of International Law* 263, 288.
[97] 1988 Convention, Art 13.
[98] Bassiouni (n 3) 317.

The United Nations Commissions on Narcotic Drugs (UNCND)

This was established in 1946 by the Economic and Social Council as the United Nations' policy-making body on drug issues. Its consists of forty members elected by the Economic and Social Council, and it reviews the international drug situation, makes drugs policy, and sponsors international conventions.

The United Nations Division of Narcotic Drugs (UNDND)

This basically functions as the administrative body, secretariat and executive arm of the Commission on Narcotic Drugs. It gives assistance to members in the implementation of various drugs conventions and provides services and facilities to the Commission. It publishes annual reports as well as the national reports required by the various relevant international treaties.

The International Narcotics Control Board (INCB)

This was established under the 1961 Single Convention. It was established to limit the cultivation, production, manufacture and use of drugs to the adequate amounts required for medical and scientific purposes. It has the right to arrange quotas for countries based on their estimates of need for licit chemical and scientific purposes. It consists of thirteen members elected from the state parties.

The United Nations Fund for Drug Abuse Control (UNFDAC)

This is the only multilateral agency established to provide technical assistance and funding for crop substitution. In recent times, it has played a more important role by assisting actions against drug abuse and illicit trafficking. This organisation was established by the Secretary-General in 1971 and relies heavily on contributions by member states.[99]

The United Nations International Drug Control Programme (UNIDC)

Before 1990, there were many separate United Nations agencies dealing with responsibilities arising from the international drug control treaties and specific mandates of the General Assembly, the Economic and Social Council, and the Commission on Narcotic Drugs. By Resolution 45/179, the General Assembly combined the separate agencies in 1990 and established the United Nations International Drug Control Programme.

The United Nations Office on Drugs and Crime (UNODC)

In 1997, the United Nations Drug Control Programme and the Centre for International Crime Prevention were merged to form the UNODC. UNODC's roles are to

[99] Bassiouni (n 3) 317–18.

provide technical assistance in the form of expert advice and training to help governments set up adequate drug control structures and create comprehensive national strategies.[100] UNODC works with member state legislatures to ensure compliance. As a result, most of the national drug statutes now stored in the UNODC's legal library conform closely with the Single Convention and its supplementary treaties, the 1971 Convention and the 1988 Convention.

Critiques of International Drug Control

For over a hundred years since the International Opium Commission was established in 1909, international drug control agreements have pursued prohibitions on the production, distribution and use of some psychoactive substances with increasing rigour and ambition. There is much debate, however, about their efficacy and whether the regime they have created should be maintained.[101] The international community has spectacularly failed to achieve its rhetorical aim of a 'drug-free world'. It has not even been able to create a significantly reduced illegal market in plant-based drugs such as cocaine, heroin and cannabis, and synthetically produced drugs such as ecstasy, amphetamines, and LSD (lysergic acid diethylamide).[102] In fact, the opposite is true.

The current United Nations comprehensive framework on narcotic drugs—represented by the 1961 Single Convention—is now over half a century old, and was drafted in a very different political and social environment. International organised criminal drug trafficking did exist at the time of the Single Convention but was nowhere near as common as it is today. Similarly, drug use was much less widespread, and illegal drug markets were more geographically confined and less diverse. The use of cocaine was not endemic and HIV (human immunodeficiency virus) and its widespread transmission through injecting drug use was not even imagined.[103]

As noted above, many countries responded aggressively to the rapidly expanding trade in illicit drugs in the 1970s and 80s. In the United States—which had the fastest growing illicit drugs market—the political response was to 'declare war' on the foreign providers rather than analyse and address the reasons for growing domestic demand. President Richard Nixon popularised the term 'War on Drugs' in 1971, declaring drug abuse to be 'public enemy No 1'. Initially the main target of his hard-line policy was Mexico, which was the chief supplier of cannabis, and later heroin, to the United States market.[104]

Other countries soon followed the United States' lead, whether willingly or not. In 1986, the United States Congress enacted a disciplinary mechanism of drug

[100] Ghodse (n 1) 24.

[101] Mike Trace, 'Drug Policy—Lessons Learnt, and Options for the Future' (2011) Global Commission on Drug Policies Working Paper, www.globalcommissionondrugs.org/wp-content/themes/gcdp_v1/pdf/Global_Com_Mike_Trace.pdf, 2.

[102] Trace, 'Drug Policy' 2.

[103] Trace (n 102) 2.

[104] Jelsma (n 6) 6.

certification. Countries that did not fully co-operate with the anti-narcotics efforts and, thus, failed to qualify for certification would face mandatory sanctions.[105] These could include withdrawal of most foreign aid funded by the United States, along with opposition to loans sought from multilateral development banks.[106] The most recent attempt at a similarly aggressive approach was in Afghanistan, where opium production has rapidly increased since 2004. It has now been realised, however, that these tactics are ineffective while alternative income sources are unavailable, and only drive Afghan farmers into the hands of the Taliban.[107]

The aggressive 'zero tolerance' approach to combating drug production and trafficking propagated by the United States since the 1970s is now widely questioned. Some of the more socially regressive consequences of the escalation of the 'war on drugs' in the last two decades include a nearly worldwide and rapid increase in the prison populations; human rights violations; restricted access to essential medicines; and criminalisation of users, creating obstacles for health care, including as regards strategies for HIV/AIDS prevention. As we show in this book, all these problems are present in contemporary Southeast Asia and are exacerbated by the developing status of most economies in that region.

It has been suggested that the UNODC, and its predecessor, the UNDCP, were the 'defacto UN equivalent for an international policy ministry on issues relating to illicit drug use.'[108] After UNODC joined the UN Programme on HIV/AIDS (acquired immune deficiency syndrome) in 1999, it recalibrated its approach to illicit narcotics to include harm reduction.[109] In opting for an alternative approach that places more emphasis on harm reduction and even decriminalisation, a small number of states that were early adopters of the harm reduction strategy triggered what would become a widespread 'soft defection' from the zero-tolerance repressive model. Some European states, Canada and Australia had all become reluctant to continue prosecuting the 'war on drugs' in the bellicose way the United States wants. They were among the first to shift policy, followed more recently by several Latin American countries.[110]

The following is a brief summary of some of the most common criticisms of the United Nation conventions on drug control made by opponents of the 'war on drugs' approach that the conventions are seen as facilitating.

Punishment vs Harm Reduction: Decriminalisation and Depenalisation

Strictly repressive approaches to drug abuse typically rely on increasing the severity of the detrimental consequences of drug use in the expectation that this will halt

[105] Bill Spencer, 'Drug Certification' (1998) 3(24) *Foreign Policy in Focus*, 1 September, http://fpif.org/drug_certification/.

[106] Spencer, 'Drug Certification'.

[107] Jelsma (n 6) 7–8.

[108] SS Lee; David Jack; and Nick Crofts, 'Harm Reduction is Good Public Health' in Fifa Rahman and Nick Crofts (eds), *Drugs Law Reform in East and Southeast Asia* (Lanham, Lexington Books, 2013), 15–25, 20.

[109] Lee, Jack and Crofts 'Harm Reduction' 20.

[110] Jelsma (n 6) 8.

drug consumption. Authorities act to raise the chance of detection by police and impose longer prison sentences for those who are caught. Zero-tolerance policies do offer benefits, one of which is limiting the spread of HIV among drug users using needles. Singapore's AIDS prevalence rate is, for example, lower than that in the Netherlands, which adopts a far less punitive approach.[111]

It is now widely accepted, however, that increasing the severity of sanctions for drug users is, in fact, unlikely to significantly reduce overall levels of drug abuse.[112] Instead, it is more likely that severe punishment for drug use will cause drug users to variously develop severe health problems, live in slums, have high debt, be in prison for lengthy periods, or lose custody of their children, among other unfortunate outcomes. The International Red Cross argues that 'from a humanitarian perspective, repressive laws that imprison and harass drug users merely serve to drive them away from health and social support services ... Changing policies and reforming the justice system are central to harm reduction'.[113] The relatively harsh drug laws in Singapore, for example, are said to lead addicts to become 'isolated from the general population'.[114] This prevents former drug addicts from living normal lives and being fully reintegrated into society. As a consequence, they miss many opportunities for employment and education. This lack of alternatives often leads ex-users to return to their old habits.[115] Singapore must also deal with the high cost of housing up to 9,000 illicit drug users in treatment facilities at a time.[116]

Harm reduction is an approach that attempts to minimise the negative impacts associated with drug use, individually and socially.[117] It does not advocate drug use. Rather, the advocates of this approach believe drug use is inevitable, although the harm it causes can be reduced. As mentioned, this alternative approach to prohibition gained support in the 1980s, especially in Europe and Australia.[118] The harm reduction approach is intended, in theory at least, to provide drug users with a high standard of health and social services, the opportunity to work and study, freedom from arbitrary detention, and freedom from cruel, inhuman and degrading treatment. It is seen as enabling a 'rights-centred' policy for illicit drug users.[119]

[111] Michael Fahey, 'Home Grown: An Economic Examination of the Origins and Effectiveness of Radical Drug Policies' (2006) 20(3) *The Region* 53, 53–54.

[112] Alex Wodak, 'Demand Reduction and Harm Reduction' Global Commission on Drug Policies Working Paper prepared for the First Meeting of the Commission, Geneva, 24–25 January 2011, www.globalcommissionondrugs.org/wp-content/themes/gcdp_v1/pdf/Global_Com_Alex_Wodak.pdf, 9.

[113] International Federation of Red Cross and Red Crescent Societies 'Out of Harm's Way: Injecting Drug Users and Harm Reduction', IFRC Advocacy Report (December 2010) www.ifrc.org/Global/Publications/Health/Harm-reduction-report-EN.pdf, 20.

[114] Fahey, 'Home Grown' 53–54.

[115] Fahey (n 111) 53–54.

[116] These are figures reported as current in 2006. Fahey (n 111) 54.

[117] See generally, Lee, Jack and Crofts (n 109) 15–25.

[118] Steve Bolt, 'Drugs and the Law' (2007) Hot Topics: Legal Issues in Plain Language Series, No 59 (New South Wales, Legal Information Access Centre), www.legalanswers.sl.nsw.gov.au/hot_topics/pdf/drugs_59.pdf, 2.

[119] Joanne Csete and Fifa Rahman, 'Turning a Page: Human Rights and Drugs Policy in Southeast Asia' in Fifa Rahman and Nick Crofts (eds), *Drugs Law Reform in East and Southeast Asia* (Lanham, Lexington Books, 2013) 27–33, 31.

Harm reduction approaches require significant reforms to remove the harsh criminal sanctions that are the foundation of the zero-tolerance approach. This is often done by legislative reforms that deliver depenalisation and decriminalisation. 'Decriminalisation' removes particular conduct or activity from the sphere of criminal law, while 'depenalisation' is the relaxation of penal sanctions imposed by law for such activities.[120]

A harm reduction approach that concurrently recognises human rights, is in fact, possible within the framework of the United Nations drugs conventions, because they do not actually require that any penalty (criminal or administrative) be imposed for consumption per se. This is clearly stated in the official Commentary to the 1988 Convention: 'It will be noted that, as with the 1961 and 1971 Conventions, paragraph 2 does not require drug consumption as such to be established as a punishable offence'.[121] There is, therefore, now an increasing number of countries where possession of a quantity of drugs for personal use has been decriminalised or is no longer a priority for law enforcement. Alternatively, sentences for such offences have been reduced. As shown in the following chapters, however, Indonesia and Singapore have not legislated to decriminalise drug use, although Vietnam has.

These changes can have positive impacts on overburdened penal systems and overcrowding in prisons.[122] A number of countries have also introduced a more tolerant approach in relation to cannabis consumption, despite it being classified in the same category as heroin in the Single Convention.[123]

Problems with the Schedules

The prohibition of cannabis use and possession is the provision that most critics of the narcotics conventions agree most urgently needs re-examination. They are, however, other substances the classification of which is also questionable. One example is the coca leaf, which in Schedule I of the 1961 Convention is placed under the same controls as cocaine. Compared to the way other plants containing psychoactive alkaloids (such as ephedra or khat) are classified, coca, critics argue, is unnecessarily strictly controlled.

The zero-tolerance approach of the 1971 Convention only added to the confusion by introducing the dubious category of 'psychotropic' drugs, which included not only opioids such as buprenorphine and pentazocine but also THC, the active ingredient of cannabis (scheduled in the 1961 Convention), and cathinone, the active ingredient of the khat plant, which has never been included in the schedules.[124]

Further, while the 1961 Convention includes precursors of narcotic drugs, precursors and plants are excluded from the 1971 Convention. Some appear later in the lists attached to the 1988 Convention.

120 Jelsma (n 6) 7–8.
121 United Nations, Commentary on the United Nations Convention Against Illicit Traffic in Narcotic Drugs and Psychotropic Substances Done at Vienna, 20 December 1988, UN Doc E/CN7/590 (New York, United Nations, 1998).
122 Jelsma (n 6) 9.
123 Jelsma (n 6) 11–12.
124 Jelsma (n 6) 14–15.

In any case, it is clear that the drug schedules under the 1961 and 1971 Conventions suffer from significant inconsistencies and need to be revised.[125]

Supply Reduction vs Demand Reduction

Following the adoption of the 1988 Convention, there was a strong call by various countries to adopt a convention on demand reduction. This was particularly popular among the so called 'drug-producing nations', particularly Mexico. The producer states, in particular most of the Group of Latin America and Caribbean Countries (GRULAC), proposed that demand reduction be the subject of an international agreement. Previous treaties had focused mainly on supply reduction and many nations were tired of being criticised as drug producers. They believed consumer nations must also accept responsibility for driving the drug trade through their high consumption levels. The argument was 'if you did not consume the drugs, we would not be producing them'.[126] The United States, the United Kingdom, Germany and many other Western European countries believed, however, that such a convention might infringe upon national sovereignty, and objected. This proved decisive.[127]

The demand reduction approach is nonetheless gaining popularity and is typically done in two ways: prevention of drug use and treatment of drug users seeking help.[128] Prevention is usually attempted by providing drug education through school-based and mass education programmes, although some would argue that this strategy has not been successful in significantly reducing demand for drugs. The second approach, drug treatment, is based on evidence that when a substantial proportion of drug users receive an effective form of drug treatment for long enough for it to work, demand for drugs in that community reduces.[129] One example is Switzerland. The provision of high quality and affordable drug treatment led the number of new heroin users in Zurich to decrease from an estimated 850 in 1990 to 150 in 2002.[130]

This approach has yet to gain significant institutional support in Singapore. It is, however, more often applied (albeit alongside, rather than in place of, harsh criminal penalties) in Indonesia and Vietnam. This is shown in the more detailed accounts of drug law and practice in each country that follow this chapter.

Implementation of the UN Drugs Conventions in Indonesia, Singapore and Vietnam

The three United Nations conventions on drugs described above oblige state parties to take such administrative and legislative measures as may be necessary to give

[125] Jelsma (n 6) 16.
[126] Bewley-Taylor and Fazey, 'The Mechanics and Dynamics'.
[127] Bewley-Taylor and Fazey (n 81) 14.
[128] Wodak, 'Demand Reduction' 3.
[129] Wodak (n 112) 4.
[130] Carlos Nordt and Rudolf Stohler, 'Incidence of Heroin Use in Zurich, Switzerland: A Treatment Case Register Analysis' (2006) 367 *Lancet* 1830.

effect to, and implement, the provisions of the conventions. Indonesia, Singapore, and Vietnam have done so by ratifying and incorporating the three conventions into their respective domestic laws.

The 1961 Single Convention has, in fact, been very effective in standardising national drug control laws in these countries. Indonesia's Law on Narcotics No 35 of 2009, Singapore's Misuse of Drugs Act of 1973, and Law on Drug Prevention and Control 2000[131] were designed to perform these treaty obligations. All include analogous schemes of drug scheduling, based on the model established by the Conventions, along with broadly similar procedures for adding, removing, and transferring listed drugs.

The three United Nations Conventions on drugs also contain a number of mandatory requirements for state parties. These are set out in the United Nations Drug Control Conventions Checklist, most of which have been met by the three countries. In the Appendix to this book we offer a short account of Indonesia, Singapore and Vietnam's obligations under the Conventions Checklist and a brief summary of their key responses. A more detailed account of drugs law in each of these countries and the measures they have taken to comply with the Conventions is provided in the rest of this book.

The next section offers a short account of other international arrangements made by these three countries regarding narcotics law, principally in relation to Southeast Asian regional co-operation.

II. REGIONAL FRAMEWORKS

ASEAN

One of the fundamental principles of the Association of Southeast Asian Nations (ASEAN), enshrined in the Bangkok Declaration of 8 August 1967, was 'strengthen[ing] the foundation for a prosperous and peaceful community of Southeast Asian Nations.'[132] Transnational crime is clearly a threat to the political, economic and social wellbeing of ASEAN and its members have made extensive efforts to combat it since the early 1970s.[133] These have generally been focused on the prohibition of drug abuse and drug trafficking. The Declaration of ASEAN Concord of 24 February 1976 called, for example, for the 'intensification of cooperation among

[131] Narcotics Law No 35 of 2009 (Indonesia); Misuse of Drugs Act 1973 (Singapore); Law on Drug Prevention and Control No 23/2000/QH10 passed by the National Assembly on 9 December 2000 (Vietnam).

[132] Association of Southeast Asian Nations (ASEAN), Association of Southeast Asian Nations Declaration (Bangkok Declaration) (signed 8 August 1967), Art 1, www.asean.org/news/item/the-asean-declaration-bangkok-declaration.

[133] ASEAN, 'ASEAN Plan of Action to Combat Transnational Crime' (nd), www.asean.org/communities/asean-political-security-community/item/asean-plan-of-action-to-combat-transnational-crime. See also ASEAN, 'Manila Declaration on the Prevention and Control of Transnational Crime' (1998).

member states as well as with the relevant international bodies in the prevention and eradication of the abuse of narcotics and the illegal trafficking of drugs.'[134] Since then, all the ASEAN Summits have expressed concerns about narcotics abuse and illegal drug trafficking in the region, albeit to little avail, as regional drug use has, in fact, significantly increased in that time.[135]

ASEAN foreign ministers have also called for closer co-operation and co-ordinated action to tackle transnational crime among ASEAN countries. ASEAN finance ministers echoed the sentiments of ASEAN leaders and foreign ministers regarding illicit drug trafficking when they signed the ASEAN Agreement on Customs at their inaugural meeting in Phuket on 1 March 1997.[136] One of the recommendations from that meeting was to strengthen co-operation in combating trafficking in narcotics and psychotropic substances to facilitate joint efforts in anti-smuggling and customs control.[137]

To strengthen ASEAN collaboration in combating transnational crime, ASEAN member countries have also agreed to the establishment of the ASEAN Ministerial Meeting on Transnational Crimes. The ASEAN Senior Officials on Drug Matters (ASOD) group was then established. Its mandate includes enhancing the implementation of the ASEAN Declaration of Principles to Combat the Abuse of Drugs of 1976; consolidating and strengthening collaborative efforts in the control and prevention of drug problems in the region; bringing about the eventual eradication of narcotic plant cultivation in the region; and, designing, implementing, monitoring and evaluating all ASEAN programmes of action in relation to drug abuse prevention and control.[138]

Another significant development took place at the 31st ASEAN Ministerial Meeting in July 1998, which announced the Joint Declaration for a Drug-Free ASEAN by 2020, affirming ASEAN's commitment to eradicate illicit drug production, processing, trafficking and abuse in the region by 2020. At the 33rd ASEAN Ministerial Meeting in July 2000, regional governments reiterated their concern about the threat posed by the manufacturing, trafficking and abuse of illicit drugs to the security and stability of the ASEAN region. They agreed to advance the target year for realising a drug-free ASEAN to 2015.[139] This, like most other prohibitive drugs control targets, has not been met.

[134] ASEAN, 'Declaration of ASEAN Concord' (signed 24 February 1976), www.asean.org/news/item/declaration-of-asean-concord-indonesia-24-february-1976.

[135] ASEAN, 'ASEAN Plan of Action'.

[136] ASEAN, 'Agreement on Customs' (signed 1 March 1997), www.asean.org/communities/asean-economic-community/item/asean-agreement-on-customs.

[137] ASEAN (n 133).

[138] ASEAN, 'Cooperation on Drugs and Narcotics Overview', www.asean.org/communities/asean-political-security-community/item/cooperation-on-drugs-and-narcotics-overview.

[139] UNODC Regional Centre for East Asia and the Pacific, 'Drug Free ASEAN 2015: Status and Recommendations' (2008), www.unodc.org/documents/southeastasiaandpacific//Publications/ASEAN_2015.pdf, iii.

Regional Co-operation Outside ASEAN

There are other regional arrangements to combat illicit drugs in Southeast Asia that were established outside the main ASEAN framework, although some are associated with it. Few have had the sort of impact their proponents hoped.[140]

AIFOCOM (AIPA Fact-finding Committee to Combat the Drug Menace)

AIPA (The ASEAN Inter-Parliamentary Assembly) established this committee (AIFOCOM), which meets once a year. To date AIFOCOM has held 12 meetings, with the most recent held in June 2015 in Kuala Lumpur, with the theme of empowering people for a drug-free ASEAN.[141] The meeting resolved to bring the attention of member parliaments to the importance of promoting a 'people-oriented and people-centred approach that embraces information, education, public awareness, early intervention, counselling, treatment, rehabilitation, relapse prevention, aftercare and social reintegration'.[142]

ASEANAPOL: ASEAN Chiefs of Police

The various ASEAN police forces co-operate to combat the use and trafficking of drugs, although it seems clear that some police in the region are involved in drug trafficking. In any case, the police forces meet annually in the ASEAN Chiefs of Police Conference and hold an annual Joint ASEAN Senior Police Officers Course (JASPOC). The 35th conference was hosted by the Indonesian National Police in Jakarta in August 2015, and vowed to strengthen ties in combating transnational crimes, including drug trafficking, terrorism, human trafficking and financial crimes. Previous conferences have set up action plans that include information exchange, coordinated operations and investigations, co-operation in regional training and intelligence sharing for the identification, tracing, freezing, forfeiture, and confiscation of assets derived from the proceeds of drug trafficking.[143]

[140] Jason Eligh, 'Illicit Drugs in East and Southeast Asia: Situation and Response', presentation to the Seventh Meeting of the AIPA (ASEAN Inter-Parliamentary Assembly) Fact-Finding Committee (AIFOCOM) to Combat the Drug Menace, 22–25 April 2010, Ho Chi Minh City, Viet Nam.

[141] ASEAN Inter-Parliamentary Assembly, 'Report of the 12th Meeting of the AIPA Fact-Finding Committee (AIFOCOM) to Combat the Drug Menace', 7–11 June 2015, Kuala Lumpur, Malaysia. www.aipa36malaysia.gov.my/wp-content/uploads/2015/06/00_Report-of-the-12th-Meeting-of-AIFOCOM-to-Combat-the-Drug-Menace.pdf.

[142] ASEAN Inter-Parliamentary Assembly, 'Resolution on Making a Drug Free ASEAN Post-2015 Through a People-Oriented and People-Centred Approach', ASEAN Inter-Parliamentary Assembly, 12th Meeting of the AIPA Fact-Finding Committee (AIFOCOM) to Combat the Drug Menace, 7–11 June 2015, Kuala Lumpur, Malaysia.

[143] The 2008 communique is the most recent available online. ASEANAPOL, 'The 35th ASEANAPOL Conference at Borobudur Hotel', Jakarta, Indonesia (13 August 2015) www.aseanapol.org/display/2015/08/13/the-35th-aseanapol-conference-at-borubudur-hotel-jakarta-indonesia. ASEAN, 'Joint Communique of the 28th ASEAN Chiefs of Police Conference', Brunei Darussalam, 25–29 May 2008, www.asean.org/communities/asean-political-security-community/item/joint-communique-of-the-28th-asean-chiefs-of-police-conference-brunei-darussalam-25-29-may-2008.

HONLEA: Heads of National Drug Law Enforcement Agencies

To further co-operation in drug law enforcement activities at the regional level, the UN Economic and Social Council established HONLEA as a subsidiary body of the Commission on Narcotic Drugs. The regions covered include Europe, Latin America and the Caribbean, Asia and the Pacific and Africa. The meetings usually take place annually to identify salient policy and enforcement issues in their regions, establish working groups to analyse the issues, and bring reports and recommendations to the attention of the Commission.[144]

Greater Mekong Subregion Memorandum of Understanding (MOU)

The Greater Mekong Subregion (GMS) is made up of Cambodia, the People's Republic of China (PRC, specifically Yunnan Province and the Guangxi Zhuang Autonomous Region), the Lao People's Democratic Republic (Lao PDR), Myanmar, Thailand, and Vietnam. In 1993, these countries signed a MOU with the United Nations Office on Drugs and Crime (UNODC) on drug control in the region, although this area remains a major source of drug production and trafficking.[145]

ACCORD: ASEAN-China Co-operative Operations in Response to Dangerous Drugs

ASEAN and China co-operate through the ASEAN-China Cooperative Operations in Response to Dangerous Drugs (ACCORD), which was signed by members on 13 October 2000 to advance regional cooperation in combating drugs. ACCORD establishes a Plan of Action that rests on four pillars:

1. promoting civic awareness and social responses on the dangers of drugs;
2. reducing illicit consumption of drugs by building consensus and sharing best practices on demand reduction;
3. strengthening the rule of law by an enhanced network of control measures and improved law enforcement co-operation and legislative review; and,
4. eliminating the supply of illicit drugs by increasing alternative development programmes and community participation in the eradication of illicit crops.[146]

[144] UNODC, 'Commission on Narcotic Drugs Vienna: Subsidiary Bodies' www.unodc.org/unodc/en/commissions/CND/Subsidiary_Bodies/Subsidiary-Bodies_Index.html.

[145] UNODC Regional Centre for East Asia and the Pacific, 'A Decade of Cooperative Partnership and Progress in the Greater Mekong Subregion through the Memorandum of Understanding (MoU) on Drug Control' (2013), http://en.oncb.go.th/document/MOU-2003.pdf; UNODC, 'Memorandum of Understanding on Drug Control' (Greater Mekong Sub-region), 1993.

[146] ASEAN and China 'Joint Regional Plan to Achieve a Drug-Free ASEAN by 2015', Press Release, Bangkok, Thailand, 13 October 2000, www.asean.org/communities/asean-political-security-community/item/press-release-of-asean-and-china-on-a-joint-regional-plan-to-achieve-a-drug-free-asean-by-2015-bangkok-thailand-13-october-2000.

3

Indonesia

With a population of about 255 million,[1] Indonesia is the largest domestic market for narcotics in Southeast Asia. As it comprises more than 17,000 widely scattered islands, with a staggering 54,000 kilometres of coastline,[2] tight border controls are almost impossible in the Indonesian archipelago. This makes it vulnerable to the illicit narcotics trade.[3] Proximity to both regional narcotics producers in the Golden Triangle (Laos, Thailand and Myanmar) and neighbouring narcotics markets, such as Australia, makes Indonesia a strategic transit hub for the international drug trade. Although Indonesia is not a major producer of narcotics for export, significant quantities of cannabis are cultivated for the local market in the province of Aceh in northern Sumatra.[4] The domestic production of amphetamine-type stimulants (ATS), primarily crystalline methamphetamine and ecstasy, is also rapidly rising.[5]

The government of Indonesia portrays narcotics trafficking and drug abuse as a major threat to the lives and cultural values of Indonesia's people, and even the nation's security.[6] It has, therefore, been eager to be seen as adopting a hardline approach to the drug trade.[7] The country's official stance has, however, often been

[1] See Indonesia, Badan Perencanaan Pembangunan Nasional [National Development Planning Agency], Badan Pusat Statistik [Central Statics Agency] and United Nations Population Fund, 'Proyeksi Penduduk Indonesia 2010–2035' [Indonesian Population Projection 2010–2035], (Jakarta, Badan Pusat Statistik, 2013), 23.

[2] CIA, 'The World Factbook: Indonesia' (22 June 2014), www.cia.gov/library/publications/the-world-factbook/geos/id.html.

[3] US Department of State, Bureau for International Narcotics and Law Enforcement Affairs, *International Narcotics Control Strategy Report. Volume I: Drug and Chemical Control* (March 2010), 346; Prodita Sabarini, 'Coastline Vulnerable to Smuggling', *The Jakarta Post* (6 September 2006), www.thejakartapost.com/news/2006/09/06/coastline-vulnerable-smuggling.html; Raymundus Rikang, 'BNN: Laut Jadi Jalur Baru Peredaran Narkoba [BNN: seas new route for narcotics distribution]', *Tempo Online* (23 November 2014), www.tempo.co/read/news/2014/11/23/064623813/BNN-Laut-Jadi-Jalur-Baru-Peredaran-Narkoba.

[4] UNODC (United Nations Office on Drugs and Crime), *Indonesia: Situation Assessment on Amphetamine-Type Stimulants* (UNODC, February 2013), 1.

[5] UNODC, *Indonesia: Situation Assessment*, 11–12, 226; Rebecca McKetin, Nicholas Kozel, Jeremy Douglas, Robert Ali, Balasingam Vicknasingam, Johannes Lund, Johannes and Li Jih-Heng, 'The Rise of Methamphetamine in Southeast and East Asia' (2008) 27 *Drug and Alcohol Review* 220, 226.

[6] See, for example, the Preambles to Law No 22 of 1997 on Narcotics [*Narkotika*] and Law No 35 of 2009 on Narcotics.

[7] Indra Akuntono, 'Kepada Semua Kepala Daerah, Jokowi Minta Tak Ada Toleransi untuk Kasus Narkoba [To all regional leaders, Jokowi requests zero tolerance for narcotics cases]', *Kompas* (4 February 2015), http://nasional.kompas.com/read/2015/02/04/11061801/Kepada.Semua.Kepala.Daerah.Jokowi.Minta.Tak.Ada.Toleransi.untuk.Kasus.Narkoba.

undermined by ongoing problems with corrupt and ineffective law enforcement institutions.[8]

This chapter presents an overview of the laws and institutional arrangements for the regulation of narcotics within Indonesia. It draws from a range of sources including legislation, cases, official policy documents, reports, media articles, government statistics and academic analysis. The first section offers a brief summary of the history of the narcotics trade in Indonesia, as well as current drug use and state responses to it. The next section describes the main drug-related offences under Indonesian law and the elements of criminal responsibility. The third section considers jurisdictional issues in relation to drug-related offences. The fourth section describes criminal procedure for drugs crimes from arrest to trial, paying particular attention to the relevant sections of Indonesia's Criminal Procedure Code (*Kitab Undang-undang Hukum Acara Pidana*, KUHAP). The fifth section examines the rights of the accused during the investigation process, while the sixth section examines trial and sentencing. The seventh section details Indonesia's approach to rehabilitation of drugs users, a growing area of concern for the Indonesian government. The eighth section examines the ways in which Indonesia has sought to tackle financial aspects of the illicit drug trade. Finally, the last section examines selected decisions of the district courts, the provincial-level High Courts and the Supreme Court, to provide case studies of how the law is actually applied in practice.

I. OVERVIEW OF DRUG TRADE AND CONSUMPTION IN INDONESIA

The emergence of a significant narcotics trade in Indonesia was linked to colonialism in the region. It is likely that the market for opium in Java and other parts of the archipelago predated colonialism[9] but it developed rapidly under the influence of European merchants, for whom the trade was a strategic means to fund Europe's appetite for products from the east. Before British domination of the opium trade, Dutch and Portuguese traders shipped raw opium from Bengal to Java and the Spice Islands (Maluku) from the seventeenth century, often exchanging it for spices.[10] As the Dutch consolidated control over many parts of the Dutch East Indies (present day Indonesia), they sought to secure a monopoly over opium trading within the colony. In the early nineteenth century, the Dutch introduced a 'vice tax' on the consumption of opium. This was intended not so much to reduce the use of opium as to implement a system whereby its consumption was controlled by the state. The colonial authorities, therefore, operated a franchise-type arrangement by which dealers paid for the exclusive right to prepare and sell opium in their respective territories.[11]

[8] United States Department of State, Bureau of International Narcotics and Law Enforcement Affairs, *International Narcotics Control Strategy Report: Volume I*, 203–04.

[9] James R Rush, 'Opium in Java: A Sinister Friend' (1985) 44(3) *The Journal of Asian Studies*, 549.

[10] Warren Bailey and Lan Truong, 'Opium and Empire: Some Evidence from Colonial-Era: Asian Stock and Commodity Markets' (2001) 32(2) *Journal of Southeast Asian Studies* 173, 174.

[11] Jan C van Ours, 'The Price Elasticity of Hard Drugs: The Case of Opium in the Dutch East Indies, 1923–1938' (1995) 103(2) *Journal of Political Economy* 261, 263.

Opium consumption increased throughout Java during the 1800s. Compared to the situation in British Malaya and Singapore, it appears that the number of serious addictions was, however, relatively low.[12] By the end of the nineteenth century this began to change and pressure mounted within the Netherlands to prohibit opium use in its colonies. The East Indies government did not support a ban, citing concerns that it would result in increased smuggling, particularly given the archipelago's extensive coastlines, which then, as now, were considered impossible to patrol.[13]

As an alternative to a ban, the government introduced a government opium control system, the *Opium-Regie*, a complete state monopoly on the import, preparation and distribution of opium. The official aims of *Opium-Regie* were to reduce criminality and the power of syndicates, lower health risks by guaranteeing clean product, and limit net opium consumption through a system of quotas and minimum price controls. The system of control it established was progressively implemented throughout the Dutch East Indies and different practices and policies were adopted in accordance with the conditions present in particular regions. In some Muslim regions of West Java, for example, where opium smoking was limited, the state promoted complete prohibition.[14] At the same time, Chinese communities and Chinese labourers working on large agricultural estates were subjected to less strict controls than their indigenous or European counterparts.[15]

The main form of opium consumed into the twentieth century was known as *tjandoe* (*candu*), which contained about 11–13 per cent morphine, and the *Opium-Regie* had mixed impacts on rates of its consumption. There is significant scholarly debate as to whether it achieved an overall decrease in opium consumption or conversely promoted higher rates of morphine consumption use.[16] There is evidence that opium became more widely available under the *Opium-Regie* and by 1905 accounted for 15.9 per cent of all colonial revenues.[17] Among communities of Chinese descent, rates of opium consumption were quite high and, while they constituted only 2 per cent of the total population in 1930, they represented almost half (47 per cent) of the total number of opium users.[18] Further, the average Chinese user consumed three times as much as indigenous users.[19]

In addition to the local processing of opium, from the 1870s, coca was also cultivated in Java. By 1912, more than 1,000 tonnes was exported to Amsterdam, where

[12] Bailey and Truong, 'Opium and Empire', 176.

[13] For this paragraph generally, see Ours, 'The Price Elasticity', 261–66.

[14] Ours (n 11), 266.

[15] Ours (n 11), 266.

[16] Van Luijk and Ours demonstrate that, measured in kilograms per year, there was a continued decline in opium use in the first decade after the introduction of the *Opium-Regie.* See Eric W Van Luijk and Jan C van Ours, 'The Effects of Government Policy on Drug Use: Java, 1875–1904' (2001) 61(1) *The Journal of Economic History* 1. By contrast, Chandra argues that if consumption is measured by the quantity of actual morphine consumed, rather than the net weight of the substance, there was an overall increase, as opium distributed under the *Opium-Regie* had a 50% higher morphine content than revenue farm opium. See Siddharth Chandra, 'The Role of Government Policy in Increasing Drug Use: Java, 1875–1914' (2002) 62(4) *The Journal of Economic History* 1116.

[17] James R Rush, *Opium to Java: Revenue Farming and Chinese Enterprise in Colonial Indonesia, 1860–1910: Asia, East by South* (Ithaca, Cornell University Press, 1990), 236–37.

[18] Ours (n 11), 266.

[19] Ours (n 11), 266.

it was processed into cocaine. Coca cultivation was short-lived, however, and from the 1930s[20] the market declined, eventually ceasing in the 1960s.[21] Local production has not been revived.

Under the Japanese occupation from 1942 to 1945, opium farms continued to operate and were taxed by the occupying forces. After the end of World War II, the distribution and sale networks that had been controlled by the colonial government were taken over by the new Indonesian republic and the revenues provided a significant source of funds for its independence struggle against the Dutch.[22] In the early years of the Indonesian republic, the consumption of opium and other drugs was not considered a major national problem or a priority for law reform. It was only from the 1970s that narcotics control rose to prominence on the national agenda, largely in response to the United States' wider efforts to promote a global 'war on drugs'.

Domestic Drug Consumption in Contemporary Indonesia

As this account suggests, drug use patterns have shifted significantly since independence in 1945. High economic growth rates in the 1970s and 1980s led to declining poverty rates and an increase in both disposable incomes and the size of the middle and upper classes. This was accompanied by the first significant post-independence increase in the consumption of so-called 'recreational drugs', including phencyclidine, mushrooms, marijuana, hypnotics/sedatives and heroin.[23] The late 1990s saw a fast rise in the use of heroin, particularly via needles, prompting the rapid spread of HIV (human immunodeficiency virus).[24] Since its first detection in Jakarta in 1998, the use of crystalline methamphetamine has also increased rapidly.[25]

Accurate estimates of the number of drug users in Indonesia are scarce. A 2011 National Survey conducted by Indonesia's National Narcotics Agency, BNN (Badan Narkotika Nasional), estimated there were between 3.7 and 4.7 million drug-users in Indonesia.[26] BNN predicted a sharp rise in the number of users[27] and in a recent report projected users to reach 5.1 to 5.6 million by 2015,[28] equivalent to about

[20] David Musto, 'International Traffic in Coca through the Early 20th Century' (1998) 49(2) *Drug and Alcohol Dependence* 145.

[21] UNODC, 'A Century of International Drug Control' in UNODC, *World Drug Report 2008* (Vienna, United Nations, 2008), 83.

[22] Robert Cribb, 'Opium and the Indonesian Revolution' (1988) 22(4) *Modern Asian Studies* 701.

[23] Irwanto, 'Indonesia: Facing Illicit Drug Challenges' (2006) 69 *Development Bulletin* 44.

[24] John McBeth, 'A New Menace' *Far Eastern Economic Review*, 19 August 2004.

[25] UNODC, *Indonesia: Situation Assessment on Amphetamine-Type Stimulants* (UNODC, February 2013), 3.

[26] Indonesia. BNN (Badan Narkotika Nasional), 'Survei Nasional Perkembangan Penyalahgunaan Narkoba [National survey of developments in narcotics abuse]' (BNN, 2011), www.bnn.go.id/portal/_uploads/post/2012/05/29/20120529145842-10263.pdf, 19.

[27] Indonesia. BNN, 'Survei Nasional Perkembangan', 1.

[28] Indonesia. BNN, 'Jurnal Data Pencegahan dan Pemberantasan Penyalahgunaan dan Peredaran Gelap Narkoba (P4GN) for 2013 [Data on Prevention and Elimination of Illicit Narcotics Trafficking and Abuse (P4GN) in 2013]' (BNN, 2014), http://103.3.70.3/portal/_uploads/post/2014/08/19/Jurnal_Data_P4GN_2013_Edisi_2014_Oke.pdf, 3.

2.1 per cent of the population. BNN has faced considerable criticism of the methodology used to justify these claims.[29] The 2011 National Survey did not, for example, cite the sources, dates, sample sizes or methodological techniques of the various surveys that were compiled to achieve its estimate of user numbers. This makes it impossible to have any confidence in the estimate or the number of users BNN predicted.

Of the 2,210 drug users surveyed by BNN in 2011, 37 per cent were classified as experimental users, 45 per cent were regular users, 27 per cent were non-needle-based addicts and 2 per cent were needle-based addicts. Again, these figures should also be interpreted with some caution because of the highly problematic definition of 'addiction' used by BNN. The survey defines 'experimental users' as those who have used narcotics less than five times in the year prior to the survey. Those who have used drugs between 5 and 49 times in that year are classified as 'regular users'. 'Non-needle based addicts' are defined as those who used drugs more than 49 times in the previous year. More problematically, anyone who has injected themselves with a narcotic substance at any time in the past year, regardless of the amount of times, is considered a needle-based addict.[30]

That said, the survey suggests cannabis remains the most commonly consumed drug in Indonesia, used by 64 per cent of drug users.[31] Consumption of crystalline methamphetamine (referred to as *shabu* or *sabu*) is rising sharply, and was consumed by 38 per cent of drug users surveyed.[32] It is now identified as the main drug threat in Indonesia.[33] The survey also found that ecstasy was consumed by 18 per cent of drug users, followed by heroin at 13 per cent and methadone at 9 per cent.[34] Cocaine is not a major drug of concern in Indonesia. According to BNN, the median age at which people first try drugs is 16 years, with 75 per cent of first-time users consuming marijuana.[35]

Drug seizures broadly reflect these patterns of use. In 2014, BNN confiscated 8,417 kilograms of marijuana and 60 marijuana plants, 447 kilograms of crystalline methamphetamine, 37,277 ecstasy pills, and 7.9 kg of heroin. In 2014, approximately 80 per cent of suspects in drug-related crimes were male.[36]

Amphetamine-type stimulant use has expanded throughout Indonesia in recent years and is now increasingly prevalent across many provinces and a wide demographic range.[37] Usage is most prevalent, however, among labourers, students

[29] Claudia Stoicescu, 'Indonesia Uses Faulty Stats on 'Drug Crisis' to Justify Death Penalty' *The Conversation*, 5 February 2015, https://theconversation.com/indonesia-uses-faulty-stats-on-drug-crisis-to-justify-death-penalty-36512.

[30] Indonesia. BNN (n 26), 6, 7 and 22.

[31] Indonesia. BNN (n 26), 45.

[32] Indonesia. BNN (n 26), 29.

[33] UNODC, *Indonesia: Situation Assessment on Amphetamine-Type Stimulants* (UNODC, February 2013) 1.

[34] Indonesia. BNN (n 26), 45.

[35] Indonesia. BNN (n 26), 28.

[36] Indonesia. BNN, 'Lampiran Press Release Akhir Tahun, Badan Narkotika Nasional [National Narcotics Agency end of year press release]', Press Release, 23 December 2014, http://103.3.70.3/portal/_uploads/post/2014/12/23/Press_Release_Akhir_Tahun_2014_LAMPIRAN_22122014_20_08.pdf, 1.

[37] UNODC, 'Indonesia: Situation Assessment', 2.

and commercial sex workers.[38] In 2011, drug users in Indonesia were estimated to have consumed approximately 12.5 metric tonnes of crystalline methamphetamine and 16 million ecstasy pills.[39] Methamphetamine is now a more prevalent drug than cannabis in terms of recent drug arrests and new admissions for treatment. Methamphetamine consumption is, again, overwhelmingly a male preoccupation, with 89 per cent of methamphetamine users being men.[40]

Domestic producers are responsible for supplying 60 per cent of crystalline methamphetamine seized in Indonesia. Most of the rest is trafficked into the country from Iran, China, Malaysia and the Philippines (see Figure 1, below).[41] Over recent years, an increase in drug trafficking operations by syndicates based in West Africa has been identified.[42] Both large and small-scale manufacture of ATS has been recorded in Indonesia since 2002. Outbound trafficking of locally manufactured ATS is limited and much greater quantities are imported into Indonesia. This seems to be due to the size of the market and the relatively high prices available in Indonesia compared to some neighbouring countries.[43]

BNN estimates that costs to the Indonesian economy from narcotics are as much as Rp 48.2 trillion (US$ 3.8 billion) but the techniques and accuracy of data used to obtain this estimate are, as mentioned, highly questionable.[44]

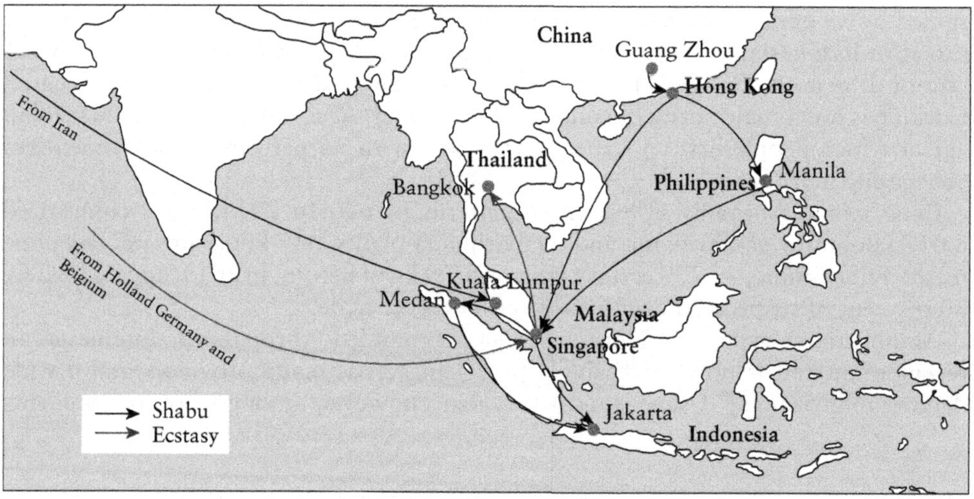

Figure 1: Amphetamine-type Stimulant (ATS) Trafficking Routes to Indonesia, BNN 2011

[38] UNODC (n 25), 2.
[39] UNODC (n 25).
[40] UNODC (n 25), 8.
[41] UNODC (n 25), 18.
[42] US Department of State, Bureau for International Narcotics and Law Enforcement Affairs (n 3).
[43] UNODC (n 25), 3.
[44] Indonesia. BNN (n 26), 49.

State Responses to Narcotics

Although Indonesia does invest in a growing number of prevention and rehabilitation programs, the state's approach to narcotics is primarily punitive in nature.[45] Drug use is widely perceived as a problem of crime and morality, and there is broad societal and political support for a harsh law enforcement approach.

Indonesia has ratified all three major UN conventions on drug control and entered into a number of bilateral agreements, including memoranda of understanding with China, Nigeria, Lao, Pakistan, Iran, Australia, Timor-Leste and Mexico. It is a member of the Asia/Pacific Group on Money Laundering (APG). BNN also takes part in a range of bilateral co-operation programs. In 2012, it co-hosted the International Drug Enforcement Conference, the world's largest international drug enforcement event, with participants from more than 70 countries.[46] The United States operates a Drug Enforcement Administration Office in Jakarta and has collaborated in cannabis eradication programs and training for counter narcotics officers.[47]

The overarching framework for narcotics control in Indonesia has undergone major changes in the past 40 years. Following independence, the new republic adopted many elements of existing Dutch colonial law,[48] and the narcotics legislation implemented as part of the Opium-Regie remained in effect. This included the first consolidated narcotics ordinance, which was passed in 1927 (Staatsblad 1927 No 278-536 Verdovende Middelen Ordonantie), in conjunction with regulations on the preparation of opium (Staatsblad 1927 No 514, Opium Verpakkings Bepalingen). It was not until the 1970s that Indonesia addressed the need to reform narcotics control.

From the 1970s on, the Indonesian government has consistently portrayed narcotics use as a major threat to individuals, communities and the state. In 1971, President Soeharto issued an instruction to the National Intelligence Coordination Agency (Badan Koordinasi Intelijen Negara, BAKIN). This stated that the mitigation of narcotics abuse was one of six national priorities, alongside the eradication of counterfeit currency, the prevention of smuggling, youth delinquency, subversion, and the surveillance of foreign nationals.[49] In response, BAKIN formed a small interdepartmental agency to deal with narcotics abuse. The agency had no direct allocation in the national budget, however, and only limited operational authority. Throughout this period, regulation of narcotics was weak, due to the lack of uniform definitions,

[45] Gloria Lai, Fransiska Asmin and Ruth Birgin, 'Drug Policy in Indonesia', International Drug Policy Consortium Briefing Paper, 5 January 2013, 1.

[46] US Department of State, Bureau for International Narcotics and Law Enforcement Affairs (n 3), 201.

[47] US Department of State, Bureau for International Narcotics and Law Enforcement Affairs (n 3), 201.

[48] Articles I and II of the Transitional Provisions of the 1945 Constitution provided that existing colonial laws and institutions remained in place until such time as replaced in accordance with the Constitution.

[49] Presidential Instruction No 6 of 1971 on the Coordination of Actions and Activities from and/or Relevant Agencies in Efforts to Control, Prevent and Eliminate the Problem of Violations Related to the Management of Narcotics [*Koordinasi Tindakan dan Kegiatan dari Instansi yang Bersangkutan dalam Usaha Mengatasi, Mencegah dan Memberantas Masalah Pelanggaran yang Berkenan dengan Masalah Penanggulangan Narkotika*].

little law enforcement action aimed at trafficking or consumption, contradictions in criminal law, and the absence of a national body responsible for narcotics control or even a narcotics investigation unit within law enforcement agencies.[50]

In 1976, a new Narcotics Law was finally enacted to replace the antiquated Dutch laws. This prohibited the cultivation, production, extraction, conversion, storing, trafficking, transport, transit or personal use of narcotics without explicit authority from the Minister of Health.[51] The Law also introduced much stricter penalties, including the death penalty or life imprisonment for importation and trafficking offences in relation to most narcotic substances.[52] It also introduced a rudimentary framework for drug rehabilitation. The general elucidation[53] to the 1976 Narcotics Law characterises the abuse of narcotics as a 'form of subversion' that can have a 'wide-reaching and fatal impact' as addicts are driven 'to do anything possible to obtain those narcotics, without heed to social, religious or legal norms'.[54]

In 1997, a new statute was introduced to replace the 1976 Law. The revision sought to align Indonesian legislation with the provisions of the 1988 UN Convention against Illicit Traffic in Narcotic Drugs and Psychotropic Substances, which Indonesia had signed in 1989.[55] The 1997 Narcotics Law introduced a more sophisticated system for categorisation of drugs drawn from that convention, and included an initial listing of 127 narcotic substances.

The 1997 Narcotics Law was, in turn, replaced by the current Narcotics Law, which came into force on 12 October 2009. This Law was designed to strengthen Indonesia's ability to tackle contemporary drug crimes, which increasingly involve sophisticated technology, support from vast international networks, and significant capital investment. The 2009 Law listed 164 narcotics substances, and introduced a number of new provisions that aimed to more effectively target organised drug crime, including new money laundering offences and increased powers for BNN. The preamble to the 2009 Narcotics Law declares that narcotics 'represent an enormous danger to human life, society, our nation and the state as well as Indonesia's national security'.

The principle law enforcement agency for drug control, BNN, was created in 2002 and is governed by a 2007 presidential regulation.[56] It has significant powers

[50] Parasian Simanungkalit, *Globalisasi Peredaran Narkoba dan Penanggulangannya di Indonesia* [The Globalisation of Narcotics Trafficking and Prevention in Indonesia] (Jakarta, Yayasan Wajar Hidup, 2011), 241–42.

[51] 1976 Narcotics Law, Art 23.

[52] 1976 Narcotics Law, Art 26.

[53] The 'elucidation [*penjelasan*]' is the explanatory memorandum that routinely accompanies Indonesian regulation and is usually read with it. The text of the regulation prevails in the event of any inconsistency but the elucidation guides interpretation and application.

[54] Elucidation to the 1976 Narcotics Law.

[55] United Nations, United Nations Convention against Illicit Traffic in Narcotic Drugs and Psychotropic Substances, (status as at 19 June 2015), https://treaties.un.org/pages/viewdetails.aspx?src=treaty&mtdsg_no=vi-19&chapter=6&lang=en.

[56] Presidential Regulation [*Peraturan Presiden*] No 83 of 2007 on the National Narcotics Agency, Provincial Narcotics Agencies and Regency/Municipality Narcotics Agencies [*Badan Narkotika Nasional, Badan Narkotika Provinsi, dan Badan Narkotika Kabupaten/Kota*]. See also Jun Honna, 'Orchestrating Transnational Crime: Security Sector Politics as a Trojan Horse for Anti-Reformists' in Ed Aspinall and Gerry van Klinken (eds), *The State and Illegality in Indonesia*, (Leiden, KITLV Press, 2011) 261.

under the 2009 Narcotics Law. The agency is independent of government ministries and directly accountable to the president. Its 2012 annual budget was Rp 806 billion (US$ 64 million)[57] and it employed around 3,350 staff.[58] It has five main sections, including departments of mitigation, eradication, social empowerment, rehabilitation, and law and co-operation. The agency has regional offices in 33 provinces and more than 100 offices at the district and municipality level. It plans to progressively increase its regional representation.[59]

BNN has signed a Memorandum of Understanding with the Indonesian National Police to more effectively co-ordinate the enforcement of drug law throughout the archipelago, including through the development of a national drug crime database, information exchange, and co-ordination on money laundering and precursor chemical control.[60] BNN has also co-operated with the Corruption Eradication Commission (Komisi Pemberantasan Korupsi, KPK) to investigate money laundering and financing aspects of drug crimes, although no formal arrangement exists between the two institutions.[61]

In addition to BNN, the provincial commands of the National Police each have a directorate for narcotics, and district-level commands also have a narcotics investigation unit. The Directorate General of Customs has responsibility for monitoring narcotic substances that transit through international airports and other custom zones, and has played a significant role in seizing narcotics and making arrests in recent years.[62] The Ministry of Health also has an important role under the 2009 Narcotics Law and is responsible for the classification of drugs,[63] the regulation of drugs for medical use, and setting standards for rehabilitation and treatment programs.[64]

The high levels of corruption that exist at all levels of the Indonesian government have been identified as a major obstacle to the nation's counter-narcotics strategy.[65] The 2013 arrest of Constitutional Court Chief Justice Akil Mochtar for corruptly fixing decisions on electoral disputes in his court revealed, for example, that

[57] Indonesia. BNN, 'Laporan Akuntabilitas Kinerja Instansi Perintah: Badan Narkotika Nasional [Government agency efficiency and accountability report: National Narcotics Agency]' (2013), www.bnn.go.id/portal/_uploads/post/2013/04/23/LAKIP%20BNN%202013%20OKE.pdf.

[58] US Department of State, Bureau for International Narcotics and Law Enforcement Affairs (n 3), 199.

[59] Indonesia. BNN, 'Sejarah BNN [History of the BNN]', 23 November 2010, www.bnn.go.id/portal/index.php/konten/detail/bnn-pusat/profil/8005/sejarah-bnn.

[60] Indonesia. BNN, 'Penandatangan Nota Kesepahaman antara Badan Narkotika Nasional (BNN) dengan Korps Lalu Lintas Polri', [Signing of the Memorandum of Understanding between the National Narcotics Agency and the Traffic Police Corps] Press Release (27 February 2012), www.bnn.go.id/portal/index.php/konten/detail/humas/pressrelease/10152/penandatangan-nota-kesepahaman-antara-badan-narkotika-nasional-bnn-dengan-korps-lalu-lintas-korlantas-polri.

[61] Rinaldy Sofwa Fakhrana, 'KPK-BNN Kerjasama Tangani Cuci Duit Narkotik [KPK-BNN co-operate to handle narcotics money laundering]' *CNN Indonesia*, 21 October 2014, www.cnnindonesia.com/nasional/20141021123009-20-7174/kpk-bnn-kerjasama-tangani-cuci-duit-narkotik/.

[62] Law No 17 of 2006 on Amendment to Law No 10 of 1995 on Custom Zones, Art 115A and elucidation.

[63] Law No 35 of 2009 on Narcotics, Art 6 states that changes to the categorisation of narcotics substances are to be regulated by ministerial regulation. One such regulation is Health Ministerial Regulation No 13 of 2014 on Changes to Narcotics Categories [*Perubahan Penggolongan Narkotika*].

[64] Law No 35 of 2009 on Narcotics, Arts 53–59, 60–63.

[65] US Department of State Bureau for International Narcotics and Law Enforcement Affairs (n 3), 200.

corruption had reached the highest levels of the Indonesian judicial system. He was later also charged with narcotics offences after drugs were found in his office.[66] In fact, corruption plagues law enforcement efforts in relation to drugs in Indonesia, to the extent that narcotics defendants have been referred to as 'walking ATMs'.[67] In 2014 alone, there were numerous corruption scandals involving BNN staff, mainly in regional offices.[68] In the same year, Indonesian police officers were also arrested in Malaysia for alleged involvement in regional smuggling syndicates.[69] Early in 2015, a member of the West Jakarta Police's narcotics unit was arrested with 9,700 ecstasy pills and more than 800 grams of methamphetamine.[70]

II. NARCOTIC-RELATED CRIMES

Legislative Framework

The Indonesian Criminal Code (*Kitab Undang-undang Hukum Pidana*, KUHP) does not contain provisions dealing specifically with drug offences.[71] These are largely regulated by the 2009 Narcotics Law and, to a lesser extent, by the 1997 Law on

[66] See, for example: Yenni Kwok, 'Top Indonesian "Anticorruption" Judge Is Arrested for Graft' *Time*, 4 October 2013, http://world.time.com/2013/10/04/arrest-of-antigraft-judge-shows-depth-of-indonesias-corruption-crisis/; and, Dian Maharani, 'Akil Mochtar Jadi Tersangka Kasus Narkotika' *Kompas*, 17 January 2014, http://nasional.kompas.com/read/2014/01/17/1903457/Akil.Mochtar.Jadi.Tersangka.Kasus.Narkotika. Akil Mochtar was eventually sentenced to life imprisonment.

[67] Andri Haryanto, 'Wakapolri Minta BNN Seret Polisi yang Terlibat Korupsi di Kasus Narkotika [Deputy police chief asks BNN to haul in police involved in narcotics corruption' *Detik News*, 16 December 2014, http://news.detik.com/read/2014/12/16/113907/2778730/10/wakapolri-minta-bnn-seret-polisi-yang-terlibat-korupsi-di-kasus-narkotika?nd771104bcj.

[68] A Syalaby Ichsan, 'Duh, Tiga Pegawai BNN Jadi Tersangka Korupsi [Ouch, three BNN staff declared corruption suspects]' *Republika*, 8 May 2014, www.republika.co.id/berita/nasional/hukum/14/05/08/n58vtd-duh-tiga-pegawai-bnn-jadi-tersangka-korupsi; *Berita Satu*, 'Pekan Depan Kejati NTT Ekspose Dugaan Korupsi di BNN [Next week NTT prosecutor's office to expose suspected corruption in the BNN]', 5 August 2014, www.beritasatu.com/nasional/200870-pekan-depan-kejati-ntt-ekspose-dugaan-korupsi-di-bnn.html.

[69] Two Indonesian police officers were arrested in Kuching, Malaysia, with 6 kg of narcotics, following a tip-off from one of their associates who had been caught in Kuala Lumpur. One of the officers, Idha Endri Prastiono, was serving as the head of the narcotics division in the West Kalimantan Police. Although they were eventually released by the Malaysian authorities, Idha was charged by the West Kalimantan police for, among other things, taking a car originally confiscated from a narcotics dealer. For a full coverage, see the topic page on Tempo online: www.tempo.co/topik/tokoh/1716/Idha--Idha-Endri-Prasetyono.

[70] Chief Brig Sudirman was arrested in a hotel parking lot in West Jakarta, apparently attempting to conduct a narcotics transaction. Following the arrest, police stressed that the drugs in question were not the result of police confiscations: Indra Budiari, 'Cops Could Face Death Sentence for Drug Trafficking' *The Jakarta Post* (20 January 2015), www.thejakartapost.com/news/2015/01/20/cops-could-face-death-sentence-drug-trafficking.html; Nur Azizah, 'Kata Kasat Narkoba Polres Jakarta Barat Soal Anggotanya yang Tertangkap [This is what the head of West Jakarta Police Narcotics Unit had to say about the member of his team who was arrested]' *Kompas*, 19 January 2015, http://megapolitan.kompas.com/read/2015/01/19/18223481/Kata.Kasat.Narkoba.Polres.Jakarta.Barat.soal.Anggotanya.yang.Tertangkap.

[71] Articles 204 and 205 of the Criminal Code make it an offence to provide, whether intentionally or otherwise, another person with any harmful substance without disclosing its harmful nature. These provisions could arguably be applied to a person supplying illegal drugs where the recipient was unaware of the effects. Indeed, Art 204 was apparently used to prosecute ecstasy dealers in at least two cases before Law No 35 of 2009 on Narcotics was enacted, as ecstasy was not previously included in the list of prohibited drugs.

Psychotropic Substances. Activities regulated include the production, importation, exportation and distribution of drugs; their use for medical, therapeutic, academic and other scientific purposes; the treatment and rehabilitation of addicts; licensing and accreditation for all these activities; reporting requirements of related parties; government supervision; and the role of the public in preventing narcotics abuse. Technical regulations for the implementation of the 2009 Narcotics Law are set out in subordinate government regulations and ministerial regulations.[72] These include specific rules regarding the classification of substances and rules regarding authorisation of the legal import and export of controlled substances.

Offences in relation to the financial aspects of the drug trade are set out in the 2010 Anti-Money Laundering Law.[73] Additionally, BNN has published additional rules regarding some of its key functions, such as narcotics testing.[74] More fundamental principles regarding criminal liability and procedures for the investigation and prosecution of drug offences are set out in the Criminal Code and the 1981 Criminal Procedure Code (KUHAP). These include regulations dealing with the roles of the police and prosecutors (*jaksa*), arrests, warrants, detention, searches, and the provision of legal aid.

A draft bill to reform both the Criminal Code and the Criminal Procedure Code has been discussed in the legislature since 2010,[75] although the slow pace of negotiations means it remains unclear when, if ever, they will be passed, or what form they might finally take.

Definition of Narcotics

Under the 2009 Narcotics Law, a narcotic substance (*narkotika*) is defined as 'an addictive synthetic or semi-synthetic drug or substance derived from a plant or non-plant material that has the potential to alter or decrease one's awareness, impair or extinguish feeling, or reduce or extinguish fear'.[76] An exhaustive appendix to the 2009 Narcotics Law categorises narcotics substances as Group I, II or III narcotics. The elucidation to the law sets out the detail of this typology, as follows.[77]

Group I covers narcotics that have a very high potential to lead to addiction, are not used in therapy, and are only used in the development of scientific knowledge. Group I narcotics include, among others, any part of the opium poppy (*papaver somniferum L)* other than its seeds; heroin and opium; cocaine and any part of

[72] Government Regulation No 40 of 2013 on the Implementation of Law No 35 of 2009 on Narcotics.

[73] Law No 8 of 2010 on Prevention and Elimination of Money Laundering [*Pencegahan dan Pemberantasan Tindak Pidana Pencucian Uang*].

[74] See, for example, BNN Director's Regulation No 11 of 2011 on Revision to BNN Director's Regulation No 5 of 2010 on Technical Guidelines for Narcotics Testing Laboratory Services for BNN [*Pedoman Teknis Penyelenggaraan Pelayanan Laboratorium Pengujian Narkoba pada Badan Narkotika Nasional*].

[75] A version of the bill can be downloaded from the website of the Directorate General of Legislation, Ministry of Law and Human Rights, Republic of Indonesia, ditjenpp.kemenkumham.go.id/files/doc/1008_RUU%20KUHAP.doc.

[76] 2009 Narcotics Law, Art 1(1).

[77] 2009 Narcotics Law, elucidation to Art 6.

the coca plant; cannabis, THC and any part of the marijuana plant; and ecstasy (MDMA), MDA, LSD, mescaline, PCP, amphetamine, dexamphetamine (which is used to treat attention deficit hyperactive disorder (ADHD)), and methamphetamine.

Group II narcotics are medicines that may be used as a last resort, in therapy and in the development of scientific knowledge, and which have a high potential to lead to addiction. They include morphine and codeine.

Group III narcotics are medicines that are frequently used in therapy, and in the development of scientific knowledge and have a low potential to lead to addiction.

In the 2009 Narcotics Law, there were 65 substances in Group I, 85 substances in Group II, and 14 substances in Group III. Chemical salts containing any of the substances listed in Group II and Group III were also considered narcotic substances. Changes to the categories are regulated via ministerial regulation and do not require amendment by legislative process. Precursor substances are listed in the second appendix to the Narcotics Law, which included 23 substances in 2009. In accordance with the 2009 Narcotics Law, the precursor substance list can also be amended via ministerial regulation, in co-ordination with related ministries.[78]

On 1 April 2014, a ministerial regulation was introduced to update the 2009 listing, increasing the number of substances in Group I to 82.[79] The preamble to the regulation notes an increase in the use of new highly addictive substances that were not included in the original Group I list. The Group I list now contains substances that were previously classified as Group I and II psychotropic substances under Law No 5 of 1997 on Psychotropic Substances. The 1997 Psychotropic Substances Law now applies exclusively to those substances listed in Groups III and IV of its appendix. Under the law, a psychotropic substance is defined as:

> a natural or synthetic drug or substance that is not a narcotic that has a psychoactive effect through selective influence on the central nervous system that causes particular changes to behavioural and mental activity.[80]

Categories of Drug Offences

The 2009 Narcotics Law creates offences for a wide range of drug-related activities, including production, possession, trafficking and consumption, as well as breaches of licensing, reporting and other legal obligations. Separate offences apply in relation to particular categories of drugs but the same types of activities are typically criminalised. The lack of precise explanations of the physical acts that constitute particular offences creates significant ambiguity in the 2009 Narcotics Law, as some conduct may fall within multiple separate categories of offences, each of

[78] 2009 Narcotics Law, Art 49(3).

[79] Health Ministerial Regulation No 13 of 2014 on Changes to Narcotics Categories [*Perubahan Penggolongan Narkotika*].

[80] Law No 5 of 1997 on Psychotropic Substances, Art 1(1).

which attract different penalties. This leaves police and prosecutors with significant discretion in determining the charges that are laid.

Unlawfully Planting, Cultivating, Owning, Storing, Possessing or Providing Narcotics (Arts 111, 112, 117, 122)[81]

This offence applies to all narcotics, although penalties differ depending on the categories and quantity of narcotics in question. The 2009 Narcotics Law does not contain precise definitions of cultivation, storing, possession or any other activity prohibited by these provisions. There are, in fact, very few cultivation convictions reported by Indonesia (only 32 in 2012, and 35 in 2011), and all were in relation to the cultivation of cannabis.[82] As explained further below, the possession aspect of this offence has been problematic, since it can apply to amounts that are for personal use and can, thus, lead to the prosecution of drug addicts rather than those involved in the drug trade.[83]

Unlawfully Producing, Importing, Exporting or Distributing Narcotics (Arts 113, 118, 123)

This offence also applies to all groups of narcotics and is considered more serious than the offences relating to planting and cultivation. Producing is defined as:

> the activity or process of preparing, manufacturing, creating and producing narcotics directly or indirectly via extraction or non-extractive means from natural sources or synthetic chemicals or a combination, including packaging and/or altering the form of narcotics.[84]

The total number of manufacturing convictions is, again, small (39 in 2012, 64 in 2011).[85] 'Importing' is defined as 'the act of bringing narcotics or precursor substances into Indonesia's custom zone',[86] while 'exporting' is 'taking narcotics or precursor substances out from Indonesia's custom zone'.[87] The definition of 'distribution' is vague, referring simply to 'any activity or series of activities carried out without authority or in contravention of the law that stipulates narcotics and precursor offences'.[88] A related offence applies to authorised drug holders who distribute drugs for unauthorised purposes.[89]

[81] In this part, 'Categories of Drug Offences', all references to Articles are to provisions of the 2009 Narcotics Law.

[82] ASEAN Inter-Parliamentary Assembly (AIPA), 'Indonesia Country Progress Report of Drug Control', presented during the 10th Meeting of the ASEAN Inter-Parliamentary Assembly (AIPA) Fact-Finding Committee (AIFOCOM), Bandar Seri Begawan, 2013, 3.

[83] In Supreme Court case No 1174 K/Pid.Sus/2012, for example, the Court found that where an offender is a drug addict and has purchased narcotics for personal use, and is in possession of them, he or she should be dealt with under the consumption offence rather than the Art 111 offence, which includes a minimum penalty of four years in prison and an Rp 800 million fine.

[84] 2009 Narcotics Law, Art 1(3).

[85] AIPA, 'Indonesia Country Progress Report'.

[86] 2009 Narcotics Law, Art 1(4).

[87] 2009 Narcotics Law, Art 1(5).

[88] 2009 Narcotics Law, Art 1(6).

[89] 2009 Narcotics Law, Art 147.

Unlawfully Offering to Buy, Sell, Be an Intermediary in the Purchase or Sale of, Acceptance, Giving or Trading of Narcotics (Arts 114, 119, 124)

This trafficking offence applies to each group of narcotics and attracts the heaviest penalties under the 2009 Narcotics Law. There were 23,214 distribution and selling convictions in 2012, amounting to 65 per cent of total convictions.[90] It is unclear, however, which provision of the Law was applied in relation to these offences. This is because of the potential for significant overlap between offences for distribution and offences for offering to sell or acting as an intermediary in the drug trade.

Unlawfully Carrying, Sending, Shipping or Transiting Narcotics (Arts 115, 120, 125)

'Transiting' is defined as transporting narcotics from one country to another through Indonesia, whether the method of shipment changes or not.[91] There is no definition provided for the other aspects of this offence ('carrying', 'sending' or 'shipping'). There is some potential for overlap between this 'transporting' offence and separate offences that cover distribution and trafficking.

The penalties attached to this offence are lighter than those that apply to production and trafficking offences and vary depending on the type and quantity of drug. In relation to Category I drugs, heavier penalties apply for the transport of plant material in excess of one kilogram or in excess of five trees. The article prescribing penalties for transporting narcotics does not deal with non-plant substances over five grams. This seems to be an anomaly and is perhaps the result of legislative error or mistake made when the 2009 Narcotics Law was being drafted.[92]

Precursor Offences (Art 129)

The drug offences and corresponding penalties just described apply also where the substance in question is a narcotics precursor, although not an actual narcotic.[93] Narcotics precursors (*prekursor narkotika*) are defined as 'any substance or chemical or initial material that can be used to produce narcotics'.[94] In other words, the 2009 Narcotics Law stipulates that the production, possession or trafficking of preparatory materials for the purposes of producing narcotics are offences.

Consumption Offences (Art 127)

The 2009 Narcotics Law prohibits personal use of drugs. A drug abuser (*penyalahguna)* is defined as anyone who uses narcotics without authorisation or

[90] AIPA (n 82), 3.

[91] 2009 Narcotics Law, Art 1(12).

[92] The phrase 'non-plant substances' appears to be missing from the text, as Art 115 describes 'plant material in excess of one kilogram or in excess of five trees of more than five grams': 2009 Narcotics Law, Art 115.

[93] 2009 Narcotics Law, Art 129.

[94] 2009 Narcotics Law, Art 1(2).

otherwise in breach of the law.[95] It is unclear from the Law what precise physical acts constitute this offence.

Penalties depend on the category of narcotics consumed but no minimum sentencing requirements apply. Judges are directed to refer to rehabilitation clauses when determining cases of personal consumption.[96] Users who are found to be 'victims' of drug abuse or 'addicts' must undergo medical and social rehabilitation,[97] a process that is discussed further below. According to the 2009 Narcotics Law, a 'victim' of drug abuse is a person who 'unintentionally' uses narcotics because he or she has been coaxed, deceived, tricked, forced or threatened into using narcotics.[98] An 'addict' is a person who uses or abuses narcotics and is in a state of dependency on narcotics, including both physical and psychological dependency.[99]

The 2009 Narcotics Law is significant in that it introduces non-custodial sentences for drug users. Article 103 of the law states that time spent in rehabilitation is considered equivalent to serving a prison sentence.[100] In practice, however, prosecutors and police continue to display a strong preference for punitive sentencing. According to BNN, there were 12,168 convictions for consumption offences in 2012, equivalent to 34 per cent of all drug-related convictions in that year.[101]

Third Party-Administered/Induced Narcotics Use (Arts 116, 121, 126)

Unlawfully administering narcotics to other people or providing another person with narcotics to use is a major offence under the 2009 Narcotics Law, and subject to strict penalties.[102] Where the unlawful administration or provision of narcotics results in death or permanent injury, heavier punishments apply.[103]

Offences in Relation to Children (Arts 128, 133)

The Elucidation to the 2009 Narcotics Law notes a trend towards increased consumption of drugs, particularly among children, teenagers and young people. Accordingly, the Law includes provisions that target the involvement of children in the consumption and trade of narcotics. Involving a child in any way, and by any means, in the commission of an offence attracts separate liability and serious penalties may be imposed, including the death penalty or life imprisonment, or imprisonment for a minimum of five years and a maximum of 20 years, with a fine of Rp[104] 2 to 20 billion.[105]

[95] 2009 Narcotics Law, Art 1(15).
[96] 2009 Narcotics Law, Art 127(2)–(3).
[97] 2009 Narcotics Law, Art 54, 127(3)
[98] 2009 Narcotics Law, elucidation to Art 54.
[99] 2009 Narcotics Law, Art 1(13).
[100] 2009 Narcotics Law, Art 103(2): '*Masa menjalani pengobatan dan/atau perawatan bagi Pecandu Narkotika sebagaimana dimaksud pada ayat (1) huruf a diperhitungkan sebagai masa menjalani hukuman.*' ['Time spent in treatment and/or care as a Narcotics Addict as intended in paragraph (1) sub-paragraph (a) is calculated as time spent serving a sentence.']
[101] AIPA (n 82).
[102] 2009 Narcotics Law, Arts 116(1), 121(1) and 126(1).
[103] 2009 Narcotics Law, Arts 116(2), 121(2) and 126(2).
[104] At the time of writing, Rp 10,000 was roughly equivalent to US$ 1.
[105] 2009 Narcotics Law, Art 133(1).

A third party may be liable even if he or she has had no role in supplying or administering narcotics, if he or she 'allows, encourages, facilitates or forces' a child to use drugs.[106] In some circumstances, the user's parents may also be liable to criminal prosecution. Where the user is under the age of consent (18 years),[107] the parent or guardian must report the child's addiction to a government rehabilitation clinic.[108] If the parent or guardian 'intentionally' fails to do so, he or she is liable to a maximum of six months *kurungan* imprisonment (a form of light imprisonment, discussed further below), or a fine of Rp 1 million.[109] An underage addict who is reported by his or her parents will not be liable to criminal prosecution.[110]

Third Party Obligations: Reporting on Narcotics Crimes (Arts 131, 139)

Under the 2009 Narcotics Law, the broader community has 'the opportunity to participate' in efforts to prevent and eradicate the trade and use of narcotics.[111] In fact, the Law appears to impose positive reporting obligations on any person who becomes aware of narcotics offences taking place (not just the parents or guardians of underage users). For example, it is an offence to 'intentionally' fail to report criminal offences listed in Chapter XV of the 2009 Narcotics Law.[112] It is unclear precisely how this duty applies. It may be intended to target those who are approached as witnesses or questioned by police and intentionally fail to disclose information. On the other hand, it might extend further, to catch any individual who fails to voluntarily offer up information in relation to an offence.

An additional reporting offence applies to captains or pilots who fail to report the presence of narcotics in their ship/aircraft cargo where required to do so by relevant regulations.[113]

Other Psychotropic Substances (Arts 60, 61, 62, 63, 64, 65)

A similar range of offences are also established under Chapter XIV of the 1997 Law on Psychotropic Substances.[114] Articles 60–65 cover a range of production, possession, importation, exportation, distribution and transportation offences that apply to Groups III and IV psychotropic substances.

Proceeds of Crime and Money Laundering (Art 137)

Under the 2009 Narcotics Law, it is an offence to conduct any transaction (giving, receiving, trading, storing, hiding, bequeathing or inheriting) with property

[106] 2009 Narcotics Law, Art 133(2).
[107] 2009 Narcotics Law explanatory memorandum to Art 55(1).
[108] 2009 Narcotics Law, Art 55(1).
[109] 2009 Narcotics Law, Art 128(1).
[110] 2009 Narcotics Law, Art 128(2).
[111] 2009 Narcotics Law, Art 104, 105.
[112] 2009 Narcotics Law, Art 131.
[113] 2009 Narcotics Law, Art 139.
[114] 1997 Law on Psychotropic Substances, Art 1(1).

in any form, tangible or intangible, derived from an offence involving narcotics or preparatory materials.[115] Further offences are contained in the 2010 Law on the Prevention and Eradication of Money-Laundering, which is discussed further below.

Basis for Criminal Responsibility

Indonesia's Criminal Code states that no action can be punished unless it constitutes a criminal offence under the laws of Indonesia.[116] Under the Code, a person can be found criminally responsible for a serious offence (*kejahatan*, or felony) on one of three bases: as a principal perpetrator (*pelaku tindak pidana*); as an accessory (*pembantu pelaku*); or for attempting to commit an offence.

There is no overriding requirement to demonstrate a guilty mind or criminal intent in order to establish criminal liability under Indonesian law. Some offences, however, may require that, in addition to the physical commission of a certain act, the defendant was in possession of a particular mental state. In other cases, the law is much more ambiguous regarding the level of knowledge, awareness or intent required to establish liability.

A person will be tried as a principal perpetrator if he or she committed the offence, ordered the offence to be committed, or took part in the offence; or if he or she intentionally encouraged the commission of the offence through duress, facilitation (that is, providing materials, information or opportunity), or by unlawfully offering or promising something in return for the commission of the offence.[117] In such cases, a person may only be held responsible for those acts that he or she intentionally encouraged, and the consequences of those acts.[118]

There are a number of factors that can free a defendant from criminal responsibility under the Criminal Code. A person who commits an act because of mental illness or insanity is not criminally liable.[119] In such cases, judges have the discretion to instead send the defendant to a mental health care facility for a period of up to one year. Judges have a broad discretion when dealing with child defendants below the age of 16 and may decide not to punish the offender.[120] Where the court decides against sentencing a minor, the child must be either returned to his or her parents or guardians or sent to the applicable government agency as a ward of the state. The 2009 Narcotics Law does not make any distinction between offenders under the age of 18 and adult offenders.

Criminal liability can be imposed on corporate entities under the Indonesian Criminal Code[121] and on both a company and its directors. Article 130 of the 2009 Narcotics Law also sets out punishments for corporate entities found guilty of committing offences described in Arts 111–126 and 129 of the Law.

[115] 2009 Narcotics Law, Art 137.
[116] Criminal Code, Art 1(1).
[117] Criminal Code, Art 55(1).
[118] Criminal Code, Art 55(2).
[119] Criminal Code, Art 44(1).
[120] Criminal Code, Art 45.
[121] Criminal Code, Arts 47–53.

Aiding and Abetting

Under the Criminal Code, a person will be found guilty on the basis of complicity if he or she intentionally provides assistance at the time the offence is committed, or provides opportunity, facilities, or information for commission of the offence.[122] The Criminal Code also creates liability for 'accessories after the fact' where it is an offence to assist a person who has committed a crime to avoid prosecution or to assist in 'covering up' the offence in any way.[123] The maximum sentence for this crime is nine months imprisonment.

Under the Criminal Code, the maximum prison sentence for complicity or an attempt is two-thirds that of the corresponding principal or completed offence.[124] For offences attracting the death penalty or life imprisonment, complicity or attempt will attract a maximum of 15 years.[125] An attempt to commit a less serious offence (*pelanggaran*, or misdemeanour) is not punishable,[126] and neither is complicity in such an offence.[127] The Criminal Code considers that exculpatory, mitigating and aggravating factors particular to one person are only relevant to determining the liability of that person. They are not taken into consideration in determining the liability of a principal or an accessory to that person.[128]

The 2009 Narcotics Law, however, departs from these general rules for certain narcotics-related offences. According to the Law, a person who attempts to commit, or conspires in the commission of, any major offence[129] under the Law is to be punished as if they had committed the offence.[130] This means the maximum sentence is not reduced by one third, as with other offences involving attempt or complicity. Criminal conspiracy (*pemufakatan jahat*) is defined as:

> the action of two people or more who conspire or agree to commit, implement, assist, contribute, order, encourage, facilitate, consult, become a member of a narcotic criminal organisation, or organise a narcotics crime.[131]

This definition is broad and unclear in a number of respects. It could potentially include within its scope the acts of a principal perpetrator, an accessory, or individuals associated more generally with organised crime (*kejahatan terorganisir*). 'Narcotic criminal organisation' is not defined in the 2009 Narcotics Law. Organised crime, however, is defined as:

> crime carried out by a structured group that consists of three or more people that has been in existence for a certain period of time and [where the people have] acted in cohort with the intention of carrying out a narcotics related offence.[132]

122 Criminal Code, Art 56.
123 Criminal Code, Art 221(1).
124 Criminal Code, Arts 53(2), 57(1).
125 Criminal Code, Arts 53(3), 57(2).
126 Criminal Code, Art 54.
127 Criminal Code, Art 60.
128 Criminal Code, Art 58.
129 2009 Narcotics Law, Arts 111–126, 129.
130 2009 Narcotics Law, Art 132(1).
131 2009 Narcotics Law, 1(18).
132 2009 Narcotics Law, Art 1(20).

Case No 772.K/Pid/2007, discussed below, considers the issue of 'organised' crime in some detail. Although the prosecution in this case was based on the 1997 Law on Psychotropic Substances, the judges in their decision also referred to the definition of organised crime in the 1997 Narcotics Law.

Attempt

An attempt to commit a serious offence (*kejahatan*) is punishable under the Criminal Code if the intent to commit the crime is apparent from preparatory actions taken, and the failure to go through with the offence is due to circumstances independent of the offender's own will.[133] The maximum punishments for an attempted crime are one-third less than the primary punishment that would apply if the crime had been committed.[134] In cases where the primary offence attracts a maximum punishment of capital punishment or life imprisonment, an attempt will attract a maximum punishment of 15 years.[135]

Defences

The Criminal Code also recognises the defence of duress, that is, where the accused has been compelled to commit the act by force.[136] According to accepted jurisprudence, duress applies only where the pressure is such that it can in no way be avoided.[137] Duress can be established in situations where there is absolute physical compulsion, as well as in situations where the power exerted over the defendant is such that the defendant is left with little choice (for example, because he or she is threatened with being immediately shot).[138]

Legal scholar Raden Soesilo argues that duress must be assessed from various perspectives, including the relative weakness of the defendant or the power of the person compelling the offence; whether the defendant had any means to escape or avoid the situation; and the balance between the level of force or threat and the act committed.[139]

An additional defence exists where an act is committed in relation to implementing provisions of a law, or on the basis of commands from a superior.[140] In the latter case, the superior must be a government official for the defence to apply and have

[133] Criminal Code, Art 53(1).

[134] Criminal Code, Art 53(2).

[135] Criminal Code, Art 53(3).

[136] Criminal Code, Art 48.

[137] See, for example, Raden Soesilo, *Kitab Undang-undang Hukum Pidana Serta Komentar-komentarnya Lengkap Pasal Demi Pasal* [The Criminal Code and its complete article by article commentary] (Bogor, Politeia, 1974), 54.

[138] R Sugandhi, *Kitab Undang-Undang Hukum Pidana Berikut Penjelasannya* [The Criminal Code Followed by its Elucidation] (Usaha Nasional, 1980).

[139] Soesilo, *Kitab Undang-undang Hukum* Pidana, 54.

[140] Criminal Code, Arts 50, 51.

authority to give such a command, while the person who receives the order must be in a position where they have an obligation to comply with that order.[141]

There is no defence of entrapment in the Criminal Code. In fact, the 2009 Narcotics Law explicitly provides for the use of some entrapment-like techniques in setting out the investigative authorities of BNN staff. BNN investigators are, for example, empowered to carry out undercover purchasing and transfer of narcotics under supervised conditions.[142]

There have been reports of entrapment by police in drugs cases, and even the planting of evidence.[143] The courts, however, have been critical of police who rely excessively on entrapment techniques. In the 2012 case of Ita Mega Sari Binti Matsuri,[144] for example, an undercover policeman approached the accused and demanded that she find him someone who could supply methamphetamine. The accused was reportedly hesitant and was heavily pressured into co-operating. In reviewing the case on appeal, the Supreme Court found that the police had overstepped their powers by so forcefully initiating and driving the transaction. The Court found that practices of entrapment used by the police in the case were 'very concerning'. In particular, the Court said that it was problematic that the police officer had acted as the 'brains' behind the deal and had 'ordered' the accused to participate, in which case the accused should have been tried together with the buyer (the undercover officer) and the seller, who had, in fact, been the primary offenders in the case.[145] The Court did not overturn the conviction, however. Instead, it relied on Art 253 of the Criminal Procedure Code to find that, as an appellant court, it could not re-examine issues of evidence, and could only decide issues of law.[146]

Penalties

Punishments under the 2009 Narcotics Law range from administrative sanctions, to fines, imprisonment and the death penalty. The death penalty is the maximum sentence available to a judge. It applies only in relation to a small number of offences and is never mandatory. The extent of the punishment available depends on the category of drug the offence relates to, with more serious punishments imposed where greater quantities of the drug are involved.

The following table provides examples of the various production, possession and trafficking offences related to narcotics under the 2009 Narcotics Law.

141 Soesilo (n 137), 57.

142 2009 Narcotics Law 75(j); 1997 Law on Psychotropic Substances 55(a).

143 Lai et al, 'Drug Policy in Indonesia', 2. See also Case No 02/Pid/2010/PN.TGL, discussed, below. p 73.

144 Supreme Court Decision No 815 K/Pid.Sus/2012 (26 June 2012), http://putusan.mahkamahagung.go.id/putusan/456fad390f2cc8afc48f7caaea5bc954; *Public Prosecutor v Ita Mega Sari Binti Matsuri* (26 June 2012).

145 Ibid, 23–24.

146 Ibid, 24.

Table 1: Offences and Penalties under the Narcotics Law 2009: production, possession and trafficking

Articles	Offence	Quantity	Penalty		
			Group I	Group II	Group III
111 112 117 122	Unlawfully plants, owns, stores, possesses or prepares	No quantity specified	Imprisonment for 4–12 years or Fine of Rp 800 million–8 billion	Imprisonment for 3–10 years or Fine of Rp 600 million–5 billion	Imprisonment for 2–7 years or Fine of Rp 400 million–3 billion
		>1 kg/5 plants (for plants) >5 g (for non-plant substances)	Imprisonment for 5–20 years or life or Fine of Rp 800 million–10.67 billion	Imprisonment for 5–15 years or Fine of Rp 600 million–6.67 billion	Imprisonment for 3–10 years or Fine of Rp 400 million–4 billion
113 118 123	Unlawfully produces, imports, exports or channels	No quantity specified	Imprisonment for 5–15 years or Fine of Rp 1–10 billion	Imprisonment for 4–12 years or Fine of Rp 800 million–8 billion	Imprisonment for 3–10 years or Fine of Rp 600 milllion–5 billion
		>1 kg/5 plants (for plants) >5 g (for non-plant substances)	Death penalty or Imprisonment for 5–20 years or life or Fine of Rp 1–13.34 billion	Death penalty or Imprisonment for 5–20 years or life or Fine of Rp 800 million–10.67 billion	Imprisonment for 5–15 years or Fine of Rp 600 million–6.67 billion

(continued)

Table 1: *(Continued)*

Articles	Offence	Quantity	Penalty		
			Group I	Group II	Group III
114 119 124	Unlawfully offers to buy, sell, be an intermediary in the purchase or sale of, accept, give or trade	No quantity specified	Imprisonment for 5–20 years or life or Fine of Rp 1–10 billion	Imprisonment for 4–12 years or Fine of Rp 800 million–8 billion	Imprisonment for 4–10 years or Fine of Rp 600 million–5 billion
		>1 kg/5 plants (for plants) >5 g (for non-plant substances)	Death penalty or Imprisonment for 5–20 years or life or Fine of Rp 1–13.34 billion	Death penalty or Imprisonment for 5–20 years or life or Fine of Rp 800 million–10.67 billion	Imprisonment for 5–15 years or Fine of Rp 600 million–6.67 billion
115 120 125	Unlawfully carries, sends, ships or 'transits'[147]	No quantity specified	Imprisonment for 4–12 years; or fine of Rp 800 million–8 billion	Imprisonment for 3–10 years or fine of Rp 600 million–5 billion	Imprisonment for 2–7 years; or fine of Rp 400 million–3 billion
		>1 kg/5 plants (for plants) >5 g (for non-plant substances)	Imprisonment for 5–20 years or life or Fine of Rp 800 million–10.67 billion	Imprisonment for 5–15 years or Fine of Rp 600 million–6.67 billion	Imprisonment for 3–10 years or Fine of Rp 400 million–4 billion

[147] 'Transiting' is defined in the 2009 Narcotics Law, Art 1 (12), as shipping from one country to another through Indonesia, regardless of whether the method of shipping changes.

The next table outlines the penalties for consumption and third party-administered or induced narcotics use.

Table 2: Offences and Penalties under the Narcotics Law 2009: consumption and third party-administered or induced use

Articles	Offence	Penalty		
		Group I	Group II	Group III
116(1) 121(1) 126(1)	Unlawfully uses narcotic on other person or provides other person with narcotic to use	Imprisonment for 5–15 years or Fine for Rp 1–10 billion	Imprisonment for 4–12 years or Fine for Rp 800 million–8 billion	Imprisonment for 3–10 years or Fine for Rp 600 million–5 billion
116(2) 121(2)	Unlawfully uses narcotic on other person or provides other person with narcotic to use, resulting in that other person's death or permanent injury	Death penalty or Imprisonment for 5–20 years or life or Fine for Rp 1–13.34 billion	Death penalty or Imprisonment for 5–20 years or life or Fine for Rp 800 million–10.67 billion	Imprisonment for 5–15 years or Fine for Rp 600 million–6.67 billion
127(1)	Personal abuse of narcotics	Up to 4 years	Up to 2 years	Up to 1 year

The punishment for committing any of these offences with preparatory materials is imprisonment for a minimum of four and a maximum of 20 years, or a maximum fine of Rp 5 billion.

III. JURISDICTION

As mentioned, under Indonesia's Criminal Code, no act may be punished unless it is an offence under the criminal laws of Indonesia.[148] Indonesian criminal law applies to:

— anyone within the territorial limits of Indonesia;[149]

[148] Criminal Code, Art 1(1).
[149] Criminal Code, Art 2.

— anyone beyond the territorial limits of Indonesia aboard an Indonesian airplane or sea vessel;[150]
— Indonesian citizens beyond the territorial limits of Indonesia who commit a serious offence (*kejahatan*) in breach of the Criminal Code that is also a criminal offence in the jurisdiction where it took place.[151] The death penalty may not be applied in Indonesia if the offence does not attract the death penalty in the jurisdiction where the offence took place;[152] and
— other people beyond the territorial limits of Indonesia who commit certain offences, unrelated to drugs, in breach of Indonesia's Criminal Code.[153]

Where there is an amendment of the applicable Law after a crime has taken place, the version of the Law to be applied to the defendant is the one that most benefits him or her.[154]

In relation to drug offences, Art 145 of the 2009 Narcotics Law provides that the majority of offences (that is, under Arts 111–26, and 129) apply to anyone beyond the territorial limits of Indonesia. Article 145 does not limit the meaning of 'anyone' to Indonesian citizens nor does it require the offence to have any nexus with Indonesia at all. It appears, therefore, that the Indonesian legislature sought to apply a universal jurisdiction to drug production, possession, use and trafficking.

Courts

The Indonesian justice sector is comprised of four main branches, all under the administration of the Supreme Court (*Mahkamah Agung*): the State Courts of general jurisdiction; the Religious (Islamic) Courts; the Administrative Courts; and the Military Courts. Sitting outside this structure is the Constitutional Court (*Mahkamah Konstitusi*), which makes decisions on the constitutional validity of laws, hears electoral disputes and resolves disputes between state bodies. It has no trial or appeal function. Its decisions are prospective in nature and, although they are binding as regards interpretation of the Constitution, they cannot alter existing judgments or sentences imposed by other courts. There is also a Judicial Commission, an oversight body charged with proposing candidates for judicial office to the House of Representatives and investigating allegations of judicial misconduct.

Turning first to the State Courts (*Pengadilan Negeri*), often referred to as 'general courts' (*pengadilan umum*) or 'District Courts', these are the courts of first instance for civil and criminal cases. They have jurisdiction for any matter that does not fall under the jurisdiction of the other lower-level courts and are, therefore,

150 Criminal Code, Art 3. 'Aboard the airplane' means from the time the doors are closed after passengers have embarked until the time the doors are opened to allow passengers to disembark: Criminal Procedure Code, Art 95b.

151 Criminal Code, Art 5.

152 Criminal Code, Art 6.

153 Criminal Code, Art 4, 5, 7 and 8.

154 Criminal Code, Art 1(2).

responsible for handling drug-related offences, all of which are first heard in these courts, including those that might attract the death penalty. There are more than 350 of these courts operating at the district (*kabupaten*) and municipal (*kota*) level across the country[155] and criminal cases dominate their work. In 2013, for example, 3,334,226 criminal cases were lodged with the District Courts and just 142,196 civil cases.[156]

The District Courts also house a number of specialised courts, including the Human Rights Courts, Anti-Corruption Courts, Commercial Courts, Industrial Relations Courts, Fisheries Courts, and Taxation Courts.

The Religious Courts (*Pengadilan Agama*) also operate at the district and municipality level. These deal with divorce, inheritance, and custody matters for Indonesia's Muslim community, with divorces comprising more than 95 per cent of their work. The Administrative Courts (*Pengadilan Tata Usaha Negara*), which are tasked with hearing disputes between Indonesian citizens and state officials or institutions after other administrative avenues have been exhausted, are also represented at the district and municipality level, as are the Military Courts (*Pengadilan Militer*), which deal with matters involving military officials.

Appeals (*banding*) from the State Courts are heard at one of Indonesia's 31 High Courts (*Pengadilan Tinggi*), which are located in the capital city of most provinces in the country. The High Court can send a case back to the district and municipality level for further examination if it deems it necessary; uphold the original decision in full or in part; quash the decision; or re-decide the case itself and alter orders as it sees fit.

Cassation appeals (*kasasi*) from the High Court are heard by the Supreme Court, which is located in Jakarta. Cassation is brought on grounds of error of law and the applicable time limits are always rigorously enforced by the courts. Any breach of such limits usually results in the appeal being rejected out of hand, regardless of its merits. Once the time limit for a *banding* appeal or cassation has expired, the judgment is considered to be of 'binding legal force' (*kekuatan hukum tetap*).[157]

The Supreme Court also has authority for reconsideration (*peninjauan kembali,* commonly referred to by its initials, 'PK') of a case, if, for example, a judicial error, inconsistent decisions or new evidence is found. This is a power to reopen and, if necessary, redetermine, any previous decision of any court (other than the Constitutional Court) that is of 'binding legal force', including the Supreme Court's own cassation decisions.[158]

[155] Supreme Court of the Republic of Indonesia www.mahkamahagung.go.id/daftarweb2.asp?jns=Umum.

[156] Indonesia. Mahkamah Agung [Supreme Court], *Laporan Tahunan 2013* [2013 Annual Report] (Jakarta, Mahkamah Agung, 2013), www.mahkamahagung.go.id/images/ltmari-2013.pdf.

[157] The last section of this chapter, on judicial decisions, looks at grounds of appeal, cassation and reconsideration in further detail.

[158] See Criminal Procedure Code, Art 263. See also Simon Butt and Tim Lindsey, *The Constitution of Indonesia: A Contextual Analysis* (Oxford, Hart Publishing, 2012), 89.

Foreigners and Extra-territorial Jurisdiction

Despite considerable evidence of domestic production of narcotics, there remains a widespread perception in Indonesia that all drugs enter from outside the country.[159] According to Indonesian National Police and BNN data, authorities investigated 43,885 Indonesian suspects and 127 foreign suspects in relation to drug-related crime in 2013.[160] These are stark figures but narcotics offences are nonetheless frequently described as a 'foreign influence' on Indonesian culture, and the role of foreigners in the drug trade is heavily emphasised by public officials and in the Indonesian media. In June 2015, for example, the head of BNN, Anang Iskandar, even urged Indonesian women not to communicate with, or date, foreigners, suggesting that foreigners could trick them into becoming drug couriers.[161]

This may explain why foreign nationals constitute two-thirds of all prisoners on death row for narcotics offences in Indonesia and why recent executions have overwhelmingly targeted them.[162] Twelve of the 14 people executed by Indonesia in January and April 2015 were foreigners, and all were convicted for drug-related offences. In fact, a defendant's status as a foreign national has even been found by the Supreme Court to be an aggravating factor in sentencing.[163] This targeting of foreign nationals of course only reinforces the popular perception that drugs are a problem caused by foreigners.

Although public officials and the media emphasise the role of foreigners (and despite the fact that Art 145 of the 2009 Narcotics Laws appears to apply universal jurisdiction to drug production, possession, use and trafficking), there are no known cases of Indonesia asserting its extra-territorial jurisdiction overseas to pursue foreign nationals involved in the narcotics trade in Indonesia.

[159] To give just one example of this perception, Indonesia's national news agency, *Antara,* published an opinion article in March 2015 stating that Australia needs to realise that a 'variety of narcotics, from methamphetamine to marijuana and other addictive chemicals, keep pouring in from overseas'. See Arnaz Firman, 'Kenapa Mesti Takluk Terhadap Upaya Australia [Why should we submit to Australia's efforts]' *Antara*, 7 March 2015, www.antaranews.com/berita/483888/kenapa-mesti-takluk-terhadap-upaya-australia. See also, Randy Ferdy Firdaus, 'Menteri Marwan Awasi Desa Rawan Jadi Pintu Penyelundupan Narkoba [Minister Marwan supervises villages vulnerable to becoming entry points for narcotics trade]', *Merdeka*, 23 February 2015, www.merdeka.com/peristiwa/menteri-marwan-awasi-desa-rawan-jadi-pintu-penyelundupan-narkoba.html.

[160] Indonesia. BNN, 'Analisa Data Pencegahan dan Pemberantasan Penyalahgunaan dan Peredaran Gelap Narkoba (P4GN) [Data analysis on the prevention and eradication of illicit narcotics trafficking and abuse (P4GN)]' (BNN, 2013).

[161] See Resty Armenia, 'Rentan Jadi Kurir Narkotik Perempuan Diimbau Tak Pacari WNA [Vulnerable to being made into drug couriers, women urged not to date foreigners]' *CNN Indonesia*, 26 June 2015, www.cnnindonesia.com/nasional/20150626130321-12-62575/rentan-jadi-kurir-narkotik-perempuan-diimbau-tak-pacari-wna/.

[162] Of the four death penalty cases examined later in this chapter, all involved foreigners. See also Diane Zhang, 'By the Numbers: Indonesia's Executions of Foreigners' *The Drum, ABC*, 27 February 2015, www.abc.net.au/news/2015-02-26/zhang-indonesia-likely-to-execute-more-foreigners/6263122.

[163] See Case No 772.K/Pid/2007, discussed below, p 131.

Extradition

Extraditions are regulated under Law No 1 of 1979 on Extradition in Indonesia, which sets out the underlying principles for extradition both to and from Indonesia, including the principles of dual criminality and double jeopardy. Most extraditions that take place between Indonesia and other countries are based on treaties. Indonesia now has extradition treaties with Australia, Hong Kong, India, Malaysia, Papua New Guinea, the Philippines, Republic of Korea, and Thailand.[164] It has also signed an extradition treaty with Singapore but this has still not been ratified by the national legislature, the DPR (*Dewan Perwakilan Rakyat*, People's Representative Assembly), which considers the treaty to be biased in favour of Singapore and has called repeatedly for it to be renegotiated.[165]

Where no treaty between Indonesia and the requesting state exists, an extradition may nonetheless proceed if it is deemed to be in Indonesia's best interests overall.[166]

Persons who may be extradited are those requested by authorised officials from the requesting foreign country on the basis that they are alleged to have committed crimes or face legal prosecution or arrest orders.[167] Persons who are suspected, or convicted, of having assisted, attempted or agreed to initiate the same criminal acts may also be extradited where the acts of assistance, attempt and criminal consent may be prosecuted under the laws of the country requesting the extradition and are punishable under Indonesian law.[168] A non-exhaustive list of crimes to which an extradition process may apply is contained in an appendix to the 1979 Extradition Law and includes narcotics and other 'dangerous drug' crimes.

[164] See Margareth Aritonang, 'RI Targets Fugitives in PNG and Vietnam' *The Jakarta Post* (3 February 2015), www.thejakartapost.com/news/2015/02/03/ri-targets-fugitives-png-and-vietnam.html; *The Jakarta Post*, 'House Ratifies Extradition Treaty with South Korea' (26 September 2007), www.thejakartapost.com/news/2007/09/26/house-ratifies-extradition-treaty-south-korea.html; and *Radio New Zealand International*, 'PNG MP Plays Down Indonesia-PNG Extradition Treaty', 29 May 2015, www.radionz.co.nz/international/pacific-news/274909/png-mp-plays-down-indonesia-png-extradition-treaty. See also Law No 8 of 1994 on the Ratification of the Extradition Treaty between Indonesia and Australia [*Pengesahan Perjanjian Ekstradisi antara Indonesia dan Australia*]; Law No 1 of 2001 on Ratification of the Agreement Between the Government of the Republic of Indonesia and the Government of Hong Kong for the Surrender of Fugitive Offenders [*Pengesahan Persetujuan antara Pemerintah Republik Indonesia dan Pemerintah Hong Kong untuk Penyerahan Pelanggar Hukum yang Melarikan Diri*]; Law No 13 of 2014 on the Ratification of the Extradition Treaty between the Republic of Indonesia and the Republic of India [*Pengesahan Perjanjian Ekstradisi Antara Republik Indonesia dan Republik India*]; Law No 9 of 1974 on Ratification of the Agreement between Indonesia and the Government of Malaysia on Extradition [*Pengesahan Perjanjian Antara Pemerintah Republik Indonesia Dan Pemerintah Malaysia Mengenai Ekstradisi*]; Law No 10 of 1976 on Ratification of the Extradition Treaty Between Indonesia and the Philippines [*Pengesahan Perjanjian Ekstradisi Antara Republik Indonesia Dan Republik Philippina*]; and Law No 42 of 2007 on Ratification of the Extradition Treaty Between the Republic of Indonesia and the Republic of Korea [*Pengesahan Perjanjian Ekstradisi Antara Republik Indonesia dan Republik Korea*].

[165] See Hasyim Widhiarto, 'Singapore Refuses to Renegotiate Extradition Treaty with Indonesia' *The Jakarta Post* (29 September 2011), www.thejakartapost.com/news/2011/09/29/s%E2%80%99pore-refuses-renegotiate-extradition-treaty-with-ri.html.

[166] 1979 Extradition Law, Art 2.

[167] 1979 Extradition Law, Art 3(1).

[168] 1979 Extradition Law, Art 3(2).

Extradition requests may be refused where, in the view of competent authorities, there are substantial grounds for believing that the person subject to the extradition order will be prosecuted, sentenced or subjected to other measures on account of his or her religion, political opinion or nationality, or because he or she belongs to a certain race or population group.[169] As a general rule Indonesian citizens may not be extradited.[170] Interestingly, although Indonesia itself applies the death penalty, Indonesia may also refuse to extradite a person where the crime for which extradition is requested is punishable by death under the law of the requesting state but does not attract the death penalty under Indonesian law, unless the requesting country provides a sufficient guarantee that the death penalty will not be carried out.[171]

The 1979 Extradition Law also provides authority to reject requests where the offence has been perpetrated completely or partially on Indonesian territory;[172] the requested person is being investigated or prosecuted for similar crimes under Indonesia's jurisdiction;[173] or the requested person has been tried and acquitted, or has served a penal term, in another country for the crimes on which an extradition request is based.[174]

Articles 19 to 21 of the 1979 Extradition Law set out detailed procedures for requesting extradition and provisional requests. Generally, provided the arrest is not contrary to Indonesian law, the requesting country may request a provisional arrest in urgent circumstances, such as where there are grounds for believing that the person in question might abscond.[175] If a request for provisional arrest is made, the requesting country must submit the original legal documents on the extradition case through diplomatic channels or via Interpol, or directly by post or telegram, to the Chief of Police or the Prosecutor General (*Jaksa Agung*, also known as the Attorney-General). For states that have an extradition treaty with Indonesia, this must be done within 45 days of the provisional arrest; for states with no treaty it must be done within 20 days. If the requesting country fails to meet these obligations, the person who has been arrested will be released from custody.

Requests for extradition must be lodged in writing through diplomatic channels with the Indonesian Minister of Law and Human Rights (formerly the Minister of Justice), to be submitted to the President.[176] Extradition requests are handled by a number of authorities but the main ones are the Ministry of Foreign Affairs and the 'central authority', the Ministry of Law and Human Rights, which generally coordinates communication between the requesting country and the other Indonesian authorities involved throughout the extradition process. The police conduct any necessary search for, and arrest and indictment of, the requested person. The Prosecutor General's Office then issues a summons for the arrested person to attend a hearing in

169 1979 Extradition Law, Art 5.
170 1979 Extradition Law, Art 7(1).
171 1979 Extradition Law, Art 13.
172 1979 Extradition Law, Art 8.
173 1979 Extradition Law, Art 9.
174 1979 Extradition Law, Art 11.
175 1979 Extradition Law, Arts 19–21.
176 1979 Extradition Law, Art 22.

a District Court, which, if it determines that the person can be extradited, produces a supposedly final court order for the person's extradition.

Upon receiving an extradition request, the police conduct an investigation based on information and evidence supplied by the requesting country. The investigation findings are recorded in a formal statement that is submitted to the Prosecutor General.[177] Within seven days of receiving the statement, the Prosecutor General will make a written request to the District Court in the location where the person is apprehended to conduct an investigation to determine whether the person should be extradited.[178] The District Court then decides whether to extradite the requested person and submits its decision, together with relevant documents, to the Minister of Law and Human Rights for further consideration and action.[179] The President has final say on whether the extradition request is granted.[180]

The nature of this process means that extradition cases can be vulnerable to political considerations or pressure from the requesting country. As the final decision is in the hands of the President, there is a greater opportunity for political pressure to influence extradition decisions than might perhaps be the case in common law (British tradition) countries, where the final decision is usually in the hands of the courts. Missbach argues this difference in extradition procedure has been a source of tension in recent years between Indonesian and Australian law enforcement agencies.[181]

IV. CRIMINAL PROCEDURE

Criminal procedure is regulated in the 1981 Criminal Procedure Code[182] but is subject to some significant additions and exceptions created by the 2009 Narcotics Law.

Criminal procedure is divided into four distinct stages. The first is the preliminary investigation (*penyelidikan*), which is an investigation to determine whether a crime has been committed.[183] This is followed by the primary investigation (*penyidikan*), which aims to obtain more information and find evidence of the crime, and to identify suspects so they may be prosecuted.[184] The third stage is prosecution or indictment (*penuntutan*), in which the prosecution presents the case to the judge.[185] This is followed by the trial (*pemeriksaan*), the final stage, during which a panel of three judges examines the case and rules on the guilt or innocence of the

177 1979 Extradition Law, Art 26.

178 1979 Extradition Law, Art 27.

179 1979 Extradition Law, Art 33.

180 1979 Extradition Law, Art 36(2).

181 Antje Missbach, 'The Extradition of People Smugglers from Indonesia to Australia: Political and Legal Challenges' (2014) 15(2) *Australian Journal of Asian Law* 2.

182 Criminal Procedure Code, Law No 8 of 1981 on Criminal Procedure Law [*Kitab Undang-Undang Hukum Acara Pidana, Undang-Undang Nomor 8 Tahun 1981 tentang Hukum Acara Pidana*], abbreviated to KUHAP in Indonesian.

183 Criminal Procedure Code, Art 1 (4 and 5), Arts 4, 5, and Chapter XIV Part 1.

184 Criminal Procedure Code, Art 1 (1, 2, and 3), Arts 6–8, and Chapter XIV Part 2.

185 Criminal Procedure Code, Art 1 (6 and 7), Arts 13–15 and Chapter XV.

accused in a judgment (*putusan*). The strict divisions within the criminal justice process, particularly between the investigation and prosecutorial stages, have led to a compartmentalised approach and, in some cases, a lack of co-operation between police and prosecutors.[186]

The Criminal Procedure Code does not contain a clear, comprehensive articulation of a defendant's fundamental rights or the principles that underpin many criminal justice systems, such as the right to remain silent or the presumption of innocence.[187] Law No 48 of 2009 on Judicial Powers states that every person suspected, arrested, detained, prosecuted or summoned before the courts must be considered not guilty until there is a judicial decision of binding legal authority that establishes fault.[188] The Criminal Procedure Code adds that the burden of proof to establish such fault shall not be borne by the accused or the defendant.[189] That onus is, however, reversed in some instances. This is true, for example when an accused is charged with an offence under the 2009 Narcotics Law, in which case he or she becomes responsible for demonstrating that certain assets are not proceeds of drug-related crime.[190]

Some commentators have identified a major gap between procedural rules and actual practice, partly stemming from vague or inadequate regulations on important procedural issues.[191] This is detrimental not only to the rights of defendants but also significantly detracts from the rigour and quality of police investigations.[192]

Investigation

As mentioned, investigatory powers are principally regulated under the Criminal Procedure Code but there are also a number of more specific laws relevant to criminal investigations. These include Law No 2 of 2002 on the National Police and Law No 16 of 2004 on Prosecution. The Indonesian police are, in fact, responsible for the majority of investigations under Indonesia's Criminal Code. Like a number of other civil law (European tradition) countries, Indonesia no longer has a role for the investigating magistrate.[193]

[186] See, for example, Benjamin B Wagner and Leslie Gielow Jacobs, 'Retooling Law Enforcement to Investigate and Prosecute Entrenched Corruption: Key Criminal Procedure Reforms for Indonesia and Other Nations' (2008) 180 *University of Pennsylvania Journal of International Law* 183, 201–02.

[187] Defendants' rights are discussed in greater detail, below.

[188] Law No 48 of 2009 on Judicial Power [*Kekuasaan Kehakiman*], Art 8(1).

[189] Criminal Procedure Code, Art 66.

[190] 2009 Narcotics Law, Art 98.

[191] See, for example, Robert R Strang, 'More Adversarial, But Not Completely Adversarial: Reformasi of the Indonesian Criminal Procedure Code' (2009) 32 *Fordham International Law Journal* 188, 197; and Daniel Fitzpatrick 'Culture, Ideology and human rights: The Case of Indonesia's Code of Criminal Procedure' in Tim Lindsey (ed) *Indonesia: Law and Society* (Sydney, Federation Press, 2008) 499–514.

[192] For example, there is no overarching legislation or procedures authorising police use of wiretapping, although they are known to use it without legal authority. This means that when police use phone tapping in investigations they cannot use the evidence obtained in court but, at the same time, citizens whose privacy is violated by such actions have little protection or remedy. See Strang, 'More Adversarial', 198.

[193] Strang (n 191), 195–96.

The Criminal Procedure Code dictates that the preliminary investigation (*penyelidikan*), which determines whether or not a crime has been committed, must be conducted by junior investigators who are police officers.[194] The primary investigation (*penyidikan*) is conducted by members of the police or civil servants who are authorised to conduct such investigations in accordance with specific laws.[195] The 2009 Narcotics Law dispenses with this distinction, however, and officers from BNN are provided with both preliminary and primary investigation powers.[196]

When undertaking preliminary investigations, police officials (and BNN investigators under the 2009 Narcotics Law) have the authority to receive reports and complaints of crimes, search for information and evidence, and order a suspicious person to stop and to provide their identification card for inspection.[197] On the order of a primary investigator, junior investigators may also arrest and detain a person; conduct body and property searches; seize property; inspect and seize documents; take fingerprints and photos; and bring a person before a prosecutor.[198] When conducting primary investigations, the powers are essentially the same but without the requirement of more senior investigator approval.

Alongside the general powers contained in the Criminal Procedure Code, the 2009 Narcotics Law sets out a range of specific powers that may be exercised by BNN officers investigating narcotics crimes. These include powers to:

— receive and investigate reports and complaints of crimes;
— order suspects to stop and inspect their identification documents;
— arrest and detain;
— conduct body and property searches;
— seize property;
— inspect and seize documents;
— take fingerprints and photos;
— call witnesses and suspects;
— call expert witnesses and employ expert assistance;
— wiretap people, buildings, objects, telephones or any other form of electronic communication, where there is sufficient initial evidence;
— purchase narcotics as undercover agents;
— test urine, blood, hair, DNA and other body parts;
— scan people, objects, animals, or plants;
— test samples of narcotics and preparatory narcotic materials seized;
— open and inspect mail or any other communications; and
— destroy narcotics or preparatory narcotic materials.[199]

194 Criminal Procedure Code, Art 4.
195 Criminal Procedure Code, Art 6(1).
196 Ibid.
197 Criminal Procedure Code, Art 5(1)(a).
198 Criminal Procedure Code, Art 5(1)(b).
199 2009 Narcotics Law, Art 75.

Testing

Urine, blood, hair and other tests 'must be conducted according to scientific and technological developments' in order to determine whether or not narcotics have been consumed.[200] DNA testing is also authorised under the 2009 Narcotics Law to identify victims, addicts or suspects.[201] BNN has produced a number of technical regulations dealing with how laboratories must conduct narcotics testing.[202] BNN does not need any reason to suspect narcotics consumption as a prerequisite for carrying out a test on an individual, and can, therefore, carry out random or routine testing programs. It now conducts a number of regular testing programs with various government ministries, departments and agencies, private enterprises, and secondary schools and universities.[203]

Wiretapping

There is no general provision for wiretapping under the Criminal Procedure Code. A 2006 Constitutional Court decision held that wiretapping is only permissible when conducted under express statutory authority and in such a way that avoids abuse of authority in breach of human rights.[204] More specifically, the court found that although the Indonesian Constitution does not expressly recognise a right to privacy, it does contain protections that encompass privacy.[205] The court held that regulation of wiretapping must detail who has the authority to order wiretapping, and authorisation should be granted only if there is sufficient evidence to support its use. It held that further regulation of wiretapping should outline whether evidence obtained through wiretapping may be relied upon in its own right or whether it can only be used to support other forms of evidence.[206]

The 2009 Narcotics Law appears to respond to the Constitutional Court's recommendations. It provides that where there is sufficient initial evidence, wiretapping may be used in the preliminary or primary investigation stages by either a

[200] 2009 Narcotics Law, elucidation to Art 75(l).

[201] 2009 Narcotics Law, elucidation to Art 75(l).

[202] See BNN Director's Regulation No 11 of 2011 on Revision to BNN Director's Regulation No 5 of 2010 on Technical Guidelines for Narcotics Testing Laboratory Services for BNN.

[203] See, for example, Afif, 'Perangi Narkoba, BNN Aceh Tes Urine Anak SMA [To combat drugs, Aceh BNN conducts urine tests for high school kids]', 4 February 2015, www.merdeka.com/peristiwa/perangi-narkoba-bnn-aceh-tes-urine-anak-sma.html; Kurnia Sari Aziza, 'Kejutan Ahok di Pelantikan, Ribuan Pejabat Langsung Tes Urine Narkoba [Ahok's inauguration surprise, thousands of officials undergo urine drug tests]' *Kompas*, 2 January 2015, http://megapolitan.kompas.com/read/2015/01/02/09452221/Kejutan.Ahok.di.Pelantikan.Ribuan.Pejabat.Langsung.Tes.Urine.Narkoba.

[204] Constitutional Court Decision No 012-016-019/PUU-IV/2006 (18 December 2006), www.mahkamahkonstitusi.go.id/putusan/putusan_sidang_Putusan012-016-019PUUIV2006ttgKPKtgl20122006.pdf.

[205] For instance, the right to privacy was found to be a component of the right to communicate under Art 28F (and wiretapping interferes with that right), and the right to safety and security under Art 28G of the Constitution; see Constitutional Court Decision No 012-016-019/PUU-IV/2006, 209.

[206] Constitutional Court Decision No 012-016-019/PUU-IV/2006, 275–76.

BNN investigator or a police primary investigator. Wiretapping is only permitted where authorised in writing by the head of a District Court and must be carried out within three months of receiving authorisation.[207] The wiretapping may be conducted for an initial 30 days, and may be extended for another 30 days. In 'emergency' situations, an investigator may use wiretapping without written permission but must apply to the head of the District Court for permission within 24 hours.[208] No explanation of what constitutes an emergency is given in the text of the Law or its accompanying elucidation.

The general elucidation attached to the Law does state that wiretapping or surveillance can use a range of electronic devices 'in accordance with technological developments', and includes a non-exhaustive list of devices and procedures, including planting 'bugging' devices, transmitting devices, intercepting internet, pagers, SMS, fax, and closed-circuit television (CCTV). The statute explains that the adoption of this broad understanding of wiretapping is intended to anticipate developments in the technology used by drug offenders in national and international syndicates.

Undercover Operations

The 2009 Narcotics Law allows for undercover purchasing and transfer of drugs where written authorisation is provided by a supervisor.[209] As mentioned, there is no express defence of entrapment in Indonesian criminal law but courts have been very critical of prosecutions where police have relied heavily on entrapment techniques to instigate participation in narcotics offences.[210]

The 2009 Narcotics Law also contains a range of investigative powers that aim to enhance BNN's capacity to target the financial aspects of drug offences, including powers to:

— request information from the Financial Transaction Reports and Analysis Centre (Pusat Pelaporan dan Analisis Transaksi Keuangan, PPATK) on financial transactions related to drug crimes;
— receive information on a suspect's bank accounts;
— order a bank to block a suspect's account or the account of a related party;
— prohibit a person from leaving the country;
— receive from the relevant institution a suspect's property and tax information;
— block a suspect's financial transactions, trade agreement, any other agreement, licence or concession; and
— request aid from Interpol Indonesia or any other law enforcement agency from another country to help search for and arrest a suspect and seize evidence.[211]

207 2009 Narcotics Law, Art 77.
208 2009 Narcotics Law, Art 78.
209 2009 Narcotics Law, Art 79.
210 See Supreme Court Decision No 815 K/Pid.Sus/2012, discussed below.
211 2009 Narcotics Law, Art 80.

Under the 2009 Narcotics Law it is an offence for anyone to 'obstruct or hinder the investigation as well as the prosecution and trial of a narcotics offence or preparatory narcotics material offence in the court'.[212] This provision is ambiguous in a number of respects. For example, does the offence require that, to be liable, a person must hinder each of the stages of investigation, prosecution, and trial, or only one? Need all the obstruction be done in the courtroom? It is also unclear whether it might apply to those seeking diplomatic or other non-legal avenues to assist a defendant to escape conviction.

Witness and Informant Protection

A 2013 government regulation on the implementation of the 2009 Narcotics Law provides that protection must be afforded to witnesses, informants, their families and various state authorities involved in narcotics cases (BNN investigators, police investigators, prosecutors and so on) against any threats to their safety, lives or property prior to, during or after the investigation process.[213] Police are required to provide protection in the form of: security for individuals, their families and property; suppression of the identity of witnesses and informants; and provide information for witnesses and informants about the progress of the investigations without requiring them to meet face to face with the suspect or the accused.[214]

The Witness and Victim Protection Agency (Lembaga Perlindungan Saksi dan Korban, LPSK) is an independent government agency established in 2006 to provide protection to witnesses and victims of crimes who request their services during criminal investigations.[215] The process of registering a request for LPSK protection is straightforward (an online form is available on the agency's website) and does not involve any costs. Law No 13 of 2006 on Witness and Victim Protection provides that the agency must make a decision on providing protection within seven days of receiving a written request for protection.[216] The LPSK has a range of initiatives designed to assist witnesses and victims, including safe houses, medical and psychological services and support with procedural law. It struggles, however, with ongoing budgetary constraints.[217]

In 2010, the LPSK signed a memorandum of understanding with BNN on the protection of witnesses, victims and informants in cases involving the misuse or distribution of narcotics and precursors. Two years later, however, the LPSK

[212] 2009 Narcotics Law, Art 138.

[213] 2009 Narcotics Law, Art 35.

[214] Government Regulation No 40 of 2013 on the Implementation of Law No 35 of 2009 on Narcotics [*Pelaksanaan Undang-Undang Nomor 35 Tahun 2009 tentang Narkotika*], Art 37.

[215] Law No 13 of 2006 on Witness and Victim Protection [*Perlindungan Saksi dan Korban*].

[216] Law No 29 of 2014 on the Revision of Law No 13 of 2006 on Witness and Victim Protection, Art 29, www.lpsk.go.id/assets/uploads/files/fde1db3d249db2abfb1ea61f8579d45e.pdf.

[217] Indra Wijaya 'LPSK Keluhkan Minimnya Anggaran 2014 [LPSK complains about its small 2014 budget]' *Tempo* (27 December 2013), www.tempo.co/read/news/2013/12/27/078540529/LPSK-Keluhkan-Minimnya-Anggaran-2014.

said that it had received just one request for protection in a narcotics case since 2008.[218]

In 2011, the head of BNN signed a Joint Regulation with the Minister of Law and Human Rights, the Prosecutor General, the Chief of Police and the head of the Corruption Eradication Commission (*Komisi Pemberantasan Korupsi*, KPK) on the protection of informants and 'justice collaborators'. The regulation was intended to improve collaboration among these agencies in uncovering 'serious and/or organised crime',[219] including narcotics offences. Under the regulation, perpetrators are offered physical and legal protection in return for collaborating with law enforcement officials. Such protection can involve: being detained separately from the accused or others involved in the case; having their case filed separately to the accused; delay in the prosecution of their case; and the right to conceal their identity when providing witness statements to the court. The regulation also provides for lighter sentencing demands or additional remissions for perpetrators who collaborate. The LPSK, for example, can submit a recommendation to the Prosecutor General suggesting that a justice collaborator receive a lighter sentence.[220]

Arrest and Interrogation

The Criminal Procedure Code allows police and BNN officials to arrest a person who is 'heavily suspected' of a crime where there is 'sufficient preliminary evidence'.[221] There is considerable debate about what constitutes adequate preliminary evidence.[222] In 1984, a meeting between the Chief Justice of the Supreme Court, the Prosecutor General, the Minister of Justice and the Chief of Police decided that 'adequate preliminary evidence' constituted a police report and one other piece of

218 Maharani Siti Shopia, 'LPSK: Saksi dan Pelapor Narkotika Wajib Dilindungi [LPSK: witnesses and informants of drug crime must be protected]', Lembaga Perlindungan Saksi dan Korban, Press Release (5 July 2012), www.lpsk.go.id/berita/berita_detail/482.

219 Joint Regulation of the Minister of Law and Human Rights, Prosecutor General, Chief of the National Police, Head of the Corruption Eradication Commission, and Head of the Witness and Victims Protection Agency [*Peraturan Bersama Menteri Hukum dan Hak Asasi Manusia Republik Indonesia, Jaksa Agung Republik Indonesia, Kepala Kepolisian Negara Republik Indonesia, Ketua Komisi Pemberantasan Korupsi Republik Indonesia, dan Ketua Lembaga Perlindungan Saksi dan Korban Republik Indonesia tentang Perlindungan Bagi Pelapor, Saksi Pelapor dan Saksi Pelaku yang Bekerjasama*], 2011, (M.HH-11.HM.03.02.th.2011, PER-045/A/JA/12/2011; No 1 of 2011; KEPB-02/01-55/12/2011; No 4 of 2011), www.lpsk.go.id/upload/Peraturan%20Bersama%20Perlindungan%20Saksi%20Pelaku%20Bekerjasama%20141211%20FIXED.pdf, Art 2.

220 Joint Regulation of the Minister of Law and Human Rights, Prosecutor General, Chief of the National Police, Head of the Corruption Eradication Commission, and Head of the Witness and Victims Protection Agency, 2011, Art 10.

221 Criminal Procedure Code, Arts 16–17. In the accompanying elucidation, 'adequate preliminary evidence' is defined as 'preliminary evidence to suspect a crime' in accordance with Art 1(14). This states that a 'suspect' is a person who, based on preliminary evidence, is suspected of committing an offence.

222 See Chandra M Hamzah, 'Penjelasan Hukum (Restatement) Tentang Bukti Permulaan Yang Cukup [Legal Explanation (Restatement) of Sufficient Preliminary Evidence]' (Jakarta, Pusat Studi Hukum dan Kebijakan [Centre for Legal and Policy Studies], Jakarta, 2014), http://pshk.or.id/site/sites/default/files/Dokumen%20penelitian/Penjelasan%20Hukum%20Tentang%20Bukti%20Permulaan%20Yang%20Cukup.pdf.

evidence.[223] Arrest ordinarily requires a warrant, which must identify the person to be arrested, provide a reason for arrest and a brief description of the suspected crime, and state the place of interrogation.[224] The police must provide a copy of the warrant to the family of the person arrested immediately following the arrest.[225] Where an offender is caught in the act, however, no warrant is required.[226]

According to the Criminal Procedure Code, a suspect has the right to be interrogated promptly after arrest by a relevant police officer.[227] The suspect or accused person has the right to be clearly informed, in a language he or she understands, of what is alleged against him or her at the beginning of the interrogation.[228] The Criminal Procedure Code also requires that the testimony of suspects and witnesses be provided without pressure.[229] Testimonies of suspects and witnesses are recorded in their own words, and must be signed by the police investigator and then approved by the person giving the statement. If the suspect refuses to sign, the police investigator is required to record the reason for the refusal in the police report.[230]

There is, unfortunately, considerable evidence that the standards these provisions impose are not routinely followed. The rights of the accused and shortcomings in their application in practice are discussed in more detail below.

Searches

The Criminal Procedure Code states that a primary investigator may conduct a search of the body or the house of a suspect for the purposes of investigation.[231] To conduct a search of a house, the investigator must first obtain a search warrant from the Chief Judge of the local District Court.[232] When required, police officers may, on written orders from an investigator, enter the house.[233] If the resident of the house gives permission for the search to be conducted, two witnesses must be present. Where permission is not provided, the search must be witnessed by the village or neighbourhood head and two other witnesses.

Within two days of entering or searching a house, a case file must be prepared and delivered to the owner or occupant of the house.[234] Under urgent circumstances, the investigator may conduct a search without a warrant. The investigator may search the yard of the house where the suspect resides, other places where the suspect lives or stays, the location where the crime occurred, and other 'relevant' public places.

223 Hamzah, 'Penjelasan Hukum', 9.
224 Criminal Procedure Code, Art 18(1).
225 Criminal Procedure Code, Art 18(3).
226 Criminal Procedure Code, Art 18(2).
227 Criminal Procedure Code, Art 50.
228 Criminal Procedure Code, Art 51.
229 Criminal Procedure Code, Art 117.
230 Criminal Procedure Code, Art 118.
231 Criminal Procedure Code, Art 32.
232 Criminal Procedure Code, Art 33(1).
233 Criminal Procedure Code, Art 33(2).
234 Criminal Procedure Code, Art 33(3–5).

The Criminal Procedure Code provides that if there is a strong suspicion that the suspect is carrying items that should be confiscated, junior investigators have the authority to search the clothing of the suspect and any items carried by him or her.[235] The primary investigator may also search the body of the suspect.[236]

Confiscation

Under the Criminal Procedure Code, confiscation of goods can only be conducted by an investigator with written approval from the local District Court. In immediate and pressing circumstances, investigators may confiscate movable objects but the investigator must immediately file a report to the local District Court for approval.[237] The items that may be confiscated include:

— items of the suspect or accused that are suspected to be partially or completely obtained through criminal means;
— items that have been directly used to conduct or prepare for a criminal offence;
— items used to impede a criminal investigation;
— items made to conduct crime; and
— other items that are directly connected to the crime.[238]

When a person is caught in the act, the investigator may confiscate items used, or suspected to have been used, to conduct crime, as well as other items that may be used as evidence.[239]

The 2009 Narcotics Law contains detailed procedures for the storage and destruction of seized narcotics and precursors. BNN or police investigators who confiscate narcotics must seal the confiscated drugs and prepare a report on the confiscation on the day it occurred. The report must detail the name, type, nature and amount of narcotics seized, the location and time of confiscation, and the identity details of the owner or holder of the drugs, as well as the confiscating officer. The report must also be signed by the owner or holder of the drugs. The confiscation report must be prepared and delivered within 72 hours to the head of the local prosecution service office, the head of the local District Court, the Minister, and the head of the Food and Drug Monitoring Agency (Badan Pengawas Obat dan Makanan, BPOM).[240]

The investigator is responsible for the storage and security of the seized goods. For the purposes of investigation and trial, police, BNN and civil servant investigators must retain a small portion of the seized narcotics for laboratory examination, which must be conducted within 72 hours of confiscation.[241]

[235] Criminal Procedure Code, Art 37.
[236] Criminal Procedure Code, Art 37.
[237] Criminal Procedure Code, Art 38.
[238] Criminal Procedure Code, Art 39.
[239] Criminal Procedure Code, Art 40.
[240] Law No 35 of 2009 on Narcotics, Art 87.
[241] Law No 35 of 2009 on Narcotics, Art 90.

On receiving a report of confiscation of narcotics or precursors, the head of the local prosecution service office must decide within seven days whether the confiscated narcotics will be used as evidence in court, for scientific research, for education and training, and/or be destroyed.[242] If the narcotics are to be destroyed, the investigator must do so within seven days of receiving the decision (under certain circumstances this limit can be extended by another seven days). The investigator must prepare a case file on the destruction within 24 hours of the event and deliver it to the local police or BNN investigator, as well as the local prosecution service office, the head of the local District Court, the Minister, and the head of the Food and Drug Monitoring Agency.[243]

If the seized item is a plant, police and BNN investigators must destroy it within 48 hours, after reserving a small portion for the purposes of investigation and trial, research, or education and training. If there are many plants, or they are located in an area that is difficult to access, investigators have 14 days to destroy them. Investigators must prepare a case file on the destruction that includes the name, type, nature and amount of narcotics seized, the location and time of confiscation, and the identity details and signatures of the owner or holder of the drugs and the officials who witnessed the destruction.[244]

If the seized goods are to be used for scientific research they must be handed over to the Minister, or if they are to be used for education and training, to the head of BNN and the Police Chief, within five days of receiving the prosecutor's decision. The police and BNN are required to prepare a report for the Minister on the use of seized goods for education and training.[245]

Custody (Temporary Detention)

Under the Criminal Procedure Code, detention may only be ordered where there is 'sufficient evidence' to 'strongly suspect' a person of having committed an offence, and circumstances give rise to fear that the suspect will not attend trial, will damage or dispose of evidence, or will repeat the offence.[246] The relevant offence must carry a penalty of at least five years imprisonment or be one of a number of specified offences, including, notably, Arts 36 (7), 41, 42, 43, 47 and 48 of the 1976 Narcotics Law.[247]

Detention is not mandatory under the Criminal Procedure Code. If a person is to be detained, the Code describes three forms of detention: detention in a state facility; home confinement under observation from authorities; and city detention, with the suspect or accused person required to report to authorities at agreed intervals.[248]

[242] 2009 Narcotics Law, Art 91.
[243] 2009 Narcotics Law, Art 90(3).
[244] 2009 Narcotics Law, Art 92.
[245] 2009 Narcotics Law, Art 92.
[246] Criminal Procedure Code, Art 21(1).
[247] Criminal Procedure Code, Art 21(4).
[248] Criminal Procedure Code, Art 22(1–3).

The Criminal Procedure Code includes clear provisions regarding the limits to detention under each stage of the criminal procedure, as set out below.

Table 3: Criminal Procedure Code and Limits to Detention

Phase of criminal procedure	**Limits of detention**	**Relevant legislation**
Arrest and preliminary investigation (*penyelidikan*)	24 hours	Criminal Procedure Code, Art 19(1)
	BNN investigators may detain a person for 72 hours, with possibility of extension for a further 72 hours	2009 Narcotics Law, Art 76
Investigation (*penyidikan*)	20 days, with possibility of extension for a further 40 days	Criminal Procedure Code, Arts 20(1), 24
Indictment (*penuntutan*)	20 days, with possibility of extension for a further 30 days	Criminal Procedure Code, Arts 20(2), 25
Trial (*pemeriksaan*)	30 days, with possibility of extension for a further 60 days. Any detention must be ordered by a District Court judge.	Criminal Procedure Code, Arts 20(3), 26
Appeal (*banding*)	30 days, with possibility of extension for a further 60 days. Any detention must be ordered by a High Court judge.	Criminal Procedure Code, Arts 20(3), 27
Cassation (*kasasi*)	50 days, with possibility of extension for a further 60 days. Any detention must be ordered by the chief justice of the Supreme Court.	Criminal Procedure Code, Arts 20(3), 28

In addition to these conditions, detention can be extended further for up to 60 days for the purposes of investigation if the suspect or accused is suffering from a serious physical or mental disturbance as evidenced by a doctor's certificate, or if the case being examined carries a penalty of nine years imprisonment or more. This extension may be applied for at any of the investigation, prosecution or trial stages. It must be ordered by a District Court judge, a High Court judge or the Supreme Court, according to the stage the process has reached.[249]

Unfortunately, there is a huge difference between these limits and what occurs in practice. The process results in many incentives and opportunities for rent-seeking, and there is widespread evidence of the abuse of the pre-trial detention process, with serious violations of human rights. For many years, police had discretion to impose

249 Criminal Procedure Code, Art 29.

detention for any crime punishable with a fine of at least Rp 250 (equivalent to about US$ 0.02).[250] Police frequently overused this provision, leading to very high rates of pre-trial detention throughout Indonesia.[251] Although the Supreme Court recently issued a regulation[252] raising the minimum threshold for pre-trial detention to Rp 2.5 million (about US$ 200), the old threshold continues to be used.

Pre-trial detention in Indonesia is often lengthy. Some drug users are detained for up to nine months before sentencing, although in most cases they are held for a period of between two to four months. During a visit to Indonesia in 2007, the UN special rapporteur on torture, Manfred Nowak, found that it was standard procedure among Indonesian police to detain suspects for the full 61 days provided by Indonesian law, a much longer period than is permitted under international law.[253] He noted that prolonged detention not only increases opportunities for abuse but also means that signs of any physical abuse have often disappeared by the time detainees are released or transferred. Nowak expressed concern that in many of Indonesia's prisons, pre-trial detainees and convicted prisoners are not housed separately, another clear violation of international standards.[254]

Reports of death in police custody are not uncommon, including among minors.[255] The UN special rapporteur on torture reported receiving significant numbers of allegations of torture and ill-treatment perpetrated by the police.[256] He concluded that torture was 'routine practice' in police stations in Jakarta and other metropolitan areas of Java, including Yogyakarta.[257] In some police stations, beatings were even taking place at the time of his visit. Nowak received reports, corroborated by forensic medical analysis, of beatings, including with wooden sticks, chains, iron bars and hammers, kicking with heavy boots, electrocution, and shots fired into detainees' legs. Other reports have described sexual violence.[258] Detainees interviewed by

[250] This amount is so small because the figure was fixed directly by a provision of the Criminal Code dating from 1960.

[251] Leopold Sudaryono, 'Overcrowding Crisis' (2013) 113 *Inside Indonesia*, July-September, www.insideindonesia.org/current-edition/overcrowding-crisis.

[252] Supreme Court Regulation No 2 of 2012 on Adjustment of Limits for Minor Crimes and Fines in the Criminal Code [*Penyesuaian Batasan Tindak Pidana Ringan dan Jumlah Denda dalam KUHP*], Art 1.

[253] United Nations, General Assembly, Human Rights Council, 'Report of the Special Rapporteur on Torture and Other Cruel, Inhuman or Degrading Treatment or Punishment, Manfred Nowak, Addendum: Mission to Indonesia', A/HRC/7/3/Add.7 (10 March 2008), http://daccess-dds-ny.un.org/doc/UNDOC/GEN/G08/114/90/PDF/G0811490.pdf?OpenElement.

[254] United Nations, General Assembly, Human Rights Council, 'Report of the Special Rapporteur', 14.

[255] Ulma Haryanto, 'Police in West Sumatra Tortured Brothers to Death: Komnas HAM' *The Jakarta Globe* (25 January 2012), http://thejakartaglobe.beritasatu.com/archive/police-in-west-sumatra-tortured-brothers-to-death-komnas-ham/493409/; Indra Budiari, 'Cleaners' Families Reveal Police Torture to Kompolnas' *The Jakarta Post* (18 February 2015), www.thejakartapost.com/news/2015/02/18/cleaners-families-reveal-police-torture-kompolnas.html.

[256] United Nations, General Assembly, Human Rights Council (n 253), 12.

[257] United Nations, General Assembly, Human Rights Council (n 253), 12.

[258] Perkumpulan Lembaga Bantuan Hukum Masyarakat [Association of Community Legal Aid Foundations] and Open Society Foundations, 'Revealing the Practice of Violations of the Rights of the Accused during the Investigation Stage: Case Study of the Accused of Drug Offense in Jakarta' [sic] (Jakarta, LBH Masyarakat, 2012), http://lbhmasyarakat.org/admin/dataupload/Documentation%20on%20the%20Violation%20of%20the%20Rights%20of%20the%20Suspect,%20July%202012.pdf).

Nowak reported that abuse was used primarily to elicit confessions or information on drug suppliers. In a number of cases, beatings were used to extract bribes.[259]

In May 2015, the Directorate General of Corrections electronic database system recorded 172,911 prisoners in state detention, including 54,078 (32 per cent) pre-trial detainees. Data on the number of detainees in police detention facilities, meanwhile, is almost impossible to obtain.

Challenges to Arrest and Investigation

Challenges to arrest or detention and any seizure of property may be made at a pre-trial (*pra-peradilan*) hearing.[260] A pre-trial hearing is a mechanism that allows a suspect, or his or her family or legal counsel to challenge the legality (in a narrow and formal sense) of an arrest or detention, such as when an arrest was made without a valid warrant.[261] It has been loosely compared to the principle of *habeas corpus* in common law countries but is much more restricted. A single judge hears the challenge, and a decision must be reached within 10 days of the application being made.[262] Importantly, there is no right of appeal from a pre-trial determination to a High Court or the Supreme Court, and if an issue relating to arrest or detention is not raised in a pre-trial hearing, it cannot be raised at all at trial.[263] If the arrest or detention is found to be unlawful, the accused is released.[264] A suspect or accused person has the right to receive compensation for unlawful detention.[265]

Scholars have documented a number of serious shortcomings with the pre-trial hearing process in practice. Chief among these is the fact that any complaints about arrest or detention are to be lodged with the police, the very body that is the subject of the complaint.[266] A further concern is an undersupply of lawyers, especially in rural areas, and the fact that detainees often report being intimidated by police into not seeking legal counsel,[267] which (as discussed below) is their right. There are also no regulations that govern the appearance of government officials at pre-trial hearings. This means that hearings can sometimes be delayed because officials fail to appear, with some not showing up until after the trial itself has started and others never attending at all. Finally, because pre-trial hearings are decided by a single judge and determinations cannot be appealed, this encourages low standards of decision-making, with outcomes notorious for lack of uniformity and predictability.[268]

[259] United Nations, General Assembly, Human Rights Council (n 253), 12.
[260] Criminal Procedure Code, Arts 77–83.
[261] Criminal Procedure Code, Arts 77, 79.
[262] Criminal Procedure Code, Arts 78, 82(1).
[263] Criminal Procedure Code, Art 83.
[264] Criminal Procedure Code, Art 82(3)(a).
[265] Criminal Procedure Code, Art 95.
[266] Daniel Fitzpatrick, 'Culture, Ideology and Human Rights', 506.
[267] Fitzpatrick (n 191), 506; and Perkumpulan Lembaga Bantuan Hukum Masyarakat and Open Society Foundations, 'Revealing the Practice'.
[268] Fitzpatrick (n 191), 506.

On 28 April 2015, the Constitutional Court issued a ruling expanding the arena covered by pre-trial motions, to allow suspects to challenge the legality of law enforcement officials' actions in naming them a suspect.[269] This remains a new development at the time of writing, so it is difficult to assess its impact beyond a handful of early decisions. There are indications, however, that the decision has provided an avenue for corruption suspects to challenge their investigations. A number of high-profile corruption suspects have done so, and won.[270]

Bail

Article 31 of the Criminal Procedure Code provides for bail under certain conditions. It states that an investigator, prosecutor or judge may, at the request of the suspect or the accused, suspend or postpone detention—with or without bail money or personal guarantee—on the basis of stipulated conditions. The general elucidation to the Criminal Procedure Code provides examples of such conditions, namely a requirement to report regularly to authorities (for example daily, or once every three days) or a requirement not to leave home or the city. The suspension of detention may be revoked by the investigator or prosecutor if the suspect or accused fails to adhere to the agreed conditions.[271]

Government Regulation, No 27 of 1983 on the implementation of the Criminal Procedure Code offers further detail regarding bail procedures.[272] Article 35 states that the relevant authority (depending on the stage of investigation) determines the amount of bail payable.[273] The accused or his or her legal representative must deliver the bail money directly to the clerk of the District Court, who is then required to sign a form confirming receipt of the funds.[274] If the suspect or accused flees, and cannot be found after three months, the money is handed over to the state.

The personal guarantee may be made by a legal representative, family member or anyone who has a relationship with the suspect or accused. The guarantor is required to sign a statement to the effect that they are willing to bear the risk of the accused fleeing. If the accused does abscond, the guarantor must pay a sum to the relevant authorities. If the suspect or accused cannot be found within three months, the money becomes the property of the state.[275]

[269] Constitutional Court [Makahmah Konstitusi] Decision No 21/PUU-XII/2014, www.mahkamahkonstitusi.go.id/putusan/21_PUU-XII_2014.pdf.

[270] *The Jakarta Post*, 'Former Makassar Mayor Wins Pre-trial Court Decision' (12 May 2015), www.thejakartapost.com/news/2015/05/12/former-makassar-mayor-wins-pretrial-court-decision.html; Bagus BT Saragih, 'Hadi's Pre-Trial Victory a "Disaster" for KPK' *The Jakarta Post* (26 May 2015), www.thejakartapost.com/news/2015/05/26/hadi-s-pretrial-victory-a-disaster-kpk.html. See also Rifqi Assegaf, 'Pretrial Hearings: Who Will Fix the Mess?' *Indonesia at Melbourne* (7 July 2015), http://indonesiaatmelbourne.unimelb.edu.au/pretrial-hearings-who-will-fix-the-mess/.

[271] Criminal Procedure Code, Art 31.

[272] Government Regulation No 27 of 1983 on the Implementation of the Criminal Procedure Code.

[273] Government Regulation No 27 of 1983 on the Implementation of the Criminal Procedure Code [*Pelaksanaan Kitab Undang-Undang Hukum Acara Pidana*], Art 35.

[274] Government Regulation No 27 of 1983, Art 35.

[275] Government Regulation No 27 of 1983, Art 36.

In practice, there are reports that District Court clerks do not always sign the form confirming receipt of bail money and rarely return the funds if the suspect or accused is found guilty, as is required. There are further reports that bail money is often handed to the investigating police officer or prosecutor with the expectation that they will then deliver it to the court, although they often do not do so. Given these inconsistencies, legal aid organisations report a preference for personal guarantees.[276]

Prosecutorial Discretion

At the prosecution stage, the police (or BNN) investigator must present the dossier of evidence to the prosecutor who then determines whether to accept it or return it for further investigation.[277] The prosecutor must inform the investigator whether the results of investigation are complete or incomplete within seven days.[278] If the investigation is considered incomplete, the prosecutor provides instructions on what should be done to make it complete. The investigator then has 14 days to return the dossier to the prosecutor. The formal roles of the investigators and prosecutors are distinct, as the prosecutor can only accept or reject a finished product. In some cases, police choose to drop the returned case rather than embark upon further investigations.[279]

Following the receipt of a completed dossier, the prosecutor is required to deliver it to the District Court, and prepare a formal indictment. Indonesian law recognises prosecutorial discretion to decline to prosecute or to terminate a case where it is deemed not to be in the public interest.[280] A prosecutor may decide to terminate the prosecution process because there is an absence of sufficient evidence, the alleged offence does not constitute a criminal act, or the case is considered closed by law (*ditutup demi hukum*),[281] that is, it cannot legally proceed, for example, because the accused has died.

The procedures for joinder of defendants involved in the same crime are very restrictive, which means that defendants party to the same conspiracy are often tried separately, at times leading to quite inconsistent outcomes.

While there is no formal provision for plea-bargaining, the police often exercise discretion at the stage of laying charges through an informal system referred to as 'reserve cases' (*kasus cadangan*). Under this practice, police may charge a suspect with only one of multiple potential crimes for which they are believed to be responsible but reserve the right to press further charges in order to secure the suspect's co-operation. This usually takes place without court or prosecutor involvement.

[276] *Hukum Online*, 'Penangguhan Penahanan Dengan Uang Jaminan Perlu Diperjelas [Suspension of detention with bail money needs clarification]' (28 July 2005), www.hukumonline.com/berita/baca/hol13271/penangguhan-penahanan-dengan-uang-jaminan-perlu-diperjelas.

[277] Criminal Procedure Code, Arts 110s(1) and 138.

[278] Criminal Procedure Code, Art 137.

[279] See Strang (n 191), 198.

[280] Law No 16 of 2004 on the Public Prosecution [*Kejaksaan*], Art 35(c) and elucidation to Art 35(c).

[281] Criminal Procedure Code, Art 140(2a).

Limitations on Prosecution

Limitation Periods

Articles 78 to 80 of Criminal Procedure Code set fixed times within which a defendant may be prosecuted. After the relevant period expires, no prosecution may be brought. For crimes carrying a prison sentence of three years or less, the limitation period (*daluwarsa*) is six years. For crimes carrying a prison sentence of more than three years, the period is 12 years. For crimes carrying the death penalty or life imprisonment, it is 18 years. For people under the age of 18 years at the time the offence was committed, the period is reduced by one third. Limitation periods run from the day the offence is committed[282] and cease as soon as any prosecutorial action is taken.[283]

Double Jeopardy and Reconsideration

Indonesian law provides protection against double jeopardy (*nebis in idem*). Article 76 of the Criminal Procedure Code provides that:

> Except where it still possible for a judge's decision to be reconsidered a person may not be prosecuted twice for an act regarding which an Indonesia judge has adjudicated with a decision that has become binding.

This 'double jeopardy' prohibition is repeated again in Art 18(5) of Law No 39 of 1999 on Human Rights:

> No person can be prosecuted for a second time for the same case for an act that has been the subject of a court decision that has legally binding force.

These provisions have the effect that once an Indonesian judge has handed down a decision that has acquired 'binding legal force', that is, one in respect of which no further appeal is possible,[284] the defendant may not be prosecuted again for an act in respect of which that decision was made. The same prohibition applies under certain circumstances where the person in question has been prosecuted outside Indonesia.

Article 76 of the Criminal Procedure Code does, however, contain an important exception to the rule against double jeopardy, in that it specifically allows for reconsideration of a decision that has acquired binding legal force. This power of reconsideration (PK) in criminal cases is principally regulated by Art 263 of the Criminal Procedure Code. It is exercised by the Supreme Court and, although it is sometimes described as a final appeal, it is better understood as the reopening of a case.[285] As mentioned earlier, the Supreme Court can reconsider almost all judgments that have become final and binding, including its own decisions and can, if necessary, re-decide them.

[282] Criminal Procedure Code, Art 79.
[283] Criminal Procedure Code, Art 80.
[284] On this, see p 65.
[285] Butt and Lindsey, *The Constitution of Indonesia*, 89.

Under Art 263(2) of the Criminal Procedure Code, a request for reconsideration of a criminal case may only be made:

1. where there is a new situation that gives rise to a strong suspicion that if that situation had been known at the time the case was being heard, the result would have been an acquittal or dismissal of all charges or the charges laid by the general prosecutor would not be accepted or a lighter punishment would have been imposed in the case;[286]
2. where in several cases something has been found to be proven but it appears that the proven issues or situations forming the basis and reason for the decisions conflict with each other;
3. where the decision clearly shows a judicial error or an obvious mistake.[287]

The reconsideration process was originally intended to only be available in extraordinary cases but it has now become a common procedure,[288] contributing to the Supreme Court's heavy caseload. In 2013, for example, 12,337 cases were lodged with the Supreme Court, including 2,426 (19.7 per cent) reconsideration requests.[289] These cases were added to a backlog of 10,112 cases carried over from 2012, of which 2,261 cases were reconsideration requests, leaving a total 4,687 reconsideration cases to be decided. The Court reached a decision in 3,242 of these cases, rejecting applications for reconsideration in 78.2 per cent of cases.

There are two aspects of the reconsideration power that have been controversial in recent years. The first is the question of whether the prosecution may apply for reconsideration where a defendant has not been found guilty. The second is whether more than one reconsideration can be sought in the same case.

Can the Prosecutor Request a PK?

Turning to the first of these issues, Art 263(1) of the Criminal Procedure Code seems to exclude the prosecution from seeking reconsideration and prohibits reconsideration of acquittals and dismissals altogether:

> As regards a court decision that has obtained binding legal force, except for an acquittal or dismissal, a convicted person or his or her heir may bring a request for reconsideration to the Supreme Court.

This reflects the notion that the reconsideration mechanism was originally intended as a remedy for defendants who had been wrongly convicted but had exhausted the appeal process.[290]

[286] Such a new situation is known in Indonesian law as a *novum.*

[287] Criminal Procedure Code, Art 263.

[288] Simon Butt 'Surat Sakti: The Decline of the Authority of Judicial Decisions in Indonesia' in Tim Lindsey (ed) *Indonesia: Law and Society* (Sydney, The Federation Press, 2008) 350.

[289] Indonesia, Mahkamah Agung, *Laporan Tahunan 2013*, 17.

[290] The reconsideration process in the Criminal Procedure Code is a revised version of earlier colonial mechanisms (which did allow application for reconsideration by the prosecution). The new process was specifically inserted into the Code to assist defendants who had suffered injustice: see Martiman Prodjohamidjojo, *Komentar atas Kitab Undang-Undang Hukum Acara Pidana (KUHAP)* [Commentary on The Code of Criminal Procedure (KUHAP)] (Jakarta, Pradnya Paramita, 1984). For the legislators'

Although the Supreme Court has not been consistent in its interpretation of Art 263, it has allowed applications by prosecutors to reopen acquittals and dismissals in a series of high-profile decisions since 1996.[291] It doing so, it has usually relied on Art 263(3) of the Criminal Procedure Code, which provides:

> As regards a court decision that has obtained binding legal force, a request for reconsideration may be brought ... if in that decision an act as charged was declared proved but was not followed by a punishment.

The Court argues that only a prosecutor would have an interest in changing such a decision. It therefore finds that although Art 263(1) may be intended only for use by a convicted person or his or her heirs, Art 263(3) must implicitly be intended for use by the prosecutor, even though the prosecutor is not mentioned. This ignores the fact that it is quite conceivable that a defendant found to have committed acts but who has received no punishment for them might still wish to seek a reconsideration of that decision to challenge the finding that he or she had committed those acts. This could be for reasons of reputation or because such acts might form the basis of other legal action against him or her, whether criminal or civil. On this view, Art 263(3) is necessary because Art 263(1) only applies where a person has been convicted. Conviction is not a requirement for Art 263(3), because it only applies where no punishment has been imposed. On this alternative reading, which the Supreme Court has followed in another, smaller, group of decisions beginning in 2007,[292] Art 263(3) of the Criminal Code does not, in fact, give power to the prosecution to apply for reconsideration.

views of the purpose of Art 263 see Indonesia, Direktorat Jenderal Hukum dan Perundang-Undangan [Directorate General of Law and Legislation], 'Sejarah Pembentukan Undang-Undang Republik Indonesia No 8 Tahun 1981 tentang Hukum Acara Pidana [The history of the Formation of Law of the Republic of Indonesia No 8 Year 1981 on the Laws of Criminal Procedure]', (Jakarta, Direktorat Jenderal Hukum dan Perundang-Undangan [Directorate General of Law and Legislation], 1981). In short, it was a response to a notorious case of injustice involving two men who had exhausted their appeals and could not secure release despite another man later confessing to the murder for which they were imprisoned: Bekasi District Court Decision; *Sengkon Bin Yakin dan Karta alias Karung alias Encep Bin Salam (Sengkon dan Karta)* (20 October 1977, Bekasi District Court Decision No 2/K.T.S/Bks/1977); Bandung High Court Decision: *Sengkon Bin Yakin dan Karta alias Karung alias Encep Bin Salam (Sengkon dan Karta)* (25 May 1978, No 38/1978/Pid/PTB). Reconsideration (PK): *Sengkon Bin Yakin dan Karta alias Karung alias Encep Bin Salam (Sengkon dan Karta)* (31 January 1981, No 6 PKK/Kr/1980).

[291] These decisions include: *Muchtar Pakpahan* (Supreme Court Decision No 55 PK/Pid/1996, 25 October 1996, pp 362–66); *Ram Gulumal Alias v Ram* (Supreme Court Decision No 3 PK/Pid/2001 2 August 2001); *Dr Eddy Linus and others* (No 54PK/Pid/2006); Soetiyawati Alias Ahua Binti Kartaningsih (Supreme Court Decision No 15 PK/Pid/2006, 19 June 2006, pp 5–14); *Pollycarpus Budihari Priyanto* (Supreme Court Decision No 109 2008: PK/Pid/2007, 25 January 2008, pp 17–26; Supreme Court Decision No 109PK/Pid/2007); *Dr Edhy Sudjono Muliadi* (No 8 PK/Pid/2008, p 13); 2009: *Joko Tjandra* (No 12PK/Pid.Sus/2009, 11 June 2009, p 126); *Syahril Sabirin* (No 07 PK/Pid. Sus/2009, 8 June 2009, pp 41–50); and *Ny. Nyayu Saodah bin (alm) KA Kosim* (No 41 PK/Pid/2009, 13 October 2009, pp 24–25).

[292] This alternative line of Supreme Court authority includes: *Sdr. Mulyar bin Samsi* (84/PK/Pid/2006, 2007, 18 July 2007, pp 7–8); *Johan Imago al Guan Kabir* (Supreme Court Decision No 69 PK/Pid. Sus/2010); *Anggodo Widjojo and the Head of Police* (Supreme Court Decision No 152 PK/Pid/2010, 7 October 2010, pp 64–66); and *Zaki Toya Bawazir*; (No 16 PK/Pid/2010, 29 November 2011, pp 23–24).

In the (more numerous) decisions in which it allows applications for reconsideration by the prosecution, the Supreme Court also cites Art 24(1) of Law No 48 of 2009 on Judicial Powers, which provides that:

> As regards a court decision that has acquired binding legal force, parties involved may bring a reconsideration to the Supreme Court, whenever there is particular matter or situation as provided for in statute.

The Court takes the view that the phrase 'parties involved' is broad and covers prosecutors. This, however, takes no account of the fact that this Article is expressed to be restricted by what is otherwise provided for in statute, including, of course, Art 263 of the Criminal Procedure Code, which make no reference to prosecutors or 'parties involved'.[293] It also ignores the fact that the Elucidation to Art 263 explicitly states that the Article is intended to limit the grounds on which reconsideration may be brought, and should, therefore, not be construed broadly.[294]

The Court likewise often refers to one its own internal regulations, introduced to 'clarify' Art 263. This provides that applications for reconsideration may be lodged by 'the prosecutor, the defendant or a party involved'.[295] Pulling itself up by its own bootstraps, the Court argues that the grant of this power to prosecutor would be largely meaningless if the prosecutor could not seek the reopening of acquittals.

In summary, although the reasoning used by the Supreme Court in decisions allowing prosecutors to seek reconsideration is far from coherent, it does seem more likely to follow this line of authority rather than the contrary, and more convincing, view it has sometimes expressed in a smaller number of decisions.

More than One PK?

Turning to the second issue, Art 268 of the Criminal Procedure Code originally stated that reconsideration requests may only be made once. This provision was, however, recently successfully challenged in the Constitutional Court. It found in March 2014 that there could be no limit to the number of applications for reconsideration, as that could cause injustice to defendants who only found evidence to support their claim after a first application was refused.[296] The Constitutional Court held that preventing more than one reconsideration application was a violation of fundamental constitutional principles of substantive justice, rule of law and guarantees of citizen's rights.

The Supreme Court continues, however, to refuse to allow second reconsideration applications, relying on the fact that there are regulatory bases for the restriction

[293] This is reinforced by Art 76 of Law No 14 of 1985 on the Supreme Court, which makes it clear that Criminal Procedure Code is the key reference point for reconsideration in criminal cases: 'In deciding an application for a reconsideration [PK] of a criminal case that has binding legal force the procedure for reconsideration [PK] as provided for in the Code of Criminal Procedure shall be used.'

[294] The Elucidation to Art 263 states: 'This Article contains limited [*limitatif*] grounds for requesting a reconsideration [PK] of a criminal case that has obtained binding legal force'.

[295] Supreme Court Regulation No 1 of 1980 on Reconsideration [PK], Art 10.

[296] Constitutional Court Decision 34/PUU-XI/2013.

to a single reconsideration application other than the provision struck down by the Constitutional Court.[297] It is motivated in this, in part at least, by a concern to avoid a flood of new reconsideration applications that might swamp the Court's already backlogged case list. In fact, in December 2014, the Supreme Court published a 'Circular Letter' (effectively a Practice Note) restating its position that reconsideration requests could still only be filed once.[298] At the time of writing, discussions had been held involving the two courts and other government law enforcement officials to see if a compromise could be reached, but so far without result.

V. RIGHTS OF THE ACCUSED

The Criminal Procedure Code contains a number of safeguards intended to protect the rights of suspects and the accused, including the presumption of innocence, the right to legal counsel, and the right to be free of the burden of proof. In practice, however, such rights are often denied. This is particularly the case for suspected narcotics offenders, who are typically subject to frequent and serious violations of their rights.

Right to Silence

The Code of Criminal Procedure does not provide for a clear right against self-incrimination. Although Art 66 of the code states that a suspect or the accused shall not bear the burden of proof, there is some debate as to whether this constitutes the right to silence.[299] If it is present at all, the right to silence is implicit at best.

Right to Counsel

The Code of Criminal Procedure states that the accused has the right to receive assistance from legal counsel of his or her choice during the period of investigation, and at every stage of examination.[300] Under the code, the state is obliged to provide free legal assistance for persons accused of crimes that carry the death penalty or at least 15 years imprisonment, or for those of insufficient means accused of a crime that attracts a sentence of five years imprisonment or more.[301] If detained, the suspect or the accused has the right to contact his or her legal counsel, and foreign citizens may contact diplomatic representatives.[302]

[297] Law No 14 of 1985 on the Supreme Court, Art 66 (amended through Law No 5 of 2004 and Law No 3 of 2009) and Law No 48 of 2009 on Judicial Powers, Art 24(2).
[298] Supreme Court Circular Letter No 7 of 2014 (165/Bua.6/Hs/SP/XII/2014).
[299] Fitzpatrick (n 191), 507.
[300] Criminal Procedure Code, Art 54, 55.
[301] Criminal Procedure Code, Art 56.
[302] Criminal Procedure Code, Art 57.

In practice, most detainees do not have a lawyer present during police questioning. In many instances, they are not even aware of their right to legal counsel and, unfortunately, police are not obliged to inform them of this right.[303] Detainees have reported that police threaten violence or harsher sentencing demands if they request legal aid. This has resulted in many detainees declining legal counsel during investigation—even in the rare event that investigators do offer them the opportunity to obtain legal assistance.[304]

The right to legal assistance was strengthened considerably with the passage of Law No 16 of 2011 on Legal Aid. Before the passage of the Law, legal aid and public interest law organisations operated largely without legislative or regulatory controls. Now 'legal aid' is defined in the new Law as 'legal assistance that is given by a legal aid provider free of charge to the recipient of legal aid'.[305] A person who receives legal aid is defined as a 'poor' person or group;[306] and the provision of legal aid includes criminal, civil and administrative matters, both litigious and non-litigious.[307] A person who receives legal aid has certain rights and obligations.[308] He or she must, first, satisfy certain conditions in the law, such as putting his or her complaint in writing, and providing evidence of poverty from the *lurah*, the head of his or her village, or other local official.[309] A legal aid provider must respond to receipt of request from a qualified person within the very short period of just three days.[310] It is a criminal offence for a legal aid provider to receive money from a client or any other party related to a case, and the maximum penalty is set at imprisonment for one year or a Rp 50 million [US$ 4,400] fine.[311]

The delivery of legal aid and its funding is overseen by the Ministry of Law and Human Rights, and the Minister is required to establish a committee to oversee the administration and verification and accreditation process.[312] A legal aid provider must be accredited every three years by meeting certain requirements—for example, it must be a legal entity or *badan hukum* and have an office. The obligations imposed on legal aid providers include reporting requirements and education of lawyers.[313]

The roll-out of the new legal aid system has not been as smooth as many hoped. It is, however, still too soon to say how the new Law will work in practice, and whether it will, in fact, be effective and fully implemented. If it is, that could significantly improve protection for detainees against violence and excessive pre-trial detention. Success might also lead to greater government funding being made available for legal aid, as it would show the extent of demand for such services. In any case, subject to the amount of funding offered and how it is distributed and regulated, the Law

303 Fitzpatrick (n 191), 508.
304 Perkumpulan Lembaga Bantuan Hukum Masyarakat and Open Society Foundations (n 258).
305 Law No 16 of 2011 on Legal Aid [*Bantuan Hukum*], Art 1(1).
306 Law No 16 of 2011 on Legal Aid, Art 1(2).
307 Law No 16 of 2011 on Legal Aid, Art 4.
308 Law No 16 of 2011 on Legal Aid, Art 12–13.
309 Law No 16 of 2011 on Legal Aid, Art 14(1).
310 Law No 16 of 2011 on Legal Aid, Art 15.
311 Law No 16 of 2011 on Legal Aid, Art 21.
312 Law No 16 of 2011 on Legal Aid, Arts 6 and 7.
313 Law No 16 of 2011 on Legal Aid, Art 10.

certainly has the potential to strengthen legal non-governmental organisations in Indonesia—310 of which have already been accredited by the Ministry of Law and Human Rights as Eligible Legal Aid Providers (*Organisasi Bantuan Hukum,* OBH) under Law No 16 of 2011.[314]

Accredited legal aid organisations are not evenly distributed across Indonesia, with only 22 per cent of Indonesia's 508 districts (or equivalent) currently home to one. Even if all the legal aid organisations that applied to the Ministry of Law and Human Rights in 2012 were successfully accredited, 338 districts would still be left without an accredited legal aid organisation.[315] The only viable solution in the medium term is for accredited legal aid organisations to provide services in more than one district. Together with initiatives such as mobile legal clinics, paralegals can be an effective way for legal aid organisations to expand their coverage and ensure more citizens can access their services. The Ministry has floated the idea of 'one village one paralegal' in anticipation of significantly greater resources being available under the new Village Law.[316] While this proposal would face enormous practical difficulties if adopted as official policy, it does signal openness to initiatives aimed at increasing the number of paralegals and improving their skills.

Another problem is that most funding received by accredited legal aid organisations from the Ministry of Law and Human Rights is earmarked for litigation. The reimbursement-based funding system (which is overly-complex, inefficient and difficult to access) creates an additional obstacle for the small percentage of funding allocated for non-litigious activities, including training. Obtaining reimbursement is very costly in terms of time and effort, and anecdotal evidence suggests that, in any case, many poorly-resourced legal aid organisations are simply unable to pre-finance training and, therefore, cannot access government funding. Even if they could, it is unlikely to be sufficient to cover needs. While the government is aware of the problem, fixing the system will not be quick or easy. There may be other sources of funding, for example, pursuant to regional regulations on legal aid or through institution-specific budgets for legal aid, but it is likely training will, unfortunately, remain underfunded in the medium term.

Other Rights of the Accused

Under the Criminal Procedure Code, an accused has the right to:

1. be clearly informed, in a language that he or she understands, about what is alleged against him or her (Art 51);

[314] Justice for the Poor, the World Bank and the Ministry of Law and Human Rights, *Legal Aid Organisations in Indonesia: A Survey of 230 Legal Aid Organisations* (Jakarta, Justice for the Poor, 2014), iii. There are, at the very least, 623 legal aid organisations across Indonesia, predominantly in Java and Sumatra, where most of the population is located. The real numbers are, however, likely much higher than this.

[315] Justice for the Poor, The World Bank and The Ministry of Law and Human Rights, *Legal Aid Organisations*, viii.

[316] Law No 6 of 2014 on Villages [*Desa*].

2. freely provide investigators, prosecutors and the court with information (Art 52);
3. use an interpreter (Art 53(1));
4. contact, and receive visits from, a private doctor for health purposes, whether connected with the case or not (Art 58);
5. contact, and receive visits from, his or her family, people of the same household or anyone else whose assistance is required, or have them informed of the detention by a relevant officer, in order to receive legal assistance or security for bail or for any other family or business purpose (Arts 59, 60, 61);
6. correspond with his or her family or legal counsel at any time and receive writing materials for this purpose. Investigators, prosecutors, judges and state officials are not permitted to examine this correspondence, except in instances where there is reason to suspect that correspondence is being abused. In such circumstances, documents must be stamped and returned to the accused to indicate that they have been scrutinised (Art 62);
7. contact and receive visits from a member of the clergy of any religion (Art 63);
8. be tried in public/open court (Art 64); and
9. endeavour to present witnesses beneficial to his or her cause (Art 65).

VI. CRIMINAL PROCEDURE: TRIAL

As the Indonesian legal system is a civil law system, nearly all cases that come before the District Courts are heard by a panel of three judges. There are no juries. One of the judges is the chair (*ketua*) and is usually more senior than the other two. Typically, the judges produce a single, joint judgment (*putusan*).

Civil law systems are 'inquisitorial' in nature, meaning the judges conduct an inquiry into the truth of what has occurred. The judges control the proceedings and can directly question witnesses if they choose. As civil law systems do not follow the principle of precedent (*stare decisis*) as do common law countries, judicial decisions are generally not considered a source of law. Indonesian courts are, therefore, not bound by the decision of courts at the same level or higher. While an Indonesian judge may follow a previous decision from a higher court with respect to the interpretation of any given provision, he or she is not usually required to do so. Only a tiny number of Supreme Court decisions are considered highly influential (*yurisprudensi tetap* or 'fixed jurisprudence'), that is, decisions that have been followed consistently over time, such that it would be unusual for a lower court to ignore them. In the absence of a formal system of precedent, reliance is placed largely on statutes and other regulations, usually referred to as 'positive law' (*hukum positif*), in determining applicable law in Indonesia. Likewise, common law notions of 'equity' as a means of interpreting or modifying the application of statute do not exist, and a system of remedies similar to equitable remedies in British common law have never been developed in Indonesia. These issues are discussed further at the end of this chapter in the section on judicial decisions.

Trial is regulated by Chapter XVI of the Criminal Procedure Code, and is modified in some respects in relation to drug offences by the 2009 Narcotics Law, which specifies that drug crimes are to be prioritised and expedited in every stage of the trial, including appeals and the execution of the judgment.[317] As discussed above, the Criminal Procedure Code provides a number of important protections for suspects, including the presumption of innocence;[318] a right to be present in person at trial;[319] and a right to be tried promptly, although these rights are often not respected in practice.[320]

Evidence—Admissibility of Statements and Confessions

The Criminal Procedure Code generally requires that at least two different categories of legitimate evidence must be present in order to establish guilt.[321] The 2009 Narcotics Law greatly expands the types of evidence that may be cited in a narcotics case.[322] While the code only permits a narrow range of evidence, such as witness and expert testimony, statements of the accused and documents,[323] the 2009 Narcotics Law allows all forms of electronic information and communications, pictures, sound recordings, videos and other kinds of physical and non-physical data. It is an offence under the 2009 Narcotics Law for investigators, police or prosecutors to breach provisions related to the handling of drug evidence.[324]

During investigation and trial, defendants are obliged to provide the court with all information about their own property and finances, as well as any belonging to their family, any partnerships in which they are involved, and any person connected with the crime.[325] They may also be required by the court to prove their property and finances were not derived from proceeds of drug-related offences.[326]

Witness statements are admissible where adduced in court[327] but a witness statement alone is insufficient to establish the guilt of the accused unless accompanied by another form of evidence.[328] Opinion and conjecture may not form part of a witness statement.[329] The statement of the accused is fully admissible where stated before the court but statements by the accused made outside the trial may be used as a form of supporting evidence, provided there is at least one other form of evidence. The prosecution may not rely on a confession or witness statement alone to establish

[317] Law No 35 of 2009 on Narcotics, Art 74.
[318] Criminal Procedure Code, Art 66.
[319] Criminal Procedure Code, Art 152 and 154.
[320] Criminal Procedure Code, Art 50. See also Fitzpatrick (n 191), 508.
[321] Criminal Procedure Code, Art 183.
[322] Law No 35 of 2009 on Narcotics, Art 86.
[323] Criminal Procedure Code, Art 184(1).
[324] Law No 35 of 2009 on Narcotics, Arts 140–41.
[325] Law No 35 of 2009 on Narcotics, Art 97.
[326] Law No 35 of 2009 on Narcotics, Art 98.
[327] See Case No 612.K/Pid/2005, discussed in Section IX, below.
[328] Criminal Procedure Code, Art 185(1)–(3).
[329] Criminal Procedure Code, Art 185(5).

guilt and must adduce at least one other form of evidence.[330] The results of urine and other drug tests are admissible in court but must be supplemented by another form of evidence in order to establish guilt.[331]

Appeal

The defendant and prosecution have the right to appeal a decision, except a decision of not guilty, or a decision in an expedited procedure.[332] Despite this provision, the Supreme Court regularly hears appeals against not-guilty decisions, for example in Case No 1521.K/Pid/2002, discussed below.

As mentioned, appeals from the first instance District Courts are heard in Indonesia's High Courts, which are located in provincial capitals. Appeals must be lodged at the District Courts where the case was first heard within seven days of the first instance decision.[333] If the defendant does not lodge an appeal within seven days of receiving his or her decision, then the defendant is deemed to have accepted the decision.[334] This time limit is usually strictly applied, and the courts routinely reject late applications.

Appeals to the High Court are reviewed by a panel of at least three judges.[335] If the High Court believes that there was negligence in application of the law during examination in the District Court, a mistake was made, or examination was incomplete, the High Court may order the District Court to correct the matter, or it may do so itself.[336] If necessary, the High Court may cancel a determination made by the District Court before it makes its own decision on a case.[337]

Following a decision by the High Court, dissatisfied parties may lodge an appeal to the Supreme Court within 14 days[338] but on issues of law alone.[339] This is known as a cassation (*kasasi*, discussed above). The main function of cassation hearings is to ensure that lower courts have applied the law in the correct manner.[340] The Supreme

330 Criminal Procedure Code, Art 189(3).

331 The 2009 Narcotics Law, Art 75(l), states that a BNN head can conduct tests of urine, blood, hair, DNA and other body parts for the purposes of investigation. This is outlined further in BNN Chief Regulation No 5 of 2010, which states that examination of biological specimens suspected of containing narcotics can be conducted for the purposes of obtaining evidence. The result of the urine test is considered a document (or *surat*) under Art 184(1) of the Criminal Procedure Code on admissible evidence.

332 Criminal Procedure Code, Art 67. See above, pp 85–87, for the question of whether the prosecution has the right to apply to the Supreme Court for the re-opening or reconsideration (PK) of a case involving an acquittal or dismissal.

333 Criminal Procedure Code, Art 233. Article 236 of the Code states that the clerk of the District Court is required to send a copy of the decision, the case file and evidence to the High Court within 14 days of the defendant lodging an appeal. The defendant must be provided with seven days to review these documents before they are sent to the High Court.

334 Criminal Procedure Code, Art 234(1).

335 Criminal Procedure Code, Art 238(1).

336 Criminal Procedure Code, Arts 240(1).

337 Criminal Procedure Code, Art 240(2).

338 Criminal Procedure Code, Arts 244, 245(1).

339 Criminal Procedure Code, Art 253(1).

340 Butt and Lindsey (n 158), 87.

Court may overturn the decisions of lower courts if, for example, a lower court lacked or exceeded its jurisdiction, or wrongly applied or broke the law. Although the Supreme Court is not required to reconsider the facts of a case, it often does so, usually by defining the issue in question as a legal one.[341] The Supreme Court's decision has permanent binding force, and is immediately executable, although problems with enforcement are very common.[342]

Although not strictly an appeal, the Criminal Procedure Code also allows for reconsideration (PK) of a case at the Supreme Court, a process discussed in more detail above. Requests for reconsideration are lodged with the court of first instance, and there is no time limit before which an appeal must be lodged.[343] The grounds for a reconsideration request are often easily met. If new evidence is required, for example to establish a *novum* ('new situation') under Art 263(a) of the Code, then the case will be remitted temporarily to the District Court that originally heard the matter. It will examine any witnesses before returning the case to the Supreme Court, along with a summary of evidence taken. Any sentence imposed by the Supreme Court in a reconsideration decision may not exceed that of the original decision, although in practice this rule is often ignored.[344] The recent decision of the Constitutional Court to place no limits on the number of reconsideration requests[345] could have a significant impact on legal certainty and contribute to the already heavy caseload at the Supreme Court if the Supreme Court decides to follow the decision, which, as mentioned, it has so far refused to do.

The annual report of the Supreme Court details the number of cases lodged with the courts under its authority, allowing calculation of the rates of appeal. In 2013, for example, 119,876 criminal cases (*pidana biasa*) were lodged with the District Courts.[346] These were added to 51,874 cases carried over from 2012, bringing the total number of criminal cases handled by the courts in 2013 to 171,750.[347] District Courts reached decisions in 104,554 of these cases. Meanwhile, High Courts heard 6,128 criminal cases in 2013, suggesting that appeals were lodged in respect of about 6 per cent of criminal cases decided in District Courts.[348]

The Supreme Court, meanwhile, received 9,799 cassation requests in 2013. Combined with the 7,784 cases carried over from 2012, this resulted in a total of 17,583 cassation requests for the Court to handle in 2013.[349] It reached decisions on 12,655 cases, including 713 cases relating to narcotics and psychotropic substances.[350] In 2013, the Court received 2,426 reconsideration requests, which were added to

341 Law No 14 of 1985 on the Supreme Court, Art 30.
342 Butt and Lindsey (n 158), 87.
343 Criminal Procedure Code, Art 264(3).
344 Criminal Procedure Code, Art 266(3).
345 Constitutional Court Decision 34/PUU-XI/2013. See above, 87–88.
346 A total of 3,334,226 cases were lodged with District Courts in 2013, although most of these were expedited cases, or *pidana cepat*, which cannot be appealed to higher courts.
347 Mahkamah Agung (n 156), 61.
348 Mahkamah Agung (n 156), 61.
349 Mahkamah Agung (n 156), 17.
350 Mahkamah Agung (n 156), 27.

2,261 requests carried over from 2012.[351] It decided 3,242 cases, including 37 cases relating to narcotics and psychotropic substances.[352]

Sentencing

The Criminal Code recognises two categories of punishment: primary and additional penalties.[353] Primary penalties comprise the death penalty, imprisonment and fines. Additional penalties consist of the revocation of a particular right or rights, seizure of property, and publication of the court's verdict. The court may impose a sentence but order that it does not need to be implemented so long as the defendant adheres to certain conditions, primarily related to good behaviour.[354] Non-custodial sentences were only introduced with the passage of the 2009 Narcotics Law but, in practice, prosecutors and police show a strong preference for punitive sentencing. Sentences are only considered to be valid and of legal force if read in an open and public court.[355] The last section in this Part, which discusses decision-making in District and High Courts, describes the sentencing process in further detail.

Imprisonment can either be for life or for a 'fixed period of time'.[356] During imprisonment, the convict must perform all work assigned to him or her.[357] The fixed period is between one day and 15 years,[358] although imprisonment of up to 20 years may be imposed as an alternative to life imprisonment or the death penalty.[359] Similarly, imprisonment of more than 15 years may be imposed where the primary sentence is increased due to aggravating factors.[360] Under no circumstances may the 'fixed period' of imprisonment exceed 20 years.[361]

There are also less severe forms of imprisonment known as *kurungan* and *tutupan*. *Kurungan* may be for a maximum period of one year,[362] or one year and four months in the case of aggravating circumstances.[363] A convicted person may elect to serve a *kurungan* term instead of paying a fine,[364] and a person will be sentenced to *kurungan* if they are unable to pay a fine,[365] although generally for not longer than six months.[366] The workload imposed on people serving a *kurungan* term is

351 Mahkamah Agung (n 156), 31.
352 Mahkamah Agung (n 156), 37.
353 Criminal Code, Art 10.
354 Criminal Code, Art 14A.
355 Criminal Procedure Code, Art 195.
356 Criminal Code, Art 12(1).
357 Criminal Code, Art 14.
358 Criminal Code, Art 12(2).
359 Criminal Code, Art 12(3).
360 Criminal Code, Art 12(3).
361 Criminal Code, Art 12(4)).
362 Criminal Code, Art 18(1).
363 Criminal Code, Art 18(2).
364 Criminal Code, Art 31(1).
365 Criminal Code, Art 30(2).
366 Criminal Code, Art 30(3).

lighter than regular imprisonment,[367] and prisoners are allowed certain privileges.[368] *Tutupan* is similar to house arrest and is for 'respected' prisoners.[369] A person who is unable to pay a fine imposed under the 2009 Narcotics Law may be imprisoned (*penjara*, the heavier form of imprisonment) for up to two years.[370]

Chapter VI of the Criminal Code deals with whether punishments are cumulative or alternative in cases where a person has breached a number of criminal provisions. Essentially, this chapter provides that where a particular action is punishable under more than one provision, the defendant is to be charged with only one offence, either the most specific or that which carries the harshest penalty.[371] The same is true where the defendant has committed a number of actions in breach of several criminal provisions that are best viewed as one continuous crime.[372] Where the individual breaches are more properly seen as separate offences, the punishments may be cumulative but may not exceed a third more than the harshest penalty.[373] These rules are of particular significance in prosecutions under the 2009 Narcotics Law, as so many of the offences overlap.

The period a defendant has spent in prison, awaiting and during trial, is to be deducted in full from any sentence later imposed. Only the portion of the time spent under house arrest or 'city arrest' is deducted from the sentence.[374] The judge may order the accused, if he or she is a drug addict, to undergo treatment or rehabilitation.[375] The period of treatment or rehabilitation is, as mentioned, considered part of the sentence period.

The time period in which any punishment must be carried out[376] is counted from the day after the court order becomes enforceable.[377] For all non-serious offences (*pelanggaran*, or misdemeanours), the period is two years.[378] For serious offences, the period is one third more than the period for prosecution to be initiated.[379] Under no circumstances may the period be less than the length of any prison term imposed.[380]

There is no time limit for carrying out a death sentence fixed in the Criminal Code.[381] The Supreme Court has, however, issued a practice ruling asking the prosecutor's office set a limit of 180 days for the condemned to file a reconsideration motion or seek clemency, after which execution will take place.[382] As noted above, it

[367] Criminal Code, Art 19.
[368] Criminal Code, Arts 20, 21 and 23.
[369] For more on *tutupan* see Government Regulation No 8 of 1948 on House Arrest [*Rumah Tutupan*].
[370] 2009 Narcotics Law, Art 148.
[371] Criminal Code, Art 63.
[372] Criminal Code, Art 64.
[373] Criminal Code, Arts 65, 66.
[374] Criminal Procedure Code, or 'KUHAP', Art 22(4), (5).
[375] 2009 Narcotics Law, Art 103.
[376] Criminal Code, Art 84(1).
[377] Criminal Code, Art 85.
[378] Criminal Code, Art 84(2).
[379] Criminal Code, Art 84(2).
[380] Criminal Code, Art 84(3).
[381] Criminal Code, Art 84(4).
[382] Supreme Court Chief Justice Guidance on Death Penalty No 029/KMA/III/2009 [*Fatwa Ketua Mahkamah Agung Tentang Pidana Mati*] (17 March 2009), www.mahkamahagung.go.id/images/uploaded/Fatwa_29_09.pdf. This limit is based on Art 69 of Law No 14 of 1985 on the Supreme Court

is not uncommon, however, for those facing the death penalty to spend long periods in jail (over ten years, for example) pending resolution of any appeals and cassation, reconsideration or clemency applications.

Exonerating and Aggravating Considerations

The 2009 Narcotics Law creates a number of special aggravating circumstances. Where a person repeats the same offence within three years, the maximum punishment is increased by one third.[383] Similarly, where the commission of certain offences[384] is said to be 'organised', the maximum punishment is increased by one third.[385] An 'organised crime' is defined as a crime involving a 'structured group' of three or more people that is 'in existence for a certain period of time, acting in concert, with the aim to commit a narcotics offence'.[386] In addition, extra punishments and larger fines may be imposed where corporations are found liable for an offence.[387] As shown below, the courts have held that being a foreigner is an aggravating factor in sentencing for narcotics offences.[388]

A foreign citizen who has committed an offence under the 2009 Narcotics Law, and has served his or her sentence, is to be deported from Indonesia and is not permitted to return.[389] A foreign citizen who has been convicted of a narcotics-related offence overseas is also prohibited from entering Indonesia.[390] The 1997 Law on Psychotropic Substances provides, however, that foreign citizens found guilty of an offence involving psychotropic substances shall be deported from Indonesia after serving their sentence but may return after a prescribed period.[391]

Co-operative Defendants

The 2006 Law on Witness and Victim Protection originally stated that a defendant who co-operates with the authorities by acting as a witness:

> cannot be released from any legal charges if he/she is proven legally and convincingly guilty; nevertheless, his or her testimony can be used by the judge as a consideration to lessen the sentence.[392]

This provision was deleted in the recently passed revision of the law, Law No 31 of 2014, and replaced by a new provision that further clarifies what is meant by

(as amended by Law No 5 of 2004 and Law No 3 of 2009), which sets a limit of 180 days for the filing of reconsideration requests. For more detail regarding the death penalty, see below, at pp 103–08.

383 2009 Narcotics Law, Art 144(1).
384 Offences under the 2009 Narcotics Law, Arts 111–126, 129.
385 2009 Narcotics Law, Art 132(2).
386 2009 Narcotics Law, Art 1(20).
387 2009 Narcotics Law, Art 130.
388 See below, at p 133.
389 2009 Narcotics Law, Art 146(1), (2).
390 2009 Narcotics Law, Art 146(3).
391 Law No 5 of 1997 on Psychotropic Substances, Art 67.
392 Law No 13 of 2006 on Witness and Victim Protection [*Perlindungan Saksi dan Korban*], Art 10(2).

a 'co-operative defendant' or 'justice collaborator'. It provides that such a person has the right to be detained separately from the suspect or accused, and have his or her examination, prosecution and trial conducted separately.[393] Justice collaborators may also be eligible for lighter sentences or be considered for parole, additional remissions, or other inmates' rights, in accordance with relevant regulation.[394]

For a justice collaborator to be eligible, the LPSK must provide a written recommendation for a sentence reduction to the state prosecutor (who is then required to include it in the sentencing demand handed to the judge), or the relevant Ministry, in the case of parole and remission considerations.[395] This Law repeats provisions outlined in a joint regulation signed in 2011 by the head of the LPSK, the Minister of Law and Human Rights, the Prosecutor General, the Chief of Police and the head of the Corruption Eradication Commission, discussed above.[396]

It is too early to assess the impact of this greater legal clarity. The LPSK is under-resourced and, as a result, nowhere near as effective as its proponents had hoped. Its 2013 budget of Rp 148.7 billion was, for example, cut to Rp 66.6 billion in the following year. The number of witnesses seeking protection has grown from less than 500 in 2010–2011 to 1,555 in 2013 and, while this may be a positive sign of rising public trust, 'the increasing number of demands contrasts with the LPSK's actual capacity to efficiently protect people'.[397] Its capacity is also limited by its reliance on the police for protection personnel, who can be recalled at any time by the police, and may have an interest in preventing the LPSK from doing its job in particular cases.[398] The LPSK's ability to respond effectively to requests for protection from regions across Indonesia is likewise greatly constrained by the fact that its relatively few staff members are based solely in Jakarta.[399]

Historically, poor collaboration among the police, prosecutors and the LPSK has hampered legal protection for justice collaborators. In one recent case, police contacted a judge directly to object to a sentencing recommendation submitted by prosecutors because they felt it was too high given the co-operation provided by the defendant.[400] As mentioned above, in practice, police sometimes exercise discretion to not press certain charges early in the criminal process, to 'reward' co-operative

[393] Law No 31 of 2014 on Revisions to Law No 13 of 2006 on Witness and Victim Protection [*Perlindungan Saksi dan Korban*], Art 10A, 2.

[394] Law No 31 or 2014 on Revisions to Law No 13 of 2006 on Witness and Victim Protection, Art 10A, 3.

[395] Law No 31 or 2014 on Revisions to Law No 13 of 2006 on Witness and Victim Protection, Art 10A, 4, 5.

[396] Joint Regulation of the Minister of Law and Human Rights, Prosecutor General, Chief of the National Police, Head of the Corruption Eradication Commission, and Head of the Witness and Victims Protection Agency, 2011, (M.HH-11.HM.03.02.th.2011, PER-045/A/JA/12/2011; No 1 of 2011; KEPB-02/01-55/12/2011; No 4 of 2011).

[397] Asian Human Rights Commission, 'Indonesia: Lack of Effective Witness and Victim Protection' (18 February 2010), www.humanrights.asia/news/ahrc-news/AHRC-STM-029-2010.

[398] Yeremia Sukoyo, 'Rise in Criminal Case Witnesses Seeking Protection' *The Jakarta Globe* (30 December 2013), http://thejakartaglobe.beritasatu.com/news/rise-in-criminal-case-witnesses-seeking-protection/.

[399] Amir Tejo, 'Witness Care Body Pushes Change' *The Jakarta Globe* (18 September 2013), http://thejakartaglobe.beritasatu.com/news/witness-care-body-pushes-change/.

[400] Wagner and Jacobs 'Retooling Law Enforcement'.

witnesses. It remains to be seen if the recent amendments will allow the LPSK to be more effective in the years ahead.

Imprisonment

The Directorate General of Corrections, under the Ministry of Law and Human Rights, is responsible for the management of Indonesia's prisons. As of May 2015, there were 477 prisons and detention centres throughout the country,[401] including 21 specifically designed for the incarceration of drug offenders and five 'general' prisons used by the Directorate General of Corrections to house drug offenders.[402] In the years following the fall of the Soeharto regime, considerable amounts of government attention and foreign development assistance were devoted to reforming and restructuring the justice sector. The corrections system, however, was relatively neglected. Consequently, Indonesian prisons suffer from overcrowding, poor governance and institutionalised corruption, dismal health facilities, and pervasive violence.

Since 2008, there have been greater efforts to reform the corrections system, in particular under the leadership of former President Susilo Bambang Yudhoyono's Deputy Minister for Law and Human Rights, Denny Indrayana. The system remains crippled, however, by budgetary constraints, and struggles to provide even the most basic facilities for inmates. The prison population increased from 71,500 to about 144,000 between 2004 and 2011, while prison capacity increased only 2 per cent over the same period.[403] Although a recently introduced electronic prisons database system has improved oversight, poor administration within the prison system leads to many prisoners being detained longer than the duration of their sentence.[404]

In May 2015, there were a total of 172,911 detainees in Indonesian prisons, according to the Directorate General of Corrections' online database.[405] The overcrowding rate was about 40 per cent across the entire corrections system but climbed above 400 per cent in several prisons. In one of the worst examples, the Bagansiapiapi detention centre housed 707 detainees, despite having capacity for just 98.[406] In that month, detainees held for drug-related charges or convictions comprised more than one-third of the total prison population (63,329 detainees). This figure included

[401] Indonesia. Direktorat Jenderal Pemasyarakatan [Directorate General of Corrections], 'Sistem Database Pemasyarakatan [Corrections Database System]' (May 2015), http://smslap.ditjenpas.go.id/public/grl/current/monthly/kanwil/all/year/2015/month/5.

[402] Indonesia. Direktorat Jenderal Pemasyarakatan, 'Penanganan Narapidana dan Tahanan Tindak Pidana Narkotika [Management of inmates and narcotics criminals]', presentation for a Coordination meeting with the Minister of Law and Human Rights (4 February 2015), http://103.3.70.3/portal/_uploads/post/2015/02/03/Paparan_MENKUMHAM_04_02_2015.ppt), slide 7.

[403] Sudaryono 'Overcrowding Crisis'.

[404] Sudaryono (n 251).

[405] Indonesia. Direktorat Jenderal Pemasyarakatan, 'Sistem Database Pemasyarakatan'.

[406] Indonesia. Direktorat Jenderal Pemasyarakatan (n 401).

38,836 who were held for drug trafficking (61 per cent), and 24,493 who were drug users (39 per cent).[407]

Health conditions in Indonesian prisons are poor, and rates of HIV are much higher than the general population.[408] According to the 2014 Annual Report of the Directorate General of Corrections, the annual budget for health care across the entire prison system was Rp 1 billion (US$ 74,900).[409] This is equivalent to less than US$ 0.50 per prisoner per annum. Although an HIV prevalence study conducted by the Directorate General of Corrections in 2010 found rates of only 1.1 per cent in male inmates and 6.0 per cent in female inmates,[410] previous studies have reported much higher prevalence rates. A report by the Indonesian National AIDS Commission in 2009 claimed, for example, that HIV prevalence rates were as high as 80 per cent in the Jakarta narcotics prison and even claimed that 90 per cent of inmates who die in prison are drug users.[411]

Beyond the poor conditions for inmates, corruption within the prison sector facilitates the ongoing use, distribution, and trafficking of illicit substances.[412] Reports regularly emerge of inmates and prison guards participating in the illegal drug trade.[413] In February 2015, a spokesperson for BNN announced that as much as 70 per cent of all narcotics networks in Indonesia are managed from within the prison system.[414]

At the same time, however, some Indonesian prisons have a good reputation for facilitating various rehabilitation programs and allowing prisoners significant freedom to participate and even instigate various social and creative initiatives within the prison community. In 2011, for example, nine Indonesian prisons were implementing harm reduction initiatives, such as opioid substitution therapy. Bali's Kerobokan Prison has reportedly been a leader in the provision of harm reduction services among Indonesian prisons, and has offered opioid substitution therapy and anti-retroviral therapy, as well as condoms and bleach for the cleaning of syringes.[415]

[407] Indonesia. Direktorat Jenderal Pemasyarakatan (n 401).

[408] Erni J Nelwan, Reinout van Crevel, Bachti Alisjahbana, Agnew Indrati, Reiva F Dwiyana, Nissa Nuralam, Herdiman T Pohan, Ilham Jaya, Andre Meheus, and Aandre van der Ven, 'Human Immunodeficiency Virus, Hepatitis B and Hepatitis C in an Indonesian Prison: Prevalence, Risk Factors and Implications of HIV Screening' (2010) 15(12) *Tropical Medicine and International Health* 1491–98.

[409] Indonesia. Direktorat Jenderal Pemasyarakatan, '2014 Annual Report' (December 2014), 19.

[410] Indonesia. Direktorat Jenderal Pemasyarakatan, 'HIV and Syphilis Prevalence and Risk Behaviour Study among Prisoners in Prisons and Detention Centres in Indonesia' (April 2011), 9.

[411] Indonesia, National Aids Commission, 'Republic of Indonesia Country Report on the Follow Up to the Declaration of the Commitment on HIV/AIDS (UNGASS)': Reporting Period 2008–2009, National AIDS Commission (2010), www.unaids.org/sites/default/files/en/dataanalysis/knowyourresponse/countryprogressreports/2010countries/indonesia_2010_country_progress_report_en.pdf, 21.

[412] US Department of State, Bureau for International Narcotics and Law Enforcement Affairs (n 3), 200.

[413] Agus Maryono, 'More Guards Suspected of Assisting Drug Trade in Prisons' *The Jakarta Post* (4 December 2014), www.thejakartapost.com/news/2014/12/04/more-guards-suspected-assisting-drug-trade-prisons.html; Fana FS Putra, 'Inmates Accused of Running Meth Ring from Indonesian Prisons' *The Jakarta Globe* (13 June 2014), http://thejakartaglobe.beritasatu.com/news/inmates-accused-running-meth-ring-indonesian-prisons/.

[414] Moyang Kasih Dewimerdeka, 'Ironis, Mafia Narkotik Banyak Diatur dari Penjara' *Tempo* (5 February 2015), www.tempo.co/read/news/2015/02/05/063640030/Ironis-Mafia-Narkotik-Banyak-Diatur-dari-Penjara.

[415] Lai (n 45), 8.

Prison Transfers

Indonesia does not have a law regulating the international transfer of prisoners. The Ministry of Law and Human Rights has prepared a policy paper on the transfer of prisoners[416] but it is yet to be debated in the national legislature. The policy paper is intended to respond to the problem of the large numbers of Indonesians (mainly domestic workers and labourers) serving sentences abroad, as well as the issue of foreigners in Indonesian prisons. The policy paper notes that Malaysia, China/Hong Kong, Thailand, the Philippines, France, Nigeria, Iran, Bulgaria, Romania, Brazil, Australia, Syria, India and England have all approached Indonesia with proposals for co-operation on the transfer of sentenced persons.[417]

Prisoner transfer legislation is included in the list of priority bills for discussion for the 2015–2019 period, although not for 2015.[418] Bills sometimes languish on the priority list for many years, so its inclusion does not necessarily indicate a Law on international transfers will be passed before 2019.

Under the 1995 Law on Corrections, inmates can be moved within Indonesia from one correctional institution to another for the purposes of guidance or rehabilitation (*pembinaan*), for safety and security, court procedures, or other reasons if considered necessary.[419] The process for transfer is described in further detail in a 1999 government regulation. The head of a corrections institution may move an inmate if the following requirements are met: written permission is obtained from the relevant authorities; and the request for transfer includes the inmate's rehabilitation records (*berkas-berkas pembinaan*) and results of the deliberations of a Corrections Observation Team.[420]

Australia's International Transfer of Prisoners Scheme

To give one example of the difficulties in this area, Indonesia does not participate in Australia's International Transfer of Prisoners scheme.[421] As discussed briefly above,

[416] Indonesia. Direktorat Jenderal Peraturan Perundang-Undangan [Directorate General of Legislation], Kementerian Hukum dan Hak Asasi Manusia [Ministry of Law and Human Rights], 'Sosialisasi Rancangan Undang-Undang Tentang Pemindahan Narapidana' [Socialisation of the bill on transfer of prisoners] (1 November 2014), http://ditjenpp.kemenkumham.go.id/harmonisasi-peraturan-lainnya/43-sosialisasi/2749-sosialisasi-rancangan-undang-undang-tentang-pemindahan-narapidana.html. The document can be downloaded at www.bphn.go.id/data/documents/na_tentang_transfer_narapidana_final.pdf.

[417] Indonesia. Badan Pembinaan Hukum Nasional [Agency for National Legal Development], Kementerian Hukum dan Hak Asasi Manusia [Ministry of Law and Human Rights], 'Naskah Akademik RUU Tentang Pemindaan Narapidana [Policy paper on the bill on the transfer of prisoners]' (no date), www.bphn.go.id/data/documents/na_tentang_transfer_narapidana_final.pdf, 3-4.

[418] House of Representatives of the Republic of Indonesia, 'Priority Bill Long List', *House of Representatives*, www.dpr.go.id/uu/prolegnas-long-list.

[419] Law No 12 of 1995 on Corrections [*Pemasyarakatan*], Art 16.

[420] Government Regulation No 31 of 1999 on Guidance of Prisoners [*Pembinaan dan Pembimbingan Warga Binaan Pemasyarakatan*], Art 46(2).

[421] Source, *ComLaw* website, search of Legislative Instruments for 'transfer country', consultation of CETS 112. As of 18 May 2011, it was not listed as a participant state on the Commonwealth Attorney-General's ITP information website: www.ag.gov.au/Internationalrelations/Internationalcrimecooperationarrangements/TransferOfPrisoners/Documents/List%20of%20participating%20countries.pdf.

Indonesia does have an extradition agreement with Australia that came into force in 1995 but this does not touch on the international transfer of prisoners.[422] Australia also has a treaty with Indonesia on Mutual Assistance in Criminal Matters.[423] This expressly disclaims transfer of persons in custody to serve sentences as a form of assistance contemplated by the treaty,[424] although temporary transfer for the purpose of giving evidence is contemplated.[425]

Australia has previously made concerted efforts to bring Indonesia into the International Transfer of Prisoner scheme and there are indications that the matter was discussed as early as July 2004.[426] During the 8th Australia-Indonesia Ministerial Forum in Bali in 2006, the Australian press quoted the then Indonesian Minister of Law and Human Rights, Hamid Awaludin, as saying that he expected a bilateral agreement to be in place by September.[427] Negotiations stalled, however, in December of that year.[428] Sticking points included whether or not judicial review could be sought by repatriated prisoners.

There have been periodic revivals of interest in the scheme in the press, and it has often been mentioned in connection with the cases of Schapelle Corby and the Bali Nine. A March 2008 article[429] explained that negotiations were still stalled on issues of minimum imprisonment periods in the sentencing state and whether those convicted of drug or terrorism offences would qualify.[430] Questions were asked in Australia's parliament about the negotiations in February 2010.[431] Negotiations were still underway in 2011 but their status at the time of writing is less clear, given bitter bilateral recrimination over the execution by Indonesia in May 2015 of Australian 'Bali Nine' drug offenders Andrew Chan and Myuran Sukumaran.

[422] Australian Statutory Rules No 441 of 1994.

[423] Australian Statutory Rules No 50 of 1999.

[424] Australian Statutory Rules No 50 of 1999, Art 1(5(c)).

[425] Australian Statutory Rules No 50 of 1999, Art 12.

[426] This press release was one of the first public mentions of such negotiations: Australia, Minister for Justice and Customs, Hon Christopher Ellison, 'Australia and Indonesia Agree to Seek Prisoner Transfer Agreement', Press Release (7 April 2005), http://parlinfo.aph.gov.au/parlInfo/download/media/pressrel/4BOF6/upload_binary/4bof62.pdf;fileType=application%2Fpdf. Although in a reply to a parliamentary question in 2006, the then Attorney-General, Phillip Ruddock, indicated that the matter had been discussed as early as July 2004. Australia, House of Representatives, 'Parliamentary Debates', Phillip Ruddock, Attorney-General (30 October 2006).

[427] *ABC News*, 'Govt Close to Finalising Prisoner Exchange Treaty with Indonesia' (29 June 2006), www.abc.net.au/news/2006-06-29/govt-close-to-finalising-prisoner-exchange-treaty/1789216.

[428] Olivia Rondonuwu, 'ASIA: Indon Rejects Aust Draft fror [sic] Prisoner Exchange' *The Australian Associated Press* (29 December 2006).

[429] Karen Michelmore, 'ASIA: Bali Nine, Corby Dealt Blow on Transfer Chances' *The Australian Associated Press* (11 March 2008). Available online as 'Bali Nine, Corby Dealt Transfer Blow' *NineMSN* (11 March 2008), http://news.ninemsn.com.au/article.aspx?id=151980.

[430] Interestingly, the then Attorney-General Phillip Ruddock's response to a 2006 Parliamentary Question was that universal applicability to all offences was a settled matter between the parties as early as June 2006: Australia, House of Representatives, 'Parliamentary Debates', Phillip Ruddock, Attorney-General (30 October 2006), 170.

[431] Australia, Senate, 'Parliamentary Debates', David Johnson (22 February 2010), 789; Australia. House of Representatives, 'Parliamentary Debates', Julie Bishop (3 February 2010).

The Death Penalty

The death penalty can be applied to a variety of crimes in Indonesia but in the post-Soeharto democratic era it has only been used in cases of terrorism, premeditated murder and narcotics crimes.[432] As mentioned, the death penalty in Indonesia is never mandatory and it is always up to the discretion of the judge whether or not to impose it. In relation to drug offences, the death penalty applies as the maximum sentence available for a range of offences, including producing and trafficking of group I and group II narcotics. As also mentioned, Indonesian law does not impose a time limit within which executions must take place but the Supreme Court has published a practice ruling that asks the Prosecutor General to set a time limit of 180 days for the condemned to file a reconsideration request or seek clemency, failing which the execution will take place.[433]

The means by which the death penalty is carried out is regulated by a 1984 Presidential Decree[434] and a 2010 Chief of Police Regulation details the exact procedures for execution.[435] Prisoners are given 72 hours' notice. Dressed in white, they are transported together with any co-offenders from prison at night to a remote location (often a forest or beach), accompanied by a chaplain or other religious adviser if they wish. Once they arrive, their handcuffs are removed, their hands and legs bound, and they are tied to upright poles (usually with cross-pieces) next to each other. They can choose whether to stand, sit or kneel for their execution, unless the prosecutor determines otherwise. They are given three minutes to 'calm themselves', again accompanied by a chaplain if they wish. They are then offered blindfolds, and a doctor marks the location of their heart in black on their clothes.

A firing squad of 12 officers stands between five and ten metres away. Only three of these 12 officers have live bullets, the rest have blanks. On the commander's signal, all 12 officers fire. If the prisoners still show signs of life, the commander shoots them above the ear. If still not dead, this finishing shot may be repeated until the doctor decides they are dead. Afterwards, their corpses are handed over to their families.

Clemency

Under Art 14 of the Indonesian Constitution, the President is granted a number of powers that he or she may use to free prisoners or reduce their sentence. These

[432] Dave McRae, 'A Key Domino? Indonesia's Death Penalty Politics', *Lowy Institute for International Policy*, (March 2012), www.lowyinstitute.org/publications/key-domino-indonesias-death-penalty-politics, 5.

[433] Supreme Court Chief Justice Guidance on Death Penalty, No 029/KMA/III/2009 (17 March 2009). The limit is based on Art 69 of Law No 14 of 1985 on the Supreme Court (as amended by Law No 5 of 2004 and Law No 3 of 2009).

[434] Presidential Decree No 2 of 1964 [Penpres 02-PNPS-1964] on the Means of Implementation of the Death Penalty Imposed by the General and Military Courts [*Tata Cara Pelaksanaan Hukuman Mati Yang Dijatuhkan di Lingkungan Peradilan Umum dan Peradilan Militer*].

[435] Police Chief Regulation [*Peraturan Kepala Kepolisian*] No 12 of 2010 on the Implementation of the Death Penalty [*Tata Cara Pelaksanaan Pidana Mati*]. See especially, Art 15.

include rehabilitation (*rehabilitasi*), which restores 'the reputation of the person accused of criminal offences who is then acquitted'; amnesty (*amnesti*), which is a form of clemency intended 'to release an entire class of prisoners from incarceration'; and abolition (*abolisi*), which 'resembles amnesty but is granted before conviction, while the case against the prisoner is still pending'. The most commonly exercised of all the powers is, however, clemency (*grasi*), which 'involves the alteration, reduction or abrogation of criminal punishment and is sometimes used to convert a death sentence to life imprisonment'.[436] The only constitutional requirement for the exercise of clemency is that the president must 'consider the views of' (*memperhatikan pertimbangan*) of the Supreme Court.[437]

The 2002 Law on Clemency, as amended in 2010,[438] provides more detail of how the clemency process operates. It provides that clemency may be granted in cases where a person is sentenced to the death penalty, life imprisonment or imprisonment for at least two years. No indications are given as to the types of crimes that will or will not be treated favourably. The President has the right to grant clemency by ordering a lighter or alternative sentence, reducing the sentence or quashing the sentence.[439] The Law reiterates the provision in Art 14(1) of the Constitution that the President has the authority to either grant or reject a clemency application only after considering the views of the Supreme Court. The President is not, however, bound by the Supreme Court's recommendations.

Clemency applications may be lodged once a decision is final and binding and must be lodged within one year of such a decision.[440] This timeframe was introduced by the 2010 amendment to the 2002 Clemency Law. Previously there was no time limit on the preparation of clemency applications, and this was used as a delaying tactic by prisoners in some cases.[441]

Clemency appeals to the President may be lodged by the convicted person, his or her legal representative or his or her family.[442] The Minister for Law and Human Rights has authority to research and facilitate the clemency application process and to submit requests to the President.[443] Copies of the application must be sent to the court of first instance (that is, the District Court that first heard the case), which must forward the application to the Supreme Court.[444] The Supreme Court must, forward a written opinion to the President regarding the application within

[436] The quotations in this paragraph are from Daniel Pascoe, 'Jokowi's Dilemma: Amnesty or Clemency for Political Prisoners?' *Indonesia at Melbourne* (20 July 2015), http://indonesiaatmelbourne.unimelb.edu.au/jokowis-dilemma-amnesty-or-clemency-for-political-prisoners/.

[437] Constitution, Art 14(1). Article 14 also provides that before granting rehabilitation, the president must consider the views of the Supreme Court, and that before granting amnesty or abolition he or she must consider the views of the national legislature, the DPR.

[438] Law No 5 of 2010 on the Amendment of Law No 22 of 2002 on Clemency.

[439] Law No 22 of 2002 on Clemency, Art 4(2).

[440] Law No 22 of 2002 on Clemency, Art 7.

[441] See Daniel Pascoe 'Clemency in Southeast Asian Death Penalty Cases', Centre for Indonesian Law, Islam and Society Policy Paper No 4; Asian Law Centre Briefing Paper No 1 (CILIS and ALC, Melbourne Law School, the University of Melbourne, 2014), 15.

[442] Law No 22 of 2002 on Clemency, Art 8(1).

[443] Law No 5 of 2010 on the Amendment of Law No 22 of 2002 on Clemency, Art 6A(2).

[444] Law No 22 of 2002 on Clemency, Art 8(2).

30 days.[445] After paying regard to the Supreme Court's opinion, the President must issue a decision regarding the clemency application within 30 days, although this time limit is routinely ignored.[446] Should the case be subject to an application for judicial reconsideration (PK) within a similar time frame, the application for reconsideration must be decided by the Supreme Court before the President may decide the clemency application.[447]

The authority to grant or deny clemency is an executive prerogative. The Law clearly states that the President must give due consideration to the Supreme Court's opinion but there is no other provision setting out what particular factors he or she must take into consideration. The general elucidation to the 2010 amendment to the 2002 Clemency Law merely states that:

> in issuing a decision in relation to a clemency application, the president needs to wisely and judiciously consider matters in relation to the crime committed by the convicted, particularly in cases where the crime has been commissioned repeatedly, is a crime against morality and crimes that are sadistic or premeditated in nature.

In recent decisions, the Administrative Court has held that the President's exercise of his wide discretion in clemency cases cannot be reviewed by that court. In April 2015, for example, the Jakarta Administrative Court ruled that it could not hear an appeal brought by drugs offenders Andrew Chan and Myuran Sukumaran against President Joko 'Jokowi' Widodo's refusal to properly consider their clemency requests.[448] Chan and Sukumaran's application was based on the fact that the President had failed to read their applications for clemency, as he was widely reported to have stated publicly. Lawyers for the pair had argued unsuccessfully that, because the President was the head of administration in Indonesia, his refusal to grant clemency was an administrative process that could be challenged in the court.[449] This decision seems to put the President's exercise of his discretion to grant or refuse clemency beyond the reach of the courts, with the result that there seems now to be no way to test whether such a decision complies with the Clemency Law or Art 14 of the Constitution.

Death Penalty and Clemency in Practice

Indonesian government policy on the death penalty is inconsistent and has seen considerable change in recent times. Although its use remains popular with the

[445] Law No 22 of 2002 on Clemency, Art 10.
[446] Law No 22 of 2002 on Clemency, Art 11.
[447] For details of the reconsideration process, see above p 136.
[448] George Roberts, 'Bali Nine: Indonesian Court Rejects Andrew Chan, Myuran Sukumaran's Last-Ditch Appeal against Execution' *ABC News* (7 April 2015), www.abc.net.au/news/2015-04-06/court-decides-on-bali-nine-pair-appeal-against-execution/6373032. Note that President Joko Widodo has formally asked to be known as 'Jokowi'. See Tika Primandari, 'Presiden Minta Disapa "Bapak Jokowi"' [The president asks to be called "Mr Jokowi"]', *Tempo* (7 February 2015), http://nasional.tempo.co/read/news/2015/02/07/078640602/presiden-minta-disapa-bapak-jokowi.
[449] George Roberts, 'Bali Nine: Law Expert Says Indonesian Court Has Power to Hear Execution Challenge for Andrew Chan, Myuran Sukumaran' *ABC News* (30 March 2015), www.abc.net.au/news/2015-03-30/expert-says-indonesian-court-can-hear-execution-challenge/6359910.

public,[450] there are forces within the government advocating both for and against its retention.

For many years, Indonesia was considered a low application, even reductionist, state but the government's stance has hardened significantly after President Jokowi took office in late 2014. Between 1999 and 2014, Indonesia executed 27 people, with executions peaking in 2008, when 10 people were executed, including the three Islamist terrorists known as the Bali bombers. Under President Jokowi, 14 people were put to death in January and April of 2015, with plans announced to execute a total of up to 60 in that year.

Former President Susilo Bambang Yudhoyono reportedly had a deep personal dislike for the death penalty and between 2008 and early 2013, Indonesia observed a de facto moratorium on its use, although this was never officially confirmed. In October 2012, President Yudhoyono granted clemency to four narcotics criminals sentenced to death, including one foreign national.[451] Yudhoyono was pilloried for this decision, particularly by BNN. In the 30 years before this, there was only one known case of a death sentence in a narcotics case being commuted as a result of an application clemency.[452]

The trend towards abolition, or at least reduction, seems to have been driven, in part at least, by large numbers of Indonesians facing the death penalty abroad. In recent years, the Indonesian government has come under intense public pressure to protect its citizens on death row overseas and its bargaining position is severely compromised by continued application of the death penalty at home. The popular understanding is that most of the Indonesians on death row abroad are domestic workers who have killed their employers following rape or abuse. While many of them are indeed migrant workers, the majority of Indonesians on death row abroad may, in fact, be narcotics offenders.[453] Under Yudhoyono, the government set up a highly effective taskforce to provide legal assistance to Indonesians on death row abroad. In at least one case in Saudi Arabia, the government paid 'blood money' to have a sentence commuted to imprisonment.[454]

A significant shift in government policy on executions took place, however, once Yudhoyono left office. Just ten days after the inauguration of President Jokowi, BNN began applying pressure, with Anang Iskandar, the then head of the agency, publicly stating that BNN had written to the Prosecutor General's Office requesting

[450] Yohannie Linggasari, 'Mayoritas Publik Setuju Pengedar Narkotika Divonis Mati [A majority of the public support the death penalty for drug traffickers]' *CNN Indonesia* (6 April 2015), www.cnnindonesia.com/nasional/20150406164718-12-44574/mayoritas-publik-setuju-pengedar-narkotika-divonis-mati/.

[451] Bagus BT Saragih, 'SBY Approves Clemency for 19 Drug Convicts' *The Jakarta Post* (17 October 2012), www.thejakartapost.com/news/2012/10/17/sby-approves-clemency-19-drug-convicts.html.

[452] McRae, 'A Key Domino?' 6.

[453] Panca Nugraha, 'Many Indonesians on Death Row Abroad for Drug Charges' *The Jakarta Post* (10 December 2013), www.thejakartapost.com/news/2013/12/10/many-indonesians-death-row-abroad-drug-charges.html.

[454] *BBC News*, 'Blood Money Spares Indonesian Maid from Saudi Execution' (3 April 2014), www.bbc.com/news/world-asia-pacific-26872447.

that all narcotics prisoners on death row be executed.[455] BNN has long called for the harshest penalties to be imposed for narcotics crimes, and often publicly criticises courts for failing to hand down the death penalty.[456] Although they cannot be entirely attributed to BNN's efforts, recent developments suggest that those convicted of drug-related offences will now rarely, if ever, be considered for clemency. President Jokowi has publicly committed his government to a hardline approach to drugs. He appears to genuinely believe that his country is in the grips of a drug 'emergency'[457] and sees the death penalty as a crucial element in the eradication of narcotics. In December 2014, for example, President Jokowi declared that he would show no mercy to drug offenders facing execution.[458] He then withstood intense international pressure to proceed with the execution of 14 narcotics offenders in January and April 2015.

Accurate figures on the number of prisoners on death row in Indonesia are difficult to obtain. Immediately following the execution of six prisoners in January 2015, the Minister of Law and Human Rights, Yasonna H Laoly, claimed there were 133 prisoners still awaiting execution in Indonesia, including 57 narcotics offenders.[459] Statements from some other government officials suggested that the government was determined to press on with the execution of narcotics criminals. Following the January executions, the Prosecutor General said that the government still had a 'stock' of 60 people to execute.[460] A draft amended Criminal Code is currently before the national legislature (DPR), which would make execution conditional upon a condemned prisoner failing to 'rehabilitate' while on death row. If of good behaviour, his or her sentence would be commuted to a term of imprisonment, form 20 years to life (Article 91). It is too soon to say whether this Bill will be passed and, if so, whether this provision will be included.

[455] Ninis Chairunnisa, '66 Terpidana Mati Narkoba Belum Dieksekusi' *Tempo* (30 October 2014), http://nasional.tempo.co/read/news/2014/10/30/063618293/66-terpidana-mati-narkoba-belum-dieksekusi; Dave McRae, '"Jokowi" and His Firing Squads' *Strategic Review* (July-September 2015), www.sr-indonesia.com/in_the_journal/view/jokowi-and-his-firing-squads?pg=all.

[456] See, for example: *Rappler.com*, 'Hukuman Mati Dua Penyelundup Narkoba asal Iran Dibatalkan [Death sentence of two Iranian drug traffickers cancelled]' (20 April 2015), www.rappler.com/world/regions/asia-pacific/indonesia/90562-hukuman-mati-dua-penyelundup-narkoba-asal-iran-dibatalkan.

[457] Gadjah Mada University, 'Four State Problem Have [sic] to Be Resolved Immediately', *Gadjah Mada University* (10 December 2014), http://ugm.ac.id/en/news/9558-president.jokowi:.four.state.problem.have.to.be.resolved.immediately.

[458] *Antara News*, 'No Mercy for Drug Dealers: President' (9 December 2014), www.antaranews.com/en/news/96848/no-mercy-for-drug-dealers-president.

[459] Indra Akuntono, 'Menkumham Sebut Ada 133 Terpidana Mati di Indonesia [Minister of Law and Human Rights says there are 133 prisoners on death row in Indonesia]' *Kompas* (21 January 2015), http://nasional.kompas.com/read/2015/01/21/11482491/Menkumham.Sebut.Ada.133.Terpidana.Mati.di.Indonesia.

[460] Fabian Januarius Kuwardo, 'Jaksa Agung: Kita Punya "Stok" 60 Orang Yang Akan Dieksekusi Mati [Attorney General: We Have a "Stock" of 60 People Still to Execute]' *Kompas* (20 January 2015), http://nasional.kompas.com/read/2015/01/20/12023981/Jaksa.Agung.Kita.Punya.Stok.60.Orang.yang.Akan.Dieksekusi.Mati.

Remissions

Prisoners may apply for conditional release or a sentence reduction (remission). Remission is regulated by Law on Corrections No 12 of 1995 and a series of related regulations.[461]

According to a 2012 regulation, all prisoners have the right to remissions,[462] which may be granted to prisoners who demonstrate good behaviour and have served at least six months of their sentence. To be considered for 'good behaviour', the inmate must not have been served a disciplinary sentence in the previous six months, and must have participated to a satisfactory level in a rehabilitation program run by the corrections institution.[463] Inmates convicted of narcotics crimes face additional requirements, including providing a written statement that they are willing to co-operate with law enforcement officials to reveal details of their case.[464] This additional requirement only applies to narcotics criminals serving a prison sentence of at least five years.[465]

Presidential Decision No 174 of 1999 provides further details of the procedures regulating the granting of remission. Remissions are granted by the Minister of Law and Human Rights (previously the Minister of Law and Legislation, as described in the decision).[466] 'General' remissions are granted on Independence Day (17 August),[467] and 'special' remissions are granted on religious holidays, such as *Idul Fitri* (*Eid al-Fitr*), and Christmas, according to the religion of the inmate.[468] Inmates may be eligible for 'additional' remissions if they demonstrate: service to the country; behaviour that will benefit the country or humanity; or behaviour that assists in rehabilitation activities in prison.[469] The length of remission granted depends on the type of remission and the length of the sentence served, as below.[470]

[461] Presidential Decision No 174 of 1999 on Remissions; Government Regulation No 99 of 2012 on Changes to Government Regulation No 32 of 1999 on Conditions and Requirements of Inmates Rights [*Syarat dan Tata Cara Pelaksanaan Hak Warga Binaan Pemasyarakatan*], as amended by Government Regulation No 28 of 2006 and Government Regulation No 99 of 2012; and Regulation of the Minister of Law and Human Rights No 21 of 2013 on the Requirements and Procedure for Granting Remission, Assimilation, Family Leave, Conditional Release, Leave Approaching Release and Conditional Leave [*Syarat dan Tata Cara Pemberian Remisi, Asimilasi, Cuti Mengunjungi Keluarga, Pembebasan Bersyarat, Cuti Menjelang Bebas, dan Cuti Bersyarat*].

[462] Government Regulation No 99 of 2012 on the Amendment of Government Regulation No 32 of 1999 on Conditions and Requirements on Inmates' Rights [*Syarat dan Tata Cara Pelaksanaan Hak Warga Binaan Pemasyarakatan*], Art 34.

[463] Article 34(2), (3).

[464] Article 34A(1), (3). These requirements are also detailed in Arts 3 and 7 of Regulation of the Minister of Law and Human Rights No 21 of 2013 on the Requirements and Procedure for Granting Remission, Assimilation, Family Leave, Conditional Release, Leave Approaching Release, and Conditional Leave.

[465] Article 34A(2).

[466] Presidential Decision No 174 of 1999 on Remissions [*Remisi*], Art 1.

[467] Presidential Decision No 174 of 1999 on Remissions, Art 2(a).

[468] Presidential Decision No 174 of 1999 on Remissions, Art 2(b).

[469] Presidential Decision No 174 of 1999 on Remissions, Art 3(1).

[470] Presidential Decision No 174 of 1999 on Remissions.

Table 4: Remissions in Sentences

Sentence served	General remission (Art 4)	Special remissions (Art 5)
6–12 months	1 month	15 days
1 year	2 months	1 month
2 years	3 months	1 month
3 years	4 months	1 month
4–5 years	5 months	1 month and 15 days
6 years +	6 months	2 months

Additional remissions are half the length of the general remission for that year for prisoners who have demonstrated service to the country or behaviour that provides benefits to the country and humanity, and one-third of the length of the general remission for behaviour that assists in rehabilitation activities in prison.[471]

Applications for remissions are made to the Minister of Law and Human Rights by the head of the correctional institution, through the office of the Ministry of Law and Human Rights. The Minister informs inmates of remission decisions each year on Indonesian Independence day, 17 August, or on the relevant religious holiday.[472] Convicted Australian drug smuggler Schapelle Corby had more than two years cut from her sentence through this process of general and special remissions.[473]

Conditional Release and Leave

Before serving their full term of imprisonment, a prisoner may be eligible for conditional release. According to the Criminal Code, to qualify for conditional release a prisoner must have served at least nine months in prison or two-thirds of their term, whichever is greater.[474] For the purposes of determining this minimum period, multiple prison sentences are counted as one term.[475] The parole period will be one year longer than whatever time the person had left to serve of their sentence.[476] A number of conditions may be imposed during this period, including a requirement of good behaviour.[477]

Probation is the responsibility of the Minister for Law and Human Rights (previously the Minster for Judicial Affairs (*Kehakiman*), as described in the Criminal Code).[478] Persons convicted of drug offences who are sentenced to death or life

471 Presidential Decision No 174 of 1999 on Remissions, Art 6.
472 Presidential Decision No 174 of 1999 on Remissions, Art 13.
473 Kate Lamb, 'Schapelle Corby Release Has Irked Some in Indonesia' *The Guardian* (10 February 2014), www.theguardian.com/world/2014/feb/10/schapelle-corby-release-irked-some-indonesia.
474 Criminal Code, Art 15(1).
475 Criminal Code, Art 15(2).
476 Criminal Code, Art 15(3).
477 Criminal Code, Arts 15(2), 15A(1), and see generally Arts 15A, 15B and 16 for other requirements of probation.
478 Criminal Code, Art 16.

imprisonment do not qualify for conditional release. In 2009, the Directorate General of Corrections introduced a pilot program in order to reduce overcrowding in prisons by relaxing the requirements for applications for parole or reduced sentencing. The program was short-lived, however, because of public backlash, particularly over concerns around the early release of prisoners convicted with corruption and terrorism offences.[479]

Five forms of release are outlined in detail in a 2013 Minister of Law and Human Rights regulation:

1. **Assimilation.** This is the process of reintroducing inmates and child detainees into community life.[480] Inmates must have completed at least half of their sentence to be eligible for assimilation, have demonstrated good behaviour,[481] and actively participated in rehabilitation programs.[482] Inmates convicted of narcotics offences must have completed at least two-thirds of their sentence to be eligible for assimilation.[483] Assimilation can take the form of education, work skills training, community work, or other rehabilitation activities.[484] Inmates convicted of narcotics offences are, however, restricted to community work in government or non-governmental institutions, including in religious organisations, and sectors such as agriculture, education and culture, health and sanitation.[485]
2. **Conditional release.** This is a rehabilitation program to integrate inmates and child detainees into community life after fulfilling certain requirements. As noted above, to be eligible for conditional release, inmates must have served two-thirds of their sentence, or at least nine months.[486] The inmate must have demonstrated good behaviour in the previous nine months and have participated in rehabilitation activities with enthusiasm and diligence. The community must also 'be able to accept' the inmate.[487] Inmates convicted of narcotics offences serving a sentence of five years or more face additional requirements, including co-operating with law enforcement officials to reveal details of their case and 'prior participation in assimilation activities for a length of time equivalent to at least half of the time remaining of his or her sentence'.[488]
3. **Family leave.** This is a rehabilitation program to allow inmates and child detainees to assimilate with their families and the community.[489] Family leave is a maximum of two days (or two times 24 hours) every three months.[490] Family

[479] Sudaryono (n 251).
[480] Regulation of the Minister of Law and Human Rights No 21 of 2013 on the Requirements and Procedure for Granting Remission, Assimilation, Family Leave, Conditional Release, Leave Approaching Release, and Conditional Leave, Art 1(2).
[481] To be considered for 'good behaviour' the inmate must not have served a disciplinary sentence in the previous six months, Art 21(3).
[482] Regulation No 21 of 2013, Art 21(1).
[483] Regulation No 21 of 2013, Art 22.
[484] Regulation No 21 of 2013, Art 30.
[485] Regulation No 21 of 2013, Art 34.
[486] Regulation No 21 of 2013, Art 49.
[487] Regulation No 21 of 2013, Art 49(1).
[488] Regulation No 21 of 2013, Art 49: '*telah menjalani Asimilasi paling sedikit ½ (satu per dua) dari sisa masa pidana yang wajib dijalani*'.
[489] Regulation No 21 of 2013, Art 1(3).
[490] Regulation No 21 of 2013, Art 44.

leave is available to inmates serving a sentence of at least 12 months.[491] Inmates must demonstrate good behaviour, with no procedural violations in the current year.[492] They should have served at least half of their sentence, or six months for child detainees.[493] Family leave is not available to narcotics offenders with a sentence of five years or more, inmates sentenced to death or life in prison, inmates whose lives are under threat, or inmates who might reoffend.[494]

4. **Leave approaching release.** This is a rehabilitation program to integrate inmates and child detainees into community life after fulfilling certain requirements.[495] The inmate must have served two-thirds of his or her sentence, with at least nine months of good behaviour. The length of the leave is the same as the last remission granted, and can be no longer than six months.[496] For inmates convicted of narcotics offences, leave can be no longer than three months, and the application must also be approved by the Director General of Corrections.[497]
5. **Conditional leave.** This is a rehabilitation program to integrate inmates and child detainees into community life after fulfilling certain requirements.[498] Conditional leave can be granted for a maximum of four months.[499] To be eligible for conditional leave, an inmate must be serving a sentence of 15 months or less, have served at least two-thirds of his or her sentence, and have demonstrated good behaviour for the past six months.[500] For persons convicted of narcotics offences, this good behaviour requirement is extended to nine months. If the person in question commits a new offence while on leave, the time spent outside prison does not contribute towards serving the sentence.[501]

The procedure for granting leave and conditional release has been simplified since the introduction of an electronic database across the Indonesian corrections system, although there are still multiple layers of approval before leave or release can be granted. In all cases, a corrections observation team examines the inmate's data and makes a recommendation to the head of the corrections institution.[502] The head of the corrections institution can, in some cases publish a decision immediately (for example, for some forms of assimilation),[503] although in other cases, the decision must be approved by the minister.[504] For conditional release of persons convicted

[491] Regulation No 21 of 2013, Art 35(b).
[492] Regulation No 21 of 2013, Art 35(a).
[493] Regulation No 21 of 2013, Art 35(c), (e).
[494] Regulation No 21 of 2013, Art 36.
[495] Regulation No 21 of 2013, Art 1(4).
[496] Regulation No 21 of 2013, Art 60.
[497] Regulation No 21 of 2013, Art 61.
[498] Regulation No 21 of 2013, Art 1(4).
[499] Regulation No 21 of 2013, Art 71.
[500] Regulation of the Minister of Law and Human Rights No M.2.PK.04-10 of 2007 on the Requirements and Procedure for Assimilation, Conditional Release, Leave Approaching Release, and Conditional Leave [*Syarat dan Tata Cara Pelaksanaan Asimilasi, Pembebasan Bersyarat, Cuti Menjelang Bebas, dan Cuti Bersyarat*], Art 1(4).
[501] M.2.PK.04-10 of 2007, Art 6(1)(f)(4).
[502] Regulation No 21 of 2013, Art 25–27, Art 63–65.
[503] Regulation No 21 of 2013, Art 27(2).
[504] Regulation No 21 of 2013, Art 29.

of narcotics offences, for example, the head of the corrections institution makes a recommendation to the head of the regional corrections office. The regional corrections office chief then makes a recommendation to the Director General of Corrections, and the latter makes a recommendation to the Minister of Law and Human Rights, based on the recommendations of his team, and the recommendations of the Police, BNN, and the Prosecutor General's office. Leave may then granted by ministerial decision.[505]

Decisions on conditional release may be revoked if there are indications that the crime will be repeated or the person in question breaks the law, fails to report to prison officials on three consecutive occasions, fails to report a change in address, does not participate in a development program set by prison officials, or 'causes unrest in the community' (*menimbulkan keresahan dalam masyarakat*). It was this last condition that led narcotics offender Schapelle Corby to cancel a highly publicised interview on her release from Kerobokan Prison in Bali in 2014. The then Deputy Minister for Law and Human Rights, Denny Indrayana, had stressed that if Corby gave an interview, she would likely breach the conditions of her release.[506]

Life Imprisonment

A question arises as to whether a life sentence in Indonesia necessarily means the prisoner must die in jail. In fact, life imprisonment may be reduced by a grant of clemency (*grasi*) or remission (*remisi*), the procedures for which are regulated by different instruments.

Law No 22 of 2002 on Clemency states that a person who receives a life sentence may appeal for clemency for *perubahan hukuman*, or sentence amendment (Arts 2 and 4(2)). Remission for those sentenced to life imprisonment is, however, regulated by Presidential Decision No 174 of 1999 on Remission.[507] Article 9 provides:

(1) Inmates subjected to a life sentence who have served at least five years of the sentence consecutively, as well as demonstrated good behaviour, may have their sentence amended to a fixed period of time, with 15 years the maximum time remaining to be served.
(2) Amendment of life imprisonment to a fixed sentence as stipulated in paragraph (1) is granted by a Presidential Decision.
(3) A request for amendment of life imprisonment to a fixed sentence shall be submitted by the inmate to the President via the Minister of Law and Legislation [now the Minister of Law and Human Rights].

[505] Regulation No 21 of 2013, Art 59.

[506] Tim Lindsey and Simon Butt, 'Schapelle Corby Should Not Give Interviews. To Do So Would Be Foolhardy' *The Guardian* (17 February 2014), www.theguardian.com/commentisfree/2014/feb/17/schapelle-corby-should-not-give-interviews.

[507] The President's power to regulate remissions derives from Government Regulation No 32 of 1999, Art 35 on the Requirements and Procedures for implementing the Rights of Inmates, which states that 'regulation of remissions is determined by Presidential Regulation'.

(4) Provisions on the procedures for submission of a request for amendment of life imprisonment to a fixed sentence as stipulated in paragraph (3) will be further regulated by a Decision of the Minister of Law and Legislation [Minister of Law and Human Rights].

A prisoner whose life sentence has been reduced to at least 15 years of imprisonment may then apply for further remission and, if their age permits, assimilation and full release.[508]

VII. REHABILITATION AND DIVERSIONARY PROGRAMS

The 2009 Narcotics Law contains a number of provisions that aim to channel drug users into rehabilitation programs as an alternative to imprisonment.[509] Under the Law, addicts and 'victims of drug abuse' are required to undergo therapy at a rehabilitation or treatment clinic.[510] Although the Law states that time spent in treatment or rehabilitation is considered equivalent to a prison term,[511] use of these new provisions remains uncommon and inconsistent. There is poor awareness among many judges, prosecutors and defence lawyers, regarding the courts' discretion to order rehabilitation as an alternative form of sentencing.[512] Many judges apply a sentence of imprisonment plus rehabilitation. This pattern has contributed to the high levels of incarceration of drug users in the Indonesian prison system.[513]

Efforts have been made to rectify this situation. A 2010 Supreme Court Circular Letter (a form of practice note) directs that, where possible, users should undergo rehabilitation and be kept out of prison.[514] It also contains further guidance as to when a suspect qualifies as a drug user (as opposed to, for example, a dealer). The Circular Letter stipulates that to be classified as a 'user', suitable for a rehabilitation sentence, the following five elements must be satisfied:

— The person was caught 'red handed'. There is no explanation of what it is that the person must be caught doing but presumably this refers to either being caught using drugs or caught committing the offence with which the person is charged.
— When the person was caught, evidence of one day's use of drugs was found. No explanation is given of whether the person must be in possession of the drugs at the time, whether the 'evidence found' must be linked to the person, or how this provision would operate when multiple users are caught at the same time.

[508] Regulation of the Minister of Law and Human Rights No 21 of 2013 on the Requirements and Procedure for Granting Remission, Assimilation, Family Leave, Conditional Release, Leave Approaching Release and Conditional Leave, Art 11.
[509] 2009 Narcotics Law, Arts 54, 103(2).
[510] 2009 Narcotics Law, Arts 103(1).
[511] 2009 Narcotics Law, Arts 103(2).
[512] Lai (n 45), 2.
[513] Lai (n 45), 2.
[514] Supreme Court Circular [*Surat Edaran Mahkamah Agung*] No 4 of 2010 on the Internment of Narcotics Users into Rehabilitation and Therapy Institutions [*Menempatkan Pemakai Narkoba ke Dalam Panti Terapi dan Rehabilitasi*].

According to an older Circular Letter,[515] the maximum quantity of drugs a person could be found with to satisfy this requirement was extremely low. The 2010 Circular Letter dramatically increased these maximums, and added more drugs to the list.

Table 5: Maximum Quantity of Drugs to Be Defined as a 'User'

Drug	2009 Circular	2010 Circular
Cannabis	0.05 g	5 g
Heroin	0.15 g	1.8 g
Cocaine	0.15 g	1.8 g
Ecstasy	1 tablet	2.4 g or 8 tablets
Methamphetamine	—	1 g
LSD	—	2 g
PCP	—	3 g
Mescaline	—	5 g

— The person tests positive to drug use by a laboratory report requested by the police investigator or prosecutor.
— A report is provided by a judge-appointed government psychologist or psychiatrist. What such a report must show is not stated.
— No evidence is found that the person is involved in the unlawful production or distribution of drugs.[516]

Further, a joint regulation on the rehabilitation of drug addicts was signed in 2014 by the Chief Justice of the Supreme Court, the Minister for Law and Human Rights, the Minister of Health, the Minister of Social Affairs, the Prosecutor General, the Chief of Police, and the head of BNN. The regulation is aimed at improving co-ordination among these institutions, and ensuring that addicts and victims of drug abuse are provided with treatment and rehabilitation services during investigation and trial, as well as following sentencing. Under the regulation, a co-ordinated team, comprising a medical team (a doctor and psychologist) and a legal team (representatives of the police, BNN, the prosecutor's office and the Ministry of Law and Human Rights) is responsible for conducting an assessment of the accused. The medical team determines the severity of drug use and provides recommendations for therapy and rehabilitation.[517] As of December 2014, assessments had been conducted on

[515] Supreme Court Circular No 7 of 2009 On the Internment of Narcotics Users into Rehabilitation and Therapy Institutions [*Menempatkan Pemakai Narkoba ke Dalam Panti Terapi dan Rehabilitasi*].
[516] Supreme Court Circular No 4 of 2010 on the internment of narcotics users into rehabilitation and therapy institutions [*Menempatkan Pemakai Narkoba ke Dalam Panti Terapi dan Rehabilitasi*].
[517] Joint Regulation of the Chief Justice of the Supreme Court, the Minister of Law and Human Rights, the Minister of Health, the Minister of Social Affairs, the Prosecutor General, the Chief of Police and Head of the National Narcotics Agency on Addicts and Victims of Drug Abuse in Rehabilitation

163 people, with 94 directed into rehabilitation programs, 40 people imprisoned, and 25 still undergoing investigation or trial.[518]

The 2009 Narcotics Law describes two forms of rehabilitation: social and medical. Medical rehabilitation is to be conducted in a hospital, community health centre (*puskesmas*) or rehabilitation institution appointed by the Minister, and social rehabilitation is conducted by government or community institutions. Where a court orders a drug user to undergo treatment at a state-run rehabilitation centre, the drug user may access those facilities free of charge. If, however, they are allocated to a privately managed centre (such as community or religious organisations), they must pay for their own treatment.

The quality of rehabilitation and treatment programs throughout Indonesia is highly variable.[519] Rehabilitation services are managed by the Ministry of Health, which manages hospitals and community health centres, the Social Affairs Ministry, which oversees community and religious rehabilitation services, and BNN. Concerns have been raised about the lack of consistency between these Ministries and agencies and the lack of consensus around 'best practice' models.[520] The 2009 Narcotics Law allows rehabilitation services and therapy to be delivered via a 'religious or traditional approach'.[521] There are questions as to whether this allows for treatment that is religious or traditional in character but may fall short of accepted medical and scientific approaches.

In 2014, BNN reported that there were 366 institutions where drug users could report for rehabilitation and treatment,[522] including 316 health facilities managed by the Ministry of Health and 50 rehabilitation institutions managed by the Ministry of Social Affairs.[523] BNN now has four compulsory drug treatment centres, which are located in Bogor, Makassar, Samarinda and Batam, and together serve around 1,000 drug users. In 2013, there were 6,111 individuals being treated for drug addiction in facilities co-operating with BNN, of whom 88 per cent were men and 12 per cent were women.[524] In 2012, 14,510 drug users accessed rehabilitation services.[525]

Institutions [*Peraturan Bersama Ketua Mahkamah Agung, Menteri Hukum dan Hak Asasi Manusia, Menteri Kesehatan, Menteri Sosial, Jaksa Agung, Kepala Kepolisian Negara dan Kepala Badan Narkotika Nasional tentang Penanganan Pecandu Narkotika Dan Korban Penyalahgunaan Narkotika Ke Dalam Lembaga Rehabilitasi*] (No 01/PB/MA/III/2014; No 03 of 2014; No 11 of 2014; No 03 of 2014, No Per 005/A/JA/03/2014; No 1 of 2014; No Perber/01/III/2014/BNN), Art 9(2).

518 Indonesia. BNN, 'Lampiran Press Release' 14.

519 Lai (n 45) 6.

520 Lai (n 45) 6.

521 2009 Narcotics Law, Art 57.

522 Indonesia, BNN (n 36).

523 The actual number may be higher than this. The Minister of Social Affairs, Khofifah Indar Parawansa, has repeatedly stated that her ministry oversees 105 compulsory reporting institutions (IPWL), although the Ministry of Social Affairs website lists just 50. See Ari Suprianti Rikin, 'Kemsos Siap Rehabilitasi Social 10,000 Korban Penyalahgunaan Narkoba [Social Affairs Ministry prepared to rehabilitate 10,000 victims of drug abuse]' *Berita Satu* (30 January 2015), www.beritasatu.com/nasional/245070-kemsos-siap-rehabilitasi-sosial-10000-korban-penyalahgunaan-narkoba.html.

524 Indonesia, BNN, 'Jurnal Data', 10.

525 Fana Suparman, 'BNNP dan BNNK Diminta Aktif Ajak Pecandu untuk Direhabilitasi [BNNP and BNNK asked to actively encourage addicts to join rehabilitation activities]' *Berita Satu* (29 April 2014), www.beritasatu.com/nasional/180846-bnnp-dan-bnnk-diminta-aktif-ajak-pecandu-untuk-direhabilitasi.html.

BNN has recently declared ambitious plans to rehabilitate 100,000 drug users in 2015,[526] a figure that will be difficult to achieve given actual rates of drug use and existing disincentives for accessing treatment (see below).[527]

Compulsory Reporting Requirements

Under the 2009 Narcotics Law, addicts over the age of 18 are required to self-report to designated rehabilitation institutions appointed by the government.[528] Failure to report can result in fines of up to Rp 2 million (US$ 150) or up to six months imprisonment. As noted earlier in this chapter, the families, parents or guardians of addicts under age 18 are also required to report them to these institutions, and face a fine of up to Rp 1 million (US$ 75) or up to six months imprisonment for failure to comply.

This oppressive requirement was further elaborated in a 2011 government regulation on mandatory reporting. Under the regulation, the receiving institution assesses the addict to determine the degree of addiction and formulates a treatment plan, which is also agreed to by the addict (or his or her family or guardian).[529] After the addict has agreed to the treatment plan, he or she is provided with a self-reporting card, which is valid for two treatment cycles of one to six months.[530] The 2009 Narcotics Law states that addicts who are already registered with a rehabilitation institution should not be charged with an offence.[531]

Despite the protection provided to drug users by these compulsory reporting provisions, uptake of self-reporting has, unsurprisingly, been sluggish. In 2013, for example, BNN reported that only 1,370 drug users voluntarily reported to rehabilitation institutions.[532] A history of criminalisation of drug use and possession for personal consumption, as well as 'routine' abuse by law enforcement officials, has undoubtedly played a role in dissuading addicts from seeking rehabilitation services.

The 2011 government regulation states that health service providers must send registration data to BNN, which must store it in a database.[533] Civil society groups

[526] Fedina S Sundaryani, 'Govt Wants to Rehabilitate 100,000 Drug Addicts in 2015' *The Jakarta Post* (1 February 2015), www.thejakartapost.com/news/2015/02/01/govt-wants-rehabilitate-100000-drug-addicts-2015.html.

[527] Claudia Stoicescu, 'Forced Rehabilitation of Drug Users in Indonesia not a Solution' *The Conversation* (2 July 2015), https://theconversation.com/forced-rehabilitation-of-drug-users-in-indonesia-not-a-solution-43184. In 2011, BNN introduced a policy known as P4GN (Prevention and Eradication of Illicit Drug Abuse and Trafficking). The program aims to inculcate anti-drug attitudes and behaviours among the population of non-drug users to make them 'immune' to the trade and ensure that existing drug users receive medical treatment and social rehabilitation. The program further aims to work towards 'the total eradication of local and foreign syndicates' through forfeiture of assets as well as 'harsh and severe law enforcement measures'. See AIPA (n 82) 7–8.

[528] 2009 Narcotics Law, Art 55(2).

[529] Government Regulation No 25 of 2011 on Compulsory Reporting of Drug Addicts [*Pelaksanaan Wajib Lapor Pecandu Narkotika*], Art 9.

[530] Government Regulation No 25 of 2011 on Compulsory Reporting of Drug Addicts, Art 10(2), including accompanying explanation.

[531] 2009 Narcotics Law, Art 128(2), (3).

[532] Indonesia. BNN (n 28) 76.

[533] Lai (n 45) 6.

have expressed deep concern over the potential for misuse of this data for the investigation of drug offences.[534] There are already numerous reports of law enforcement officials demanding access to private client records at methadone substitution clinics and other organisations working with drug users.[535]

VIII. REGULATIONS ON FINANCE AND THE DRUG TRADE

The United States' State Department's International Narcotics Control Strategy Report observes that although Indonesia is not a major financial centre or tax haven, it is vulnerable to money laundering because of major loopholes in financial legislation and regulation, its cash-based economy, the weak rule of law, and the lack of effective enforcement institutions.[536] While the report lists the finances of other criminal activities as far more significant than those associated with the illicit drug trade,[537] BNN maintains that drug-related money laundering is a major challenge.

BNN has found that syndicates use a variety of means to deal with the proceeds of their crimes, including transferring funds in the guise of remittances from overseas Indonesian workers and using private banking facilities.[538] The Financial Reports and Analysis Centre (PPATK) reported that of all money laundering cases prosecuted between January 2005 and January 2013, 27 involved narcotics, while 16 cases involved corruption and 14 related to fraud.[539]

Provisions dealing with proceeds of crime from the illicit drug trade are largely contained in the 2009 Narcotics Law and the 2010 Law on the Prevention and Eradication of Money Laundering.[540] Under the 2009 Narcotics Law, it is an offence to transact in any way with property (including giving, receiving, trading, storing, hiding, bequeathing or inheriting) in any form, tangible or intangible, derived from an offence involving narcotics or precursor substances.[541] The offence requires that the recipient know that the transaction involved benefits derived from a narcotics or precursor offence.[542] The Law does not provide details of the level of knowledge required but it appears actual knowledge is necessary, rather than just a strong suspicion. The offence attracts minimum imprisonment of five years or a minimum fine of Rp 1 billion for those instigating such transactions, and a three year minimum sentence or Rp 500 million for those receiving funds.[543]

534 Lai (n 45) 6.
535 Stoicescu, 'Forced Rehabilitation of Drug Users'.
536 United States Department of State, Bureau of International Narcotics and Law Enforcement Affairs, 'International Narcotics Control Strategy Report: Volume II Money Laundering and Financial Crimes' (March 2014), www.state.gov/j/inl/rls/nrcrpt/2014/vol2/index.htm. 125.
537 United States Department of State, Bureau of International Narcotics and Law Enforcement Affairs, 'International Narcotics Control Strategy Report: Volume II'.
538 Indonesia. BNN, 'Mayoritas Kasus Pencucian Uang Berasal Dari Sindikat Narkoba' (25 November 2013), www.bnn.go.id/portal/index.php/konten/detail/humas/pressrelease/11605/mayoritas-kasus-pencucian-uang-berasal-dari-sindikat-narkoba.
539 Ibid.
540 Law No 8 of 2010 on Prevention and Elimination of the Crime of Money Laundering, Art 2(1)(c).
541 2009 Narcotics Law, Art 137.
542 2009 Narcotics Law, Art 137(b).
543 2009 Narcotics Law, Art 137.

In accordance with the 2009 Narcotics Law, proceeds of narcotics and precursor crimes that are seized by the state are to be used for the purpose of funding efforts to prevent and eradicate the illicit trade and abuse of narcotics, and to fund medical and social rehabilitation.[544]

Provisions that apply to the proceeds of drug crimes are also contained in the 2010 Law on the Prevention and Eradication of Money Laundering. Under this Law, the proceeds of crime are defined as benefits that are obtained from an exhaustive list of offences, including narcotics offences.[545]

Any person who deals in assets that they know, or should reasonably suspect, to be the proceeds of crime with the purpose of hiding the source of those assets is liable to a prison sentence of up to 20 years and/or a fine of up to Rp 10 billion.[546] This offence covers depositing, transferring (including overseas transfers), spending, exchanging for foreign currency or a letter of credit, and other changes to the form of the assets.[547] Anyone who hides or obfuscates the origin, source, location, purpose, transfer of rights or beneficial ownership of assets that are known to be, or are reasonably suspected of being, proceeds of crime is also liable to up to 20 years imprisonment and a fine of up to Rp 5 billion.[548] Anyone who accepts or takes control of a deposit, transfer, payment, grant, donation, allocation or exchange, or uses assets that he or she knows to be, or should reasonably suspect, to be the proceeds of crime is liable to a prison sentence of up to 5 years and a fine of up to Rp 1 billion.[549] These provisions do not apply where that individual is an informant who has fulfilled his or her reporting obligations in accordance with the law.[550] Where a corporate entity is implicated in a money laundering offence, liability may be imposed on both the entity and its management, and increased fines and a range of other penalties apply.[551]

The provisions of the 2010 Law on the Prevention and Eradication of Money Laundering are stricter than the proceeds of crime provisions in the 2009 Narcotics Law. Under the Money Laundering Law, an individual who receives benefits will be liable if he or she should reasonably have suspected the assets in question to be proceeds of crime. 'Should reasonably suspect' refers to a situation where the individual is aware of an intention or purpose at the time of the transaction that would (on an objective analysis) indicate a breach of law.[552] A person who was aware of the circumstances of a transaction will be liable, even where the prosecution falls short of demonstrating that the accused had actual knowledge that the funds were proceeds of crime. It appears more likely that a suspect would be charged under the 2010 Law on the Prevention and Eradication of Money Laundering than the 2009 Narcotics Law, given it contains stricter provisions and was enacted more recently.

[544] Law No 35 of 2009 on Narcotics, Art 101(3).
[545] Law No 8 of 2010 on Prevention and Elimination of the Crime of Money Laundering, Art 2(1)(c).
[546] Law No 8 of 2010 on Prevention and Elimination of the Crime of Money Laundering, Art 3.
[547] Ibid.
[548] Law No 8 of 2010 on Prevention and Elimination of the Crime of Money Laundering, Art 4.
[549] Law No 8 of 2010 on Prevention and Elimination of the Crime of Money Laundering, Art 5(1).
[550] Law No 8 of 2010 on Prevention and Elimination of the Crime of Money Laundering, Art 5(2).
[551] Law No 8 of 2010 on Prevention and Elimination of the Crime of Money Laundering, Arts 6 and 7.
[552] Law No 8 of 2010 on Prevention and Elimination of the Crime of Money Laundering, explanatory note to Art 5(1).

The Money Laundering Law also creates a range of compulsory reporting requirements for financial service providers. These encompass a wide range of institutions, such as banks, finance companies, insurance companies, pension funds, listed companies, investment managers.[553] Both BNN and police officers are empowered to undertake investigations in relation to money-laundering for drug offences where they find sufficient evidence.[554]

There are many examples of prosecutions for narcotics-related money laundering under the 2010 Money Laundering Law and the 2009 Narcotics Law.[555] In some cases examined, only one of the relevant pieces of legislation is referred to, while in others both laws are mentioned. Case number 438/Pid.Sus/2013/PN.Jkt.Sel, for example, involved a woman caught by two BNN officers attempting to deliver a bag containing methamphetamine to another woman. Multiple transactions had also been made into her bank account, suspected to be as a result of narcotics. The prosecution charged the defendant with purchasing or selling or receiving category I narcotics under Art 114(2) of the 2009 Narcotics Law, and with possession under Art 112(2) as a secondary charge. The prosecution also offered two alternative money laundering charges under Art 137(b) of the 2009 Narcotics Law, or Arts 5(1) and 2(1)(c), of the 2010 Money Laundering Law. The first alternative of the two charges relating to money laundering was proven, so no attempt was made to prove the second. The woman was found guilty under Arts 114(2) and 137(b) of the 2009 Narcotics Law and sentenced to 15 years prison, with a fine of Rp 1 billion.

IX. JUDICIAL DECISIONS

As mentioned, Indonesia has a very traditional civil law system, and judicial decisions are generally not considered a source of law in themselves. There is, thus, no formal system of precedent or independent body of judge-made law in the way these are understood in British tradition common law countries. Although an Indonesian judge may follow a previous decision from a higher court, he or she is not usually required to do so. Legislation and regulation form the overwhelming bulk of the applicable sources of law in criminal cases.

The courts are sometimes required to make important decisions to fill a gap that is not regulated by drawing principles relating to other sources, such as general principles of scholarly writing, or, more often, on the interpretation or application of legislation. As explained above, decisions of this kind can be influential as what is known as *yurisprudensi* (jurisprudence). Only a very small number of Supreme Court decisions are considered *yurisprudensi tetap* (fixed jurisprudence) that is, decisions that

[553] Law No 8 of 2010 on Prevention and Elimination of the Crime of Money Laundering, Chapter IV.

[554] Law No 8 of 2010 on Prevention and Elimination of the Crime of Money Laundering, explanatory note to Art 74.

[555] 2009 Narcotics Law, Art 137 and 2010 Law on the Prevention and Eradication of Money-Laundering Arts 3, 4 and 5. See for example, Decision No.603/Pid.Sus/2013/PN.Sda, No 42/Pid/2014/PT.DKI, No 132/Pid/2013/PT.BTN, No 438/Pid.Sus/2013/PN.Jkt.Sel., 149/Pid/2012/PT.BTN, 191/Pid.Sus/2014/PN.Jbi, among many others.

it would be unusual for a lower court not to follow. These *yurisprudensi* decisions are sometimes much more rigidly defined than is 'case law' in common law countries. The Supreme Court routinely publishes short books containing lists of the very small number of cases that it regards as *yurisprudensi* and the principles, typically narrowly defined, for which they stand. These books are the only official and authoritative sources of *yurisprudensi* or case law in Indonesia.

There are very few principles that have emerged as fixed jurisprudence from the courts in the field of narcotics law. This is not altogether surprising, as Indonesia's courts are notorious for the brevity and inconsistency of their decision-making. Drugs-related decisions are no exception and most display a lack of analysis or reasoning and a high degree of inconsistency. These judgments are, in fact, primarily devoted to recounting the factual narrative proposed by the prosecution, with little space reserved for the courts' opinion. Even where reasoning is provided, very little of it amounts to useful legal analysis or interpretation that could be used to better understand the way drug offences are dealt with, let alone predict the outcome of future cases.

The one area in which some clear tendencies or trends can be adduced is in relation to sentencing. For example, the cases discussed below show that a person's status as a foreign citizen may be considered an aggravating circumstance that can be relied upon to impose the death penalty. Equally, however, it seems clear that honesty, remorse, politeness, youth and parental status are usually significant mitigating factors. To give another example, courts have expressly sidelined the mandatory minimum sentencing requirements, holding that they are, in fact, not mandatory at all, yet many courts continue to adhere to them. Faced with a number of alternative offences applicable to the defendant's conduct, as the courts typically are, they tend to find the defendant guilty of the most serious offence, with possession as a kind of default offence. Life or death sentences are typically only imposed for importing or production offences. Defendants who have been lured into committing an offence by a police informant will likely receive a sentence closer to the minimum than the maximum.

A total of 94 decisions in criminal prosecutions of drug-related offences were reviewed for this book. Of these, 44 were from the District Court (*Pengadilan Negeri*, or first-instance court) level, eight from provincial appeal courts, the High Courts (*Pengadilan Tinggi*), 36 were cassation appeals at the Supreme Court, and six were reconsideration (PK) decisions, also at the Supreme Court. Of the 94 cases, 12 involved foreign citizens; the other 82 concerned Indonesian citizens. The overall conviction rate out of this small random sample was 90 out of 94, or 95.7 per cent. All foreign citizens were convicted. The cases took, on average, 6.4 months from the date the trial was registered to the date the decision was handed down.

Despite the fact that the principle of precedent does not apply in Indonesia, it is still possible to gain some insight into court practice in drug trials by examining recent cases, although this can only be impressionistic in nature, given most decisions are not formally binding on courts in future cases. This is, of course, a common difficulty Indonesian lawyers face when preparing defence cases in drugs trials. In any case, the decisions discussed here are not limited to *yurisprudensi* but also include non-*yurisprudensi* judgments.

The Supreme Court

The style and quality of decision-making by Indonesian courts in drug cases is consistent with that in most other cases they hear. Contrary to what is usually the case in common law countries, the Supreme Court generally offers the least amount of reasoning of any Indonesian court involved in drug cases, typically providing far less legal analysis than the first instance courts. Its reasoning can also often be somewhat circular, or at least gnomic. The court's standard basis for dismissing cassation applications—typically explained in just one line—is simply that the lower court 'did not err in its application of the law'. Occasionally, the court offers one or two extra lines of reasoning, such as that the arguments raised on appeal did not fall within the grounds for appeal listed in the legislation but usually no explanation is given for why this is so.

One reason for the Supreme Court adopting a standard formula for dismissing cassation applications is that the grounds for overturning a decision of a lower court are limited. According to Art 253 of the Criminal Procedure Code, the Supreme Court is limited in cassation decisions to deciding the following questions: Was a Law not applied or applied incorrectly? Was the judicial process not implemented in accordance with statute? Did the court exceed its jurisdictional limits? The Supreme Court adheres strictly to these questions and will usually consider no others.

In reconsideration decisions, the relevant questions are different:

1. Is there a new situation [*novum*] that gives rise to a strong belief that, if it had been known at the time of the trial, the result would have been not guilty or the prosecutor's submissions would not have been accepted or a less serious offence would have been applied?
2. Were there, in a number of (related) decisions, statements that something has been proven, but the circumstances or things that form the basis or reason for the decisions that were claimed to be proven were, in fact, in contradiction with one and other?
3. Did the decision clearly exhibit a judicial mistake or a real error?[556]

Many case review submissions by those convicted of crimes expressly address these grounds but are nonetheless rejected for not doing so, without little or no explanation by the court.

The following cases provide illustrations of all these issues.

Case No 612.K/Pid/2005

The defendant in case No 612.K/Pid/2005, Jallow Mustafa, was accused of selling 50 g of heroin through intermediaries. The only evidence against him was the testimony of the alleged intermediaries. Mustafa was found guilty of importing/distributing by the District Court and was sentenced to 10 years imprisonment with a fine of Rp 10 million. On appeal to the High Court his sentence was increased to 15 years, with a fine of Rp 20 million.

[556] Criminal Procedure Code, Art 263.

Jallow filed a cassation appeal to the Supreme Court on all three possible grounds. He claimed that the lower courts had erred in their application of the law, because there was no evidence that he had committed the crimes alleged. By 'no evidence', he meant he had not been caught red handed and had not been found with any narcotics. Second, he claimed that the trial had not been implemented in accordance with law, because he had refuted all witness testimony and there was no other supporting evidence. Third, he claimed that the lower courts had exceeded their jurisdiction by convicting him on the basis of witness testimony that was merely read out in court, not spoken by the witness.[557]

The Supreme Court dismissed these arguments in its usual formulaic way, holding that 'these objections cannot be accepted, because the lower court did not err in its application of the law'.[558] Indeed, in a narrow legalistic sense, the lower courts did follow Indonesian law. Witness testimony is a valid form of evidence according to Indonesian criminal law,[559] whether refuted or not.

Case No 111.PK/Pid/2006

The Supreme Court also gave no reasons for rejecting the reconsideration application of John Sabastian, a citizen of Nigeria, in this case. It began with the arrest of a young female Indonesian student, Nova, at the University of Indonesia. She was caught providing a third person with 300 g of heroin. She claimed Sabastian had given her the heroin that morning outside his hotel in Central Jakarta. Sabastian was charged with distribution of narcotics and sentenced to life imprisonment, with a Rp 75 million fine.

In his application, Sabastian claimed that he had a written statement from Nova, claiming that she had been given the heroin by a man named Newman but had been pressured by law enforcement officials to identify Sabastian. Sabastian's application was rejected as having no legal basis, despite the fact that, if supported by evidence, it would seem, prima facie, to fall within the first of the three prerequisites for case review in Art 263 of the Criminal Procedure Code.

Case No 15.PK/Pid/2004

The defendant in this case was sentenced to 20 years in prison by the High Court for importing heroin. Prosecutors filed a cassation appeal to the Supreme Court, and his sentence was increased to the death penalty. The defendant applied to the Supreme Court, for reconsideration, arguing that the court had overstepped its jurisdiction by imposing the death penalty. According to the defendant, overturning a lower court's decision merely to impose a harsher penalty constituted an error. The Supreme Court dismissed the application, stating that the defendant's reasons did not fall within the grounds of review mentioned in Art 263(2) of the Criminal Procedure Code.[560] No further explanation was given.

557 Supreme Court Decision 612.K/Pid/2005, pp 11–12.
558 612.K/Pid/2005, pp 12–13.
559 Criminal Procedure Code, Art 184(1)(a). See also the discussion of evidence at pp 92–93.
560 Case No 15.PK/Pid/2004, p 10.

These brief and poorly explained dismissals by the Supreme Court make it difficult for scholars or practitioners to draw legal doctrine or principles from the Supreme Court's decisions. As mentioned, a principle will occasionally emerge in the form of the *yurisprudensi* but this is rare, and typically only concerns technical or procedural aspects of the law. Those who wish to study the Supreme Court's jurisprudence are reduced to searching, often fruitlessly, for general trends or tendencies in the court's pattern of rejecting or accepting particular arguments. One such trend is the Supreme Court's strong tendency to favour concrete, technical arguments over more abstract arguments of injustice or arguments that particular elements of an offence were not satisfied. The Supreme Court did not, in any of the cases studied, endorse a particular interpretation of an offence or uphold an argument that the evidence did not satisfy the elements of the alleged crime.

Case No 202.K/Pid/2001

This case is an example of the kind of argument the Supreme Court does tend to accept. The defendant in that case admitted to, and was charged with, possession of cannabis. In its statement of the crime, however, the prosecution had described the offence as, 'owning, storing for the purpose of owning … or possessing category I narcotics not in plant form'.

On cassation, the Supreme Court pointed out that it was common knowledge that cannabis was a plant material and, due to this discrepancy, the prosecution's indictment was 'unclear' (*kabur*). The Supreme Court declared the indictment to be invalid, quashed the decisions of the lower courts and struck out the records of the lower court proceedings.

Case No 35.PK/Pid/2005

By contrast, more abstract arguments, such as that in this case are typically dismissed with the briefest of consideration. This case involved Nigerian national Hansen Anthony Nwaolisa, who was caught by customs officials at Soekarno-Hatta International Airport after swallowing 43 heroin capsules with a total weight of 600 g. He was sentenced to death by the Bandung High Court.

In his reconsideration application, the condemned, inter alia, pleaded remorse as a reason for reducing his death sentence, an argument that the Supreme Court stated 'could not be considered'. His case is discussed further below, in the section on cases involving the death penalty.

Case No 1690.K/Pid/1987

This decision is another illustration of the sort of arguments the Supreme Court will accept and demonstrates its pre-occupation with procedural formalities. The defendant was sentenced to 20 years in prison with a fine of Rp 500,000 by the West Jakarta District Court for dealing heroin, a decision that was upheld by the High Court. The defendant applied for cassation on the grounds, among others, that the High Court had based its decision completely on the police report and had not properly considered the defendant's submissions; that the police report had never been read to the defendant and he had been forced into signing it; and that the defendant had been detained for five days without lawful authority (a detention order, *surat perintah penahanan*) and had been tortured.

The Supreme Court accepted the application but not on the grounds put forward by the defendant nor to his advantage. The Supreme Court was concerned with one line of the High Court's decision, where it claimed it did not have authority to detain the defendant. The Supreme Court held that the High Court did have the authority to order a defendant detained. It, therefore, cancelled the High Court's decision but decided the case anew, sentencing the defendant to the same penalties of 20 years imprisonment and a fine of Rp 500,000.

In fact, the applicant was successful in just 12 of the 36 Supreme Court decisions studied, and, of these, nine were brought by prosecution[561] and only three by the defendant.[562] For the reasons outlined above, dismissals by the Supreme Court add little to our understanding of Indonesian drugs law. The next section will, therefore, focus on the minority of cases where applications were accepted.

Case No 645.K/Pid/2007

As mentioned, the majority of appeals accepted by the Supreme Court were brought by the prosecution on the issue of sentencing, typically arguing that the sentence imposed by the lower courts was too light, and did not 'fulfil the community's sense of justice' (*belum memenuhi rasa keadilan*).[563] In this decision, for example, the Supreme Court accepted the cassation application brought by the defendant, holding that the decision of the High Court was 'incomplete and less than perfect in its application of the law'.[564] The defendant, found guilty of 'carrying' (*membawa*) marijuana, was sentenced to four years and eight months imprisonment by the Takengon District Court. This was increased to nine years by the Banda Aceh High Court. The Supreme Court found that the reasoning of the High Court (which was that the sentence imposed by the District Court) did not fulfil the community's sense of justice was too vague to support such a drastic increase in the sentence. This, in the Supreme Court's opinion, was sufficient grounds to accept the appeal. It, accordingly, reinstated the lighter sentence originally imposed by the Tekengon District Court.

561 Cases 49.K/Pid/1977; 1230.K/Pid/2002; 1521.K/Pid/2002; 15.PK/Pid/2004; 412.K/Pid/2005; 568.K/Pid/2006; 2268.K/Pid/2006; 2491.K/Pid/2006; 1245.K/Pid/2007. In Case No 49.K/Pid/1977, however, which has been declared *yurisprudensi*, the issue on appeal was whether a car belonging to the defendant, used to store and transport the 46 kgs of cannabis seized from him, should be confiscated on behalf of the state. The Supreme Court held that it should, and ordered accordingly. The defendant, a 27-year-old Australian citizen, had been sentenced by the District Court to 18 months imprisonment.

562 Cases 1690.K/Pid/1987; 202.K/Pid/2001; 645.K/Pid/2007.

563 See, for example, cases 412.K/Pid/2005; 2491.K/Pid/2006; 1245.K/Pid/2007; 1245.K/Pid/2007; see also case 558.K/Pid/2006.

564 Case No 1521.K/Pid/2002, p 7.

Case No 1521.K/Pid/2002

This decision is notable because it is an example of the Supreme Court overturning a not guilty verdict of the district court. The police had caught a man in possession of cannabis. The man claimed he had been given the cannabis by the defendant. When searched, the defendant was not found in possession of any proscribed substances. The district court found the defendant not guilty and, in doing so, disregarded testimony by police of verbal admissions allegedly made by the defendant at the time of arrest.

Notwithstanding Art 244 of the Criminal Procedure Code, which holds that no appeal may be made against a verdict of not guilty, the Supreme Court heard a cassation application brought by the prosecution. The court relied on its own jurisprudence to hold that, despite Art 244, the Supreme Court nevertheless was obliged, as the highest court in the land with a responsibility to ensure that law is applied correctly and justly, to hear any cassation application, even against an acquittal, so it could determine whether the decision to acquit was correct and just.[565] The court did, however, draw a distinction, though perhaps an illusory one, between absolute acquittals, in respect of which it would under no circumstances permit cassation, and acquittals based on erroneous interpretations of the relevant law, against which it would entertain cassation. In this case, the Supreme Court determined the acquittal fell into the latter category. The distinction would seem to be largely illusory, because a case can only fall into first category if it is not within the second one, that is, the court would usually need to review any acquittal to determine if it contains errors in law, which it interprets in a wide sense. Only if it does not contain such errors can it be considered 'absolute' and, therefore, immune from appeal. This means the court must at least consider almost any appeal against acquittal that comes before it.

In this case, the prosecution argued that the defendant's admissions out of court were admissible as evidence according to Art 189(2) of the Criminal Procedure Code, so long as they were corroborated by other evidence. In this case, the out-of-court admissions were corroborated by, first, the testimony of the witness who claimed he had been given the cannabis by the defendant; second, the police report in which the investigating officer recounted the admission by the defendant; and, third, the inferences (*petunjuk*) drawn from these. All of these were valid evidence according to Arts 184(1)(a), (c), (d), 187(a), 188(2) of the Criminal Procedure Code.

This, according to the Supreme Court, was sufficient to show that the acquittal in question was not absolute but based on an error, namely 'difference in interpretation of the crime'.[566] The court further held that the prosecution had also proven that the defendant had committed the crime of handing over (*menyerahkan*) category I narcotics. Accordingly, the Supreme Court was 'convinced that a crime really had taken place and that the defendant was the perpetrator, and that, based on the trial transcripts, there was no reason why the defendant should be absolved of criminal

[565] Case No 1521.K/Pid/2002, p 4.
[566] Case No 1521.K/Pid/2002, p 5.

responsibility'.[567] Accordingly, the Supreme Court overturned the acquittal and sentenced the defendant to 18 months imprisonment.

Case No 1230.K/Pid/2002

This was another case in which the Supreme Court overturned a decision of not guilty. It involved a female Indonesian citizen, 46 years old, referred to as a housewife (*ibu rumah tangga*). She was found guilty of giving and receiving methamphetamine in contravention of Art 60 of Law No 5 of 1997 on Psychotropic Substances. She had allegedly received 25 g of methamphetamine and given out 1 g amounts to a number of individuals. She appealed to the High Court, which upheld her conviction for giving drugs but acquitted her of having received them.

Both the defendant and the prosecution brought cassation applications against the High Court's verdict to the Supreme Court. The prosecution appealed both against the sentencing and the High Court's decision to acquit her on the receiving charge. The prosecution was ultimately successful on both grounds. The High Court had not given adequate reasons for finding the defendant not guilty of receiving drugs. Presumably, the High Court had accepted the defendant's argument that the only evidence was sworn testimony by the person who had allegedly provided the drugs to the defendant, testimony the defendant denied. The Supreme Court, however, found that the evidence was sufficient for the District Court to have handed down a verdict of guilty.

In relation to sentencing, the High Court's decision had not clearly spelt out the mitigating and aggravating factors it had taken into consideration. It had held that in reaching its decision it had taken into consideration that the defendant had family responsibilities but it had not specified whether this was a mitigating or aggravating factor. The prosecution argued that the defendant did not have 'family responsibilities'. Instead, these lay with her husband, the father of her children; rather, she merely 'managed' the household, which, according to the prosecution, was a quite different thing. Indeed, the prosecution argued that the fact that the defendant was a mother should be an aggravating, not mitigating, circumstance. Mothers, it was claimed, should be teaching their children good morals, not setting a bad example.

The Supreme Court agreed that the mitigating and aggravating factors needed to be spelt out in more detail but did not agree entirely with the prosecution's arguments. It overturned the lower decisions and decided the case itself. It found the defendant guilty of giving and receiving methamphetamine, and sentenced her to three years imprisonment, with a fine of Rp 10 million. It found three aggravating circumstances, namely that the defendant's actions had the potential to harm the mental health of the younger generation, that she had not helped in the government's program to combat drugs, and that she had not been honest in admitting her crimes. The mitigating circumstances were that she had no previous convictions and had family responsibilities.

[567] Case No 1521.K/Pid/2002, p 5.

District and High Court Jurisprudence

While District and High Court decisions are usually much more detailed than those of the Supreme Court, they nevertheless provide little guidance as to how the various narcotic offences are to be interpreted or the law applied to the facts. This is largely due to the style of decision-writing that is routinely adopted. The prosecution's case typically consists of a narrative that it compiles on the basis of the police reports and investigation. It is almost always a pure narrative, and does not argue how particular facts relate to the various elements of the relevant offence or how the offence should be interpreted or applied. The prosecution typically charges a defendant with a number of alternative offences of varying severity. To support the charge, the prosecution recounts the prepared narrative. The same narrative is repeated verbatim to support each charge, without additional argument or analysis, notwithstanding that the constituent elements of each offence differ.

The court then breaks the offence down into its constituent elements, and discusses each to determine whether it has been satisfied. In the case of most narcotic offences, this consists of three elements: (1) 'any person' (easily satisfied); (2) 'unlawfully or without licence' (again, easily satisfied); and (3) the description of the offence, generally a list of alternative verbs referring to the defendant's actions, followed by the category of narcotic, and in some cases the quantity. The first two are rarely, if ever, of any legal interest. The third element requires legal analysis to apply the list of verbs to the facts in question and, therefore, offers potential for the court to develop its jurisprudence. The court's discussion of this third element, however, typically consists of it again recounting the factual narrative, either verbatim from the prosecution's brief or with minor amendments. At the end of this narrative of the facts, the court simply declares whether or not, based on this narrative, the element has been satisfied. It does not give reasons why the element was or was not satisfied, nor does it explain why it accepted certain facts to be true and did not accept other evidence. It instead appears to prefer a highly simplistic and unarticulated 'common sense' approach, always choosing the most serious of the potentially applicable offences if it finds the accused guilty. As demonstrated out below, the 'sense' of the decisions is rarely apparent.

Given this paucity of analysis and explanation, it is difficult to draw conclusions from the reasons courts give in their decisions about the substance of narcotic offences. At best, only broad trends can be identified from the courts' tendency to find particular elements satisfied in particular factual scenarios. More illuminating material tends, however, to be found in relation to sentencing. Accordingly, the following section has a particular focus on sentencing issues, although questions of guilt and whether particular offences have been committed are also discussed.

Case No 11/Pid.SUS/2011/PN.SLW

This decision is worthy of note, because in it the Slawi District Court expressly addressed the issue of mandatory minimum sentences. The defendant in the case, Siti Maulidyah, a 26-year-old Indonesian woman and mother of two, bought an ecstasy tablet for a friend and had been about to purchase methamphetamine for another friend when she and the vendor were caught by police. The defendant did not object to any of the prosecution's evidence or witness testimony. She was found guilty on two counts: first, of being an intermediary in a category I narcotics transaction; and second, for attempting to be an intermediary in a category I narcotics transaction. The quantities involved were less than five grams. According to Law No 35 of 2009, this would make her liable to a minimum of five years imprisonment.

The court took issue with the prescribed minimum sentence of five years. It cited academic work by Indonesian legal academics to the effect that minimum sentences needed to be accompanied by guidelines for when the minimum sentence is to be imposed, and when it may be overlooked. The court considered it 'unjust' to apply a mandatory minimum sentence without taking in to account any mitigating circumstances. This would, according to the court, effectively amount to treating people the same (by imposing the same minimum sentence) when their culpability may be different. Accordingly, the court refused to apply the minimum sentence, rejected the prosecution's submissions on sentencing and sentenced the defendant to 30 months imprisonment. The mitigating factors for the defendant were that she had been polite, co-operative and truthful in court, had admitted to her actions and showed remorse, had no previous convictions, and was still young and, therefore, might improve her life and 'become a contributing member of society'.

This case does not appear to have been subject to appeal. There is no evidence of other courts expressly citing this decision as authority to impose a penalty less than the mandatory minimum sentence. Although there are other cases where the penalty imposed was less than the minimum sentence, the courts in those decisions did not expressly explain why this was done.[568] It is, in any case, unlikely that this decision has been influential, as first instance decisions rarely have that sort of impact on other courts in Indonesia.

Case No 05/Pid.Sus/2011/PN.TGL

The courts have been willing to reduce a sentence where they believe police may have manufactured a case.[569] This case involved a defendant who was caught by police with 21 g of cannabis following a tip-off from an informant. The defendant worked in a food stall beside a bus terminal and had been asked to purchase the cannabis by a friend, Ian. When the defendant returned to the bus terminal to give Ian the cannabis, as arranged, Ian refused to take it and said he needed to return home to get his cellular phone. Two police officers arrived soon after, searched the defendant and found the cannabis. The prosecution charged the defendant with storing (*menyimpan*) or possessing (*menguasai*) category I narcotics in the form of plants pursuant to Art 111(1) of Law No 35 of 2009, and requested a prison sentence of five years.

The Tegal District Court found that all the elements of the offence had been satisfied but disagreed with prosecution on sentencing. The court determined that

[568] Such cases include: 02/Pid.B/2010/PN.TGL; 05/Pid.Sus/2011/PN.TGL.

[569] Entrapment is reportedly not unusual in narcotics cases in Indonesia. See also above, pp 60, 73.

the defendant was the victim of a 'scenario' (*skenario*) involving the police,[570] and believed Ian had provided the tip-off. Further, Ian and the vendor of the cannabis were clearly more culpable than the defendant but were not arrested. Other mitigating factors for the defendant were that he already worked in the food stall and was, in the court's opinion, not a full time drug dealer. He was also honest and open in court. Accordingly, the defendant was sentenced to two years and six months imprisonment, and fined Rp 800 million (which could be discharged by three months *kurungan* imprisonment).

Case No 02/Pid/2010/PN.TGL

In this decision, again from the Tegal District Court, the defendant was also caught by police on the basis of an informant's report, although this time the police were more candid about the fact. He was searched and police found a packet of cannabis in his pocket. The police then searched his house and found another two packets of cannabis. The three packets were later proven to contain over 6.5 g of cannabis in total.

The defendant claimed he had bought the cannabis on behalf of a gangster (*preman*),[571] who threatened to do him harm if he refused to buy the cannabis. After the defendant had bought the cannabis, the *preman* instructed the defendant to take a portion of it and save it. The court accepted this evidence.

The prosecution charged the defendant with purchasing or selling or receiving category I narcotics (under Art 114(1) of Law No 35 of 2009), with possession (under Art 111(1)) as a *subsidair* (subsidiary offence or secondary charge) and requested he be sentenced to five years imprisonment. The defendant did not contradict any of the evidence but argued mitigating factors and asked for the lightest sentence possible.

The court found that the defendant had not purchased or sold or received the cannabis and that Art 114(1) was not made out. It found instead that the defendant had stored (*menyimpan*) and had possession (or control, *menguasai*) of the cannabis, so the Art 111(1) charges were satisfied. It took into account that the *preman*, who was a wanted person, was now at large, and this indicated to the court that the *preman* had intentionally told the defendant to store the cannabis so he could report him to the police. The court disagreed with the prosecution on the issue of the sentence, and imposed a sentence of 30 months imprisonment and a Rp 1 billion fine (or three months *kurungan* imprisonment).

No satisfactory reason was given for why the defendant's actions did not amount to purchasing or receiving, despite the defendant admitting that he had purchased the cannabis (albeit on another's behalf). Although agency could possibly excuse

[570] Case No 05/Pid.Sus/2011/PN.TGL, p 20.

[571] This term, *preman*, is usually applied to members of criminal gangs but can also be used to describe undercover police officers, for example, because they wear *preman* clothes: see Case No 11/Pid.Sus/2011/PN.SLW. Whether or not the *preman* in this case was, in fact, a police officer was not made clear in the judgment. The Court, however, was apparently convinced that it was the *preman* who informed the arresting police of the defendant's crime.

him from being charged with purchasing, it does not explain why he was not found to have received the cannabis. Perhaps it was the fact that the defendant had been a victim of manipulation by the police and the informant that led the court to impose the lesser offence but given the lack of any explanation by the court, the decision could have been purely arbitrary.

Case No 97/Pid/2011/PT.BTN

In this decision, the High Court of Banten held that a defendant's status as a foreign citizen was not a factor that could be relied on to increase his or her sentence. The defendant in this case was a citizen of Iran, caught at Soekarno Hatta International Airport with 450 g of methamphetamine in his suitcase. The prosecution charged the defendant with three alternative offences: receiving category I narcotics in excess of five grams (Art 113(2) of Law No 35 of 2009); importing category I narcotics in excess of five grams (Art 114(2) of the same Law); or possession of category I narcotics in excess of five grams (Art 112(2)). The prosecution requested a sentence of 14 years imprisonment.

The Tangerang District Court acquitted the defendant on the first charge, receiving, but found him guilty of the second charge, importing. It sentenced the defendant to life imprisonment. In so doing, it relied on an inference that the fact that the defendant was an international citizen indicated that he was part of an international organised crime syndicate.

On appeal, the High Court of Banten agreed with the District Court's finding of guilt but disagreed with the sentencing. It found that the District Court did not give sufficient reason for imposing 'the maximum sentence' (this was, in fact, an error, as the maximum is the death penalty). In particular, it took issue with the District Court's inference that the defendant should have been given a heavier sentence simply because he was a foreign citizen. It referred to another decision of the Tangerang District Court in which the court did not make such an inference or impose such a harsh penalty on a foreign citizen.[572] Moreover, the High Court held that life imprisonment could only be imposed where there were no mitigating factors, and that this was not true in this case. Accordingly, it reduced the sentence to 12 years imprisonment and a fine of Rp 1 billion (or three months *kurungan* imprisonment). The Banten High Court's decision differed to that of the Supreme Court in Case No 772.K/Pid/2007, discussed below in relation to the death sentence, in which it did explicitly find that a defendant's status as a foreign citizen was an aggravating factor.

Case No 78/Pid/2011/PT.BTN

This case also involved an Iranian defendant. The defendant and a companion, tried in separate cases,[573] were discovered at Soekarno Hatta International Airport

[572] Tangerang District Court, Case No 101/Pid.B/2011/PN.TNG of 24 May 2011, involving the defendant David Bao Duang.

[573] See Case No 1880/Pid.B/2010/PN.TNG.

with over 300 g of methamphetamine each, hidden in the handles of their suitcases. The prosecution charged the defendant with three alternative offences. The *primair* (or primary charge) was receiving category I narcotics in excess of five grams (Art 114(2)); the *subsidair* was importing category I narcotics in excess of five grams (Art 113(2)); and the *lebih subsidair* (further secondary charge) was possession of category I narcotics in excess of five grams (Art 112(2)). The prosecution requested 12 years imprisonment.

As with the previous case, the Tangerang District Court at first instance found the defendant not guilty of the first charge (receiving) but guilty of importing under Art 113(2). It sentenced him to life imprisonment, with a Rp 1 billion fine.

On appeal, the High Court upheld the District Court's finding of guilt but disagreed with the sentence imposed. The High Court held that the court could impose a heavier sentence than that requested by the prosecution but it needed sufficient reason to do so. Because the district court's reasons for imposing life imprisonment were the same as the prosecution's reasons for requesting a 12-year sentence, the High Court held that a life sentence had not been justifiable. Moreover, the High Court held that life imprisonment was only to be imposed where there were no mitigating factors but the District Court had, in fact, found mitigating factors. Finally, the same court sentenced the defendant's companion to nine years for essentially the same crime, so the High Court thought it unjust for the sentences to be so different. The defendant requested the sentence to be reduced to nine years, but the High Court imposed 11.

X. DEATH SENTENCES

Of the 94 cases studied, the death penalty was applied in only four cases.[574] All involved foreign citizens.

Case No 772.K/Pid/2007

This decision involved the most elaborate facts of all the cases studied, and was one of the only cases involving organised production. It centred on two individuals in a large, international drug production and trafficking ring. The organisation was financed out of Hong Kong and run by local Indonesian members, with experts flown in from the Netherlands, France and China to help with production. This was carried out under the cover of a front company purportedly in the business of plastics, enabling those involved to rent and use a large factory, receive large container loads of chemicals and other industrial machinery, fly in drug consultants, and hire local staff legitimately.

The two defendants in this case, one a citizen of the Netherlands and the other a French citizen, had been flown in as consultants to produce MDMA. The first,

[574] Cases Nos 44.PK/Pid/1991; 15.PK/Pid/2004; 772.K/Pid/2007; and 35.PK/Pid/2005.

Nicolaas Garnick Josephus Gerardus, Dutch, was the chemist, while the second, Serge Areski Atlaoui, French, was the mechanic for the sophisticated machinery used in MDMA production. For the several years the organisation was in operation, the defendants, particularly the first defendant, made many trips to Indonesia. They produced test batches of MDMA, tested the machinery and chemicals and suggested how the factory/laboratory could be improved. They were compensated for each of their visits.

The defendants were sentenced to life by the District Court and this was affirmed by the High Court. Both the prosecution and the defendant appealed to the Supreme Court on cassation, the prosecution arguing that the sentence was too light. There were two critical issues on appeal in relation to which the prosecution presented detailed submissions. The first was whether the defendants had, in fact, produced MDMA. The second was whether their actions were 'organised'.

Both the prosecution and the defendants agreed that the defendants had the aim of producing MDMA. The defendants, however, argued they had only ever succeeded in producing PMK (a precursor to MDMA) or, at best, some other substance that fell short of constituting MDMA. One of the arguments put forward by the first defendant in support of this was that he had no chemistry or pharmaceutical training and was, in fact, a translator by trade. He argued that it was not possible for a person without the proper expertise in chemistry to produce MDMA. In explaining why what was produced could not be considered MDMA, the defendant, or at least his lawyers, gave technical descriptions of the properties of the various chemicals they had allegedly used, and argued, again using technical language, that it was impossible for those chemicals to produce MDMA.

The prosecution allowed that some of the test batches had failed or were of poor quality, but submitted that on at least one or two occasions the defendants had succeeded in producing MDMA. This included one occasion on which the first defendant produced around one kilogram of MDMA, which was mixed by other members of the group with various other chemicals and pressed into 200 ecstasy tablets. At the time the defendants were caught by police they were in the laboratory, which was accessed through a door disguised as a bookshelf, and were in the process of making a new batch of MDMA with new machinery. Although the process was not complete when they were arrested, traces of MDMA were found on various pieces of machinery, proving, according to the prosecution, that the defendants had, in fact, succeeded in producing MDMA at some point.

The prosecution went to great length to show the elaborate and highly 'organised' nature of the operation, something the defendants tried to distance themselves from. It was an accepted fact that the operation had been financed by a man living in Hong Kong and was managed day-to-day in Indonesia by two Indonesian citizens. Many other people were also involved. Apart from their 'manager' and the president of the company, the defendants also had dealings with a driver for the organisation, who took them back and forth from the factory, and other staff who helped in the laboratory. A group of Chinese citizens were operating out of the same factory, albeit in a different laboratory, producing methamphetamine at the same time the two defendants in this case were producing (or attempting to produce) MDMA.

The defendants, however, argued that they had taken instructions from their manager, and no one else. They claimed that they had done all the production work themselves, that no one had helped pour chemicals, that they were unaware of the various tasks and actions of the other members of the alleged group, and that they were not involved with any of the other members of the group because they could not speak Indonesian. The second defendant also argued that his poor financial situation was evidence that he was not a member of an international narcotics syndicate because, according to the second defendant, no one in an international drug syndicate would be poor. Based on this, the defendants argued they should be treated as having committed a crime in concert, not an 'organised' crime.

The Supreme Court dismissed the defendants' appeal, because the district court and high court 'did not err in their application of the law' in relation to the issues the defendants raised.[575] On the other hand, it held the prosecution's application should be accepted because two courts had 'erred in their application of the law'[576] by imposing a sentence (life imprisonment) that was not proportionate to the defendants' culpability. The Supreme Court, therefore, quashed the original sentence and sentenced them both to death.

In arriving at this sentence, the Supreme Court, as is the custom, weighed up the aggravating and mitigating factors. The fact that the defendants were foreign citizens was explicitly found to be an aggravating factor and contributed to the finding that the death penalty was warranted. It held that the aggravating factors were, inter alia:

1. 'The defendants as foreign citizens committed acts which, from their legal consequences alone, damaged the mentality of, not only the Indonesian nation, but the international community as well.'[577]
2. 'The defendants as professional experts abused their expertise to commit a crime that greatly endangered the life of the Indonesian nation and state.'[578]
3. 'The defendants' actions committed in Indonesia were highly organised and could ruin the good name of the [Indonesian] nation and state in the world's eyes.'[579]

Case No 15.PK/Pid/2004

This was another case in which the death penalty was ultimately imposed. The defendant, Raheem Agbaje Salami, a citizen of Nigeria,[580] was described as an agricultural consultant. Salami was caught in 1998 by customs officials at the Juanda

[575] Case No 772.K/Pid/2007, p 185.
[576] Case No 772.K/Pid/2007, p 184.
[577] *Para Terdakwa sebagai WNA telah melakukan perbuatan yang menimbulkan akibat hukum saja merusak mental bangsa Indonesia tetapi juga masyarakat internasional* (at p 185).
[578] *Para Terdakwa sebagai tenaga ahli yang professional telah menyalahgunakan keahliannya untuk melakukan kejahatan yang sangat membahayakan kehidupan Bangsa dan Negara Indonesia* (at p 185).
[579] *Perbuatan para Terdakwa yang dilakukan di Indonesia sangat terorganisir dan dapat mencoreng nama baik Bangsa dan Negara di mata dunia* (at p 186).
[580] The Supreme Court decision oddly describes him as a citizen of the 'Republic of Cordova'.

International Airport in Surabaya, East Java, while attempting to bring more than five kilograms of heroin into the country.

Salami, 33, had arrived on a Thai Airways flight and was first detected by the luggage scan when exiting the airport. Customs officials performed an inspection of his suitcase and discovered that it had a false bottom and sides. The police were called to take over the investigation. In addition to a large quantity of women's shoes and clothing, police found two packages of white powder concealed within the sides and bottom of the suitcase. Immediate on-the-spot tests, later confirmed by laboratory testing, revealed the white powder to be heroin. The total amount was 5.280 kg.

At first instance, the Surabaya District Court found Salami guilty and sentenced him to life imprisonment with a fine of Rp 10 million. Both Salami and the prosecution appealed. On appeal to the Surabaya High Court, Salami was sentenced to 20 years imprisonment and a fine of Rp 100 million. This was appealed by the prosecution to the Supreme Court on cassation. The Supreme Court imposed the death penalty.

The defendant applied for reconsideration (PK), asking the Supreme Court to review its earlier cassation decision. The grounds were that the Supreme Court had overstepped its jurisdiction by imposing the death penalty without giving sufficient legal grounds or reasons. The defendant referred to Art 30 of the Supreme Court Law (No 14 of 1985), which provides the three grounds on which the Supreme Court may overturn a decision of a lower court, namely: (a) the court did not have jurisdiction or went beyond its jurisdiction; (b) the court erred in its application of the law; or (c) the court did not adhere to a condition imposed by law, the nonfulfilment of which causes the decision to be void. According to the defendant, overturning a lower court's decision merely to impose a harsher penalty did not fall into any of these categories and was, therefore, a judicial error of the kind that would satisfy the grounds for reconsideration in Art 263(2)(c) of the Criminal Procedure Code (set out above).[581]

The Supreme Court rejected the application, tersely holding that the defendant's reasons did not fall within any of the grounds of review mentioned in Art 263(2) of the Criminal Procedure Code.[582] No further explanation was given. Accordingly, the Supreme Court decision imposing the death penalty was upheld. Salami was executed by firing squad on 28 April 2015.

Case No 35.PK/Pid/2005

As noted above, the defendant in this case was a citizen of Nigeria. He had been caught at Soekarno Hatta International Airport with 43 capsules inside his stomach. The capsules contained a total of 600 g net of heroin. He was sentenced to death by the Tangerang District Court. This decision was upheld by the Bandung

[581] See p 85.
[582] Case No 15.PK/Pid/2004, p 10.

High Court, and his cassation application to the Supreme Court was rejected. The defendant then sought reconsideration and in his application took responsibility for his actions, showed remorse and pleaded for his sentence to be reduced from death. The Supreme Court was not moved by these arguments, which were more suited to a clemency application. It correctly held that reconsideration was only available on the basis of the three grounds in Art 263 of the Criminal Procedure Code, and not on questions of sentence. The previous court decisions were upheld.

Case No 44.PK/Pid/1991

The crime in this case was committed in 1987, so Law No 9 of 1976 on Narcotics was applied. The defendant in that case, a citizen of Taiwan, was found guilty of transporting narcotics (heroin), despite contested evidence about whether he knew of the existence of the heroin, which was hidden in the wall behind his bed on the boat he was captaining. The District Court sentenced him to death, and all appeals (including reconsideration) were dismissed with the usual virtual absence of explanation.

XI. CONCLUSION

In Indonesia, drugs are regulated within a European civil law structure inherited from Dutch colonialism. This is still strongly influenced by colonial legal culture but has followed its own trajectory since independence. An inquisitorial trial model ultimately derived from European models is followed. There is no system of precedent, at least not as it is practised in common law countries.

The collapse of Soeharto's authoritarian regime in 1998 triggered ambitious efforts to reform the legal system, including the introduction of judicial independence. The implementation of these reforms remains incomplete, however. Legal institutions have changed greatly over the last 17 years but can sometimes still be vulnerable to pressure from political elites, as well as outright corruption. Bribery of police, prosecutors and judges continues, with the justice system often dismissed by Indonesians as the *mafia peradilan* or 'judicial mafia', a reference to systems of institutionalised corruption within the bar, police, prosecutors and courts.

In recent years, lawyers and activists have frequently challenged the limits of law and the new democratic system through still-emerging institutions like the Constitutional Court, established in 2003. This court has been asked to determine a wide range of issues that touch on drugs law in Indonesia, including the application of the death penalty. Although more professional and sophisticated than most other Indonesian courts, the Constitutional Court's record to date is mixed. Its decisions also have only limited impact on the other courts.

Despite increasing oversight of law enforcement agencies, police and prosecutors continue to enjoy much discretion, which sometimes involves entrapment and corruption. Rights and procedural safeguards are often ignored during the pre-trial phase of the criminal process. The right to counsel, for example, is seldom a reality during investigations. Many detainees are unaware of this right and there are reports that some who assert it are threatened by police. The presumption of innocence certainly exists but it can be problematic in narcotics trials. Some argue there is an implicit right to silence but not all accept that this is so.

Further problems are created by the poor quality of many written decisions. This often creates real uncertainty about how laws are interpreted and applied, and serious problems of inconsistency in sentencing. Generally speaking, criminal appeal, cassation and reconsideration decisions in Indonesia are notable for brevity and lack of detail in their reasoning. They are also often inconsistent. In part, this reflects a shortage of basic skills in a newly-independent judiciary still struggling to emerge from more than three decades of repression and deliberate neglect under Soeharto. It is also, however, the result of the lack of any effective system for standardisation of the interpretation of laws and sentencing, as well as the continued influence of the so-called 'judicial mafia'.

Indonesia has a range of non-custodial sentencing options available for drug offences, although most of those convicted of trafficking are jailed or, in more serious cases, sentenced to a life in prison or executed. Courts may also order detention for medical and social rehabilitation, and detention for these purposes can substitute for jail time, at least since reforms introduced in 2009. Imprisonment remains more common, however, and only limited advantage is taken of the legislated alternatives, as the traditional punitive approach continues to dominate. The Supreme Court has held that being a foreigner is in itself an aggravating factor in sentencing.

Numbers executed fluctuate, with execution policy distorted by domestic political considerations, and a long delay of between 10 and 20 years before execution not uncommon. There is a robust debate among the elite as to whether executions are consistent with aspirations for recognition as a state that respects human rights. President Yudhoyono imposed an unofficial moratorium from late 2008 until 2013 but executions by firing squad resumed with his approval in the following year. At the end of 2014, Yudhoyono was succeeded by President Jokowi. As at the time of writing (mid-2015), Jokowi has presided over the execution of 14 people, mostly foreigners convicted of drugs offences, notwithstanding strong international criticism.

The Constitution and statute provide that clemency must be sought from the President and it has recently become clear that his or her decision is not capable of review by a court. Applications have historically been successful in 24 to 33 per cent of cases, although clemency is now very rarely granted where the death penalty is imposed for drug trafficking. Jokowi has reportedly so far refused all applications for clemency made by drugs offenders.

In summary, although Indonesia's drug law regime has undergone significant change in recent years, most reforms are only imperfectly implemented and trial outcomes remain unpredictable but generally harsh. Like most in Southeast Asia, the system in Indonesia is still characterised by the 'war on drugs' rhetoric that sees drugs as a serious social evil, for which severe punishment is necessary to 'protect the nation'.

4

Singapore

Singapore is a small island state of just over 5.5 million inhabitants[1] but it is also a global centre of finance, trade and one of Asia's leading shipping and transport hubs. Its role in the international regulation of narcotics, therefore, carries significance beyond its size. Singapore is not a narcotics producer: domestic drug consumption rates are relatively low and a large proportion of drugs seized within Singapore are in transit. Narcotics control nonetheless features very prominently in the nation's domestic political agenda. The Singaporean government prides itself on having a 'zero tolerance'[2] approach to drugs, with strict laws and a rigorous enforcement regime. The state's hard-line approach is not, however, a static one. Drugs laws are subject to frequent legislative reform, while Singaporean courts have also made important, albeit incremental, shifts in their interpretation of narcotics legislation.

This chapter provides a description of narcotics law in Singapore, drawing from legislation, case law, parliamentary speeches, official policy documents, reports, government statistics and academic analysis. It begins with a brief historic account of trading and use of drugs in Singapore before offering an overview of trade and use in contemporary Singapore and the state's response. The second part introduces the legal framework for drug control and describes the main narcotics offences. The third and fourth parts of the chapter examine jurisdictional issues and the various procedural laws that apply to drug-related criminal prosecutions. The fifth section discusses Singapore's legal framework in relation to the rehabilitation of drug users, while the final section describes Singapore's approach to regulating the financial aspects of the illicit drug trade.

I. HISTORICAL AND POLITICAL CONTEXT

Singapore was founded in 1819 as a British trading colony. After briefly joining the Malaysian Federation in 1963, it gained independence in 1965 as the Republic of Singapore. The country has a parliamentary system of government in which legislative power is vested in a legislature that consists of the President and Parliament, while judicial power is vested in the Supreme Court and subordinate courts.

[1] 5,567,301 (estimate as at July 2014). See CIA, 'World Factbook' (nd), www.cia.gov/library/publications/the-world-factbook/geos/sn.html.

[2] Teo Chee Hean, 'Second Reading on the Misuse of Drugs (Amendment) Bill. Speech by Mr Teo Chee Hean, Deputy Prime Minister for Home Affairs' (12 November 2012) 33.

Executive authority is vested in the President, while the leader who commands a majority in Parliament (in practice, the head of the ruling party) takes the role of Prime Minister. Cabinet is selected by the Prime Minister and consists of Members of Parliament. Singapore has a common law legal system that is still strongly influenced by its British colonial legacy, although appeals to the Privy Council in London were abolished between 1989 and 1994. Since Singaporean independence, the nation's economy expanded rapidly, with an average GDP growth rate of 7.6 per cent in the period from 1961 to 2012.[3] Today, Singapore is one of the world's most prosperous nations, with its 2014 per capita GDP of US$ 81,300 ranking seventh highest in the world.[4]

Patterns of drug trade and consumption in Singapore, like its drug laws, policies and social attitudes, have evolved and changed dramatically since the small island rose to prominence in the nineteenth century as South-East Asia's foremost entrepôt. The first drug recorded as imported into Singapore was opium, which in the early 1800s was traded from India and Persia to China and elsewhere in Asia by the British East India Company.[5] Singapore's strategic position along this major trade route made it a popular destination for Chinese immigration[6] and Abdullah suggests opium use was 'popular among immigrant Chinese populations, both rich and poor'.[7] Opium became sought-after within all classes of Chinese migrant communities—particularly poor labourers who experienced harsh working conditions. For them, opium was a common way to 'escape' these circumstances and a prophylactic treatment for various tropical diseases.[8] Opium was also customarily consumed within the upper echelons of the merchant community.[9]

For much of the nineteenth century, opium usage was seen as commonplace. Few regarded it as a social problem and its consumption was not regulated.[10] Further, as a regional opium distribution centre, Singapore's economy derived significant revenues from the opium trade and a number of local packing plants were established.[11] Singaporean opium 'farmers' would purchase supplies on the open market and then process the opium into *chandu*, which would be distributed for retail consumption through opium shops.[12] Between 1820 and 1914, opium revenues made up close

[3] World Bank, 'World Development Indicators: Singapore' http://data.worldbank.org/country/singapore#cp_fin.

[4] CIA 'World Factbook: Country Comparison: GDP—Per Capita (PPP)' (no date), www.cia.gov/library/publications/the-world-factbook/rankorder/2004rank.html.

[5] Noorman Abdullah, 'Exploring Constructions of the "Drug Problem" in Historical and Contemporary Singapore' 7(2) *New Zealand Journal of Asian Studies* 40, 43.

[6] *The British Empire Series Vol 1, (India, Ceylon, Straits Settlements, British North Borneo, Hong Kong)* (London, Kegan Paul, Trench, Trubner & Co Ltd, 1899) 449.

[7] Abdullah, 'Exploring Constructions', 43. See also Jean E Abshire, *The History of Singapore* (Santa Barbara CA, Greenwood ABC-CLIO, 2011) 69.

[8] CE Dumbleton, 'The Need of Reform in the Present System of Registration of Deaths in the Straits Settlements' (1892–93) 66, 69, cited in Abdullah (n 5) 43.

[9] Abdullah (n 5) 43.

[10] Ibid 43–44.

[11] Ibid 44.

[12] Carl A Trocki, 'The Rise of Singapore's Great Opium Syndicate, 1840–86' (1987) 18(1) *Journal of Southeast Asian Studies* 58, 60.

to 50 per cent of Singapore's total income and delivered major profits to Chinese commercial syndicates.[13] Some merchants also sought to exploit opium use among labourers as a method of control by encouraging the habit and even selling *chandu* on credit to their workers, as addicts would use up to two-thirds of their wages to purchase the substance.[14]

An anti-opium social movement emerged in the early twentieth century, with the formation of an Anti-Opium Society backed by a number of religious institutions.[15] The Society organised anti-opium conferences and Chinese operas on the issue, while methodist missionaries lobbied both the Straits Settlements and British governments.[16] At the same time, the Straits Settlements Governor was instructed by London to minimise and eventually eradicate 'the evil' within the colony.[17] A commission was duly appointed by the Straights Settlements government in 1907 to assess the extent of opium smoking and eradicate problems associated with its consumption.[18] The commission found insufficient grounds to impose a total ban on the substance, and instead recommended restricting its sale, including a prohibition on selling to women or children below the age of 18 and a ban on its use in brothels.[19]

In 1910, a Monopolies Department was established to restrict the manufacture and sale of opium.[20] In 1925, the colonial government created a licensing regime around opium use, limiting opium smoking to the users' own premises.[21] Within a few years, supplies were rationed.[22] As opium use became more stigmatised and users increasingly turned to contraband suppliers, a smuggling boom was created. The anti-opium movement gained further momentum in the 1930s, when the 'opium problem' was presented as a moral problem among the Chinese and characterised as 'irresponsible' and 'unfilial'.[23] The leader of the Anti-Opium Society was insistent, however, that only with the full backing of the state would its abolition be achieved. Despite this, sale of opium was not made a criminal offence until after World War II.[24]

The anti-opium movement lost ground during the Japanese occupation, and there were an estimated 16,000 opium addicts by the end of the war.[25] On

[13] Trocki, 'The Rise of Singapore's Great Opium Syndicate' 66.
[14] Trocki (n 12) 79.
[15] Abdullah (n 5) 40, 45.
[16] David W Scott, 'Alcohol, Opium, and the Methodists in Singapore: The Inculturation of a Moral Crusade' (2012) 29 *Mission Studies* 147, 157; Abdullah (n 5) 40, 45.
[17] Abdullah (n 5) 44–5, citing Straits Settlements Legislative Council Proceedings (SLCP) (1907), Singapore: Government Printing Office, 1900–1942.
[18] Abdullah (n 5) 45.
[19] Abdullah (n 5) 45–46, citing M Soo 'The Ups and Downs of Opium in Singapore', *Nanyang Siang Pau* (13–14 January 1977): 1, 18.
[20] Abdullah (n 5) 46.
[21] Abdullah (n 5) 47, citing KS Goh 'Prevention is Our Best Hope in the War on Drugs' *The Straits Times* (5 August 1976).
[22] Abdullah (n 5) 47.
[23] Abdullah (n 5) 47–48.
[24] Abdullah (n 5) 48–49, citing Soo 'The Ups and Downs of Opium' 18.
[25] UNODC (United Nations Office on Drugs and Crime), 'The Opium Problem in Singapore' (1958) 4 *Bulletin on Narcotics* 7.

instructions from London, the British Military Administration introduced the Opium and Chandu Proclamation in February 1946. This criminalised the possession of prepared or raw opium, as well as smoking utensils. Since local market demand for opium remained high, the Proclamation triggered a rise in smuggling syndicates.[26] Morphine also entered the market as a more potent, but less expensive, substitute. To deal with these challenges, the Dangerous Drugs Ordinance and regulations were enacted, coming into force in March 1951.[27] They repealed all existing controlled drug legislation; listed substances such as opium, cannabis, morphine, cocaine and heroin (diamorphine) as dangerous drugs; and criminalised unauthorised possession, introducing more severe penalties. They also mandated treatment and rehabilitation for drug addicts.[28] Singapore also established a special taskforce within its Customs Department, the Central Narcotics Intelligence Bureau, to prevent the import of drugs. In 1954 and 1955, 'twelve leading traffickers were either banished or imprisoned, while others fled the country'.[29] Between 1952 and 1958, more than 21,000 raids were conducted on opium smoking dens, while more than 53,000 tonnes of opium were seized by officials from 1947 to 1958.[30]

Following independence in 1965, Singapore introduced the Drugs (Prevention of Misuse) Act 1969, which was soon replaced by the Misuse of Drugs Act 1973.[31] The Misuse of Drugs Act was significantly stricter than the pre-existing laws and introduced the death penalty for several offences. Not long after the introduction of the Misuse of Drugs Act, heroin use escalated to the point that it was labelled the country's 'No 1 menace' and 'social scourge',[32] with an estimated 20,000 heroin users by the 1970s.[33] The Singaporean police tackled the drug problem aggressively through a combination of harsh penalties and compulsory rehabilitation, and drug use steadily declined.[34] Throughout the 1980s, the state's stance towards drug use continued to toughen as drug use was frequently linked to other serious crimes such as burglary, theft and rape.[35]

Official statistics suggest that Singapore has had significant success in curbing drug consumption in recent decades. Between the 1980s and the second decade of

[26] Abdullah (n 5) 49.

[27] Dangerous Drugs Ordinance 1951.

[28] See Ong Teck Hong *Drug Abuse in Singapore: A Psychological Perspective* (Singapore, Hillview Publications, 1989); and Ong Teck Hong and Richard E Isralowitz, *Substance Use in Singapore: Illegal Drugs, Inhalants and Alcohol* (Singapore, Toppan, 1996).

[29] UNODC, 'The Opium Problem'.

[30] UNODC (n 25) 11.

[31] Misuse of Drugs Act (Singapore, Cap 185, 2008 Rev Ed).

[32] Abdullah (n 5) 50, citing *The Straits Times*, 'Big Rise in Number of Addicts: Heroin the No 1 Menace' (21 April 1975).

[33] Abdullah (n 5) 51, citing TO Boon *Towards a Drug-Free Singapore: Strategies, Policies and Programmes against Drugs* (Singapore, National Council Against Drug Abuse, 1998); F Chia-Chow, 'Law Enforcement Action, Collection of Law Enforcement Data and Registration of Drug Offenders: Drug Abuse Situation in Singapore' paper delivered at the Workshop on the Reduction of Demand for Illicit Drugs in South-East Asia, Universiti Sains Malaysia, 14–20 May 1978; Alfred McCoy *The Politics of Heroin: CIA Complicity in the Global Drug Trade* (Chicago, Lawrence Hill Books, 2003).

[34] McCoy, *The Politics of Heroin* 409–10.

[35] Abdullah (n 5) 54.

this century, rates of drug dealing and consumption in Singapore have fallen sharply. In 1994, heroin-related arrests were 208 per 100,000 people, while in 2011 that figure fell to just 86.[36] The state's official view is that 'rigorous and effective enforcement coupled with severe penalties have allowed us to stay on top of the situation'.[37]

Drugs in Contemporary Singapore

Today, drug dealing in Singapore is generally small-scale and few sophisticated syndicates have made headway in the local market. By international standards, illegal drug use in Singapore is low. High levels of disposable income, particularly among the young, can be a factor contributing to increased drug consumption but this has not been the case in Singapore.[38] In 2013, 3,581 drug users were arrested, as were 3,507 in 2012,[39] of whom approximately 70 per cent were repeat abusers.[40] The main illicit drugs consumed in Singapore are heroin and methamphetamine, which together account for 92 per cent of drug offender arrests in the first half of 2013.[41] In recent years, there has been a major increase in the quantity of methamphetamine seized in Singapore.[42] Methamphetamine arrests doubled between 2008–12[43] and the drug is now the most commonly consumed substance among new users.[44] In 2012, methamphetamine users accounted for 42 per cent of all persons receiving drug treatment.[45] Two-thirds of drug-related arrests are persons aged below 30 years.

Most dealing is conducted by small groups of dealers who rely on cash transactions between the buyer and the seller.[46] Compared to many of its neighbouring countries, drug trafficking networks in Singapore are, therefore, small-scale and generally deal

[36] Teo Chee Hean, 'Enhancing Our Drug Control Framework and Review of the Death Penalty—Ministerial Statement by Mr Teo Chee Hean, Deputy Prime Minister, Coordinating Minister for National Security and Minister for Home Affairs', Press Release (9 July 2012) 8.

[37] Teo Chee Hean, 'Enhancing Our Drug Control' 17.

[38] UNODC, *World Drug Report 2012* (Vienna, United Nations, June 2012) www.unodc.org/documents/data-and-analysis/WDR2012/WDR_2012_web_small.pdf, 87.

[39] National Council against Drug Abuse, 'Annual Report 2013', www.cnb.gov.sg/Libraries/CNB_MediaLibrary_Files/NCADA_Annual_Report_2013.sflb.ashx, 10.

[40] Central Narcotics Bureau, 'Singapore's Country Report on Illicit Drug Trafficking'. Report for the 10th Meeting of AIFOCOM [ASEAN Inter-Parliamentary Assembly Fact Finding Committee], Brunei, 12–16 May 2013, 2.

[41] United States Department of State, Bureau of International Narcotics and Law Enforcement Affairs, 'International Narcotics Control Strategy Report. Volume I: Drug and Chemical Control' (March 2014), www.state.gov/documents/organization/222881.pdf, 283.

[42] UNODC, 'World Drug Report 2014' (Vienna, United Nations, June 2014) 48 www.unodc.org/documents/wdr2014/World_Drug_Report_2014_web.pdf, 48.

[43] UNODC, 'Patterns and Trends of Amphetamine-Type Stimulants and Other Drugs, Asia and the Pacific: A Report from the Global SMART Programme', (November 2013) 124.

[44] Central Narcotics Bureau, 'Two-Thirds of New Drug Abusers Arrested in 1st Half of 2014 were below 30 Years Old', Press Release (June 2014).

[45] UNODC, 'Patterns and Trends of Amphetamine-Type Stimulants' 12.

[46] Central Narcotics Bureau 'Singapore's Country Report' (12–16 May 2013) 3.

in limited quantities.[47] While drug-dealing is limited within Singapore, it remains a major transit point for narcotics en route to countries such as Indonesia, Australia and Malaysia, whether in parcels, maritime containers or air cargo.[48] Singapore's port is the second largest in the world by container volume and it does not screen containers unless they enter its customs territory. It now ranks as the world's fifth largest exporter and the third largest importer of ephedrine and pseudoephedrine.[49] Precursor chemicals such as ephedrine sent from India and Bangladesh to Central American countries frequently transit through Singapore. According to the United States Bureau of International Narcotics and Law Enforcement Affairs, Singapore's free trade zone and sophisticated air and maritime cargo infrastructure make it vulnerable to illegal freight forwarding activity,[50] although it is difficult to quantify the extent of this trade.

State Responses to Drugs

Politically, Singapore is dominated by the People's Action Party (PAP), which has held power since 1959. Elections are viewed as free although the government maintains tight controls on the media and censors content deemed to undermine social cohesion or criticise the government.[51] The PAP prides itself on having a 'tough stance'[52] and a 'zero tolerance'[53] approach to drugs. As the discussion above suggests, popular perceptions of drug use in Singaporean society have shifted significantly over the past two centuries, from relative acceptance and normalisation in the early 1800s to an increasingly strict moral position of censure and punitive criminalisation since World War II.[54]

At present, the Singaporean state imposes one of the world's strictest regimes for drug control, combining tough laws with active enforcement and an extensive drug-use prevention framework. Singapore is party to the three major multinational conventions that tackle drugs that were described earlier in this book: the 1961 Single Convention on Narcotic Drugs, the 1971 Convention on Psychotropic Substances, and the 1988 Convention against Illicit Traffic in Narcotic Drugs and Psychotropic Substances. It pursues, however, a more rigorous and punitive approach than many other contracting parties. Its overall strategy aims to reduce both supply and demand

[47] Central Narcotics Bureau, 'CNB's Intensified Enforcement Efforts in 2012. See Increase in Drug Abusers Arrested and Drugs Seized', Press Release, (February 2013), www.cnb.gov.sg/Libraries/CNB_Newsroom_Files/CNB_2012_Press_Release_Updated_figures_on_23_Jul_2013_2.sflb.ashx).

[48] US Department of State, Bureau of International Narcotics and Law Enforcement Affairs, 'International Narcotics Control Strategy Report: Vol I' 283.

[49] US Department of State, Bureau of International Narcotics and Law Enforcement Affairs (n 41) 62.

[50] US Department of State, '2013 INCSR: Country Reports—Moldova through Singapore' (5 March 2013), www.state.gov/j/inl/rls/nrcrpt/2013/vol1/204051.htm.

[51] See, eg, Chris Hudson and Terry Johal, 'A Chill in the Blogosphere: The State, the Internet and the Struggle for Narrative Control in Singapore' (2011) 44(1) *Communication, Politics & Culture* 33.

[52] Central Narcotics Bureau (n 46) 9.

[53] Teo Chee Hean, 'Second Reading on the Misuse of Drugs (Amendment) Bill' 33.

[54] See Abdullah (n 5) 59.

through 'tough legislation, vigorous enforcement, intensive preventive drug education and co-ordinated rehabilitation as well as aftercare in its fight against drugs'.[55]

Some argue that drug control 'disproportionately' occupies the national legislative and political agenda.[56] Noorman Abdullah suggests that this is because drug use symbolises the antithesis of the state's official values and the ideologies of the political elite in Singapore, which include productivity and 'capitalist ideals', namely sobriety, self-control, rationality and industriousness.[57] Because 'drug use' is seen to have no use in a 'success-oriented' society, it is particularly demonised by the Singaporean state.[58] Indeed, in the second reading of the Misuse of Drugs (Amendment) Bill in 1975 drug abuse was presented as causing 'irreparable damage' to the 'health and career of the drug abuser', sorrow and shame to family as well as a threat to 'national security and viability'.[59] The Minister for Home Affairs, moving the Bill, commented that:

> [i]f drug abuse were to be allowed to grow unchecked, particularly among our youths, we would eventually be faced with a dangerous national security problem. In no time we would find that it had penetrated right into the vital and sensitive institutions of the State, like the Police and the Armed Forces.[60]

The Minister even suggested that there was a 'Communist plan to use narcotics to corrupt and soften the population of the various states in South-East Asia for the purposes of subversion and eventual take-over'.[61] In fact, the drug problem was portrayed as a menacing threat to Singapore's very survival:

> Rampant drug addiction among our young men and women will also strike at the very foundations of our social fabric and undermine our economy. Once ensnared by drug dependence they will no longer be productive digits contributing to our economic and social progress. They will not be able to carry on with their regular jobs. Usually for the young men, they turn to all sorts of crime, and for the girls, to prostitution to get money to buy their badly needed supply of drugs. Thus, as a developing country, our progress and very survival will be seriously threatened.[62]

In this context, the fact that the government has effectively 'paralysed drug-trafficking in Singapore' is held up as a major national success and a testimony to the effectiveness of the Misuse of Drugs Act and a tough approach to the narcotics

[55] Central Narcotics Bureau (n 40) 2.
[56] Abdullah (n 5) 41.
[57] Abdullah (n 5) 63.
[58] Ibid.
[59] *Singapore Parliamentary Debates, Official Report* (20 November 1975) vol 34 at cols 1379–81.
[60] These comments were made by the then Minister for Home Affairs and Education during the second reading of the Bill that was ultimately enacted as the Misuse of Drugs (Amendment) Act 1975 (Act 49 of 1975) (which, most significantly, introduced the death penalty for drug trafficking for the first time). See *Singapore Parliamentary Debates, Official Report* (20 November 1975) vol 34 at cols 1379–81.
[61] Chua Sian Chin, Minister for Home Affairs and Education, *Singapore Parliamentary Debates, Official Report* (20 November 1975) vol 34, col 1380.
[62] Chua Sian Chin, *Singapore Parliamentary Debates, Official Report* (20 November 1975) vol 34 at col 1380.

trade.[63] The state has not, however, demonstrated as much progress in tackling the financial aspects of the trade. Singapore is one of the world's most popular financial service hubs and a major money-laundering destination. It has certainly introduced more stringent regulation to deal with the proceeds of drug-related crimes in recent years but it has, in the past, also been criticised for dealings with Burmese business figures closely linked to narcotics trade. This has included a notorious Burmese conglomerate, Asia World, and investments via the Myanmar Fund during the 1990s,[64] when Burma was one of the world's largest heroin exporters and the main supplier of heroin in Singapore.

Central Narcotics Bureau

The chief enforcement agency for drug related offences is the Central Narcotics Bureau (CNB). The Director of the CNB is appointed by the Minister of Home Affairs and has considerable powers under the Misuse of Drugs Act.[65] The Director and Deputy Director of CNB oversee eight divisions (the Supervision Division, Intelligence Division, Enforcement Division, Investigation Division, Policy, Planning and Research Division, Corporate Services Division, Communications Division and Staff Development Division), as well as an Office of Internal Investigations and a Psychology Unit. The CNB is a large and well-resourced organisation; its actual expenditure was in excess of S$ 107 million in financial year 2012[66] and S$ 93.87 million in financial year 2011.[67] Supported by the Singapore Police Force, the CNB conducts routine operations against drug suppliers, street-based dealers and addicts. In 2013, the CNB conducted 46 major operations against syndicates, seizing more than S$ 20.5 million worth of drugs.[68] Like most Singaporean government agencies, the CNB is considered to be a clean institution.[69] Singapore itself currently ranks as

[63] Chan Wing Cheong and Andrew BL Phang, 'The Development of Criminal Law and Criminal Justice' in Kevin Tan (ed) *Essays in Singapore Legal History* (Singapore, Marshall Cavendish, 2004) 245, 255.

[64] Dennis Bernstein and Leslie Kean, 'Singapore's Blood Money: Hanging Drug Couriers but Investing with Their Suppliers' *The Nation* (20 October 1997), 11.

[65] Misuse of Drugs Act (Singapore, Cap 185, 2008 Rev Ed) s 3. (MDA 2008 Rev Ed). The Act was originally enacted in 1973.

[66] Central Narcotics Bureau, 'Annual Bulletin 2013', www.cnb.gov.sg/Libraries/CNB_MediaLibrary_Files/CNB_Annual_Report_2013.sflb.ashx, 41.

[67] Central Narcotics Bureau, 'Annual Bulletin 2012', www.cnb.gov.sg/Libraries/CNB_MediaLibrary_Files/Central_Narcotics_Bureau_CNB_Bulletin_2012_Final_2.sflb.ashx, 39.

[68] Central Narcotics Bureau, 'Annual Bulletin 2013', 13; Central Narcotics Bureau, 'Annual Bulletin 2012', 5.

[69] The CNB director was suspended in 2012 in relation to graft charges in a major scandal but was subsequently acquitted. See Joyce Lim, 'Ng Boon Gay's "Not Guilty" Verdict: AGC Will Assess Whether to Appeal Decision' *The Straits Times* (14 February 2013), www.straitstimes.com/the-big-story/ng-boon-gay-trial/story/ng-boon-gays-not-guilty-verdict-agc-will-assess-whether-appeal; Walter Sim, 'Prosecution Not Appealing against Ex-CNB Chief Ng Boon Gay's Acquittal' *The Straits Times* (11 June 2013), www.straitstimes.com/breaking-news/singapore/story/prosecution-not-appealing-against-ex-cnb-chief-ng-boon-gays-acquittal-#sthash.ZJp2F5aJ.dpuf.

the seventh least corrupt country in Transparency International's Corruption Perceptions Index.[70]

Within the region, CNB works closely with foreign drug law enforcement agencies including the US Drug Enforcement Administration and the Australian Federal Police. Singapore also participates in multilateral programs to control precursor chemicals, tracking exports and co-operating with industry officials.[71] It has entered into a bilateral legal assistance program on narcotics offences with the United States, and Singaporean law enforcement officers frequently attend US sponsored training programs and regional drug control forums.[72] On 26 June 2012, Singapore signed a Memorandum of Understanding with the Malaysian Minister of Home Affairs to increase intelligence sharing and operational co-ordination to intensify co-operation in the fight against cross-border drug crimes. According to the CNB, its 'close and strategic collaboration' with foreign counterparts is crucial to its fight against cross-border trafficking.[73]

II. NARCOTIC-RELATED CRIMES

Legislative Framework

The Misuse of Drugs Act[74] is the primary legislation for the control of dangerous or harmful drugs and substances in Singapore. As at September 2014, it had undergone more than 50 amendments. The Act provides for the appointment of the Central Narcotics Bureau Director and officers, sets out major offences, specific rules of evidence, enforcement, punishment, and a framework for drug treatment and rehabilitation. The relevant controlled drugs, temporarily listed drugs, and equipment, materials and substances used for manufacturing appear in the Schedules to the Act. The Act also provides the Minister with authority to make specific regulations on issues such as conditions and procedures for the issuance of licences in relation to controlled drugs, as well as drug-user treatment and rehabilitation. The regulation of non-controlled substances that may cause intoxication (for example glue or paint thinners) is set out in the Intoxicating Substances Act (Singapore, Cap 146A, 2001 Rev Ed).

The broader principles and procedures relevant to Singaporean narcotics law are set out in the Penal Code 2008 Rev Ed,[75] the Criminal Procedure Code (Singapore, Cap 68, 2012 Rev Ed) (CPC 2012),[76] the Evidence Act 1997 Rev Ed[77]

[70] See Transparency International, *Corruption Perceptions Index: 2014* (Berlin, Transparency International, 2014), www.transparency.org/cpi2014/results.

[71] US Department of State, Bureau of International Narcotics and Law Enforcement Affairs (n 41) 62.

[72] US Department of State, Bureau of International Narcotics and Law Enforcement Affairs (n 41) 283.

[73] Central Narcotics Bureau (n 40) 2.

[74] MDA 2008 Rev Ed (Singapore, Cap 185 Rev Ed).

[75] Penal Code (Singapore, Cap 224, 2008 Rev Ed).

[76] Criminal Procedure Code (Singapore, Cap 68, 2012 Rev Ed) (CPC 2012 Rev Ed). The original Act was enacted in 2010.

[77] Evidence Act (Singapore, Cap 97, 1997 Rev Ed). Original enactment in 1893.

and the Criminal Law (Temporary Provisions) Act (Singapore, Cap 67, 2000 Rev Ed) (CLPTA 2000 Rev Ed).[78] The Penal Code was originally a copy of the Indian Penal Code, which was enacted there in 1860. There are now many other criminal statutes that deal with particular types of crime but the Penal Code remains the primary general statute for substantive criminal law and has undergone relatively few major amendments.[79] The Evidence Act, first introduced in 1893, was also based largely on its colonial Indian equivalent and deals with, inter alia, admissions and confessions, acceptable forms of evidence, the burden of proof and the treatment of witnesses. The Criminal Procedure Code, which was most recently re-enacted in 2012, sets out procedures that must be followed in the conduct of criminal cases. The Criminal Law (Temporary Provisions) Act,[80] which makes special provisions for powers such as temporary detention without trial, is also frequently used against suspected drug traffickers.[81] This Act was first introduced as a strategy to deal with secret societies and the communist insurgency in the 1950s.[82] It was intended as a temporary measure but has been renewed continuously, most recently in November 2013, and will remain in force until 20 October 2019. Since 1974, the Criminal Law (Temporary Provisions) Act has, again, been increasingly used to detain drug traffickers.[83] According to the Singaporean government, it is an 'effective' and 'important tool' against transnational and local organised drug syndicates.[84] Financial aspects of the drug trade are dealt with in the Corruption, Drug Trafficking and Other Serious Crimes (Confiscation of Benefits) Act (Singapore, Cap 65A, 2000 Rev Ed), which creates offences in relation to the proceeds of drug related offences (discussed at the end of this chapter).

Categories of Drug Offences

The Misuse of Drugs Act sets out most of the drug offences applicable in Singapore, including trafficking, import and export, manufacture, consumption and possession and the cultivation of 'controlled drugs'.[85] Controlled drugs are specified in the First Schedule to the Misuse of Drugs Act and include any substance or product that contains a controlled drug.[86]

[78] Criminal Law (Temporary Provisions) Act (Singapore, Cap 67, 2000 Rev Ed).

[79] Chan and Phang, 'The Development of Criminal Law' 250.

[80] Criminal Law (Singapore, Cap 67, 2000 Rev Ed).

[81] Singapore, Bureau of Democracy, Human Rights, and Labor, 'Singapore 2013 Human Rights Report' (27 February 2014), www.state.gov/j/drl/rls/hrrpt/2013/eap/220229.htm, 4.

[82] Michael Hor, 'Singapore's Innovations to Due Process' (2001) 12 *Criminal Law Forum* 25, 29.

[83] Singapore. Ministry of Home Affairs, 'Criminal Law (Temporary Provisions) Act Factsheet' (23 June 2014), www.mha.gov.sg/get_blob.aspx?file_id=d7d_RevisedCLTPACollateral23062014.pdf, 2.

[84] Singapore, 'National Report for Singapore's Universal Periodic Review', Human Rights Council, submitted to the Working Group on the Universal Periodic Review, Eleventh session, Geneva, United Nations, 2–13 May 2011, A/HRC/WG.6/11/SGP/1, www.mfa.gov.sg/content/dam/mfa/images/media_center/special_events/upr/UPR%20National%20Report_Singapore.pdf, 17 (point 127).

[85] Ibid.

[86] MDA 2008 Rev Ed, s 2.

Trafficking in Controlled Drugs

The Misuse of Drugs Act criminalises 'trafficking in controlled drugs',[87] which is defined broadly as 'to sell, give, administer, transport, send, deliver or distribute'[88] a controlled drug or 'to offer to do' any of those acts.[89] The only exceptions are where explicit authorisation has been granted in accordance with the Act. The trafficking offence also extends to those who do, or offer to do, any 'preparatory acts' for trafficking.[90] A person can be found guilty of a trafficking offence by possessing a drug for the purpose of trafficking, even where that drug is yet to undergo transport or change hands.[91] Punishments for trafficking vary significantly, depending on the specific type or classification drug and the quantity trafficked. For example, the trafficking of a Class C drug attracts a minimum penalty between 2–10 years and 2–5 strokes of the cane, while trafficking more than 250 g of methamphetamine or 15 g of heroin attracts a mandatory death penalty.[92]

Manufacture of Controlled Drugs

The Misuse of Drugs Act criminalises the 'manufacture' of a controlled drug, which is defined as 'any process of producing the drug and the refining or transformation of one drug into another' including 'any process of producing the substance and the refining or transformation of one substance into another'.[93] Penalties attached to unauthorised manufacture of a controlled drug depends on the class of the drug but range from five years to life imprisonment, together with five to 15 lashes of the cane.[94] The death penalty applies for unauthorised manufacture of morphine, cocaine and heroin.[95] Unless specific authorisation has been given, the manufacture, supply, possession, import or export of any controlled equipment, material, or substance is also an offence if the person committing the act knew, or had reason to believe, that that the equipment, material or substance was to be used in the manufacture of a controlled drug.[96]

Import and Export of Controlled Drugs

The unauthorised import into or export from Singapore of a controlled drug constitutes an offence under the Misuse of Drugs Act.[97] It is irrelevant whether the alleged offender is in transit and that Singapore is not his or her ultimate destination.[98]

[87] MDA 2008 Rev Ed, s 5.
[88] MDA 2008 Rev Ed, s 2.
[89] MDA 2008 Rev Ed, s 5(1)(a), (b).
[90] MDA 2008 Rev Ed, s 5(1)(c).
[91] MDA 2008 Rev Ed, s 5(2).
[92] MDA 2008 Rev Ed, sch 2.
[93] MDA 2008 Rev Ed, s 2.
[94] MDA 2008 Rev Ed, sch 2.
[95] Ibid.
[96] MDA 2008 Rev Ed, s 10A(1).
[97] MDA 2008 Rev Ed, s 7.
[98] *Ko Mun Cheung and another v PP (Public Prosecutor)* [1992] 1 SLR (R) 887; [1992] SGCA 30, [16], [20].

This means that all passengers who possess a controlled drug and touch down in Singapore risk being caught under the Act, even if bound elsewhere. Since more than 500,000 travellers enter or transit through Singapore every day,[99] the potential reach of this offence is significant.

The penalties that apply to the import and export of controlled drugs are stricter than those that apply to other trafficking offences. For example the maximum imprisonment for the import or export of a Class A drug is 30 years, as opposed to 20 years for the corresponding trafficking offence. Given importing or exporting is considered a more serious offence than trafficking within Singapore, the question arises as to whether there is a particular *mens rea* that attaches to the act of import or export, or whether the strict penalties apply even when the drugs are imported for a purpose other than trafficking, for instance for personal consumption.

The question of the interpretation of 'import' was examined at length in the case of *Public Prosecutor v Adnan bin Kadir*.[100] The High Court held that since the crime of unauthorised import attracts a harsher penalty than trafficking, it must be interpreted as import with the intention of trafficking, as opposed to import for personal use.[101] The prosecution referred this question of law to the Court of Appeal on public interest grounds. The Court of Appeal, however, applied the Interpretation Act 1965 and found that words and expressions have the meanings assigned, unless such a construction is inconsistent with the context or subject, or unless an alternative meaning is expressly provided.[102] The Interpretation Act provides that 'import' means 'to bring or cause to be brought into Singapore by land, sea or air'.[103] The Court of Appeal, therefore, found that the meaning of the word 'import' within the Misuse of Drugs Act was 'plain and unambiguous' and, in lieu of 'very compelling' evidence that parliament intended otherwise, there was nothing to support the view that 'import' must be read as 'import for the purpose of trafficking'.[104] The Court of Appeal noted that while the penalty for importation was heavy, the problem of increased drug supply in Singapore arises regardless of whether the drugs were intended for trafficking or for personal consumption. It therefore did not follow, the Court held, that parliament only intended the section to apply to those importing for the purpose of trafficking.[105] The Court of Appeal accordingly ruled out the possible defence to a change of importation of drugs that the import was for personal consumption or some purpose other than trafficking.[106]

[99] Teo Chee Hean (n 2) 30.
[100] *PP v Adnan bin Kadir* [2013] SGCA 34.
[101] *Adnan bin Kadir v PP* [2012] SGHC 196.
[102] *PP v Adnan bin Kadir* [2013] SGCA 34.
[103] Interpretation Act (Singapore, Cap 2, 2002 Rev Ed) s 2(1).
[104] *PP v Adnan bin Kadir* [2013] SGCA 34 [62].
[105] *PP v Adnan bin Kadir* [2013] SGCA 34 [53–54].
[106] *PP v Adnan bin Kadir* [2013] SGCA 34 [69].

Possession and Consumption of Controlled Drugs

The Misuse of Drugs Act criminalises unauthorised possession and consumption of controlled drugs.[107] The offence applies to a person who has a controlled drug in his or her possession,[108] and/or smokes, self-administers or otherwise consumes a controlled or 'specified drug'.[109] The consumption of a controlled or specified drug (as set out in the Fourth Schedule) can lead to a maximum sentence of 10 years' imprisonment and/or a fine of up to S$ 20,000. A minimum sentence of two years applies to repeat offenders. Should the defendant have certain past convictions, he or she faces an additional punishment of between five to seven years' imprisonment.[110] In 1998, the Act was amended to include new provisions that prohibited consumption of controlled or specified drugs by Singaporean citizens or residents outside of Singapore.[111] The amendment was justified as a response to 'a noticeable trend of Singaporeans consuming drugs overseas in recent years'.[112] These extra-territorial provisions apply where a person is found to have consumed a drug pursuant to urine tests conducted in compliance with the Misuse of Drugs Act. In such cases, the same liabilities and penalties apply as those that attach to the offence within Singapore's territorial jurisdiction. It is uncertain whether Singapore might seek to exercise jurisdiction where an individual who commits a drug offence outside Singapore has permanent residency in Singapore but citizenship in another jurisdiction.

Third Party Responsibility

In recent years, the Misuse of Drugs Act has been amended to include a number of offences that apply to third parties who tolerate or indirectly facilitate drug-related activities, even where the third party is not immediately involved in the trafficking, manufacturing, import and export or consumption of drugs. For example, the owner, tenant, occupier or person overseeing any premises may be found guilty of an offence where he or she allows the premises to be kept or used for the consumption, unlawful trafficking or manufacturing of any controlled drug.[113] Third party offences also apply in relation to those who organise events or gatherings where drugs are to be trafficked or consumed.[114] This amendment was based on research commissioned by the Singapore inter-ministry Taskforce on Drugs, which found that new drug users were often introduced to drugs at social gatherings where a number of friends were consuming such drugs. A 'gathering' is defined very broadly under the Misuse of Drugs Act as two or more people in any place. A person is guilty of

[107] MDA 2008 Rev Ed, s 8.
[108] MDA 2008 Rev Ed, s 8(a).
[109] MDA 2008 Rev Ed, s 8(b).
[110] MDA 2008 Rev Ed, s 33(a).
[111] MDA 2008 Rev Ed, s 8A(1).
[112] Wong Kan Seng, 'Singapore Parliamentary Debates, Mr Wong Kan Seng', Official Record, col 45 (1 June 1998).
[113] MDA 2008 Rev Ed, s 11.
[114] MDA 2008 Rev Ed, s 11A.

this offence if they know that any controlled drug is to be consumed or trafficked at that gathering.[115] Thus, criminal liability for the offence can apply regardless of whether the accused has any role in the actual supply of the controlled drug.[116] The offence attracts a penalty of between three to 20 years imprisonment and caning. Harsher penalties apply where the gathering includes any person below the age of 21 or suffering a mental impairment.[117]

Misuse of Intoxicating Substances

Singapore has made the use or inhalation of other substances (non-controlled drugs) that can cause intoxication offences under the Intoxicating Substances Act (Singapore, Cap 146A, 2001 Rev Ed).[118] This Act was introduced to tackle the use of inhalants such as glue and paint thinners. The misuse of intoxicating substances offence applies where a person uses or inhales any intoxicating substance for the purpose of inducing, or causing in himself, a state of intoxication.[119] Intoxicating substances are defined as any substance that releases toxic vapours or fumes that contain any chemical compound specified in the Schedule to the Act and which, when inhaled, induces or causes a state of intoxication.[120] The Schedule currently lists only toluene. Supplying intoxicating substances with knowledge, or reasonable cause to believe, that the substance is likely to be inhaled or used for intoxication purposes also constitutes an offence.[121] It attracts a fine of up to S$ 5,000 and/or imprisonment of up to two years.[122]

Money Laundering Offences

A number of offences apply to those who finance or in any way facilitate, maintain or deal with the proceeds of drug related offences. These are regulated under the Corruption, Drug Trafficking and Other Serious Crimes (Confiscation of Benefits) Act (Singapore, Cap 65A, 2000 Rev Ed) and are discussed in greater detail later in this chapter.

Definition of Narcotics

The First Schedule to the Misuse of Drugs Act contains a list of substances and products that constitute 'controlled drugs'. The First Schedule divides substances into

[115] MDA 2008 Rev Ed, s 11A(1).
[116] MDA 2008 Rev Ed, s 11A(2).
[117] MDA 2008 Rev Ed, s 33(4)(c).
[118] Intoxicating Substances Act (Singapore, Cap 146A, 2001 Rev Ed) (ISA 2001 Rev Ed), s 3. The Act was originally enacted in 1987.
[119] ISA 2001 Rev Ed, s 3.
[120] ISA 2001 Rev Ed, s 2.
[121] ISA 2001 Rev Ed, s 4(1).
[122] ISA 2001 Rev Ed, s 4(2).

three classes of drugs in accordance with their relative level of danger or harm.[123] Any substance that is not listed in the First Schedule but contains one or more drugs that are listed there also qualifies as a 'controlled drug' for the purposes of the Act.[124] The schedule was updated on six occasions between 2004 and 2014[125] and, as of September 2014, lists more than 260 Class A substances, 15 Class B substances and 11 Class C substances. It is seen as an exhaustive list of controlled drugs.

The emergence of new varieties of synthetic drugs is viewed as the major challenge in Singapore's 'war against drugs'[126] and has made it increasingly difficult to maintain a comprehensive drug listing. New psychoactive substances are often created by introducing slight modifications to the chemical structures of existing controlled drugs, leading to the rapid development of new substances[127] that technically are not caught by the drug control laws.[128] In 2012 alone, for example, Singaporean authorities identified 11 previously unknown psychoactive substances.[129] In contrast to the speed with which new drugs can be developed, the process of listing a new substance in the First Schedule of the Misuse of Drugs Act is time consuming, involving a detailed study of the substance and its harmful effects, and industry consultation to identify and understand potential legitimate uses. There is, thus, a real possibility that a harmful drug can remain in circulation for an extended period before the listing process is complete.

To resolve this problem, the Misuse of Drugs Act was amended in 2012 to insert a Fifth Schedule that allows authorities to list a new psychoactive substance for an initial 12 month period while they undergo further investigation, with the option of a further 12 month extension.[130] Singapore's strategy in dealing with new psychoactive substances is not unique. 'Emergency scheduling' is now used in many jurisdictions to introduce temporary bans while assessment and legislative processes are under way. Other countries that have adopted this approach include Australia, China, Croatia, Bahrain, Ghana, Hungary Ireland, Italy, Netherlands, the Russian Federation, Saudi Arabia, the United Kingdom, and the United States.[131] Trafficking,

[123] MDA 2008 Rev Ed, s 2 provides that 'Class A drug', 'Class B drug' and 'Class C drug' mean any of the substances and products for the time being specified in Parts I, II and III of the First Schedule, respectively. See also Chua Sian Chin 'Second Reading Speech by Mr Chua Sian Chin, Minister for Health and Home Affairs', vol 32, col 416 (16 February 1973).

[124] MDA 2008 Rev Ed, s 2(1) ('controlled drug').

[125] Wong Kan Seng, 'Bill No 40/2005, Second Reading Speech, Mr Wong Kan Seng' (16 January 2006), vol 80, col 2095. Note that there were amendments made with no second reading speeches: see GN No S 491/2006—Misuse of Drugs Act (Amendment of First Schedule) Order 2006; GN No S 685/2010—Misuse of Drugs Act (Amendment of First Schedule) Order 2010; GN No S 272/2013—Misuse of Drugs Act (Amendment of First and Third Schedules) Order 2013; GN No S 572/2014—(Amendment of First, Third and Fifth Schedules) Order 2014.

[126] Singapore, Ministry of Home Affairs, 'Second Reading Speech for the Misuse of Drugs (Amendment) Bill 2006, Ministry of Home Affairs' (21 June 2007).

[127] Central Narcotics Bureau (n 40) 5.

[128] See UNODC, 'The Challenge of New Psychoactive Substances: A Report from the Global SMART Programme' (March 2013), www.unodc.org/documents/scientific/NPS_2013_SMART.pdf, 26.

[129] UNODC (United Nations Office on Drugs and Crime), 'World Drug Report 2013' (Vienna, United Nations, May 2013), www.unodc.org/unodc/secured/wdr/wdr2013/World_Drug_Report_2013.pdf, 93.

[130] See Misuse of Drugs (Amendment) Act 2012 s 30.

[131] See UNODC, 'The Challenge of New Psychoactive Substances' 31.

manufacturing, importing, possessing or consuming a substance listed under the Fifth Schedule does not constitute an offence under the Misuse of Drugs Act but the CNB is empowered to seize all such substances,[132] thus restricting circulation of the drugs while further study, consultation and legislative process is under way. Since its enactment in 2012 the Fifth Schedule has been amended three times.[133]

Mens Rea in Drug Offences

To establish criminal liability in the common law tradition it is generally a requirement that the prosecution proves beyond reasonable doubt that the defendant committed the physical act constituting the offence (*actus reas*) and had the requisite knowledge or intention (*mens rea*).[134] In a number of cases, Singaporean courts have approved the English courts' position that '*mens rea*, an evil intention or a knowledge of the wrongfulness of the act is an essential ingredient in every offence'.[135] They have, nonetheless, sometimes been inconsistent in addressing the question of the nature of knowledge that a defendant must possess to satisfy the requisite *mens rea*.[136] Even where a presumption of actual knowledge applies, if the defendant establishes that he or she had no knowledge of the relevant circumstances then a literal reading of the Misuse of Drugs Act would indicate that the prosecution must fail.

In some cases, courts have nonetheless relied on an approach more akin to an objective negligence test, rather than an examination of the defendant's subjective mental state. In other words, in some drug trafficking cases the courts have accepted that the test can be satisfied where a 'reasonable person ought to have known' or 'would have made enquiries or take other steps to allay his suspicions' that they were carrying controlled substances.[137] This is the test generally used in civil law negligence cases but would appear to fall short of the 'actual knowledge' generally required to give rise to liability for a criminal offence. The confusion that this causes in evident in cases such as *Chan Heng Kong v Public Prosecutor* (discussed below),[138] where the lower court applied a negligence-type test to knowledge, while the Court of Appeal retained a subjective test approach.

[132] MDA 2008 Rev Ed, ss 24(1)(a)(i), (b), (c); 26(2)(a).

[133] GN No S 572/2014—Misuse of Drugs Act (Amendment of First, Third and Fifth Schedules) Order 2014; GN No S 323/2014—Misuse of Drugs Act (Amendment of First, Fourth and Fifth Schedules) Order 2014; GN No S 273/2013—Misuse of Drugs Act (Amendment of Fifth Schedule) Order 2013.

[134] *Chan Pean Leon v PP* [1956] 1 MLJ 237; *Chng Wei Meng v PP* [2002] 4 SLR 595.

[135] Wright J in *Sherras v Rutzen* [1895] 1 QB 918 at 921, cited in the Singapore Privy Council case of *Lim Chin Aik v R* [1963] 1 All ER 223, 227–8; [1963] MLJ 50.

[136] See discussion in Michael Hor, 'Managing *Mens Rea* in Singapore' (2006) 18 *Singapore Academy of Law Journal* 341, 331.

[137] *PP v Azman bin Mohamed Sanwan* [2010] SGHC 196 [147]. On appeal, the Court of Appeal did not criticise this passage: *Azman bin Mohamed Sanwan v PP* [2012] 2 SLR 733. See also Chan Wing Cheong, 'Culpability in the Misuse of Drugs Act: Wilful Blindness, the Reasonable Person and a Duty to Check' (2013) 25 *Singapore Academy of Law Journal* 110, 118.

[138] [2012] SGCA 18.

In the case of *Tan Ah Tee v Public Prosecutor*,[139] the Court of Appeal adopted an interpretation by Lord Pearce in relation to a House of Lords decision regarding English statutes. Under this approach, Lord Pearce argued that it was possible to establish an offence where the accused had less than actual knowledge of possession. In particular, the Court found that constructive knowledge could be imputed if: (i) someone has a reasonable opportunity to acquaint themselves with the contents of a package and fails to do so; or (ii) fails to immediately inspect its contents where there is a risk, or reason to suspect, that its contents might be illicit.[140] This argument was, however, originally put forward in the context of a legislative framework that contained no presumptions as to knowledge, whereas the Misuse of Drugs Act contains an express one. A number of cases have followed this line of reasoning.[141] Hor notes that this approach is also reflected in other areas of Singaporean law, including immigration prosecutions, where there has been a tendency to conflate concepts of actual knowledge and negligence.[142]

Other cases have nonetheless clearly dismissed a negligence-type test of knowledge.[143] For example, in the case of *Public Prosecutor v Hla Win*,[144] the defendant, who arrived in Changi Airport from Hatyai, Thailand, with 3,468 g of heroin in his bag, was under the belief that he was carrying precious stones. After close examination of the defendant's responses upon his arrest, and other documentary evidence, the High Court and Court of Appeal held that on a balance of probabilities the defendant did not know that he was smuggling drugs, and as such should not be prosecuted.[145] The Court found that the fact that the respondent knew that the contents of his bag were illicit could not be used to demonstrate that he knew the content was drugs.[146] It found that the defendant's claim of mistake could only go to the credibility of his evidence and that a proper assessment would always depend on the circumstances of the case.[147] Whether the defendant ought to have known or checked was not the key test; rather, the question was one of determining actual knowledge.[148]

In *Public Prosecutor v Tan Kiam Peng*,[149] the High Court again emphasised that the statute requires knowledge and that it is incorrect to replace actual knowledge with 'ought to reasonably know',[150] which is a test for negligence rather than criminal liability. The Court rejected arguments around a 'duty to inspect' or 'strict liability'

[139] [1978–1979] SLR 211.

[140] *Tan Ah Tee v PP* [1978-79] SLR 211, 219–220 citing Lord Pearce in *R v Warner* [1969] 2 AC 256, 306; Michael Hor, 'Misuse of Drugs and Aberrations of Drugs in the Criminal Law' (2001) 13 *Singapore Academy of Law Journal* 54, 63.

[141] See, eg, *Shan Kai Weng v PP* [2004] 1 SLR 57 at [23]–[24] ('Shan Kai Weng').

[142] Hor, 'Managing Mens Rea' 329.

[143] See majority judgment in *PP v Hla Win* [1995] 2 SLR 424; *PP v Tan Kiam Peng* [2007] 1 SLR 522.

[144] [1995] 2 SLR 424.

[145] [1995] 2 SLR 424.

[146] [1995] 2 SLR 424.

[147] [1995] 2 SLR 424 [41].

[148] Ibid.

[149] [2007] 1 SLR 522.

[150] *PP v Tan Kiam Peng* [2007] 1 SLR 522 [23].

for drug offences and found that a failure to inspect or inquire is only relevant where it goes towards establishing either that the accused knew what he was carrying or was wilfully blind to the obvious.[151] This approach was affirmed by the Court of Appeal in *Chan Heng Kong v Public Prosecutor*.[152] In this case, the High Court, in determining whether the accused knew that he was engaged in a drug deal, looked at what 'any person of average intelligence and honesty would have realised'.[153] By contrast, the Court of Appeal applied a subjective basis based on evidence that the accused had deliberately refused to 'want to go and think about it' and that in his heart he believed the packets contained illegal drugs but did not ask 'what exactly was inside'.[154]

Wilful Blindness

While the application of a negligence test approach to drugs cases is debatable under Singaporean law, the courts have certainly been willing to accept a narrow form of constructive knowledge where a defendant is 'wilfully blind' to the truth, such that he or she may be criminally responsible even where their mental state falls short of actual knowledge.[155] Once established, wilful blindness is treated as being the equivalent in law to actual knowledge.[156] 'Wilful blindness' applies where it can be demonstrated that the defendant suspects that it is highly probable that a particular drug is in his or her possession but consciously refuses to check so as to avoid confirming that strong suspicion.[157] In other words, the facts must substantiate that defendant held a suspicion, but deliberately decided against confirming that suspicion, for wilful blindness to be established.[158] Thus, the test for wilful blindness sets a higher bar than mere recklessness as to the relevant circumstances.[159] It is a subjective state, as the Court emphasised in *Nagaenthran a/l K Dharmalingam v Public Prosecutor:*[160]

> ... Wilful blindness ... is merely 'lawyer-speak' for *actual knowledge* that is *inferred* from the circumstances of the case. It is an indirect way to prove actual knowledge; ie, actual knowledge is proved because the inference of knowledge is *irresistible* and is the *only rational inference* available *on the facts*. ... It is a subjective concept, in that the extent of knowledge in question is the knowledge of the *accused* and not that which might be postulated of a hypothetical person in the position of the accused ... [emphasis in the original]

[151] *PP v Tan Kiam Peng* [2007] 1 SLR 522 [28].
[152] *Chan Heng Kong and another v PP* [2012] SGCA 18.
[153] *PP v Sng Chun Heng and another* [2010] SGHC 317 [75].
[154] *Chan Heng Kong and another v PP* [2012] SGCA 18 [21–22].
[155] Chan Wing Cheong, 'Culpability in the Misuse of Drugs Act: Wilful Blindness, the Reasonable Person and a Duty to Check', (2013) 25 *Singapore Academy of Law Journal* 110, www.sal.org.sg/digitallibrary/Lists/SAL%20Journal/Attachments/626/(2013)%2025%20SAcLJ%20110-129%20(Chan%20Wing%20Cheong).pdf.
[156] *Tan Kiam Peng v PP* [2008] 1 SLR 1; [2007] SGCA 38 [43].
[157] *Tan Kiam Peng v PP* [2008] 1 SLR 1; [2007] SGCA 38 [123].
[158] *Tan Kiam Peng v PP* [2008] 1 SLR 1; [2007] SGCA 38 [104].
[159] *Tan Kiam Peng v PP* [2008] 1 SLR 1; [2007] SGCA 38 [104].
[160] [2011] 4 SLR 1156 at [30].

A leading example of wilful blindness is, again, the case of *Chan Heng Kong v Public Prosecutor*,[161] in which the accused (Chan) was found guilty of placing a plastic bag containing a number of sachets of diamorphine (heroin) at a pavilion of 'Mamee Monster' snack packs. Chan did not dispute possession but argued that he did not possess the requisite *mens rea* since he was under the belief that he had only been engaged in an illegal money lending transaction. This argument was dismissed by the Court of Appeal, which found that that:

> The first appellant knew '*in his heart*'... that he was dealing with illegal drugs when he brought the 'Mamee Monster' snack packs from Malaysia to Singapore ... Needless to say [the accused's] refusal to 'want to go and think about it' in spite of such suspicion ... clearly attracted the application of wilful blindness.[162] [emphasis in the original]

By contrast, in *Public Prosecutor v Azman bin Mohamed Sanwan*,[163] the accused was held not to be liable for drug trafficking because the Court found that he was not at all aware of the existence of bundles containing drugs in the car and, therefore, did not intentionally refrain from making inquiries as to their contents. As such, wilful blindness could not be established. This decision shows that where a defendant can demonstrate an honest belief that precluded actual, subjective knowledge of the substances, then the fact that the defendant had opportunities to discover otherwise will not be sufficient to prove wilful blindness.[164]

Courts have acknowledged the need to more vigilantly preserve a distinction between recklessness and negligence on one hand, and actual knowledge and wilful blindness on the other.[165] A 2006 Court of Appeal case emphasised that the Misuse of Drugs Act does not impose a positive obligation on individuals to inspect containers and does not attach liability to a failure to inspect.[166] Despite this, there are inconsistencies in the approach taken by Singaporean courts on the question of which *mens rea* test should apply, and it remains subject to some uncertainty.

Extent of Knowledge: Type of Drug

This is particularly true in relation to trafficking offences. The question arises as to whether it is necessary that the accused is aware of the precise nature of the substance they have in possession, or whether it is simply enough that he or she knows it is a 'controlled drug'. The court's position is that the prosecution only needs to prove the latter case.[167]

In the case of *Public Prosecutor v Lim Boon Hiong*,[168] the two defendants were charged with drug trafficking. They argued that they did not know the nature of the

[161] [2012] SGCA 18.
[162] Ibid [22].
[163] [2010] SGHC 196.
[164] *PP v Mas Swan bin Adnan* and another appeal [2012] SGCA 29 [11(g)].
[165] See *PP v Tan Kiam Peng* [2007] 1 SLR(R) 522. This was accepted in *Tan Kiam Peng v PP* [2008] 1 SLR(R) 1, 35.
[166] *Iwuchukwu Amara Tochi v PP* [2006] 2 SLR 503 [6].
[167] *Tan Kiam Peng v PP* [2008] 1 SLR 1; [2007] SGCA 38 [19].
[168] [2010] 4 SLR 696.

substance contained in the bundles and because they were not aware it contained diamorphine they were not in 'possession', since possession requires knowledge of the thing possessed. The judge applied a narrow interpretation of 'knowledge' to require knowledge of the actual substance possessed, based on the need to resolve ambiguities in favour of the accused.[169] He found, however, that knowledge as to the precise nature of the substance becomes less important where the court finds the defendant has been wilfully blind:

> ... since the accused *knows* (whether by actual knowledge *simpliciter* or by wilful blindness) that the package contains controlled drugs, if he does not take sufficient steps (and it is clear from the Court of Appeal's observations above that merely asking for, and receiving assurances is not sufficient), he is *wilfully blind* as to the specific nature of the drug, ie, the narrow approach.[170] [emphasis in the original]

The Court held that because the defendant in this case knew he was carrying controlled drugs, he ought to have taken reasonable steps to investigate by making further inquiries, such as opening the packets and satisfying himself that it did not contain heroin.[171] By refraining from such steps, the accused was wilfully blind to the fact that the drugs were diamorphine.[172] This reflects the approach in *Tan Kiam Peng*, where the High Court held that for liability to be imposed, the law does not require that an accused know details such as the name of the drug, its classification, its exact chemical or physical properties, or the punishment associated with that particular type of drug.[173]

Presumptions

Presumptions apply in relation to the *mens rea* for most offences under the Misuse of Drugs Act. Where a legislative presumption applies under the Act such that the requisite *mens rea* is presumed to exist, the burden then falls on the defendant to show that, on the balance of probabilities, he or she was not in possession of the relevant knowledge or intention and that the *mens rea* element of the offence was not made out.

Singaporean courts have recognised the presumption of innocence as the 'cornerstone' of the criminal justice system and the 'bedrock of the law of evidence'.[174] The cumulative effect of the many mechanisms under the Act that shift the onus to the defendant to disprove his or her guilt raises the question, however, of whether the presumption of innocence still has much relevance for Singaporean narcotics law.[175]

[169] Ibid [62].
[170] [2010] SGHC 205 [66].
[171] [2010] SGHC 205 [84].
[172] Ibid.
[173] [2010] SGHC 205 [37].
[174] *XP v PP* [2008] 4 SLR(R) 686 [90]. See also *Took Leng How v PP* [2006] 2 SLR 70 [27].
[175] See discussion in Chen Siyuan and Nathaniel Yong-Ern Khng, 'Possession and Knowledge in the Misuse of Drugs Act' (2012) 13 *Singapore Law Review* 181, 189.

Presumptions Concerning Trafficking and Possession

In trafficking cases where a presumption of *mens rea* does not apply, the prosecution must prove, beyond reasonable doubt, that the defendant was not only in possession of the controlled drugs in question but also had an intention to traffic them. Possession of certain drugs above a set quantity gives rise, however, to a presumption that the accused possessed the drug for the purpose of trafficking, unless the defendant can prove the contrary. For example, the Misuse of Drugs Act provides that if a person if found to possess more than two grams of heroin, 100 g of opium or 15 g of cannabis, then he or she is presumed to possess such an amount for the purpose of trafficking.[176] The onus is on the defendant to demonstrate that his possession of that drug was not for that purpose.

The Misuse of Drugs Act also provides that the defendant is presumed to have possessed a drug, unless proven otherwise, where the defendant has in his or her possession, custody or control: (a) anything that holds or includes a controlled drug; (b) the keys to anything that holds or gives access to a controlled drug; (c) the keys to any location where a controlled drug is discovered; or (d) a 'document of title' associated with a controlled drug or any other document meant for the drug's delivery.[177] The Act also provides that if a controlled drug is discovered on any ship, aircraft or vehicle that will trigger a presumption that the drug is in possession of the master or captain of the ship or aircraft or the owner or 'person in charge' of the vehicle.[178] Merely demonstrating that the defendant never had physical possession of the substance will not necessarily rebut the presumption.[179] Likewise, where a person possesses a controlled drug with the 'knowledge and consent' of one or more others, 'each and all' will be deemed to possess that drug.[180]

Another presumption under the Misuse of Drugs Act is that any person who has possession, custody or control of anything containing a controlled drug is presumed to be in possession and to have known the nature of the drug, unless they are able to prove to the contrary.[181] The presumption of knowledge can operate in conjunction with the presumption of possession, and, thus, extends to anyone who possesses the keys to anything containing a controlled drug, the keys to any premises where a controlled drug is found, or a document of title relating to the controlled drug.[182] The impact of this presumption is that, provided the prosecution can prove possession of a drug, or trigger a presumption of possession, there is no need to demonstrate that the defendant knew its nature. In such a case, the burden shifts to the defence to prove that on the balance of probabilities the accused did not actually know, and was not wilfully blind to, the nature of the relevant drug in his or her possession. In

[176] MDA 2008 Rev Ed, s 17.
[177] MDA 2008 Rev Ed, s 18(1).
[178] MDA 2008 Rev Ed, ss 20–21.
[179] MDA 2008 Rev Ed, s 18(3).
[180] MDA 2008 Rev Ed, s 18(4).
[181] MDA 2008 Rev Ed, s 18(2).
[182] MDA 2008 Rev Ed, s 18(1)(b)–(d).

the case of *Nagaenthran a/l K Dharmalingam v Public Prosecutor*,[183] the Court held that an accused can overturn such a presumption of knowledge by:

> proving, on a balance of probabilities, that he genuinely believed that what was in his possession was something innocuous (e.g. washing power, when it was in fact heroin (see *Warner v Metropolitan Police Commissioner* [1969] 2 AC 256)), or that he thought it was a controlled drug other than the one actually found in his possession (e.g. where he genuinely believed he was carrying 'ice' rather than heroin (see *Khor Soon Lee v PP* [2011] 3 SLR 201)).[184]

In *Mervin Singh v Public Prosecutor*,[185] the Court of Appeal emphasised that to rebut the presumption of knowledge the accused did not have to present a 'compelling evidence' and that the lower threshold of 'on a balance of probabilities' would be enough.[186]

Importantly, the presumptions in relation to trafficking and possession cannot be applied simultaneously. In *Tang Hai Liang v Public Prosecutor*, the Court of Appeal reiterated that the presumption of possession of heroin 'for the purpose of trafficking' and the presumption of knowledge 'of the nature of the drug' upon proof of possession of a controlled drug or presumption of possession of a controlled drug cannot apply concurrently or cumulatively.[187]

Presumptions Concerning Premises and Drug Consumption

Under the Misuse of Drugs, where any 'pipe, syringe, utensil, apparatus' or other accessories meant for consuming a controlled drug are discovered in any location or property, it is presumed that the location is used to consume a controlled drug.[188] Further, any individual discovered in such a place or 'escaping' from a place that is proved or presumed to be a place for the consumption of a controlled drug will be presumed to have been consuming such a drug there.[189] The onus is then on the defendant to demonstrate that he or she was not present for such a purpose.

In relation to tests administrated under the Misuse of Drugs Act, if a controlled drug is found in an accused person's urine sample, and he or she fails a drug test, that person will be presumed to have knowingly consumed that drug.[190] Thus, a positive test triggers a presumption that the accused had both the requisite *mens rea* and *actus reus* for consuming that controlled drug.[191] He or she then bears the burden of rebutting the presumption on the balance of probabilities. For example, the accused could invoke the 'spiker defence' by leading evidence that he or she was not aware of

[183] *Nagaenthran a/l K Dharmalingam v PP* [2011] 4 SLR 1156.
[184] *Nagaenthran a/l K Dharmalingam v PP* [2011] 4 SLR 1156, 1166 [27].
[185] [2013] SGCA 20.
[186] Ibid [35].
[187] [2011] SGCA 38 [18].
[188] MDA 2008 Rev Ed, s 19(1).
[189] MDA 2008 Rev Ed, s 19(2).
[190] MDA 2008 Rev Ed, s 22.
[191] See *Vadugaiah Mahendran v PP* [1996] 1 SLR 289.

taking a controlled drug and that another person had 'slipped the drugs into his (sic) drinks or cigarettes'.[192] In *Public Prosecutor v Tan Chui Yun Joselyn*,[193] the accused was acquitted partly because it was held to be 'extremely unlikely' that she would take the controlled drug knowing that the following day she faced a police interview regarding drug-related practices. Further, there was 'some evidence' that she knew who had spiked her drink.[194] The Court emphasised that in applying presumptions under the Misuse of Drugs Act, the courts had to strike 'a delicate balance' and should not impose too heavy a burden on the accused to displace the presumption, as that could effectively turn the crime into one of strict liability.[195] Once the presumption of consumption is triggered, however, it is not sufficient for the defence counsel to merely raise doubts about whether the accused consumed the relevant drug. There is an obligation to prove to the contrary by adducing evidence giving rise to facts and not simply raising doubts about the prosecution's case theory.[196]

Aiding, Abetting and Criminal Conspiracy

A person who abets the commission of an offence, and a person who attempts to commit, or engages in 'preparatory acts in furtherance of', any crime under the Misuse of Drugs Act is deemed to be guilty of that crime and may receive the punishment applicable to it.[197] An offender who abets the trafficking of a controlled drug can, therefore, be prosecuted and punished in the same way as a person who actually trafficked it.

In interpreting abetment under the Misuse of Drugs Act, the Court of Appeal in *Iwuchukwu Amara Tochi v Public Prosecutor*[198] adopted the Penal Code definition. That includes any person who: (a) instigates any person to do that thing; (b) engages with one or more person or persons in any conspiracy for the doing of that thing, if an act or illegal omission takes place in pursuance of that conspiracy, and in order to aid the doing of that thing; or (c) intentionally aids the doing of that thing by any act or illegal omission.[199] Under the Misuse of Drugs Act, the aiding and abetment offence extends to offences that take place outside of Singapore where a person 'aids, abets, counsels or procures' a crime committed and 'punishable' under a 'corresponding law' in another jurisdiction, or carries out a 'preparatory act' that would constitute a crime under the Misuse of Drugs Act had such an act taken place in Singapore.[200]

192 See *Cheng Siah Johnson v PP* [2002] 2 SLR 481; *PP v Tan Chui Yun Joselyn*.
193 [2003] 2 SLR 85.
194 *PP v Tan Chui Yun Joselyn* [2003] 2 SLR 85, 87.
195 *PP v Tan Chui Yun Joselyn* [2003] 2 SLR 85, 90.
196 See Glenn Seah Kim Ming (2003) 'Criminal Procedure, Evidence and Sentencing' *Singapore Academy of Law Annual Review* 192, 207.
197 MDA 2008 Rev Ed, s 12.
198 *Iwuchukwu Amara Tochi v PP* [2006] 2 SLR 503 [8].
199 See Penal Code 2008 Rev Ed, s 107.
200 MDA 2008 Rev Ed, s 13.

This is now also the position of the Penal Code,[201] and new section in the Code also provides for the converse—where a person outside Singapore abets the commission of an offence that takes place in Singapore.[202] The purpose of this amendment was to ensure a more 'holistic' approach to tackling transnational crime, particularly in a context where technological advances make it easier to abet criminal offences from a remote location.[203]

In 2012, the Misuse of Drugs Act was also amended to include a more specific offence targeting those who recruit drug couriers. This makes it a crime for any person above the age of 21 to cause a young or vulnerable person to engage in the trafficking, import or export of drugs.[204]

The Court of Appeal clarified the law of criminal conspiracy in 2012, in *Quek Hock Lye v Public Prosecutor*.[205] In this case, the two defendants (Quek and Winai) possessed different quantities of heroin (62.14 g and 14.99 g respectively). They were both charged with possession of the relevant amounts as well as criminal conspiracy to traffic the combined quantity of drugs. In the prosecution of Quek, the question arose as to whether the fact that each defendant held a different quantity of drugs was relevant to whether they could be found party to the same criminal conspiracy when they had also been charged separately in relation to different quantities. The Court found that the fact one defendant had a smaller quantity of a controlled drug did not affect the underlying question of whether there was an agreement between Quek and Winai to traffic a total of 62.14 g of heroin.[206] That they held different quantities did not change the nature of the agreement because both defendants knew the full quantity they collectively possessed. The Court did not expand on what might happen if one criminal conspirator had no knowledge of the precise quantity of drugs possessed and whether this is an integral element of an underlying agreement.

Attempt

Attempt is also punishable under the Misuse of Drugs Act and carries the same penalties that would apply in the event that the crime actually took place.[207] To be found guilty of attempt, the defendant must have had the intention to commit the primary offence and must have 'embarked on the crime proper'.[208]

201 Penal Code 2008 Rev Ed, s 108A

202 Penal Code 2008 Rev Ed, s 108B.

203 Ho Peng Kee, 'Second Reading Speech of the Penal Code (Amendment) Bill, by Senior Minister of State A/P Ho Peng Kee' (22 October 2007), 26–27.

204 MDA 2008 Rev Ed, s 12A.

205 [2012] 2 SLR 1012.

206 Ibid [37].

207 MDA 2008 Rev Ed, S 12.

208 See *PP v Mas Swan bin Adnan and another appeal* [2012] SGCA 29, [34], citing *Chua Kian Kok v PP* [1999] 1 SLR(R) 826 [36].

In the case of *Public Prosecutor v Mas Swan bin Adnan and another appeal*,[209] the question arose as to whether it is possible to establish attempt in a case where the factual circumstances were such that the commission of the crime was, in fact, impossible. On appeal, the prosecution sought to convict the defendant for attempting to import an unspecified quantity of ecstasy. Three bundles containing heroin were discovered in a car in his possession. The defendant admitted he knew the bundles contained a controlled drug but claimed that he thought it was ecstasy. The Court found that according to section 511 of the Penal Code, which establishes the general rule for attempt, impossible attempts are punishable under certain circumstances.[210] The Court held that a similar view should apply in relation to attempt under section 12 of the Misuse of Drugs Act.[211] The *actus reus* was satisfied, since Mas Swan had imported the bundles into Singapore and had done everything possible to complete the offence of importing ecstasy.[212] The only reason he could not complete the commission of the offence was that he was factually mistaken as to the nature of the controlled drugs in the three bundles—he thought they were ecstasy when they were actually diamorphine.[213]

Defences

Duress

The defence of duress is recognised in limited circumstances in Singaporean law under the Penal Code.[214] It does not apply to murder or other acts punishable by death and, therefore, does not apply in relation to drug offences that carry capital punishment. Duress can only be established where the act constituting the offence is committed by a person compelled to do so by threats that cause the apprehension 'that instant death to that person or any other person will otherwise be the consequence'.[215] This must be proved by the defendant on the balance of probabilities.[216]

It is generally difficult to make out the defence of duress and it does not apply to those who put themselves in a situation where they are likely to be subject to threats, for example by joining gangs. The example cited in the Penal Code is of a person seized by gang robbers and forced by threat of instant death to commit an offence (for example, a smith made to use his tools to force open a door for a gang of robbers to enter and rob). By contrast, a person who knowingly joins a gang of robbers of his own accord or due to a threat of being beaten is not entitled to rely on the defence of duress.

209 *PP v Mas Swan bin Adnan and another appeal* [2012] SGCA 29.
210 *PP v Mas Swan bin Adnan and another appeal* [2012] SGCA 29 [38].
211 *PP v Mas Swan bin Adnan and another appeal* [2012] SGCA 29 [41].
212 *PP v Mas Swan bin Adnan and another appeal* [2012] SGCA 29 [44].
213 *PP v Mas Swan bin Adnan and another appeal* [2012] SGCA 29 [44].
214 Penal Code 2008 Rev Ed, s 94.
215 Ibid.
216 See, eg, *Chu Tak Fai v PP* [1998] 4 MLJ 246.

Justice Chan Seng Onn, in *Public Prosecutor v Ng Pen Tine*,[217] set out five elements that must be established to demonstrate duress: (i) the harm with which the accused was threatened was death; (ii) the threat was directed at the accused or other persons, which would include any of his family members; (iii) the threat was of 'instant' death; (iv) the accused reasonably apprehended that the threat would be carried out; and (v) the accused had not, voluntarily or from a reasonable apprehension of harm to himself short of instant death, placed himself in that situation.[218] The threat must also be 'imminent, persistent and extreme'[219] although it is not necessary that the harm would be carried out immediately.[220] In *Ng Pen Tine*,[221] a Malaysian gangster made threats that he would kill the accused and his family members if the accused refused to drive from Malaysia to Singapore. The threat was uttered the day before the alleged crime. The accused claimed that he had attempted to stay away from the gangster by moving to Pahang but to no avail. The accused said that he was followed closely in motor vehicles. The prosecution argued that the accused was not under a threat of 'instant' death since he had reasonable opportunity to escape by running away or alerting a custom or immigration officer. Chan J found, however, that given threats were made against family members, the involvement of violent criminal organisations, and the limitations of police protection, alerting officials would not have ameliorated any threat to the lives of the accused and his family.[222] In this case, the defence of duress was, therefore, established because the coercer was believed to be a 'very influential and powerful' gangster whose gang members were 'very closely' observing the conduct of the accused, creating a reasonable apprehension of harm of the part of the defendant.[223]

By contrast, duress cannot be made out in situations where the facts are not such as to establish 'reasonable apprehension' that the threat would be carried out. In *Nagaenthran*, the defendant claimed that a man by the name of King had threatened to kill his girlfriend should he fail to deliver the package of drugs. On the facts of the case there was, however, no evidence of likely harm befalling to his girlfriend, or that the threat was acting significantly on the mind of the accused. There was no evidence that King was a powerful or influential gangster who had the capacity to keep watch over the accused or that the accused thought that King was the kind of person to deal in illicit activities.[224] Unlike the case of *Ng Pen Tine*, there was no evidence suggesting that the accused was being watched closely in such a way that the threat was so 'imminent, persistent and extreme'[225] that it would act on his mind so as to make him break the law.

[217] [2009] SGHC 230.

[218] *PP v Ng Pen Tine* [2009] SGHC 230 [*Ng Pen Tine*] [154].

[219] See, eg, *PP v Goh Hock Huat* [1994] 3 SLR(R) 375; *Wong Yoke Wah v PP* [1995] 3 SLR(R) 776; *Shaiful Edham bin Adam and another v PP* [1999] 1 SLR(R) 442; *Teo Hee Heng v PP* [2000] 2 SLR(R) 351.

[220] *Ng Pen Tine* at [155].

[221] [2009] SGHC 230.

[222] [2009] SGHC 230 [160].

[223] [2009] SGHC 230 [158], [160].

[224] [2011] 4 SLR 1156 [21]–[22].

[225] [2011] 4 SLR 1156 [28].

Entrapment Defence

The defence of *agent provocateur* or entrapment does not exist in Singapore.[226] The Penal Code defines 'abetment of doing a thing' to include circumstances where a person instigates any person to do that thing.[227] There is, however, no separate provision that covers 'entrapment'. Entrapment may go to mitigation of the sentence[228] and, in some cases, courts have exercised discretion to exclude the evidence of an agent provocateur, if that evidence would operate unfairly against the accused.[229] In *Law Society of Singapore v Tan Guat Neo Phyllis*,[230] the Court of Appeal held unequivocally, however, that the position in Singapore was that the courts have no discretion under the Evidence Act to exclude illegally obtained evidence and that a prosecution founded upon entrapment evidence was not an abuse of process.[231]

The issue of entrapment has become controversial in cases where the death penalty applies, such as *Rozman bin Jusoh*.[232] In this case, the accused (Rozman) was a 22-year-old Malaysian of subnormal intelligence. He was approached by an undercover CNB officer who asked if he had any cannabis. The accused replied that he did not, to which the officer responded by insisting that he find some cannabis for him. The following day, the officer approached Rozman again. Rozman then consulted with his friends and arranged to hand the drug to the officer than evening. Rozman was charged with trafficking more than one kilogram of cannabis, an offence that attracts the death penalty.

The Court received evidence that Rozman's cognitive reasoning was poor, he was vulnerable to being hurt or misused by others, and could not easily discern right from wrong. The High Court held that this did not constitute a defence, as poor intellect is not equivalent to 'unsoundness of mind'.[233] Given the role of the CNB operative and the intellectual disability of the accused, the trial judge nonetheless thought it 'unsafe for the court to proceed to convict him on the charge of trafficking' and instead sentenced him to seven years' imprisonment on the lesser charge of possession.[234]

The Court of Appeal disagreed with acquittal on the trafficking charge. It held that the finding of subnormal intellect and the intervention of the CNB were not sufficient to negate Rozman's intention to traffic drugs and could only be taken into account in mitigating the sentence.[235] It also found that the court may only take mitigating factors into account where sentencing discretion applies, and because

[226] *How Poh Sun v PP* [1991] SLR 220; *Mohamed Emran bin Mohamed Ali v PP* [2008] 4 SLR 411; [2008] SGHC 103.

[227] Penal Code 2008 Rev Ed, s 107.

[228] *Tan Boon Hock v PP* [1994] 2 SLR 150 [7], [9].

[229] *PP v Teo Ai Nee* (MA No 111/94/01-02).

[230] [2008] 2 SLR 239.

[231] [2008] 2 SLR 239 [124], [138].

[232] [1995] 3 SLR 317; See Sylvia Lim, 'Speech on Misuse of Drugs Amendment Bill—MP Sylvia Lim' (12 November 2012).

[233] *PP v Rozman bin Jusoh* [1994] SGHC 251.

[234] Ibid.

[235] The decision of the Court of Appeal is recorded in *PP v Rozman bin Jusoh* [1995] 2 SLR(R) 879.

trafficking cannabis in excess of one kilogram attracted a mandatory death sentence there was no room for mitigation.[236] Rozlan was executed on 12 April 1996.[237]

Penalties

As Rozlan's fate suggests, penalties for drug-related crimes in Singapore are heavy and the mandatory death penalty is applied to a wide range of offences. In fact, the mandatory death sentence has been characterised as the 'cornerstone' of the drug-control regime in Singapore.[238]

The main rationale presented for Singapore's very harsh penalties for drug trafficking is the concept of deterrence.[239] Singapore claims that the mandatory death penalty has had a tangible impact in reducing drug trafficking, although it is difficult to empirically access such claims.[240] The harsh approach also reflects the view within government that drugs represent a threat to the welfare of its general population as well as an issue of national security and economic survival.[241]

Punishments under the Misuse of Drugs Act are categorised by the type of controlled drug and quantity involved, and have been held to differ in 'kind rather than degree'[242] and it is often the case that 0.1 g may be determinative of life and death.[243] Stricter penalties apply for repeat offenders,[244] as well as those responsible for crimes targeting young or vulnerable persons.[245]

This penalty framework has been criticised for not having the flexibility required to ensure fairness and consistency in dealing with drug cases. As discussed below, an amendment was introduced in 2012 creating an exception to the mandatory imposition of the death penalty where specific conditions are satisfied.

236 *PP v Rozman bin Jusoh* [1995] 2 SLR(R) 879.

237 www.amnesty.org/fr/library/asset/ASA36/001/2004/fr/6de04440-d64e-11dd-ab95-a13b602c0642/asa360012004en.html.

238 See 'Second Reading of the Misuse of Drugs (Amendment) Bill', *Singapore Parliamentary Debates, Official Report* (20 November 1975) vol 34 at col 1379ff and 'Second Reading of the Misuse of Drugs (Amendment) Bill', *Singapore Parliamentary Debates, Official Report* (12 November 2012) vol 89.

239 Chan and Phang (n 63) 274.

240 See Rick Lines, *The Death Penalty for Drug Offences: A Violation of International Human Rights Law* (London, International Harm Reduction Association, 2007) 14.

241 See *Singapore Parliamentary Debates, Official Report* (20 November 1975) vol 34, cols 1379–81.

242 *Reyes v The Queen* [2002] UKPC 11 [34].

243 *PP v Ang Soon Huat* [1990] 2 SLR(R) 246.

244 MDA 2008 Rev Ed, ss 33(4)(a), 33A.

245 MDA 2008 Rev Ed, s 33(4)(b), (c).

Table 6: Summary of Penalties for Major Offences under Misuse of Drugs Act[246]

Article	Offence	Minimum Penalty	Maximum Penalty
5	Unauthorised traffic in Class A Drug	5 years and 5 strokes	20 years and 15 strokes
	Unauthorised traffic in Class B Drug	3 years and 3 strokes	20 years and 10 strokes
	Unauthorised traffic in Class C Drug	2 years and 2 strokes	10 years and 5 strokes
	Unauthorised traffic in 800–1200 g opium	20 years and 15 strokes	30 years or imprisonment for life and 15 strokes
	Unauthorised traffic in >1,200 opium	Death	
	Unauthorised traffic in controlled drug containing 10 g–15 g diamorphine	20 years and 15 strokes	30 years or imprisonment for life and 15 strokes
	Unauthorised traffic in controlled drug containing >15 g diamorphine	Death	
	Unauthorised traffic in controlled drug containing 20–30 g cocaine	20 years and 15 strokes	30 years or imprisonment for life and 15 strokes
	Unauthorised traffic in controlled drug containing >30 g cocaine	Death	
	Unauthorised traffic in controlled drug containing 167–250 methamphetamine	20 years and 15 strokes	30 years or imprisonment for life and 15 strokes
	Unauthorised traffic in controlled drug containing >250 g methamphetamine	Death	
	Unauthorised traffic in 330–500 g cannabis	20 years and 15 strokes	30 years or imprisonment for life and 15 strokes
	Unauthorised traffic in >500 g cannabis	Death	
	Unauthorised traffic in controlled drug containing 20–30 g cocaine	20 years and 15 strokes	30 years or imprisonment for life and 15 strokes
6	Unauthorised manufacture in Class A Drug	10 years and 5 strokes	30 years or imprisonment for life and 15 strokes
	Unauthorised manufacture in Class B Drug	10 years and 5 strokes	30 years or imprisonment for life and 15 strokes

(*continued*)

246 This list is a summary of major offences and does not include all offences listed in the Second Schedule of the Misuse of Drugs Act. The general penalty provisions for Class A, B or C drugs apply unless a more specific provision applies in relation to a specific drug and its quantity.

Table 6: *(Continued)*

Article	Offence	Minimum Penalty	Maximum Penalty
6	Unauthorised manufacture in Class C Drug	5 years and 2 strokes	20 years and 15 strokes
	Unauthorised manufacture of diamorphine or any salt of diamorphine	Death	
	Unauthorised manufacture of cocaine or any salt of cocaine	Death	
	Unauthorised manufacture of methamphetamine or any salt of methamphetamine	Death	
7	Unauthorised import or export of Class A Drug	5 years and 5 strokes	30 years and 15 strokes
	Unauthorised import or export of Class B Drug	5 years and 5 strokes	30 years and 15 strokes
	Unauthorised import or export of Class C Drug	3 years and 5 strokes	20 years and 15 strokes
	Unauthorised traffic in 800–1200 g opium	20 years and 15 strokes	30 years or imprisonment for life and 15 strokes
	Unauthorised traffic in >1,200 opium	Death	
	Unauthorised traffic in controlled drug containing 10 g–15 g diamorphine	20 years and 15 strokes	30 years or imprisonment for life and 15 strokes
	Unauthorised traffic in controlled drug containing >15 g diamorphine	Death	
	Unauthorised traffic in controlled drug containing 20–30 g cocaine	20 years and 15 strokes	30 years or imprisonment for life and 15 strokes
	Unauthorised traffic in controlled drug containing >30 g cocaine	Death	
	Unauthorised traffic in controlled drug containing 167–250 methamphetamine	20 years and 15 strokes	30 years or imprisonment for life and 15 strokes
	Unauthorised traffic in controlled drug containing >250 g methamphetamine	Death	
	Unauthorised traffic in 330–500 g cannabis	20 years and 15 strokes	30 years or imprisonment for life and 15 strokes
	Unauthorised traffic in >500 g cannabis	Death	
	Unauthorised traffic in controlled drug containing 20–30 g cocaine	20 years and 15 strokes	30 years or imprisonment for life and 15 strokes

(*continued*)

Table 6: ***(Continued)***

Article	Offence	Minimum Penalty	Maximum Penalty
8(a)	Unauthorised possession of a controlled drug	2 years for a second or subsequent offence	10 years or S$ 20,000 or both
10(a)	Manufacture, supply, possession, import or export of equipment, materials or substances useful for manufacture of controlled drugs		20 years or S$ 200,000 or both
11	Being the owner, tenant, occupier or person concerned in the management of premises and permitting or suffering certain activities to take place there: Class A Drug	2 years or S$ 4,000 or both	10 years or S$ 40,000 or both
	Being the owner, tenant, occupier or person concerned in the management of premises and permitting or suffering certain activities to take place there: Class B Drug	2 years or S$ 4,000 or both	10 years or S$ 40,000 or both
	Being the owner, tenant, occupier or person concerned in the management of premises and permitting or suffering certain activities to take place there: Class C Drug	12 months or S$ 2,000 or both	5 years or S$ 10,000 or both
12A	Causing or procuring a young person or vulnerable person to commit certain offences: Class A Drug	30 years and 15 strokes	10 years and 10 strokes
	Causing or procuring a young person or vulnerable person to commit certain offences: Class B Drug	30 years and 15 strokes	6 years and 6 strokes
	Causing or procuring a young person or vulnerable person to commit certain offences: Class C Drug	20 years and 15 strokes	4 years and 4 strokes
13	Abetting or procuring the commission outside Singapore of an offence punishable under a corresponding law	3 years or S$ 5,000 or both	10 years or S$ 40,000 or both

Table 7: Corruption, Drug Trafficking and Other Serious Crimes (Confiscation of Benefits) Act 2000 Rev Ed

Section	Offence	Minimum Penalty	Maximum Penalty
43	Assisting in the retention of benefits from drug-related offences—Individuals		S$ 500,000 or imprisonment for a term not exceeding 10 years or both
	Assisting in the retention of benefits from drug-related offences—Body Corporates		A fine not exceeding S$ 1 million
46	Acquiring, possessing, using, concealing or transferring benefits of drug dealing		S$ 500,000 or imprisonment for a term not exceeding 10 years or both
	Acquiring, possessing, using, concealing or transferring benefits of drug dealing—Body Corporates		A fine not exceeding S$ 1 million

III. JURISDICTION

This section provides an overview of the court hierarchy, Singapore's jurisdiction in relation to both domestic and extra-territorial drug crimes, and its framework for extradition.

Courts

The Supreme Court is Singapore's highest court and consists of two tiers: an upper Appeal Court and a lower-tier High Court.[247] Judges are appointed by the President of the Supreme Court from candidates recommended by the Prime Minister. The subordinate courts include District Courts, Magistrates' Courts and a range of specialist courts. The High Court has original jurisdiction over criminal matters including murder and drug trafficking. Its jurisdiction for criminal trials is divided into 'capital and non-capital cases', including crimes attracting over 10 years' imprisonment.[248] This means that criminal trials involving drug offences attracting the death penalty and those that carry a penalty of over 10 years' imprisonment are heard in the High Court as the court of first instance. The Court of Appeal is the court of last resort for the accused.

247 http://app.supremecourt.gov.sg/default.aspx?pgID=43.

248 Supreme Court of Judicature Act (Singapore, Cap 322, 2007 Rev Ed). Original enactment was in 1969. For details see www.supremecourt.gov.sg/rules/court-processes/criminal-proceedings/types-of-criminal-proceedings/criminal-trials.

The subordinate courts of Singapore comprise: (i) District Courts; (ii) Magistrates' Courts; (iii) Commercial Criminal Courts and Special Trial Courts; and (iv) Criminal Mentions Courts. Both District Courts and Magistrates' Courts have civil and criminal jurisdiction but the former has broader powers in both areas. The criminal jurisdiction of the District Courts is, in principle, limited to cases punishable by up to seven years' imprisonment, a fine of up to S$ 10,000, and up to 12 cane lashes. Generally, Magistrates' Courts are only empowered to exercise criminal jurisdiction over offences carrying up to two years' imprisonment, a fine of up to S$ 2,000 and up to six cane lashes. District and Magistrates' Courts have, however, been granted prescribed jurisdiction by certain statutes (including the Misuse of Drugs Act) to hear criminal cases involving offences punishable with higher sentences. In fact, District and Magistrates Courts can now try all drug offences and impose all penalties under the Misuse of Drugs Act other than capital punishment.[249]

Foreigners and Extraterritorial Jurisdiction

In the absence of express statutory authority, the courts have affirmed a presumption at common law against the extraterritorial application of Singapore's laws beyond its geographic borders.[250] The Misuse of Drugs Act contains, however, a number of express offences that significantly extend Singapore's extraterritorial jurisdiction in relation to drug offences. As mentioned above, these provisions cover not only Singaporeans and permanent residents who allegedly commit these crimes outside Singapore[251] but also non-Singaporeans who participate in such activities by aiding, abetting, counselling or procuring the commission of any drug offence within Singapore.[252] This could include members of organised criminal syndicates based abroad.

These extra-territorial offences were introduced in the late 1990s, as the government became increasingly concerned about legal 'loopholes' in the regulation of transnational aspects of drug offences taking place in Singapore or implicating Singaporeans abroad.[253] Singapore does not publish statistics on the number of foreigners prosecuted under the Misuse of Drugs Act or the number of extra-territorial offences pursued, so it is difficult to ascertain how actively Singapore enforces its extra-territorial authority in relation to drugs.

Extradition for Drug Offences

The extradition of fugitives to and from foreign countries is principally regulated by the Extradition Act (Singapore, Cap 103, 2000 Rev Ed).[254] For extradition to take

249 MDA 2008 Rev Ed, s 53.
250 See, eg, *PP v Taw Cheng Kong* [1998] 2 SLR 410; [1998] SGCA 37.
251 MDA 2008 Rev Ed, s 8A.
252 MDA 2008 Rev Ed, s 13(aa).
253 CL Lim, 'Singapore Crimes Abroad' (2001) *Singapore Journal of Legal Studies* 494, 495.
254 Extradition Act (Singapore, Cap 103, 2000 Rev Ed). First enacted in 1968.

place there must be an extradition treaty or arrangement between Singapore and the requesting state. At present, Singapore has extradition relations with 39 Commonwealth countries under the Extradition Declaration, including Australia, Canada, New Zealand and the United Kingdom.[255] It also has an extradition treaty with Hong Kong and China, as well as the United States. Singapore does not, however, have an extradition treaty with a number of other ASEAN (Association of South East Asian Nations) states. It signed an extradition treaty with Indonesia in 2007 but it has still not been ratified by that country's national legislature, which wishes to renegotiate it. Singapore refuses, so the treaty is currently ineffective.[256]

Depending on whether the request is made by a foreign state with which Singapore has an extradition treaty, a member of the Commonwealth or by Malaysia, the Extradition Act provides for three different types of extradition, and a number of general principles also apply. Extradition is only possible where the offence for which the extradition is requested is classified as an 'extradition crime' and where the requirement of 'dual criminality' is satisfied (that is, the offence is a crime in both countries).[257] The first schedule to the Extradition Act lists various types of offences that constitute 'extradition crimes' including offences 'against the law relating to psychotropic substances, dangerous drugs or narcotics'[258] and offences 'against the law relating to benefits derived from corruption, drug trafficking and other serious crimes'.[259]

Determinations regarding the legality of any apprehension and extradition requests are left to the judicial arm of government. Specifically, a Singaporean magistrate must decide whether there is sufficient evidence to justify the apprehension of the suspect according to the standards that would apply if the act or omission constituting the crime was conducted within Singapore's jurisdiction.[260] Once the suspect is apprehended, the magistrate must then determine whether the evidence presented is such that it would justify the trial of the fugitive if the act or omission constituting an offence had taken place within Singapore's jurisdiction.[261] If the magistrate considers the evidence sufficient to justify a trial, the suspect will be imprisoned pending ministerial approval of his or her surrender. The suspect has a period of 15 days from the date of committal to appeal the decision to the High Court by applying for a writ of *habeus corpus*,[262] failing which the Minister decides whether to issue a surrender order.

[255] Extradition (Commonwealth Countries) (Consolidation) Declaration (2009 Rev Ed), Extradition Act (Cap 103, 2000 Rev Ed), s 19.

[256] See Hasyim Widhiarto, 'Singapore Refuses to Renegotiate Extradition Treaty with Indonesia' *The Jakarta Post* (29 September 2011), www.thejakartapost.com/news/2011/09/29/s%E2%80%99pore-refuses-renegotiate-extradition-treaty-with-ri.html.

[257] Extradition Act 2000 Rev Ed, s 2(1). See also *Wong Yuh Lan v PP and other matters* [2012] SGHC 161.

[258] Extradition Act 2000 Rev Ed, sch 1 s 25.

[259] Extradition Act 2000 Rev Ed, sch 1 s 26.

[260] Extradition Act 2000 Rev Ed, s 10(1).

[261] Extradition Act 2000 Rev Ed, s 11(7).

[262] Extradition Act 2000 Rev Ed, s 12(1).

The Minister's power to issue an order for surrender is subject to a number of restrictions. Surrender is not allowed where the Minister has substantial grounds to believe that the real reasons for requesting extradition are for the purpose of prosecuting or punishing the suspect on account of his or her race, religion, nationality or political opinions.[263] Surrender to a foreign state is similarly restricted where it would result in a prejudicial trial or punishment by reason of race, religion, nationality or political opinions,[264] and a fugitive may not be extradited where the offence is of a 'political character'.[265]

A fugitive must not be extradited for the purpose of surrender to another country or for an offence (or acts/commissions constituting the offence) for which the suspect has previously been tried. The Minister must also refuse surrender where the requisition is in respect of a person held in custody or on bail in Singapore for an offence alleged to have taken place in Singapore, or who is serving a sentence for a conviction in Singapore.[266] Thus, while there have been some attempts by lawyers to use extradition as a strategy to assist foreign drug offenders avoid the death sentence in Singapore,[267] such an approach is very unlikely to succeed.

The Extradition Act sets out numerous detailed procedural and evidentiary requirements regarding the relevant process for requesting states. These rules differ depending on the specific category of extradition request and the content of the relevant extradition treaty. In general, requesting states are advised to make contact with the Attorney-General's Chambers (AGC) or Interpol Singapore at the earliest stage possible to inform relevant agencies of their intention to request provisional arrest or extradition. They are also advised to liaise with Singaporean authorities as quickly as possible.[268] The central authority for dealing with extradition requests in Singapore is, as this suggests, the AGC. There are no consolidated statistics available for extradition requests and surrenders lodged with, or made by Singapore. Foreign government data shows, however, that, in recent years, Singapore has granted extradition requests to countries including Australia,[269] the United States[270] and the United Kingdom.[271]

[263] Extradition Act 2000 Rev Ed, ss 8(a), 21(1).

[264] Extradition Act 2000 Rev Ed, s 8(b).

[265] Extradition Act 2000 Rev Ed, ss 7(1), 21(1).

[266] Extradition Act 2000 Rev Ed, ss 7(3), 21(2).

[267] See, eg, AAP (Australian Associated Press), 'Nguyen "Loophole" Rejected' *The Age* (23 November 2005) www.smh.com.au/articles/2005/11/23/1132421693497.html?from=rss.

[268] Nor'ashikin Samdin, 'International Co-operation: The Extradition Framework in Singapore—A General Overview', paper delivered at the Sixth Regional Seminar on Good Governance for Southeast Asian Countries: International Co-operation Mutual Legal Assistance And Extradition, Tokyo, 12–14 December 2012 (Tokyo, UNAFEI—United Nations Asia and Far East Institute for the Prevention of Crime and the Treatment of Offenders, 2013), www.unafei.or.jp/english/pdf/PDF_GG6_Seminar/04-3_SP3.pdf.

[269] Singapore. Attorney-General's Department, 'Annual Report 2010–2011: Appendix 11—Extradition and Mutual Assistance', www.ag.gov.au/Publications/AnnualReports/Annualreport201011/Pages/Appendixes/Appendix11Extraditionandmutualassistance.aspx.

[270] US Attorney's Office, Two Extradited from Singapore in Connection with Plot to Illegally Export Military Antennas' 21 December 2012, www.fbi.gov/washingtondc/press-releases/2012/two-extradited-from-singapore-in-connection-with-plot-to-illegally-export-military-antennas.

[271] UK Home Office, 'Extradition Requests Received and Made by the UK from January to December 2013' (24 October 2014), www.gov.uk/government/publications/extradition-requests-

IV. CRIMINAL PROCEDURE

Traditionally, criminal procedure in Singapore has had a strong focus on prosecutorial powers. In recent years, however, there has been increasing attention paid to international norms relating to procedural fairness and defendants' rights, and even some movement towards reform in these areas.[272] A revised Criminal Procedure Code was introduced in 2010 with the aim of striking a balance between the interests of society at large in tackling criminal activity and the interests of the individual criminal defendant in avoiding wrongful conviction.[273] It was re-enacted in 2012. Its underlying principles are stated to be the presumption of innocence, procedural fairness, and an emphasis on providing a system for 'arriving at the truth'.[274] Whether Singapore's current criminal procedure has satisfied these aims remains controversial. Singapore's Minister for Law, K Shanmugam, was candid about this in his second reading speech of the Criminal Procedure Code, where he stated that:

> I will admit freely that there can be reasonable debate as to whether that balance has been rightly struck ... The procedure to be adopted for administration of criminal justice is an area where there are diverse and often contentious viewpoints. This is an evolutionary process and we will have to continue to be open to amending our criminal procedures to meet changing norms.[275]

The following sections provide an overview of the main aspects of criminal procedure law relevant to the investigation and prosecution of drug offences in Singapore as it now stands.

Investigation

Most drug-related investigations in Singapore are conducted by the investigation division of the Central Narcotics Bureau (CNB) with significant support from the Singapore Police Force and the Immigration and Checkpoints Authority. In relation to cases involving the commission of any offence under the Misuse of Drugs Act, CNB officers have all powers available to police officers under the Criminal Procedure Code that pertain to investigations into both seizable and non-seizable offences.[276] Under the Criminal Procedure Code, 'seizable offences' are now referred to as 'arrestable offences', which are defined as an offence for which a police officer

received-and-made-by-the-uk-in-2013/extradition-requests-received-and-made-by-the-uk-from-january-to-december-2013.

[272] Michael Hor, 'The Future of Singapore's Criminal Process' (2013) 25 *Singapore Academy of Law Journal* 847.

[273] K Shanmugam, 'Second Reading Speech by Law Minister K Shanmugam on the Criminal Procedure Code Bill' (18 May 2010), www.mlaw.gov.sg/news/parliamentary-speeches-and-responses/second-reading-speech-by-law-minister-k-shanmugam-on-the-criminal-procedure-code-bill.html.

[274] Shanmugam, 'Second Reading Speech' (18 May 2010) 4–8.

[275] Shanmugam (n 273) 11.

[276] MDA 2008 Rev Ed, s 32(1).

may ordinarily arrest without warrant in accordance with the First Schedule of the Criminal Procedure Code or any other written law.[277] A 'non-seizable offence' is equivalent to a 'non-arrestable offence'.[278]

Under the Misuse of Drugs Act, officers of the CNB or authorised police officers may at any time, and without warrant, enter and search any premises reasonably suspected of containing any controlled drug, temporarily listed drug, or a person reasonably suspected of committing a drug offence.[279] They may also search any person found on such a premises.[280] Officers are likewise authorised to stop, board and search any ship, hovercraft, aircraft, vehicle or train, if an authorised officer has reason to believe that a controlled drug/substance or seizable item is inside the relevant carrier.[281] This power extends to searching any person in such a vehicle or any person arriving in or departing from Singapore.[282] Authorised officers may confiscate any controlled drug or temporarily listed drug seized as a result of a search, as well as any carrier used in the commission of a drug offence.[283] The Internal Security Act 1985 Rev Ed contains similar provisions for search without warrant of any premises reasonably suspected to contain articles liable for seizure.[284]

Obstruction of inspections and failure to comply with lawful requests from officers in the course of investigations are offences under the Misuse of Drugs Act.[285] This creates criminal liability for individuals who resist being searched, fail to give information or volunteer wrong or misleading information that the person knows, or has reason to believe, is not true.[286] Hindering investigations and failing to comply with lawful requirements or provide information may attract penalties of between three to six years' imprisonment and/or a fine of between S$ 1,000 and S$ 5,000.[287] Furnishing false information carries a maximum penalty of 12 months' imprisonment and/or a fine of S$ 5,000.[288]

An authorised officer who confiscates the controlled drug, substance or seizable item is obliged to give written notice to the owner unless the seizure is witnessed by the accused, the owner, or her or his agent.[289] If no prosecution takes place, the relevant drug or item will be treated as forfeited one month from the date it was confiscated, unless a claim is made within that period. The Misuse of Drugs Act provides for the disposal and/or handling of the controlled drug, substance or item at the relevant Minister's discretion, including dealing with any claims after forfeiture.[290] In 2014, the CNB conducted 46 major operations and 1,526 general

277 CPC 2012 Rev Ed, ss 2, 429(19).
278 CPC 2010, s 429(19).
279 MDA 2008 Rev Ed, s 24(1)(a).
280 MDA 2008 Rev Ed, s 24(1)(b).
281 MDA 2008 Rev Ed, s 26(1).
282 MDA 2008 Rev Ed, s 26(1).
283 MDA 2008 Rev Ed, s 26(2).
284 Internal Security Act 1985 Rev Ed, s 8.
285 MDA 2008 Rev Ed, s 30.
286 MDA 2008 Rev Ed, s 30(1).
287 MDA 2008 Rev Ed, sch 2.
288 Ibid.
289 MDA 2008 Rev Ed, s 27.
290 MDA 2008 Rev Ed, s 29.

operations at checkpoints with the Singapore Police Force and the Immigration and Checkpoints Authority.[291] The estimated value of the total quantity of drugs seized in 2013 was approximately S$ 20.5 million.[292] A significant quantity of seizures account for drugs not intended for the domestic market. So, for example, of all crystal methamphetamine confiscated in 2013, approximately 80 per cent was found to be in transit.[293]

To investigate cases of suspected drug consumption, Singapore enforces an extensive regime of both urine and hair tests. The Misuse of Drugs Act authorises a CNB official, immigration official or a police officer holding at least the rank of a sergeant to order an individual she or he reasonably suspects of consuming a controlled or specified drug to submit a urine sample for testing.[294] Failure to do so without reasonable excuse is a crime.[295] Pursuant to the Misuse of Drugs Act, Singaporeans who test positive are admitted to a Drug Rehabilitation Centre for compulsory treatment and rehabilitation (discussed further below). An individual who is not a Singaporean citizen or a permanent resident and fails, without reasonable excuse, to submit a urine sample to an immigration official for testing, or tests positive for consuming a controlled drug, may be banned from entering Singapore or deported.[296]

In addition to targeted and random drug testing conducted by the state, a number of international schools in Singapore also conduct mandatory hair and urine sample drug tests for their students, although the tests are conducted offshore and operate separately to the programs run by the CNB.[297] Media reports suggest that schools deal with students found to have consumed drugs through 'in-house' sanctions such as suspension, rather than involving the police.[298]

The Misuse of Drugs Act was amended in 2012 to give powers to law enforcement officers to undertake hair analysis as well as urine testing.[299] Whereas urine samples are generally only indicative of drugs for a few days following consumption, hair analysis can detect drug intake several months after consumption.[300] The power to conduct hair analysis applies where an officer of the CNB, police or immigration officer reasonably suspects that a person may have consumed a controlled

[291] Central Narcotics Bureau, 'Annual Bulletin 2013' 13.

[292] Ibid.

[293] Ibid.

[294] MDA 2008 Rev Ed, s 31(1).

[295] MDA 2008 Rev Ed, s 31(2).

[296] MDA 2008 Rev Ed, s 31(3).

[297] Zul Othman, 'Hair Analysis Used by CNB, Schools to Fight Drug Abuse' *AsiaOne* (13 November 2013), http://education.asiaone.com/content/hair-analysis-used-cnb-schools-fight-drug-abuse/page/0/3#sthash.OII8e3da.dpuf.

[298] *Asia Sentinel*, 'Singapore's Leaky Drugs Enforcement' (26 September 2011), www.asiasentinel.com/society/singapores-leaky-drugs-enforcement/.

[299] MDA 2008 Rev Ed, s 31A. See also Masagos Zulkifli, 'Second Reading Speech of the Senior Minister of State for Home Affairs, Mr Masagos Zulkifli BMM' (14 November 2012).

[300] See, R Wenning, 'Potential Problems with the Interpretation of Hair Analysis Results' (2000) 107 *Forensic Science International* 5, 8; Fritz Pragst and Marie A Balikova, 'State of the Art in Hair Analysis for Detection of Drug and Alcohol Abuse' (2006) 370(1–2) *Clinica Chimica Acta* 17, 18; and Robert L DuPont, Werner A Baumgartner, 'Drug Testing by Urine and Hair Analysis: Complementary Features and Scientific Issues' (1995) 70 *Forensic Science International* 63, 64 and 66.

drug.[301] Failure to provide a specimen without reasonable excuse also constitutes an offence[302] and attracts a penalty of up to two years imprisonment and/or a S$ 5000 fine.[303] Once a sample is taken, it is tested by an approved analyst.[304] Where a test is positive, the director may make a supervision order for up to two years.[305] Similar provisions in the Internal Security Act 1985 Rev Ed authorise mandatory blood testing of individuals who have inhaled, or are suspected to have inhaled, an intoxicating substance, if an authorised officer so requests.[306]

Arrest and Interrogation

Singaporean law prohibits arbitrary arrest and detention. The Singaporean Constitution states that no person shall be deprived of his life or personal liberty save in accordance with law.[307] The Criminal Procedure Code, however, sets out a number of circumstances under which a police officer may carry out an arrest without warrant,[308] and confirms the authority to arrest without warrant where conferred by other more specific laws.[309] The Misuse of Drugs Act and the Criminal Law (Temporary Provisions) Act (CLTPA) are two of four specific laws that include provisions for arrest without warrant.[310]

The Misuse of Drugs Act provides that an individual may be arrested and searched without warrant if he or she is 'reasonably suspected' of having committed a drug offence under the Act or a seizable offence under the regulations.[311] Any controlled drug or seizable item found on a person may be confiscated.[312] The suspect can be brought to the CNB police or customs office.[313] Authorised law enforcement officers empowered to do so include Bureau officers, police officers, customs officers, and specifically authorised Vigilante Corps members.[314] A person arrested under the Misuse of Drugs Act, together with the relevant controlled drug or seizeable item, is taken to the CNB or police or customs office to be searched.[315] Only female officers may search female suspects.[316] In 2013, the Bureau arrested 3,581 drug abusers, a slight increase from 3,507 arrests in 2012.[317]

301 MDA 2008 Rev Ed, s 31A(1).
302 MDA 2008 Rev Ed, s 31A(2).
303 MDA 2008 Rev Ed, sch 2.
304 MDA 2008 Rev Ed, s 31A(3)–(4).
305 MDA 2008 Rev Ed, s 34(2A).
306 Internal Security Act 1985 Rev Ed, s 13.
307 Constitution of the Republic of Singapore (1999 reprint) Art 9(1).
308 CPC 2010 s 64 (1).
309 CPC 2010 s 64(2).
310 Singapore, Bureau of Democracy, Human Rights, and Labor, 'Singapore 2013 Human Rights Report'.
311 MDA 2008 Rev Ed, s 25(1).
312 MDA 2008 Rev Ed, s 25(4).
313 MDA 2008 Rev Ed, s 25(2).
314 MDA 2008 Rev Ed, s 25(1).
315 MDA 2008 Rev Ed, s 25(2).
316 MDA 2008 Rev Ed, s 25(3).
317 Central Narcotics Bureau, 'Drug Situation Report 2013' www.cnb.gov.sg/drugsituationreport/drugsituationreport2013.aspx.

The Intoxicating Substances Act (Singapore, Cap 146A, 2001 Rev Ed) similarly authorises arrest without warrant of any person who has committed, or whom an officer reasonably suspects to have committed, an offence under the Internal Security Act 1985 Rev Ed.[318] In addition to this statute and the Misuse of Drugs Act, arrest powers under the Criminal Law (Temporary Provisions) Act are frequently deployed against suspected drug traffickers.[319] Under this Act, a police officer may arrest and detain any person without warrant where he or she has reason to believe there are grounds that justify the person's detention on the basis of public safety, peace and good order.[320] Whether the court has any ability to review the grounds of arrest and detention under this statute remains an area of legal uncertainty. The High Court in *Re Ong Yew Teck*, held that the exercise of arrest powers under s 44(1) of the CLTPA could only be reviewed on the basis of a subjective test, that is, whether the police officer actually believed there were grounds to justify arrest. By contrast, in *Kamal Jit Singh v Minister for Home Affairs* which looked at preventative detention powers under of the CLTPA, the Court of Appeal reviewed the grounds for detention on an objective basis. It was subsequently held by the High Court in *Re Wong Sin Yee* [2007] SGHC 147 that the judicial process is unsuitable for reaching decisions on questions of public safety, peace and good order.[321]

Custody (Temporary Detention)

The Criminal Procedure Code provides that a person who has been arrested without warrant cannot be detained for more than 48 hours and must be produced before a magistrate.[322] When a person has been arrested with a warrant issued for arrest, he or she must be produced in court 'without unnecessary delay', subject to applicable surety requirements.[323] Further protections against arbitrary arrest and detention are found in the Constitution, which requires that an arrested person will 'without unreasonable delay' and, in any event, within 48 hours, appear before a magistrate 'in person' or via 'videoconferencing' and cannot be imprisoned further without the magistrate's approval.[324]

Under the Criminal Law (Temporary Provisions) Act (CLTPA), however, a police officer is permitted to detain a person pending enquiries where he or she has

[318] Internal Security Act 1985 Rev Ed s 7.

[319] S Iswaran, 'Second Reading of the Criminal Law (Temporary Provisions) (Amendment) Bill: Speech by Mr S Iswaran, Minister in Prime Minister's Office and Second Minister for Home Affairs and Trade & Industry' (11 November 2013), www.mha.gov.sg/news_details.aspx?nid=MzAyNQ%3D%3D-GoI2I5kqrAg%3D, 14; Singapore. Bureau of Democracy, Human Rights, and Labor (n 81), 4.

[320] Criminal Law (Temporary Provisions) Act (Cap 67, 2000 Rev Ed), particularly s 30.

[321] *Re Ong Yew Teck* [1960] 1 *Malayan Law Journal* 67; *Kamal Jit Singh v Minister for Home Affairs* [1993] 1 SLR 24; *Re Wong Sin Yee* [2007] SGHC 147.

[322] CPC 2012 Rev Ed, ss 67, 68.

[323] CPC 2012 Rev Ed, s 74.

[324] Constitution of the Republic of Singapore (1999 reprint) Art 9(4).

reason to believe there are grounds to justify the detention of such a person by the Minister in the interests of 'public safety, peace and good order'.[325] This extremely broad authority extends also to officers of the CNB.[326] Singapore uses the CLTPA almost exclusively for narcotics or organised crime cases. Detention may not exceed 24 hours unless there is explicit authorisation from a police officer of, or above, the rank of assistant superintendent. The maximum period of detention under the Act is 48 hours.[327] In 2014, there were 707 people held in remand on drug-related charges.[328]

Notwithstanding the general prohibition on detention in excess of 48 hours, the Minister of Home Affairs may order preventative detention with agreement from the Public Prosecutor for an initial period of up to one year.[329] Preventative detention without trial must be justified on the grounds of public security, safety or the maintenance of public order. Detention orders may be extended for a maximum period of 12 months at any time but there is no limitation on the number of extensions.[330] Preventative detention is not restricted to offenders with a history of violent behaviour and has been used in relation to drug offences.[331] In 2013, there was one detainee who had been held for almost 11 years under the CLPTA for involvement in drug trafficking activities but the Singaporean government maintains that most inmates are detained for less than four years.[332]

As discussed further below, the Misuse of Drugs Act also allows for detention without trial in approved institutions for the purposes of rehabilitation and treatment of drug addicts.[333] Pursuant to the Intoxicating Substances Act (Singapore, Cap 146A, 2001 Rev Ed), the CNB may also order treatment of a person believed to be an inhalant drug addict for a period up to six months.[334] These powers are certainly used. In 2012, as many as 1,384 people were committed to rehabilitation centres pursuant to the Misuse of Drugs Act and the Internal Security Act[335]

Interrogation and the Right to Silence

The law in Singapore grants 'comprehensive and potent powers of interrogation'[336] to police officers in the course of investigations. Despite numerous calls for

[325] CLPTA (Singapore, Cap 67, 2000 Rev Ed) s 44(1) and s 30.
[326] CLPTA 2000 Rev Ed, s 47.
[327] CLPTA 2000 Rev Ed, s 44(2)–(3).
[328] Singapore Prison Service, 'Strong Community Efforts Essential in Preventing Re-offending', News Release (23 January 2015), www.sps.gov.sg/sites/default/files/Press%20Release_PRIS%20Annual%20Statistics%20Release%202014_SG%20PRESS%20CENTRE_0.pdf, 5.
[329] CLPTA 2000 Rev Ed, s 30(a).
[330] CLPTA 2000 Rev Ed, s 38(1).
[331] See *Jeyapalan s/o Bhanoo v PP* [2002] SGDC 136.
[332] Second Reading of the Criminal Law (Temporary Provisions) (Amendment) Bill: Response Speech by Mr S Iswaran, Minister in Prime Minister's Office and Second Minister for Home Affairs and Trade & Industry, 11 November 2013 [19–20].
[333] MDA 2008 Rev Ed, (Singapore, Cap 185, 2008 Rev Ed) s 34(2)(b).
[334] Intoxicating Substances Act (Singapore, Cap 146A, 2001 Rev Ed) s 17(1)–(3).
[335] Singapore, Bureau of Democracy, Human Rights, and Labor (n 335) 6.
[336] See *Muhammad bin Kadar v PP* [2011] 3 SIR 1205 [57]–[60].

legislative reform to require the video-recording of pre-trial interrogations,[337] no such requirement currently applies. This makes the right to silence a crucial issue in Singaporean criminal procedure, since the right encompasses the right of a person being questioned by police not to answer incriminating questions.

There is no constitutional protection of the right to silence in Singapore[338] nor is there a positive obligation on the police to inform suspects or accused persons that they may decline to respond to a question that might incriminate them.[339] Generally, the court will not allow adverse inferences in instances where a defendant chooses to exercise the right to silence but this protection is far indeed from absolute. For example, a judge may draw an adverse inference where a defendant fails to mention a fact in his or her defence at the time of police questioning.[340] In the drug trafficking case of *Kwek Seow Hock*,[341] the Court of Appeal held that an adverse inference could be drawn from the failure of the accused to mention that he intended to keep half the quantity of diamorphine in question for his personal consumption.[342] The Court held that while the right to silence precluded adverse inferences, the same did not apply to where a person subject to investigation withheld information that might support their case.[343]

The Criminal Procedure Code (CPC) also expressly stipulates a power to draw adverse inferences where the accused fails to mention a matter relevant to his defence 'on being charged with an offence, or informed by a police officer ... that he may be prosecuted for an offence'.[344] The CPC provides that the Court may, draw such inferences as 'appear proper' from the accused person's failure to reveal any fact which she or he could 'reasonably have been expected to mention', and later uses it in his or her defence.[345] For this reason, criminal defendants are usually advised that if they choose to remain silent they risk certain information or facts that 'should have been revealed' being disbelieved at a later stage.[346] The statutory basis for drawing adverse inferences from a defendant's silence is not unlimited. It is strictly confined to the situation where the police have set out the charge in writing, read it to the accused, and cautioned the accused prior to making a statement that the court may be less likely to believe him if he or she withholds any information in his defence and reveals it only at the trial.[347] It is nonetheless a significant qualification of the right to silence.

[337] See, eg, Chin Tet Yung, 'Confessions and Statements by Accused Persons Revisited' (2012) 24 *Singapore Academy of Law Journal* 60.

[338] See *PP v Mazlan bin Maidun & Another* 1 SLR 512.

[339] In *Lim Thian Lai v PP* [2006] 1 SLR 319; [2005] SGCA 50 [17].

[340] See *Kwek Seow Hock v PP* [2011] 3 SLR 157.

[341] [2011] 3 SLR 157.

[342] *Kwek Seow Hock v PP* [2011] 3 SLR 157 [5].

[343] Ibid [18–19].

[344] CPC 2012 Rev Ed, s 261(1).

[345] CPC 2012 Rev Ed, s 261(1).

[346] Lyn Tok and Hugh Turnbull, 'Know the Law NOW! 2015' (Singapore, Law Society of Singapore, 2015), http://probono.lawsociety.org.sg/Documents/pdf/Know%20the%20Law%20NOW-FINAL.pdf, 82.

[347] See CPC 2012 Rev Ed, s 23.

Right to Counsel

The right of access to counsel is protected under the Constitution, which provides that 'where a person is arrested, he (sic) shall be informed as soon as may be of the grounds of his arrest and shall be allowed to consult and be defended by a legal practitioner of his choice'.[348] In practice, this right has proved to be very weak.

The value of the right is reduced, for example, by the fact that a criminal suspect does not have the right to be informed of his or her constitutional right to counsel. The High Court has taken the view that this would amount to inserting a 'further right' into the existing provision.[349] Since there is no obligation for an investigating officer to inform the accused of the right to counsel, in practice the right to counsel is often only realised if the defendant already knows that the right exists, and can either afford a lawyer or qualifies for the Law Society's Criminal Legal Aid Scheme. This means that during initial arrests and investigations prior to the filing of official charges, access to counsel is often very limited. In fact, a brochure on 'Basic Criminal Procedure' for accused persons, produced by the Law Society of Singapore, even suggests that suspects may not contact a lawyer until formal charges are laid.[350]

The law also does not stipulate a specific time within which a suspect must be provided with access to legal representation. Several decisions have emphasised that the right to counsel is 'not an immediate one'.[351] In *Lee Mau Seng v Minister for Home Affairs*, the Court held that the constitutional right to counsel was satisfied if the defendant is allowed to consult a lawyer 'within a reasonable time after his arrest'.[352] The courts have generally taken a flexible view as to what constitutes a 'reasonable time', permitting a delay of two weeks in the case of *Jasbir Singh v Public Prosecutor*[353] and a 19 day delay in the case of *Public Prosecutor v Leong Siew Chor (Leong Siew Chor)*.[354]

The courts have also accepted the argument that a delay is 'reasonable' where allowing the suspect to access legal counsel at an earlier stage might obstruct the police investigation.[355] In *Leong Siew Chor*, the trial court accepted that it was legitimate for the police to deny access to legal counsel to mitigate the risk of 'external parties impeding the investigations and resulting in the accused shutting up'.[356] The Court of Appeal rejected the defence counsel's argument that it was unreasonable to refuse to grant the accused counsel once he had filed an application for one.[357] In this case, the accused had filed the application for access to legal advice on 24 June 2005. The lawyer offered to meet in the presence of the deputy Public Prosecutor

[348] Constitution of the Republic of Singapore (1999 reprint) Art 9(3).
[349] See *Rajeevan Edakalavan v PP* [1998] 1 SLR(R) 10; *Sun Hongyu v PP* [2005] 2 SLR(R) 750 [34].
[350] Law Society of Singapore, Pro Bono Services Office, 'Basic Criminal Procedure'.
[351] See, eg, *Jasbir Singh v PP* [1994] 2 SLR 18 and *Lee Mau Seng v Minister for Home Affairs, Singapore* [1969–71] SLR 508.
[352] [1971–1973] SLR(R) 135 at [12].
[353] [1994] 1 SLR(R) 782 at [49].
[354] [2006] 3 SLR(R) 290 at [87].
[355] *PP v Leong Siew Chor* [2006] 3 SLR 290.
[356] *PP v Leong Siew Chor* [2006] 3 SLR 290; [2006] SGHC 81 [61].
[357] *Leong Siew Chor v PP* [2006] SGCA 38.

and the investigating officer in order to advise the accused of his rights but even this request was denied.[358] The accused then gave a statement that contained several incriminating admissions, on 26 June 2005.[359] He was eventually given access to legal advice on 7 July 2005.[360] The Court held that it was not appropriate to discuss whether the accused should be able to seek legal advice, particularly advice on the right to remain silent, before the completion of investigations. As this decision suggests, access to legal representation is, in practice, often permitted only after the investigation process is concluded. This has led to concerns that the right to counsel is frequently denied to decrease the likelihood that the accused would become aware of, and exercise, the privilege against self-incrimination.[361]

Although the Constitution provides that an arrested person may be defended by a legal practitioner of his or her choice, the right to counsel is generally limited to access to local lawyers. Foreign lawyers are generally forbidden from practising Singapore criminal law, although recent reforms to the Legal Profession Act 2009 Rev Ed have made it easier for parties to retain services of Queen's Counsel or foreign lawyers through ad hoc admission provisions.[362] These have the effect that, when considering requests for the admission of QCs or other foreign lawyers, the court must take into account:

> (a) the nature of the factual and legal issues involved in the case; (b) the necessity for the services of a foreign senior counsel; (c) the availability of any Senior Counsel or other advocate and solicitor with appropriate experience; and (d) whether, having regard to the circumstances of the case, it is reasonable to admit a foreign senior counsel for the purpose of the case.[363]

Criminal defendants who are unable to afford legal representation may be eligible for the Singapore Criminal Legal Aid Scheme, administered by the Law Society of Singapore, which covers drug offences under the Misuse of Drugs Act. Applicants must be either Singaporean citizens or permanent residents and are subject to means-testing. Defendants are not permitted to access legal aid for offences to which capital punishment applies but where a criminal defendant accused of a capital offence cannot afford a lawyer, the state assigns one under the Legal Assistance Scheme for Capital Offences. A criminal defendant is also allowed to waive the right to counsel and elect to represent him or herself.[364] In deciding whether such a waiver was legitimate, Singaporean courts will consider the totality of circumstances, including weighing conflicting interests and whether the defendant is 'unduly prejudiced' by being unrepresented.[365]

[358] *PP v Leong Siew Chor* [2006] 3 SLR 290; [2006] SGHC 81 [61].

[359] See *PP v Leong Siew Chor* [2006] 3 SLR 290; [2006] SGHC 81 [58]–[67].

[360] *PP v Leong Siew Chor* [2006] 3 SLR 290; [2006] SGHC 81 [68].

[361] See Ho Hock Lai, 'The Privilege against Self-Incrimination and Right of Access to a Lawyer' (2013) 25 *Singapore Academy of Law Journal* 826, 840.

[362] Legal Profession Act (Singapore, Cap 161, 2009 Rev Ed) s 15(1). Original enactment in 1981.

[363] Legal Profession Act 2009 Rev Ed; Legal Profession (Ad Hoc Admissions) Notification 2012, s 132.

[364] See, eg, *Tan Chor Jin v PP* [2008] 4 SLR 306 [54].

[365] *Tan Chor Jin v PP* [55].

Thus very limited interpretation of the right to counsel reflects the courts' view that it functions 'not only to protect the rights of the accused' and that it has 'an equally strong duty to protect the rights of the public and the state'.[366] There has, however, been significant debate as to whether or not this narrow interpretation satisfies the constitutionally protected right. In *Ong Ah Chuan v Public Prosecutor*, the Privy Council, then the highest court of appeal for adjudicating Singapore cases, stated that Part IV of the Constitution, which sets out fundamental liberties, should be given 'a generous interpretation, avoiding what has been called "the austerity of tabulated legalism", suitable to give to individuals the full measure of the [fundamental liberties] referred to'.[367] Likewise, in *Taw Cheng Kong v Public Prosecutor*, Karthigesu JA stated that 'Constitutional liberties are enjoyed as fundamental liberties—not stick and carrot privileges. To the extent that the Constitution is supreme, those rights are inalienable'.[368] During Parliamentary debates in 2005, however, the then Minister for Home Affairs said that 'immediate access to legal counsel or family members could compromise police investigations' and favoured the existing far more restrictive approach.[369]

Bail

The procedures that apply in relation to bail depend on whether the crime with which the defendant is charged qualifies as a 'bailable offence'. Bailable and non-bailable offences are listed in the First Schedule to the Criminal Procedure Code. Where the defendant is charged with a 'bailable crime' he or she has an 'absolute right to bail'.[370] The First Schedule states that for all criminal offences other than those dealt with in the criminal code, a bailable offence is one that carries a sentence of less than three years' imprisonment. As a result, most offences under the Misuse of Drugs Act are not bailable. Where a defendant is charged with a non-bailable crime, he or she has only a discretionary right to bail.[371] The discretionary right does not, however, apply to offences punishable by death or at least 20 years imprisonment,[372] although the court does retain discretion where defendants are young or have a medical condition.[373]

In the case of bailable offences, the accused may be released on bail by a police officer or the court, on a personal bond.[374] If at any stage of investigation or trial it

[366] *Leong Siew Chor v PP* [2006] SGCA 38 [9].
[367] *Ong Ah Chuan v PP* [1981] AC 648, 670.
[368] *Taw Cheng Kong v PP* [1998] 1 SLR 78.
[369] Chin Tet Yung, 'Remaking the Evidence Code: Search for Values' (2009) 21 *Singapore Academy of Law Journal* 52, www.sal.org.sg/digitallibrary/Lists/SAL%20Journal/Attachments/468/2009-21-SAcLJ-52-Chin.pdf, 67.
[370] See Low Siew Ling, 'A Re-examination of Bail Law in Singapore' (2005) 17 *Singapore Academy of Law Journal* 869.
[371] CPC 2012 Rev Ed, ss 92(1), 93(1).
[372] CPC 2012 Rev Ed, s 95(1)(a).
[373] CPC 2012 Rev Ed, s 95(2).
[374] CPC 2012 Rev Ed, s 92(1).

becomes evident that there are no reasonable grounds for believing a person accused of a non-bailable offence has, in fact, committed the offence in question, he or she must be released.[375] A police officer of or above the rank of sergeant or the court may also release a person accused of a non-bailable offence,[376] subject to any conditions deemed necessary.[377] The Criminal Procedure Code does not set out guidelines that must be taken into account in deciding whether a defendant charged with a non-bailable crime may be released on bail. In practice, it is normally refused for drug crimes that attract 20 years' imprisonment or more, unless the accused is below 18 years of age or successfully raises medical concerns.

There are two policy arguments frequently accepted by courts as a basis for refusing bail applications from those accused of drug offences. First, recidivism rates are highest for drug offenders.[378] Second, given the heavy penalties attached to most drug convictions the flight risk in relation to drug crimes is viewed as relatively high.[379] There have been a number of high-profile cases where criminal defendants charged with drug crimes have skipped bail.[380] Overall, 122 persons absconded while on bail in 2013, and 99 in 2012.[381] Absconding does not constitute a further criminal offence under Singaporean law.

At the time of writing in 2015, Singapore was undertaking a comprehensive review of its bail system.[382]

Prosecutorial Discretion

The power to prosecute resides exclusively with the Attorney-General and the Public Prosecutor. There is debate as to whether or not this power is subject to any form of judicial oversight. In the recent case of *Ramalingam Ravinthran v Attorney-General*,[383] the applicant, who was convicted of drug trafficking, argued that the Public Prosecutor's decision to prosecute was in breach of Article 12(1) of the Constitution, which protects equality before the law, because the defendant's accomplice was charged with far less severe offences in relation to the same act. The Court of Appeal dismissed the submission.[384] The Chief Justice Chan Sek Keong held

[375] CPC 2012 Rev Ed, s 93(2).

[376] CPC 2012 Rev Ed, s 93(1).

[377] CPC 2012 Rev Ed, s 94(1).

[378] Low Siew Ling, 'A Re-examination of Bail Law' 885, n 58.

[379] See Lee Lit Cheng, 'Criminal Procedure, Evidence and Sentencing', (2010) *Singapore Academy of Law Annual Review of Singapore Cases*, Annual Review 2010, 332–54.

[380] For example, between December 2004 and February 2005, drug offence suspects Jeremy Mahen Chanmugam (District Arrest Case No 45377 of 2004), Hamdan bin Mohd (District Arrest Case Nos 45355 of 2004, 48185–48187 of 2004), and Guiga Lyes Ben Laroussi (District Arrest Case Nos 53126 of 2004, 55524–55538 of 2004 and 55512–55513 of 2004) absconded while on bail: Fiona Low, '22 years, 12 Strokes for Man who Jumped Bail' *The Straits Times* (6 April 2012), A3.

[381] Remy Choo Zheng Xi, '2015 Bail Review: Striking the Right Balance' *The Straits Times* (13 January 2015), www.straitstimes.com/news/opinion/more-opinion-stories/story/2015-bail-review-striking-the-right-balance-20150113?page=2.

[382] Remy Choo Zheng Xi, '2015 Bail Review'.

[383] [2012] 2 SLR 49.

[384] *Ramalingam Ravinthran v Attorney-General* [2012] SGCA 2.

that, given the constitutional position of the Attorney-General, there is a general presumption that prosecutorial powers are exercised in the public interest and according to law.[385] This presumption may be rebutted where an offender can demonstrate a prima facie breach of fundamental liberty, in which case the burden may fall on the Attorney-General to justify a prosecutorial decision.[386] Mere differentiation of charges laid against different offenders involved in the same criminal enterprise was not, of itself, sufficient to demonstrate the biased or arbitrary exercise of prosecutorial power.[387]

There is some evidence that over the past two decades prosecutorial discretion has increasingly been exercised to reduce the number of prosecutions for charges to which the mandatory death penalty applies.[388] The approach used to achieve this is referred to as the '14.99 charge', and involves formally recording the quantity of drugs in the charges laid as just below the weight that would attract the mandatory death penalty (15 g, in the case of heroin). Given that, first, the courts obviously have no sentencing discretion once the mandatory death sentence provisions are invoked, and, second, that successful appeals for clemency are very low, prosecutorial decisions appear to play a very significant role in determining the number of executions carried out in Singapore.[389]

Pre-Trial Discovery

In 2012, new pre-trial discovery provisions were introduced into the Criminal Procedure Code to facilitate transparency and 'level the playing field' during the discovery process.[390] For cases to be tried in the High Court (where the sentence may involve capital punishment or life imprisonment), some of the prosecution's case must now be disclosed in the pre-trial committal proceedings process, which is presided over by a magistrate.[391] Prior to the committal proceeding, there is an initial criminal case disclosure conference where the prosecution must set out the charge or charges with which it intends to proceed, while the accused must stipulate whether he or she intends to plead guilty or to 'claim trial'.[392] The court sets a date for the committal hearing.[393]

[385] *Ramalingam Ravinthran v Attorney-General* [2012] SGCA 2 [46].

[386] *Ramalingam Ravinthran v Attorney-General* [2012] SGCA 2 [28].

[387] *Ramalingam Ravinthran v Attorney-General* [2012] SGCA 2 [73].

[388] See Michael Hor, 'Singapore's Death Penalty: The Beginning of the End?' in Roger Hood and Surya Deva (eds) *Confronting Capital Punishment in Asia: Human Rights, Politics and Public Opinion* (Oxford University Press, 2003) 163; and Daniel Pascoe, 'Clemency in Southeast Asian Death Penalty Cases' (2014) *CILIS Policy Paper, ALC Briefing Paper* 19.

[389] See Hor, 'Singapore's Death Penalty' 162–63; and Pascoe, 'Clemency in Southeast Asian Death Penalty Cases' 19.

[390] See Ho Peng Kee, 'Singapore Parliamentary Debates, Hansard Reports, Budget, Minister of State for Law, Associate Professor Ho Peng Kee' (27 February 2008).

[391] CPC 2012 Rev Ed, ss 176(1), 177(1).

[392] CPC 2012 Rev Ed, s 176(1).

[393] CPC 2012 Rev Ed, s 176(1).

At least seven days prior to the committal hearing, the prosecution must furnish details of the charge that will form the basis of the trial, a list of witnesses and exhibits to be admitted at trial, written statements from witnesses to be admitted and any statement of the accused the prosecution attends to adduce in evidence.[394] In the committal proceeding, the prosecution must satisfy the examining magistrate that there are 'sufficient grounds for committing the accused for trial'.[395] If the accused is committed to stand trial, the accused and prosecution must attend a further criminal case disclosure conference.

Cases to be tried in the subordinate courts must also undergo a criminal case disclosure process. Under this process, prosecutors must serve on the defence documents that support their case within two weeks of the first case disclosure conference, if the accused refuses to plead or claims trial.[396] Defence counsel must then file a summary of the defence and the evidence supporting its case within two weeks and serve such submissions on the Attorney-General's Chambers.[397] Once this is done, prosecutors must, within two weeks, turn over to defence lawyers all other statements taken from the accused, any criminal records, and any other exhibits.[398]

In the first instance, the court will ask the accused how she or he wishes to plead. If the accused does not want to plead or wants to go to trial, the court is required to set the date for the 'first criminal case disclosure conference' eight weeks or more from then, unless there are sound reasons not to do so.[399] At the criminal case disclosure conference, both prosecution and the accused must agree on such matters as the submission of the respective cases for prosecution and defence; the legal or factual issues for the trial judge to determine; the witnesses who will be called at trial; 'statements, documents or exhibits' to be tendered; and the commencement date of the trial.[400]

Where the accused does not wish to plead guilty to the relevant charges, the prosecution is required to submit the case for the prosecution to court and issue a copy to the accused and any co-accused within two weeks of the conference.[401] The case for the prosecution must include the charges the prosecution intends to pursue; a synopsis of facts giving rise to the charges; witnesses' names; the records of exhibits the prosecution wishes to adduce at trial; and any of the accused person's statements recorded by the relevant authorities upon which the prosecution wishes to rely.[402] While the prosecution must produce a record of the witnesses they intend to call, they are not required to disclose witness statements, not even those that might favour the accused.

[394] CPC 2012 Rev Ed, s 176(4).
[395] CPC 2012 Rev Ed, s 185(b).
[396] CPC 2012 Rev Ed, s 161(2).
[397] CPC 2012 Rev Ed, s 163(1).
[398] CPC 2012 Rev Ed, s 166(1).
[399] CPC 2012 Rev Ed, s 161(1).
[400] CPC 2012 Rev Ed, s 160(1).
[401] CPC 2012 Rev Ed, s 161(2).
[402] CPC 2012 Rev Ed, s 162.

The court may schedule another criminal case disclosure conference one week from the date the prosecution is scheduled to submit its case against the accused.[403] If, at this conference, the defendant does not indicate whether or not she or he wishes to plead guilty, the defence must submit its 'case for the defence' to the court.[404] The defendant must issue a copy to the prosecution, and every co-defendant who wishes not to plead guilty, within two weeks of the date of the conference, or within two weeks of the next disclosure conference, should it be adjourned.[405] Special court procedures apply where the defendant has no counsel.[406] The 'case for the defence' must include: (a) a synopsis of the defence and the facts that substantiate it; (b) a record of names of defence witnesses; (c) a record of the exhibits the defence wishes to adduce at trial; and (d) whether the defence objects to 'any issue of fact or law' relevant to the case for the prosecution, together with a statement explaining the objection, factual matters relating to evidence to be adduced and legal arguments substantiating the objection.[407]

The new disclosure regime puts defence counsel in a better position to advise their clients, given they have access to the prosecution's case and the defendant's statements. Under the reformed Criminal Procedure Code, the defence will normally obtain all the defendant's statements ('long' statements) made to the police within two weeks of the first case disclosure conference. Before these changes, defence counsel would only become aware of such evidence against their clients just before the trial commenced.[408]

In addition to the Criminal Procedure Code requirements, the courts have sometimes accepted non-statutory disclosure obligations in accordance with those recognised by other major common law jurisdictions on the basis of the 'right to a fair trial' and the 'rules of natural justice'.[409] The courts have, for example, found that such obligations encompass a duty to disclose: (a) any unused material that is likely to be admissible and that might reasonably be regarded as credible and relevant to the guilt or innocence of the accused; and (b) any unused material that is likely to be inadmissible but would provide a real (not fanciful) chance of pursuing a line of inquiry that leads to material that is likely to be admissible and that might reasonably be regarded as credible and relevant to the guilt or innocence of the accused.[410]

The pre-trial discovery process in Singapore has been described as rudimentary, as there is no general statutory obligation on either party to assist the other or obtain insight into the evidence held by their counterpart prior to the trial beginning.[411]

403 Pursuant to CPC 2012 Rev Ed, s 161(4).
404 CPC 2012 Rev Ed, s 163(1).
405 CPC 2012 Rev Ed, s 163(1).
406 See CPC 2012 Rev Ed, s 161(5).
407 CPC 2012 Rev Ed, s 165(1).
408 See Ho Peng Kee, 'Singapore Parliamentary Debates, Budget' (27 February 2008); Kimberly Spykerman, 'Trial Run to Prep Lawyers for Changes: From Next Year, Defence Team Will Have Access to More Information', *The Straits Times* (13 October 2010).
409 See, eg, *Muhammad bin Kadar v PP* [2011] 3 SLR 1205.
410 *Muhammad bin Kadar v PP* [2011] 3 SLR 1205 [113].
411 Hor, 'The Future of Singapore's Criminal Process' 862.

In other words, there is no mandatory access to evidence in the possession of the other party. According to Hor, this results in considerable procedural unfairness, given the imbalance of resources between the police and prosecutorial bodies on the one hand, and the accused and his or her legal representatives on the other.[412]

Evidence—Admissibility of Statements and Confessions

The laws of evidence in Singapore are set out in detail in the Evidence Act 1997 Rev Ed, which includes rules on the relevance of facts, admissions and confessions, acceptable forms of evidence, burden of proof, and treatment of witnesses. This section will focus specifically on the rules regarding witness statements and confessions, and the admissibility of those statements and confessions.

To comply with procedural rules, investigating officers must ensure that any witness or suspect statements are taken down in writing, read back to the witness, translated into an understandable language (if the witness does not speak English), and signed by the witness.[413]

Further procedures apply when a suspect is formally charged. A suspect who is charged must be served a written notice to the following effect:

> You have been charged with [or informed that that you may be prosecuted for] [set out the charge]. Do you want to say anything about the charge that was just read to you? If you keep quiet now about any fact or matter in your defence and you reveal this fact or matter in your defence only at your trial, the judge may be less likely to believe you. This may have a bad effect on your case in court. Therefore it may be better for you to mention such fact or matter now. If you wish to do so, what you say will be written down, read back to you for any mistakes to be corrected and then signed by you.[414]

If after being cautioned the accused person remains silent or communicates that she or he declines to give a statement, the police or authorised investigating officer must record that response.[415] If the accused person makes a statement, the statement must be recorded in writing, read back to him or her, translated into an understandable language (if she or he does not speak English) and signed by him or her.[416] The accused must also be provided with a copy of the cautioned statement after its completion.[417] The investigating officer is required to follow this protocol but failure to do so will not necessarily render the accused person's statement inadmissible in court.[418] Statements are inadmissible where made to a police officer of a rank lower than sergeant.[419]

412 Ibid.
413 Evidence Act (Singapore, Cap 97, 1997 Rev Ed) s 22(3). Original enactment was in 1893.
414 Evidence Act 1997 Rev Ed, s 23(1).
415 Evidence Act 1997 Rev Ed, s 23(2).
416 Evidence Act 1997 Rev Ed, s 23(3).
417 Evidence Act 1997 Rev Ed, s 23(4).
418 See *Lim Thian Lai v PP* (Court of Criminal Appeal).
419 CPC 2012 Rev Ed, s 258(2).

If the accused person is cautioned, the statement cannot be deemed the result of a threat, inducement or promise, so long as it is offered voluntarily.[420] An accused person's statement will, however, be inadmissible if the court finds that it appears to have, in fact, been made under an 'inducement, threat or promise' relevant to the charge, enough to give him or her reasonable grounds to believe that by making that statement, she or he would gain any advantage or avoid 'any evil of a temporal nature'.[421] If a police officer ranked as a sergeant or above behaves in such a way that his acts 'tend to sap', or 'in fact sapped', the free will of the accused (such that the accused reasonably believes that she or he would gain any advantage or avoid any evil of a temporal nature by making a particular statement) that behaviour will constitute a threat, inducement or promise and be inadmissible in court.[422] A court may admit a statement made following an 'inducement, threat or promise' if the court is satisfied that the influence of the inducement, threat or promise had been fully removed.[423]

A statement will not be inadmissible simply because it is obtained in dubious circumstances. For example, the court may accept a statement made under a promise of secrecy or as a result of deception, under intoxication, or in response to questions that the accused was not obliged to answer.[424] The court may also admit a statement made without the accused being forewarned that it might be used as evidence against him or her, or without the relevant officer fully complying with protocols for the formal recording of witness or cautioned statements.[425] Put simply, the position is that even if the investigating officer fails to caution the accused in accordance with Criminal Procedure Code protocol, a statement will not necessarily be rendered inadmissible.

As mentioned, a voluntary statement is admissible[426] and the prosecution must prove that any statement on which it relies was voluntary. In practice, however, where there is a contradiction between the prosecution and the defendant regarding the voluntariness of a statement, the courts usually accept the credibility of submissions made by the police.[427] More generally the court has taken the position that it is not the court's responsibility in criminal trials to discipline police misbehaviour.[428]

As discussed above, the Criminal Procedure Code permits adverse inferences to be drawn against an accused person who fails to disclose a material fact at various stages of the pre-trial and trial process. This includes such inferences as appear proper from the accused person's failure to reveal any fact in his or he defence that the defendant could 'reasonably have been expected to mention'.[429] The court may

[420] CPC 2012 Rev Ed, s 258(3).
[421] CPC 2012 Rev Ed, s 258(3).
[422] CPC 2012 Rev Ed, s 258 (Explanation 1).
[423] CPC 2012 Rev Ed, s 258(4).
[424] CPC 2012 Rev Ed, s 258(3).
[425] CPC 2012 Rev Ed, s 258(3).
[426] CPC 2012 Rev Ed, s 258(3).
[427] See Hor (n 272) 854.
[428] See *Law Society of Singapore v Tan Guat Neo Phyllis* [2008] 2 SLR (R) 239.
[429] CPC 2012 Rev Ed, s 261(1).

also draw such inferences that, where relevant, may support or corroborate evidence given against the accused.[430] In addition, inference may be drawn from the accused person's 'silence or other reaction' in response to allegations about his behaviour that are relevant to the charge.[431]

Any of an accused person's verbal or written statements made at any time are admissible as evidence at his or her trial.[432] This means that an individual's statements made during questioning prior to being cautioned and formally charged are admissible as evidence, even where such statements were only made in his or her capacity as a witness. The Criminal Procedure Code explicitly states that if the accused is willing to testify in his defence from the dock, any statements made can be used in cross-examination to 'impeach his (sic) credit'.[433]

The courts have held that a confession can be sufficient to sustain a conviction even if without corroboration, and even in circumstances where the accused retracts the statement at trial.[434] Where accused persons are jointly tried for the same crime, and one of them confesses and, in so doing, implicates the others involved, the court may take into confession into account in determining the guilt of all defendants.[435] This applies even where separate trials are held.

Appeal

The High Court has jurisdiction to hear appeals from District Courts or Magistrates' Courts, as well as points of law submitted by those courts (Criminal References), and appeals from Family or Youth Courts when exercising their criminal jurisdiction.[436]

The Criminal jurisdiction of the Court of Appeal consists of appeals against any decisions issued by the High Court in the exercise of its original criminal jurisdiction.[437] There is, however, no appeal to the Court of Appeal from decisions made by the High Court in its appellate or revisionary jurisdiction. In other words, there can be no appeal from an order made by the High Court in a Magistrate's Appeal or Criminal Reference.

The prosecution has the right to appeal against the acquittal of an accused, a sentence imposed on an accused, or an order of the trial court.[438] A convicted defendant may appeal against his conviction by a trial court, a sentence imposed, or an order of the trial court.[439] Where an accused has pleaded guilty, however, and is convicted in accordance with that plea, he or she may only appeal against the extent or legality of

430 CPC 2012 Rev Ed, s 261(1).
431 CPC 2012 Rev Ed, s 261(2).
432 CPC 2012 Rev Ed, s 258(1).
433 CPC 2012 Rev Ed, s 258(1).
434 See *Ismail bin UK Abdul Rahman v PP* [1974–1976] SLR (R) 91.
435 CPC 2012 Rev Ed, s 258(5).
436 Supreme Court of Judicature Act 2007 Rev Ed, s 19.
437 Supreme Court of Judicature Act 2007 Rev Ed, s 29A(2).
438 CPC 2012 Rev Ed, s 374(3).
439 CPC 2012 Rev Ed, s 374(3).

the sentencing.[440] Appeals against convictions and sentencing must be made within 14 days of the issuance of the sentence.[441]

Sentencing

For drug trafficking offences, the factors a court may consider in determining an appropriate sentence include: the quantity and type of drug in the possession of the offender; the time and sophistication involved in planning and carrying out the offence; and the relative levels of participation in cases where there are accomplices.[442] Aggravating factors are those factors that indicate the 'level of gravity of the crime in specific relation to the offence upon which the accused was charged.'[443] Aside from the seriousness of the category of the offence generally, the gravity of the particular offence can be determined from the manner and mode in which it was commissioned, the degree of seriousness of the consequences of the criminal act, and the impact it has on 'the public interest'.[444]

A mitigating factor is defined as something that reduces the severity of the sentence passed. It can relate to matters such as the offender's past and circumstances (for example, good character); the offender's response to the offence and prosecution (for example, remorse, co-operation with authorities); or the offender's present and future prospects (for example, family responsibilities, capacity to address issues driving criminal behaviour, etc).[445] Singaporean courts generally consider personal hardship to have no mitigating value, other than in exceptional circumstances.[446] Offending to feed drug addiction has likewise been held to have no mitigating value.[447]

In relation to the considerations that apply when sentencing for drug offences, the courts have placed a strong emphasis on the public interest in deterring the drug trade and the need to take into account that:

> drugs impact (in the most adverse manner possible) actual lives in real place and time—with (in many instances) equally adverse consequences for the future as well.[448]

Rates of incarceration for convicted drug offenders in Singapore are high. Drug offenders constitute around two thirds of inmates in Singaporean prisons,[449] and

[440] CPC 2012 Rev Ed, s 365.
[441] CPC 2012 Rev Ed, s 377(2)(a).
[442] See *Jeffery bin Abdullah v PP* [2009] 3 SLR(R) 414 per Chan Sek Keong CJ at [7] citing Judge Jasvender Kaur et al, *Sentencing Practice in the Subordinate Courts* (Singapore, LexisNexis, 2nd edn, 2003) 638–39.
[443] *PP v Huang Hong Si* [2003] 3 SLR 57 per Choo Han Teck J [8].
[444] *PP v Huang Hong Si* [2003] 3 SLR 57 [8–11].
[445] See Kow Keng Siong, *Sentencing Principles in Singapore* (Singapore, Academy Publishing, 2009) 344.
[446] See *Tan Kiam Peng v PP* [2008] 1 SLR 1 at [182].
[447] *PP v Ng Bee Ling Lana* [1992] 1 SLR 635 at [16].
[448] *Tan Kiam Peng v PP* [2008] 1 SLR 1 at [181].
[449] Teo Chee Hean (n 36) 8.

four-fifths of the prison population have prior drug charges.[450] At the end of 2014, there were 6,527 people imprisoned on drug-related convictions, compared to 6,510 at the end of 2013, and 6,287 at the end of 2012.[451] At 31 December 2014, there were a further 707 people held in remand for drug related offences and 1,400 were interned at Drug Rehabilitation Centres, of whom 82 per cent were male.[452] It is generally accepted that Singaporean prisons and detention centres meet international standards.[453]

Death Penalty

Singapore's use of the mandatory death penalty has attracted criticism from both local and international observers.[454] Singapore first introduced the death penalty for drug offences when it enacted the Misuse of Drugs Act in 1973. According to the Singapore Prison Service statistical data, there were two executions for drug related offences in 2011, three in 2009, none between 2010–13,[455] and two in 2014.[456] Since 2004, there have not been more than 10 people executed in any year.[457]

Historically rates have been much higher. According to Amnesty International, more than 70 people were executed in both 1994 and 1995, including more than 50 per year for drug trafficking.[458] Between 1991 and 2004 more than 400 prisoners were hanged in Singapore, giving the small city-state what may be the highest execution rate in the world relative to its small population, now around 5.5 million people.[459] Those who support the death penalty argue that it is Singapore's

[450] Teo Chee Hean, Deputy Prime Minister and Minister for Home Affairs, 'Response Speech on the Misuse Of Drugs (Amendment) Bill' (14 November 2012).

[451] Singapore Prison Service, 'Strong Community Efforts' 3.

[452] Singapore Prison Service (n 328), 6.

[453] US Department of State, '2010 Country Reports on Human Rights Practices—Singapore' (8 April 2011), www.refworld.org/docid/4da56d8ba5.html.

[454] See KS Rajah 'Death Penalty: The Unconstitutional Punishment', *The Straits Times* (28 August 2013); Amnesty International, eg, Amnesty International, 'Singapore: The Death Penalty: A Hidden Toll of Executions', ASA 36/001/2004 (January 2004), www.amnesty.org/en/documents/asa36/001/2004/en/; Michael Hor (2004) 'The Death Penalty in Singapore and International Law' 8 *Singapore Year Book of International Law* 105.

[455] Singapore Prison Service, 'Greater Community Involvement Contributes to Lower Re-Offending Rates: Concerted Focus on Stronger Rehabilitation for Drug Offenders' (30 January 2013), www.sps.gov.sg/sites/default/files/2013%20Singapore%20Prison%20Service%20Annual%20Statistics%20Release.pdf; Singapore Prison Service, 'Stronger Community and Family Support Help Keep Recividism Rates Low as SPS Maintains Focus on its "Through-Care" Philosophy' (1 February 2012), http://160.96.2.181/content/dam/sps/publication_latest/2012%20Prisons%20Annual%20Statistics%20Release%201%20Feb%202012.pdf.

[456] Singapore Prison Service (n 328) 9.

[457] Amnesty International USA, 'Amnesty International Implores Singapore to Join Global Trend toward Abolition of the Death Penalty', Press Release (2 May 2012), www.amnestyusa.org/news/press-releases/amnesty-international-implores-singapore-to-join-global-trend-toward-abolition-of-death-penalty.

[458] Amnesty International 'Public Statement: Singapore Should Join Global Trend and Establish a Moratorium on Executions', AI Index: ASA 36/004/2012 (2 May 2012).

[459] Amnesty International, 'Singapore: The Death Penalty: A Hidden Toll of Executions', ASA 36/001/2004 (January 2004), www.amnesty.org/en/documents/asa36/001/2004/en/, 3.

tough stand—including its use of the death sentence—that has allowed the state to achieve one of the lowest rates of drug abuse in the world.[460] Others, including some Singaporean parliamentarians, are very critical of capital punishment and, in particular, the mandatory death sentence that applies to a number of narcotics offences.[461]

In December 2010, the Ministry of Home Affairs launched a study into the implementation of the death penalty in Singapore. The study prompted a review of the death penalty in relation to drug offences in 2011. The study found that the death penalty should continue to apply to drug traffickers but should not be a mandatory sentence, promoting greater discretion for the courts.[462] Singapore did not alter its overall support for retaining the death sentence as result of the study. An amendment to the Misuse of Drugs Act was introduced, however, in 2012, which increased judicial discretion regarding the imposition of the death penalty for drug trafficking and drug importation offences to 'strike the right balance'.

Although its discretion is tightly restricted,[463] the court may now, in certain circumstances, decide whether to impose a sentence of life imprisonment and caning rather than the death sentence, where the court is satisfied of two specific conditions. The first is that the offender proves on the balance of probabilities that his or her role in the commissioning of the offence was restricted to being a courier, that is, transporting, sending or delivering a controlled drug, or offering to do one such act, or carrying out or offering to carry out preparation for such acts.[464] The second condition is that the offender has provided substantive assistance to the Central Narcotics Bureau in disrupting drug trafficking activities within or outside Singapore, which must be demonstrated through certification by the Public Prosecutor.[465] This substantive assistance requirement was introduced to enhance the operational effectiveness of the Bureau and aims to increase the likelihood that investigators can more effectively target higher levels within drug syndicates.[466] Accordingly, assistance that does not result in any enhanced enforcement effectiveness is not sufficient to attract certification.[467] Indeed, the policy intent behind the reforms was not to be more lenient on couriers but rather to enable the Bureau to obtain more information about drug trafficking activities.[468] Thus, while some have argued that it is unfair that those couriers who know little about the drug hierarchies, suppliers or kingpins cannot benefit from the amendments, it is clear from parliamentary records that the legislative intent was to maintain a tight regime in which couriers would continue to be 'vigorously targeted'.[469]

460 Michael Teo, 'Singapore's Policy Keeps Drugs at Bay' *The Guardian* (6 June 2010), www.theguardian.com/commentisfree/2010/jun/05/singapore-policy-drugs-bay.

461 See NMP Laurence Lien, Parliamentary Speech (12 November 2012).

462 Teo Chee Hean (n 36).

463 Teo Chee Hean, 'Second Reading on the Misuse of Drugs (Amendment) Bill' (12 November 2012) 32.

464 MDA 2008 Rev Ed, s 33B(2)(a).

465 MDA 2008 Rev Ed, s 33B(2)(b).

466 Teo Chee Hean (n 2) 23.

467 Ibid.

468 Teo Chee Hean, 'Response Speech on the Misuse of Drugs (Amendment) Bill' (14 November 2012) 36.

469 Ibid [37].

In a separate amendment, parliament has also given the court discretion to sentence an offender to life in prison in place of death, without caning, where the defendant can demonstrate that his or her role was restricted to that of a courier and he or she was suffering from an abnormality of mind that substantially impaired his or her mental responsibility for the offence.[470] This reform is intended to deal with cases 'worthy of special consideration' where the accused has shown such an abnormality of mind that it substantially impairs his or her mental responsibility for the acts constituting his offences.[471]

Clemency

If the High Court convicts a defendant of a drugs offence that carries the mandatory death penalty, and the Court of Appeal upholds the conviction, the only recourse available is to seek clemency or pardon from the President. Clemency has its basis in Article 22P of the Singaporean Constitution, which holds that an individual who has been convicted of an offence may seek pardon from the President of Singapore who, acting on the advice of Cabinet, may grant such pardon with or without conditions, or a reprieve from the execution of any sentence pronounced on the offender.[472] The Court of Appeal has held that Article 22P is clear that the President is to act on the advice of Cabinet and does not have independent discretion in exercising the clemency power,[473] and that there is a presumption of legality that applies to the clemency process on the basis of the high constitutional office held by those responsible for dealing with clemency petitions.[474]

Precise data on the number of clemency applications and the success rate is not published and is very difficult to obtain. Observed clemency rates are, however, very low.[475] There is evidence to suggest that prisoners sentenced to the death penalty are often only held in prison for two years prior to execution and that petitions for clemency are generally considered on the basis of retribution,[476] rather than factors such as significant rehabilitation, religious piety or remorse. As indicated above, there is some evidence that prosecutorial discretion in framing charges plays a much more influential role in determining the overall impact of the death penalty in Singapore than the clemency process established by the Constitution.[477]

[470] MDA 2008 Rev Ed, s 33B(1)(b), (3).
[471] Teo Chee Hean (n 450) 33.
[472] Constitution of the Republic of Singapore Art 22P.
[473] *Yong Vui Kong v AG* [2011] 2 SLR 1189 at [149]–[150].
[474] *Yong Vui Kong v AG* [2011] 2 SLR 1189 at [135]–[139].
[475] Pascoe (n 388) 17.
[476] Pascoe (n 388) 15.
[477] Pascoe (n 388) 19.

Reduced Sentencing/Parole

Where an inmate has demonstrated good conduct and behaviour in prison and has not committed any breach of prison discipline, he or she may be eligible for a one-third remission of his or her sentence.[478] Further, where prisoners have served 20 years of a life sentence or a long-term prison sentence, the Minister has discretion to direct the Commissioner to make a remission order.[479] Inmates released on parole are issued a Conditional Remission Order, which requires that the person not commit an offence during the remission period that would result in a sentence of imprisonment, corrective training, reformative training or preventative detention.[480] If such a breach occurs, an enhanced sentence applies with the maximum term of the remaining remission period applied in addition to any other sentence of imprisonment.[481] In deciding the length of the enhanced sentence, the court must consider the gravity of the new offence, whether the new offence is of a similar nature to the previous offence, the amount of time the offender remained offence-free, and any other relevant aggravating or mitigating circumstances.[482]

Supervision Orders

With approval from the Public Prosecutor, the Minister may direct that a person be subject to supervision by the police for a period of up to three years.[483] Any person subject to a supervision order must comply with conditions imposed under the Criminal Procedure Code and any further restrictions imposed by the Minister. These may include restrictions in relation to place of residence, change of address, ability to leave Singapore, regular reporting to the police station, curfews, and restrictions on entering certain areas.[484]

There is a supervision program for drug-users, tiered according to their age and the risk of re-offending (see below). Supervisees who have more than two prior drug convictions and are assessed as having a high-risk of re-offending are subject to the more intensive Enhanced Supervision Scheme, under which they may be subject to electronic monitoring, routine urine tests, curfew requirements, and compulsory counselling.[485] In 2013 and 2014, it was expected that around 500 high-risk

[478] See Prisons Act (Singapore, Cap 247, 2000 Rev Ed) s 50I. Original enactment in 1933.
[479] Prisons Act 2000 Rev Ed, ss 50J, 50P.
[480] Prisons Act 2000 Rev Ed, s 50S(1).
[481] Prisons Act 2000 Rev Ed, s 50T(1).
[482] Prisons Act 2000 Rev Ed, s 50T(3).
[483] Criminal Law (Temporary Provisions) Act 2000 Rev Ed, s 30(b).
[484] Criminal Law (Temporary Provisions) Act 2000 Rev Ed, s 33(1).
[485] Central Narcotics Bureau (n 40) 8.

long-term offenders would be subject to this scheme.[486] Supervision orders also apply under the Intoxicating Substances Act (Singapore, Cap 146A, 2001 Rev Ed).[487]

V. REHABILITATION AND DIVERSIONARY PROGRAMS

Drug users arrested for the first or second time are usually detained at rehabilitation centres for treatment. Under the Misuse of Drugs Act, the Central Narcotics Bureau (CNB) has the power to commit a suspected drug-user who has tested positive to a verified urine test to Drug Rehabilitation Centres (DRC) under the management of the Singapore Prison Service.[488] Committal to a DRC does not automatically result in a criminal record but drug-users who are arrested more than twice are liable for long-term imprisonment.

A 2012 amendment to the Misuse of Drugs Act introduced provisions for a Community Rehabilitation Centre, which is intended as a 'step-down arrangement' for young drug-users following a short period of detention at a DRC.[489] In the centres, young drug-users are allowed to continue their education and employment during the day. This also segregates young users from more seasoned repeat abusers among the detainees. The focus on rehabilitating young drug users is aimed at breaking 'the cycle of addiction' and to provide support to those 'who have a genuine desire to rid themselves of their addiction'.[490]

Drugs-users are usually detained in the DRC for a minimum of six months unless discharged earlier by the institution's director or a review committee.[491] If the review committee is of the opinion that the inmate requires further treatment after the initial six months, it may direct that he or she be detained for a further period of up to six months, with a maximum combined extension period of two years.[492] The DRC runs a compulsory treatment and rehabilitation program involving an initial detoxification stage, followed by a behavioural change program including an individualised 'relapse prevention plan'.[493] Each detainee has a case manager who oversees progress. The release process can involve job placements and half-way houses designed to help drug-users reintegrate into the community. Upon discharge, drug-users are generally subject to a supervision period of up to two years, which entails regular compulsory urine tests.[494]

486 Singapore Prison Service, 'Greater Community Involvement Contributes to Lower Re-Offending Rates: Concerted Focus on Stronger Rehabilitation for Drug Offenders', News Release (30 January 2013), www.sps.gov.sg/sites/default/files/2013%20Singapore%20Prison%20Service%20Annual%20Statistics%20Release.pdf, 2.

487 Intoxicating Substances Act 2001 Rev Ed, s 17.

488 MDA 2008 Rev Ed, s 34(2)(b).

489 MDA 2008 Rev Ed, s 38(2)(b).

490 Teo Chee Hean (n 2) 29.

491 MDA 2008 Rev Ed, s 34(3).

492 MDA 2008 Rev Ed, s 34(4)(4A).

493 Central Narcotics Bureau (n 40) 8.

494 Central Narcotics Bureau (n 40) 8.

The Singapore Prison System co-operates with Singapore Corporation of Rehabilitative Enterprises (SCORE), which runs programs to improve the vocational skills of inmates detained in DRCs. It also has a program to find employers for inmates upon release. The recidivism rate of people released from DRCs was 30.5 per cent in 2008, 27.1 per cent in 2009 and 27.5 per cent in 2010.[495]

In addition to its law enforcement efforts, the CNB invests significant resources in prevention programmes. It co-ordinates a national Preventative Drug Education programme, targeting students and high-risk youth. The CNB also collaborates with the National Council against Drug Abuse to promote a 'national consensus' regarding Singapore's zero tolerance framework for drug use. The CNB's program includes anti-drug talks, performances and exhibitions. They also hold a range of youth activities intended to promote a 'healthy, social lifestyle', such as dance contexts, essay-writing and art competitions, sports carnivals, and gaming competitions.

The National Council against Drug Abuse also plays a role in Singapore's efforts to prevent drug abuse. Established in 1995, it is a citizens' advisory body on national anti-drug strategies and initiatives and aims to engage the community to support the government's zero tolerance policy on drugs. The government also frequently convenes inter-ministerial or cross agency taskforces on drugs to issue recommendations on the most appropriate strategies for tackling drug abuse.

VI. REGULATIONS ON FINANCE AND THE DRUG TRADE

Singapore is one of the world's leading offshore financial centres, with major private banking and asset management sectors. Its financial institutions are estimated to manage funds and assets of approximately US$ 1.3 trillion.[496] The size and growth in this market, combined with secrecy protections and limited routine large-scale currency reporting requirements, make Singapore a major potential target for money laundering by drug traffickers. Singapore also has two casinos that generate large profits and are believed to be used for money laundering purposes.[497] As a result, the US Bureau for International Narcotics and Law Enforcement Affairs has identified Singapore as a major money laundering destination 'whose financial institutions engage in currency transactions involving significant amounts of proceeds from international narcotics trafficking'.[498]

The Corruption, Drug Trafficking and Other Serious Crimes (Confiscation of Benefits) Act (Singapore, Cap 65A, 2000 Rev Ed) (CDSC Act 2000 Rev Ed) creates a range of offences in relation to the proceeds of drug related offences.[499] These

[495] Singapore Prison Service, 'Greater Community Involvement' 1 (Table 2).

[496] US Department of State, Bureau of International Narcotics and Law Enforcement Affairs, 'Money Laundering and Financial Crimes: Country Database' (June 2014) 370, www.state.gov/documents/organization/222881.pdf.

[497] US Department of State, Bureau of International Narcotics and Law Enforcement Affairs, 'Money Laundering' (June 2014) 370.

[498] US Department of State, Bureau of International Narcotics and Law Enforcement Affairs (n 41) 6.

[499] CDSC Act (Chapter 65A Rev Ed 2000, Singapore). Original Act was enacted in 1992.

include assisting another to retain benefits of drug dealing, where a person enters, or is concerned in, an arrangement 'knowing or having reasonable grounds to believe' that the arrangement facilitates the retention of benefits obtained through drug dealing, including by concealment, removal from jurisdiction or transfer to nominees.[500] It is an offence to enter an arrangement through which benefits of drug dealing are used to secure funds or to acquire property where there are reasonable grounds to believe that the other person is, or was, engaged in drug dealing or has benefited from drug dealing.[501] It is also an offence to conceal, disguise, convert or transfer property which, whether partially or wholly, directly or indirectly, represents a benefit of drug dealing where the person knows, or has reasonable grounds to believe, that this is the case.[502] Acquiring property that, whether partially or wholly, and directly or indirectly, comprises the proceeds of drug dealing also constitutes an offence.[503]

The CDSC Act allows authorities to trace, freeze and confiscate the assets of convicted drug traffickers and creates a criminal offence of laundering the proceeds of drug-related offences. It also imposes positive obligations in a person who knows, or has reasonable grounds to suspect, that a property is the proceeds of, or was, or is to be, used in connection with, drug dealing to disclose that knowledge or suspicion to a Suspicious Transaction Reporting Officer as soon as reasonably practicable.[504] Failure to do so constitutes an offence and attracts a fine of up to S$ 20,000.[505] The Act contains provisions to protect the identity of informers.[506]

The money laundering laws are strict in that the *mens rea* required can be less than actual knowledge—it is sufficient that the accused had 'reasonable grounds to believe' that the acts in question involved money laundering.[507] Parliament adopted this standard on the basis that proof of actual knowledge would be very difficult to produce.[508] There are also significant challenges involved in tracing particular funds back to a drug deal but the courts have held that proving that an asset is a proceed of crime does not necessarily require that a specific offence can be attributed to the funds in question. In *Ang Jeanette v Public Prosecutor*,[509] the Court held that in proving that certain property constitutes 'benefits of criminal conduct' it must:

> adduce some evidence linking the moneys in question with particular criminal conduct, i.e., some act that may constitute one or other of the offences (or classes thereof) listed in the Second Schedule, from which the moneys dealt with in an arrangement under s 44(1)(a) are derived, and in which the other person is engaged or had engaged, or from which he has benefited.[510]

[500] CSDC Act 2000 Rev Ed, s 43.
[501] CSDC Act 2000 Rev Ed, s 43.
[502] CSDC Act 2000 Rev Ed, s 46.
[503] CSDC Act 2000 Rev Ed, s 46(3).
[504] CSDC Act 2000 Rev Ed, s 39(1).
[505] CSDC Act 2000 Rev Ed, s 39(2).
[506] CSDC Act 2000 Rev Ed, s 40A.
[507] CSDC Act 2000 Rev Ed, ss 43, 47A.
[508] Wong Kan Seng, 'Second Reading Speech by Minister for Home Affairs Mr Wong Kan Seng Drug Trafficking (Confiscation of Benefits) (Amendment) Bill' (6 Jul 1999).
[509] [2011] 4 SLR 1.
[510] Ibid [58].

The CDSC Act also provides for the confiscation of benefits of drug dealing, including a presumption that unaccounted wealth is derived from drug dealing when assessing third party financial transactions.[511] It, likewise, imposes numerous obligations on financial institutions, such as production orders and 'know your customer rules'.[512] Under these rules, banks, financial institutions, insurers, brokers, securities dealers, investment advisors, trust companies and money changers have a duty to conduct due diligence and report. This applies where a person 'reasonably suspects' the property to be the proceeds of an offence.[513]

In addition to domestic money laundering efforts, Singapore participates in the Financial Action Task Force, an inter-governmental body established in 1989 to promote and develop both national and international policies to combat money laundering. It is also a member of the Asia Pacific Group on Money Laundering.

VII. CONCLUSION

Singapore has an adversarial common law system in which each party can lead and contest evidence. A system of precedent applies, and there are established and firmly enforced rules of evidence derived from British common law practice.

Singapore's legal system has, however, also developed its own characteristics. Many of these reflect the overwhelming political and social dominance of the People's Action Party (PAP), the party that has ruled since independence in 1965, and, in particular, its conservative social policies and tough 'law and order' approach. Singapore appears, for example, to have some of the most extensive and coercive rehabilitation regimes in the region. Offenders arrested for drug use can be compulsorily detained in a rehabilitation centre managed by the Singapore Prison Service. There is also an extensive program of post-release monitoring and supervision to minimise relapse into drug use.

Defence lawyers often push back against the PAP's position that the rights of the criminal defendants are always to be qualified by the interests of society in punishing criminal activity, particularly by invoking constitutional guarantees, for example the right to counsel. They have had limited success, however, given the far-reaching authority the state has accrued as a result of extensive regulatory reform, usually supported by the judiciary.

Accordingly, while Singapore's criminal law is practised in open court, complete with due process and procedural safeguards, substantial unreviewable power is retained by law enforcement authorities. In particular, decisions whether to prosecute, and for what crimes, are generally matters of the exercise of prosecutorial discretion.

This is also true of decisions about whether a defendant has provided sufficient assistance to the authorities to escape the death sentence that is otherwise mandatory

[511] CSDC Act 2000 Rev Ed, ss 4–4A.
[512] CSDC Act 2000 Rev Ed, ss 48H-K.
[513] CSDC Act 2000 Rev Ed, s 47A.

for most drug offences. Between 1991 and 2004, the small nation state reportedly executed more than 400 prisoners but it appears the current number of executions is markedly lower, with perhaps only five executions in the five years from 2009 to 2014.[514] The Constitution provides that clemency can be sought from the President, acting on the advice of the Cabinet. Clemency rates generally are the lowest here in Southeast Asia[515] and it is very unusual in drug trafficking cases. There is, in fact, little sign that Singapore will abandon its retentionist approach to capital punishment, notwithstanding criticism even within PAP.

Singapore's 'tough on drugs' rhetoric presents drugs as a serious social evil, for which severe punishment is appropriate, and this policy saturates its legal regime. It is unlikely that it will change in the near future.

[514] Note also Simon Rogers and Mona Chalabi, 'Capital Punishment', Data Blog (nd), https://docs.google.com/spreadsheet/ccc?key=0AonYZs4MzlZbdGJiUzRwTVhlM25DWDlPdjBmNURjOUE&hl=en#gid=0.

[515] Pascoe (n 388) 5.

5

Vietnam

This chapter examines criminal law and practice relevant to the regulation of drug use, cultivation and trade in contemporary socialist Vietnam.[1] It draws on law, policy statements, legal commentary and reports from court, procuracy and ministry websites, the Supreme People's Courts Annual Reports and Vietnamese legal journals to describe criminal law and criminal procedure law relevant to drugs cases. It is also based on interviews with twenty legal professionals, selected judgments and dossiers,[2] and media reporting.

Following a brief introduction to the Vietnamese legal system, the patterns of drug use in Vietnam and the history of drug regulation, the chapter describes drugs law and practice in relation to drug offences including: their investigation; evolving presumptions and defendants' rights; the jurisdiction of courts; trial practices; penalties; the appeals processes (including appeal, cassational appeals, and the 're-opening' procedure); types of clemency; and death penalty law and practice in Vietnam. It concludes with an account of the role of the media in Vietnamese trials.

At the time of writing, the Criminal Code and the Criminal Procedure Code[3] were under review, with changes expected in late 2015. As explained below in more detail, reduced use of the death penalty is one of the changes anticipated. The following discussion is, therefore, based on the 2003 Criminal Procedure Code and 1999 Penal Code but considers many of the debates over their amendments. A postscript setting out the major relevant changes is included at the conclusion of this chapter.

As in all matters, the Party-state in Vietnam leads the development of drugs policy and regulation. As a matter of course, initiatives are first articulated as policy by the Communist Party of Vietnam (CPV). Campaigns against social evils are an example of this, as are statements of new directions in the management of drugs. Following

[1] This study does not analyse imperial or colonial drugs policy and practice. For an excellent survey of drug use in Vietnam, see Nguyễn Thị Phương Hoa, 'Legislative Implementations by Vietnam of its Obligations under the United Nations Drug Control Convention' (Doctoral Thesis, University of Wollongong, 2007) 32–34.

[2] Criminal law judgments are not freely available in Vietnam, having been deemed 'sensitive'. General court reporting is also limited, albeit growing. Eighteen drug-related judgments were, however, obtained informally, and these involved a total of 5 foreigners and 50 Vietnamese defendants. Some judgments dealt with the trials of large numbers of defendants, up to 18 in one case. While these are only a fraction of the total number of drug trials for the years they cover, the sample does offer some insight into what arguments are raised in court and how courts state their decisions.

[3] Criminal Code No 15/1999/QH10 passed by the National Assembly on 21 December 1999 (the Criminal Code 1999); Criminal Procedure Code No 19/2003/QH11 passed by the National Assembly on 26 November 2003 (the Criminal Procedure Code 2003).

these pronouncements, the National Assembly, central government ministers or local provincial governments pass implementing legislation. These sources of legislation operate hierarchically, with the National Assembly having the greatest legislative authority, including the power to make and amend the constitution. At the lowest level are implementing circulars and resolutions issued by state institutions, either alone or in combination.

As a civil law country, Vietnam shares commonalities with the Indonesian legal system but has its own distinct practices. In particular, as a socialist country, Vietnam does not aspire to an independent court system, although it does currently aim to achieve a better-managed and more open, transparent and accessible one.[4] There is no system of precedent officially acknowledged but there is very strong leadership by the highest central court, the Supreme People's Court (SPC)[5] and current reforms indicate that at least some within the SPC are enthusiastic about adopting a system of guiding or published cases.[6] To date, however, discussion of the publication of court decisions has excluded publication of criminal law decisions, which are often regarded as inherently sensitive. The SPC nonetheless publishes Annual Reports setting out trial experience and providing guidelines on the adjudication of particular types of cases including drugs cases.[7] Further, recent surveys make plain that there is a high level of both formal and informal consultation by lower courts with higher courts about how to determine cases, as well as consultations with local government.[8]

The Vietnamese system of criminal law generally reflects the more 'inquisitorial or investigatory' qualities of civil law systems.[9] This is evident, for example, in the ongoing use of the dossier (*hồ sơ*) as the repository of the evidence amassed before trial, and the procuracy-supervised investigation of the matter by police. As shown below, there have, however, been some attempts to adapt the inquisitorial model in the recent past, particularly with respect to rights to counsel and rights to access and contest evidence.

[4] Pip Nicholson, 'Renovating Courts: The Role of Courts in Contemporary Vietnam' in Jiunn-rong Yeh and Wen-Chen Chang (eds), *Asian Courts in Context* (Cambridge, Cambridge University Press, 2015) 528–65.

[5] See Pip Nicholson, *Borrowing Court Systems: The Experience of Socialist Vietnam* (Leiden, Brill Academic Publishers, 2007).

[6] Socialist Republic of Vietnam (SRVN) Constitution 2013, Art 104(3) introduces the constitutional basis for the courts to lead the development of a system of model cases or case law, 'ensuring the uniform application of law in trial'. See also, Decision No 74/QD–TANDTC dated 31 December 2012 of the Supreme People's Court on Approval of Official Project for Development of Case Law of the Supreme People's Court in Vietnam.

[7] Nicholson, *Borrowing Court Systems*, 126–28, 260–63, 266–67.

[8] UNDP (United Nations Development Programme), *Report on the Survey of Needs of District People's Courts Nationwide* (Hanoi, Justice Publishing House, 2007), 250–52. This report notes that 68.5 per cent of District Court judges say they are influenced by Provincial Court judges. The Provincial Court judges, however, dispute this. It is also alleged that District Courts seek the advice of local government in 25 per cent of cases (at 305). See also UNDP, *Report on the Survey of the Reality of Local Court Governance in Vietnam* (2014), www.vn.undp.org/content/vietnam/en/home/library/democratic_governance/reality_of_local_court_governance_in_viet_nam.html.

[9] See William Burnham and Jeffrey Kahn, 'Russia's Criminal Procedure Code Five Years Out' (2008) 33 *Review of Central & East European Law* 1, 1.

A particular feature of the Vietnamese criminal justice system is the procuracy. Broadly speaking, this is an institution borrowed from the Soviet Union in 1960. The procuracy originally had enormous powers to supervise the observance of law by government agencies and their staff, economic and social organisations, people's armed units, and citizens.[10] Although this 'general supervision' power was removed by the 2001 amendments to the SRVN Constitution 1992,[11] the procuracy should not be confused with the office of public prosecutions typical of common law countries, as its role is much wider than that. In addition to being the prosecuting authority of the state, the procuracy is also the supervisor of judicial activities, including investigation and trial. It is additionally responsible for the enforcement of sentences and the operation of detention houses and prisons.[12] The procuracy also has a review function that continues to extend to the courts, raising concern about their independence. Despite repeated calls for further reduction of its functions, the procuracy has successfully resisted further dimunition of its authority and its powers were, in fact, reaffirmed in the most recent amendment of the SRVN Constitution in 2013.[13]

In short, Vietnam remains socialist and various aspects of its criminal justice system reflect their Soviet roots. As with most socialist legislation, offences are not merely set out in Vietnamese regulation but preceded by general provisions in the Criminal Code about the impact of offending on the socialist state and society. More particularly, legal institutions are led by the Party-state; courts are not independent; the procuracy arguably dominates the prosecution, trial and appeal processes; and legal counsel hold an inferior position to judges and the procuracy (although they are gradually expanding their role in criminal defence work). A lack of transparency permeates the system generally. While legal institutions are being reformed, Vietnam is not in transition to a rights-based, open, adversarial legal system—at least not yet.

It is critical to realise that there is also a law-practice gap in Vietnam. This is widely documented.[14] There are a range of plausible explanations for this phenomenon, ranging from lack of technical training for all actors (police, procurators, judges, and counsel), changes to the law and lack of access to laws, to deliberate corruption and manipulation of law by those in power, either for personal gain or political reasons. In this chapter, the applicable law is set out but with the caveat that there is much inconsistency in levels of compliance. Where compliance is generally absent or incomplete, it is noted.

This study is not focused on corruption of police, procuracy or judges. That said, the new Constitution 2013 provides that 'interference in the trials by judges and assessors by bodies, organisations, and individuals is strictly prohibited.'[15] This

[10] DRVN Constitution 1959, Art 105. This was reaffirmed by the DRVN Constitution 1980, Art 138 and the SRVN Constitution 1992, Art 137 (before its 2001 Amendment).

[11] Resolution No 51/2001/QH10 dated 25 December 2001 of the National Assembly on Amending and Supplementing a Number of Articles of the SRVN Constitution 1992, Art 1(23).

[12] Ibid.

[13] SRVN Constitution 2001, Art 107.

[14] UNDP, 'Appointed Counsel in Vietnamese Criminal Law and Practice' (Hanoi: UNDP, 2013) and UNDP, 'Appointed Counsel in Vietnamese Criminal Law and Practice' (Hanoi: UNDP, 2013).

[15] See SRVN Constitution 2013, Art 103(2).

very specific prohibition on interference with courts' work is a new addition to the Constitution. Arguably, its insertion ought to reduce 'interference' within trials, given the specific prohibition of corruption it contains, cast here as seeking to influence court work.

It will be interesting to see if, over time, it provokes greater scrutiny of the behaviour of judges and people's assessors (lay judges). In the context of drug prosecutions, it is suggested that the taking of bribes by either judges or people's assessors is, in fact, rare.[16] This may be attributable to the relative clarity of the evidence in those cases that proceed to trial (for example where defendants are caught red-handed) or to the well-understood moral opprobrium with which the Party-state, and society generally, treat drug offending in Vietnam. Counsel keep in close contact with judges (and the procuracy) during the progress of a case. This practice of close consultation, however, is not necessarily corrupt. In a system where even the trial date may have to be elicited through contact with the courts, counsel must ensure excellent working relationships with judges and court staff.

Finally, it is noted that there is little publication of judgments in Vietnam, although there have been increases in what is available, driven by the statements in Resolutions 48 and 49 about the need to publish judgments.[17] Initially, publication was limited to hardcopy, donor-supported publication of cassational review judgments.[18] More recently, the Supreme People's Court has commenced limited publication online of economic and civil judgments, searchable by date and location only.[19] Criminal judgments are still not publicly available in Vietnam.

I. DIMENSIONS OF THE DRUG PROBLEM

The so-called 'golden triangle' where Myanmar, Laos and Thailand meet is proximate to China, while the Mekong River, which flows through this area, continues into Vietnam. In 2015, senior official delegates from Cambodia, China,

[16] Interviewee 13 (14 August 2012).

[17] Resolution No 48 NQ/TW dated 24 May 2005 of the Politburo of the Vietnamese Communist Party on the Strategy for Development and Improvement of Vietnam's Legal System to the Year 2010 and Direction for the Period 2020 (Resolution 48). The translation used is that supported by the UNDP and published under VIE/02/015 in 2006); Resolution No 49 NQ/TW dated 2 June 2005 of the Central Committee of the Vietnamese Communist Party of Vietnam on the Judicial Reform Strategy (Resolution 49).

[18] See Pip Nicholson, 'Access to Justice in Vietnam: State Supply—Public Distrust' in John Gillespie and Albert Chen (eds), *Legal Development in East Asia: China and Vietnam Compared* (London, Routledge, 2010) 188–215. See also Tòa Án Nhân Dân Tối Cao, *Quyết định giám đốc thẩm của Hội đồng Thẩm phán Tòa án nhân dân tối cao 2006* [Supreme People's Court, Cassational review decisions of the Supreme People's Court Justice Council 2006] (Hanoi, 2008); Tòa Án Nhân Dân Tối Cao, *Quyết định giám đốc thẩm của Hội đồng Thẩm phán Tòa án nhân dân tối cao 2005* [Supreme People's Court, Cassational review decisions of the Supreme People's Court Justice Council 2005] (Hanoi, 2008); Tòa Án Nhân Dân Tối Cao, *Quyết định giám đốc thẩm của Hội đồng Thẩm phán Tòa án nhân dân tối cao 2003–2004, Quyển 1* [Supreme People's Court, Cassational review decisions of the Supreme People's Court Justice Council 2003–2004, Volume 1] (Hanoi, 2004); Tòa Án Nhân Dân Tối Cao, *Quyết định giám đốc thẩm của Hội đồng Thẩm phán Tòa án nhân dân tối cao 2003–2004, Quyển* 2 [Supreme People's Court, Cassational review decisions of the Supreme People's Court Justice Council 2003–2004, Volume 2] (Hanoi, 2004).

[19] This database is available at (Vietnamese) Supreme People's Court, toaan.gov.vn/portal/page/portal/tandtc/5477127?action=1.

Laos, Myanmar, Thailand and Vietnam met in Hanoi with officials from the United Nations Office on Drugs and Crime (UNODC) to restate their commitment to a regional plan to counter the development of the drug trade.[20] While this book does not offer a study of drugs trade patterns and players, or the role of diaspora communities,[21] it must be acknowledged that Vietnam's geographic position makes it a vitally significant regulator of the developing trade in precursors, as well as the long-standing trade in heroin and opium.[22]

Although this book is not a study of the health and social impacts of drug use,[23] it is useful to briefly consider the dimensions of drug use in Vietnam to understand how they inform the development of Vietnamese law and policy on drugs. Drug use trends are always speculative, at least in part, given that they report on a 'hidden population'[24] but a brief survey gives some sense of the ways in which drug use has changed over time in Vietnam. It also highlights the ways in which criminal laws struggle to cope with new forms of drug use.[25]

Vietnam's population is over 90 million, and there were reportedly more than 172,000 registered drug users in 2012, a rise of 8.5 per cent from mid-2011.[26] The United Nations Office on Drugs Use and Crime reports that the majority (96 per cent) of drug users in Vietnam are men,[27] with heroin the most commonly used drug, followed by amphetamine-type stimulants (ATS), opium and cannabis.[28] The use of

[20] UNODC, 'Mekong Region Officials Vow to Counter Drug Threat', 21 May 2015, www.unodc.org/unodc/en/frontpage/2015/May/mekong-region-officials-vow-to-counter-drug-threat.html?ref=fs3.

[21] Lê Thị Kim Vy, 'Understanding the Operational Structure of Southeast Asian Drug Trafficking Groups in Australia' (Doctoral Thesis, QUT, 2013) [Copy on file with authors]; Hai Thanh Lương, 'Based on the "Ethnic" Factor to Understanding the Distinct Characteristics of Cannabis Cultivation: A Review of Overseas Vietnamese Drug Groups' (2014) 3 *GSTF International Journal of Law and Social Sciences* 75, 75–85.

[22] See more generally, Ko-lin Chin and Sheldon X Zhang, *The Chinese Connection: Cross-border Drug Trafficking between Myanmar and China* (US Department of Justice, April 2007).

[23] See UNODC, 'World Drug Report 2014' (Vienna, United Nations, June 2014), www.unodc.org/wdr2014/, 2–13. See also Fifa Rahman and Nick Crofts (eds), *Drug Law Reform in East and Southeast Asia* (Lanham, Lexington Books, 2013).

[24] Rajat Ray, 'National Drug Abuse Situation in Vietnam—How Accurate are the Projections?' 103 *Addiction* 544, 544–55. Ray notes there is no population survey or time series studies informing data on Vietnam.

[25] Regrettably, there are no government-reported statistics for 2011 drug use (UNODC, 'Patterns and Trends of Amphetamine-Type Stimulants and Other Drugs: Asia and the Pacific 2012', 12 December 2012, www.unodc.org/southeastasiaandpacific/en/ats-2012.html).

[26] UNODC, 'Patterns and Trends of Amphetamine-Type Stimulants and Other Drugs: Challenges for Asia and the Pacific, November 2013, www.unodc.org/southeastasiaandpacific/en/ats-2013.html, 135. UNODC bases its findings on data supplied to the Drug Abuse Information Network for Asia and the Pacific (DAINAP) by Vietnamese drug control agencies and other institutions. This information is supplemented with other research gathered from government sources such as national reports and primary and secondary research, where available. UNODC also works in collaboration with the Vietnamese Standing Office on Drug Control, located within the Ministry of Public Security, and other government departments to produce estimates based upon the results of surveys and interviews. In preparing its 2010 report on ATS, the UNODC undertook a number of qualitative and quantitative surveys with samples drawn from cities across Vietnam including Hà Nội, Hồ Chí Minh City, Đà Nẵng, Hải Phòng, and Quảng Ninh. Interviews were also undertaken with police, hospital staff and owners/managers of popular nightclubs. Arrest, seizure and forensic data of 63 cities and provinces from 2005–10 for ATS was collected and analysed.

[27] UNODC, 'Patterns and Trends 2013'.

[28] Ibid.

cannabis, heroin and opium has decreased, while the use of ATS has increased significantly over the past decade.[29] Estimates suggest that synthetic drugs users account for just 6.5 per cent of all drug users.[30] Heroin has long been the most commonly used drug in Vietnam. In 2012, heroin users accounted for an estimated 85 per cent of all drug users aged between 30–45 years of age, representing 54 per cent of the total number of drug users.[31] Heroin is primarily administered via injection.[32]

ATS first appeared in Vietnam in the late 1990s, with use increasing markedly since 2003.[33] In 2010, ATS replaced opium as the second most commonly used drug type.[34] ATS is primarily found in cities, border areas and industrial zones[35] but use is increasing in rural areas.[36] The most popular types of ATS are ecstasy and crystalline methamphetamine (or 'ice').[37] ATS use is high among targeted risk groups (including sex workers, homosexuals, taxi and construction workers and wealthy nightclub goers). The use of ice ranged from 70–97 per cent across all risk groups in Hanoi and Ho Chi Minh City,[38] with the most common users of ecstasy being homosexual men (82 per cent) and nightclub goers (86 per cent).[39] Use is primarily recreational, as most of the persons surveyed reported having used different types of ATS several times a month (70 per cent).[40] A significantly smaller percentage (20 per cent) reported using ATS weekly.[41] In contrast, use of ATS remains very low among school and university students. Among school students, 1 per cent had used methamphetamine tablets, 1.6 per cent had used ecstasy, and 1.1 per cent had used ice.[42] University students reported even less ATS use, with 0.9 per cent reporting use of methamphetamine tablets, 0.7 per cent ecstasy and 0.4 per cent ice.[43]

Ketamine use has also increased as a result of the increased use of ATS, with which it is often taken.[44] Its use is, however, not yet widespread and seems to be largely restricted to nightclubs.[45]

29 UNODC, 'Patterns and Trends 2012', 116; UNODC, 'Patterns and Trends 2013', 136; US Department of State, *International Narcotics Control Strategy Report: Volume I Drug and Chemical Control* (March 2013), www.state.gov/j/inl/rls/nrcrpt/2013/, 318. The International Narcotics Control Strategy Report ('INCSR') obtains its estimates from official Vietnamese government data. By way of background, the INCSR is prepared by the Department of State for Congress in accordance with the 1961 American Foreign Assistance Act. It describes the efforts of key countries to attack all aspects of the international drug trade.

30 UNODC (n 27) 136.

31 There is a discrepancy between reports on heroin use. The UNODC report states 85 per cent of all drugs users use heroin, while the UNODC Report on Amphetamine–Type Stimulants in Vietnam indicates heroin is used by 85 per cent of those aged between 30–45 years of age.

32 UNODC (n 27) 136.

33 UNODC, 'Patterns and Trends 2012' 115.

34 UNODC (n 27) 136.

35 UNODC (n 33) 116.

36 Ibid.

37 Ibid.

38 Ibid.

39 Ibid.

40 Ibid.

41 Ibid.

42 Ibid.

43 Ibid

44 Ibid.

45 Ibid.

In the past few years, the Vietnamese government has reported an increase of international drug syndicate activity,[46] particularly via south-west air traffic.[47] It has highlighted the rising role of African-based operators in drug trafficking and sale networks in Vietnam's Southern provinces, especially in Ho Chi Minh City.[48] Police have also stated that cross-border trade is of particular significance in terms of the quantity of narcotics trafficked. In 2008, for example, police reported that 60–70 per cent of total confiscated drugs were seized in border provinces.[49] In 2012, Vietnam also reported a large amount of illicit drug trafficking along the land border routes (north-west, central-northern and south-west) allegedly orchestrated by foreign nationals and Vietnamese fugitives hiding abroad.[50]

State Responses to Drug Trade and Use

Imperial Vietnam condemned both drug use and its trafficking, and the death penalty was applied to traffickers.[51] Vietnamese accounts stress that the use of drugs (particularly opium) and trade in them radically increased after the arrival of the French. This is largely attributed to the colonial government's enthusiasm for taxes derived from the sale of opium.[52] Drugs at this time were grown in the northern, mountainous provinces, as had long been the case.

Before 1945, the French Penal Codes existed in each of the three colonial zones of Vietnam, and applied to French nationals and Vietnamese.[53] The French revised their Penal Code to replace the imperial Gia Long Code.[54] From 1945, southern Vietnam experienced an unstable administration of criminal justice as a result of the war.[55] With the escalation of the war, and continuing after the partition of the country in

[46] ASEAN Inter-Parliamentary Assembly (AIPA) Fact Finding Committee (AIFOCOM) to Combat the Drug Menace, 'Country Progress Report of Viet Nam: Prevention and Combat against Drug and Drug-related Crimes in the Period 2011–2013: Process and Outcomes', 11th Meeting, (12–16 May 2014, Vientiane, Lao People's Democratic Republic), www.na.gov.la/docs/AIPA/aifocom11/Doc_for_AIFOCOM/COUNTRY%20REPORT/(16)%20Annex%20R-%20Country%20Report%20of%20Vietnam.pdf, 7; ASEAN Inter-Parliamentary Assembly (AIPA) Fact Finding Committee (AIFOCOM), 'Country Progress Report of Vietnam' (8–12 July 2012, Yogyakarta, Indonesia) [1.1], The 9th Meeting, www.aipasecretariat.org/wp-content/uploads/2014/02/CP-Vietnam-Formatted.pdf.

[47] ASEAN Inter-Parliamentary Assembly (AIPA) Fact-Finding Committee (AIFOCOM) to Combat the Drug Menace: Annex O, 'Vietnam Country Report, Drug Situation in Vietnam in 2009 and the First Months of 2010', the 7th Meeting, 9 June 2010.

[48] AIPA AIFOCOM, 'Country Progress Report Vietnam', 2012, Yogyakarta.

[49] *Viet Nam News*, 'Drug Crime Fuelled by Foreigners, Expats' (5 January 2008), www.vietnamnews.vn/society/172605/drug-crime-fuelled-by-foreigners-expats.htm.

[50] AIPA AIFOCOM, 'Country Progress Report Vietnam', 2012, Yogyakarta.

[51] Nguyễn Thị Phương Hoa, 'Legislative Implementations' 32–34.

[52] Ibid 33.

[53] See Nicholson (n 7) 323–24. See also more generally MB Hooker, *Legal Pluralism: An Introduction to Colonial and Neo Colonial Laws* (Oxford, Clarendon Press, 1975) and MB Hooker, *A Concise Legal History of South-East Asia* (Oxford, Clarendon Press, 1978).

[54] Ibid.

[55] Ordinance No 4 dated 18 October 1949 relative to the Judiciary Organisation, including articles dealing with criminal procedure. See Ministry of Justice Vietnam, *The Legal System of Vietnam* (Saigon, 1967) 30–31. See also Harvey Smith et al, *Area Handbook for North Vietnam* (Washington DC, US Government Printing House, 1967) 409–26.

1956, policing was fragmented and highly localised,[56] although it is suggested work on a single criminal code began in 1962.[57] Commentators note that drug use by military personnel in the South was very high throughout the war years.[58] The Republic of Vietnam introduced a Penal Code in 1972 but with uniufication of the country in 1975, the northern system of drugs regulation applied.

In the northern Democratic Republic of Vietnam there were 'individual penal statutes' that criminalised smuggling and trafficking in narcotics.[59] More specifically, on 3 September 1945, a day after the Provisional Revolutionary Government of Vietnam declared its independence in the north, President Ho Chi Minh announced that the new revolutionary government 'strictly forbids opium smoking'.[60] Since that time, both Vietnamese policy and law on prevention and prosecution of drug offences have fluctuated, with periods of apparent inconsistency,[61] although a strict approach to drugs cultivation, storage and trade has been maintained officially since 1945.

Laws were passed early in the life of the new government to regulate opium smuggling.[62] Laws promulgated in the period 1945–87 also permitted the cultivation of opium but on condition that it was sold to state-run traders and tax levied on the basis of opium resin output.[63] Drug production is core to the socio-economic activities of ethnic minorities including the H'mong, who, as mentioned, are located in the North. Vietnamese commentators point out that the ethnic minorities are very poor and cultivate opium not only as a product for sale but also as a hunger suppressant

[56] Ibid pp 409–12.

[57] Smith et al, *Area Handbook* 421.

[58] Alfred McCoy, 'South Vietnam's Heroin Trade' in Alfred McCoy (ed), *The Politics of Heroin—CIA Complicity in the Global Drug Trade: Afghanistan, Southeast Asia, Central America, Columbia*, 2nd edn (New York, Lawrence Hill Books, 2003) 193, 222–26. See also Nguyễn Thị Phương Hoa (n 1) 33.

[59] John Quigley, 'Vietnam at the Legal Crossroads Adopts a Penal Code' (1988) 36 *American Journal of Comparative Law* 351, 351. See also on opium smuggling: Decree No 150/TTg dated 5 March 1952 of the Prime Minister; Decree No 580/TTg dated 15 September 1955 of the Prime Minister; Circular No 635/HS dated 29 March 1958 of the Ministry of Justice on Depositing for Illegal Purchase of Opium; and Circular No 33/VHH/HS dated 5 July 1958 of the Ministry of Justice on the Prosecution and Adjudication of Opium Smuggling Cases. These laws are set out in *The System of Criminal Laws—promulgated up to 31/12/1974*, 1974, unknown publishing house (in Vietnamese). The publication is, in turn, cited on Governmental Committee for Ethnic Minorities, the website on HIV/AIDS, Narcotics and Prostitution Evil Prevention, pcmt.ubdt.gov.vn/modules.php?name=CMS&op=details&mid=31.

[60] Hồ Chí Minh, 'Những nhiệm vụ cấp bách của Nhà nước Việt Nam Dân chủ Cộng hòa [Urgent duties of the Democratic Republic of Vietnam]' (3 September 1945), pcmt.ubdt.gov.vn/modules.php?name=CMS&op=details&mid=31.

[61] Governmental Committee for Ethnic Minorities, The Site on HIV/AIDS, Narcotics and Prostitution Evil Prevention, pcmt.ubdt.gov.vn/modules.php?name=CMS&op=details&mid=31.

[62] On opium smuggling: Decree No 150/TTg dated 05 March 1952 of the Prime Minister; Decree No 580/TTg dated 15 September 1955 of the Prime Minister; Circular No 635/HS dated 29 March 1958 of the Ministry of Justice on Depositing for Illegal Purchase of Opium; and Circular No 33/VHH/HS dated 5 July 1958 of the Ministry of Justice on the Prosecution and Adjudication of Opium Smuggling Cases. These laws are set out in *The System of Criminal Laws—promulgated up to 31/12/1974*, 1974, unknown publishing house (in Vietnamese). The publication is, in turn, cited on Governmental Committee for Ethnic Minorities (n 61).

[63] Governmental Committee for Ethnic Minorities (n 59). More particularly reference is made to Decree No 150/TTg dated 5 March 1952 of the Prime Minister and Decree No 225/TTg dated December 1952 of the Prime Minister. COMECON, the Council of Mutual Economic Assistance, also noted Vietnam was authorised to cultivate opium for pharmaceutical reasons.

and a stimulant at weddings, funerals and local festivals.[64] It was, and continues to be, used medicinally.[65] Commentators note that drug sales were encouraged by the leadership to earn foreign currency.[66] These regulations did not prohibit the use of narcotics—primarily opium at the time—notwithstanding Ho Chi Minh's call for an end to drug use.

The Criminal Code 1985, which applied to the whole of now-unified Vietnam, included only one drug-related provision, namely the 'organisation of the use of narcotic substances'. This carried a maximum punishment of five years imprisonment, and up to ten years if it 'entails serious consequences or constitutes a serious case of recidivism'.[67] In his analysis of this statute, Quigley argues it shows a 'strong influence' from both socialist China and the USSR, although he then details greater Soviet influence.[68] Quigley also notes that the French categorisation of crimes into '*crime* (more serious offences) and *delit* (less serious offences)', which did not appear in the Soviet Criminal Code, was adopted,[69] and that the categories and structures in the Vietnamese Code generally reflect those of continental criminal codes, not communist ones.[70] Quigley also argues one of the biggest changes brought about by the introduction of this Criminal Code 1985 was the elimination of punishment 'based on analogy'.[71] Put another way, after the introduction of the Criminal Code behaviour was not subject to criminal punishment unless specifically proscribed in the Code.

From 1987, the regulation of narcotics escalated, moving from the introduction of appeals for good behaviour to extensions and revisions of then limited drug-focussed laws. This move to regulate drugs was no doubt partially reflective of the official move to a law-based state, although that was not formally adopted until the 1991 Seventh Party Congress.[72] After 1986, the adoption of the *đổi mới* (literally 'renovation') policy, which allowed a transition to a socialist-oriented market economy, led the Party-state to revisit much of its legislation, including the 1985 Criminal Code.

More particularly, in 1987, the Secretariat of the Communist Party of Vietnam's Central Party Committee issued a Directive requesting Provincial Party Committees

[64] Nguyễn Thị Phương Hoa (n 1) 35.

[65] Ibid.

[66] Christopher S Wren, 'China Says Vietnam Grows Opium to Earn Funds', *The New York Times* (26 July 1983), 3. See also, Toi Van Doan and David Chanoff, 'Vietnam Turns to Narcotics to Pay its Bills', *The Wall Street Journal* (8 March 1984), 30.

[67] Criminal Code No 17-LCT/HĐNN7 passed by the National Assembly on 27 June 1985 ('Criminal Code 1985'), Art 203.

[68] Quigley, 'Vietnam at the Legal Crossroads' 352.

[69] Ibid 353.

[70] Ibid. More specifically, criminal responsibility is articulated up-front, together with the state of mind relevant to all types of crime (all require some form of *mens rea*), penalties are related to particular offences, and rules are set out for complicity. Liability for 'attempting' a crime is also included.

[71] Ibid 354. Quigley refers to Art 24(1) of Ordinance No 149-LCT dated 21 October 1970 of the Standing Committee of the National Assembly on the Repression of Infringements on Socialist Property. This stated that 'As for infringements against socialist property not foreseen in this decree-law, the dispositions of this decree-law shall be applied by analogy.'

[72] For a discussion of the Seventh Party Congress, see John Gillespie, 'Concepts of Law in Vietnam: Transforming Statist Socialism' in Randall Peerenboon (ed), *Asian Discourses of the Rule of Law* (London & New York, Routledge Curzon, 2004) 46.

and Provincial People's Committees to campaign to persuade people not to grow poppy plants or inject or smoke poppy products, and to prevent trade in poppy products.[73] Moving to formalise these moral appeals, the National Assembly amended the Criminal Code on 28 December 1989 to include a new Art 96a. This regulated the crime of illegally 'manufacturing, storing, trafficking, or transporting narcotic substances', and applied a range of penalties, including capital punishment, for proven offences. Subsequently, the then Ministerial Council (today called 'the Government'), issued a Directive that state-supported bodies (including officials generally, Provincial People's Committees, the Vietnam Fatherland Front Committee, the Vietnam Women's Union, the Ho Chi Minh Communist Youth Union, and the Farmers' Association) should 'mobilise the Vietnamese people to desist from involvement with drugs'.[74]

From that period on, Vietnam promulgated an increasing amount of regulation on drug-related crimes. The Constitution of 1992 saw a new provision introduced in the section on 'health protection' stating that 'it is strictly forbidden to produce, transport, deal in, store, and use unlawfully opium and other narcotics'.[75] Following a 1992 constitutional amendment, the government introduced a resolution detailing strategies to prevent and control drug use, and a social campaign against drugs was launched in 1998.[76] The timing of these reforms is consistent with Vietnam's accession to the three United Nations Drug Control Conventions in 1997: the Single Convention on Narcotic Drugs 1961; the Convention on Psychotropic Substances 1971; and the Convention Against Illicit Trafficking of Narcotic Drugs and Psychotropic Substances 1988[77] (all discussed in Chapter 2).

On 26 March 2008, the Politburo issued a policy directive on the 'fight against' drugs.[78] On 27 June 2011, a new National Strategy, drafted by the Ministry of Public Security, announced plans to reduce drug use by 30–40 per cent, with 70 per cent of communes to be drug-free by 2030.[79] In October 2011, the Ministry of Interior issued a Decision comprising a Plan for the Implementation of the National Strategy for Prevention, Fighting, and Control of Drugs in Vietnam to 2020, extending out to 2030.[80] In April 2014, the Politburo issued a request to Party committees,

[73] Directive No 13/CT-TW dated 30 August 1987 of the Secretariat Committee of the Central Committee of the Vietnamese Communist Party; Governmental Committee for Ethnic Minorities (n 59).

[74] Directive No 99/CT dated 8 April 1991 of the Council of Ministers on Propagandising the People not to Plant Marijuana.

[75] SRVN Constitution 1992, Art 61.

[76] Resolution No 06/CP dated 29 January 1993 of the Government on Improving the Prevention and Control of Drugs; Decision No 139/1998/QD-TTg dated 31 July 1998 of the Prime Minister Approving the 1998–2000 Plan on Drug Prevention and Fight.

[77] Nguyễn Thị Phương Hoa (n 1).

[78] Directive No 21-CT/TW dated 26 March 2008 of the Vietnamese Communist Party on Continuing to Promote Leading and Directing Prevention, Fighting, and Control of Drugs in the New Context.

[79] Simon Baldwin, 'Emerging from a Black Box' in Fifa Rahman and Nick Crofts (eds), *Drug Law Reform in East and Southeast Asia* (Lanham, Lexington Books, 2013) 211–19. See also Decision No 1001/QD-TTg dated 27 June 2011 of the Prime Minister on Approval of the National Strategy for Prevention, Fighting, and Control of Drugs in Vietnam to 2020 with the Vision to 2030.

[80] Decision No 1803/QD-BNV dated 24 October 2011 of the Ministry of Internal Affairs on the Issuance of the Plan on Implementation of the National Strategy for Prevention, Fighting, and Control of Drugs in Vietnam to 2020 with the Vision to 2030.

governments and mass organisations to continue the fight against drugs and identify 'focal tasks' to be carried out.[81] While there has been escalating momentum to regulate drugs over the last ten years, use of narcotics was decriminalised in 2010 and the Constitution was amended to reflect this change in 2013, with the prohibition on drug use contained in Art 61 of the SRVN Constitution 1992 removed. Article 38 of the SRVN Constitution 2013 still provides, however, that '[a]ny acts threatening the life and health of other people are strictly prohibited'. This remains the basis of Vietnam's generally robust anti-drug laws, although they no longer target drug use.

As we shall see, court decisions have, unsurprisingly, reflected these anti-drugs policies, which, as mentioned, emanate first from the Communist Party and are then taken up by organs of the state. In 1999, the Supreme People's Court, which sits at the apex of the Vietnamese court system and has a duty to guide lower courts, requested that all courts settle drug-related cases strictly in accordance with the law and contribute to the battle against drugs:

> ...after the Government's Resolution 06/CP dated 29 Jan 1993 on improving the prevention and control of drugs, the SPC has instructed all courts to implement it. [...] After the Prime Minister issued an official letter to open a campaign against drugs in 1998, the tribunal sector has actively responded though its adjudication activities [...] All courts consider drug crimes to be key and serious cases and cooperate actively with Police and Prosecution, also receiving support from local governments.[82]

Later in the same report the SPC noted:

> Last year, the courts severely sanctioned crimes relating to drugs. [...] Most courts have refused to suspend sentences where the accused has committed such a crime.[83]

In 2000, the SPC reaffirmed its view that drugs cases should be dealt with severely:

> The drug-related cases increase day by day and are a high proportion of all criminal cases handled by all courts. The tribunal sector is determined to handle these narcotic criminal cases severely. All courts need seriously to review errors and the wrong application of laws in the adjudication of narcotic-related crimes in order to strictly apply sanctions in narcotic-related crimes. [...] In the settlement of drug-related cases, all local courts should co-operate actively with Police and Prosecution, receive support from local governments, and overcome financial difficulties to organise mobile trials. [...] In general, all courts have sanctioned severely all narcotic-related crimes ... SPC has instructed all courts to quickly bring all big drug-related cases to trial for propaganda.[84]

The SPC's recent annual reports have not explicitly detailed how drugs cases should be handled, in some cases merely exhorting court personnel to do so with severity.[85]

[81] Conclusion No 95/KL-TW dated 2 April 2014 of the Politburo of the Vietnamese Communist Party on Continuing to Implement Politburo Directive No 21-CT/TW on Continuing to Promote Leading and Directing Prevention, Fighting, and Control of Drugs in the New Context.

[82] SPC's Annual Report of 1999, 14.

[83] Ibid 15. The same sentiment to avoid suspended sentences was restated in the following year. See SPC's Annual Report of 2000, 41.

[84] SPC's Annual Report of 2000, 41–42. See also SPC's Annual Report of 2001, 59–60.

[85] See, for example, SPC's Annual Report of 2011, 3; SPC's Annual Report of 2012, 4; SPC's Annual Report of 2013, 5; and SPC's Annual Report of 2014, 5.

This is intended as an exhortation to the lower courts to abide by an anti-drugs policy and not suspend sentences that ought to be imposed by law. The court journal has long been a forum in which the SPC sets out its policy and directs court propaganda (*tuyên truyền*) activity.[86]

Statistics for Crime and Drug Offences

By way of background, court criminal case numbers have grown marginally across time, with 91.7 cases per 100,000 of the population in 1999, rising to 93.88 in 2013.[87] Regrettably, there are no official court reports on the number of drugs cases publicly available. Data have, however, been obtained by Vietnamese researchers

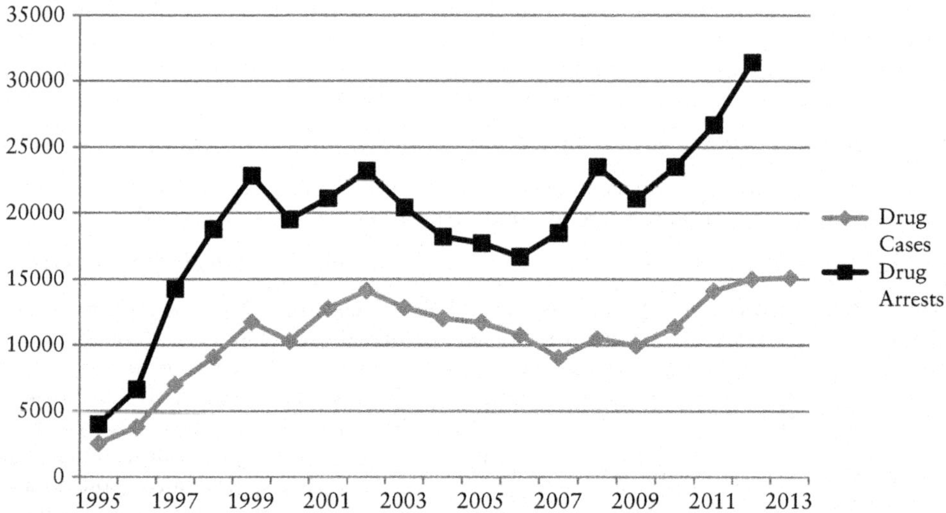

Figure 2: Drug-related Cases and Arrests in Vietnam (1995–2013)[88]

[86] See Nicholson (n 7) 129–32, 267–79.

[87] Source for Population Numbers: World Bank, *Total Population*, data.worldbank.org/indicator/SP.POP.TOTL.

[88] Nguyễn Thị Phương Hoa (n 1) 41–42. Dr Nguyễn's data has been augmented by SPC report data for the year 2010 and 2011; Supreme People's Procuracy, Criminal Statistics Bureau, 'Annual Statistics 2007–2013'; ASEAN Inter-Parliamentary Assembly Fact Finding Committee (AIFOCOM) 'Country Progress Report, Vietnam (2009–2011)' [Copies on file with author].

from the Standing Office of Drug Control and we have combined them with data from the UNODC and the Supreme People's Procuracy (see Figure 2).

The data reveal that the number of drugs arrests increased significantly, by 7 per cent in 2006 and 10.8 per cent in 2007.[89] The UNODC also reports an increase in the number of drug-related arrests in Vietnam from 26,680 in 2011 to 31,412 in 2012, an increase of 17 per cent.[90] The rate of drug-related arrests continues to increase even after use was decriminalised in 2009.

Foreigners' Participation in Drug Crimes

Official statistics on drug-offence arrests involving foreigners are not routinely reported but, according to one source, in 2009, the Counter-Narcotics Division of the Police investigated 45 drug cases involving a total of 125 foreign suspects.[91] While this is only around 0.34 per cent of the 13,219 cases investigated by the counter-narcotics police in that year, authorities have emphasised that cases with a foreign aspect are generally far more complex.[92] Recent foreign arrests for drug offences in Vietnam have involved people from Thailand, Cambodia, the Philippines, Indonesia, China, Burma, Nigeria, Australia, the USA, Russia, and Canada.[93] Another source of data for the period 2008 to 2010, suggests there were 90 criminal cases relating to foreigners, some of which had multiple defendants. One hundred and eighty eight defendants in all were prosecuted in these cases, of which 127 were foreigners. The breakdown of foreigners by country involved in drugs prosecutions over this 3-year period is supposedly 49 Laotians; 31 Chinese; 15 Cambodians; 13 Nigerians; 13 Australians; and 3 people from each of the Philippines, Zimbabwe, the Czech Republic, and the United States.[94]

89 SPC's Annual Report of 2006, 2 and SPC's Annual Report of 2007, 3.

90 UNODC (n 27) 137. The 2012 data upon which UNODC relies is not disaggregated by drug-type, gender or nationality.

91 ASEAN Inter-Parliamentary Assembly (AIPA) Fact Finding Committee (AIFOCOM) to Combat the Drug Menace: Annex O, 'Vietnam Country Report, Drug Situation in Vietnam in 2009 and the First Months of 2010', 7th Meeting, 9 June 2010.

92 *Viet Nam News*, 'Drug Crime Fuelled by Foreigners, Expats'.

93 This information was obtained from a survey of Vietnamese media on drug arrests since 2010, drawing upon *Tuoi Tre News* and *Vietnam News*. See also, AIPA, 'Country Progress Report of Viet Nam Prevention and Combat against Drug and Drug-Related Crimes between 2010 and 2012: Process and Outcomes' (2014), www.aipasecretariat.org/wp-content/uploads/2014/03/Country-Report_Vietnam.pdf.

94 Supreme People's Procuracy, 'Viện kiểm sát nhân dân tối cao: Kiến nghị Bộ Công an về việc quản lý người nước ngoài tại Việt Nam [The supreme people's procuracy: Suggestion to Ministry of Public Security in relation to the management of foreigners in Vietnam]' (2 August 2011), Viện kiểm sát nhân dân tối cao (Việt Nam) [(Vietnamese) Supreme People's Procuracy], www.vksndtc.gov.vn/tin-chi-tiet-1995.

Drug Use and Detention

As mentioned, drug use was a crime in Vietnam until 2009,[95] and a system of compulsory detention of users operated.[96] The applicable law authorised urine testing for drug addiction and enabled the temporary consignment of drug addicts and prostitutes without a stable residence to medical treatment establishments.[97] Apart from this provision for urine testing, there is no other legal document providing for compulsory testing for 'drug concentration in urine' or by other methods.

The 2008 amendment to the Law on Drug Prevention and Control encourages individuals, families, agencies and organisations to arrange voluntary detoxification for drug addicts.[98] Drug addicts who are 18 years or older and remain addicted to drugs after having been subject to education measures within their commune, ward or township, or those who have not been subject to this measure but have no stable residence, remain subject, however, to compulsory detoxification.[99] In addition, measures for post-detoxification management are governed by law.[100] Human Rights Watch reports shocking abuse of human rights in detention centres, for example, through forced labour.[101]

II. NARCOTIC-RELATED CRIMES

As indicated above, the first Criminal Code of Vietnam, introduced ten years after the 1975 unification of the country, provided for just one narcotic-related crime, namely 'organisation of the use of narcotic substances'.[102] The 1989 amendment of the Code introduced one more crime: 'illegally producing, storing, trafficking, and transporting narcotic substances'.[103] This criminalisation of drug use occurred in the

[95] Law No 37/2009/QH12 passed by the National Assembly on 19 June 2009 on Amending and Supplementing a Number of Articles of the Criminal Code 1999, Art 1(36) ('Law No 37/2009').

[96] See Guidance No 1160/VKSTC_KSDTTA dated 18 May 2001 of the Supreme People's Procuracy on Implementation of the Law on Drug Prevention and Control.

[97] Decree No 43/2005/ND-CP dated 05 April 2005 of the Government Providing the Temporary Consignment of Drug Addicts, Prostitutes without Stable Residential Places to Medical Treatment Establishments and on testing see Art 10.

[98] Law No 16/2008/QH12 passed by the National Assembly on 3 June 2008 on Amending and Supplementing a Number of Articles of Law on Drug Prevention and Control, Art 1(25)(3) ('Law on Drug Prevention and Control').

[99] Law No 15/2012/QH13 passed by the National Assembly on 20 June 2012 on Administrative Sanctions, Art 96(1).

[100] Circular No 33/2010/TT-BLĐTBXH dated 1 November 2010 of the Ministry of Labour, Invalid and Social Affairs Guiding a Number of Articles of Decree No 94/2009/ND-CP dated 22 December 2009 of the Government Implementing the Law on Drug Prevention on Management of Drug Detoxification ('Circular 33') and Decree No 94/2009/ND-CP dated 22 December 2009 of the Government Implementing the Law on Drug Prevention on Management of Drug Detoxification ('Decree 94').

[101] Human Rights Watch, *The Rehab Archipelago Forced Labour and Other Abuses in Drug Detention Centres in Southern Vietnam* (Report, 2011).

[102] Criminal Code 1985, Art 203.

[103] Criminal Code 1985 as amended by Law No 30-LCT/HĐNN8 dated 28 December 1989, Art 96(a).

face of a long history of legal use, and between 1985 and 1999, legislation relating to drug offences increased significantly, reflecting a policy change and delivering much closer regulation of drugs.

It was not until the Criminal Code 1999 entered into force, however, that a fuller set of narcotic-related offences were introduced. Chapter XVIII of that Code contained prohibitions on: (1) growing opium poppy and other kinds of plant bearing narcotic substance;[104] (2) illegal production of narcotic substances;[105] (3) illegally stockpiling, transporting, trading in or appropriating narcotic substances;[106] (4) stockpiling, transporting, trading in or appropriating pre-substances for use in the illegal production of narcotic substances;[107] (5) manufacturing, stockpiling, transporting and/or trading in means and/or tools used in the illegal production or use of narcotic substances;[108] (6) organising the illegal use of narcotic substances;[109] (7) harbouring the illegal use of narcotic substances;[110] (8) illegal use of narcotic substances;[111] (9) forcing, inducing other persons into illegal use of narcotic substances;[112] and (10) breaching regulations on management and use of addictive drugs or other narcotic substances.[113] As mentioned earlier, the offence of drug use has recently been repealed.[114] By way of background, the Criminal Code 1999 stipulated the crime of 'illegal use of narcotics'[115] but did not explain the circumstances in which this crime would be made out. Inter-circular 17, which provides details on drug offences, offered no further guidance on the meaning of 'use'.[116]

Definition of 'Narcotic Substance'

The term 'narcotic substance' (*chất ma tuý*, with narcotics translated as *ma tuý*) has been widely used in various Vietnamese legal instruments but was not clearly defined until recently. The Criminal Code 1985, for example, was silent on its definition, although a later Joint Circular listed opium, cannabis, heroin, codeine, pentanyl and pethidine as narcotic substances.[117] The Criminal Code 1999 likewise did not further define narcotics. The Law on Drug Prevention and Control 2000 stipulates that

[104] Criminal Code 1999, Art 192.
[105] Ibid Art 193.
[106] Ibid Art 194.
[107] Ibid Art 195.
[108] Ibid Art 196.
[109] Ibid Art 197.
[110] Ibid Art 198.
[111] Ibid Art 199.
[112] Ibid Art 200.
[113] Ibid Art 201.
[114] Law No 37/2009.
[115] Criminal Code 1999, Art 199(8).
[116] Inter-circular No 17/2007/TTLT-BCA-VKSNDTC-TANDTC-BTP dated 24 December 2007 of the Ministry of Public Defence, the Supreme People's Procuracy, the Supreme People's Court and the Ministry of Justice Providing Guidelines for Application of a Number of Articles in Chapter XVIII 'Crimes Related to Narcotic Drugs' of the Criminal Code 1999 ('Inter-circular 17').
[117] See Joint Circular No 07/TTLN dated 5 December 1992 of the Ministry of Internal Affairs, the Supreme People's Procuracy and the Supreme People's Court Guiding the Application of Arts 96(a) and 203 of the Criminal Code 1985, cited in Nguyễn Thị Phương Hoa (n 1) 79.

'narcotic substances are addictive substances, centripetalneurotropic substances, prescribed in the lists promulgated by the Government.'[118] 'Addictive substances' are defined as 'neurogenic or neurosuppressible substances easily causing addiction to users'[119] and 'centripetalneurotropic substances' are 'those which stimulate or inhibit nerves or cause illusion, [and] may cause addiction to users if they are used repeatedly for many times.'[120]

Until recently, the Vietnamese legal definition of 'narcotic substances' was thus an indirect one, based on the definitions of 'addictive substances' and 'centripetalneurotropic' substances. In July 2013, however, the government issued a list of narcotic substances and pre-substances.[121] This list divides narcotic substances and pre-substances into four groups: (i) narcotics that are absolutely prohibited in medical and social life, the use of which in scientific research and criminal investigation must comply with special regulations of competent authority; (ii) narcotics that are strictly used in scientific research, criminal investigation or in the medical field as regulated by competent authority; (iii) centripetalneurotropic substances which are used in scientific research, criminal investigation or in the medical field as regulated by the competent authority; and (iv) pre-substances. With the promulgation of the list in Decree 82, narcotic substances and pre-substances were listed and re-organised.[122] The names and scientific names of all listed substances were also revised to be consistent with international legal nomenclature,[123] and Chemical Abstract Service numbers based on regulations of the International Narcotics Control Board were added as well. The list still fails, however, to distinguish between addictive substances and centripetalneurotropics, creating an inconsistency with the general definition provided in the Law on Narcotics Prevention and Control.

[118] Law on Drug Prevention and Control, Art 2(1). See also Inter-circular 17, Art 1(1).

[119] Law on Drug Prevention and Control, Art 2(2).

[120] Ibid Art 2(3).

[121] Decree No 82/2013/ND-CP dated 19 July 2013 of the Government Promulgating the List of Narcotic Substances and Pre-substances ('Decree 82').

[122] Before Decree 82 was promulgated, narcotic substances and pre-substances were listed in a number of documents, namely, Decree No 67/2001/ND-CP dated 1 October 2001 of the Government Promulgating the List of Narcotic Substances and Pre-substances ('Decree 67'); Decree No 133/2003/ND-CP dated 6 November 2003 of the Government Adding a Number of Substances to the List of Narcotics and Pre-substances, Issued together with Decree No 67/2001/ND-CP dated 1 October 2001 of the Government ('Decree 133'); Resolution No 17/2011/ND-CP dated 22 February 2011 of the Government Adding and Modifying Common Names and Scientific Names of a Number of Substances on the List of Narcotic Substances and Pre-substances Issued together with the Decree No 67/2001/ND-CP dated 1 October 2001 of the Government; and Decree No 163/2007/ND-CP dated 12 November 2007 of the Government Amending and Supplementing Decree No 67/2001/ND-CP of 1 October 2001.

[123] For more detail about the list of narcotic substances and pre-substances promulgated by Decree 82 see Tra Vinh Public Security, 'Một số điểm mới trong việc triển khai thực hiện Nghị định số 82/2013/NĐ-CP ngày 19/7/2013 của Chính phủ [Some changes in implementing Decree No 82/2013/ND-CP dated 19 July 2013 of the Government]', www.travinh.gov.vn/wps/portal/congan/!ut/p/c0/04_SB8K8xLLM9MSSzPy8xBz9CP0os3gDIws_QzcPIwN3CwNLA0dnD-dQY5MwYwsXU_2CbEdFANFfNB4!/?WCM_PORTLET=PC_7_028N1FH20GNG80ACH2VG1I30K0_WCM&WCM_GLOBAL_CONTEXT=/wps/wcm/connect/Cong%20an/cong+an+tra+vinh/phong+chong+toi+pham+va+bai+tru+te+nan+xa+hoi/phong+chong+toi+pham+ma+tuy/mot+so+diem+moi+trong+viec+trien+khai+thuc+hien+nghi+dinh+so+82.2012.nd.cp+ngay+19.7.2012+cua+chinh+phu.

Basis for Criminal Liability

Vietnamese criminal law has four constituent elements: object, subject, physical elements, and mental elements. The analysis of any crime traverses each of these components and all must be present before a crime can be made out. The 'object' refers to the aim of the crime (murder, drug trafficking for example). The 'subject' is a reference to the perpetrator of the crime. The 'physical elements' of a crime can be formal or material, as discussed below. Finally, there is a need to consider the mental elements of a crime: intention and lack of intention, and the relevance of each to the crime under scrutiny (also discussed below).

Capacity and Drug Offences

To be convicted of a narcotic-related crime, the defendant must have full capacity for criminal liability and have reached the age of criminal liability as stipulated by the Criminal Code 1999. Accordingly, Art 12 provides that '[p]ersons aged a full 16 years or older shall have to bear criminal liability for all crimes they commit,' and '[p]ersons aged a full 14 years or older but under 16 years shall have to bear criminal liability for very serious crimes intentionally committed or especially serious crimes.'[124] Under the Criminal Code 1999, crimes are classified into less serious crimes, serious crimes, very serious crimes, and especially serious crimes.[125] The seriousness of a crime is determined by the penalties and the range of imprisonment is: up to three years; up to seven years; up to 15 years; over 15 years; and life imprisonment or capital punishment.[126] Additionally, a defendant has no capacity for criminal liability 'while suffering from mental disease or a disease which deprives them of their capability to be aware of or to control their acts.'[127]

The age of criminal liability is an issue currently under debate as part of the ongoing review of the Criminal Code. It is currently proposed that, rather than rely on the terms 'very serious crimes intentionally committed or especially serious crimes', the Code should clearly identify those crimes for which persons aged between 14 and 16 years should bear full criminal liability,[128] to improve the transparency of the Code and increase its capacity to deter.[129] Specifically, it is suggested that Art 12(2) of the Criminal Code be revised as follows:

> [p]ersons aged a full 14 years or older but under 16 years shall have to bear criminal liability for the following crimes: [....] unlawful manufacturing of narcotic substances (Article 249(2)–(4), unlawful stockpiling of narcotics (Article 250(2)–(4),

124 Criminal Code 1999, Art 12.
125 Criminal Code 1999, Art 8(2).
126 Criminal Code 1999, Art 8(3).
127 Criminal Code 1999, Art 13.
128 Drafting Committee, 'Bản Thuyết Minh Chi Tiết Về Dự Thảo Bộ Luật Hình Sự (Sửa Đổi) [Detail explanation about the Draft (Amended) Criminal Code]', duthaoonline.quochoi.vn/DuThao/Lists/DT_DUTHAO_LUAT/View_Detail.aspx?ItemID=526&TabIndex=2&TaiLieuID=1949, pt I(9).
129 Ibid.

unlawful transporting of narcotics (Article 251(2)–(4), unlawful trading of narcotics (Article 252(2)–(4), unlawful appropriating of narcotics (Article 253(2)–(4).[130]

It remains to be seen if this proposal will be approved, as opponents argue that it would be too narrow and may, in some cases, allow serious criminals to escape appropriate punishment.

Physical Elements

As mentioned, the Vietnamese Criminal Code divides the physical element of drug crimes into two kinds: 'formal crimes' (*tội phạm có cấu thành hình thức*) and 'material crimes' (*tội phạm có cấu thành vật chất*).[131] With formal crimes, the legislature punishes particular conduct or behaviour regardless of what results from it. Put another way, harm resulting from the alleged criminal act does not need to be made out. An example of a formal crime is the manufacturing of drugs. The mere fact of manufacture establishes the offence. Conversely, for material crimes, the legislature criminalises 'ways of being' (*hành vi khách quan*), that is, behaviour that presents a risk of serious harm to other people or for property, when it is coupled with realisation or causation of a harm.[132] If causation can be demonstrated, the actor is subject to criminal liability. For example, if 'A' stabs a man and death results, murder is made out. In addition, material crimes must be completed. Put another way, if 'A' stabs a man and he does not die, the crime of murder is incomplete. A different offence of stabbing would be made out but not murder.

Under Vietnamese law, narcotic-related crimes are formal. Thus, a crime will be complete if there is an act committed that is of a kind described in the Criminal Code 1999, regardless of the consequences. Consequences, however, are relevant to sentencing (see below).[133]

Mental Elements

Under the Vietnamese Criminal Code, 'intention' (*cố ý*), can be either 'direct' (*trực tiếp*) or 'indirect' (*gián tiếp*). One Vietnamese criminal law expert suggests that direct intention reflects 'actual intention' and indirect intention resembles 'constructive intention' as those terms are understood in other jurisdictions.[134] Drug crimes require direct intention.[135]

[130] See Draft (Amended) Criminal Procedure Code, duthaoonline.quochoi.vn/DuThao/Lists/DT_DUTHAO_LUAT/View_Detail.aspx?ItemID=561&LanID=1070&TabIndex=1 ('Draft (Amended) Criminal Procedure Code').

[131] Trần Minh Hưởng, *Bình luận khoa học Bộ luật Hình sự (đã được sửa đổi, bổ sung)* [Comments on Criminal Code (amendment)] (Hong Duc Publishing House, 2011) 25.

[132] Ibid 26.

[133] Ibid 402.

[134] Nguyễn Thị Phương Hoa (n 1) 155.

[135] Nguyễn Thị Phương Hoa (n 1) 162.

Drug Crimes

'Cultivating' is not defined in the Vietnamese Criminal Code but the word is understood in a broad sense. It is said to cover a range of activities from 'preparation of the soil before planting' to 'harvesting.'[136]

The precise acts that constitute 'manufacturing' are also not elucidated in the Criminal Code. However, it is defined to, again, include a very broad range of activities involved in the production of narcotics, such as the extraction of the drug from plant parts, compounding and refinement processes.[137] The offence applies in relation to the exhaustive list of controlled substances set out in the newly introduced Decree 82.[138] To be criminally liable, the offender must, in addition to being involved in the physical act of manufacturing, know that he or she is participating in the manufacture of illicit substances.[139] It is irrelevant whether the ultimate purpose of that manufacturing is to produce drugs for personal consumption or for trafficking.[140] As shown below, the penalties that apply vary depending on the quantity of drugs manufactured.[141]

As well as the crime of manufacturing narcotics, the Criminal Code also creates distinct offences in relation to precursor substances, equipment and tools used in the production of illicit drugs. The unlawful stockpiling, transporting, trading or appropriating of precursors for the manufacture of narcotics constitutes a criminal offence.[142] Criminal liability also applies to the unlawful manufacturing, stockpiling, transporting, and trading or appropriating of equipment or tools that are to be used in the illicit manufacture of drugs.[143]

'Stockpiling' can only be established where the offender either has direct physical control over the objects in question or the power to exercise control over the objects at a later stage. It is, therefore, not necessary that the immediate physical location of the stockpiled objects be under the direct control of the accused. Knowledge and control are sufficient to demonstrate criminal liability.[144]

'Transporting' is the act of carrying or moving the objects in question between locations and can include both domestic and international movement. Cross-border

136 Nguyễn Thị Phương Hoa (n 1) 156.

137 Inter-circular 17, s II(2)(2)(1). See Nguyễn Thị Phương Hoa, 'Drug-Related Crimes under Vietnamese Criminal Law: Sentencing and Clemency in Law and Practice' (ALC Briefing Paper, No 2, 2014) 8.

138 Decree 82 2013.

139 See, eg, Nguyễn Ngọc Hòa, *Giáo trình Luật Hình sự Việt Nam* [Textbook on criminal law] (Ha Noi, Police Publishing House, 2001) 498.

140 Nguyễn Thị Phương Hoa, 'Drug-Related Crimes under Vietnamese Criminal Law', 12.

141 Criminal Code 1999, Arts 193(1),(2(e), 3(c) and 4(d).

142 Ibid Art 195.

143 Ibid Art 196.

144 See Inter-circular 17, s II(3)(3)(2). See also Đinh Văn Quế, *Bình luận khoa học Bộ luật Hình sự, phần các tội phạm về ma túy* [Scientific commentary on the Criminal Code, crime part: drug-related crimes] (Ho Chi Minh, Ho Chi Minh Publishing House, 2004) 86; Trần Văn Luyện, *Trách nhiệm hình sự đối với các tội phạm về ma túy* [Criminal liability for drug-related crimes] (Hanoi, National Politics Publishing House, 1998) 55; Trần Minh Hưởng, *Tìm hiểu bộ luật hình sự nước Cộng Hòa Xã Hội Chủ Nghĩa Việt Nam: Bình luận và chú giải* [Studying the criminal code of Vietnam: Comments and annotations] (Hanoi, Public Security Publishing House, 2002) 361.

transportation creates an aggravating offence that attracts harsher punishments.[145] The offence of stockpiling or transportation of narcotic substances does not apply for those who hold narcotics substances of less than a specified minimum quantity and had no intention of engaging in illegal narcotics trade or manufacture.[146] This means that those who store very small amounts of drugs for personal consumption will not be liable under these provisions. 'Manufacturing' equipment or tools used in the production or consumption of drugs is also broadly defined.[147] It is important to note, however, that there is no specific offence for manufacturing precursor substances in Vietnam, a notable point of departure from the supply-related provisions of the 1988 Convention.[148] 'Appropriating' refers to all manner of illegally obtaining the object in question, including theft and fraud.[149]

These offences can only be established where the prosecution demonstrates the offender was engaged in manufacturing, stockpiling or transporting with knowledge that the objects in question were to be used in drug manufacture or consumption.[150] For example, to be liable for trading and transporting precursors, the offender must have prior knowledge that the substances were to be used in the manufacture of narcotics.

As noted, the manufacture of precursors is not currently a crime under Vietnamese law, although commentators are calling for its criminalisation.[151] The Ministry of Public Security also proposes to criminalise the stockpiling, transporting, trading and appropriating of opium poppy and other kinds of plant containing narcotic substances.[152] Other proposed changes to drug offences include breaking the current Art 194 into different provisions and retaining the death penalty only for the crime of unlawful trading in narcotic substances. There are also calls to review the ways in which penalties are ascribed to particular concentrations of drugs.[153] It is suggested these changes would assist with crime prevention and ensure greater fairness.[154]

[145] Criminal Code 1999, Arts 194(2)(d), 195(2)(e) and 196(2)(e).

[146] See Inter-circular 17 2007, s II(3)(3)(6).

[147] Nguyễn Thị Phương Hoa (n 137) 11.

[148] Nguyễn Thị Phương Hoa (n 137) 12.

[149] See Inter-circular 17, s II(3)(3)(4). See also Đinh Văn Quế, *Bình luận khoa học*, 97 and Nguyễn Ngọc Hòa, *Giáo trình Luật Hình sự Việt Nam* [Textbook on Criminal Law] 501. According to Arts 133, 138 and 139 of the Criminal Code 1999, 'theft' is the unlawful taking or removing of things that are under the control of another in a secret manner; 'robbery' is the unlawful taking or removing of things that are under the control of another with violence (that is, physical force) or the immediate threat of violence; and 'fraud' is the unlawful taking or removing of things that are under the control of another, by deception.

[150] Nguyễn Thị Phương Hoa (n 1) 11.

[151] Nguyễn Thị Phương Hoa (n 1) 8–12.

[152] Drafting Committee, 'Bản Thuyết Minh Chi Tiết Về Dự Thảo Bộ Luật Hình Sự (Sửa Đổi) [Detail explanation about the Draft (Amended) Criminal Code]' (n 128) pt II(8).

[153] Ibid.

[154] Ibid.

Multiple Offences

Chapter XVIII of the Criminal Code includes several articles (194, 195 and 196) which contain multiple offences. This raises the question of how different offences constituting multiple breaches arising out of the one article of the Code are treated. Further, Art 193 ('illegally producing narcotics') is made out where a person stockpiles, transports, trades in or appropriates narcotics.[155] Like Arts 194 to 196, Art 193, therefore, requires a determination as to whether one or more offences have been committed in assessing whether 'illegally producing narcotics' is made out. The distinction is that if the offences under Art 193 are made out, it amounts to a single breach of the Code, with one sentence resulting.

If an offender commits a single crime under Arts 194 (illegally stockpiling, transporting, trading in or appropriating narcotics), 195 (stockpiling, transporting, trading in or appropriating pre-substances for use in the illegal production of narcotics) or 196 (manufacturing, stockpiling, transporting and/or trading in means and/or tools used in the illegal production or use of narcotics) of the Criminal Code 1999, she or he will be prosecuted under the relevant clause of that article. For example, a person trading pre-substances will be prosecuted for trading pre-substances for use in the illegal production of narcotics under Art 195 of the Criminal Code 1999.

Where an offender commits a number of crimes under any one of Arts 194, 195 or 196 of the Criminal Code 1999 and such crimes are closely related to each other (for example, one crime is a condition for committing the other crime, or is the obvious consequence of it), she or he will be prosecuted for all the crimes but will be subject to only one penalty. So, for example, a person who trades pre-substances that are used to produce narcotic substances and then transports them to a new place and stockpiles them will be prosecuted for the crimes of trading, transporting and stockpiling pre-substances for use in the illegal production of narcotics under Art 195 of the Criminal Code 1999, but will be subject to only one penalty.

Where offences carry penalties of differing severity, the offender will be prosecuted for the 'heavier crime' (*tội nặng hơn*),[156] namely that carrying the heaviest penalty.[157] For example, if a man who grew opium poppy has been regularly re-educated and administratively sanctioned, and he continues to illegally produce narcotic substances, he will be prosecuted for illegal production of narcotic substances under Art 193 of the Criminal Code. This is because the crime of illegally producing narcotic substances involves higher penalties than the crime of growing opium poppies.[158] Where the crimes bear equal penalties, the offender will be prosecuted for the crime committed first.[159]

[155] Inter-circular 17, s I(3)(3)(2).
[156] Inter-circular 17, s I(3)(3)(1).
[157] Resolution No 04/2004/NQ-HDTP dated 05 November 2004 of the Judges' Council of the Supreme People's Court Providing Guidelines for Implementation of Some Regulations in Section III 'First Instance Adjudication' of the Criminal Procedure Code 2003 ('Resolution 04').
[158] Inter-circular 17, s I(3)(3)(1).
[159] Inter-circular 17, s I(3)(3)(2).

Where the offender commits several crimes under Arts 194, 195 or 196 of the Criminal Code 1999 and such acts are performed independently of each other, she or he will be prosecuted for each. Upon adjudication, the court will determine a 'common penalty' (*hình phạt chung*).[160] For example, if a person was arrested on charges of illegally trading one type of pre-substance for use in the illegal production of narcotics and, upon examination of his or her house, it is discovered that she or he also stockpiled another kind of pre-substance (but not for trading), the offender would then be prosecuted for trading a pre-substance for use in the illegal production of narcotics, and for the crime of stockpiling a pre-substances for use in the illegal production of narcotics under Art 195 of the Criminal Code 1999.

Complicity

Under the Vietnamese Penal Code, where 'two or more persons intentionally commit a crime', that is, the same crime, they are deemed to be accomplices.[161] 'Accomplice' is defined to include 'organisers, executors, instigators and helpers'.[162] There are two types of complicity: simple and complex.[163] Simple complicity is a situation where all persons committing a crime are 'executors'.[164] Complex or organised complicity is a situation where there is close collusion between persons committing a crime (organisers, executors, instigators and helpers).[165] Organised complicity is an aggravating circumstance under the Criminal Code.[166]

Defences

The issue of 'defences' is vexed in Vietnam. As we show below, defendants' rights to counsel and the recognition of presumption of innocence indicate increasing momentum for recognition of adversarial elements in trials. There is, however, still very limited opportunity available to defendants to adduce evidence. The status of counsel is lower than that of the judge and procurator and both the right to counsel and a presumption of innocence are relatively new. In short, despite the reforms discussed below, trials still generally proceed on the basis that the accused is guilty,

[160] Criminal Code 1999, Art 50 sets out the principles for judges to use in determining the common penalty for an offender who has committed more than one crime.

[161] Criminal Code 1999, Art 20. See also Đinh Văn Quế, 'Một số vấn đề về đồng phạm quy định tại Điều 20 Bộ luật Hình sự [Some issues about complicity as regulated at Art 20 of the Criminal Code]', Tòa Án Nhân Dân Tối Cao (Việt Nam) [(Vietnamese) Supreme People's Court], toaan.gov.vn/portal/page/portal/tandtc/Baiviet?p_page_id=1754190&p_cateid=1751909&article_details=1&item_id=10931636.

[162] Criminal Code 1999, Art 20.

[163] Đinh Văn Quế, 'Một số vấn đề về đồng phạm', Tòa Án Nhân Dân Tối Cao (Việt Nam) [(Vietnamese) Supreme People's Court], toaan.gov.vn/portal/page/portal/tandtc/Baiviet?p_page_id=1754190&p_cateid=1751909&article_details=1&item_id=10931636.

[164] Ibid.

[165] Ibid.

[166] Criminal Code 1999, Art 48(1)(a).

at least in the eyes of the state, with it usually assumed that innocence or guilt was established before trial. For this reason, the pleading of extenuating circumstances becomes the key role of counsel in most trials.

The Criminal Code provides that where a person commits an act of 'legitimate defence' they have not committed a crime:

> Legitimate defence is an act of persons who, for the purpose of protecting the interests of the State and/or organisations, as well as the legitimate rights and interests of their own or other persons, fight in a necessary manner against persons who are committing acts infringing upon the interests of the above-mentioned.[167]

A person who acts beyond the limits of legitimate defence, for example, by 'fighting back' in a manner unnecessary and inappropriate to the nature and the extent of danger posed by the act of infringement, will be criminally liable.[168]

It is important to note that the Criminal Code explicitly provides that drunkenness or being intoxicated by drugs is not a valid defence.[169]

Penalties

Penalties in Vietnam comprise principal *(hình phạt chính)* and supplementary/additional penalties *(hình phạt bổ sung)*.[170] Principal penalties range from a warning to the death penalty.[171] For each crime committed, courts may impose one or more supplementary penalties in addition to a single principal penalty. Supplementary penalties can range from a ban on performing certain kinds of work;[172] a ban on residence (for example, requiring people not to live in a particular locality for up to five years from completion of a custodial sentence);[173] 'probation', that is, a requirement to live in a particular locality for rehabilitative reasons, again for up to five years from completion of a custodial sentence;[174] loss of the right to work for the state for up to five years;[175] and confiscation of property.[176]

Where more than one offence is involved, a penalty is first imposed in respect of each, and then a common penalty for all the offences is determined.[177] For example, if the penalties are all non-custodial *(cải tạo không giam giữ)* or all custodial, the penalties are consolidated into a single term of imprisonment or single non-custodial sentence, referred to as the 'common penalty.' If the penalties are both custodial and

[167] Criminal Code 1999, Art 15.
[168] Criminal Code 1999, Art 15(2).
[169] Criminal Code 1999, Art 14.
[170] Criminal Code 1999, Art 28.
[171] Criminal Code 1999, Art 28(1).
[172] Criminal Code 1999, Art 36.
[173] Criminal Code 1999, Art 37.
[174] Criminal Code 1999, Art 38.
[175] Criminal Code 1999, Art 39.
[176] Criminal Code 1999, Art 40.
[177] Criminal Code 1999, Art 50.

non-custodial, the non-custodial sentence is converted into imprisonment at a ratio of one day of imprisonment for every three days of non-custodial reform. The common penalty must not exceed three years for non-custodial reform, or thirty years for a jail term.[178] If the heaviest penalty applicable is life imprisonment it will be the common penalty. This principle of applying the most severe penalty applies also to the death penalty.

The proposed amendments to the Criminal Code will encourage the imposition of warnings, fines, and non-custodial reform as principal penalties and reduce the frequency with which imprisonment and the death penalty are imposed.[179]

III. INVESTIGATION

The Criminal Procedure Code 2003 classifies people involved in criminal matters in three categories. First, persons 'held in custody' are 'persons arrested in urgent cases, offenders caught red-handed, persons arrested as wanted offenders, or confessing or self-surrendering offenders against whom a custodial decision has been issued.'[180] Second, the 'accused' (*bị can*) is a person 'against whom criminal proceedings have been initiated,'[181] that is, a person who has been detained and is subject to investigation but has not yet been charged. Third, defendants (*bị cáo*) are those facing trial in respect of whom a decision has been made to prosecute and charges have been laid.[182] The status of the person involved is important, as it affects their rights generally, their access to counsel particularly (see below), and the place where they are held.

In order to better protect the rights of people involved in criminal matters, including their right to counsel, the current draft amendments to the Criminal Procedure Code introduce two new categories: (i) persons who are denounced, (where offences are alleged on the basis of supplied information and criminal proceedings requested);[183] and (ii) persons who are arrested (persons arrested in urgent cases, persons caught red handed, and persons arrested as wanted offenders).[184] It is anticipated that the amended Criminal Procedure Code will not only more clearly specify the bases upon which people can be investigated but will also specify the rights attached to these categories of people, such as their right to counsel.

Under the Criminal Procedure Code, 'expert conclusions' (*kết luận giám định*, literally the findings of a survey or investigation) are considered evidence for the purposes of determining 'whether or not criminal acts have been committed, whether persons charged have committed such acts as well as other circumstances necessary

[178] Ibid.

[179] Drafting Committee, 'Bản Thuyết Minh Chi Tiết Về Dự Thảo Bộ Luật Hình Sự (Sửa Đổi) [Detail Explanation About The Draft (Amended) Criminal Code]' (n 128) pt I(6).

[180] Criminal Procedure Code 2003, Art 48.

[181] Criminal Procedure Code 2003, Art 49.

[182] Criminal Procedure Code 2003, Art 50.

[183] Draft (Amended) Criminal Procedure Code, Art 39.

[184] Draft (Amended) Criminal Procedure Code, Art 40.

for the proper settlement of the cases.'[185] In effect, the procuracy reaches a decision about the merits of the case and determines whether an accused should become a defendant.

Search

Searches arising during investigations are generally provided for in Arts 140 to 143 of the Criminal Procedure Code. These provisions set out grounds for: searches of residences; searches of working places; searches of other premises, objects, correspondence, telegraphs, postal parcels and matters;[186] competence to issue search warrants;[187] and body searches.[188]

Generally those who have the right to order the arrest of an accused for temporary detention under Art 80(1) of the Criminal Procedure Code have competence to issue search warrants in all cases.[189] They include the chairmen and vice-chairmen of people's procuracies and military procuracies at all levels; presidents and vice-presidents of people's courts and military courts at all levels; judges holding the post of president or vice-president of the Court of Appeal of the Supreme People's Court; trial panels; and heads and deputy heads of investigating bodies at all levels. Arrest warrants must be approved by the procuracy of the same level before they are executed.[190]

In urgent cases, the following have the right to issue search warrants: heads and deputy heads of investigating bodies at all levels; commanders of independent military units of a regimental or equivalent level; commanders of border posts in islands or border areas; and commanders of aircraft and sea-going ships that have left airports or seaports.[191]

Others who have the right to issue search warrants including: border guard investigation bodies;[192] customs;[193] rangers;[194] coast guards,[195] other agencies of the police force in the People's Police;[196] other agencies of the security force in the People's Police;[197] and other agencies in the People's Army.[198]

185 Criminal Procedure Code 2003, Art 64(2).
186 Criminal Procedure Code 2003, Art 140.
187 Criminal Procedure Code 2003, Art 141.
188 Criminal Procedure Code 2003, Art 142.
189 Criminal Procedure Code 2003, Art 141(1).
190 Criminal Procedure Code 2003, Arts 141(1) and 141(2).
191 Criminal Procedure Code 2003, Art 141(2).
192 Ordinance No 23/2004/PL-UBTVQH11 dated 20 August 2004 of the Standing Committee of National Assembly on Organisation of Criminal Investigations, as amended by Ordinance No 09/2009/PL-UBTVQH12 dated 27 February 2009 of the Standing Committee of National Assembly ('Ordinance on Organisation of Criminal Investigations 2004') Art 19.
193 Ibid Art 20.
194 Ibid Art 21.
195 Ibid Art 22.
196 Ibid Art 23.
197 Ibid Art 24.
198 Ibid Art 25.

Search of aircraft, ships, vehicles, or trains is not provided for in the Criminal Procedure Code nor the Ordinance on Organisation of Criminal Investigation. Instead, it appears in a range of other instruments, such as the Law on Vietnamese Seas,[199] the Law on Civil Aviation,[200] and the Law on Customs.[201] The latter stipulates that:

> When there are grounds to believe that illegal goods are hidden on the transport means on exit, entry, in transit or going from one border gate to another, or signs of serious law violation are revealed, the directors of the border-gate customs sub-departments, the directors of the customs sub-departments of the outside-of-border gate sites of customs-procedures completion and the heads of the customs control squads may decide to temporarily postpone the departure or stop the means of transport for search. Such search must comply with the law and the decision issuers must take responsibility before law for their decisions.[202]

With respect to searches of aircraft, the Law on Civil Aviation provides that:

1. Directors of airport authorities and other competent agencies shall decide to search an aircraft in the following cases:
    a. Signs of violating national sovereignty, national security, aviation security or safety are detected;
    b. Members of the flight crew, passengers or the carriage of baggage, cargo, postal items or other articles in the aircraft violate regulations on entry, exit, customs and quarantine.
2. Persons deciding to search an aircraft shall notify the aircraft commander and concerned agencies and organisations before conducting search.
3. Competent state agencies shall notify aircraft search decisions to the directors of airport authorities for co-ordination.[203]

For searches of ships or vessels, the Law on Vietnamese Seas states:

> When having grounds that vessels, organisations, or individuals are trading in people or illegally transporting, stockpiling, or trading in narcotics, the Sea Patrol and Control Forces of Vietnam shall be entitled to search, inspect, arrest, escort to ports, harbors or shelters of Vietnam or escort, transfer to foreign ports, harbors or shelters as prescribed by Vietnamese law or international treaties to which the Socialist Republic of Vietnam is a signatory.[204]

Resisting Inspection or Search

There is no specific provision that deals with the consequences of resisting inspection or search during the investigation process. Those who do obstruct an inspection or

[199] Law No 18/2012/QH13 passed by the National Assembly on 21 June 2012 on Vietnamese Sea ('Law on Vietnamese Sea 2012').

[200] Law No 66/2006/QH11 passed by the National Assembly on 29 June 2006 on Vietnam Civil Aviation ('Law on Civil Aviation 2006').

[201] Law No 29/2001/QH10 passed by the National Assembly on 29 June 2001 on Customs ('Law on Customs 2001').

[202] Law on Customs 2001, Art 51(3).

[203] Law on Civil Aviation 2006, Art 45.

[204] Law on Vietnamese Seas 2012, Art 39(2).

search may, however, be considered to be 'resisting persons in the performance of their official duties' under the Criminal Code:

> Those who use force, threaten to use force or use other tricks to obstruct persons in the performance of their official duties or coerce them to perform illegal acts, shall be sentenced to non-custodial reform for up to three years or between six months and three years of imprisonment.[205]

This provision bestows a wide discretion on persons performing official duties to determine the seriousness of the resistance. This can be of great significance. For example, if the action is not serious, the offender may receive only administrative sanctions and escape criminal punishment.[206]

In some cases, obstruction of search or inspection may also constitute 'concealment of crimes' under the Criminal Code:

> Any person who, though having not earlier promised anything, knows a crime has been committed and conceals the offender, traces and/or exhibits of the crime or commits the act of obstructing the detection, investigation and/or handling of the offender, shall bear criminal liability for the concealment of crime as provided for by this Code.[207]

Concealment of crimes is considered an infringement of judicial activities and may be punished with imprisonment.[208]

Arrest

Arrest is seen as a deterrent measure to prevent the commission of a crime. It can also be used when there are grounds indicating that the accused could cause difficulties for an investigation, prosecution or adjudication, or that he or she will continue committing offences. Arrest can also take place when necessary to secure the execution of a judgment. Other deterrent measures comprise: custody (in theory, at least, limited to three days unless formally extended to enable investigation and limited to a total of nine days); temporary detention (detention approved by officials in more serious cases and lasting for longer periods); the banning of travel outside one's residence; provision of a guarantee; or the deposit of money or valuable property as bail.[209] The 'regime' of custody and temporary detention are distinguished from the 'regime' that applies to those serving sentences, with different rights to visits, receipt of gifts and care for the property of the accused.[210]

[205] Criminal Code, 1999, Art 257(1).

[206] For example, if a person resisted a search in the context of a road transport investigation they could be dealt with as having merely committed an administrative violation and simply be fined: Decree No 34/2010/ND-CP dated 02 April 2010 of the Government on Sanction of Administrative Violations in the Field of Road Transport, as amended by Decree No 71/2012/ND-CP dated 19 September 2012 of the Government on Amendments and Supplements to a Number of Articles of Decree No 34/2010/ND-CP, Art 5(1).

[207] Criminal Code 1999, Art 21.

[208] Criminal Code 1999, Art 313.

[209] Criminal Procedure Code 2003, Art 79. See also Arts 87 and 88.

[210] Criminal Procedure Code 2003, Arts 89 and 90.

There are three circumstances in which arrest is permitted: for remand or temporary detention;[211] in urgent circumstances;[212] and where offenders are caught red-handed or are wanted persons.[213] These are now explained in more detail.

The Draft (Amended) Criminal Procedure Code separates arresting offenders caught red-handed from arresting wanted persons, and adds a provision on arresting persons being required for extradition.[214] The specific rules, competent authorities and procedure for arresting in each circumstance appear in separate provisions of the Draft Code.[215]

Arresting the Accused or Defendants for Remand (Art 80—Criminal Procedure Code)

The Criminal Procedure Code does not specify the circumstances in which accused persons or defendants (that is, persons formally charged by the People's Procuracy) may be arrested or be placed on remand or temporary detention. Investigating bodies, therefore, usually refer to Art 79 of the Criminal Procedure Code. This provision allows detention: to 'stave off crimes'; where there is an apprehension that a defendant could cause 'difficulties in the investigation, prosecution or adjudication' of a crime; where there is a risk of ongoing offending; or where there is a need for detention to 'secure judgment execution'.[216]

Criminal procedures for arrest must comply with Art 80 of the Criminal Procedure Code. Broadly speaking, those authorised to approve a search may also authorise an arrest, provided the People's Procuracy has approved it too (that is, chairmen and vice-chairmen of people's procuracies; presidents, vice-presidents of people's courts; and judges holding the post of president or vice-president of the Court of Appeal of the Supreme People's Court; and trial panels).[217] Importantly, in the event that the heads or deputy heads of investigating bodies order the arrest, an arrest warrant *(lệnh bắt giữ)* must be approved by the procuracy of the same level in advance.[218] The warrant must set out who has issued it, the identity of the arrestee, and the reasons for the arrest.[219]

When persons are arrested at their residence, representatives of the local administration and the neighbours of the arrestees must be present as witnesses.[220] When

211 Criminal Procedure Code 2003, Art 80.
212 Criminal Procedure Code 2003, Art 81.
213 Criminal Procedure Code 2003, Art 82.
214 Draft (Amended) Criminal Procedure Code, Art 83.
215 For detail see Draft (Amended) Criminal Procedure Code, Arts 84–87.
216 Criminal Procedure Code 2003, Art 79.
217 The Draft (Amended) Criminal Procedure Code also allows presiding judges to order the arrest of an accused or defendant for temporary detention—see Draft (Amended) Criminal Procedure Code, duthaoonline.quochoi.vn/DuThao/Lists/DT_DUTHAO_LUAT/View_Detail.aspx?ItemID=561&LanID=1070&TabIndex=1, Art 87(1)(c).
218 Criminal Procedure Code 2003, Art 80(1).
219 Criminal Procedure Code 2003, Art 80(2).
220 Ibid.

persons are arrested at their place of work, the witnesses must be representatives of the agencies or organisations where such persons work. When persons are arrested at other places, witnesses must be representatives of local administrations of the places where the arrests are made. Arrest at night is not permitted,[221] except in urgent cases, arrest red-handed or arrest of wanted persons.[222] 'Night' is defined as beginning at 22:00 and finishing at 6:00 the following day.[223]

Any arrest under Art 80 must be accompanied by the taking of minutes that set out the date, time and place of arrest and note what is seized and any complaints made by the arrested person.[224]

Arresting Persons in Urgent Cases (Art 81—Criminal Procedure Code)

Urgent arrests can be made in the following cases:

a. When there exist grounds to believe that such persons are preparing to commit very serious or exceptionally serious offenses;
b. When victims or persons present at the scenes where the offenses occurred saw with their own eyes and confirmed that such persons are the very ones who committed the offenses and it is deemed necessary to immediately prevent such persons from escaping;
c. When traces of offenses are found on the bodies or at the residences of the persons suspected of having committed the offenses and it is deemed necessary to immediately prevent such persons from escaping or destroying evidences.[225]

In the Draft (Amended) Criminal Procedure Code, the grounds for urgent arrests are revised as follows (amendments in bold):

a. When there exist grounds to **confirm** that such persons are preparing to commit very serious or exceptionally serious offenses;
b. When **accomplices**, victims or persons present at the scenes where the offenses occurred saw with their own eyes and confirmed that such persons are the very ones who committed the offenses and it is deemed necessary to immediately prevent such persons from escaping;
c. When traces of offenses are found on the bodies, at the residences, **working places, or vehicles** of the persons suspected of having committed the offenses and it is deemed necessary to immediately prevent such persons from escaping or destroying evidence.[226]

Heads and deputy heads of investigating bodies at all levels, commanders of independent military units and commanders of aircraft, sea-going ships that have left airports or seaports have the power to order the arrest of persons in urgent cases.[227] The contents of, and procedure for, arrest warrants in urgent cases are generally

[221] Criminal Procedure Code 2003, Art 80(3).
[222] Ibid. See also Arts 81 and 82.
[223] Criminal Procedure Code 2003, Art 96(1).
[224] Criminal Procedure Code 2003, Art 84.
[225] Criminal Procedure Code 2003, Art 81(1).
[226] Draft (Amended) Criminal Procedure Code, Art 84.
[227] Criminal Procedure Code 2003, Art 81(2).

similar in practice to warrants for temporary detention, but they do have some special features:

> A request for urgent arrest, enclosed with relevant documents, is required to be approved by the People's Procuracy of the same level. This approval is not required before the arrest but the procuracies must strictly examine all bases for urgent arrest and decide whether to approve such arrests within 12 hours after receiving the requests. If the procuracies decide not to approve, the issuers of the arrest warrants must immediately release the arrestees.[228]

As mentioned, urgent arrests may be made at any time, even at night.

Arresting people in this way arguably frees investigation bodies from the need to apply for approval from the procuracy before arrest, even though they must still prepare a dossier to request the procuracy at the same level for approval subsequent to the arrest. This may also enable arbitrariness in arresting, despite the proviso that 'The People's Procuracy must strictly examine all bases for urgent arrest before deciding whether or not to approve the Arrest warrant'.[229]

To further guide the preparation of dossiers required for urgent arrest requests, as well as the procedure for approval of warrant in urgent arrests, agencies involved must prepare a detailed dossier: 'arresting persons in urgent cases is only permitted where there are sufficient documents evidencing that such arrest belongs to one of the circumstances provided in Art 81(1) of the Criminal Procedure Code.'[230] Where there exist grounds to believe that persons are preparing to commit very serious or exceptionally serious offences, the dossier must contain documents evidencing this.

In the event that there are witnesses present at the scenes where the offences occurred who can confirm who committed them, and it is deemed necessary to immediately prevent the offender from escaping, the dossiers must contain a minute of the testimony of the witnesses, and other materials or evidence suggesting that the offender may escape.

Where traces of offences are found on the bodies or at the residence of the persons suspected of having committed the offences, and it is deemed necessary to immediately prevent such persons from escaping or destroying evidence, evidence, documents, or other materials relating to the crime should be collected and certified before the urgent arrest takes place.[231]

When considering an application to approve a warrant for an urgent arrest, the official authorised to issue the warrant and the procuracy shall 'rely on and comprehensively evaluate all matters' in order to make an accurate assessment of whether the suspected person may attempt to escape.[232] The matters to be taken into account include: the personal record of the person under suspicion; the seriousness of the

[228] Criminal Procedure Code 2003, Art 81(4).

[229] Ibid.

[230] Inter-circular No 05/2005/TTLT-VKSNDTC-BCA-BQP dated 07 September 2005 of the Supreme People's Procuracy, the Ministry of Public Security and the Ministry of National on the Coordination Relation between Investigation Body and Procuracy in Implementing Some Provisions of the Criminal Procedure Code 2003 ('Inter-circular 05'), Art 3(1).

[231] Criminal Procedure Code 2003, Art 81(1).

[232] Inter-circular 05, s 3(1).

crime; and whether those offending in this manner often flee, as is said to be the case with thieves, swindlers, robbers, murderers, or those involved in the illegal trading of narcotic substances.[233]

In urgent cases, an investigating body can 'entrust' (*uỷ thác*) another body to complete the arrest. Once this is done, that body must immediately deliver the arrested person and relevant documents to those who gave them that authority, that is, the 'entrusting investigating body'. The primary investigating body must promptly transfer the dossiers containing the decision to so entrust to the People's Procuracy at the same level for approval.[234] The dossiers must include:

a. Official letter requesting the Procuracy to approve the Warrant of urgent arrest;
b. Warrant of urgent arrest, clearly specifying the circumstance of the urgent arrest in accordance with regulations of Art 81(1);
c. Minutes of urgent arrest;
d. Information or denunciation regarding the offence; proposal for prosecution by state bodies;
e. Other relevant supporting documents for the decision on urgent arrest for each particular circumstance provided in point 3(1) of this section.
f. Documents regarding the personal record of the arrested;
g. Testimony of the arrested (if any);
h. List of all documents included in the dossiers.[235]

As noted, the procuracy must approve a warrant for urgent arrest within 12 hours of receipt of the request.[236] This applies even if the procuracy needs to meet and question the arrested person as a result of a suspicion of an abuse of the urgent arrest procedure, and regardless of whether it must approve several cases of urgent arrest at the same time.[237] This time limit includes both working and non-working hours, so the procuracy must always assign prosecutors to be responsible for this function around the clock.[238] The minutes of the detainee's testimony prepared by the prosecutor must be handed to the investigating body 'to add to the case file.'[239]

Arresting Offenders Red-handed or Wanted Offenders (Art 82—Criminal Procedure Code)

Unlike the forms of arrests just decribed, there is a power of citizens' arrest in the case of wanted persons (*khi bắt giữ 'người đang bị truy nã'*) and persons who are detected or pursued while committing offences or immediately after having committed offences. The Criminal Procedure Code provides that all persons 'shall have the right to arrest and take [such persons] to police agencies, the procuracy or

233 Ibid.
234 Criminal Procedure Code 2003, Art 118. See Inter-circular 05, Arts 3(2), 3(3).
235 Inter-circular 05, Art 3(3).
236 Criminal Procedure Code 2003, Art 81(4).
237 Inter-circular 05, Art 3(4).
238 Ibid.
239 Inter-circular 05, Art 3(5).

People's Committees at the nearest location.'[240] Particular powers of arrest are also given to border guards,[241] customs officers,[242] rangers[243] and the coast guard.[244]

Where the crime is less serious and the investigating agencies (including those just mentioned) arrest offenders caught red-handed in circumstances where the evidence and personal identity of the offender is clear, and the crime took place in an area under the management or authority of the arresting bodies, they have authority to prosecute the case and conduct other relevant investigation activities. In other circumstances, they must transfer the case file to the competent investigating bodies.[245]

Within 24 hours of delivering an arrested person to the investigating body's office, the investigating body must take a statement from that person and make a decision whether to keep the arrested person in custody or release him or her.[246] This decision may be made before obtaining approval of an urgent arrest warrant by the procuracy.[247] If the procuracy subsequently finds that there is no basis for a warrant, it may order the investigating bodies to immediately release the arrested person. If the investigating body decides to release an arrested person, after itself determining there is no basis for the arrest, it must immediately notify the procuracy that it does not approve the arrest warrant.[248]

When arresting a wanted person, the investigating bodies must take a statement from the person, compile personal records, take a photograph and immediately send these to the body issuing the 'wanted decision' (*quyết định truy nã*) so it can take custody of the arrested person. The latter body must then verify whether the person arrested is, in fact, the person sought and decide whether to take custody or request the investigating bodies to release him or her.[249] If the body that issued the original 'wanted decision' is not able to immediately take custody of the arrested person, it must issue a temporary detention warrant and send this warrant, together with the original wanted decision, to the procuracy of the same level for consideration and approval.[250] The time limit for such approval may not exceed 24 hours from its receipt.

After receiving a temporary detention warrant approved by the procuracy, the investigating body must escort the person arrested to the nearest temporary detention centre. Minutes shall be made on the receipt of the person jointly by the investigating body and the centre, and between the temporary detention centre and the body that issued the 'wanted decision'.[251]

[240] Criminal Procedure Code 2003, Art 82(1).
[241] Ordinance on Organisation of Criminal Investigations, Art 19.
[242] Ordinance on Organisation of Criminal Investigations, Art 20.
[243] Ordinance on Organisation of Criminal Investigations, Art 21.
[244] Ordinance on Organisation of Criminal Investigations, Art 22.
[245] Ordinance on Organisation of Criminal Investigations, Arts 19–22.
[246] Criminal Procedure Code 2003, Art 83(1).
[247] Inter-circular 05, Art 4(1).
[248] Ibid.
[249] Inter-circular 05, Art 4(3).
[250] Ibid.
[251] Inter-circular 05, Art 4(4).

If the latter is unable to attend immediately or issue a temporary detention warrant, the investigating body holding the arrested person must issue a custody decision and notify the procuracy of the same level of it.[252] If the body that issued the 'wanted decision' cannot take custody of the arrested person within 12 hours, the investigating body must transfer the case file, with an Official Letter, to the procuracy at the same level to seek approval to extend the time limit for custody.

Custody and Temporary Detention

People or agencies with the right to issue urgent arrest warrants may also issue custody decisions.[253] As noted, these currently include heads and deputy heads of investigating bodies at all levels; commanders of independent military units; and commanders of aircraft, sea-going ships that have left airports or seaports.[254] Local authorities and police agencies at communal, ward, and township level, and other forces do not have the right to make custody decisions in criminal cases.

As also noted, the time in custody must not exceed three days, commencing from the time the investigating body receives a detainee.[255] This may be extended for not more than three days where deemed necessary, and an extra three days in special cases.[256]

Interviews we conducted with investigators and procurators indicated that the detention power was particularly vulnerable to abuse, with detention without proper approval or in excess of time limits common.[257] Estimates for the duration of delays varied but it was suggested 'it was unsurprising if the actual time taken exceeded the prescribed limit by a couple of months'.[258] It was also noted that detention may take place under administrative measures[259] to avoid the strict detention provisions that are set out in the Criminal Procedure Code and the risk of compensation arising if improper detention can be proved.[260]

[252] Inter-circular 05, Art 4(2).

[253] Inter-circular 05, Art 86(2).

[254] Inter-circular 05, Art 81(2).

[255] Inter-circular 05, Art 87(1).

[256] Inter-circular 05, Art 87(2). The general regime of custody is provided under Arts 89 and 90 of the Criminal Procedure Code 2003. See also Decree No 89/1998/ND-CP dated 7 November 1998 of the Government Promulgating the Regulations on Temporary Custody and Detention (Decree 89) and Decree No 98/2002/ND-CP dated 27 November 2002 of the Government Amending and Supplementing a Number of Articles of the Regulation on Custody and Detention Issued together with Decree No 89/1998/ND-CP dated 7 November 1998 of the Government.

[257] Interviewee 8 (4 June 2012); Interviewee 9 (5 June 2012); and Interviewee 15 (16 August 2012).

[258] Interviewee 15 (16 August 2012).

[259] Ibid. Administrative measures are defined as 'measures applied to individuals who commit acts that violate security, social order and safety, however, these acts do not constitute crimes. Rather they attract administrative measures including: education at communes, wards, towns; sending to a reform institution; sending to compulsory education establishments; and sending to compulsory detoxification establishments', Law No 15/2012/QH13 passed by the National Assembly on 20 June 2012 on Administrative Sanctions, Art 2(3). Administrative measures include warnings, fines, expulsion and other measures.

[260] See Resolution No 388/2003/NQ-UBTVQH11 dated 17 March 2003 of the Standing Committee of the National Assembly on Compensation for Damage Caused to Unjustly Condemned People by Competent People in Criminal Proceedings. Compensation is discussed further below.

Bail

Bail is defined as a deterrent measure that replaces temporary detention.[261] Bail may be determined by investigating bodies, the procuracy or the courts, depending on the nature of the offence, the extent of danger to society and the personal circumstances of the person seeking it.[262] The requirements for persons offering bail on behalf of an accused or a defendant are set out in the Criminal Procedure Code.[263] Bail must be offered by at least two persons who are relatives of the person seeking bail and they must be of good conduct and morality, and strictly observe the law.[264] If an organisation offers bail, the accused or defendant must be a member of that organisation, and the head of the organisation must certify that.[265]

The Criminal Procedure Code provides that bail must also be 'certified' by local authorities at the places where the person to be bailed resides or by the agency or organisation for which he or she works. It is not clear, however, what has to be certified. More particularly, it is unclear whether the certification relates to the residence, working place or morality and behaviour of the persons giving or making bail.[266]

Although the Criminal Procedure Code provides that individuals and organisations that stand bail are responsible for their pledges,[267] there are no other sanctions for a person who has put up bail where the person granted bail escapes or commits other offences.[268] At the time of writing, an amendment is proposed to the Criminal Procedure Code that would make those who stand bail pay a fine of up to 50 million Vietnam Dong (USD $2,300.00) if bail is violated.[269] It is also proposed that individuals offering bail must be at least 18 years old, in a 'good condition' to manage the bailed person, and have a stable income.[270]

Admissibility of Statements and Confession

Rules relating to statements made by an accused or a defendant are set out in the Criminal Procedure Code:

1. The accused or defendant shall present circumstances related to being suspected of having committed criminal acts.

[261] Criminal Procedure Code 2013, Art 92(1). Again see also Decree 89.
[262] Criminal Procedure Code 2013, Art 92(1).
[263] Criminal Procedure Code 2013, Art 92.
[264] Criminal Procedure Code 2013, Art 92(2), (4).
[265] Ibid.
[266] Criminal Procedure Code 2013, Art 92(4).
[267] Criminal Procedure Code 2013, Art 92(5).
[268] Phạm Ngọc Ánh, 'Băn khoăn chuyện bảo lãnh trong án hình Sự [Concerns about bail in criminal cases]', *Pháp Luật Thành Phố Hồ Chí Minh* [*Ho Chi Minh Law Newspaper*] (9 September 2011), plo.vn/phap-luat/ban-khoan-chuyen-bao-linh-trong-an-hinh-su-106315.html.
[269] Draft (Amended) Criminal Procedure Code. See www.xe.com/currencyconverter/convert/?Amount=50%2C000%2C000&From=VND&To=USD for the currency conversion as at 16 July 2015.
[270] Ibid.

2. Confessions of an accused or a defendant shall only be regarded as evidence if consistent with other evidence in the case.
3. Confessions of an accused or a defendant must not be used as sole evidence for conviction (*chứng cứ duy nhất để kết tội*).[271]

Such statements are acceptable by the courts, as they form a part of the case dossier.[272]

If an offender confesses, the agency involved is required to produce minutes clearly setting out the details of the confession and immediately inform the investigating bodies or the procuracy of the statement.[273] Under the Criminal Code, confessions may mitigate criminal liability (Art 46(1)(o)), although the Criminal Procedure Code provides that they may also be a ground for instituting criminal cases.[274]

There is, in fact, some debate about the extent to which confessions can be used as an extenuating factor in criminal trials. According to Đinh Văn Quế, the Chief Judge of Criminal Court of the SPC, Art 46(1)(o) of the Criminal Code 1999 clearly allows an act of a confession to be grounds for extenuating criminal liability.[275] The Supreme People's Court agrees, at least when the confession is volunteered by a party for an offence about which the authorities are unaware. The Court does not, however, extend the benefits of confession to circumstances where the confession arises in the context of an investigation, unless there are additional indicators of remorse.

Upon promulgation of the Criminal Code in 1999, the Supreme People's Court explained its position on confessions in an Official Letter to guide the courts on the use of 'confessions', which it defined as follows.

> Confession *(Tự thú)* is the act of offenders who plead guilty themselves and make a declaration about their crime even though the crime has not been detected. Where persons who are arrested for a certain criminal offence, but in the course of investigation plead guilty to other crimes and make declarations about such crimes that have not been detected, they will also be considered as confessing their crimes.
>
> Self-surrender *(Đầu thú)* is the act of an offender who knows that his or her crimes have been detected and that he or she is unable to escape, and so they surrender to the competent agencies as responsible for the offences.[276]

[271] Criminal Procedure Code 2003, Art 72.

[272] See *Quyết định giám đốc thẩm số 17/2003/HĐTP-HS ngày 29/07/2003 về vụ án Nguyễn Công La phạm tội 'cố ý gây thương tích* [Cassation-trial decision No 17/2003/HDTP-HS dated 29/07/2003 on the case of Nguyen Cong La committing the crime of 'intentionally inflicting injury]'; *Quyết định giám đốc thẩm số 20/2003/HĐTP-HS Ngày 26/08/2003 về vụ án lê thu huyền phạm tội 'mua bán trái phép chất ma túy* [Cassation-trial decision No 20/2003/HDTP-HS dated 26/08/2003 on the case of Le Thu Huyen committing the crime of 'illegally trading narcotics]'.

[273] Criminal Procedure Code 2003, Art 102.

[274] Criminal Procedure Code 2003, Art 100(5).

[275] See also Đinh Văn Quế, 'Một số vấn đề khi áp dụng tình tiết 'tự thú' và 'đầu thú' trong thực tiễn xét xử [Some issues for application of 'confession' and 'surrender]', Tra Cứu Pháp Luật [Law Reference], www.tracuuphapluat.info/2010/09/ap-dung-tinh-tiet-tu-thu-va-au-thu.html.

[276] Official Letter No 81/2002/TANDTC dated 10 June 2002 of the Supreme People's Court in Response to Professional Queries, s 7.

The Official Letter goes on to deal specifically with the benefit an offender can obtain from confession.

> If offenders plead guilty and clearly make a statement about their crime even though the crime has not been detected, such offenders have the benefit of the extenuating circumstances of 'confession' under Art 46 (1) of the Criminal Code 1999.
>
> If the criminal offence of the offender is known, and the offenders present themselves at the competent agencies just because they know that they are unable to escape, Article 46(2) of the Criminal Code 1999 shall be applied to consider the extenuation of criminal liability of the offenders.[277] It is also noted that if, in such a case, the offenders make honest declarations and reports and show their repentance or do something else which is deemed as circumstances of extenuating criminal liability, they shall be entitled to the benefit of the circumstances of extenuating criminal liability as provided under Article 46(1) of the Criminal Code 1999.[278]

The Chief Judge of the Criminal Court also argues that the Criminal Code allows a confession to be the basis for exempting an accused entirely from criminal liability.[279] This, however, is contentious and not all commentators accept his interpretation.[280]

Drug Testing

There is no special procedure for drug testing. Article 33 of the Criminal Procedure Code defines 'procedure-conducting agencies' to include investigating bodies, the procuracy and courts. Article 34 of the Criminal Procedure Code gives these procedure-conducting agencies the power to order investigators to 'carry out investigation measures'.[281]

Despite the provisions of Article 34, other provisions of the Code only suggest that the heads of investigating bodies or the chief procurators have this power, not courts.[282] Investigators, therefore, usually seek approval of their heads to order expert tests. Procurators, however, have the power to set investigation requirements for investigators, which effectively means they can also require investigators to order expert tests.[283] As we have seen, the Criminal Procedure Code does not empower judges to directly order expert tests but since 2014 they have had the power to return case

[277] Article 46(2) of the Criminal Code 1999 provides 'When deciding penalties, the court may also consider other circumstances as extenuating, but must clearly inscribe them in the judgment.'

[278] Official Letter No 81/2002/TANDTC dated 10 June 2002 of the Supreme People's Court in Response to Professional Queries, s 5.

[279] Criminal Code 1999, Art 25(2).

[280] Đinh Văn Quế, 'Một số vấn đề khi áp dụng tình tiết 'tự thú''.

[281] Criminal Procedure Code 2003, Art 34. See also the general power to order tests set out in Law No 13/2012/QH13 passed by the National Assembly on 20 June 2012 on Judicial Expertise.

[282] Criminal Procedure Code 2003, Art 34: Tasks, powers and responsibilities of heads and deputy heads of investigating bodies, and Art 36: Tasks, powers and responsibilities of chief procurators.

[283] Criminal Procedure Code 2003, Art 37.

files for further investigation when important evidence needs further examination.[284] Unfortunately, if the procuracy does not carry out such further investigation (which may include testing), the courts are required to proceed with the trial.[285]

In practice, investigating bodies are usually the ones who order expert tests but in recent times courts have been begun to be more assertive about this. For example, a procurator of the Bac Giang Provincial Procuracy reports that since the Supreme Court promulgated Official Letter No 234 (requiring that local courts only adjudicate drug cases after expert tests have been conducted to determine the concentration of drugs), the case files of all drug cases previously sent to trial in Bac Giang were returned to investigators so they could order expert tests.[286]

Drug tests, like all other expert tests that determine criminal liability, may not be ordered by an accused person or defendant.[287] Accused persons may only request notification of test results, and may then express opinions about results, although they do have the right to request additional tests or re-tests.[288] Such requests may, however, be rejected.[289] In fact, additional expert tests are usually only conducted in cases where the expert conclusions remain unclear or incomplete, or if new matters related to the circumstances of the case arise.[290] Re-tests are undertaken only if there is suspicion about the test results or the results are contradictory.[291]

Evidence in Foreign Jurisdictions

An interesting issue arises where evidence exists in another jurisdiction that goes to an issue before the Vietnamese courts. For example, if a defendant has a mental incapacity and this is known in Canada, can expert evidence of this be put before the court in Vietnam? There seem to be no clear rules on this point but such information could, at the very least, be put to the procuracy as grounds to order testing or additional testing. Further, if the procuracy resisted ordering tests, it may be possible to argue the fact of such 'extra' evidence before the court, either formally or informally. This would usually be done ahead of trial, although the defence would need to agitate for recognition if the procuracy took a cavalier attitude to the case. More generally, character evidence for foreign defendants often needs to be assembled abroad and sent to Vietnam so that local counsel can bring it to the attention of the procuracy and the court, including in advance of the trial.

[284] Criminal Procedure Code 2003, Arts 39 and 179; Official Letter No 234/TANDTC-HS dated 17 September 2014 of the Supreme People's Court, requiring that local courts only adjudicate drug cases after expert tests have been conducted to determine the concentration of drugs (the percentage of drugs in the seized substance or liquid). See also Inter-circular 17.

[285] Criminal Procedure Code 2003, Art 179.

[286] Vũ Thanh Tùng, 'Vấn đề giám định hàm lượng ma túy và những bất cập cần giải quyết [The evaluation of drug concentration and problems that need to be solved]', Viện Kiểm sát Bắc Giang (Việt Nam) [(Vietnam) Bac Giang Procuracy], vksbacgiang.gov.vn/chuyendephapluat/61/3545.

[287] See Law on Judicial Expert Tests 2012, Art 2(3).

[288] Criminal Procedure Code 2003, Arts 158(1) and 158(2).

[289] Criminal Procedure Code 2003, Art 158(2).

[290] Criminal Procedure Code 2003, Art 159(1).

[291] Criminal Procedure Code 2003, Art 159(2).

IV. PRESUMPTIONS AND RIGHTS

Presumption of Not Guilty and the Presumption of Innocence

Until 2013, a right to be presumed not guilty (*suy đoán vô tội)*,[292] was constitutionally established and reaffirmed in the Criminal Procedure Code 2003:

> No one shall be considered guilty nor be punished until there is a final and conclusive judgment from the Court.[293]
>
> No person shall be considered guilty and be punished until a court judgment on his/her criminality takes legal effect.[294]

There is also a legal obligation on investigating bodies, the prosecution and the court to collect exculpatory evidence and clarify both aggravating and extenuating circumstances.[295]

These provisions confirmed the supreme decision-making power of the Court as the 'sole governmental agency'[296] with the power to determine the innocence or guilt of a person. Their wording suggested that it was not only those charged who were entitled to the right but also those arrested or detained pending formal charging[297]—that is, conviction was not a prerequisite for the existence of the right.[298] The provisions also make clear that the presumption of not guilty ceased when a guilty judgment became final and conclusive, that is, when the right to appeal expired without having been exercised (15 days from judgment)[299] or when an appeal judgment or a decision to stay the appeal was handed down.[300]

The literature suggests, however, that the operation of the 'not guilty' principle was less concerned with protecting a fundamental right[301] and more with ensuring and maintaining the 'required attitude' of impartiality and independence on the part of 'judicial staff'.[302] As bodies that administer criminal procedures,[303] Vietnamese

[292] The 'presumption of innocence' has also been translated as *giả định vô tội* instead of *suy đoán vô tội*, as the former better reflects the meaning of 'presumption' in this context, which is, in fact, 'assumption'. See Bùi Tiến Đạt, 'Vì sao 'suy đoán có tội' phổ biến? [Why is the presumption of guilt popular?]' *Vietnamnet* (Vietnam, 20 June 2015), vietnamnet.vn/vn/tuanvietnam/245080/vi-sao--suy-doan-co-toi--pho-bien-.html.

[293] SRVN Constitution 1992, Art 72.

[294] Criminal Procedure Code 2003, Art 9.

[295] Criminal Procedure Code 2003, Art 10.

[296] Nguyễn Ngọc Anh, *Bình luận khoa học Bộ luật Tố tụng Hình sự 2003* [Scientific commentary on the 2003 Criminal Procedure Code] (Ha Noi, National Politics Publishing House, 2004) 23–24. See also Nguyễn Quốc Việt, *Bình luận khoa học Bộ luật Tố tụng Hình sự 2003* [Scientific commentary on the 2003 Criminal Procedure Code] (Hanoi, National Politics Publishing House, 2005) 23–25.

[297] Criminal Procedure Code 2003, Arts 239 and 240. Mai Thanh Hiếu, 'The Scope within Which a Subject is Entitled to Presumption of Innocence in Criminal Procedure of Vietnam' (2004) 01/2004 *Jurisprudence Magazine* 27, 27–31.

[298] Mai Thanh Hiếu, 'The Scope' 27–31.

[299] Criminal Procedure Code 2003, Art 240.

[300] Criminal Procedure Code 2003, Arts 238 and 240. Mai Thanh Hiếu (n 297) 27–31.

[301] Ibid. See also Nguyễn Quốc Việt, *Bình luận khoa học* 23–25.

[302] Hoàng Thị Sơn and Bùi Kiên Điện, *Những nguyên tắc cơ bản của luật tố tụng hình sự Việt Nam* [Fundamental principles of the Criminal Procedure Code of Vietnam] (Hanoi, Public Security Publishing House, 2003), 69–81.

[303] Criminal Procedure Code 2003, Art 33.

judges and courts have an active role to identify and assert the 'truth' of a case in an objective, comprehensive and complete manner[304] so that the process will not 'wrongly convict the innocent' or 'let any crime go unpunished'.[305] Such an approach or 'spirit' is considerably different to the fundamental principle of presumption of innocence long celebrated in common law countries. Put another way, Vietnamese judges (and judicial staff) have not, to date, regarded accused persons as 'innocent' when they administer their cases.[306] They are, instead, entitled to trust and follow their 'inner faith' (*niềm tin nội tâm)* regarding the culpability or innocence of the accused.[307]

The presumption of not guilty is, therefore, usually seen as simply requiring that judges (and other people involving in the proceeding, such as the procuracy or the police) do not formally treat the accused as a criminal until the court decides he or she is one.[308] One well-known Vietnamese barrister reports, however, that the principle of the presumption of not guilty is, in practice, simply not accepted by many officials in charge of criminal proceedings.[309] This has the effect that detainees or accused persons are, in fact, often treated as if they were convicted already.[310] This weak presumption of not guilty was nevertheless seen as useful in cases where there was a lack of clear proof. For example, where suspicions remain but they are not supported by the evidence available, this should be interpreted to the benefit of the accused (*giải thích theo chiều hướng có lợi)*.

Perhaps in response to the concerns just described, the new SRVN Constitution 2013 has replaced the presumption of not guilty with a more robust presumption of innocence:

> 1. A person charged with a criminal offence shall be presumed innocent until proven guilty according to a legally established procedure and the sentence of the court takes legal effect.[311]

A proposal has been put to give this brief constitutional provision more concrete form in the Draft (Amended) Criminal Procedure Code:

> 1. An accused person shall not be considered guilty until proven guilty in accordance with the procedure stipulated by law and a guilty verdict has been reached by the Court and has come into effect.

[304] Criminal Procedure Code 2003, Art 10. Such objectivity is nevertheless questionable. See Phạm Hồng Hải, *Mô hình lý luận Bộ luật Tố tụng Hình sự Việt Nam* [Analytical framework for the Criminal Procedure Code of Vietnam] (Ha Noi, Public Security Publishing House, 2003) 180, stating that, in practice, many people still consider a judge's decision to bring a case to the court as his/her approval of the opinions expressed by the investigators and the prosecutors with respect to the case.

[305] Criminal Procedure Code 2003, Art 1.

[306] Interviewee 12 (13 August 2012).

[307] Hoàng Thị Sơn and Bùi Kiên Điện, *Những nguyên tắc cơ bản*, 69–81.

[308] Ibid.

[309] Phạm Hồng Hải, *Mô hình lý luận,* 125; Interviewee 12 (13 August 2012).

[310] Ibid.

[311] SRVN Constitution 2013, Art 31.

2. An accused person shall have the right but no obligation to prove his/her innocence. Procedure-conducting agencies bear the responsibility to prove guilt.
3. Any doubts about the guilt/innocence of the accused person that cannot be clarified by the procedure stipulated by this Code must be interpreted positively in favour of the accused person.[312]

These three clauses would formally embed a presumption of innocence in Vietnamese criminal law, although it remains unclear to what extent practice would alter. Coupled with the development of a separate 'judicial power' in the SRVN Constitution 2013, these amendments would, however, at the very least offer increased scope for the courts to insist on the right to the presumption of innocence in criminal cases.

Right to Silence

While there may now be a basis for a new presumption of innocence in Vietnam, accused persons do not to enjoy a right to silence (*quyền im lặng*). Vietnamese law makes no provision for people in custody or an accused or defendant to exercise such a right. Although the Criminal Procedure Code provides that the accused and defendants have a right, but no obligation, to prove their innocence, there is, as discussed above, also a requirement that the accused make a statement or 'present the circumstances of the case.'[313] Further, 'remaining silent' may be the basis of an adverse implication, or reflect poorly on the integrity of an accused, by suggesting that they are withholding information and not making 'honest' declarations. This may also compromise any claim of extenuating or mitigating circumstances.[314]

Even if a right to silence exists as a corollary of the new presumption of innocence, its exercise is, in any case, unlikely to be effective as a defence. Rather it would be regarded as just one of a number of possible sources of evidence from which inferences, positive or adverse, could be drawn by the court.

As debate over revision of the Criminal Procedure Code continues, the introduction of the right to silence is, unsurprisingly, strongly opposed by government agencies, particularly representatives of the Ministry of Public Security. They argue that the right will hinder investigation activities and, thus, adversely affect the fight against crime.[315] As a result, no right to silence currently appears in the Draft Criminal Procedure Code and it is unlikely it will be introduced.

[312] Draft (Amended) Criminal Procedure Code, Art 10.
[313] Criminal Procedure Code 2003, Arts 10, 71 and 72.
[314] Criminal Code 1999, Art 46.
[315] Thu Hằng and Minh Thăng, 'Im lặng thành quyền độc lập khó chống tội phạm? [Recognising the right to silence adversely affects the fight against crimes?]' *Vietnamnet* (17 June 2015), vietnamnet.vn/vn/chinh-tri/244691/im-lang-thanh-quyen-doc-lap-kho-chong-toi-pham-.html.

Right to Counsel

There have recently been moves at the policy level to escalate the adversarial nature of trials. This has directly affected the right to counsel during the investigation and trial, as well as the standing of counsel. More particularly, the Vietnamese court system has undergone substantial reforms based on the policy directions set out in the Communist Party of Vietnam's Resolution 49, which, in turn, referenced its 2002 Resolution 08.[316] Resolution 08 called for reforms requiring the legal system and the organs responsible for its implementation to reform to deliver 'strictness [in legal enforcement], justice and democracy'.[317] More particularly, Resolution 08 called for an increase in the role of lawyers including ensuring the development of an adversarial practice (cast as 'democratic') 'between prosecutors at trial and lawyers'.[318] Lawyers, Resolution 08 noted, were to be able to assist at the interrogation and have access to the court dossier.[319] In subsequent, more detailed, Politburo policy statements similar changes were foreshadowed[320] and Resolution 49 identified 'improving the quality of adversarial elements at hearings' as a priority.[321]

A formal right to legal representation was introduced, as a matter of law (if not practice), in the 2003 amendments to the Criminal Procedure Code and was supported by statements about the role of lawyers in the Law on Lawyers of 2006.[322] In particular, there must now be counsel when: (i) 'The accused or defendants [are] charged with offences punishable by death as the highest penalty prescribed by the Criminal Code'; or (ii) 'The accused or defendants [are] minors or persons with physical or mental defects.'[323]

Before exploring the Vietnamese provisions on right to counsel and their limited take-up, it is useful to briefly canvas the civil law approach to a right to counsel. This highlights the ways in which the Vietnamese have sought to hybridise civil and common law practice. It also explains the fundamental nature of the Vietnamese reforms, and may, in part, explain their lack of implementation.

Traditionally civil law countries have not granted a right to counsel in criminal proceedings. Instead, the interests of the accused are seen as safeguarded by the state's role in judicial investigation and supervision, integral to an inquisitorial system.[324]

[316] Resolution No 08-NQ/TW dated 2 January 2002 of the Politburo of the Vietnamese Communist Party on Forthcoming Principal Judiciary Tasks and Resolution No 49 NQ/TW dated 2 June 2005 of the Central Committee of the Vietnamese Communist Party of Vietnam on the Judicial Reform Strategy.

[317] Resolution 08.

[318] Ibid.

[319] Ibid.

[320] See in particular, Resolution No 900/UBTVQH11 dated 12 March 2007 of the Standing Committee of the National Assembly on the Action Plan to Implement Resolution No 48-NQ/TW dated 24 May 2005 of the Politburo of the Vietnamese Communist Party on the Strategy for Development and Improvement of Vietnam's Legal System to the Year 2010 and Direction for the Period 2020.

[321] Resolution 49.

[322] See Criminal Procedure Code 2003, Arts 11, 49 and 50 and Law No 65/2006/QH11 passed by the National Assembly on 29 June 2006 on Lawyers.

[323] Criminal Procedure Code 2003, Art 57(2).

[324] Jacqueline Hodgson, 'The Detention and Interrogation of Suspects in Police Custody in France: A Comparative Account' (2004) 1 *European Journal of Criminology* 169, 171–73.

In France, for example, the system is based on the magistrate (usually a procurator with the status of a magistrate) supervising the police investigation.[325] The procurator is able to call the accused before him or her at any time, and interviews in non-serious cases that last beyond 24 hours must be approved by the procurator. In drug trafficking cases, an accused may be held and interrogated for 72 hours before seeing counsel.[326]

In France, the treatment of a person in custody is supposed to be monitored, and there is a duty to record all interview times, rest periods and when food is taken.[327] Until 2012, there was no right for the accused to have a lawyer present during an interview, or for the lawyer to have access to the court dossier.[328] An accused could only meet briefly with their lawyer (half an hour) before interview and then again after 20, and then 36, hours of interrogation.[329] Only after June 2000 (and then only for three years) was a detainee in France entitled to be informed of his or her right to silence.[330]

This treatment of the accused during investigation came under attack from the European Court of Human Rights in the 2008 case of *Salduz v Turkey*.[331] As Hodgson explains, the Salduz decision called for lawyers to be present from the commencement of any investigation, unless there were 'compelling reasons to restrict this right'.[332] In her most recent analysis of this issue in France, Hodgson describes how the European Court of Human Rights challenged French practices fundamentally but eventually received the support of both the French Conseil Constitutionnel, which called for legislative amendments with effect from July 2011, and the Cour de Cassation, which decided in a subsequent 2011 case that the right to counsel took effect immediately.[333]

In this context, the Vietnamese reforms to the right to counsel are wide-ranging and fundamental. The Constitution now gives arrested persons, persons in custody and defendants a broad right to legal representation:

> Any person who has been arrested, held in custody, prosecuted, brought to trial in violation of the law has the right to self-defend or to seek the assistance of defence from lawyers or other people.[334]

[325] Ibid 171.

[326] Jacqueline Hodgson, 'The Impact of Salduz in France: Making Custodial Legal Advice More Effective' (Legal Studies Research Paper No 2013-08) 3.

[327] Hodgson, 'The Detention and Interrogation' 172.

[328] Hodgson, 'The Detention and Interrogation' 173.

[329] Ibid.

[330] Ibid. This right was repealed in 2003.

[331] *Salduz v Turkey* (App No 36391/02) ECHR 27 November 2008.

[332] *Salduz v Turkey* (27 November 2008, No 36391/02), [55] extracted in Hodgson, 'The Impact of Salduz', 1. See also Hodgson, Jacqueline, 'Making Custodial Legal Advice More Effective in France' (2013) 92 *Criminal Justice Matters* 14, 14–15.

[333] See also Hodgson, 'Making Custodial Legal Advice' 14–15. See also, Hodgson, 'The Impact of Salduz' 2–3.

[334] SRVN Constitution 2013, Art 31(4).

It also confirms they may exercise the right during investigation and in court:

> The right of the internee and the defendant to be defended is guaranteed; the right of the persons concerned to defend their legitimate interests is guaranteed.[335]

These constitutional changes made concrete rights that had been introduced in the Criminal Procedure Code 2013 and a Circular the Ministry of Public Security issued in 2011.[336]

The court, procuracy and investigating authorities must now ensure the appointment of counsel (either through the Bar Association or the Vietnam Fatherland Front) in cases involving the death penalty, minors or people with mental disabilities.[337] Criminal lawyers report, however, that in cases where counsel are mandatory, such as the death penalty, the quality of representation is often low. This is because young and inexperienced counsel often accept such cases to gain work experience and develop connections with the court, procuracy and investigating authorities, accepting they will be very poorly compensated and possibly even make a loss on the brief.[338]

A recent analysis by the UNDP reveals uneven practices on the part of legal institutions in Vietnam regarding access to lawyers. For example, while courts frequently work to see that a party has a lawyer (at least in the cities), the investigating police and the procuracy have frustrated the new legislation, frequently preventing detainees from obtaining early or timely legal advice.[339] The UNDP Report notes that there is rarely an explicit refusal of the right to counsel, as this could lead to termination of the proceeding and an order for a new hearing. An investigator notes, however, that 'investigators may not provide all materials' when needed by the defence, instead providing them in 'a gradual way', rationalising it as a way to protect their investigation.[340] It can also be hard for counsel to obtain the Certificate of Defence needed to access the court dossier and attend interviews by the authorities with those suspected of crimes.[341] The same UNDP report also notes that it is even harder to access a lawyer in rural and mountainous regions.[342]

[335] SRVN Constitution 2013, Art 103. Compare this with the limited wording in the DRVN Constitution 1959, Art 101: 'The right to defence is guaranteed to the accused'. In the DRVN Constitution 1980, the wording echoed that of 1959, adding that: 'a jurist organisation may be formed to give legal assistance to the defendants and other persons concerned' (Art 133).

[336] Criminal Procedure Code 2013, Art 11. See also Circular No 70/2011/TT-BCA dated 10 October 2011 of the Ministry of Public Security on Detailing the Implementation of the Articles of the Criminal Procedure Code Regarding the Guarantee of the Right to Defence at the Stage of the Criminal Investigation.

[337] Criminal Procedure Code 2013, Art 57.

[338] UNDP, 'Appointed Counsel' (n 14) 37.

[339] UNDP, 'Right to Counsel' (n 14) 37, 43. Commenting on the impossibility of obtaining a Certificate of Defence during the investigation phase of a criminal case, all 45 lawyer interviewees noted that such a Certificate had never been granted. As mentioned, the certificate is required for a lawyer to access either his or her client or the dossier.

[340] Interviewee 3 (23 and 29 May 2012).

[341] UNDP, 'Right to Counsel' (n 14) 47. On how to obtain a certificate of defence counsel, see Circular 70, Art 5.

[342] UNDP, 'Right to Counsel' (n 14) 66–67 and 77. One judge interviewed for the Report noted that in 2008 counsel only assisted in 2 or 3 out of 40 criminal cases (p 67).

There is no agreement about how many defendants have had access to a lawyer at a criminal trial. The Ministry of Justice reports a much higher rate of lawyer involvement than does the Supreme People's Court, claiming that 60,000 of 70,000 criminal cases proceeded with a defence lawyer.[343] Data from the Supreme People's Court suggests, however, that only about 10 per cent of criminal cases involved a defence lawyer.[344]

Some counsel told us that they have had improved access to clients in recent years, although prior relationships with investigators or prosecutors (such as having taught them) may have been a factor here.[345] Most counsel report that access only improved after the introduction of the Ministry of Public Security's circular was issued in 2013,[346] confirming the right to counsel during the investigation phase. One lawyer even said that the Ministry of Public Security circular had an 'unbelievable' impact, radically improving access to counsel, at least when in big cities.[347] While the debate about access continues, representation of defendants in criminal trials will continue to be hampered by the relatively small number of lawyers in Vietnam, given its population of over 90 million.[348]

Legal Aid

Legal aid in Vietnam was established in 1997 by the Ministry of Justice and was initially provided as a largely advisory service.[349] After 2007, legal aid expanded its reach from just 6 of 64 provinces to all of them, together with representation, albeit uneven, at the district level.[350] After 2007, legal aid was extended to include court work. It is now provided either by legal aid centres or by private lawyers who can register as providers of legal aid with the Ministry of Justice[351] and, once registered, are available for hire by state legal aid at a fee set by the state.[352] Legal aid is

343 UNDP, 'Appointed Counsel' (n 14) 33. This figure was provided to the researchers by the Ministry of Justice, although no official source was cited.

344 Ibid.

345 Interviewee 10 (25 May 2012). This interviewee was a former lecturer who had taught many judges and prosecutors.

346 Circular 70.

347 Interviewee 9 (5 June 2012).

348 Nguyễn Thị Minh, 'Legal and Professional Challenges Confronting Practising Lawyers in Contemporary Vietnam' (Doctoral Thesis, The University of New South Wales, 2008), pp 110–13. Minh notes that the number of national lawyers has increased as follows: 1991–369; 1996–727; 2001–2,100; 2007–4,357. The national bar association suggests that in 2010, there were 5,250 lawyers: Vietnam Bar Association, Report on Access to Justice Research, 2010, [copy on file with author]. In 2012, the Ministry of Justice estimated there were 7,200 lawyers nationally: Anh Luu 'Vietnam Legal Research', *New York University Update* (May 2013), www.nyulawglobal.org/globalex/Vietnam1.htm#_edn33.

349 Nicholson, 'Access to Justice in Vietnam' (2010) 188–215.

350 Law on Legal Aid, Law No 69/2006/QH11, 29 June 2006 (Law on Legal Aid).

351 Decision No 358/2003/QD-BTP, 15 August 2003 of the Ministry of Justice Promulgating the Regulation on Collaborators of Legal Aid Organisations.

352 UNDP, 'Appointed Counsel' (n 14) 29–30. The UNDP report notes that the set fee was 120,000 Vietnam Dong/day (US$ 5.40/day).

provided to the poor, the elderly, ethnic minorities from poor areas, and those who 'served the revolution'.[353] In the case of poor clients, provincial governments determine what amounts to financial difficulty.[354] Commentators note the lack of independence of state-approved and institutionally appointed counsel,[355] and research describes the capacity of the Party-state to sanction lawyers that 'appear' to push their case too hard by prosecuting them, for example, in disciplinary proceedings.[356]

The involvement of legal aid-funded lawyers in trial work is uneven but not extensive. In Hanoi, for example, 524 of 7,000 (7.48 per cent) criminal cases benefited from legal aid in 2009, while in the northern mountainous province of Lạng Sơn 82 of 700 (11.71 per cent) cases were assisted.[357] The Vietnam Bar Association reports that advocates face an 'evasive attitude [from] law enforcement officers.'[358] The result is that legal aid lawyers (often, as indicated above, some of the most inexperienced members of counsel) have to deal with both clients and legal institutions that are confused about their role in a trial.

V. JURISDICTION

Vietnam's judiciary previously comprised three levels: District Courts (about 700); Provincial Courts (64); and the final appellate courts, located in the Supreme People's Court (three in total). The new Law on the Organisation of People's Courts of 2014 introduced a new Superior or High Court (*tòa án cấp cao*)[359] but it remains to be seen when the resulting 4-tiered structure will be fully implemented. There are still some significant regulatory gaps as a result of the new Law on the Organisation of People's Courts being introduced while amendment of the Criminal Procedure Code was incomplete. As mentioned, the Criminal Procedure Code is still under review, with a new Code anticipated in late 2015.

The current Criminal Procedure Code 2003 (which replaced that of 1988) provides that District Courts should hear almost all criminal trials, except for those involving national security, disruption of the peace, war crimes and crimes involving human lives.[360] The new Law on the Organisation of People's Courts provides that District Courts 'may' have a 'criminal tribunal' or specialist division[361] and it is anticipated that this will be the case.

353 Law on Legal Aid 2006, Arts 3, 10 and 14.

354 Regulations on Legal Aid, adopted 16 July 2003 at the 15th executive meeting of the State Council, Art 11 and 13.

355 UNDP, 'Appointed Counsel' (n 14) 29–30.

356 Anonymous, 'Assessment on the Real Situation of the Protection of Legitimate Rights and Interests of Lawyers 1999–2009, Annex 1' [copy on file with author].

357 UNDP, 'Appointed Counsel' (n 14) 14.

358 Vietnam Bar Association, Report on Access to Justice Research, 2010, [copy on file with author].

359 There is also a system of military courts in Vietnam. Ordinarily, Military Courts hear cases involving members of the armed forces, including criminal cases.

360 Criminal Procedure Code 2003, Art 170(1).

361 Law No 62/2014/QH13 passed by the National Assembly on 24 November 2014 on the Organisation of People's Courts, Art 45.

Previously the District Courts had jurisdiction where the applicable penalty was seven years or less and foreigners were not involved.[362] By a Letter, the Supreme People's Court had specifically instructed that matters involving foreigners (whether as 'foreign defendants, victims, persons whose rights or obligations are involved, civil plaintiffs or foreign organisations') should be heard in the Provincial Courts.[363] This Letter is still in effect,[364] and the new Draft Criminal Procedure Code confirms that Provincial Courts will hear cases 'in which defendants, victims, civil plaintiffs, civil defendants, or persons whose rights and obligations are involved in the cases are residing overseas, or assets involved in the cases are overseas.'[365]

The Criminal Procedure Code 2003 provides that: District Courts shall conduct first-instance trials of criminal cases involving less serious offences, serious offences and very serious offences, excluding certain specific offences; and the Provincial Courts shall conduct first-instance trials of the those criminal cases not dealt with by the District Court or other cases that they decide to take for trial.[366] This reflects the classification of crimes by the Criminal Code 1999 into less serious crimes, serious crimes, very serious crimes and especially serious crimes.[367] The seriousness of a crime is determined by its penalty and, as noted, the range for imprisonment is: up to three years; up to seven years; up to 15 years; over 15 years; up to life imprisonment or capital punishment.[368] Narcotics crimes, therefore, proceed at first instance either in a District People's Court, or in a Provincial People's Court if the matter attracts life imprisonment or the death penalty.

The territorial jurisdiction of the courts under the Criminal Procedure Code is established by reference to where the offences were allegedly committed.[369] Where an offence is committed in different places, or if the place where an offence was committed is unknown, jurisdiction is with the court where the investigation was completed.[370] Where a defendant allegedly committed an offence abroad but is to be

362 Criminal Procedure Code 1988, Art 145. See also Resolution No 1036/2006/NQ-UBTVQH11 dated 27 July 2006 of the Standing Committee of the National Assembly on Assigning the Jurisdiction of Criminal Cases Stipulated at Art 170(1) of the Criminal Procedure Code and Jurisdiction of Civil Cases Stipulated at Art 33 of the Civil Procedure Code to the District-Level Courts.

363 Official Letter No 81/2002/TANDTC dated 10 June 2002 of the Supreme People's Court in Response to Professional Queries.

364 See, eg, Trần Đức Long, 'Bàn về thẩm quyền giải quyết, xét xử vụ án hình sự có bị cáo là người nước ngoài [Regarding the jurisdiction to process and adjudicate criminal cases with foreign defendants]', Tòa Án Nhân Dân Tối Cao (Việt Nam) [Vietnam. Supreme People's Court], toaan.gov.vn/portal/page/portal/tandtc/Baiviet?p_page_id=1754190&p_cateid=1751909&Article_details=1&item_id=13493581; Thanh Tùng, 'Có nên cho tòa huyện xử án có yếu tố nước ngoài? [Should District Courts be allowed to adjudicate cases involving foreign factors?]', Pháp Luật Thành Phố Hồ Chí Minh [Ho Chi Minh Law Newspaper] (online), 14 January 2011, plo.vn/phap-luat/co-nen-cho-toa-huyen-xu-an-co-yeu-to-nuoc-ngoai-150138.html. The Criminal Code 1999 only adds that District Courts do not hear cases in which the offences are committed outside the territory of Vietnam (Art 6).

365 Draft (Amended) Criminal Procedure Code, Art 258.

366 Criminal Procedure Code 2003, Art 170.

367 Criminal Code 1999, Art 8.

368 Criminal Code 1999, Art 8(3).

369 Criminal Procedure Code 2003, Art 171(1).

370 Ibid.

tried in Vietnam, the Provincial Court of their last residence in Vietnam has jurisdiction. If the defendant's last residence in Vietnam cannot be determined, the President of the Supreme People's Court will assign the trial to the People's Court in Hanoi or Ho Chi Minh City on a case-by-case basis.[371]

Offences committed on board aircraft or sea-going ships of the Socialist Republic of Vietnam operating outside the airspace or the territorial seas of Vietnam fall under the jurisdiction of the Vietnamese courts of the locality where the relevant ships or planes were due to return or where such aircraft or sea-going ships are registered.[372]

In the event that a defendant commits a number of offences, and one falls under the jurisdiction of a court at higher level, that court (not the lower level court) will hear the entire case.[373]

Foreigners and Jurisdiction

Diplomatic Immunity

The Criminal Code 1999 provides that

> for foreigners who commit offences in the territory of Vietnam, but are entitled to diplomatic immunities or consular privileges and immunities under Vietnamese laws, international treaties that the Socialist Republic of Vietnam has signed or acceded to or international practices, their criminal liability shall be settled through diplomatic channels.[374]

To be more specific, according to the Ordinance on the Privileges and Immunities Relating to Diplomatic Missions, Consular Posts and Representative Offices of International Organisations in Vietnam issued by the Standing Committee of the National Assembly in 1993, a diplomatic agent is inviolable and not liable to any form of arrest or detention. The Vietnamese government is required to treat him or her with due respect and prevent any attack on his or her person, freedom or dignity.[375] If a diplomatic agent commits a crime, Vietnamese authorities are, therefore, only able to make a record, seize physical evidence, and then immediately report the incident to the Ministry of Public Security and the appropriate diplomatic agency.

Other Foreigners

The Criminal Procedure Code does not deal specifically with foreigners who are not diplomats. There are, however, special procedures applicable to foreigners that

[371] Criminal Procedure Code 2003, Art 171(2).
[372] Criminal Procedure Code 2003, Art 172.
[373] Criminal Procedure Code 2003, Art 173.
[374] Criminal Code 1999, Art 5.
[375] Ordinance No 25-L/CTN dated 23 August 1993 of the Standing Committee of National Assembly on the Privileges and Immunities Relating to Diplomatic Mission, Consular Posts and Representative Offices of International Organisations in Vietnam, Art 10.

derive from legal documents issued by other bodies, such as the Ministry of Public Security. Until relatively recently, unless caught red-handed[376] a foreigner who committed a crime in Vietnam could only be arrested with the approval of the head of the Ministry of Public Security.[377] If arrested red-handed, a report had to be sent to the head of the Ministry of Public Security as soon as possible afterwards.[378] In 1993, the Party Central Committee Secretariat also decided that '[t]he arrest and detention of academics, artists, leaders of religious communities or ethnic minorities, foreigners, and Vietnamese citizens who also hold foreign citizenship must be approved by the Supreme People's Procuracy and the Ministry of Interior'.[379]

A recent increase in the number of foreigners visiting Vietnam and, it is claimed, of offences committed by them, led to resistance to these policies, which, it was argued, hindered investigations and hampered the fight against crime.[380] As a result, the Politburo passed a directive in 2000 to the effect that those investigating crimes and wishing to make an arrest of a foreigner need only seek approval of (Party) executive committees where the foreigner has 'political influence',[381] a term that is not further defined. In such cases, the Board of Directors of Provincial Public Security must report to the Secretary of the Provincial Party Committee and the Central Party Committee to seek guidance.[382]

Provincial investigation agencies are also responsible for investigating criminal cases within the jurisdiction of the Provincial People's Court[383] and they, therefore, typically arrest foreigners.[384] The agencies involved then usually send written notification to the provincial office of the Department of Foreign Affairs so diplomatic missions can be notified.[385] Together, these procedures have the effect that the arrest of foreigners can be subject to the exercise of significant discretion at the provincial level.

376 Ibid.

377 Official Letter No 318/CV-BNV (V11) dated 29 March 1992 of the Ministry of Public Security on Reporting and Seeking Approval before Arresting Special Subjects (Including Foreigners).

378 Ibid.

379 Conclusion No 212/BBT dated 25 May 1993 of the Central Committee Secretariat of the Vietnamese Communist Party.

380 Nguyễn Văn Phú and Nguyễn Tiến Nam, 'Quy định của pháp luật Việt Nam về việc bắt người nước ngoài phạm tội [Regulations of Vietnamese law on arresting foreign offenders]', *Tạp Chí Công An Nhân Dân* [People's police journal] (Vietnam), www.pup.edu.vn/vi/Tap-chi-CAND/Quy-dinh-cua-phap-luat-Viet-Nam-ve-ap-dung-bien-phap-bat-nguoi-nuoc-ngoai-pham-toi--567.

381 Directive No 52-CT/TW dated 16 March 2000 of the Politburo of the Vietnamese Communist Party on the Scope of Responsibilities and Powers between Party Committees with Party Unit in the Police, Party Unit in the People's Supremacy, and Party Unit in the People's Courts in Protecting the Party and Dealing with Crimes Involving Party Members.

382 Ibid.

383 Criminal Procedure Code 2003, Art 110(4).

384 Decision No 1044/QD-BCA (C11) dated 5 September 2007 of the Ministry of Public Security on the Division of Responsibilities and Co-ordination in Investigating Activities of Public Security Investigating Police Agencies.

385 Nguyễn Văn Phú and Nguyễn Tiến Nam, 'Quy định của pháp luật'.

Extradition

Regulation of the extradition of people to and from Vietnam is dealt with in Chapter XXXVII of the Criminal Procedure Code 2003 and the Law on Legal Assistance 2007.[386] Together, they grant competent authorities in Vietnam (including investigation agencies, the procuracy and courts) the right to rely on international treaties to which Vietnam is a party or the principle of reciprocity to make a request for extradition or perform an extradition at the request of a counterpart in another country.[387]

To date, Vietnam has entered into 15 bilateral treaties on 'legal assistance' that allow extradition to and from Vietnam,[388] and it has executed six bilateral treaties specifically on extradition with Republic of Korea, Australia, Laos, Indonesia, Hungary and Cambodia.[389] Vietnam has been negotiating with France for a similar bilateral treaty on extradition since 2014.[390] The Law on Legal Assistance provides, however, that even without reciprocity with another country or a treaty authorising extradition, Vietnam's competent authorities may still exercise their rights to extradite or make extradition requests.[391] Vietnam has acceded to a number of multinational conventions that also impose certain obligations on it when conducting extradition, although it has also declared reservations in respect of all these obligations.[392]

In 2005, the Politburo adopted Resolution 48 recommending the 'prompt adoption' of a law on extradition and transfer of the convicts. Despite this, a draft law is yet to be submitted to the National Assembly, although in 2011 the Assembly itself suggested the finalisation of regulations on extradition.[393] As a result, the sources outlined above remain the principal legal bases for extradition to and from Vietnam. Not all the bilateral treaties are in identical terms and there are also differences between them and the Law on Legal assistance 2007. The general principles that apply in relation to extradition in Vietnam are, however, summarised below.

[386] Criminal Procedure Code 2003; Law No 08/2007/QH 12 passed by the National Assembly on 22 November 2007 on Legal Assistance.

[387] Criminal Procedure Code 2003, Art 343.

[388] See Ngô Thanh Xuyên, 'Dẫn độ tội phạm trong hiệp định tương trợ tư pháp giữa Việt Nam với một số quốc gia trên thế giới [Extradition in bilateral treaties on legal assistance between Vietnam and several countries in the world]' (16 April 2015) Bộ Tư Pháp (Việt Nam) [(Vietnamese) Ministry of Justice], www.moj.gov.vn/ct/tintuc/Pages/nghien-cuu-trao-doi.aspx?ItemID=6788#_edn6.

[389] Ibid.

[390] Ibid.

[391] Law on Legal Assistance 2007, Art 32.

[392] A discussion of these conventions is published on the official website of the Ministry of Justice, see Ngô Thanh Xuyên, 'Dẫn độ tội phạm'.

[393] National Assembly issued Resolution No 10/2011/QH13 dated 8 November 2011 of the National Assembly on the 2011–2015 Socio-economic Development Plan.

Right to Extradite and Request Extradition

Competent agencies may extradite a person from Vietnam, or request the extradition of a person to Vietnam, if that person:

- is in the territory of Vietnam or the country to which Vietnam makes the extradition request, and
- has committed an offence which is punishable under both the laws of Vietnam and the requesting country by imprisonment for a minimum of one year, or a more severe penalty;[394] or
- is wanted for enforcement of a sentence of imprisonment and a period of at least six months to one year of that sentence remains to be served[395] (this stipulation is generally not included in bilateral treaties on legal assistance involving Vietnam concluded before 2000.)

When the person in respect of whom extradition is sought has allegedly committed a crime outside Vietnam, the extradition can be granted if that conduct is a crime at Vietnamese law.[396] An equivalent principle applies when Vietnam requests the extradition of a person to Vietnam in cases where that person has committed a crime outside the territory of the requesting country, that is, the extradition can be granted if the crime is punishable under the law of the requesting country.[397]

Right to Refuse to Extradite

Extradition of a person to and from Vietnam will generally be refused if:

- the person is a citizen of the requested country;[398]
- the person has been convicted in a legally valid judgment or the case has been discontinued in the requested country;[399]

[394] Law on Legal Assistance 2007, Art 33(1); Treaty between the Socialist Republic of Vietnam and Australia on Extradition, signed on 10 April 2012 (entered into force on 10 October 2012), Art 2(1); Treaty between the Socialist Republic of Vietnam and the Republic of Korea on Extradition, signed on 15 September 2003 (entered into force on 19 April 2004), Art 2(1); and Treaty between the Socialist Republic of Vietnam and the People's Democratic Republic of Lao on Legal Assistance in Civil and Criminal Matters, signed on 6 July 1998 (entered into force on 19 February 2000), Art 60; Treaty between the Socialist Republic of Vietnam and the Republic of Hungary on Legal Assistance in Matrimonial, Civil and Criminal Matters, signed on 18 January 1985 (entered into force on 26 March 1985), Art 58(2). Note that Art 2(1) of the Treaty between the Socialist Republic of Vietnam and the Kingdom of Cambodia on Extradition, signed on 23 December 2013 (entered into force on 9 October 2014) requires imprisonment of two years.

[395] Law on Legal Assistance 2007, Art 33(1); Treaty between Vietnam and Australia on Extradition, Art 2(2); Treaty between Vietnam and South Korea on Extradition, Art 2(2); Treaty between Vietnam and Cambodia on Extradition, Art 2(2).

[396] Law on Legal Assistance 2007, Art 33(3).

[397] Treaty between Vietnam and Australia on Extradition, Art 2(5); Treaty between Vietnam and South Korea on Extradition, Art 2(5); Treaty between Vietnam and Cambodia on Extradition, Art 2(4).

[398] Law on Legal Assistance 2007, Art 35(1)(a); Treaty between Vietnam and Lao on Legal Assistance, Art 61(1)(a); Treaty between Vietnam and Hungary on Legal Assistance, Art 58(3); Treaty between Vietnam and Australia on Extradition, Art 4(1); Treaty between Vietnam and South Korea, Art 6(1); Treaty between Vietnam and Cambodia on Extradition, Art 2(4).

[399] Criminal Procedure Code 2003, Arts 344(1)(a) and Art 344(1)(c); Law on Legal Assistance 2007, Art 35; Treaty between Vietnam and Australia on Extradition, Art 4; Treaty between Vietnam and South

— the person becomes immune from prosecution or punishment by reason of lapse of the applicable limitation period or for other 'legitimate reasons';[400]
— there is substantial ground for a belief that a request for extradition for a criminal offence has been made for the purpose of prosecuting or penalising a person on account of that person's race, religion, nationality, ethnic origin or political opinion; or[401]
— the offence for which the extradition is sought is a political offence under the law of the requesting country[402] (treaties on legal assistance that Vietnam entered into before 2000 generally do not include this basis for refusal of extradition).

Additionally, Vietnam (or the country from which Vietnam has requested an extradition) may refuse to extradite a person if that person is being prosecuted in Vietnam or the requesting country for the same offence on which the extradition request is based.[403]

Limitations on the Prosecution of Extradited Person

Limits on the prosecution of an extradited person appear in the Law on Legal Assistance 2007 and bilateral treaties on legal assistance or extradition. These limits vary significantly, however. The two most common are that, first, prosecution of an extradited person is restricted to offences for which the extradition was granted, unless the requested country agrees otherwise;[404] and, second, when a person has been extradited to the requesting country, that person shall not be extradited to a third country.[405] Extradition to a third country can take place where the requesting

Korea on Extradition, Art 6; Treaty between Vietnam and Cambodia on Extradition, Art 4; Treaty between Vietnam and Lao on Legal Assistance, Art 61; Treaty between Vietnam and Hungary on Legal Assistance, Art 59(1)(a).

[400] Criminal Procedure Code 2003, Art 344(1)(b); Law on Legal Assistance 2007, Art 35(1)(b); Treaty between Vietnam and Australia on Extradition, Art 3(1)(c); Treaty between Vietnam and South Korea on Extradition, Art 3(1)(c); Treaty between Vietnam and Cambodia on Extradition, Art 3(1)(e); Treaty between Vietnam and Lao on Legal Assistance, Art 61(1)(c); Treaty between Vietnam and Hungary on Legal Assistance, Art 59(1)(a).

[401] Criminal Procedure Code 2003, Art 334(1)(d); Law on Legal Assistance 2007, Art 35(1)(d); Treaty between Vietnam and Australia on Extradition, Art 3(1)(a); Treaty between Vietnam and South Korea on Extradition, Art 3(1)(d); Treaty between Vietnam and Cambodia on Extradition, Art 3(1)(c).

[402] Treaty between Vietnam and Australia on Extradition, Art 3(2)(a); Treaty between Vietnam and South Korea on Extradition, Art 3(1)(a); Treaty between Vietnam and Cambodia on Extradition, Art 3(1)(a).

[403] Criminal Procedure Code 2003, Art 344(2)(b); Law on Legal Assistance 2007, Art 35(2)(b); Treaty between Vietnam and Australia on Extradition, Art 3(2)(d); Treaty between Vietnam and Cambodia on Extradition, Art 3(2)(a).

[404] Law on Legal Assistance 2007, Art 34; Treaty between Vietnam and Australia on Extradition, Art 16(1)(a); Treaty between Vietnam and South Korea on Extradition, Art 15(1)(a); Treaty between Vietnam and Cambodia on Extradition, Art 17(1)(a); Treaty between Vietnam and Lao on Legal Assistance, Art 72(1); Treaty between Vietnam and Hungary on Legal Assistance, Art 69(1).

[405] Law on Legal Assistance 2007, Art 34; Treaty between Vietnam and Australia on Extradition, Art 17; Treaty between Vietnam and South Korea on Extradition, Arts 15(2) and 15(3); Treaty between Vietnam and Cambodia on Extradition, Art 18; Treaty between Vietnam and Lao on Legal Assistance, Art 72(2); Treaty between Vietnam and Hungary on Legal Assistance, Art 69(2).

country consents to an additional extradition, and the extradited person has had an opportunity to leave the requesting country's territory (but has not done so in certain time period) or that person has voluntarily returned to the requesting country after leaving it.[406]

VI. TRIALS

Pre-trial Practice

Chapter XVII of the Criminal Procedure Code 2003 deals with pre-trial procedures, and requires judges presiding to 'study the files, settle complaints and requests of the participants in the procedure and perform other tasks necessary for opening court sessions.'[407] The Judges' Council of the SPC has also promulgated guidelines on the receipt and handling of case files, trial preparation time limits and the extension of time limits for consistent application by judges at all levels.[408]

The Criminal Procedure Code provides that:

> Within thirty days for less serious offences, 45 days for serious offences, two months for very serious offences and three months for especially serious offences, counting from the date of receipt of the case files, the judges assigned to preside over court sessions must issue one of the following decisions:
>
> a) Bring the case for trial;
> b) Return the file for additional investigation;
> c) Cease or suspend the case.[409]

In complicated cases, the president of a court may 'decide to prolong the trial preparation time limits for no more than 15 days for less serious offences and serious offences, and for no more than 30 days for very serious offences and especially serious offences.'[410] It is said that judges need to discuss with the president of the relevant court what to do before reaching any decision about whether or not to try a case. There is also capacity for a judge to consult with the procuracy about particular aspects of a case at this time and also to talk with counsel. This is common practice.

As shown above, judges may also return a case file for additional investigation[411] but '[p]rocuracies or courts shall only return case files for additional investigation twice or less'.[412] An official of the SPC we interviewed was of the opinion that if

406 Ibid.

407 Criminal Procedure Code 2003, Art 176.

408 Resolution 04.

409 Criminal Procedure Code 2003, Art 176.

410 Criminal Procedure Code 2003, Art 176(2).

411 See Criminal Procedure Code 2003, Art 179; Inter-circular No 01/2010/TTLT–VKSNDTC-BCA-TANDTC dated 27 August 2010 of the Supreme People's Court, the Ministry of Public Security, and the Supreme People's Court Guiding a Number of Articles of the Criminal Procedure Code in Relation to Returning Case Files for Additional Investigation.

412 Criminal Procedure Code 2003, Art 121(2).

a case file does not contain sufficient evidence, the court should decide that the accused is not guilty, without returning the case file for additional investigation.[413]

During the first year of implementation of Inter-circular 01, the Supreme People's Procuracy suggested that the court abused its power to return case files for additional investigation.

> Some judges who are assigned to preside over the first instance trials have not carefully researched the case files, do not comprehensively evaluate the available evidence; or do not coordinate well with other relevant bodies. Therefore, they decide to return case files that contain only tiny mistakes capable of easy rectification by the courts. [...][414]

The procuracy has also claimed that judges evade their 'responsibilities and time pressures' by returning files for further investigation, where technically not possible, alleging the expiration of limitations periods.[415] Sometimes, courts do this multiple times in a single case, despite the formal limit of two returns.[416] In short, delays in going to trial are common place, often extending beyond a year,[417] and the procuracy argues that the courts ought to take responsibility for the ways in which some judges frustrate the prosecution of drugs cases.[418]

Mass Trials

The courts in Vietnam do not have the power to separate related criminal cases or determine which parties will appear in one trial, although they may do so in civil and administrative matters.[419] As a result, 'mass trials' where many defendants appear together are not uncommon. In 2015, a trial involving 89 defendants was reported, with 29 of the 89 receiving the death penalty.[420]

[413] Nguyễn Thị Hải Châu, 'Góp ý sửa đổi những quy định pháp luật tố tụng hình sự về 'trả hồ sơ điều tra bổ sung [Comments on the Provisions of Criminal Procedures in Relation to Returning Case Files for the Additional Investigation]' *Tạp Chí Pháp Lý* [*Legal Journal*] (Vietnam, 19 April 2011), phaply.net.vn/dien-dan-phap-luat/gop-y-sua-doi-nhung-qui-dinh-phap-luat-to-tung-hinh-su-ve-%E2%80%9Ctra-ho-so-de-dieu-tra-bo-sung%E2%80%9D.html.

[414] Supreme People's Procuracy, 'Kết quả một năm thực hiện thông tư liên tịch số 01 về điều tra bổ sung giữa các cơ quan tiến hành tố tụng [Results of one year implementation of Inter-Circular no 01 on returning case files for additional investigation among litigation authorised agencies]' (10 January 2012), Viện kiểm sát nhân dân tối cao (Việt Nam) [(Vietnamese) Supreme People's Procuracy], www.vksndtc.gov.vn/tin-chi-tiet-2263.

[415] Ibid.

[416] Ibid.

[417] Of 32 cases scrutinised involving Australian nationals between 1999 and 2013, arrest dates and first instance trial dates were not confirmed in 6 cases. Of the 26 cases with dates, 15 or 41.6 per cent waited more than a year for a trial. Delays in trials are common globally but in the case of Vietnam this breaches the Criminal Procedure Code.

[418] Ibid.

[419] See Civil Procedure Code No 24/2004/QH11 passed by the National Assembly on 15 June 2004, Art 38; Law No 64/2010/QH12 passed by the National Assembly on 24 November 2010 on Administrative Procedure ('Law on Administrative Procedure 2010'), Art 33.

[420] Phạm Hải Sâm, 'Vietnam Court Upholds Death Sentences against 29 Drug Smugglers' *Thanh Nien News* (20 June 2014), www.thanhniennews.com/society/vietnam-court-upholds-death-sentences-against-29-drug-smugglers-27474.html.

Decisions about how to run trials rest with the procuracy and the indictments it issues indicate the number of co-accused to be tried in any one hearing.[421] Usually that number will reflect procedures adopted during the investigation, which is the only point at which decisions about joinder and separation can be made.[422] The Criminal Procedure Code does allows separation of cases by the procuracy relating to the same matter in cases of 'extreme necessity',[423] such as when undue delays concerning certain evidence might justify treating one of the defendants differently, but even then only if it 'would not affect the determination of the objective and comprehensive truths of the cases'.[424] In other words, all people charged in the one case file will usually be heard together, and the court is generally powerless to change this.

This approach also reflects a common understanding in Vietnam that trial is merely a stage in a wider criminal process, the carriage of which rests largely with the investigating body and the procuracy. Given the recent changes to the Constitution and the Law on the Organisation of People's Courts 2014 (which, as noted, imposed a responsibility on the courts to protect human rights and assess the legality of the work of investigation agencies), the judiciary may adopt a more interventionist approach to trials in the future. It is too early, however, to know if this will, in fact, happen, or how.

Trials: Inquisitorial or Adversarial?

We argued above in the context of the discussion of rights to counsel that Vietnamese trials essentially remain inquisitorial, although Communist Party policy and laws now reflect a more adversarial approach. This tension between current trial practice and apirations for a more adversarial system is evident also in the role and attitudes of judges and the procuracy, and the limited power of counsel to challenge evidence at trials.

A people's assessor we interviewed claimed, for example, that defence counsel only have the status of a person 'participating in criminal proceedings (*người tham gia tố tụng*)', compared to procurators who have 'the status of a person conducting

[421] Vietnam. Judicial Training School, 2011 Professional Discussion, tcbta.toaan.gov.vn/portal/page/portal/tcbta/27676686/27677465?p_page_id=27676686&p_cateid=28316919&item_id=30581267&Article_details=1, pt I—Criminal Matters, Question 6.

[422] See Criminal Procedure Code 2003, Art 117. Criticisms of this practice can be found on the website of the Ministry of Justice: See Hoàng Duy Hiệp, 'Hoàn thiện quy định của bộ Luật tố tụng hình sự về nhập hoặc tách vụ án hình sự để tiến hành điều tra [Perfecting the provisions of the Criminal Procedure Code regarding joining or separating criminal case(s) to conduct investigation]' (22 April 2013) Bộ Tư Pháp (Việt Nam) [(Vietnamese) Ministry of Justice], www.moj.gov.vn/ct/tintuc/Pages/nghien-cuu-trao-doi.aspx?ItemID=5922; and Nguyễn Trọng Nghĩa, 'Thực tiễn áp dụng Điều 117 Bộ luật Tố tụng hình sự về việc tách, nhập vụ án hình sự để tiến hành điều tra [Implementation of Article 117 of the Criminal Procedure Code joining or separating criminal case(s) to conduct investigation]', Trường Đại Học Kiểm Sát Hà Nội (Việt Nam) [(Vietnamese) Hanoi Procuracy University], tks.edu.vn/thong-tin-khoa-hoc/chi-tiet/79/247.

[423] Criminal Procedure Code 2003, Art 117(2).

[424] Ibid.

criminal proceedings (*người tiến hành tố tụng*)'.[425] This latter status is equivalent to that of a judge or people's assessor, while participant status is equivalent to that of a witness or defendant.[426] The current draft of the Criminal Procedure Code retains this lower status for counsel, despite lobbying for change from the Vietnamese Bar Council.[427]

Further, a judge noted that some judges have a 'negative attitude' toward counsel, seeing them as a 'disturbance' (*gây rối*) in criminal cases.[428] These persistent attitudes tend, of course, to undermine the recent changes to the law. It is also suggested that older judges 'are very conservative' and some of them 'have strongly rejected the idea that judge must be impartial'.[429] These older judges, it is said, cannot countenance taking a neutral position as between counsel and the procuracy.[430]

Many of the lawyers, judges, people's assessors and procurators interviewed acknowledged that procedural laws have changed very rapidly in recent years, in many cases producing improvements to trial practice.[431] Some, however, reiterated that most Vietnamese judges are still not independent but remain Party-led.[432] As noted at the outset, it remains CPV policy for judges to be Party-led. According to the Law on the Organisation of People's Courts 2014, judges are appointed initially for a five-year term.[433] If appointed for a second term, a reform to the duration of appointments introduced in 2014 means they will remain in office for a further 10 years.[434] While this extension of the second term may contribute to a more fearless judiciary over time, it is suggested that many judges still remain 'afraid of senior officials and the relevant executive committee of the Communist Party'.[435] A strategy adopted by judges to avoid conflict over reaching the 'right' decision is to seek consensus (*đồng thuận*) with seniors and political leaders to ensure their reappointment in the future.[436] The current reforms would not seem to upset this practice.

Composition of the Court

Until 2013, trials comprised a trial panel made up of a judge and two people's assessors. People's assessors can be understood as lay judges, nominated by the Vietnam Fatherland Front[437] according to criteria that include loyalty to the Fatherland and

425 Interviewee 12 (13 August 2012). See also Criminal Procedure Code 2003, Ch III on bodies and persons conducting criminal proceedings and Ch IV on persons participating in criminal proceedings.
426 Ibid.
427 Draft (Amended) Criminal Procedure Code, Art 50. Interviewee 17 (17 August 2012).
428 Interviewee 6 (27 May 2012).
429 Interviewee 12 (13 August 2012).
430 Ibid.
431 Interviewee 7 (5 June 2012); Interviewee 9 (5 June 2012).
432 Interviewee 9 (5 June 2012), Interviewee 11 (10 August 2012) and Interviewee 15 (16 August 2012). See more generally Nicholson, 'Renovating Courts', 528–65 and Nicholson (n 5).
433 Law on the Organisation of People's Courts 2014, Art 74.
434 Ibid.
435 Interviewee 9 (5 June 2012).
436 Ibid.
437 Law on the Organisation of People's Courts 2014, Art 86(1).

Constitution, 'good ethical qualities, firm political stance', and capacity to 'safeguard justice'.[438]

People's assessors ostensibly have the authority to reach a decision independently[439] but the new Law on the Organisation of People's Courts does not give them equal authority to judges, as was previously the case. In fact, it is often claimed that judges frequently use their superior expertise to manage and lead decision-making at trials, at the expense of the assessors.[440] Despite this, the new law mandates the use of people's assessors in all first-instance trials,[441] in principle at least. The amended Criminal Procedure Code is likely to do the same. The role assessors will actually play in practice remains unclear, however.

It is often claimed that Vietnamese judges are open to taking bribes in relation to sentencing.[442] The introduction of state compensation for parties who have been wrongly treated by the authorities in criminal proceedings, including where there has been a subsequent finding of innocence, conviction on a lesser charge or an annulment of a detention order,[443] has allegedly improved the performance of investigation bodies, the procuracy and the courts.[444] Certainly the case of Nguyen Thanh Chan, a poor farmer wrongly accused and sentenced to life for murder, attracted a great deal of publicity when the Supreme People's Court ordered compensation of US$ 360,000 for his 10 years in jail.[445] It is contended that there is increasingly less support for judges maintaining the view that 'wrongfully accusing a person is better than missing a criminal (*thà bắt nhầm hơn bỏ sót*)'.[446]

Finally, the Constitution now states that 'interference in the trials of the judges and assessors by bodies, organizations, and individuals is strictly prohibited',[447] and a similar prohibition appears as well in the new Law on the Organisation of People's

[438] Law on the Organisation of People's Courts 2014, Art 85.

[439] People's assessors must be 'independent impartial and objective in adjudication and contribute to ... the socialist regime, interests of the State'. Law on the Organisation of People's Courts 2014, Art 89(3).

[440] Interviewee 13 (14 August 2012).

[441] Law on the Organisation of People's Courts 2014, Art 8.

[442] Interviewee 10 (8 June 2012). See also Pip Nicholson, 'Good Governance and Institutional Accountability: The Role of the Vietnamese Courts' in Tim Lindsey and Howard Dick (eds), *Corruption in Asia: Rethinking the Good Governance Paradigm* (Sydney, Federation Press, 2002) 201–18.

[443] See Law No 35/2009/QH12 passed by the National Assembly on 18 June 2009 on Compensation Liability, Art 26. See also Resolution No 388/2003/NQ-UBTVQH11 dated 17 March 2003 of the Standing Committee of the National Assembly on Compensation for Damage Caused to Unjustly Condemned People by Competent People in Criminal Proceedings; and Joint Circular No 05/2012/TTLT-VKSNDTC-TANDTC-BCA-BTP-BQP-BTC-BNNPTNT dated 2 November 2012 of the Supreme People's Procuracy, the Supreme People's Court, the Ministry of Public Security, the Ministry of Justice, the Ministry of National Defence, the Ministry of Finance, the Ministry of Agriculture and Rural Development Guiding the Performance of State Compensation Liability in Criminal Proceedings.

[444] Interviewee 7 (5 June 2012).

[445] See Tâm Lụa, 'Vụ án oan Nguyễn Thanh Chấn: xuất hiện nhân chứng mới [Nguyen Thanh Chan case: New witnesses appear]' *Tuoi Tre* (Vietnam, 30 June 2015), tuoitre.vn/tin/phap-luat/20150630/vu-an-oan-nguyen-thanh-chan-bat-ngo-xuat-hien-nhan-chung-moi/769023.html; See Nghia Trung, 'Criminal Justice System in Vietnam: Compassionate Communists' *The Economist* (20 June 2015), www.economist.com/news/asia/21654643-party-allows-smidgen-penal-reform-compassionate-communists.

[446] Ibid.

[447] See SRVN Constitution 2013, Art 103(2).

Courts.[448] These very specific prohibitions arguably buttress the anti-corruption agenda, although they certainly do not deliver an end to judicial misconduct.

Evidence in Trial: Experts and the Role of Argument

Earlier reforms to the Criminal Procedure Code 2003 included allowing the presentation of defence arguments in court by defence counsel, as well as the questioning of evidence. More particularly, the Criminal Procedure Code provides that all documents and reports of 'agencies and organisations' (in this case, the procuracy in particular) are to be presented in court. If they are not, the court must specifically declare any reliance it places on such documents or reports.[449] The Code adds that:

> Procurators, defendants, defence counsels and other participants in court sessions shall have the right to give remarks on such documents and inquire further about related matters.[450]

These provisions give more substance to the constitutional right to counsel, discussed above, including the right to be informed of the bases of evidence and a right of response to that evidence.[451]

More particularly, the defence technically has a range of rights to test evidence and present opinions, (as outlined below) but there is a core tension between the influence of the dossier—with which the procuracy and the judges are familiar—and what later takes place in court. As mentioned, the court and the procuracy gather in advance of trials in a joint meeting (*họp liên ngành*) to discuss and determine the approach to the case. This allows judges to seek advice or receive instructions from their superiors[452] or the Party about how to decide the case.[453]

As explained above, the procuracy continues to determine the contents of the case dossier. While lawyers have the right to submit documents and or materials to investigators and the procuracy and ask them to take the testimony of a particular witness, the final decision whether to include evidence remains with these agencies.[454] The investigation body, the procuracy and the court are also able to 'whittle' (*đẽo gọt*) the dossier or 'pack' (*gói*) it with evidence in ways that support the position of the authorities.[455]

The dossier has always formed the basis of judges' understanding of a case. Before the changes recently introduced into the Criminal Procedure Code, it was usually the meetings about the content of the dossier that determined the outcome of a case, not the trial. More particularly it was said that the dossier played a 'crucial role', having considerable impact on the 'inner faith (*niềm tin nội tâm*) of the judge'.[456] 'Inner

[448] Law on the Organisation of People's Courts 2014, Art 77.
[449] Criminal Procedure Code 2003, Art 214.
[450] Ibid.
[451] SRVN Constitution 2013, Arts 103(7) and 31(4).
[452] Interviewee 11 (10 August 2012) and Interviewee 15 (16 August 2012).
[453] Interviewee 11 (10 August 2012).
[454] Interviewee 12 (13 August 2012).
[455] Ibid.
[456] Ibid.

faith' is here a reference to an instinct about, or a moral evaluation of, the case, and is seen as a legitimate way to assess the facts underpinning it.[457]

At the trial, following an analysis of the evidence in the dossier by the court panel (labelled the 'inquiry' in the Criminal Procedure Code):

> the procurators shall present the arraignments, proposing the charges against the defendants on the basis of the whole or part of the indictments or conclusions on lesser offences; if deeming that there are no grounds for conviction, they shall withdraw the whole prosecution decisions and propose the trial panel to pronounce the defendants not guilty. The arraignments presented by procurators must be based on documents and evidences already examined at the court sessions and opinions of the defendants, defence counsels, defence counsels of the interests of the involved parties and other participants in the procedure at the court sessions.[458]

Following this procuratorial presentation, defence counsel has the right to 'defend the defendants including putting into evidence any 'defence opinion'.[459] Practices vary. The UNDP report on the right to counsel found that in the Hanoi District Court lawyers must present a defence submission.[460] At other courts, the UNDP report suggests neither judges nor lawyers have adopted this practice.[461] Further, lawyers claim that their contentions do not even form a part of the official record (generated by the court clerk). They report that, at best, only short versions of their submissions are noted, in marked contrast to the recording in full of the procuracy submissions.[462] Some suggest that allowing the participation of defence lawyers is still more a matter of form than substance.[463]

A review of a number of dossiers relating to narcotics offences that we were able to obtain revealed that more technical arguments are made by the procuracy in cases involving foreign defendants[464] than in those concerning local defendants. Unfortunately, because these dossiers are usually not publicly available, our conclusion can only be based on a small random sample. It is, however, supported by comments from an experienced narcotics defence lawyer who agrees that 'investigation bodies, procuracies and courts are more cautious with formalities and procedural matters' when a foreigner is involved.[465]

To conclude the hearing, the defendant has a right to 'say their final words'.[466] Those speaking can be asked to avoid irrelevancies but there is no restriction on

[457] Ibid.
[458] Criminal Procedure Code 2003, Art 217(1).
[459] Criminal Procedure Code 2003, Art 217(2).
[460] UNDP, 'Right to Counsel' (n 14) 262.
[461] Ibid.
[462] UNDP, 'Right to Counsel' (n 14) 262–63.
[463] Interviewee 12 (13 August 2012).
[464] Nicholson was able to examine dossiers containing the details of American and Australian defendants charged in 2010 for drug trafficking offences (copies on file with author). These have been compared with dossiers relating to drug trafficking charges laid against local defendants in 2009 (copies on file with author).
[465] Interviewee 9 (5 June 2012).
[466] Criminal Procedure Code 2003, Art 220.

speaking time.[467] While questions cannot be put by either party at this time, the court can decide to re-open the inquiry if the 'final words' cast doubt on the evidence.

The court must declare any reliance it decides to place on expert testimony.[468] While the defence or its counsel has no right to call competing expert evidence, 'defence counsel and other participants in court sessions shall have the right to remark on expert conclusions' and make inquiries about unclear or contradictory elements of the expert evidence.[469] Finally, a court can seek additional expert evidence if it is 'deemed necessary'.[470] As discussed above, however, there are real limitations on how counsel can challenge evidence and the dossier can often have a significant hold on judges.

A particular challenge lies in the determination of the purity of drugs. There are regulations dealing with testing for drug purity[471] but, in practice, experts usually can only accurately determine the proportion (*hàm lượng*) of a narcotic substance if it is liquid.[472] It is claimed that purity testing 'fails' where narcotics are in a solid state.[473] Whether the testing is, in fact, as limited as this, there remains little that defence counsel can do except demand that the judge order re-testing, thereby delaying trial.

One expert procurator claimed that exhibits are rarely examined at appeals but may be scrutinised at first instance trials.[474] Further, courts do summon witnesses to trial, although in drug cases witnesses are very hesitant to appear,[475] supposedly because they fear retaliation.[476] That said, another procurator claimed that the courts employ a range of strategies to consider the probity of evidence. For example, a court will consider whether the language of a statement adduced in evidence is consistent with the educational background and work experience of the witnesses whose testimony it purports to represent.[477]

Counsel generally took the view that foreigners were not treated differently in trials, except, as mentioned, that judicial agencies take great care to identify that all legal procedures are fully documented when a foreigner is involved.[478] An example of this cautious approach to the prosecution of international defendants given to us related to a trial in which the defendant was unexpectedly declared to be a Cambodian citizen by the Cambodian Consulate.[479] Although no formal evidence of the defendant's Cambodian nationality was advanced, the trial panel cancelled the case immediately to allow further investigation.[480]

467 Ibid.
468 Criminal Procedure Code 2003, Art 215(3).
469 Criminal Procedure Code 2003, Art 215(4).
470 Criminal Procedure Code 2003, Art 215(5).
471 Inter-circular 17.
472 Interviewee 7 (27 May 2012).
473 Ibid.
474 Interviewee 5 (26 May 2012).
475 Ibid; Interviewee 13 (14 August 2012).
476 Interviewee 13 (14 August 2012).
477 Interviewee 5 (26 May 2012).
478 Interviewee 19 (27 August 2012).
479 Ibid.
480 Ibid.

As argued above, there is a real possibility that a determination will often have been reached through 'guidance' before the trial commences.[481] One people's assessor maintained, for example, that there is 'debate between members of the trial panel in approximately a third of cases'[482] and that 'the final decision did not always reflect the right opinion', with decisions 'in big cases' following 'the line approved in advance by the court's leaders'.[483]

Courts' Duty to Protect Human Rights

As explained earlier, the new Constitution stipulates that courts have a particular responsibility to protect human rights and this arguably increases the prospect of adversarial elements manifesting at trials. Article 102(3) states that:

> The people's courts are responsible for the protection of justice, human rights, citizen's rights, the socialist regime, interests of the State, and legal rights and interests of organisations and individuals.[484]

This duty to protect human rights does not, however, assume those rights are absolute. Rather, it reflects an official Vietnamese notion that human rights need to be balanced against the rights of the State in order to protect the socialist regime.[485] Article 15(4), therefore, provides that citizens' rights 'cannot infringe national interests and the other's legal and legitimate rights'.[486] As argued earlier, a socialist conception of justice inevitably accords the state powers to privilege social order and stability over individual rights.

It is not yet clear how the newly-introduced human rights protections will play out, or how the existing 2003 Criminal Procedure Code might be amended in light of the new responsibilities it ostensibly imposes on the courts. Nevertheless, the new constitutional provisions, together with the new duties of courts in the new Law on the Organisation of People's Courts, empowers—and therefore potentially emboldens—the judiciary to support the rights of defendants, at least to a greater degree than in the past.

VII. SENTENCING

Vietnamese courts must give effect to the Constitution and the Criminal Code when sentencing and take into account a range of principles. The Criminal Code generally requires courts to consider the seriousness of the offence, the role in the offence

481 Interviewee 11 (10 August 2012) and Interviewee 15 (16 August 2012).
482 Interviewee 18 (20 August 2012).
483 Ibid.
484 SRVN Constitution 2013, Art 102(3).
485 Bùi Ngọc Sơn, 'What is Socialist about the Socialist Constitution of Vietnam' 2015 35–38 (forthcoming) [Copy on file with author].
486 SRVN Constitution 2013, Art 15(4).

played by the defendant, and any remorse demonstrated[487]—and they must do so in the context of the court, procuracy and police being charged with the 'struggle against crime' and the duty to 'combat' it.[488] More particularly, the Code specifically instructs the court to take into account the

> the nature and extent of danger posed to society by the acts of offence, the personal records of the offenders, and any circumstances that extenuate or aggravate the penal liability.[489]

This provision is the source of a number of bedrock sentencing principles that apply in Vietnam, which we now consider in more detail: the rule of law, proportionality, fairness, and the principle of humanity.[490]

Rule of Law or Legality (*Pháp chế*)

In Vietnam, the 'rule of law' is understood as a principle that requires courts to strictly apply the law and obey it.[491] This is to be distinguished from debates about the meaning of 'socialist rule of law' as a doctrine relating to the constitutional organisation of the state.[492] As discussed earlier, the recent introduction of tougher anti-corruption provisions bolsters the application to trials of this interpretation of the rule of law.

Proportionality

This principle requires that sentences be proportionate to the seriousness of the crime and be neither too lenient nor too harsh.

Resolution 01 is a document produced by the court that exists to guide proportionality in sentencing and it clarifies the penalties applicable to different amounts of drugs under the Criminal Code.[493] In particular, the Resolution identifies the penalties for drug-related offences where there are no aggravating or extenuating circumstances or where both are present, so that they cancel each other out. It applies when an accused faces prosecution under either Article 193 ('illegally producing narcotics') or Article 194 ('illegally stockpiling, transporting, trading in

487 Criminal Code 1999, Art 3.

488 Criminal Code 1999, Art 4.

489 Criminal Code 1999, Art 45.

490 Nguyễn Thị Phương Hoa (n 135) 20.

491 This is constitutionally enshrined. See SRVN Constitution 2013, Art 103(2): 'The trials of the judges and assessors are independent and shall only obey the law [...]'. See also Criminal Code 1999, Art 3.

492 See SRVN Constitution 2013, Art 2(1): Vietnam 'is a socialist rule of law State of the people, by the people, and for the people.' See further, Pip Nicholson with Simon Pitt 'Official Discourses and Court-Oriented Legal Reform in Vietnam' in John Gillespie and Pip Nicholson (eds), *Law and Development and the Global Discourses of Legal Transfers* (Cambridge, Cambridge University Press, 2012); John Gillespie, 'Concepts of Law' 146.

493 Resolution No 01/2001/NQ-HDTP dated 15 March 2001 of the Judges' Council of the Supreme People's Court Guiding the Implementation of Arts 139, 193, 194, 278, 279, and 289 of the Criminal Code 1999.

or appropriating narcotics) of the Criminal Code and provides more detail of penalties fixed by reference to the weight or quantity of the drugs involved.[494]

Under the Code, where less than five grams of heroin or cocaine is involved, the applicable sentence is two to seven years imprisonment;[495] where five to less than 30 grams is involved, the sentence is seven to 15 years imprisonment;[496] where 30 to less than 100 grams of heroin or cocaine is involved, imprisonment can be for up to 20 years;[497] and when more than 100 grams or more of heroin or cocaine is involved, penalties range from 20 years to life imprisonment or death.[498] The Resolution clarifies where there are neither 'aggravating circumstances' nor 'extenuating circumstances', the transportation of 100 grams to less than 300 grams of heroin or cocaine attracts a prescribed penalty of up to 20 years imprisonment, while more than 600 grams of either substance will result in the death penalty.[499] There are separate penalties for dried and fresh poppy fruit and marijuana under the Code.[500] In short, very small differences in the weight of drugs can result in radically different penalties.[501]

Table 8: Penalties applicable to drug-related offences determined by quantity of drugs for offences set out in Art 193 (manufacture) and Art 194 (stockpiling, transporting, trading or appropriating) of the Criminal Code and Resolution 01[502]

Narcotic Substances	20 years	Life Imprisonment	Death Penalty
Opium or cannabis resin, or cocaine glue	5 kg < 10 kg	10 kg < 20 kg	≥ 20 kg
Heroin or cocaine	100 mg < 300 mg	300 mg < 600 mg	≥ 600 mg
Cannabis leaf, flower and seeds	75 kg < 200 kg	200 Kg < 600 kg	≥ 600 kg
Other narcotic substances in solid form	300 mg < 900 mg	900 mg < 2500 mg	≥ 2500 mg
Other narcotic substances in liquid form	750 ml < 2000 ml	2000ml < 5000 ml	≥
Precursors	≥ 1200 mg		Not imposed

494 Criminal Code 1999, Art 8(2)—allowing for categories of offences. For particular details see Resolution 01. See also Inter-circular 17.

495 Criminal Code 1999, Art 194(1).

496 Criminal Code 1999, Art 194(2)(h).

497 Criminal Code 1999, Art 194(3)(b).

498 Criminal Code 1999, Art 194(4)(b). See also Resolution 01, Art 3, which provides detail of the interpretation of Art 194 of the Criminal Code 1999.

499 Resolution 01, Arts 3(1)(a)–(c).

500 Criminal Code 1999, Art 194.

501 Resolution 01.

502 Nguyễn Thị Phương Hoa (n 137) 44. This table summarises some of the penalties flowing from particular drug offences contravening Arts 193 and 194 of the Criminal Code 1999 and is based on the more detailed Resolution 01. The table is not exhaustive.

Extenuating Circumstances

Article 46(1) of the Criminal Code 1999, lists the following 'extenuating' or mitigating circumstance relevant to sentencing:

a) Offenders have prevented and/or reduced the harm caused by their offences;
b) Offenders volunteer to repair, compensate for the damage or overcome the consequences;
c) Crimes are committed in cases where it is beyond the limit of legitimate defence;
d) Crimes are committed in cases where it is beyond the requirements of the urgent situation;
e) Crimes are committed in cases where offenders are mentally incited by the illegal acts of the victims or other persons;
f) Crimes are committed due to particularly difficult plights not caused by the offender;
g) Crimes are committed but no damage or minor damage is caused;
h) Crimes are committed by first time offenders and in cases of less serious crimes;
i) Crimes are committed due to threats and/or coercion by other persons;
j) Crimes are committed due to ignorance;
k) Offenders are pregnant women;
l) Offenders are aged persons;
m) Offenders are persons suffering from illnesses that restrict their cognitive capability or their capability to control their acts;
n) Offenders give themselves up;
o) Offenders make honest declarations and reports and show their repentance;
p) Offenders actively help responsible bodies detect and investigate the crimes;
q) The offenders have redeemed their faults with achievements;
r) The offenders are persons who have recorded outstanding achievements in production, combat, study or work.[503]

The Criminal Code is very prescriptive about how extenuating circumstances are to be used in sentencing. If a defendant is able to convince a court that at least two of the extenuating circumstances apply, a court may apply a penalty

> under the lowest level of the penalty bracket stipulated by law which, however, must lie within the adjacent lighter penalty bracket of the law; where the law contains only one penalty bracket or such penalty bracket is the highest penalty bracket of the law, the courts may decide a penalty below the lowest level of the bracket or move to another penalty of lighter category.[504]

[503] The new Draft (Amended) Criminal Code provides a new extenuating circumstance in Art 51(1)(k): 'Committing a crime [in cases where the defendant has been] coerced or deceived into the use of alcohol or other powerful stimulants, which leads to a limitation of cognitive capacity.'

[504] Criminal Code 1999, Art 47. See also Resolution 01.

It is sometimes said that many judges are biased in favour of robust sentencing in drugs cases and, in consequence, give little weight to extenuating circumstances.[505] For example, a mental disability is considered an extenuating circumstance but the procuracy must establish it. Neither the defendant nor his or her counsel can easily seek or arrange a medical assessment when the defendant is in custody, as is often the case before trial. Similarly, an official medical report usually only indicates the nature of the mental condition suffered by the accused, leaving the court to assess how responsibility for the alleged offence should be assessed. Experienced Vietnamese counsel note that those considered to have suffered no adverse impact from a mental illness or disability will usually receive the full penalty applicable, even if that is death.[506] Where a court assesses an accused as being 70–80 per cent 'well', a life sentence may be substituted for the death penalty.[507] If the impact on accused is assessed at about 50 per cent she or he may receive a 20-year jail term in place of the death penalty.[508] There is a system of remission in Vietnam, which may result in a reduction of a 20-year term to about 12 years.

If mental impairment is made out in a particular case, for example at the level of 20 per cent impairment, and it is found that the defendant had 'actively helped' with the investigation—an extenuating circumstance under Art 46 (1)(p) of the Code—the court may sentence on the basis of the next lightest sentencing range. For example, if an offender is charged for trafficking an amount of opium (between 5 and 10 kilograms of resin) and two extenuating circumstances are made out, she or he may receive 15 to 20 years instead of 20 years.[509]

Reduction may also be sought where a defendant has sought to minimise the crime's impact,[510] and the court may radically reduce, or exempt a convicted person from, penalties where 'many' extenuating circumstances apply.[511] This 'special leniency' may not, however, entirely exempt a person from criminal liability.[512]

There are specific provisions relating to death penalty sentencing over and above the application of extenuating circumstances and these are considered in more detail below. In principle, however, the existence of at least two extenuating circumstances should be taken into account in all sentencing, including that potentially involving death.

Finally, if it relies on extenuating circumstances not set out in the Code, the court must set out its reasons for doing so.[513]

505 Interviewee 18 (20 August 2012).
506 Interviewee 20 (10 November 2014).
507 Ibid.
508 Ibid.
509 Resolution 01, Art 3(3).
510 Criminal Code 1999, Art 25.
511 Criminal Code 1999, Art 54.
512 Ibid.
513 Criminal Code 1999, Art 46 (2).

Aggravating Circumstances

Aggravating circumstances exist in the following situations:

a) Committing crimes in an organised manner;
b) Committing crimes in a professional manner;
c) Abusing position and power in order to commit crimes;
d) Committing crimes in the manner of a hooligan;
e) Committing crimes with despicable motivation;
f) Determined to complete crimes;
g) Re-offending, recidivism, dangerous recidivism;
h) Committing crimes against children, pregnant women, aged persons, persons unable to defend themselves, or persons dependent on offenders in material and/or moral conditions, work or other ways;
i) Infringing on the state's property;
j) Committing crimes causing serious, very serious or especially serious consequences;
k) Taking advantage of war conditions, emergency situations, natural calamities, epidemics or other special difficulties of society in order to commit crimes;
l) Using treachery or, cruel tricks to commit crimes and/or using means capable of causing harm to many persons;
m) Inciting juveniles to commit crimes;
n) Committing treacherous and/or violent acts in order to shirk or conceal crimes.[514]

The Criminal Code does not provide guidance on the use of aggravating circumstances. There is, however, express authority to escalate the severity with which an offence is punished if it involves 'abusing positions and/or powers'[515] or recidivism is evident.[516]

Fairness

The principle of fairness aims to ensure parity in sentencing such that like offences receive like treatment.[517] There is, in fact, some overlap between the principle of fairness and the notion of proportionality. The distinction lies in that fact that proportionality takes as its focus the elements of the offence, while the fairness principle aims to ensure that other features of the case, for example, the race and sex of the offender are treated without discrimination, except where that is specifically required by law. For example, where a defendant is pregnant or a minor particular considerations apply, as explained below.

[514] Criminal Code 1999, Art 48(1).
[515] Inter-circular 17, Art I(2)(2.1) See also Criminal Code 1999, Arts 193(2)(c), 194(2)(c), 195(2)(c), 196(2)(c) and 198(2)(a). See also Criminal Code 1999, Art 201.
[516] Criminal Code 1999, Art 49.
[517] See Nguyễn Thị Phương Hoa (n 137) 21–22.

Humanity

The principle of 'humanity' essentially requires the court to generally adopt the least severe or punitive sanctions allowed by law, given the circumstances of a particular case.[518] This is said to reflect the rehabilitative focus of the law set out in the Criminal Code as follows:

Penalties aim not only to punish offenders but also to rehabilitate them into persons useful to society and in the sense of observing laws and regulations of the socialist life, preventing them from committing new crimes. Penalties also aim to educate other people to respect laws and prevent and combat crimes.[519]

The principle of humanity is arguably also the underpinning rationale of the exemption of women and children from the death penalty (see below).

Expulsion (*trục xuất*)

It is possible to expel foreign criminals:

> Expulsion means to order sentenced foreigners to depart the territory of the Socialist Republic of Vietnam. Expulsion is applied by courts either as a principal penalty or an additional penalty, depending on each specific case.[520]

> Persons subject to expulsion must leave the territory of the Socialist Republic of Vietnam within 15 days after the decision is issued. Where the persons subject to the expulsion penalty must also serve other penalties or perform other obligations, the time limit for them to leave the territory of the Socialist Republic of Vietnam shall be prescribed by law.[521]

'Foreigners' caught by these provisions are defined as persons not having Vietnamese nationality[522] but not all foreigners who commit crimes in Vietnam are expelled.

Those expelled shall bear all the expenses of their departure[523] and are allowed to take their lawful property with them.[524] They may only extend the time limit for their departure in the event that they: i) are seriously ill and under emergency care or they cannot move on their own due to other health reasons; ii) must serve other penalties or perform other duties under the provisions of Vietnamese laws; or iii) have other plausible reasons that hinder their departure, which are certified by the head of the Exit and Entry Management Agency.[525]

Expulsion exists as a penalty additional to the principal penalty[526] and may not be 'augmented' (*tổng hợp*, that is, combined) with other penalties.[527] The court usually

[518] Nguyễn Thị Phương Hoa (n 137) 22.
[519] Criminal Code 1999, Art 27.
[520] Criminal Code 1999, Art 32.
[521] Criminal Procedure Code 2003, Art 265.
[522] Decree No 54/2001/ND-CP dated 23 August 2001 of the Government Guiding the Implementation of Expelling Penalty, Art 1.
[523] Decree 54, Art 3(5).
[524] Decree 54, Art 5.
[525] Decree 54, Art 4.
[526] Criminal Code 1999, Art 32.
[527] Criminal Code 1999, Art 50.

orders convicted foreigners to depart Vietnam after they complete imprisonment. For example, on 29 January 2013, the Ho Chi Minh City People's Court sentenced Ejike Justin Williams (a Nigerian) found guilty of trading narcotics to 18 years of imprisonment, a fine of 15 million dong, and expulsion after completing his term of imprisonment.[528]

Sentencing Practice

It is said that sentencing is often inconsistent, particularly in the District and Provincial Courts.[529] For example, it has been suggested that in the context of mass trials some will escape the death penalty where others do not and there is little to explain the different sentences.[530]

There is much disagreement about whether the nationality of the defendant affects trial and sentencing. Some commentators say all cases are treated alike but others dispute this. While foreign governments, including Australia, have sought to pressure Vietnamese courts to avoid the death penalty, the courts seem not to have succumbed to that pressure.[531] One informed observer suggested, however, that where:

> the defendant is a foreigner [that fact] may be considered when determining the severity of punishment, provided that it is still within the penalty bracket set forth by law. [...] In fact, there are cases where courts have accepted a reduction in the severity of punishment due to the pressure from foreign governments (via the Vietnamese diplomatic authorities).[532]

It has also been noted that individual defendants often fare better if they appear in cases with large numbers of co-accused.[533] As discussed, the mass trial is not uncommon in Vietnam. It has been suggested that judges dislike sentencing large numbers of people to death in one case, and that a large group trial will inevitably see a lighter sentence imposed on some of those charged with trafficking the quantity of drugs for which the death penalty is available.

Court judgments usually do not analyse evidence adduced either by the procuracy or the defence in any detail.[534] In form, criminal judgments need only comply with a Resolution of the Supreme People's Court.[535] Those we reviewed typically set out:

— the judges and people's assessors involved;
— the details of the parties involved (name, address, family and children, if any);

[528] Nguyễn Hiền, '18 năm tù dành cho người nước ngoài buôn ma túy [18 years of imprisonment for narcotics trading]' *Hải Quan Online—Tổng Cục Hải Quan (Việt Nam)* [Customs Online—(Vietnamese) General Customs Department] (Vietnam, 29 January 2013), www.baohaiquan.vn/pages/nguoi-nuoc-ngoai-buon-ma-tuy-linh-an-18-nam-tu.aspx.

[529] Interview with a criminal barrister (31 May 2008).

[530] Ibid.

[531] Interviewee 8 (4 June 2012).

[532] Interviewee 5 (26 May 2012).

[533] See, eg, Mai Nguyễn, 'Vietnam Mass Drugs Trial Sentences 30 to Death, Jails Dozen' *Reuters* (Hanoi, 20 January 2014), www.reuters.com/Article/2014/01/20/us-vietnam-court-drugs-idUSBREA0J0MK20140120.

[534] UNDP, 'Right to Counsel' (n 14) 262–63.

[535] Resolution 04.

- a detailed statement of the facts including the actions of the investigative police and the procuracy and the relationships existing between those charged;
- the bases of the charges against each defendant;
- extenuating and aggravating circumstances (where applicable);
- whether particular sentencing provisions of the code apply; and
- determinations as to guilt and sentence.

Finally, there are particular provisions guiding the diet, clothing accommodation, daily living and health of inmates of Vietnamese prisons.[536] There is provision to meet monthly with relatives for an hour, allowing up to three hours in special circumstances.[537] There is also provision for meetings with spouses of up to 24 hours for those 'inmates who properly observe prison regulations.'[538] Families are encouraged to supply cash and can do so up twice a month. It must be deposited and managed by an authorised agency (a prison, detention centre or criminal judgment execution agency for example).[539] Foreign prisoners may also be visited by their family, whether Vietnamese or foreign, after submitting an application certified by their diplomatic mission to the criminal judgment execution agency.[540]

VIII. APPEALS

An appeal must be lodged in writing with the relevant court—the provincial or High Court—within 15 days.[541] As mentioned, High Courts were introduced in 2014 to take over the Supreme People's Court's appellate function but the extent of their jurisdiction is yet to be clearly established.[542] If the appeal is to a Provincial Court, it should be commenced within 60 days.[543] If the appeal lies from the High Court or Provincial Court to the Supreme People's Court, it should be commenced within 90 days.[544] Appeals are usually heard by a panel of three judges, although two people's assessors may be added in 'cases of necessity,'[545] for example where many defendants are involved.[546] Each of the High Court and Provincial Court also offers a mechanism for the re-opening of cases and cassational review is available at the Supreme Court, the High Court and the Provincial Court, as discussed further below.

[536] Law No 53/2010/QH12 passed by the National Assembly on 17 June 2010 on the Execution of Criminal Judgments, Arts 42–48.

[537] Law No 53/2010/QH12, Art 46(1).

[538] Ibid.

[539] Law No 53/2010/QH12, Art 46(2).

[540] Law No 53/2010/QH12, Art 46(5).

[541] Criminal Procedure Code 2003, Art 234.

[542] It is expected that the Draft (Amended) Criminal Procedure Code will deal with its jurisdiction in more detail than does the current Law on the Organisation of People's Courts 2014.

[543] Criminal Procedure Code 2003, Art 242.

[544] Ibid.

[545] Criminal Procedure Code 2003, Art 244.

[546] Nguyễn Đức Mai, 'Thủ tục xét xử phúc thẩm [Appellate trial procedure]' in Vo Khanh Vinh (ed), *Bình luận khoa học Bộ luật Tố tụng Hình sự của nước Cộng Hòa Xã Hội Chủ Nghĩa Việt Nam* [Scientific commentary on the Criminal Procedure Code of the Socialist Republic of Vietnam] (Hanoi, Nhà Xuất Bản Tư Pháp [Judicial Publishing House], 2012) 538.

Appeals

A defendant or his or her legal counsel on the one hand,[547] and the procuracy on the other,[548] have the right to appeal against any conviction and sentence imposed at first instance. There is no need to apply for leave or to demonstrate that the error made at trial is substantial, parties may exercise their capacity to appeal, as a right.[549] New evidence can be introduced at an appeal by the procuracy, defence counsel or the parties.[550] An appeal court may amend or dismiss a lower court's judgment, order a re-investigation or retrial, or determine there is no case to answer and dismiss it.[551] It may also commute penalties, or substitute higher or lesser penalties.[552]

A defendant has the right to appeal against the whole first instance judgment (while other persons only have the right to appeal against part of the judgment).[553] Defence counsel have the right to appeal in order to protect the interests of a minor or a person with physical or mental defect.[554] A written appeal must be sent to the court that conducted the first instance trial or to the court of appeal.[555]

Appeals are initiated by completion of an 'appeal form' provided by the courts. Appellants must specify the judgment or part of it that is being appealed and set out detailed reasons for the appeal. Defence appeals typically claim incorrect applications of substantive law (the Criminal Code and related regulations and official documents); violations of criminal procedure (failure to comply with the Criminal Procedure Code and related regulations and official documents); and failure to take into consideration relevant matters, for example in relation to sentencing.

Where severity of sentence is the basis of the appeal, arguments may be raised about whether the trial court properly considered a defendant's situation, for example his or her medical condition. As indicated above, medical conditions must be confirmed by the Vietnamese authorities before they can be relied upon in court. Where there is evidence of a relevant medical condition and the procuracy or the defence team have suggested that the court apply the 'extenuating circumstance' provisions in Art 46(1)(n) of the Criminal Code 1999 (discussed above), the judgment should acknowledge this. A failure to do so can form the basis of an appeal against sentence. Even if such evidence is acknowledged, an appeal can still be lodged on the basis that the sentence is too severe, given the extenuating circumstances.

The 2003 Criminal Procedure Code allows the appellate court to review other parts of the judgment which are not appealed against.[556] Further, the court is able to

547 Criminal Procedure Code 2003, Art 231.
548 Criminal Procedure Code 2003, Art 232.
549 Criminal Procedure Code 2003, Art 20.
550 Criminal Procedure Code 2003, Art 246(1).
551 Criminal Procedure Code 2003, Art 248(2).
552 Criminal Procedure Code 2003, Art 249(2)–(3).
553 Criminal Procedure Code 2003, Art 231. See also Resolution No 05/2005/NQ-HDTP dated 8 December 2005 of the Judges' Council of the Supreme People's Court Guiding the Implementation of a Number of Articles in Part Four, 'Appellate Trial', of the Criminal Procedure Code.
554 Criminal Procedure Code 2003, Art 231.
555 Criminal Procedure Code 2003, Art 233.
556 Criminal Procedure Code 2003, Art 241.

reduce penalties or apply provisions of the Criminal Code that involve less serious crimes or apply less severe penalties, including retaining a sentence of imprisonment but applying probation, to defendants who do not appeal but appear in the same case.[557] This is said to demonstrate the 'humanity' principle because when the appellate court reviews first instance judgments the appellants will get outcomes better, or at least no more severe, than the first instance judgment.[558]

First instance criminal judgments become effective upon the expiration of the appeal period[559] but appellate decisions take effect the moment they are issued.[560] Within seven days of receipt of an effective first instance, or appeal or cassational judgment, the president of the first instance court must issue a decision to execute the judgment.[561] This must be sent to the procuracy at the same level as the first instance court.

If the appeal decision upholds the death penalty, the appeal court must submit the case file to the Chief Justice of the Supreme People's Court within 25 days of the date of that decision.[562]

Cassational Review (*giám đốc thẩm*)

Cassational review is brought by a protest by the Chairman of the Procuracy at a higher level than the court that decided the case.[563] The Chairman of the Supreme People's Procuracy protests judgments or decisions of courts at all levels, except for decisions of the Judges' Council of the Supreme People's Court. The Chairman of the Superior Procuracy protests judgments or decisions of Provincial courts and District Courts. The Chairman of the Provincial Procuracy protests judgments or decisions of District Courts.

Cassational review can be sought on the following grounds: a one-sided or inadequate trial; a decision that does not reflect the evidence; evidence of serious violation of the criminal procedure during the investigation, prosecution or trial; or a serious mistake made in the application of the Criminal Code.[564] Nguyễn Đức Mai explains one-sided trials as being those not conducted impartially and without bias, where trial panels are overly dependent on the dossier, focus on evidence against the defendants, or ignore evidence in their favour.[565] Further, a one-sided trial might occur where there is a focus on aggravating circumstances, while ignoring extenuating

557 Criminal Procedure Code 2003, Art 249(2).
558 Criminal Procedure Code 2003, Arts 248(2), 249(1).
559 Criminal Procedure Code 2003, Art 20; Law on the Execution of Criminal Judgements 2010, Art 2.
560 Criminal Procedure Code 2003, Art 253(4).
561 Criminal Procedure Code 2003, Art 256(1).
562 Criminal Procedure Code 2003, Art 254.
563 Criminal Procedure Code 2003, Art 275.
564 Criminal Procedure Code 2003, Art 273.
565 Nguyễn Đức Mai, 'Thủ tục xét xử phúc thẩm', 607–08. See also Dương Thanh Biểu, *Tuyển tập các quyết định giám đốc thẩm của Viện trưởng Viện Kiểm sát nhân dân* [Collection of cassation decisions of the Chairman of the Supreme People's Procuracy]' (Hanoi, Nhà Xuất Bản Tư Pháp [Judicial Publishing House], 2007).

circumstances.[566] Inadequate or one-sided trials arguably take place when the trial panels do not require expert tests that must be required by the law, do not call people whose testimony is important to a case, or do not collect important evidence and documents.[567]

There is no limit on the number of cassational reviews that can be brought, providing the President or Chairman are persuaded to lodge a request for review. If the review seeks a result that would be unfavourable to the defendant, it must be lodged within a year.[568] If it is brought on behalf of the defendant, and, if upheld, would improve their position, it can be brought anytime, including after the defendant's death.[569]

Cassation must take place within four months of being requested,[570] and involves a review of 'the whole case.' It is not restricted just to the protests forming the basis of the request.[571] A judge is assigned to 'present' the case to the cassational review panel and the procuracy will also be present.[572] Other parties may be summoned to attend, although they have no entitlement to do so.[573] The panels are differently made up depending on where they are located. The Criminal Court of the Supreme People's Court reviews judgments or decisions of the Provincial Courts. The Judges' Council of the Supreme People's Court reviews judgments or decisions of the Criminal Court or the courts of appeal of the Supreme People's Court.[574] If in the Criminal Court of the Supreme People's Court, the panel must comprise three judges.[575] If at the provincial level, it is made up of a sub-group of two-thirds of the judges' committee of that Provincial Court.[576] If in the Supreme People's Court, it comprises a sub-group of two-thirds of the judges on the judges' council of the Supreme People's Court.[577] A number equivalent to a majority of judges that sit on the committee or council must decide the cassation.[578] If this level of consensus cannot be reached, the hearing must be postponed and resumed within 30 days, with all judicial members of the committee and council attending.[579]

The Supreme People's Court, the new High Courts and the Provincial Courts all offer cassational review. It is yet to be determined whether the Supreme People's Court will only hear cassational reviews from the High Courts, or whether it will accept them from the Provincial Courts as well.

A cassational review can reject the review and reaffirm the case; accept the protest and dismiss the case; or send the case back for a retrial or further investigation.[580] In

566 Ibid.
567 Ibid.
568 Criminal Procedure Code 2003, Art 278(1).
569 Criminal Procedure Code 2003, Art 278(2).
570 Criminal Procedure Code 2003, Art 283.
571 Criminal Procedure Code 2003, Art 284.
572 Criminal Procedure Code 2003, Art 282(2).
573 Ibid.
574 Criminal Procedure Code 2003, Art 279.
575 Criminal Procedure Code 2003, Art 281(1).
576 Ibid.
577 Ibid.
578 Criminal Procedure Code 2003, Art 281(2).
579 Ibid.
580 Criminal Procedure Code 2003, Art 285.

the latter case one of the four grounds outlined above (a one-sided trial; a decision that does not reflect the evidence; evidence of serious violation of criminal procedure during the investigation, prosecution or trial; or a serious mistake in the application of the Criminal Code) must be made out.[581] To dismiss the case, the Cassational Review Board must be satisfied that there are no valid grounds on which the case could have proceeded, as set out in Art 107 of the Criminal Procedure Code.[582]

Where a case is protested and cassational review sought and the Board of Cassational Review of the Supreme People's Court upholds the death penalty, the Supreme People's Court shall immediately send the cassation decision to the convicted person[583] to enable him or her to petition for amnesty within seven days of receipt.[584]

Re-opening Procedure (*Tái thẩm*)

The re-opening procedure involves a court reopening a case to hear new evidence that was not available at the time of the trial.[585] Anyone may seek a re-opening but the procuracy at the level above that of the court that determined the case must formally alert the court to the application.[586] There are four grounds for reopening: evidence presented by witnesses, experts or interpreters at the trial is later found to be 'untruthful'; the investigators, procuracy, judges or people's assessors reached erroneous conclusions of fact on the basis of which the trial proceeded; evidence, such as exhibits, records or other documents relied upon at the trial are later found to be 'not truthful'; and, finally, any other circumstance that led to a lack of integrity in the trial.[587] This last category appears to leave the door open for claims of corrupt practice.

If the re-opening seeks a result favourable to the convicted party there is no time limit within which it must be brought—it may even be sought after the death of the convicted person.[588] Where the result might be disadvantageous to the convicted person, however, application for re-opening must be made by the procuracy within one year of becoming aware of the new information on which it is based.[589]

Re-opening can result in rejection of the existing judgment, return of the judgment for re-investigation or re-trial, or dismissal of the case.[590] The new decision takes immediate effect and must be notified to all parties within 10 days.[591] Any

581 Criminal Procedure Code 2003, Art 273.
582 Criminal Procedure Code 2003, Art 107. See also Art 285.
583 Criminal Procedure Code 2003, Art 258 (2).
584 Criminal Procedure Code 2003, Art 258 (1).
585 Criminal Procedure Code 2003, Art 290.
586 Criminal Procedure Code 2003, Arts 292–93. The Chairman of the Procuracy may not, however, seek the reopening of a case determined by the Judges' Council of the SPC: Criminal Procedure Code 2003, Art 293.
587 Criminal Procedure Code 2003, Art 291.
588 Criminal Procedure Code 2003, Art 295(2).
589 Criminal Procedure Code 2003, Art 295(1).
590 Criminal Procedure Code 2003, Art 298.
591 Criminal Procedure Code 2003, Art 299.

re-investigation or re-hearing must be notified to the 'competent' authorities within 15 days.[592]

The Draft (Amended) Criminal Procedure Code introduces a new layer of review—the 'special procedure to review decisions of the judges' council of the Supreme People's Court'. According to the draft, where there is grounds to believe that a decision made by the Supreme People's Court's judges' council seriously violates the law, or where new evidence is presented that was not available at the time the decision was made that could fundamentally change that decision, it may be reviewed at the request or recommendation of the Standing Committee of the National Assembly, the Judicial Committee of the National Assembly, the Chairman of the Supreme People's Procuracy or the Chief Justice of the Supreme People's Court.[593] It remains to be seen if this change will, in fact, be part of the new Criminal Procedure Code.

Prisoner Transfer

The Vietnamese Law on Legal Assistance 2007 deals with the transfer of prisoners between Vietnam and other countries. To date, Vietnam has signed prisoner transfer agreements with the United Kingdom and Northern Ireland (2008), South Korea (2009), Australia (2009), Thailand (2010), and Hungary (2013). We take the agreement with Australia as a case study.

Australia's International Transfer of Prisoners Scheme with Vietnam

Vietnam's decision to join Australia's International Transfer of Prisoners Scheme[594] appears to have been driven largely by the case of Mai Công Thành, who was sentenced to death in 2005,[595] although negotiations had, in fact, commenced in late 2004.[596] In any case, by the time the agreement was concluded in 2008, it was described as having been a 'priority … for a number of years'.[597]

[592] Criminal Procedure Code 2003, Art 300.

[593] Draft (Amended) Criminal Procedure Code, ch XXXI.

[594] See International Transfer of Prisoners (Vietnam) Regulations 2009 (Cth), S.L.I. 282 of 2009, commenced 12 November 2009. This scheme implements Agreement between the government of Australia and the government of the Socialist Republic of Vietnam concerning Transfer of Sentenced Persons of 13 October 2008, ATS 27. According to the Australian Treaty Database, the treaty entered into force on 12 November 2009.

[595] Australian Broadcasting Corporation, 'Death Penalty Given for Australian Man in Vietnam' *PM* (Bangkok, 10 June 2005), www.abc.net.au/pm/content/2005/s1389727.htm.

[596] Holly Nott and Paul Osborne, 'Fed: Govt to Plead for Drug Smuggler Facing Firing Squad' *The Australian Associated Press* (10 June 2005) [Copy on file with author].

[597] Joint Standing Committee on Treaties, Parliament of Australia, *Report 103: Treaties tabled on 12 March and 13 May 2009* (2009) [2.19]. See also Australian Bureau of Statistics, *Prisoner Characteristics, Australia 2014* (Data cube, 11 December 2014), Table 6, which shows there were 771 Vietnamese-born prisoners in Australian jails at the end of 2014. Many of these would be Australian residents or citizens but there is no data disaggregating them by citizenship.

Before transfer of a prisoner between Vietnam and Australia can take place, several requirements must be satisfied:[598] the prisoner's conviction must be final and not subject to appeal;[599] he or she must have at least one year left of their sentence, unless otherwise agreed between Vietnam and Australia;[600] and conduct giving rise to the offence for which the person is imprisoned must be a criminal offence in both countries.[601]

As at 2015, this scheme does not yet seem to have been used, although published details are scant. At the time of writing, the best estimate is that there are 35 Australians in Vietnamese prisons and over 700 persons born in Vietnam are held in Australian jails.[602]

IX. DEATH PENALTY LAW AND PRACTICE (*Hình phạt tử hình*)

The opening up of Vietnam to foreign investment in 1986 led to an increase in trade and commerce and large-scale law reforms. This has caused Vietnam to become increasingly engaged with international law issues, including international dialogue about human rights generally and the death penalty specifically.[603] As a result, there have been Communist Party policy statements calling for review of those crimes attracting the death penalty in Resolution 08 and Resolution 49.[604] In 2006, the Ministry of Foreign Affairs Report on Human Rights confirmed that:

> The Vietnamese State has pursued the policy of narrowing the scope of capital punishment, gearing towards its abolition in the future. Along this line, in the Penal Code 1999, the number of offences subject to capital punishment is reduced from 44 to 29.[605]

That said, while the review of the death penalty is openly discussed, it is also defended:

> To meet the needs of the fight against crimes, particularly drug-related ones, Vietnam now maintains capital punishment.[606]

[598] National Interest Analysis [2009] ATNIA 10 (13 May 2009), [16]–[17].

[599] *Agreement between Australia and the Socialist Republic of Vietnam concerning transfer of sentenced persons* [2008] ATNIF 17 (done at Canberra on 13 October 2008), Art 4(e).

[600] Ibid Art 4(d).

[601] Ibid Art 4(a).

[602] Joint Standing Committee on Treaties, Parliament of Australia, *Report 103: Treaties Tabled on 12 March and 13 May 2009* (2009) [2.29]. This report suggests 684 Vietnamese-born nationals were in Australian jails in 2009, see Australian Bureau of Statistics, *Prisoner Characteristics* (2014) Table 6 (discussed at n 597). Our research reveals that 38 Australians have been charged with drug offences in Vietnam since 2003. Of that number, we are confident three are not currently serving jail terms.

[603] Võ Văn Ái, 'Human Rights and Asian Values in Vietnam' in Michael Jacobsen and Ole Bruun (eds) *Human Rights and Asian Values Contesting National Identities and Cultural Representations in Asia*, (London & New York, Routledge Curzon, 2000) 92. This study does not take up the issue of extra judicial killings in Vietnam during the war years and after the unification of the country but before the introduction of *đổi mới* in 1986. See Daniel Pascoe, 'Explaining Death Penalty Clemency in the Socialist Republic of Vietnam' (2015) pp 7–8 [Unpublished Paper: copy on file with author].

[604] Resolution 08. See also Resolution 49, s II(2)(2.1).

[605] Ministry of Foreign Affairs, *Achievements in Protecting and Promoting Human Rights in Vietnam* (2005) (the White Book) (translation) 23.

[606] Ministry of Foreign Affairs, *Achievements* (translation) 23. See also, Law No 37/2009, Art 1.

As at 2009, the number of offences in the Criminal Code to which the death penalty applied was 22, or 8 per cent.[607] At the time of writing, Vietnam was once again reviewing the offences that attract the death penalty and how it is to be applied, with the aim of reducing its incidence.[608]

The question thus arises whether Vietnam can be said to be abolitionist. There is an argument made by optimists that the current downward trend of offences to which the death penalty applies suggests the country may be on an abolitionist trajectory. Describing this as reductionist rather than abolitionist seems, however, to better capture the reality of Vietnam's death penalty policies,[609] even if death is imposed for only seven criminal offences, as some suggest may eventually be the case.[610]

A range of reforms have been mooted to limit the application of the death penalty. In 2015, for example, Deputy Minister of Justice Đinh Trung Tụng suggested that robbery and drugs crimes other than trafficking might no longer attract the death penalty.[611] Other proposals include: an age-based exemption from the death penalty for those over 70 years old;[612] a limitation of the death penalty to 'particularly serious cases'; and the possible introduction of a suspended death penalty, as in China.[613] This would retain the death penalty but enable a court to order its suspension on various grounds. Those discussed include proof of rehabilitation or compensation paid to victims, or some combination of the two over a period of years.[614] These debates continue, as do debates about whether to introduce new sentences, such as life without parole, to reduce the incidence of the death penalty.[615]

At the time of writing the death penalty still applies to a significant range of drug offences. In particular, Resolution 01/2001, discussed above, stipulates the amounts of narcotic substances that attract particular sentences, including death. As with sentencing generally, a court is expected to apply the principles of rule of law,

[607] Hải Thanh Lương, 'The Application of the Death Penalty for Drug-Related Crimes in Vietnam: Law, Policy and Practice' (2014) 17 *Thailand Journal of Policy and Law* (1), www.thailawforum.com/articles/Vietnam-death-penalty.html.

[608] Drafting Committee, 'Bản Thuyết Minh Chi Tiết Về Dự Thảo Bộ Luật Hình Sự (Sửa Đổi) [Detail explanation about the Draft (Amended) Criminal Code]' (n 128) pt I(6).

[609] Pip Nicholson, 'The Death Penalty in SE Asia: Is There a Trend towards Abolition?', *The Conversation* (2015), theconversation.com/the-death-penalty-in-se-asia-is-there-a-trend-towards-abolition-37214.

[610] Tâm Lụa, 'Có thể dùng tiền để thoát án tử hình? [Can money be used to escape the death penalty?]' *Tuoi Tre* (Vietnam, 5 April 2015), tuoitre.vn/tin/phap-luat/20150405/co-the-dung-tien-de-thoat-an-tu-hinh/729878.html.

[611] Thái Sơn, 'Jury Out as Vietnam Holds Fast to White-collar Noose: Is Vietnam Ready to Abolish the Death Penalty' *Thanh Nien News* (25 March 2015), www.thanhniennews.com/politics/vietnam-plans-to-remove-robbery-drug-crimes-from-death-penalty-list-40275.html.

[612] Ibid.

[613] Susan Trevaskes, 'Suspending Death in Chinese Capital Cases: The Road to Reform' in Roger Hood and Surya Deva (eds), *Confronting Capital Punishment in Asia: Human Rights, Politics and Public Opinion* (Oxford, Oxford University Press, 2013) 221. See also for more details Susan Trevaskes, 'China's Death Penalty: The Supreme People's Court, the Suspended Death Sentence and the Politics of Penal Reform' (2013) 53 *British Journal of Criminology* 482, 482–99.

[614] Tâm Lụa, 'Có thể dùng tiền'. See also discussion of similar proposals currently under debate in Indonesia at p 107, above.

[615] Ibid.

proportionality, fairness and the humanity described earlier in deciding whether to apply the death penalty.

Pregnant Women and Children and the Death Penalty

The Criminal Code specifically exempts certain categories of women and minors from the death penalty. Pregnant women and nursing mothers, for example, may not be executed,[616] and their sentences should be commuted to life imprisonment.[617] It is claimed that incarcerated women have attempted to become pregnant to avoid the death penalty, and, in at least one case (in 2006), this was achieved.[618]

Children are defined in Resolution 01 'as those who are under 16 years of age'[619] with the Criminal Code allowing general penal liability for those over 16.[620] No one under the age of 16 may receive the death penalty.[621] Juvenile offenders are also exempt from life imprisonment.[622] The Criminal Code provides, however, that offenders aged 14 and 15 will be liable for 'very serious' crimes where they are committed intentionally and 'especially serious crimes'.[623] The penalties they receive will, however, be adjusted to reflect their youth. It is claimed that minors are often used to sell and transport drugs because they will, if captured, receive lighter sentences or escape liability entirely.[624]

Procedural Matters

As mentioned, a court that imposes the death penalty is obliged to then send the court file to the Chairman of the Supreme People's Procuracy and the President of the Supreme People's Court.[625] These bodies must undertake a review of the court's decision within two months.[626] The Chairman of the Supreme People's Procuracy and the President of the Supreme People's Court can then decide to reject the appeal and confirm the judgment; dismiss the judgment and the case; or find the judgment wanting (dismiss it) and send the case back to the procuracy for a re-investigation or to the relevant court for a re-trial.[627] If grounds are identified for a cassational

616 Criminal Code 1999, Art 35.
617 Ibid.
618 Trần Đình Thanh Lam, 'Death Penalty: Pregnant Woman Escapes Execution in Vietnam' *IPS News* (Ho Chi Minh City, 30 October 2006), www.ipsnews.net/2006/10/death-penalty-pregnant-woman-escapes-execution-in-vietnam/. In this case, the convicted person, Nguyễn Thị Oanh, had been in 'solitary confinement' for six months for drug trafficking when the fact of her pregnancy was medically confirmed.
619 Resolution 01, Art 2(2).
620 Criminal Code 1999, Art 12.
621 Criminal Code 1999, Arts 35 and 12.
622 Criminal Code 1999, Arts 34 and 69(5).
623 Ibid.
624 Interviewee 4 (25 May 2012).
625 Criminal Procedure Code 2003, Art 258(1).
626 Ibid.
627 Criminal Procedure Code 2003, Art 248(2).

review, the Supreme People's Court's cassation court determines the case.[628] There is no basis to appeal a Supreme People's Court cassation decision at this time.

First instance criminal judgments become effective upon the expiration of the seven-day appeal period.[629] Appellate decisions take effect once issued.[630] Within seven days of receipt of an effective first instance decision, or appeal or cassational judgment, the President of that court must issue a decision to execute the judgment, and this decision must also be sent to the procuracy at the same level as the first instance court.[631] Once a death sentence is effective, there are seven days available to file a Petition for Amnesty, effectively a petition to commute the sentence (see below).[632]

It is also possible to seek to postpone the death penalty on several bases, including, as discussed above, pregnancy or motherhood of a young child, a force majeure, or new circumstances arising in the case.[633]

Oversight of the implementation of a death sentence rests with the Death Sentence Execution Council, the establishment of which follows notification of the death sentence to the procuracy of the same level as the sentencing court and the head of the criminal judgment execution agency.[634] These councils are chaired by the President or the Vice-President of the applicable court.[635] To date that has been the Provincial Court, although High Courts may have also a role in the future. The Death Penalty Execution Council must confirm the identity of those sentenced to death just prior to execution.[636]

Incidence of the Death Penalty

Data on the incidence of the death penalty are informal, as statistics on the death penalty remain classified as a state secret.[637] Various accounts aggregating and estimating death penalty cases and executions appear from time to time in the local press, however. For example, an Amnesty Inernational Report of 2012 refers to a *Thanh Nien* newspaper report in which a senior Ministry of Public Security official was quoted as estimating there are usually around 100 people sentenced to death a year in Vietnam.[638] Such estimates appear elsewhere but are usually derivative.[639]

[628] Criminal Procedure Code 2003, Art 258(2).
[629] Criminal Procedure Code 2003, Art 240.
[630] Criminal Procedure Code 2003, Art 248(3).
[631] Criminal Procedure Code 2003, Art 256.
[632] Criminal Procedure Code 2003, Art 258(1).
[633] Law on the Execution of Criminal Judgments 2010, Art 58.
[634] Law on the Execution of Criminal Judgments 2010, Art 55(1).
[635] Law on the Execution of Criminal Judgments 2010, Art 55(2).
[636] Law on the Execution of Criminal Judgments 2010, Art 59(2).
[637] Decision No 01/2004/QD-TTg dated 5 January 2004 of the Prime Minister on the List of State Secret at Top Secret Level in the People's Court Sector, Art 1(1).
[638] Amnesty International, 'Death Sentences and Executions in 2011', Report (27 March 2012) ACT 50/001/2012, www.amnesty.org/en/library/info/ACT50/001/2012/en, 28.
[639] Amnesty International 'Death Sentences and Executions in 2011', 28; Amnesty International, 'Reported in Death Penalty World Wide' (Report), www.deathpenaltyworldwide.org/country-search-post.cfm?country=Vietnam.

Statements of this kind typically arise in the context of general government statements on the need to be tough on crime and retain tough punishments for those guilty of 'social evils'.

There is also limited data concerning penalties for drug offences. Lương Thanh Hải has compiled the most comprehensive death penalty-related data publically available. He notes that over the eight-year period from 1993 to 2001, as many as 1,179 people were sentenced to death at their first instance trial (roughly 147 people per year).[640] Between 2001 and 2010 (excluding 2003 and 2004 for which there are no data), the number sentenced to death was 1,421 (roughly 177 per year).[641] These numbers are broadly consistent with statements that about a hundred people per year are executed, as the estimates do not take into account appeals, reviews and petitions for amnesty.

Lương also notes that drug-related offences account for many of the death sentences. He suggests that between 2001 and 2010, 40.04 per cent of death penalty cases involved drug trafficking offences.[642] Lương also claims that murder accounts for most death sentences (55.52 per cent over the same 10-year period), with three other grounds for death sentences (child rape, fraud and miscellaneous) accounting for less than two per cent of the death sentences over the same period.[643] This view is echoed by reports in the Vietnamese press that many of those on death row are there for drug offences.[644]

Death by firing squad was recently replaced by death by lethal injection, with effect from 1 July 2011.[645] No executions were carried out, however, due to a shortage of the drugs used for lethal injections.[646] Vietnam planned to import the necessary drugs from Europe but, in December 2011, the European Union tightened restrictions by amending its regulations concerning trade in certain goods that could be used for capital punishment.[647] This situation prompted the Vietnamese Department of Security to ask the National Assembly to allow the resumption of firing squads.[648] The lack of resolution about how to execute, and whether to resume

[640] Lương Thanh Hải, 'The Application of the Death Penalty'.

[641] Lương Thanh Hải (n 607) webpage 4.

[642] Lương Thanh Hải (607) Figure 2, webpage 5.

[643] Ibid.

[644] See, for example, *Tuoi Tre News*, 'The End of Firing Squads in Vietnam' (no date), en.baomoi.com/Info/The-end-of-firing-squads-in-Vietnam/3/214119.epi.

[645] Law on the Execution of Criminal Judgements 2010, Art 59(1).

[646] Amnesty International, 'Death Sentences and Executions 2013' (Report) (2014) ACT 50/001/2014, www.amnesty.org.au/images/uploads/about/Death_sentences_and_executions_in_2013_Amnesty_International.pdf, 28.

[647] See Council Regulation (EC) No 1236/2005 of 27 June 2005 concerning trade in certain goods which could be used for capital punishment, torture or other cruel, inhuman or degrading treatment or punishment. See also European Commission, 'Commission Extends Control over Goods Which Could be Used for Capital Punishment or Torture' (Press Release, 20 December 2011), europa.eu/rapid/press-release_IP-11-1578_en.htm.

[648] Vũ Trọng Khánh and Nguyễn Anh Thư, 'Vietnam May Return to Firing Squads Amid Shortage of Lethal Chemicals' *The Wall Street Journal* (25 July 2013), online.wsj.com/Article/SB1000142412788732 3971204578627580713971870.html.

execution by firing squad, escalated prison crowding and the emotional distress of those on death row, according to the *Thanh Nien* newspaper. It documented prisoners 'begging' to be executed rather than live with uncertainty about when their executions would occur.[649]

Executions resumed in the second half of 2013, after Vietnamese laws were amended to allow in-country manufacture of drugs that could be used in lethal injections.[650] According to a 2014 Amnesty International Report at least seven people were executed in 2013.[651] Recent Vietnamese media reports claimed that, as of November 2013, there were 678 prisoners on death row, of whom 110 had exhausted all avenues for appeal.[652]

Some suggest, however, that both the number of people sentenced to death and the number of executions appear to have decreased. Amnesty International data suggest, for example, that in 2005 at least 65 people were sentenced to death, and 21 were executed[653] and that there were at least 23 cases resulting in the death penalty in 2011 and five executions.[654] These figures do not, however, sit well with Lương's analysis, a fact that reflects the current difficulty in obtaining clear and reliable information on the death penalty in Vietnam.

Death Penalty Practice

A series of articles were published on death penalty practices in Vietnam in 2011 by *Youth* (*Tuoi Tre*) newspaper. These depicted a brutal regimen of incarceration, with prisoners kept shackled in either single or double cells[655] and shot by a five-person firing squad.[656] Prisoners, it is noted, often live for up to a year not knowing when they will be executed—much longer in some cases, given the two-year period when

[649] *Thanh Nien News*, 'Vietnam's Death Row Inmates Enduring a Wait Worse than Death' (9 July 2013), www.thanhniennews.com/index/pages/20130704-a-wait-worse-than-death.aspx.

[650] Decree No 47/2013/ND-CP dated 13 May 2013 of the Government Amending and Supplementing a Number of Articles of Decree No 82/2011/ND-CP dated 16 September 2011 of the Government on AP Execution by Lethal Injection. See also, AFP (Agence France Presse), 'Vietnam Executes First Prisoner by Lethal Injection' *ABC News* (6 August 2013), www.abc.net.au/news/2013-08-06/vietnam-first-lethal-injection-for-prisoner/4869468.

[651] Amnesty International, 'Death Sentences and Executions 2013' 7.

[652] Lao Động, 'Vietnam Minister Wants to Restore Firing Squad' *Thanh Nien News* (11 November 2013), www.thanhniennews.com/society/vietnam-minister-wants-to-restore-firing-squad-693.html; AAP, 'Vietnam Executes First Prisoner' (2013); AP (Associated Press), 'Vietnam Executes 1st Prisoner by Lethal Injection' *Asian Correspondent* (6 August 2013), asiancorrespondent.com/111593/vietnam-executes-1st-prisoner-by-lethal-injection/. See the initial reporting at *Thanh Nien News*, 'Vietnam Executes First Prisoner with Lethal Injection' (6 August 2013), www.thanhniennews.com/society/vietnam-executes-first-prisoner-with-lethal-injection-1618.html.

[653] Amnesty International, 'Death Penalty News—January 2006' (Report) web.amnesty.org/library/Index/ENGACT530012006?open&of+ENG-392.

[654] Amnesty International (n 638) 28.

[655] *Tuoi Tre News*, 'Dead Men Walking: Back from the Brink' (4 April 2011), en.baomoi.com/Info/Dead-men-walking--P3-Back-from-the-brink/2/128573.epi.

[656] *Tuoi Tre News*, 'In Dead Men Walking: Judgment Day' [no date], en.baomoi.com/Info/Dead-men-walking--P1-judgment-day/2/123295.epi.

no executions could take place, discussed above.[657] It has since been reported that Vietnam has undertaken a program of building facilities and training in the necessary techniques to enable execution by lethal injection.[658] Pascoe estimates, drawing on Amnesty International data, that the time spent on death row in Vietnam is relatively short, between five months and four years.[659]

In fact, Vietnamese press reporting supplies vital information about death penalty practice, despite often being propagandist in nature. In 2013, for example, a series of articles that depict the brutality of death by firing squad appeared just before Vietnam publicly announced that it would cease execution by firing squad and move to death by fatal injection. In 'Dead Men Walking', the journalist records the remorse of the prisoner and the kindness of a colonel who enters the prison at 2.00 am to tell the defendant that he will be executed later that day.[660] The article also chronicles the remorse of the drug-addicted single father who leaves behind him two daughters and his mother: '… in his last letter, he apologised to his mother and daughters for not being able to take care of them. He loved them very much and deeply regretted what he had done, he said, and asked for their forgiveness.'[661] This same article also has the prisoner 'thanking the supervisors for their help,' as they accompany him to the execution grounds.[662]

The theme of support and suggestions of friendship between prisoners and their keepers is reiterated in other articles in this series:

> On death row, there is often a special friendship between supervisors and prisoners. After being incarcerated there for long, some prisoners can identify an officer just by his or her footstep. It is not unusual for them to indulge in small talk, asking about each other's health and the like.[663]

Here, the press is depicting a caring but strict Party-state, which must administer punishment for those guilty of heinous crimes. The articles frame death by firing squad as cruel but administered with compassion. These publications appear to be preparing the public to accept the announcement in the same newspaper, seven months later, in December 2011, of the move to execution by lethal injection.[664] This announcement also advised that families will now be able to bury their executed relative (provided they can cover travel costs).[665]

[657] *Tuoi Tre News*, 'Dead Men Walking: Back from the Brink'.
[658] *Tuoi Tre News*, 'Locally Made Poison to be Used for Execution' (15 May 2014), tuoitrenews.vn/society/9625/locallymade-poison-to-be-used-for-execution. Facilities have reportedly been built in Hanoi, Ho Chi Minh City, and Sơn La, Nghệ An and Đắk Lắk Provinces.
[659] Pascoe 'Explaining Death Penalty Clemency' (2015) 26.
[660] *Tuoi Tre News*, 'In Dead Men Walking: Judgment Day'.
[661] Ibid.
[662] Ibid.
[663] *Tuoi Tre News*, 'Dead Men Walking: Daybreak on Death Row' (25 March 2011), en.baomoi.com/Info/Dead-men-walking--P2-daybreak-on-death-row/2/125858.epi.
[664] *Tuoi Tre News*, 'The End of Firing Squads in Vietnam'.
[665] Ibid.

X. CLEMENCY

In Vietnam, there are five types of clemency. Some are available to those who have been convicted and sentenced and others (exemption from liability and from punishment) can be granted during the investigation or prosecution phases, reflecting the humanitarian principle of sentencing described above.[666] More specifically, the following types of clemency exist: exemption from criminal liability; exemption from punishment; suspended sentence; exemption from serving a sentence; and commutation and reprieve.[667] There are also a series of amnesties that can apply to sentencing.

The National Assembly and the courts can grant clemency through commutation or reduction of sentence but a general amnesty (granting clemency or amnesty to a range of people) can only be ordered by the National Assembly.[668]

Exemption from Criminal Liability

An exemption from criminal liability means that someone found guilty of an offence does not have to serve their sentence or any other punishment.[669] Bases for exemption from criminal liability are where: the offence or the behaviour of the offender no longer risks harm to society;[670] the offender has benefited from a general amnesty (which must be ordered by the National Assembly);[671] the confession of the accused was made before detection of the offence;[672] or a juvenile has committed a less serious offence resulting in no great harm and accompanied by at least two extenuating circumstances and his or her family or a relevant organisation can supervise him or her.

In addition, a person who voluntarily terminates the commission of a crime before it is complete shall be exempt from liability for the attempted crime (however, if the act actually committed constitutes another crime, she or he will bear liability for that offence).[673] This is controversial, as some commentators argue that if the offence is incomplete the person cannot logically be liable for the offence, as matter of law, and exemption is thus redundant. Others liken the exemption to a pardon where the convict has been found guilty but the circumstances warrant forgiveness, waiving of penalties and cancellation of the criminal record.[674]

666 Nguyễn Thị Phương Hoa (n 137) 32.
667 Ibid 38.
668 SRVN Constitution 2013, Art 70. See also Art 88 allowing the President to proclaim a special amnesty based on a resolution of the National Assembly.
669 Nguyễn Thị Phương Hoa (n 137) 32.
670 Criminal Code 1999, Art 25(1).
671 Criminal Code 1999, Art 25(3).
672 Criminal Code 1999, Art 25(2).
673 Criminal Code 1999, Art 19.
674 Nguyễn Thị Phương Hoa (n 137) 32.

Under the Draft (Amended) Criminal Code, the grounds for exemption from criminal liability are supplemented, clarified and grouped into two categories of compulsory and optional exemption as follows:

An offender shall be exempted from criminal liability in the following circumstances:

- Where during the investigation, prosecution or trial, due to a change of policy, law, the act of the offender is no longer dangerous to the society.
- Where during the investigation, prosecution or trial, due to a change of situation, the act of the offender is no longer dangerous to the society.
- Where during the investigation, prosecution or trial, the offender becomes too old, too sick or due to extremely difficult situation, so he/she is no longer dangerous to the society.
- Where after committing the offence, the offender has given himself/herself up, shown repentance and made a special contribution that is recognised by the state and the society.
- Where the offender commits the offence due to ignorance, being excited, threatened or coerced by other persons, but then, aware of their offence, made an honest declaration and report, shows repentance, and effectively contributed to the detection, investigation and dealing with the crime.
- Where there are decisions on general amnesties.

An offender may be exempted from criminal liability in the following circumstances:

- Where offender commits a less serious crime, or serious crime unintentionally causing damage to the life, health or asset of another person and the victim has voluntarily reconciled and requested exemption from criminal liability for the offenders.
- Where offender commits less serious crime intentionally causing damage to the life, health or asset of another person and the victim has voluntarily reconciled and requested exemption from criminal liability for the offenders.
- Where before the act of criminal offence is detected, the offender gives him/herself up and clearly reports the facts, thus effectively contributing to the detection and investigation of the crime and trying to minimise the consequences of the crime.[675]

Exemption from Punishment

As mentioned, the court has a sentencing discretion if any two of the extenuating circumstances are made out.[676] More particularly, the court can exempt a convict from punishment, while retaining a record of the conviction and allowing the possibility

[675] Draft (Amended) Criminal Code, Art 29.
[676] Criminal Code 1999, Art 46(1).

that 'judicial measures' such as confiscation of items or ordering compensation may apply.[677]

Only the courts can grant exemption from punishment.[678]

Suspension or Postponement of Sentence

Under certain conditions it is possible for the court to temporarily suspend or postpone a sentence. If a convict is: ill; pregnant or a nursing mother; the sole source of family income while working as a labourer (except in particular cases where the breach is of a serious or especially serious crime); or sentenced for a less serious crime and needs to attend to 'official duties', a postponement of the sentence for up to a year is possible.[679] A temporary suspension of a sentence is also available on the same grounds.[680] While a sentence is suspended or postponed the convict must obey any residency requirements imposed by the court.[681]

The courts are also able to order non-custodial reform through imposition of a suspended sentence.[682] This is only available where the sentence is for between six months and three years and the crime committed falls into the 'less serious' or 'serious' categories.[683] Further, the convict must have a stable address.[684] Discounts to a suspended sentence are available where the convict has spent time in custody, at a ratio of 1:3, that is, for every one day spent in custody the sentence suspended is reduced by three days.[685] While the sentence is suspended, the convict must be supervised by their workplace, with the family also taking on responsibility for co-ordination with state agencies.[686] Ordinarily, there is also an income levy imposed at a rate of 5–20 per cent, although this can be waived.[687]

Exemption from Serving a Sentence

There are six conditions that allow the exemption of a convicted person from serving a sentence, either in whole or in part:

1. expiry of the statutory limit for the execution of a sentence (made by order by the court);[688]

[677] Nguyễn Thị Phương Hoa (n 137) 37. See also Criminal Procedure Code 2003, Art 54.
[678] Nguyễn Thị Phương Hoa (n 137) 37.
[679] Criminal Code 1999, Art 61(1).
[680] Ibid Art 62.
[681] Criminal Procedure Code 2003, Art 263.
[682] Criminal Code 1999, Art 31(1).
[683] Ibid.
[684] Ibid.
[685] Ibid.
[686] Criminal Code 1999, Art 31(2).
[687] Criminal Code 1999, Art 31(3).
[688] Criminal Code 1999, Art 55.

2. the defendant has been sentenced to non-custodial reform or a term of imprisonment but is yet to have judgment executed and has made a 'great achievement or suffered from a dangerous disease' and is no longer a danger to society.[689] This can also apply where the 'great achievement' took place during a period of suspended sentence (see above) and the procuracy makes representations to the court to exempt the convicted person from the balance of the penalty (made by order by the court);[690]
3. the convicted person benefits from a general amnesty (made by order of the National Assembly);[691]
4. the convicted person benefits from a special amnesty (made by order of the President);[692]
5. the convicted person is ordered to pay a fine but suffers particular economic hardship as a result of circumstances beyond his or her control (such as fire or accident). He or she may then be relieved of the remaining fine[693] (made by order of the court); or
6. the convicted person is on probation or has received a ban on residence and, having served half of their sentence, demonstrates rehabilitation. The court may then exempt him or her from the serving of the balance of the sentence (made by order of the court).[694]

These exemptions are sought after there has been a decision on culpability and a sentencing order made. It is the Ministry of Public Security and the Ministry of National Defence Prisons and Detention Centres that seeks the sentence reduction.[695] This is done by sending a request in the form of a dossier to the Provincial People's Court under the authority of which the sentence is being served, accompanied by a copy of the judgment, a written request for the reduction, assessment reports on the prisoner's conduct ('monthly, quarterly biannual and annual') and any relevant medical history.[696]

Upon receipt of all the documentation the Provincial People's Court must meet and consider the request within 15 days of its receipt and notify relevant bodies of its determination.[697] The decision to reduce sentence is reached on the basis of a summary of the file prepared by the court and a response to this from the procuracy.[698] The convicted person has no right to representation.

[689] Criminal Code 1999, Art 57(1).
[690] Criminal Code 1999, Art 57(4).
[691] Criminal Code 1999, Art 57(2).
[692] Ibid.
[693] Criminal Code 1999, Art 58(2).
[694] Criminal Code 1999, Art 57(5).
[695] Law on the Execution of Criminal Judgments 2010, Art 33(1).
[696] Law on the Execution of Criminal Judgments 2010, Art 33(2).
[697] Law on the Execution of Criminal Judgments 2010, Art 33(3); Criminal Procedure Code 2003, Art 269.
[698] Criminal Procedure Code 2003, Art 269.

Commutation of Sentence (Reduction)

Commutation of sentence may be court-ordered or take place by way of a presidential grant of special amnesty. Court-ordered commutation is highly regulated, with specified reductions of sentence reflecting good behaviour.[699] The request for reduction is made to the court by the relevant prison manager. In general terms, a prisoner can benefit from more than one order for commutation of sentence. In other words, there can be multiple reductions of sentence provided that, overall, the prisoner serves at least half the ordered imprisonment sentence and at least twenty years of a sentence of life imprisonment.[700]

The Draft (Amended) Criminal Code proposes a new type of court-ordered commutation—conditional early release of prisoners (*tha tù trước thời hạn có điều kiện*). Persons serving a prison sentence can be released early if the prisoner:

— is serving a sentence for his or her first offence;
— has achieved 'much improvement', and has 'a good rehabilitation attitude';
— has served half of or her sentence, or 15 years of a term of life imprisonment that has been reduced to a term of imprisonment;
— has received a reduction of imprisonment sentence once before; and
— has a clear place of residence, has completed any supplementary penalties, and has fulfilled obligations to compensate for damage and any other relevant requirement of the sentence.[701]

This type of commutation does not apply to offenders who commit certain types of crimes, including, in particular, manufacturing, trading and appropriating narcotic substances.

Nguyễn Thị Phương Hoa points out that clemency law in Vietnam is, in fact, highly confused and is in need of three fundamental reforms. First, she notes that the exemption from serving a sentence overlaps with the commutation to reduce sentence. The distinguishing feature is the length of the commutation, with an exemption from serving a sentence usually cancelling the remaining sentence, while commutation only reduces the sentence.[702] Dr Nguyễn, therefore, recommends treating all reductions, whether in whole or in part, as commutations.[703] Secondly, Dr Nguyễn points out that the exemption from criminal liability and exemption from punishment are insufficiently distinguished from each other, although they treat the criminal record differently. The former expunges the criminal record immediately, while the latter erases the record only once all aspects of the punishment have been completed.

[699] Criminal Code 1999, Art 58. See also Resolution No 02/2010/NQ-HDTP dated 22 October 2010 of the Judges' Council of the Supreme People's Court Supplementing Some Guidance Provided in Resolutions No 01/2007/NQ-HDTP dated 2 October 2007 and No 02/2007/NQ-HDTP dated 2 October 2007 of Judges' Council of the Supreme People's Court.

[700] Criminal Code 1999, Art 58(3).

[701] See Draft (Amended) Criminal Code, Art 64; See also Drafting Committee, 'Bản Thuyết Minh Chi Tiết Về Dự Thảo Bộ Luật Hình Sự (Sửa Đổi) [Detail Explanation About The Draft (Amended) Criminal Code]' (n 128) pt I(9).

[702] Nguyễn Thị Phương Hoa (n 137) 42.

[703] Ibid.

For example, while the convicted person may be exempted from a prison term, they may still have to pay court-ordered fines. Dr Nguyễn, therefore, suggests that in cases of the exemption from punishment there should be particular provision for the criminal record to last longer.[704] Finally, it is suggested that the time limits that apply to the postponement of punishment should also apply to suspension of punishment, as the Criminal Procedure Code is silent about time limits in the case of the latter.[705]

Special Amnesty (*đặc xá*): Reducing Sentence

Convicted criminals not facing the death penalty can be eligible for clemency under the Law on Special Amnesty 2007. If clemency is granted, they will be released early. Special Amnesty in these cases is granted only by Order of the President, on the advice of a Special Amnesty Advisory Council comprising representatives from all ministries involved in criminal cases.[706] The President usually makes the announcement of special amnesty, and ordinarily does so on a Vietnamese national holiday—frequently Independence Day, 2 September.

A prisoner hopes to be recognised by the detaining authority as eligible for special amnesty and have his or her name placed on the special amnesty list. Those prisoners who consider themselves eligible for special amnesty and who are not listed may, however, 'lodge complaints about non-inclusion of their names' either personally or via a legal representative.[707] This must be lodged within five working days of the special amnesty list being posted in the prison or detention centre.[708] The Law on Special Amnesty sets out the 'principles for granting amnesty':

1. Observing the Constitution and law and ensuring the interests of the state and lawful rights and interests of organisations and individuals.
2. Ensuring democracy, objectivity, fairness, publicity and transparency.
3. Meeting the requirements in internal relations, foreign relations national security and socials order and safety.[709]

The Law on Special Amnesty also sets criteria for those applying, including requiring the prisoner to have been of good behaviour and have served at least a third of their jail term.[710] Those who have had their sentences commuted to a term of imprisonment (where, for example, they were facing the death penalty) or life imprisonment are also able to seek special amnesty.

[704] Nguyễn Thị Phương Hoa (n 137) 43.
[705] Ibid.
[706] Law No 07/2007/QH12 passed by the National Assembly on 21 July 2007 on Special Amnesty, Art 25. The Ministries represented on the Special Amnesty Advisory Council are: Ministries of Public Security, Defence, Justice, together with the Supreme People's Court, Supreme People's Procuracy, State Presidential Office, Governmental Office and the Central Committee of the Vietnam Fatherland Front.
[707] Law No 07/2007/QH12, Arts 32(1)–(2).
[708] Law No 07/2007/QH12, Art 32(3).
[709] Law No 07/2007/QH12, Art 4.
[710] Law No 07/2007/QH12, Art 10.

Article 11 sets out situations in which those otherwise eligible for special amnesty under Art 10 'will not be proposed' including where: there is an ongoing appeal or cassational review; the potential applicant is being 'examined for penal liability for other criminal acts'; special amnesty has been granted previously; the detained person has 'two or more previous convictions'; or 'other cases decided by the President.'[711] This leaves the President with a wide discretion.

In addition to the grounds outlined in the Law on Special Amnesty, counsel's advice on the handling of applications for special amnesty is that the existence of the following facts usually renders a special amnesty application likely to be rejected: the crime committed is a 'serious' or 'especially serious' crime infringing national security; the crime relates to drug dealing and the term of imprisonment is for more than one year; there are grounds to confirm illegal use of drugs by the applicant; or two crimes or more have been committed at the same time.[712] Special amnesty is also likely to be rejected in the following circumstances: the convicted person already has a criminal conviction for drug offences; homicide; property theft; property theft by snatching; depriving people of property; child rape; resisting officials in the performance of their duties; causing public disorder; intentionally spreading HIV; kidnapping for ransom; trafficking women; trafficking children; escaping from any place of detention, including a detention centre or while being escorted to trial; assisting escapees; or intentionally inflicting injury as a result of hooliganism or conflict between gangs.[713]

As a matter of principle, those who have had their death sentences commuted to life imprisonment can also seek special amnesty as explained above, or on the motion of the prison to the court. In cases where the primary offence for which they are imprisoned relates to a dugs offence, special amnesty may not be sought until less than a year remains of their sentence.

There is provision for special amnesty in 'special cases' described as those where 'in order to meet the State's domestic and foreign relation requirements the State President may decide to grant special amnesty'.[714] This is a very broad discretion that is not constrained by the operation of the articles guiding special amnesty decisions of the President described above.

Amnesty (*'ân xá'*) and the Death Penalty

Amnesty can also be sought as a basis for the revocation of the death penalty, usually resulting in an order for life imprisonment. Again, the Office of the State President makes the order. In 2014, Daniel Pascoe estimated that amnesty was granted in Vietnam in between 6 per cent and 23 per cent of cases.[715] In 2015 he revised

[711] Law No 07/2007/QH12, Art 11.
[712] Interviewee 21 (8 April 2011).
[713] Ibid.
[714] Law on Special Amnesty 2007, Art 21.
[715] Daniel Pascoe, 'Clemency in Southeast Asian Death Penalty Cases' (ALC Briefing Paper, no 1, 2014), p 5.

that estimate, finding clemency occurring in between 5 per cent and 50 per cent of cases.[716] Pascoe carefully chronicles the weakness of the data upon which these figures are based, noting that it is impossible to know with certainty what percentage of those facing the death penalty are executed.[717] We do know, however, that between 2001 and 2010 (with no data for the period from 2003 to 2004), 1,421 people were sentenced to death and, as noted above, that equates to roughly 177 death sentences per year.[718] The numbers actually executed are, however, lower by most accounts.[719]

As mentioned, a criminal who receives the death sentence has seven days from the date of the judgment becoming effective to file a Petition for Amnesty (*Đơn xin ân giảm*).[720] If there is an appeal and the conviction and penalty stand, the seven-day period runs from the date of the most recent effective judgment. As already noted, a judgment that imputes the death penalty must be forwarded to the Chairman of the Supreme People's Procuracy and the President of the Supreme People's Court.[721] As discussed, each of these bodies must review the decision and consider whether there are bases for a cassational review within two months.[722] In the event that the conviction and death penalty stand, the convicted person can file a petition for amnesty upon notification of this.[723] In other words, there are multiple dates from which the seven-day time limit for the petition for amnesty may run, This arises because not all convicted persons exercise appeal and review rights. Effectively, the seven-day limit runs from the most recent effective decision where other appeal rights have not been exercised. This means the seven-day limit runs from the date of the original judgment (not appealed) or the appellate court order (where there is no cassational review or re-opening sought); or the date of the re-opening or cassational review decision, whichever is final, provided, of course, that the death penalty still stands. Again, prisoners facing the death penalty file their amnesty petitions after the final determination of the Supreme People's Court on cassational review.

There is, however, some flexibility about the seven-day time limit for amnesty petitions in death penalty cases. Where the Office of the State President receives a petition for amnesty after the time period has expired, and there are grounds for waiving the time limit, it then falls to the court to verify if there is an acceptable cause for the delay.[724] For example, in cases where the petition has been delayed by the detention centre (such as where there is slow transport or the centre is remote)

[716] See Pascoe (n 603) 7–8.

[717] Ibid.

[718] Lương Thanh Hải, 'The Application of the Death Penalty' (2014) 5.

[719] Carlyle Thayer, 'Vietnam: Time to Abolish Capital Punishment?' *Chennai Centre for China Studies*, 17 January 2015, www.c3sindia.org/vietnam/4764. This report chronicles the variable death penalty rates between 2004 and 2013. It suggests the highest number of executions was 104 in 2007, again noting that in each year the available data were speculative and not official.

[720] Criminal Procedure Code 2003, Art 258(1).

[721] Ibid.

[722] Ibid.

[723] Resolution No 02/2007/NQ-HDTP dated 02 October 2007 of the Judges' Council of the Supreme People's Court Guiding the Implementation of a Number of Articles in Part Five 'Execution of Court's Judgments and Decisions' of the Criminal Procedure Code 2003, s II(1)(1.1)(i) ('Resolution 02').

[724] Ibid. See also Criminal Procedure Code 2003, Art 235.

or where the detained person suffers from mental incapacity or does not understand the procedures by which to petition for amnesty, this detail is set out in a verification form (*văn bản xác minh*) and this form, together with the applicable decision and the dossier, must be forwarded to the appropriate appellate court.[725]

Where there is no petition sent within the time limit, the court and the temporary detention centre are required to verify why this is the case.[726] More particularly, the evidence that there is no petition forthcoming must be in written form and include the signatures of court officials, the officials of the temporary detention centre, the convicted person, witnesses, and interpreters (if any). Where the convict does not provide his or her signature (or fingerprint), the reason for this must also be included.[727]

In the event that petitions for appeal or amnesty are verified as lost due to a fault in the mailing system, a new petition is acceptable.[728]

If the convicted person has verified that he or she does not wish to appeal during the time limit, but during the verification period he or she change their mind, he or she is permitted to appeal, provided plausible reasons can be given.[729] The court of appeal will set up a trial panel consisting of three judges to consider the reason for the late appeal and whether to accept or reject it.[730] Similarly, if the convicted person does not wish to make a petition for amnesty during the provided time limit, but wishes to do so during the verification period, the persons authorised to verify shall explain to him or her the applicable regulations on time periods during which a petition for amnesty can be lodged. They must then allow the petition and instruct the person making it how to explain the lateness of the petition. The verification form (along with the case file, if not already submitted) must be submitted to the Chief Justice of the Supreme People's Court (via the Secretariat of the Supreme People's Court).[731]

There is no specific regulation of the criteria for amnesty by the State President in death penalty cases. The Legal Department, under the Office of the State President, will consider petitions for amnesty and then prepare a report and assessment for the State President, who makes the final decision.[732] The department will base its recommendations on the petition files in which comments are provided by relevant bodies including the SPC, procuracies, and public security agencies.[733] The department will also base its recommendations on other sources of information, including media reports (or reports from the Information-Press Department) and the Foreign Affairs Department (where relevant), and the type of crime committed.[734] Ultimately, the decision on whether to replace the death penalty with imprisonment rests with the

725 Resolution 02, s II(1)(1.1). See also Criminal Procedure Code 2003, Art 235.
726 Resolution 02, s II(1)(1.1)(a).
727 Ibid.
728 Resolution 02, s II(1)(1.1)(a), (d).
729 Resolution 02, s II(1)(1.1)(c).
730 Criminal Procedure Code 2003, Art 235.
731 Resolution 02, s II(1)(1.1)(d).
732 Interviewee 21 (8 April 2011).
733 Ibid.
734 Ibid.

State President. Amnesty decisions are not widely reported in Vietnam (see further below).[735]

Foreigners and the Death Penalty

All Australian citizens who have been sentenced to death in Vietnam have had their sentences commuted to life imprisonment after the determination of a petition for amnesty. For example, in 2006, Mai Công Thành,[736] Nguyễn Văn Chinh[737] and Trịnh Hữu[738] received special amnesty, while in 2001, Lê Mỹ Linh, and, in 2005, Trần Văn Thành,[739] were granted special amnesty.[740] Some applications remain pending at the time of writing.

[735] So, for example, the only record of the pardon in the case of Nguyễn Văn Chinh that could be located electronically was on the Ministry of Foreign Affairs website: Vietnam. Ministry of Foreign Affairs, 'President of the SRV Tran Duc Lương Has Decided to Commute Tran Van Thanh's Death Sentence to Life Imprisonment' (Spokesman's Statement, 23 August 2005), www.mofa.gov.vn/en/tt_baochi/pbnfn/ns050824085221. Online sources for major Vietnamese dailies did not record the pardon at all. This suggests the publication on the Ministry's website targeted an international audience rather than a domestic one.

[736] Mai Công Thành was allegedly caught in 2003 attempting to smuggle 1.7 kilograms of heroin into Australia. Arrested in May 2003, he was sentenced to death by the Ho Chi Minh City People's Court on 9 June 2005. He was granted presidential amnesty in early February 2006. See, *Thanh Nien Daily*, 'Australian Drug Dealer Gets Death Penalty in Vietnam' (9 June 2005), thanhniennews.com/society/?catid=3&newsid=7175.

[737] Nguyễn Văn Chinh was arrested in December 2000 and sentenced to death on 22 April 2005 by the Ho Chi Minh City People's Court. He received a grant of amnesty 10 months later in February 2006. Lê Nga, 'Vietnam Upholds Death Penalty for Australian Pusher', *Thanh Nien News* (23 April 2005), thanhniennews.com/overseas/?catid=12&newsid=7790; *Sydney Morning Herald*, 'Australian Faces Firing Squad Over Trafficking' (23 April 2005), www.smh.com.au/news/World/Australian-faces-firing-squad-over-trafficking/2005/04/23/1114152356093.html?oneclick=true#; *Thanh Nien News*, 'Australian Given Death Penalty in Vietnam for Drug Trafficking' (23 April 2005), thanhniennews.com/overseas/?catid=12&newsid=6303.

[738] Trịnh Hữu was arrested in 2004 with three Vietnamese accomplices transporting 2 kg heroin into Vietnam from Cambodia. He was sentenced to death at first instance and appeal. AAP (Australian Associated Press), 'Sydney Drug Smuggler Spared Death Penalty' *Sydney Morning Herald*, 17 November 2006, www.smh.com.au/news/world/sydney-drug-smuggler-spared-death-penalty/2006/11/17/1163266778896.html. On 17 November 2006, Trịnh Hữu's death penalty was commuted to life imprisonment: Alexander Downer, 'Clemency for Huu Trinh' (Press Release, 17 November 2006) http://foreignminister.gov.au/releases/2006/fa127_06.html.

[739] Lê Mỹ Linh was caught with almost a kilogram of heroin at Tan Son Nhat International Airport in November 2001 while attempting to board a plane to Sydney. She was sentenced to death but following a successful petition for amnesty by Foreign Minister Alexander Downer her sentence was reduced to life imprisonment. See Alexander Downer, 'Death Sentence Upheld on Le My Linh' (Press Release, 23 December 2002), www.foreignminister.gov.au/releases/2002/fa198_02.html. Trần Văn Thành was sentenced to death on 5 November 2004 for drug trafficking, aged 34. He was convicted of attempting to smuggle 700 grams of heroin in a tube welded into a ship container. He was arrested in 2003 in the southern city of Dalat named as part of a drug syndicate smuggling heroin from Cambodia to Australia via Vietnam. The syndicate was exposed in June 2003 when police arrested a corrupt local Vietnamese official (*can bo*), Phạm Đại Nhơn. Trần's appeal was quashed in March 2005 but a petition for amnesty was granted in August 2005, commuting his death sentence to life imprisonment. See *ABC News Online*, 'Australian Arrested in Vietnamese Drug Trafficking Crackdown' (5 July 2003), www.abc.net.au/news/newsitems/200307/s895599.htm. [copies on file with author]

[740] The official statement by the Vietnamese MOFA spokesperson, Lê Dũng, dated 23 August 2005 cites 'humanitarian tradition' for commuting Trần Văn Thành's death sentence to life imprisonment. See Vietnam. Ministry of Foreign Affairs, 'President of the SRV Tran Duc Lương has Decided' (2005).

The granting of amnesty in the case of the Australians has been explained on the basis of 'humanitarianism' and excellent relations between Australia and Vietnam. The latter's Ministry of Foreign Affairs has said, for example, that death is:

> ... a proper punishment for drug trafficking and trading crime ...[but the special amnesty is] prompted by the humanitarian tradition, by the good relationship between Australia and Vietnam and based on the appeal for pardon' [...].[741]

There has been speculation that where a foreign national's home country does not have the death penalty, Vietnam will seek to avoid executing him or her.[742] There is also strong evidence of high-level Australia-Vietnam co-operation in the prevention and prosecution of transnational organised crime, including drugs cases. The Australian Federal Police, for example, have permanent staff in Ho Chi Minh City. They are located at the Australian Federal Police Liaison Office, which has been operating since 13 June 2003 and was relaunched as the Vietnam Australia Joint Transnational Crime Centre in 2010.[743] It is reasonable to assume that the inter-police co-operation may result in an understanding that any Australians charged may not ultimately face execution. In any event, it is fair to say that Australians are very unlikely to be executed in Vietnam for drug offences if a petition for amnesty has been made setting out compelling grounds for the petition.[744] That said, this will ultimately depend on the exercise of discretion by Vietnamese authorities and so cannot be assumed.

It has not been possible to definitively track the ultimate fate of other foreign nationals through press coverage. There have, for example, been Nigerians and Thais on death row for drugs offences in Vietnam in recent years. Media reports in 2013 indicated that their executions were imminent[745] and at least one of the Nigerians has since been killed.[746] Local press coverage that could confirm the status of the others could not, however, be located. The Nigerian government has refused to support special amnesty applications on behalf of Nigerian nationals on death row. Its Ambassador to Vietnam, Mazi Mathias Orji Okafor, has nonethless provided 'moral support' and made efforts to care for the families of prisoners.[747] Ambassador Okafor also indicated that he had appealed to the Nigerian government for funds to provide legal aid to Nigerian defendants facing death. Responding to calls in 2013 for a more humanitarian approach to Nigerians on death row, the Nigerian Senate leader, David Mark, said that Nigerians who engage in criminal offences outside the

[741] Vietnam. Ministry of Foreign Affairs (n 735).

[742] Interviewee 21 (8 April 2011).

[743] Australian Embassy, Vietnam, 'News: 10th Anniversary of the AFP Liaison Office in HCMC', ([no date] c June 2013), www.vietnam.embassy.gov.au/hnoi/Police_Liaison.html.

[744] Interview with an unnamed bureaucrat (12 June 2007).

[745] *Nigerian Eye*, 'Nigerians in Vietnam Prison will be Executed Soon' (20 March 2013), www.nigerianeye.com/2013/03/26-nigerians-in-vietnam-prisons-to-be.html.

[746] Saad Yarock, 'Drug Trafficking: Ejiogulkechukwu to Die by Lethal Injection', *Youtube* (28 October 2015), www.youtube.com/watch?v=uFCvku-DGMs. This article reports the death of Nigerian Michael Ikenna Nduanya.

[747] *Nigerian Eye*, 'Nigerians in Vietnam Prison' (2013).

country deserve to die.[748] Nigeria itself has the death penalty, mostly for murder and other violent crimes, although its use differs from state to state.[749] In Nigeria, rates of execution are overall low,[750] however, and the death penalty does not apply to any offences under its National Drug Law.[751]

Our research has also not been able to identify whether the death sentences of convicted Thai drug traffickers were commuted. In the recent case of 32-year-old Chaimongkol Suracha, a woman, the death sentence handed down by the Ho Chi Minh court was upheld on appeal by the Supreme People's Court on 4 April 2014.[752] In a petition for amnesty made to the Embassy of Vietnam on 11 April 2014, the Thai Union for Civil Liberty argued that although Thailand has sentenced women to death, most have had their sentences commuted.[753] Only three Thai women have been executed since 1935 and none in recent years.[754]

Pascoe suggests there is a higher rate of amnesty in Vietnam for foreigners from Western states than those from Asia, although he notes the latter also obtain it.[755] His research does not cover the incidence of amnesty for Africans sentenced to death.

XI. REGULATIONS ON FINANCE AND THE DRUG TRADE

Since 2009, the Criminal Code has contained a laundering offence for proceeds of crime, including where proceeds arise from drugs offences.[756] The 2009 amendments to the Criminal Code implement the money laundering offence set out under the 1988 Convention,[757] making it an offence to 'legalise' money through 'financial and/or banking operations or other transactions'.[758] This is an offence of direct intention where those charged under the offence must be aware that what they propose is illegal but do it anyway because they intend to relocate funds to 'legitimate' sources.[759] They must also know that the money derives from criminal activity.[760]

[748] *EMN News*, 'Drug Trafficking: Ejiogu Ikechukwu to Die by Lethal Injection in Vietnam' (27 October 2013), emn-news.com/drug-trafficking-ejiogu-ikechukwu-to-die-by-lethal-injection-in-vietnam-watch-video/.

[749] Death Penalty Worldwide, 'Nigeria' (Report) (19 June 2014), www.deathpenaltyworldwide.org/country-search-post.cfm?country=Nigeria.

[750] Ibid.

[751] See National Drug Law Enforcement Agency Act (Nigeria, cap 30, 1989).

[752] Lê Quang, 'Vietnam Court Upholds Death Sentence to Thai Drug Mule', *ThanhNien News* (4 April 2014), www.thanhniennews.com/society/vietnam-court-upholds-death-sentence-to-thai-drug-mule-25103.html.

[753] See also Pascoe 'Clemency in Southeast Asian Death Penalty Cases' (2014) 17 where he observes that the clemency rate is 91–92 per cent.

[754] Danthong Breen, Head of Death Penalty, Union for Civil Liberty, 'Letter Addressed to H.E. Mr Nguyen Tat Thanh, the Embassy of the Socialist Republic of Vietnam' 11 April 2014, deathpenaltythailand.blogspot.com.au/2014/04/suracha-chaimongkol-2.html. It is possible that amnesty has been granted but has not been reported, or has been reported only in the Thai language press.

[755] See Pascoe (n 603) 15–19.

[756] Nguyễn Thị Phương Hoa (n 137) 13.

[757] United Nations Convention against Illicit Traffic in Narcotic Drugs and Psychotropic Substances (opened for signature 20 December 1988, entered into force 11 November 1990) 1582 UNTS 95 (1988 Convention), Art 3(1)(b).

[758] Criminal Code 1999, Art 251.

[759] Nguyễn Thị Phương Hoa (n 137) 13.

[760] Ibid.

As with other criminal offences, there are various degrees of seriousness of the crime and corresponding levels of penalty, with the standard penalty being one to five years. If the defendant has committed the crime more than once, abuses his or her position of authority, or undertakes the offences in an organised manner, the penalty increases to three to 10 years of imprisonment.[761] If the crime is committed in a 'particularly serious way' the sentence increases to five to 15 years of imprisonment.[762] There is also a range of other penalties including: confiscation of property; a fine equating to three times the value of the laundered funds; and a ban from holding certain positions or jobs for one to five years.[763]

XII. ROLE OF THE MEDIA

The role of the state-controlled media in drugs cases needs to be understood in at least five different ways.

First, the media is explicitly used by the police, procuracy and the court to assist in educating the public about the tough approach taken to the 'social evil' of drug crimes.[764] In fact, Vietnamese trials remain show trials in some ways, in that they are often intended to contribute to the propagandist work of the courts.[765] The court's use of the press to this end occurs both during and after the trial, when reports appear on the outcome of the case, particularly any harsh sentences imposed.[766] Coverage usually includes photos of defendants on trial, depicting them in striped prison clothes and, in many cases, surrounded by police.[767] By contrast, the grant of Presidential special amnesty is not covered locally.[768] This leaves the propagandist

[761] Criminal Code 1999, Art 251(2).

[762] Criminal Code 1999, Art 251(2).

[763] Criminal Code 1999, Art 251(3).

[764] A former procurator notes that procurators can only provide information to journalists if approved by the Procurator General. Interviewee 8 (4 June 2012).

[765] Pip Nicholson and Kieu Truong 'The Modern Propaganda Trial: Drugs Prosecutions in Vietnam' (2008) 34 *Monash Law Review* 430, 430–56.

[766] Interviewee 18 (20 August 2012). The case of Chu Hoàng Mai (sentenced 4 September 2009, appeal 29 October 2012) is a good example. Her circumstances were outlined in court and reiterated in advance of her appeal: a divorced mother suffering from cancer, which led to depression and gambling debts, supported in court by her three highly emotional and distressed daughters. In this case, the appeal did not reduce the sentence and Chu Hoàng Mai's original sentence of 20 years for transporting 223 grams of heroin was confirmed. See Vũ Mai, 'Những nữ Việt kiều xách thuê heroin lấy tiền đi casino [Vietnamese female expatriates traffic in heroin for gambling]', *Việt Báo (VnExpress.net)* (25 October 2009), vnexpress.net/tin-tuc/phap-luat/nhung-nguoi-dan-ba-xach-thue-heroin-lay-tien-di-casino-2147414.html.

[767] See, *Việt Báo* (*Công An TP.HCM* [Ho Chi Minh City Police]) 'Vận chuyển 3 bánh heroin ra nước ngoài, một Việt kiều lĩnh án tử hình [Trafficking in three packages of heroin to overseas, one Vietnamese expatriate receives death penalty]' (26 April 2005), vietbao.vn/An-ninh-Phap-luat/Van-chuyen-3-banh-heroin-ra-nuoc-ngoai-mot-Viet-kieu-linh-an-tu-hinh/55062500/218/; *Việt Báo* (*Công An TP.HCM* [Ho Chi Minh City Police]) 'Phạt tử hình, tù chung thân những Việt kiều buôn lậu ma túy [Imposing death penalty, life sentence to Vietnamese expatriates trafficking drugs]' (24 March 2005), vietbao.vn/An-ninh-Phap-luat/Phat-tu-hinh-tu-chung-than-nhung-Viet-kieu-buon-lau-ma-tuy/55057392/218/.

[768] See reporting on Australians, Mai Công Thành (arrested June 2003, sentenced to death 9 June 2005) and his co-accused Nguyễn Mạnh Cường (arrested June 2003, not sent to trial due to mental incapacity). Research did not reveal reporting in Vietnam of the amnesty granted to Mai Công Thành,

and didactic aspects of the trials intact and unchallenged, at least in the eyes of the public.

An example of this is media reporting of the 38 Australian nationals who have been tried for drugs offences between 2003 and 2015. As mentioned, no Australian who has exhausted the appeal and special amnesty application process over the 16 years since 1999 has been executed for drug offences. Research over that period suggests that although nine were sentenced to death and had that sentence confirmed on appeal, their death sentences were all commuted to life jail terms through the Presidential special amnesty procedure.

Second, investigation bodies at times deploy the press to leak information, whether real or fabricated, to assist with their investigations.[769] They may, for example, deliberately obscure or overstate the evidence to mislead criminals.[770] That said, in some cases, police restrain use of the media until the investigation is complete, for fear of frightening off accomplices or losing evidence critical to the case.[771] Instead, reporting is often commenced at the time of arrest, after interview, and will typically include photos of the drug 'haul' with the defendant.[772]

The third way in which press reporting should be understood lies in its contribution to publicising the defence narrative. Local lawyers have consistently advised, over many years, that if a moral narrative exists to explain how or why a defendant became involved in drug crimes, it must be circulated in the press in advance of the trial. This strategy is intended to counter the propagandist use of media by judicial agencies to promote their anti-drug agenda. Put another way, if the court is ultimately to hand down a relatively lenient sentence, albeit within the scale of available penalties, the reasons that might justify this must be well-ventilated in the press in advance of the trial and any appeal. This strategy is used to protect against a negative view of the defendant infecting the court's decision or the President's special amnesty decisions. As noted above, the President does have regard to media reports about parties when reaching his conclusions about special amnesty.[773]

This is not to suggest that courts are necessarily directly affected by the media when sentencing.[774] It is true, however, that, 'if the media has produced an indignant attitude [in the public] towards the defendant,'[775] it is hard for the trial panel to ignore this and the defendant is 'frequently subject to harsh penalty.'[776]

although it was extensively, if derivatively, reported internationally. The search string of Mai Công Thành and Nguyễn Mạnh Cường in Vietnam revealed 135 news reports available through Newsbank and 9 through Vietbao. This pattern of reporting is replicated for research on the 9 Australians sentenced to death. Our research on these cases was limited to news stories available electronically via Vietbao and Newsbank.

769 Interviewee 18 (20 August 2012).

770 Ibid. Also Interviewee 8 (4 June 2012).

771 Interviewee 3 (25 May 2012).

772 See, eg, Vũ Mai, 'Những nữ Việt kiều'; 'Bắt quả tang 2 Việt kiều vận chuyển 1/2kg heroin [Caught two Vietnamese expatriates carrying 1/2kg heroin]' (7 July 2006), vietbao.vn/An-ninh-Phap-luat/Bat-qua-tang-2-Viet-kieu-van-chuyen-1-2kg-heroin/45200506/218/.

773 Interviewee 21 (8 April 2011).

774 Interviewee 4 (25 May 2012).

775 Interviewee 11 (10 August 2012).

776 Ibid.

Fourth, the impact of press scrutiny can be significant for those involved in trials. One defence lawyer, for example, reports that if he is involved in a high profile case, attracting a lot of press coverage, 'I am very careful with my statements at the trial. I protect my client only to the extent the evidence is strong enough.'[777] The implication here is lawyers are concerned not to be seen as defending 'social evils', and tightly moderate their own behaviour to guard against being portrayed as sympathising with criminals.

Finally, it is also suggested that press involvement keeps pressure on the judicial agencies (police, procuracy and courts) to abide by the law:[778]

> The media has an increasing role in cleaning up the environment of judicial activity. The involvement of the media helps improve the compliance with procedural laws. If an official breaches the law and it is reported in newspapers, he or she will be liable for his or her breach. When journalists attend a trial, officials will follow procedural laws more strictly and behave in a careful manner (formally dressed, punctual, etc.). In Vietnam, this is the only way for the public to supervise judicial activities. It is hard for people to otherwise directly supervise judicial activities.[779]

XIII. CONCLUSION

In conclusion, there has been fundamental and wide-ranging reform to the practice of criminal trials in Vietnam generally since the 2003 reforms to the criminal procedure laws. Drugs law has also been overhauled, particularly as a result of the introduction of detailed drug offences in the Criminal Code 1999 and new penalties in Resolution 2001. The passage of Decree 82 in 2013, which identified drugs regulated with greater precision, has also assisted reform. Tensions nonetheless continue to exist between the law and its practice in the investigation, trial, sentencing and clemency processes.

Vietnam's criminal justice system also remains fundamentally socialist, despite introducing reforms that look outside that tradition. This socialist orientation is evident in the partnership approach to decision-making adopted by the procuracy and the courts, the constrained (but developing) role allowed for counsel, and the still uncertain trajectory of greater human rights recognition and adversarial court practices. That a defendant is assumed to be guilty by many involved in the trial underlines the importance of effective advocacy during the investigation. There appears to be a reductionist trend in relation to the death penalty, and this may extend to reducing its application to drug offences in the future but it is still too soon to be confident about that.

[777] Interviewee 19 (27 August 2012).
[778] Ibid.
[779] Interviewee 18 (20 August 2012).

POSTSCRIPT: AMENDMENT OF VIETNAM'S CRIMINAL CODES[780]

In November 2015, Vietnam's National Assembly introduced new Codes that replaced and significantly amended the Criminal Code 1999 and the Criminal Procedure Code 2003.[781] These amendments followed extensive debate within the country about how to better align criminal law and criminal procedure law with constitutional changes introduced in late 2013 that enhanced the human rights of citizens and introduced more features of an adversarial trial system.

The amendments fundamentally alter the regulation of drug offences. First, the new Codes largely disaggregate narcotics offences and introduce a range of procedural changes aimed at better protecting due process and the rights of defendants, as well as those arrested, detained, or suspected of crimes. Second, the application of the death penalty has been reduced for some narcotics offences and offences involving older defendants.[782]

The extensive debates about these reforms which took place before these amendments were adopted are discussed early in this Chapter. This postscript offers a brief statement of the changes relevant to drugs law that will come into effect in July 2016, as well as the relevant transitional provisions affecting the operation of the death penalty. At the time of writing there was no official translation of the two Codes available. Our translations are of Vietnamese versions of the Criminal Code and Criminal Procedure Code published on the National Assembly website.[783]

Narcotics Offences

Under the Criminal Code 2015, crimes in general are still classified into less serious crimes, serious crimes, very serious crimes, and especially serious crimes. Penalties correspond to the category of seriousness of the offence: up to three years; up to seven years; up to 15 years; over 15 years, life imprisonment or death, respectively.[784] Categorisation of the seriousness of drug offences no longer appears in the same article that defines crimes as it did in the Criminal Code 1999. It is now a separate article in the new Code.[785]

[780] This Addendum was written by the authors on 5 February 2016.

[781] Criminal Code No 100/2015/QH13 dated 27 November 2015 (Criminal Code 2015) and Criminal Procedure Code No 101/2015/QH13 dated 27 November 2015 (Criminal Procedure Code 2015). On transitional provisions see Resolution No 109/2015/QH13 on the Implementation of the Criminal Code of the National Assembly dated 27 November 2015 and Resolution No 110/2015/QH13 on the Implementation of the Criminal Procedure Code of the National Assembly dated 27 November 2015.

[782] Criminal Code 2015, Art 249, Art 252 and Resolution No 109/2015/QH13 on the Implementation of the Criminal Code of the National Assembly dated 27 November 2015, Art, 1(2)(a).

[783] http://duthaoonline.quochoi.vn/DuThao/Lists/DT_DUTHAO_LUAT/View_Detail.aspx?ItemID=526&LanID=1189&TabIndex=1 (last accessed 3 November 2015) and http://duthaoonline.quochoi.vn/DuThao/Lists/DT_DUTHAO_LUAT/View_Detail.aspx?ItemID=561&LanID=1190&TabIndex=1 (last accessed 3 November 2015).

[784] Criminal Code 2015, Art 9.

[785] Ibid.

Narcotic-related crimes are set out in Chapter XX of the Criminal Code 2015,[786] and these offences range from less serious to extremely serious crimes. The new Criminal Code does not group narcotic offences in one article, as was previously the case, but sets out each type of narcotic crime in a single article, noting the applicable penalty. These appear below with changes noted in bold:

- Art 247—Growing opium poppy, **coca, marijuana** or other kinds of plant bearing narcotic substance (coca and marijuana added)
- Art 248—**Unlawful manufacturing of narcotic substances**
- Art 249—**Unlawful stockpiling of narcotic substances**
- Art 250—**Unlawful transporting of narcotic substances**
- Art 251—**Unlawful trading of narcotic substances**
- Art 252—**Unlawful appropriation of narcotic substances**
- Art 255—Organisation of unlawful use of narcotic substances
- Art 256—Harbouring the unlawful use of narcotic substances
- Art 257—**Forcing other persons into unlawful use of narcotic substances**
- Art 258—**Inducing other persons into unlawful use of narcotic substances**[787]
- Art 259—Breaching regulations on management and use of narcotic substances, **precursors,** addictive drugs **or centripetalneurotropic drugs** (precursors and centripetalneurotropic added to the offence).

That said, several articles still group the offences. In particular, the offences relevant to precursors remain grouped: 'Stockpiling, transporting, trading or appropriating precursors used in unlawful production of narcotic substances'.[788] The manufacture of precursors is still not a crime. The offences relating to equipment and tools are also grouped: 'Producing, stockpiling, transporting or trading equipment and tools used in the unlawful production or use of narcotic substances.'[789]

Age and Narcotics Offences

As foreshadowed in Chapter 5, the Criminal Code 2015 makes explicit the offences for which those under 16 years of age and above 14 years of age may be held criminally liable. This replaces the previous, general provision that people between 14 and 16 years of age may only be criminally liable for 'very serious crimes intentionally committed or especially serious crimes'. More specifically, the Criminal Code 2015 now provides that those who are 14 or above but under 16 years of age may be held liable for the following very serious and especially serious narcotic-related crimes:

- Art 248—Unlawful manufacturing of narcotic substances
- Art 249—Unlawful stockpiling of narcotic substances
- Art 250—Unlawful transporting of narcotic substances

[786] Criminal Code 2015, Arts 247–259.

[787] Unlike the Criminal Code 1999, forcing and inducing are now separated and attract different penalties.

[788] Criminal Code 2015, Art 253.

[789] Criminal Code 2015, Art 254.

— Art 251—Unlawful trading of narcotic substances
— Art 252—Unlawful appropriation of narcotic substances[790]

Bases of Exemption from Criminal Liability

As also foreshadowed in Chapter 5, the Criminal Code 2015 now provides for compulsory and optional exemption from criminal liability, albeit in more limited form than the exemptions than had been previously been debated. The exemptions are as follows.

1. An offender shall be exempted from criminal liability in one of the following circumstances:
   — Where during the investigation, prosecution or trial, due to a change of policy or law, the act of the offender is no longer dangerous to the society.
   — Where there are decisions on general amnesties.
2. An offender may be exempted from criminal liability in one of the following circumstances:
   — Where during the investigation, prosecution or trial, due to a change of situation, the act of the offender is no longer dangerous to the society.
   — Where during the investigation, prosecution or trial, the offender suffers from incurable disease, such that he or she is no longer dangerous to the society.
   — The offender gives him/herself up and clearly reports the facts, effectively contributes to the detection and investigation of the crime, tries to minimise the consequences of the crime and make great contribution or special dedication acknowledged by the state or society.
3. An offender who commits a less serious crime, or serious crime unintentionally, causing damage to the life, health, honour, dignity, or asset of another person may be exempted from criminal liability if the victim has voluntarily reconciled and requested exemption from criminal liability.[791]

Arrest and Detention

As was suggested in Chapter 5 might be the case, the Criminal Procedure Code has amended provisions with respect to urgent arrests. These are now called 'holding persons (*giữ người*) in urgent cases' (previously known as 'arresting persons (*bắt người*) in urgent cases'). Specific provision for holding persons pending extradition is now also made.[792] The law applicable to other categories of arrest remains similar, except that arrest of offenders caught red-handed and arrest of wanted offenders are

[790] Criminal Code 2015, Art 12(2). Those between 14 and 16 years of age may also be liable for a range of other offences that are now specified, including murder and rape, for example. See Art 12(1).
[791] Criminal Code, Art 29(1)–(3).
[792] Criminal Procedure Code 2015, Art 503.

now regulated by two separate articles.[793] In summary, the new Criminal Procedure Code 2015 categorises arrest as:

(i) holding persons in urgent cases;
(ii) arresting offenders caught red-handed;
(iii) arresting wanted offenders;
(iv) arresting an accused or defendant to remand them in custody; and
(v) arresting persons requested for extradition.[794]

The grounds for 'holding persons in urgent cases' have been changed as proposed, and now are made out:

— when there exist grounds to confirm that such persons are preparing to commit very serious or exceptionally serious offences; and/or
— when accomplices, victims or persons present at the scenes where the offences occurred saw with their own eyes and confirmed that such persons are the very ones who committed the offences and it is deemed necessary to immediately prevent such persons from escaping; and/or
— when traces of offences are found on the bodies, at the residences, working places, or vehicles of the persons suspected of having committed the offences and it is deemed necessary to immediately prevent such persons from escaping or destroying evidence.[795]

Bail

The Criminal Procedure Code 2015 stipulates that the individuals who offer bail must be at least 18 years old, have a 'good personality', strictly observe the law, have a stable income, and be in a 'good condition' to manage the bailed person.[796] Age, income and being in a 'good condition' are new requirements.

The Code also adds that the bailed persons must pledge to:

— be present when summoned unless that is not possible due to force majeure or 'objective obstacles';
— not flee or commit further offences;
— not bribe, force, incite others to make false declarations, provide false documents; not destroy, falsify evidence, documents and objects related to the case, [or] disperse assets related to the case; not threaten, control, or take revenge against witnesses, victims and persons who report the crime and their relatives.[797]

If those bailed (whether accused or defendants) violate their pledge, they may be placed in temporary detention.[798] In this case, the individuals or organisations standing bail will be fined, depending on the nature and extent of the violation. A range of fines is not provided.[799]

[793] Criminal Procedure Code 2015, Arts 111 and 112.
[794] Criminal Procedure Code 2015, Art 109.
[795] Criminal Procedure Code 2015, Art 110.
[796] Criminal Procedure Code 2015, Art 121(2).
[797] Criminal Procedure Code 2015, Art 121(3).
[798] Ibid.
[799] Criminal Procedure Code 2015, Art 121(6).

Presumption of Innocence

The new Criminal Procedure Code sets out a more robust statement of the presumption of innocence, albeit falling short of that proposed in an earlier draft of the Code.[800] The 2015 Code, like its predecessor, provides that an 'accused shall be considered not guilty' until guilt is established by the court. It adds, however, that 'where the grounds are insufficient and cannot be established [...] the agency or person with competence to conduct criminal proceedings shall conclude that the arrestee, detainee, suspect or defendant is not guilty.'

The new Criminal Procedure Code also provides that a suspect has the right not to self-incriminate,[801] as does a defendant,[802] although this still falls short of a clear right to silence.

Right to Counsel

Legal aid workers may now take an active role as defenders in criminal proceedings. This was previously unclear.

Likewise, persons acting in a defence role, whether a lawyer, representative, public defender (a person appointed by the Vietnam Fatherland Front to defend)[803] or a legal aid worker, now all have rights to meet with an 'arrestee, detainee, suspect or defendant'.[804] The new Criminal Procedure Code also provides these 'defenders' with the 'right' to be present during any interview of persons detained or charged.[805] Significantly the Code specifically states that a defender may be involved 'from the initiation of a criminal proceeding against a suspect.'[806] This affords a clearer statement of rights than previously, although again time will determine how rigorously these provisions are honoured.

Despite these changes which empower defenders to be more proactive, including a right to seek out and present evidence,[807] there is still no clear statement that defenders have standing or status in the courts equivalent to that enjoyed by judges or prosecutors.

Defenders are also subject to a series of obligations under the Code, including a duty not to 'divulge confidential investigative information',[808] nor to:

> [d]isclose information on the accused that the defender obtained from the defence without the written consent of that person; not to use information on the accused that the defender obtains from the defence for the purpose of infringing upon the state's interests, the public interest, or legitimate rights and interests of agencies, organisations and individuals.[809]

[800] Criminal Procedure Code 2015, Art 13, compare with Draft (Amended) Criminal Procedure Code Art 10, available at http://duthaoonline.quochoi.vn/DuThao/Lists/DT_DUTHAO_LUAT/View_Detail.aspx?ItemID=561&TabIndex=1&LanID=1070.

[801] Criminal Procedure Code 2015, Art 60(2)(d).

[802] Criminal Procedure Code 2015, Art 61(2)(h).

[803] Criminal Procedure Code 2015, Art 72(3).

[804] Criminal Procedure Code 2015, Art 73(1)(a).

[805] Criminal Procedure Code 2015, Art 73(1)(b).

[806] Criminal Procedure Code 2015, Art 74.

[807] Criminal Procedure Code 2015, Art 73(1)(h) and (i).

[808] Criminal Procedure Code 2015, Art 73(2)(e).

[809] Criminal Procedure Code 2015, Art 73(2)(g).

Defenders may be charged with administrative and criminal offences where they 'violate' the Criminal Procedure Code.

Together, these changes place lawyers and defenders in the difficult position of being entitled to more information about their clients but with significant constraints about how that information may be deployed.

Jurisdiction

The Criminal Procedure Code provides that the Provincial Courts shall hear specific crimes set out in Art 268(1).[810] Further, and as expected, the Provincial Courts shall hear: 'Cases in which defendants, victims, involved persons are residing overseas, or assets involved in the cases are overseas'.[811]

The new Criminal Procedure Code also specifically sets out bases on which the Provincial Courts may now hear cases that would otherwise begin in the District Courts, namely:

> Cases under the jurisdiction of District Courts that have many complicated details that make it difficult to assess and agree on the nature of the case; cases involving many levels, many sectors; cases in which the defendants are judges, procurators, investigators, key leaders at district or provincial levels, persons with religious dignitaries or high prestige in an ethnic minority.[812]

As noted in Chapter 5, the Supreme People's Court had specifically instructed that matters involving foreigners (whether 'foreign defendants, victims, persons whose rights or obligations are involved, civil plaintiffs or foreign organisations') should also be heard in the Provincial Courts.[813] This Letter remains in effect.[814]

Cassational Review and Re-opening of Cases Heard by the Judicial Council of the Supreme People's Court

As noted, the vexed question of whether a decision of the Judicial Council of the Supreme People's Court would be final is resolved in the new Criminal Procedure

[810] Criminal Code 2015, Art 268(2). These are crimes against national security; crimes undermining peace and humanity; war crimes; crimes provided in Articles 123, 125, 126, 227, 277, 278, 279, 280, 282, 283, 284, 286, 287, 288, 337, 368, 369, 370, 371, 399 and 400 of the Criminal Code 2015; and crimes committed outside the territory of Vietnam.

[811] Criminal Procedure Code 2015, Art 268(2)(b).

[812] Criminal Procedure Code 2015, Art 268(2).

[813] Official Letter No 81/2002/TANDTC dated 10 June 2002 of the Supreme People's Court in Response to Professional Queries.

[814] See, eg, Trần Đức Long, 'Bàn về thẩm quyền giải quyết, xét xử vụ án hình sự có bị cáo là người nước ngoài [Regarding the jurisdiction to process and adjudicate criminal cases with foreign defendants]', Tòa Án Nhân Dân Tối Cao (Việt Nam) [Vietnam. Supreme People's Court], toaan.gov.vn/portal/page/portal/tandtc/Baiviet?p_page_id=1754190&p_cateid=1751909&Article_details=1&item_id=13493581; Thanh Tùng, 'Có nên cho tòa huyện xử án có yếu tố nước ngoài? [Should district courts be allowed to adjudicate cases involving foreign factors?]', Pháp Luật Thành Phố Hồ Chí Minh [Ho Chi Minh Law Newspaper] (online), 14 January 2011, plo.vn/phap-luat/co-nen-cho-toa-huyen-xu-an-co-yeu-to-nuoc-ngoai-150138.html.

Code.[815] This provides that where there is reason to believe that a decision made by the Supreme People's Court's Judges' Council seriously violates the law, or where new evidence is presented that was not available at the time the decision was made that could fundamentally change that decision, a reconsideration is possible.

Such a reconsideration must, however, be sought by one of a number of state bodies, and the identity of the body that seeks the review determines how it is treated. Where the Standing Committee of the National Assembly seeks a review, it must take place. Where the Judicial Committee of the National Assembly, the Chief Procurator of the Supreme People's Procuracy or the Chief Justice of the Supreme People's Court 'recommends' a review, a meeting of the Judicial Council of the Supreme People's Court must be held to determine whether a review should proceed.[816] The Judges' Council of the Supreme People's Court may, however, decide at its meeting not to agree with the recommendation of the Judicial Committee of the National Assembly, the Chief Procurator of the Supreme People's Procuracy or the suggestion of the Chief Justice of the Supreme People's Court. In that case, the Standing Committee of the National Assembly will decide whether the decision should be reviewed.[817] In a meeting to review the decision, which must be attended by the Chief Procurator of the Supreme People's Procuracy, the Judges' Council of the Supreme People's Court can decide to uphold the decision or quash it.[818]

Drug Offences and the Death Penalty

From 1 July 2016, drug offences in Vietnam are categorised as: manufacturing, stockpiling, transporting, trading and appropriation offences, as explained in more detail above. In terms of penalties, stockpiling and appropriating narcotics no longer attract the death penalty.[819]

Under the new Criminal Code, manufacturing or producing drugs continues to attract 20 years, life imprisonment or the death penalty, with penalties allocated for the same amounts of drugs as previously.[820] Similarly, transporting and trading in narcotics still attracts 20 years, life imprisonment or the death penalty. Again penalties are allocated for the same amounts of drugs as previously.[821]

Further guidance about which penalty (20 years, life imprisonment or the death penalty) should be imposed when all are within the range for a particular offence will presumably be provided by the Supreme People's Court at a later time. In the meantime, the previous implementing legislation remains in place to guide the court in determining selection of an appropriate penalty.[822]

815 Criminal Procedure Code, Chapter XXVII.
816 Criminal Procedure Code, Art 404.
817 Criminal Procedure Code, Art 408.
818 Criminal Procedure Code, Art 411.
819 Criminal Code 2015, Arts 249, 252.
820 Criminal Code 2015, Art 248.
821 Criminal Code 2015, Arts 250, 251.
822 Resolution No 01/2001/NQ-HDTP dated 15 March 2001.

The death penalty is no longer available where the defendant is over 75 years of age either at the time of committing the offence or at trial.[823]

Transitional Provisions

The National Assembly has set out how the changes to the death penalty will be administered in the period before the new law comes into effect on 1 July 2016.

Put simply, the death penalty no longer applies for those charged with the drug offences of stockpiling and appropriating.[824] In effect, the removal of the death penalty as a penalty for these offences has been backdated to 27 November 2015, when the Criminal Code was passed.[825] Further, the Criminal Code makes it clear that offenders who had been found guilty and received the death penalty, but in circumstances where the death penalty would now not be imposed, are to have their death sentences commuted to life imprisonment by the Chief Justice of the Supreme People's Court.[826]

The abolition of the death penalty for those of a 'full 75 years or more' also takes immediate effect.[827]

Early Release

As foreshadowed, the new Criminal Procedure Code introduces a conditional early release system (*tha tù trước thời hạn có điều kiện*). Under the new Code, a person serving a prison sentence can be released early if he or she meets all the following requirements:

- is serving a sentence for his or her first offence;
- has achieved 'much improvement', and has 'a good rehabilitation attitude';
- has already received a reduction of a sentence of imprisonment, if the case involved a serious crime or more serious crime;
- has a clear place of residence;
- has paid any supplementary monetary penalty, court fee and civil compensation obligations; and
- has served at least half of his or her sentence, or 15 years of a term of life imprisonment that has been reduced to a term of imprisonment.[828]

This type of commutation does not apply to offenders who commit certain types of crimes, including, in particular, manufacturing, trading and appropriating narcotic substances.[829]

[823] Resolution No 109/2015/QH13 on the Implementation of the Criminal Code of the National Assembly dated 27 November 2015, Art 1(2)(a).

[824] Criminal Code 2015, Art 248.

[825] Resolution No 109/2015/QH13 on the Implementation of the Criminal Code of the National Assembly dated 27 November 2015, Art 2(a).

[826] Resolution No 109/2015/QH13 on the Implementation of the Criminal Code of the National Assembly dated 27 November 2015, Art 2(b).

[827] Resolution No 109/2015/QH13 on the Implementation of the Criminal Code of the National Assembly dated 27 November 2015, Art 1(2)(a)–(b).

[828] Criminal Code 2015, Art 66(1).

[829] Criminal Code 2015, Art 66(2).

Appendix

INDONESIA, SINGAPORE AND VIETNAM'S OBLIGATIONS UNDER THE UNITED NATIONS DRUGS CONVENTIONS AND THEIR KEY RESPONSES

CHECKLIST	INDONESIA	SINGAPORE	VIETNAM
Establish and maintain a special licit drug regulatory administration (**Single Convention,** *Art 17*; **1971 Convention,** *Art 6*)	**Narcotics Law No 35 of 2009** *Article 7* Appoints the Minister of Health to guarantee the availability of narcotics for the health service and development of science and technology. The Minister arranges an annual demand plan in respect of narcotics needed for health and science purposes.	**Misuse of Drugs Act 1973** *Section 10B(1)* The Minister may make regulations for: the licensing, by prescribed people or authorities, of people who intend to import or export controlled equipment, materials or substances; the regulation and control of the import and export of controlled equipment, materials or substances; the registration of premises used in connection with the import, export, manufacture, processing, storage, distribution or supply of controlled equipment, materials or substances; the documentation of transactions involving controlled equipment, materials or substances; the record keeping and furnishing of information in relation to controlled equipment, materials or substances; the inspection and production of records kept pursuant to the regulations; the labelling of consignments of controlled equipment, materials or substances.	**Law on Drug Prevention and Control No 23/2000/QH10** *Article 40* Makes the Minister of Health responsible for promulgating and implementing lists and regulations on the management of addictive medicines, centripetalneurotropic medicines and pre-substances used in public health, scientific analysis, test and research.

Checklist	Indonesia	Singapore	Vietnam
		Section 58(1) The Minister may make regulations: (a) providing for licences for the import, export, sale, manufacture, production or distribution of controlled drugs; (b) prescribing the form, duration, terms, conditions, fees, cancellation and suspension of licences; (c) authorising the sale, possession or other dealing in controlled drugs and prescribing the circumstances and conditions under which people may sell, possess and deal in controlled drugs; (d) requiring medical practitioners, dentists, pharmacists, veterinary surgeons and other people who deal in controlled drugs as may be authorised by the regulations to keep records and make returns; (e) requiring medical practitioners who attend to people they consider or have reasonable grounds to suspect are addicted to a controlled drug to furnish to the prescribed authority such particulars about those people as may be prescribed; (f) prohibiting medical practitioners from administering, supplying and authorising the administration and supply, and from prescribing, controlled drugs to people addicted to them; (g) packaging and labelling of controlled drugs; (h) regulating the transport of controlled drugs and methods for destroying or otherwise disposing of those drugs when no longer required; (i) requiring precautions for the safe custody of controlled drugs; (j) providing for the inspection of precautions taken or records kept in pursuance of regulations made under this section; (k) providing for treatment and	

CHECKLIST	INDONESIA	SINGAPORE	VIETNAM
		rehabilitation of people affected by the misuse of controlled drugs; (l) prescribing the punishment by a fine not exceeding $10,000 or imprisonment for a term not exceeding four years or both to be imposed on the conviction for a breach of the regulations; (m) providing for the management, maintenance and inspection of approved institutions; (n) prescribing the functions and procedure of Review Committees; (o) providing for the control, discipline (including the imposition of corporal punishment) and occupation of inmates, and the granting of leave to inmates for employment outside an approved institution and to return to their residences or other designated places; (p) prescribing the appointment and duties of officers of approved institutions; (q) providing for the supervision and aftercare of people referred to in section 34(2)(a), or who have undergone treatment and rehabilitation at approved or other institutions or who have been convicted of an offence under section 8(b); (qa) prescribing the circumstances under which the Director may extend the supervision of a person under this Act; (r) prescribing anything that may be prescribed; (s) prescribing the functions and procedure of advisory committees; (t) requiring fingerprinting of inmates and the dissemination of this information to the police; (u) prescribing the type of offences in the regulations which may be seizable offences for the purposes of the Criminal Procedure Code; (v) generally carrying out the purposes and provisions of this Act.	

CHECKLIST	INDONESIA	SINGAPORE	VIETNAM
Establish and maintain central offices for international co-operation (mutual legal assistance, **1988 Convention,** *Art 7*)	**Narcotics Law No 35 of 2009** *Article 70(g)* Contains provisions on the tasks and authorities of Badan Narkotika Nasional (BNN, National Narcotics Agency), and states that one of the tasks of the Agency is to co-operate bilaterally and multilaterally, regionally and internationally, in order to prevent and eradicate illicit traffic in narcotics and their precursors.	**Misuse of Drugs Act 1973** *Section 3(1)* 'The Minister may appoint a Director of the Central Narcotics Bureau and such numbers of Deputy Directors, Assistant Directors and other officers as the Minister may think fit'. The Act does not specify the Bureau's responsibilities but part of the Bureau's mission is to 'actively co-operate with local and foreign agencies on drug related matters'.[1]	**Law on Drug Prevention and Control No 23/2000/QH10** *Article 36(11)* The state management of drug prevention and control involves 'undertaking international co-operation' in drug prevention Diverse ministries have responsibility including: The Ministry of Public Security's responsible for drugs-related crime prevention (Art 28). The Ministry of Health regulates addictive medicines, centripetalneurotropic medicines and pre-substances used in the health domain (Art 40).

[1] CNB Singapore, www.cnb.gov.sg/aboutus/visionmissioncorevalues.aspx.

CHECKLIST	INDONESIA	SINGAPORE	VIETNAM
Classify each controlled drug and chemical under domestic law to ensure the minimum required convention controls apply (**Single Convention,** *Arts 2, 4*; **1971 Convention,** *Art 2*; **1988 Convention,** *Art 12*)	**Narcotics Law No 35 of 2009** *Article 6* Narcotics are categorised in three groups that loosely follow the schedules of the Single Convention.	**Misuse of Drugs Act 1973** *Schedules I, III–V*[2] The Act has established four lists of drugs that loosely follow the schedules of the Single Convention.	**Decree No 82/2013/ND-CP dated 19 July 2013 of the Government promulgating the list of narcotic substances and pre-substances** In 2013, a complete list of drugs was introduced, divided into 4 groups, broadly in line with international practice.
Limit the licit use of drugs to medical and scientific purposes (**Single Convention,** *Arts 2, 4*; **1971 Convention,** *Arts 5, 7*)	**Narcotics Law No 35 of 2009** *Article 7* Narcotics may only be consumed only for the purposes of health service and/or science and technology development.	**Misuse of Drugs Act 1973** *Sections 5–8* It is an offence to import, export, traffic in, manufacture, possess, 'smoke, administer to himself or otherwise consume' a controlled drug unless authorised by the Act. *Section 10B(1)* See above. *Section 58(1)* See above	**Law on Drug Prevention and Control No 23/2000/QH10** *Article 15* States the need to tightly control research into, expertise, production, transportation, preservation, storage, purchase, sale, distribution, use, processing, exchange, import, export and transit of narcotic substances, pre-substances, addictive medicines and centripetalneurotropic medicines.

[2] Schedule II, 'Offences Punishable on Conviction', is a list of offences rather than a list of drugs.

CHECKLIST	INDONESIA	SINGAPORE	VIETNAM
			Article 17 The Ministry of Health regulates the 'storage, preservation, prescription and sale' of narcotic substances, pre-substances, addictive medicines, and centripetalneurotropic medicines for treatment of illnesses at medical establishments. *Article 40* The Ministry of Health regulates addictive medicines, centripetalneurotropic medicines and pre-substances used in the health domain. *See also:* **Law Amending and Supplementing a Number of Articles of the Law on Drug Prevention and Control Order No 11/2008/L-CTN of 12 June 2008 (Law Amending Law on Drug Prevention and Control 2008)** **Article 13 amending Article 40(1)(a) of the Law on Drug Prevention and Control No 23/2000/QH10** Makes the Minister of Health 'assume the prime responsibility for, and co-ordinate with concerned agencies in, implementing the regulation on management of narcotic substances used in the health sector, analysis, testing and scientific research'.

Checklist	Indonesia	Singapore	Vietnam
Prohibit opium, coca and cannabis cultivation, where … prevailing conditions in the country … render … prohibition … the most suitable measure, in its opinion, for protecting … public health and welfare and preventing … diversion (**Single Convention**, *Art* 22)	**Narcotics Law No 35 of 2009** *Article 12* Opium, coca and cannabis production are prohibited unless for licit purposes, such as for research and technology.	**Misuse of Drugs Act 1973** *Section 10* The cultivation of cannabis, opium and coca plants is an offence under the Act.	**Law on Drug Prevention and Control No 23/2000/QH10** *Article 3(1)* Cultivating narcotic-bearing plants is strictly forbidden in Vietnam.
Establish and maintain a national (registration), licensing and permit systems for cultivation of controlled drugs and chemicals: (**Single Convention**, *Arts 4, 22, 23, 25–28*)	**Narcotics Law No 35 of 2009** *Article 11* *Cultivation* The Minister can issue permits to produce narcotics to certain licensed pharmaceutical industry members.	**Misuse of Drugs Act 1973** *Sections 10B(1)* See above. *Section 58(1)* See above	**Law on Drug Prevention and Control No 23/2000/QH10** *Article 36(5)* State management shall grant and withdraw permits for lawful drug-related activities. **Law Amending and Supplementing a Number of Articles of the Law on Drug Prevention and Control Order No 11/2008/L-CTN of 12 June 2008 (Law Amending Law on Drug Prevention and Control 2008)**

CHECKLIST	INDONESIA	SINGAPORE	VIETNAM
	Article 12(2) Strict supervision of the production of Group I narcotics (opium, cannabis, coca) for the purposes of science and technology development is a responsibility of the Supervisory Board on Drugs and Food.		**Article 5 amending Article 43 of the Law on Drug Prevention and Control No 23/2000/QH10** Charges the Ministry of Agriculture and Rural Development to assume the 'prime responsibility for, and co-ordination' with the Committee for Ethnic Minorities and other concerned agencies, to communicate and educate about the elimination of the cultivation of narcotic-bearing plants and also to implement a program of crop substitution.
Establish and maintain a national (registration), licensing and permit systems for the manufacture/ distribution of controlled drugs and chemicals (**Single Convention**, *Arts 4, 21, 21 bis, 24, 25, 27, 29, 30*; **1971 Convention,** *Arts 2, 3, 7, 8*; **1988 Convention,** *Art 12*)	**Narcotics Law No 35 of 2009** *Article 39* Only the pharmaceutical industry, pharmaceutical large traders, and state-owned storage facilities for pharmaceutical preparation may distribute narcotics.	**Misuse of Drugs Act 1973** *Section 10B(1)* See above. *Section 58(1)* See above.	**Law on Drug Prevention and Control No 23/2000/QH10** *Article 15* Research, expertise, production, transportation, preservation, storage, purchase and sale, distribution, use processing, exchange, import, export and transit of all narcotics, pre-substances and centripetalneurotropic medicines must be 'tightly controlled'.

Checklist	Indonesia	Singapore	Vietnam
	Article 40 Certain pharmaceutical industry members may distribute narcotics only to certain pharmaceutical large traders, certain dispensaries, certain state-owned storage facilities for pharmaceutical preparation, and hospitals.		
Establish and maintain a national (registration), licensing and permit systems for import and export of controlled drugs and chemicals (**Single Convention,** *Arts 4, 21, 23–25, 31, 32*; **1971 Convention,** *Arts 2–4, 7, 8, 12–14*; **1988 Convention,** *Art 12*)	**Narcotics Law No 35 of 2009** *Articles 15, 18* The Minister of Health may only provide a permit to a single state-owned pharmaceutical company to import or export narcotics.	**Misuse of Drugs Act 1973** *Section 10B(1)* See above. *Section 58(1)* See above.	**Law on Drug Prevention and Control No 23/2000/QH10** *Article 18* Those authorised to transport, store and sell narcotics under Arts 15–17 must keep records and notify agencies as requested. *Article 19* Only agencies and organisations that fully meet conditions prescribed by the government may import or export narcotic substances, pre-substances, addictive medicines, and centripetalneurotropic medicines.

Checklist	Indonesia	Singapore	Vietnam
	Articles 16, 19 Only under special circumstances may the Minister provide a permit to another state-owned pharmaceutical company. For every importation or exportation of narcotics, such companies must obtain a letter of approval from the Minister.		*Article 20* Transit requires permits from the Ministry of Public Security. See also Art 38 (h)(ii) *Article 21* Without a permit transportation is illegal
Establish and maintain a national (registration), licensing and permit systems for supply by health care professionals of controlled drugs and chemicals (**Single Convention**, *Arts 2, 4, 30, 32, 33*; **1971 Convention**, *Arts 2, 3, 4, 5, 9, 10, 14, 20*)	**Narcotics Law No 35 of 2009** *Article 36* Provides that 'Circulation of narcotics shall cover any activity or series of activities to supply or submit narcotics, in the framework of commerce, instead of trading or transfer, for the interest of health service and science and technology development'.	**Misuse of Drugs Act 1973** *Sections 10B(1)* See above. *Sections 58(1)* See above.	**Law on Drug Prevention and Control No 23/2000/QH10** *Article 17* The Ministry of Health regulates the 'storage, preservation, prescription and sale' of narcotic substances, pre-substances, addictive medicines, and centripetalneurotropic medicines for treatment of illnesses at medical establishments.

Checklist	Indonesia	Singapore	Vietnam
	Article 36(1) A permit from the Minister is required to circulate narcotics in the form of finished medicine.		*Article 23* Allowing a limited quantity of narcotic medicines for use in emergency situations, but these must be declared.
Prevent drug abuse; make treatment/ rehabilitation measures available (**Single Convention,** *Art 38*; **1971 Convention,** *Art 20*; **1988 Convention,** *Art 14*)	**Narcotics Law No 35 of 2009** *Articles 60, 60(2)(c)* The Indonesian government promotes activities related to the prevention of drug abuse, for example, by inserting education related to narcotics into the curriculum of primary and secondary schools.	**Misuse of Drugs Act 1973** *Article 34(1), (2)(b)* The Director of the Central Narcotics Bureau may require any person whom he or she reasonably suspects to be a drug addict to be medically examined and sent to have treatment or rehabilitation or both at an approved institution. *Article 58(1)(f)* The Minister may prohibit any medical practitioner from administering, supplying, authorising the administration or supply or prescribing, controlled drugs to persons addicted to those drugs.	**Law on Drug Prevention and Control No 23/2000/QH10** *Article 9* The Vietnam Fatherland Front and its member organisations, and other organisations, are responsible for organising and co-ordinating with competent bodies in the propagation and education of people about knowledge and legislation on drug prevention and the drug fight, and for building a healthy and civilised social environment. *Article 6(1)* Individuals and families are charged with educating family members and relatives about the harm caused by drugs and the observance of drug laws, and strictly managing and preventing family members from involvement in 'drug-related evils.'

Checklist	Indonesia	Singapore	Vietnam
	Article 53 A doctor may prescribe Group II narcotics for their patients, in limited amounts and in certain preparations, pursuant to the law and relevant regulations. *Article 54* Medical and social rehabilitation are necessary. *Article 56(1)* Medical rehabilitation for narcotics addicts will be carried out in a hospital appointed by the Minister.		**Law Amending and Supplementing a Number of Articles of the Law on Drug Prevention and Control Order No 11/2008/L-CTN of 12 June 2008 (Law Amending Law on Drug Prevention and Control 2008)** *Article 25* As to rehabilitation, the state policy is to encourage voluntary drug detoxification, particularly for drug addicts; organise compulsory detoxification establishments and encourage individuals, families, agencies and organisations to apply for family-based or community-based detoxification; and encourage domestic and foreign organisations and individuals to support drug detoxification activities. *Article 25 (2)* The state shall supply institutions for the compulsory detoxification. *Article 27* Forms of family- or community-based detoxification will apply for all drug addicts. According to the law, 'local agencies and organisations must support, inspect and supervise the family and community based detoxification activities'.

CHECKLIST	INDONESIA	SINGAPORE	VIETNAM
Establish and adequately punish drug trafficking and related conduct (money laundering, precursor trafficking) as serious crimes, co-ordinate law enforcement action, and co-operate in law enforcement training, intelligence exchange and operations (**Single Convention,** *Arts 35–37*; **1971 Convention,** *Arts 21, 22*; **1988 Convention,** *Arts 2–4, 5–19*)	The three country-specific chapters in this book explore these issues in depth, describing the offences in each jurisdiction and state attitudes to drugs, law enforcement and co-operation. In summary, all three countries have complex but robust drugs law regimes that enable the prosecution of those who traffic drugs or precursors or are involved in money laundering. Each jurisdiction also participates in intelligence exchange (with some jurisdictions at least), training and local and co-ordinated operations. In many cases this takes place under the auspices of the regional agencies for co-operation described in Chapter 2	See left.	See left.

CHECKLIST	INDONESIA	SINGAPORE	VIETNAM
Establish measures to enable the tracing, freezing, seizing and ultimate confiscation of the proceeds of drug-related crime, notwithstanding bank secrecy laws (**1988 Convention,** *Arts 3, 5*)	**Narcotics Law No 35 of 2009** *Article 80* BNN investigators have the authority to instruct banks or other financial institutions to provide information regarding the financial circumstances of a suspect and block a suspected account. BNN also has the right to request assets and taxation data from the taxation office. It may also temporarily terminate any financial transaction, commercial transactions and other agreements, or temporarily revoke any permit, license and concession made or owned by a suspect.	**Misuse of Drugs Act 1973** The Act is silent on the issue of confiscation of assets deriving from drug offences. **Corruption, Drug Trafficking and Other Serious Crimes (Confiscation of Benefits) Act** This Act gives the Central Narcotics Bureau authority to trace, freeze and confiscate assets gained from drug trafficking. This statute allows the police to prevent drug traffickers from using and enjoying financial wealth gained from illegal drug trafficking activities.	**Law on Drug Prevention and Control No 23/2000/QH10 as amended by Law Amending and Supplementing a Number of Articles of the Law on Drug Prevention and Control Order No 11/2008/L-CTN of 12 June 2008 (Law Amending Law on Drug Prevention and Control 2008)** *Article 13(1)(d)* Police drug prevention agencies may request concerned individuals, families, agencies and/or organisations to supply information, documents, information about their financial situation and bank accounts, where there are grounds to believe that drug offences have been committed. **Criminal Code 1999 Vietnam, As amended in 2009** *Article 251* In 2009, money laundering offences were introduced into the Criminal Code of Vietnam in terms similar to the 1988 Convention, echoing the position under Article 3(5) of the Law on Drug Prevention and Control that it is 'strictly forbidden' to legalise 'money and/or property acquired through the commission of drug-related crimes'.

CHECKLIST	INDONESIA	SINGAPORE	VIETNAM
Establish possession, purchase or cultivation of drugs for illicit personal consumption as a criminal offence, for which treatment, rehabilitation may be provided as alternatives to conviction and punishment (**Single Convention,** *Arts 2, 4, 36*; **1971 Convention,** *Arts 3, 5, 22*; **1988 Convention,** *Art 3*)	**Narcotics Law No 35 of 2009** *Article 127(1)* Prohibits drug use for personal consumption. Any personal consumption of Group I narcotics will be punished by imprisonment for a maximum of 4 years. *Article 127(3)* Where the narcotic falls within Group II or Group III, the term of imprisonment will be for a maximum of two years and one year, respectively. The user will also be required to undertake medical and social rehabilitation.	**Misuse of Drugs Act 1973** *Section 5* It is an offence for a person, on his own behalf or on behalf of any other person, whether or not that other person is in Singapore, to traffic in a controlled drug; to offer to traffic in a controlled drug; or to do or offer to do any act preparatory to or for the purpose of trafficking in a controlled drug, except where authorised by the Act. For the purposes of this Act, a person commits the offence of trafficking in a controlled drug if he has that drug in his possession for the purpose of trafficking. *Section 6* Renders manufacture of a controlled drug an offence, except where authorised by the Act. *Section 7* Renders the import into or export from Singapore of a controlled drug an offence, except where authorised by the Act. *Section 8* Renders unauthorised possession and consumption of a controlled drug an offence.	**Law on Drug Prevention and Control No 23/2000/QH10** *Article 3(3)* Illegal use, organising the illegal use of drugs, or inciting, coercing, inducing, harbouring and/or supporting the illegal use of narcotic substances is prohibited. **SRVN Constitution 2013** *Article 38* 'Any acts threatening the life and health of other people are strictly prohibited'. Removal of drug use as a crime as previously set out in the SRVN Constitution of 1992, Art 61. **Law No 37/2009/QH12 passed by the National Assembly on 19 June 2009 amending and supplementing a number of Articles of the Criminal Code 1999** *Article 1(36)* Personal use was legalised in 2009.

CHECKLIST	INDONESIA	SINGAPORE	VIETNAM
		Section 8A A citizen or permanent resident of Singapore, both outside and within Singapore, commits an offence under s 8(b) of the Act where he is found through urine tests conducted under section 31(4)(b) to have smoked, administered to himself or otherwise consumed a controlled drug or a specified drug. Where such an offence is committed outside Singapore, the person may be dealt with as if the offence was committed within Singapore. *Section 9* Renders the possession of any pipe, syringe, utensil, apparatus or other article intended for the smoking, administration or consumption of a controlled drug an offence, except where authorised under the Act. *Section 10* The cultivation of cannabis, opium and coca plants is an offence.	

CHECKLIST	INDONESIA	SINGAPORE	VIETNAM
		Section 10A A person who manufactures, supplies, possesses, imports or exports any controlled equipment, material or substance, knowing or having reason to believe that they may be used in or for the manufacture of a controlled drug in contravention of s 6 shall be guilty of an offence. It is not a defence for a person who contravenes sub-s (1)(d) to show that the equipment, material or substance is the subject of a licence, permit or any other form of authorisation issued or granted under regulations made under s 10B. *Section 34(1), (2)(b)* The Director of the Central Narcotics Bureau may require any person whom he or she reasonably suspects to be a drug addict to be medically examined and sent to have treatment or rehabilitation or both at an approved institution.	

Bibliography

AAP (Australian Associated Press), 'Nguyen '"Loophole" Rejected' *The Age* (23 November 2005).

——, 'Sydney Drug Smuggler Spared Death Penalty' *Sydney Morning Herald* (17 November 2006).

ABC News Online, 'Australian Arrested in Vietnamese Drug Trafficking Crackdown' (5 July 2003).

ABC News, 'Govt Close to Finalising Prisoner Exchange Treaty with Indonesia' (29 June 2006).

Abdullah, Noorman, 'Exploring Constructions of the "Drug Problem" in Historical and Contemporary Singapore' (2005) 7(2) *New Zealand Journal of Asian Studies* 40.

Abshire, Jean E, *The History of Singapore* (Santa Barbara, CA, Greenwood ABC-CLIO, 2011).

Adel, Daljit Sen, *Law of Dangerous Drugs: Cases and Commentaries* (Petaling Jaya, International Law Book Services, 2001).

Afif, 'Perangi Narkoba, BNN Aceh Tes Urine Anak SMA' [To combat drugs, Aceh BNN conducts urine tests for high school kids] *Merdeka.com* (4 February 2015).

AFP (Agence France Presse), 'Vietnam Executes First Prisoner by Lethal Injection' *ABC News* (6 August 2013).

Akuntono, Indra, 'Kepada Semua Kepala Daerah, Jokowi Minta Tak Ada Toleransi untuk Kasus Narkoba [Jokowi calls on all regional leaders not to tolerate narcotics cases]' *Kompas* (4 February 2015).

——, 'Menkumham Sebut Ada 133 Terpidana Mati di Indonesia [Minister of Law and Human Rights says there are 133 prisoners on death row in Indonesia'] *Kompas.com* (21 January 2015).

Amnesty International, 'Public Statement: Singapore Should Join Global Trend and Establish a Moratorium on Executions', AI Index: ASA 36/004/2012 (2 May 2012).

——, 'Death Penalty News—January 2006' (Report).

——, 'Death Sentences and Executions 2013' (Report) (2014) ACT 50/001/2014.

——, 'Death Sentences and Executions in 2011' (Report) (27 March 2012) ACT 50/001/2012.

——, 'Reported in Death Penalty World Wide' (Report).

——, 'Singapore: The Death Penalty: A Hidden Toll of Executions', ASA 36/001/2004 (January 2004).

Amnesty International USA, 'Amnesty International Implores Singapore to Join Global Trend toward Abolition of the Death Penalty', Press Release (2 May 2012).

Anonymous, 'Assessment on the Real Situation of the Protection of Legitimate Rights and Interests of Lawyers 1999–2009, Annex 1' [copy on file with author].

Antara News, 'No Mercy for Drug Dealers: President' (9 December 2014).

AIPA, *see under* ASEAN Inter-Parliamentary Assembly.

AIPA, 'Country Progress Report of Viet Nam Prevention and Combat against Drug and Drug-Related Crimes between 2010 and 2012: Process and Outcomes' (2014).

AP (Associated Press), 'Vietnam Executes 1st Prisoner by Lethal Injection' *Asian Correspondent* (6 August 2013).

Aritonang, Margareth, 'RI Targets Fugitives in PNG and Vietnam' *The Jakarta Post* (3 February 2015).

Armenia, Resty, 'Rentan Jadi Kurir Narkotik Perempuan Diimbau Tak Pacari WNA [Vulnerable to being made into drug couriers, women urged not to date foreigners]' *CNN Indonesia* (26 June 2015).
ASEAN (Association of Southeast Asian Nations), 'ASEAN Plan of Action to Combat Transnational Crime' (nd).
ASEAN Inter-Parliamentary Assembly (AIPA) Fact-Finding Committee (AIFOCOM) to Combat the Drug Menace: Annex O, 'Vietnam Country Report, Drug Situation in Vietnam in 2009 and the First Months of 2010', 7th Meeting (9 June 2010).
——, 'Country Progress Report of Viet Nam: Prevention and Combat against Drug and Drug-related Crimes in the Period 2011–2013: Process and Outcomes', 11th Meeting (12–16 May 2014, Vientiane, Lao People's Democratic Republic).
ASEAN Inter-Parliamentary Assembly (AIPA) Fact-Finding Committee (AIFOCOM), 'Country Progress Report of Vietnam', 9th Meeting (8–12 July 2012, Yogyakarta, Indonesia).
——, 'Indonesia Country Progress Report of Drug Control', 10th Meeting (2013, Bandar Seri Begawan).
——, 'Country Progress Report, Vietnam (2009–2011)'.
ASEAN, 'Co-operation on Drugs and Narcotics Overview' (Jakarta, ASEAN Secretariat, nd). ASEAN and China 'Joint Regional Plan to Achieve a Drug-Free ASEAN by 2015', Press Release, Bangkok, Thailand, 13 October 2000.
Asia Sentinel, 'Singapore's Leaky Drugs Enforcement' (26 September 2011).
Asian Human Rights Commission, 'Indonesia: Lack of Effective Witness and Victim Protection' (18 February 2010).
Assegaf, Rifqi, 'Pretrial Hearings: Who Will Fix the Mess?' *Indonesia at Melbourne* (7 July 2015).
Australia. Attorney General's Department, 'List of Participating Countries, International Transfer of Prisoners Scheme' (2011).
Australia. House of Representatives, 'Parliamentary Debates', Julie Bishop (3 February 2010).
——, Phillip Ruddock, Attorney-General (30 October 2006).
Australia. Minister for Justice and Customs, Hon Christopher Ellison, 'Australia and Indonesia to Seek Prisoner Transfer Agreement', Press Release (7 April 2005).
Australia. Senate, 'Parliamentary Debates', David Johnson (22 February 2010).
Australian Broadcasting Corporation, 'Death Penalty Given for Australian Man in Vietnam' *PM* (10 June 2005).
Australian Bureau of Statistics, *Prisoner Characteristics, Australia 2014* (Data cube, 11 December 2014) Table 6.
Australian Embassy—Vietnam, 'News: 10th Anniversary of the AFP Liaison Office in HCMC' (c June 2013).
Aziza, Kurnia Sari, 'Kejutan Ahok di Pelantikan, Ribuan Pejabat Langsung Tes Urine Narkoba [Ahok's inauguration surprise, thousands of officials undergo urine drug tests]' *Kompas.com* (2 January 2015).
Azizah, Nur, 'Kata Kasat Narkoba Polres Jakarta Barat Soal Anggotanya yang Tertangkap [This is what the head of the West Jakarta Police Narcotics Unit had to say about the member of his team who was arrested]' *Kompas.com* (19 January 2015).
Bailey, Warren and Truong, Lan, 'Opium and Empire: Some Evidence from Colonial-Era: Asian Stock and Commodity Markets' (2001) 32 *Journal of Southeast Asian Studies* 173.
Baldwin, Simon, 'Emerging from a Black Box' in Rahman, Fifa and Crofts, Nick (eds), *Drug Law Reform in East and Southeast Asia* (Lanham, Lexington Books, 2013).
Bassiouni, C, 'Critical Reflections on International and National Control of Drugs' (1990) 18 *Denver Journal of International Law and Policy* 311.
BBC News, 'Blood Money Spares Indonesian Maid from Saudi Execution' (3 April 2014).

Berita Satu, 'Pekan Depan Kejati NTT Ekspose Dugaan Korupsi di BNN [Next week NTT prosecutor's office to expose suspected corruption in the BNN]' (5 August 2014).

Bernstein, Dennis and Kean, Leslie, 'Singapore's Blood Money: Hanging Drug Couriers but Investing with Their Suppliers' *The Nation* (20 October 1997): 11.

Bewley-Taylor, David R and Fazey, Cindy S, 'The Mechanics and Dynamics of the UN System for International Drug Control' (London, Forward Thinking on Drugs Initiative, 2003).

Bewley-Taylor, David R, *International Drug Control: Consensus Fractured* (Cambridge, Cambridge University Press, 2012).

Boister, Neil, *An Introduction to Transnational Criminal Law* (Oxford, Oxford University Press, 2012).

——, *Drugs, International Regulation, and Criminal Liability* (New York, Oxford University Press, 2013).

——, *Penal Aspects of the UN Drug Conventions* (The Hague, Kluwer Law International, 2001).

Bolt, Steve, 'Drugs and the Law', Hot Topics: Legal Issues in Plain Language Series No 59 (New South Wales, Legal Information Access Centre, 2007).

Boon, TO, *Towards a Drug-Free Singapore: Strategies, Policies and Programmes against Drugs* (Singapore, National Council Against Drug Abuse, 1998).

Breen, Danthong, Head of Death Penalty, Union for Civil Liberty, 'Letter Addressed to HE Mr Nguyen Tat Thanh, the Embassy of the Socialist Republic of Vietnam' 11 April 2014.

Brook, Timothy and Wakabayashi, Bob Tadashi, 'Introduction: Opium's History in China', in Timothy Brook and Bob Tadashi Wakabayashi (eds) *Opium Regimes: China, Britain and Japan, 1839–1952* (Berkeley, University of California Press, 2000) 6–7.

Budiari, Indra, 'Cleaners' Families Reveal Police Torture to Kompolnas' *The Jakarta Post* (18 February 2015).

——, 'Cops Could Face Death Sentence for Drug Trafficking' *The Jakarta Post* (20 January 2015).

Bùi Ngọc Sơn, 'What is Socialist about the Socialist Constitution of Vietnam' 2015 [paper: Copy on file with authors].

Bùi Tiến Đạt, 'Vì sao 'suy đoán có tội' phổ biến? [Why presumption of guilt is popular?]' *Vietnamnet* (Vietnam, 20 June 2015).

Buitenweg, KM, 'Report Including a Proposal for a Recommendation of the European Parliament to the Council on the Reform of the Conventions on Drugs', European Parliament, Committee on Citizens' Freedoms and Rights, Justice and Home Affairs.

Burnham, William and Kahn, Jeffrey, 'Russia's Criminal Procedure Code Five Years Out' (2008) 33 *Review of Central & East European Law* 1.

Butt, Simon and Lindsey, Tim, 'Judicial Mafia: The Courts and Illegality in Indonesia' in Edward Aspinall and Gerry van Klinken, *The State and Illegality in Indonesia* (Leiden, KITLV Press, 2011) 189–216.

——, *The Constitution of Indonesia: A Contextual Analysis* (Oxford, Hart Publishing, 2012).

Butt, Simon, 'Surat Sakti: The Decline of the Authority of Judicial Decisions in Indonesia' in Tim Lindsey (ed), *Indonesia: Law and Society* (Sydney, Federation Press, 2008) 346–62.

Byrnes, A, 'The Right to Life, the Death Penalty and Human Rights Law: An International and Australian Perspective', University of New South Wales Law Research Paper No 2007–66 (Sydney, University of New South Wales, 2007).

Central Narcotics Bureau, 'Annual Bulletin 2012'.

——, 'Annual Bulletin 2013'.

——, 'CNB's Intensified Enforcement Efforts in 2012. See Increase in Drug Abusers Arrested and Drugs Seized', Press Release (7 June 2013).

——, 'Drug Situation Report 2013'.

——, 'Singapore's Country Report on Illicit Drug Trafficking'. Report for the 10th Meeting of AIFOCOM, Brunei, 12–16 May 2013.

——, 'Two-Thirds of New Drug Abusers Arrested in 1st Half of 2014 Were below 30 Years Old', Press Release (June 2014).

Chairunnisa, Ninis, '66 Terpidana Mati Narkoba Belum Dieksekusi [66 narcotics criminals waiting to be executed]' *Tempo.co* (30 October 2014).

Chan Wing Cheong, 'Culpability in the Misuse of Drugs Act: Wilful Blindness, the Reasonable Person and a Duty to Check' (2013) 25 *Singapore Academy of Law Journal* 110.

Chan Wing Cheong and Phang, Andrew, *The Development of Criminal Law and Criminal Justice in Singapore* (Singapore, National University of Singapore, 2001).

Chan Wing Cheong and Phang, Andrew BL, 'The Development of Criminal Law and Criminal Justice' in Kevin Tan (ed), *Essays in Singapore Legal History* (Singapore, Marshall Cavendish, 2004).

Chan Wing Cheong, Yeo, Stanley and Hor, Michael, *Criminal Law for the 21st Century: A Model Code for Singapore* (Singapore, Academy Publishing, 2013).

Chandra, Siddharth, 'The Role of Government Policy in Increasing Drug Use: Java, 1875–1914' (2002) 62 *The Journal of Economic History* 1116.

Chatterjee, SK, *Legal Aspects of International Drug Control* (The Hague, Nijhoff, 1981).

Cheang, Molly, *Criminal Law of Malaysia and Singapore: Principles of Liability* (Kuala Lumpur, Professional Law Books Publishers, 1990).

Chen Siyuan and Khng, Nathaniel Yong-Ern, 'Possession and Knowledge in the Misuse of Drugs Act' (2012) 13 *Singapore Law Review* 181.

Chia-Chow, F, 'Law Enforcement Action, Collection of Law Enforcement Data and Registration of Drug Offenders: Drug Abuse Situation in Singapore'. Paper delivered at the Workshop on the Reduction of Demand for Illicit Drugs in South-East Asia, Universiti Sains Malaysia, 14–20 May 1978.

Chin Tet Yung, 'Confessions and Statements by Accused Persons Revisited' (2012) 24 *Singapore Academy of Law Journal* 60.

Chin Tet Yung, 'Remaking the Evidence Code: Search for Values' (2009) 21 *Singapore Academy of Law Journal* 52.

Chin, Ko-lin and Zhang, Sheldon X, *The Chinese Connection: Crossborder Drug Trafficking between Myanmar and China* (US Department of Justice, April 2007).

CIA, 'The World Factbook: Indonesia' (22 June 2014).

——, 'World Factbook: Country Comparison: GDP—Per Capita (PPP)'.

Clifford, William, 'Some Characteristics of the Application of the Criminal Justice System in Japan and Singapore' in *Selected Issues in Criminal Justice*, HEUNI Publication Series 4 (Helsinki, Helsinki Institute for Crime Prevention and Control affiliated with the United Nations, 1985).

CNB, *see under* Central Narcotics Bureau.

Cornell Law School, 'Death Penalty Worldwide', Online Database (2015).

Cribb, Robert, 'Opium and the Indonesian Revolution' (1988) 22 *Modern Asian Studies* 701.

Csete, Joanne and Rahman, Fifa 'Turning a Page: Human Rights and Drugs Policy in Southeast Asia' in Fifa Rahman and Nick Crofts (eds), *Drugs Law Reform in East and Southeast Asia* (Lanham, Lexington Books, 2013), 27–33.

Death Penalty Worldwide, 'Nigeria' (Report) (19 June 2014).

Dewimerdeka, Moyang Kasih, 'Ironis, Mafia Narkotik Banyak Diatur dari Penjara [Surprisingly, the narcotics mafia is being directed from behind bars]' *Tempo.co* (5 February 2015).

Đinh Văn Quế, 'Một số vấn đề khi áp dụng tình tiết 'tự thú' và 'đầu thú' trong thực tiễn xét xử [Some issues for application of 'confession' and 'surrender]', Tra Cứu Pháp Luật [Law Reference].

——, 'Một số vấn đề về đồng phạm quy định tại Điều 20 Bộ luật Hình sự [Some issues about complicity as regulated at Art 20 of the Criminal Code]', Tòa Án Nhân Dân Tối Cao (Việt Nam) [(Vietnamese) Supreme People's Court].

——, *Bình luận khoa học Bộ luật Hình sự, phần các tội phạm về ma túy* [Scientific commentary on the Criminal Code, crime part: drug-related crimes] (Ho Chi Minh, Ho Chi Minh Publishing House, 2004).

Doan, Toi Van and Chanoff, David, 'Vietnam Turns to Narcotics to Pay its Bills', *The Wall Street Journal*, 8 March 1984.

Downer, Alexander, 'Clemency for Huu Trinh' (Press Release, 17 November 2006).

——, 'Death Sentence Upheld on Le My Linh' (Press Release, 23 December 2002).

Dumbleton, CE, 'The Need of Reform in the Present System of Registration of Deaths in the Straits Settlements' (1892–93) 4 *Journal of the Straits Medical Association* 66.

Dương Thanh Biểu, *Tuyển tập các quyết định giám đốc thẩm của Viện trưởng Viện Kiểm sát nhân dân* [Collection of cassation decisions of the Chairman of the Supreme People's Procuracy]' (Hanoi, Nhà Xuất Bản Tư Pháp [Judicial Publishing House], 2007).

DuPont, Robert L and Baumgartner, Werner A, 'Drug Testing by Urine and Hair Analysis: Complementary Features and Scientific Issues' (1995) 70 *Forensic Science International* 63.

Eligh, Jason, 'Illicit Drugs in East and Southeast Asia: Situation and Response' (23 April 2010), presentation to the Seventh Meeting of the AIPA (ASEAN Inter-Parliamentary Assembly) Fact-Finding Committee (AIFOCOM) to Combat the Drug Menace, 22–25 April 2010, Ho Chi Minh City, Viet Nam.

EMN News, 'Drug Trafficking: Ejiogu Ikechukwu to Die by Lethal Injection in Vietnam' (27 October 2013).

European Commission, 'Commission Extends Control over Goods Which Could be Used for Capital Punishment or Torture' (Press Release, 20 December 2011).

Fahey, Michael, 'Home Grown: An Economic Examination of the Origins and Effectiveness of Radical Drug Policies' (2006) 20(3) *The Region* 53.

Fakhrana, Rinaldy Sofwa, 'KPK-BNN Kerjasama Tangani Cuci Duit Narkotik [KPK-BNN co-operate to handle narcotics money laundering]' *CNN Indonesia* (online) (21 October 2014).

Firdaus, Randy Ferdy, 'Menteri Marwan Awasi Desa Rawan Jadi Pintu Penyelundupan Narkoba [Minister Marwan supervises villages vulnerable to becoming entry points for narcotics trade]' *Merdeka.com* (23 February 2015).

Firman, Arnaz, 'Kenapa Mesti Takluk Terhadap Upaya Australia [Why should we submit to Australia's efforts]' *Antara* (7 March 2015).

Fitzpatrick, Daniel, 'Culture, Ideology and Human Rights: The Case of Indonesia's Code of Criminal Procedure' in Tim Lindsey (ed), *Indonesia: Law and Society* (Sydney, Federation Press, 2008) 499–514.

Foreign Prisoner Support Service, 'Exclusive Look inside Kerobokan Prison' (2012).

Gadjah Mada University, 'President Jokowi: Four State Problem Have to Be Resolved Immediately' (sic), (10 December 2014).

Ghodse, Hamid (ed), *International Drug Control into the 21st Century* (Aldershot, Ashgate, 2008).

Gillespie, John, 'Concepts of Law in Vietnam: Transforming Statist Socialism' in Randall Peerenboom (ed), *Asian Discourses of the Rule of Law* (London, Routledge Curzon, 2004).

Goh, KS, 'Prevention is Our Best Hope in the War on Drugs' *The Straits Times* (5 August 1976).

Governmental Committee for Ethnic Minorities, the website on HIV/AIDS, Narcotics and Prostitution Evil Prevention.

Hai Thanh Luong 'The Application of Death Penalty for Drug-Related Crimes in Vietnam: Law, Policy, and Practice' (2014) 17(1) *Thailand Journal of Law and Policy*.

Hamzah, Chandra M, 'Penjelasan Hukum (Restatement) tentang Bukti Permulaan yang Cukup [Legal explanation (restatement) of sufficient preliminary evidence]', Pusat Studi Hukum dan Kebijakan [Centre for Legal and Policy Studies], 2014)

Haq, M Emdad-ul, *Drugs in South Asia: From the Opium Trade to the Present Day* (London, Macmillan, 2000).

Haryanto, Andri, 'Wakapolri Minta BNN Seret Polisi yang Terlibat Korupsi di Kasus Narkotika [Deputy police chief asks BNN to haul in police involved in narcotics corruption]' *Detik.com* (16 December 2014).

Haryanto, Ulma, 'Police in West Sumatra Tortured Brothers to Death: Komnas HAM' *The Jakarta Globe* (25 January 2012).

Hồ Chí Minh, 'Những nhiệm vụ cấp bách của Nhà nước Việt Nam Dân chủ Cộng hòa [Urgent duties of the Democratic Republic of Vietnam]' (3 September 1945).

Ho Hock Lai, 'The Privilege against Self-Incrimination and Right of Access to a Lawyer' (2013) 25 *Singapore Academy of Law Journal* 826.

Hoàng Duy Hiệp, 'Hoàn thiện quy định của bộ Luật tố tụng hình sự về nhập hoặc tách vụ án hình sự để tiến hành điều tra [Perfecting the provisions of the Criminal Procedure Code regarding joining or separating criminal case(s) to conduct investigation]' (22 April 2013) Bộ Tư Pháp (Việt Nam) [(Vietnamese) Ministry of Justice].

Hoàng Thị Sơn and Bùi Kiên Điện, *Những nguyên tắc cơ bản của luật tố tụng hình sự Việt Nam [Fundamental principles of the criminal procedure code of Vietnam]* (Hanoi, Public Security Publishing House, 2003).

Hodgson, Jacqueline, 'Making Custodial Legal Advice More Effective in France' (2013) 92 *Criminal Justice Matters* 14.

——, 'The Detention and Interrogation of Suspects in Police Custody in France: A Comparative Account' (2004) 1 *European Journal of Criminology* 169.

——, 'The Impact of Salduz in France: Making Custodial Legal Advice More Effective' (Legal Studies Research Paper No 2013– 08).

Hong Lu and Miethe, Terance D, *China's Death Penalty: History, Law, and Contemporary Practices* (New York, Routledge, 2007).

Hood, Roger and Deva, Surya (eds), *Confronting Capital Punishment in Asia: Human Rights, Politics and Public Opinion* (Oxford, Oxford University Press, 2013).

Hood, Roger and Hoyle, Carolyn, *The Death Penalty: A Worldwide Perspective*, 5th edition (Oxford, Oxford University Press, 2015).

Hood, Roger, '*The Death Penalty in Malaysia: Public Opinion on the Mandatory Death Penalty for Drug Trafficking, Murder and Firearms Offenses*', A Report for the Death Penalty Project (London, The Death Penalty Project, 2013).

Hooker, MB, *A Concise Legal History of South-East Asia* (Oxford, Clarendon Press, 1978).

——, *Legal Pluralism: An Introduction to Colonial and Neo Colonial Laws* (Oxford, Clarendon Press, 1975).

Hor, Michael, 'Managing *Mens Rea* in Singapore' (2006) 18 *Singapore Academy of Law Journal* 314.

——, 'Misuse of Drugs and Aberrations of Drugs in the Criminal Law' (2001) 13 *Singapore Academy of Law Journal* 54.

——, 'Singapore's Death Penalty: The Beginning of the End?' in Roger Hood and Surya Deva (eds), *Confronting Capital Punishment in Asia: Human Rights, Politics and Public Opinion* (Oxford, Oxford University Press, 2013) 141–67.

——, 'Singapore's Innovations to Due Process' (2001) 12 *Criminal Law Forum* 25.

——, 'The Death Penalty in Singapore and International Law' (2004) 8 *Singapore Year Book of International Law* 105.
——, 'The Future of Singapore's Criminal Process' (2013) 25 *Singapore Academy of Law Journal* 847.
Hudson, Chris and Johal, Terry, 'A Chill in the Blogosphere: The State, the Internet and the Struggle for Narrative Control in Singapore' (2011) 44(1) *Communication, Politics & Culture* 33.
Hukum Online, 'Penangguhan Penahanan dengan Uang Jaminan Perlu Diperjelas [Suspension of detention with bail money needs clarification]' (28 July 2005).
Human Rights Watch, *The Rehab Archipelago Forced Labor and Other Abuses in Drug Detention Centers in Southern Vietnam* (Report, 2011).
Ichsan, A Syalaby, 'Duh, Tiga Pegawai BNN Jadi Tersangka Korupsi [Ouch, three BNN staff declared corruption suspects]' *Republika Online* (8 May 2014).
Indonesia. Badan Pembinaan Hukum Nasional [Agency for National Legal Development], Kementerian Hukum dan Hak Asasi Manusia [Ministry of Law and Human Rights], 'Naskah Akademik RUU Tentang Pemindaan Narapidana' [Policy paper on the bill on the transfer of prisoners] (no date).
Indonesia. Badan Perencanaan Pembangunan Nasional [National Development Planning Agency], Badan Pusat Statistik [Central Statics Agency] and United Nations Population Fund, 'Proyeksi Penduduk Indonesia 2010–2035' [Indonesian Population Projection 2010–2035], Badan Pusat Statistik (2013).
Indonesia. BNN (Badan Narcotika Nasional) [National Narcotics Agency], 'Mayoritas Kasus Pencucian Uang Berasal Dari Sindikat Narkoba' [The majority of money laundering cases stem from narcotics syndicates] (25 November 2013).
——, 'Jurnal Data Pencegahan dan Pemberantasan Penyalahgunaan dan Peredaran Gelap Narkoba (P4GN) 2013' [Data on prevention and elimination of illicit narcotics trafficking and abuse (P4GN) in 2013] (2014).
——, 'Analisa Data Pencegahan dan Pemberantasan Penyalahgunaan dan Peredaran Gelap Narkoba (P4GN)' [Data analysis on the prevention and eradication of illicit narcotics trafficking and abuse (P4GN)] (2013).
——, 'Lampiran Press Release Akhir Tahun, Badan Narkotika Nasional' [National Narcotics Agency end of year press release], Press Release (23 December 2014).
——, 'Laporan Akuntabilitas Kinerja Instansi Perintah: Badan Narkotika Nasional' [Government agency efficiency and accountability report: National Narcotics Agency] (2013).
——, 'Penandatangan Nota Kesepahaman antara Badan Narkotika Nasional (BNN) Dengan Korps Lalu Lintas Polri' [National Narcotics Agency (BNN) and Traffic Police sign a memorandum of understanding], Press Release (27 February 2012).
——, 'Sejarah BNN' [History of the BNN], (23 November 2010).
——, 'Survei Nasional Perkembangan Penyalahgunaan Narkoba di Indonesia Tahun 2011' [National survey of developments in narcotics abuse in Indonesia 2011], (2011).
Indonesia. Direktorat Jenderal Hukum dan Perundang-Undangan [Directorate General of Law and Legislation], 'Sejarah Pembentukan Undang-Undang Republik Indonesia No 8 Tahun 1981 Tentang Hukum Acara Pidana [The history of the formation of law of the Republic of Indonesia No 8 Year 1981 on the Laws of Criminal Procedure]', (Jakarta, Direktorat Jenderal Hukum dan Perundang-Undangan [Directorate General of Law and Legislation], 1981).
Indonesia. Direktorat Jenderal Pemasyarakatan [Directorate General of Corrections], 'Penanganan Narapidana dan Tahanan Tindak Pidana Narkotika [Management of inmates

and narcotics criminals]', presentation for a co-ordination meeting with the Minister of Law and Human Rights (4 February 2015).
——, '2014 Annual Report' (December 2014).
——, 'HIV and Syphilis Prevalence and Risk Behaviour Study among Prisoners in Prisons and Detention Centres in Indonesia' (April 2011).
——, 'Sistem Database Pemasyarakatan [Corrections Database System]' (May 2015).
Indonesia. Direktorat Jenderal Peraturan Perundang-Undangan [Directorate General of Legislation], Kementerian Hukum dan Hak Asasi Manusia [Ministry of Law and Human Rights], 'Sosialisasi Rancangan Undang-Undang Tentang Pemindahan Narapidana' [Socialisation of the bill on transfer of prisoners] (1 November 2014).
Indonesia. House of Representatives, 'Priority Bill Long List' (2015).
Indonesia. Mahkamah Agung [Supreme Court], *Laporan Tahunan 2013* [2013 annual report], Mahkamah Agung (2014).
Indonesia. National Aids Commission, 'Republic of Indonesia Country Report on the Follow Up to the Declaration of the Commitment on HIV/AIDS (UNGASS)': Reporting Period 2008–2009, National AIDS Commission (2010).
International Federation of Red Cross and Red Crescent Societies, 'Out of Harm's Way: Injecting Drug Users and Harm Reduction', IFRC Advocacy Report (December 2010), 20, www.ifrc.org/Global/Publications/Health/Harm-reduction-report-EN.pdf.
Irwanto, 'Indonesia: Facing Illicit Drug Challenges' (2006) 69 *Development Bulletin* 44.
Jayasuria, DC, *Regulation of Pharmaceuticals in Developing Countries: Legal Issues and Approaches* (Geneva, WHO Publications Centre, 1985).
Jelsma, M, 'The Development of International Drug Control: Lessons Learned and Strategic Challenges for the Future' (2011) Global Commission on Drug Policies Working Paper, prepared for the First Meeting of the Commission, Geneva, 24–25 January 2011.
Jianhong Liu; Hebenton, Bill and Jou, Susyan (eds), *Handbook of Asian Criminology* (New York, Springer-Verlag, 2013).
Johnson, David T and Zimring, Franklin E, *The Next Frontier: National Development, Political Change and the Death Penalty in Asia* (New York, Oxford University Press, 2009).
Johnson, David T, 'The Jolly Hangman, the Jailed Journalist, and the Decline of Singapore's Death Penalty' (2013) 8 Asian Criminology 41.
Judges of the Subordinate Courts of Singapore, *Practitioners' Library: Sentencing Practice in the Subordinate Courts* (Singapore, LexisNexis, 2013).
Justice for the Poor, The World Bank and The Ministry of Law and Human Rights, *Legal Aid Organisations in Indonesia: A Survey of 230 Legal Aid Organisations* (Jakarta, Justice for the Poor, 2014)
Kaur, Judge Jasvender et al, *Sentencing Practice in the Subordinate Courts* (Singapore, LexisNexis, 2nd edn, 2003).
Keng Siong Kow, *Sentencing Principles in Singapore* (Singapore, Academy Publishing, 2009).
Kheng Lian Koh; Clarkson, Christopher MV and Morgan, Neil A, *Criminal Law in Singapore and Malaysia: Text and Materials* (Singapore, Malayan Law Journal, 1989).
Kow Keng Siong, *Sentencing Principles in Singapore* (Singapore, Academy Publishing, 2009).
Kuwardo, Fabian Januarius, 'Jaksa Agung: Kita Punya "Stok" 60 Orang Yang Akan Dieksekusi Mati [Attorney General: We Have a "Stock" of 60 People Still to Execute]' *Kompas.com* (20 January 2015).
Kwok, Yenni, 'Top Indonesian "Anticorruption" Judge Is Arrested for Graft' *Time* (4 October 2013).
Lai, Gloria; Asmin, Fransiska and Birgin, Ruth, 'Drug Policy in Indonesia' International Drug Policy Consortium Briefing Paper (5 January 2013).

Lamb, Kate, 'Schapelle Corby Release has Irked Some in Indonesia' *The Guardian* (10 February 2014).

Lande, Adolf, *Commentary on the Protocol Amending the Single Convention on Narcotic Drugs, 1961* (New York, United Nations, 1973).

Lao Động, 'Vietnam Minister Wants to Restore Firing Squad' *Thanh Nien News* (11 November 2013).

Law Society of Singapore, Pro Bono Services Office, 'Basic Criminal Procedure'.

Lê Nga, 'Vietnam Upholds Death Penalty for Australian Pusher', *Thanh Nien News* (23 April 2005).

Lê Quang, 'Vietnam Court Upholds Death Sentence to Thai Drug Mule' *Thanh Nien News* (4 April 2014).

Lê Thị Kim Vy, 'Understanding the Operational Structure of Southeast Asian Drug Trafficking Groups in Australia' (Doctoral Thesis, QUT, 2013).

Lee Lit Cheng, 'Criminal Procedure, Evidence and Sentencing', *Singapore Academy of Law Annual Review of Singapore Cases*, Annual Review 2010, 332.

Lee, Gregory, *Global Drug Enforcement: Practical Investigative Techniques* (Boca Raton, CRC Press, 2004).

Lee, SS; Jack, David; and Crofts, Nick 'Harm Reduction is Good Public Health' in Fifa Rahman and Nick Crofts (eds), *Drugs Law Reform in East and Southeast Asia* (Lanham, Lexington Books, 2013), 15–25.

Leechaianan, Yingyos and Longmire, Dennis R, 'The Use of the Death Penalty for Drug Trafficking in the United States, Singapore, Malaysia, Indonesia and Thailand: A Comparative Legal Analysis' (2013) 2 *Laws* 115.

Lev, Daniel, 'Between State and Society: Professional Lawyers and Reform in Indonesia' in Daniel Lev and Ruth Mcvey (eds), *Making Indonesia* (Ithaca, Cornell University Press, 1996).

Lexotre, Pierre-Louis, *International Co-operation, Convergence and Harmonization of Pharmaceutical Regulations: A Global Perspective* (Oxford, Elsevier, 2014).

Lim, CL, 'Singapore Crimes Abroad' (2001) *Singapore Journal of Legal Studies* 494.

Lim, Joyce, 'Ng Boon Gay's "Not Guilty" Verdict: AGC Will Assess Whether to Appeal Decision' *The Straits Times* (14 February 2013).

Lindsey, Tim and Butt, Simon, 'Schapelle Corby Should Not Give Interviews. To Do So Would Be Foolhardy' *The Guardian* (17 February 2014).

Lines, Rick, *The Death Penalty for Drug Offences: A Violation of International Human Rights Law* (London, International Harm Reduction Association, 2007).

Linggasari, Yohannie, 'Mayoritas Publik Setuju Pengedar Narkotika Divonis Mati [A majority of the public support the death penalty for drug traffickers]' *CNN Indonesia* (6 April 2015).

Linnan, David, 'Commercial Law Enforcement in Indonesia: The Manulife case' in Tim Lindsey (ed), *Indonesia: Law and Society* (Sydney, Federation Press, 2008) 596–619.

Lloyd, Peter, *Inside Story: From ABC Foreign Correspondent to Singapore Prisoner #12988* (Sydney, Allen & Unwin, 2010).

Low Siew Ling, 'A Re-examination of Bail Law in Singapore' (2005) 17 *Singapore Academy of Law Journal* 869.

Low, Fiona, '22 Years, 12 Strokes for Man Who Jumped Bail' *The Straits Times* (6 April 2012): A3.

Luijk, Eric W van and Ours, Jan C van, 'The Effects of Government Policy on Drug Use: Java, 1875–1904' (2001) 61 *The Journal of Economic History* 1.

Lương Thanh Hải, 'Based on the "Ethnic" Factor to Understanding the Distinct Characteristics of Cannabis Cultivation: A Review of Overseas Vietnamese Drug Groups', 3 *GSTF International Journal of Law and Social Sciences* 75 (2014).

Luu, Anh 'Vietnam Legal Research' New York University Update (May 2013).
Lynch, Colman, 'Indonesia's Use of Capital Punishment for Drug-Trafficking Crimes: Legal Obligations, Extralegal Factors, and the Bali Nine Case' (2009) 40 *Columbia Human Rights Law Review* 523.
Maharani, Dian, 'Akil Mochtar Jadi Tersangka Kasus Narkotika [Akil Mochtar declared suspect in narcotics case]' *Kompas.com* (17 January 2014).
Mai Nguyễn, 'Vietnam Mass Drugs Trial Sentences 30 to Death, Jails Dozen' *Reuters* (Hanoi, 20 January 2014).
Mai Thanh Hiếu, 'The Scope within Which a Subject is Entitled to Presumption of Innocence in Criminal Procedure of Vietnam' (2004) 01/2004 *Jurisprudence Magazine* 27.
Marie, Jennifer (ed in chief); Faizal, Mohamed; and Kadir, Mohamed Abdul (general eds), *The Criminal Procedure Code of Singapore: Annotations and Commentary* (Singapore, Academy Publishing, 2012).
Maryono, Agus, 'More Guards Suspected of Assisting Drug Trade in Prisons' *The Jakarta Post* (4 December 2014).
McBeth, John, 'A New Menace' *Far Eastern Economic Review* (19 August 2004).
McCoy, Alfred, *The Politics of Heroin: CIA Complicity in the Global Drug Trade* (Chicago, Lawrence Hill Books, 2003).
——, 'South Vietnam's Heroin Trade' in Alfred McCoy (ed), *The Politics of Heroin—CIA Complicity in the Global Drug Trade: Afghanistan, Southeast Asia, Central America, Columbia*, 2nd edn (Brooklyn, NY, Lawrence Hill Books, 2003).
McKetin, Rebecca; Kozel, Nicholas; Douglas, Jeremy; Ali, Robert; Vicknasingam, Balasingam; Lund, Johannes and Jih-Heng Li, 'The Rise of Methamphetamine in Southeast and East Asia' (2008) 27 *Drug and Alcohol Review* 220.
McRae, Dave, '"Jokowi" and His Firing Squads' *Strategic Review* (July–September 2015).
——, 'A Key Domino? Indonesia's Death Penalty Politics', Lowy Institute for International Policy (March 2012).
Miao, Michelle, 'Examining China's Responses to the Global Campaign Against the Death Penalty' in Roger Hood and Surya Deva (eds), *Confronting Capital Punishment in Asia: Human Rights, Politics and Public Opinion* (Oxford, Oxford University Press, 2013) 46–67.
Michelmore, Karen, 'ASIA: Bali Nine, Corby Dealt Blow on Transfer Chances' *Australian Associated Press* (11 March 2008).
Ming, Glenn Seah Kim, 'Criminal Procedure, Evidence and Sentencing' (2003) 4 *Singapore Academy of Law Annual Review of Cases* 192.
Ministry of Foreign Affairs Vietnam, *Achievements in Protecting and Promoting Human Rights in Vietnam* (2005) (the White Book) [translation].
Ministry of Justice Vietnam, *The Legal System of Vietnam* (Saigon, 1967).
Missbach, Antje, 'The Extradition of People Smugglers from Indonesia to Australia: Political and Legal Challenges' (2014) 15 *Australian Journal of Asian Law* 2.
Musto, David, 'International Traffic in Coca through the Early 20th Century' (1998) 49 *Drug and Alcohol Dependence* 145.
——, *The American Disease: Origins of Narcotic Control*, 3rd edn (New York, Oxford University Press, 1999).
National Council against Drug Abuse, 'Annual Report 2013', www.cnb.gov.sg/Libraries/CNB_MediaLibrary_Files/NCADA_Annual_Report_2013.sflb.ashx.
Nelwan, Erni J; Crevel, Reinout van; Alisjahbana, Bachti; Indrati, Agnes K; Dwiyana, Reiva F; Nuralam, Nisaa Nuralam; Pohan, Herdiman T; Jaya, Ilham; Meheus, Andre and Ven, Andre van der, 'Human Immunodeficiency Virus, Hepatitis B and Hepatitis C in an Indonesian Prison: Prevalence, Risk Factors and Implications of HIV Screening' (2010) 15 *Tropical Medicine and International Health* 1491.

Nghia Trung, 'Criminal Justice System in Vietnam: Compassionate Communists' *The Economist* (20 June 2015).
Ngô Thanh Xuyên, 'Dẫn độ tội phạm trong hiệp định tương trợ tư pháp giữa Việt Nam với một số quốc gia trên thế giới [Extradition in bilateral treaties on legal assistance between Vietnam and several countries in the world]' (16 April 2015) Bộ Tư Pháp (Việt Nam) [(Vietnamese) Ministry of Justice].
Nguyễn Đức Mai, 'Thủ tục xét xử phúc thẩm [Appellate trial procedure]' in Vo Khanh Vinh (ed), *Bình luận khoa học Bộ luật Tố tụng Hình sự của nước Cộng Hòa Xã Hội Chủ Nghĩa Việt Nam* [Scientific commentary on the Criminal Procedure Code of the Socialist Republic of Vietnam] (Hanoi, Nhà Xuất Bản Tư Pháp [Judicial Publishing House], 2012).
Nguyễn Hiền, '18 năm tù dành cho người nước ngoài buôn ma túy [18 years of imprisonment for narcotics trading]' *Hải Quan Online—Tổng Cục Hải Quan (Việt Nam)* [*Customs Online—(Vietnamese) General Customs Department*] (Vietnam, 29 January 2013).
Nguyễn Ngọc Anh, *Bình luận khoa học Bộ luật Tố tụng Hình sự 2003* [Scientific commentary on the 2003 Criminal Procedure Code] (Ha Noi, National Politics Publishing House, 2004).
Nguyễn Ngọc Hòa, *Giáo trình Luật Hình sự Việt Nam* [*Textbook on Criminal Law*](Ha Noi, Police Publishing House, 2001).
Nguyễn Quốc Việt, *Bình luận khoa học Bộ luật Tố tụng Hình sự 2003* [Scientific commentary on the 2003 Criminal Procedure Code] (Hanoi, National Politics Publishing House, 2005).
Nguyễn Thị Hải Châu, 'Góp ý sửa đổi những quy định pháp luật tố tụng hình sự về 'trả hồ sơ điều tra bổ sung [Comments on the Provisions of Criminal Procedures in Relation to Returning Case Files for the Additional Investigation]' *Tạp Chí Pháp Lý* [*Legal Journal*] (Vietnam, 19 April 2011).
Nguyễn Thị Minh, 'Legal and Professional Challenges Confronting Practising Lawyers in Contemporary Vietnam' (Doctoral Thesis, The University of New South Wales, 2008).
Nguyễn Thị Phương Hoa, 'Drug-Related Crimes under Vietnamese Criminal Law: Sentencing and Clemency in Law and Practice' (ALC Briefing Paper, No 2, 2014).
——, 'Legislative Implementations by Vietnam of its Obligations under the United Nations Drug Control Convention' (Doctoral Thesis, University of Wollongong, 2007).
Nguyễn Trọng Nghĩa, 'Thực tiễn áp dụng Điều 117 Bộ luật Tố tụng hình sự về việc tách, nhập vụ án hình sự để tiến hành điều tra [Implementation of Article 117 of the Criminal Procedure Code joining or separating criminal case(s) to conduct investigation]', Trường Đại Học Kiểm Sát Hà Nội (Việt Nam) [(Vietnamese) Hanoi Procuracy University].
Nguyễn Văn Phú and Nguyễn Tiến Nam, 'Quy định của pháp luật Việt Nam về việc bắt người nước ngoài phạm tội [Regulations of Vietnamese Law on Arresting Foreign Offenders]', *Tạp Chí Công An Nhân Dân* [*People's Police Journal*] (Vietnam).
Nicholson, Pip, 'Access to Justice in Vietnam: State Supply—Public Distrust' in John Gillespie and Albert Chen (eds), *Legal Development in East Asia: China and Vietnam Compared* (London, Routledge, 2010).
——, *Borrowing Court Systems: The Experience of Socialist Vietnam* (Leiden, Brill Academic Publishers, 2007).
——, 'Good Governance and Institutional Accountability: The Role of the Vietnamese Courts' in Tim Lindsey and Howard Dick (eds), *Corruption in Asia: Rethinking the Good Governance Paradigm* (Sydney, Federation Press, 2002).
——, 'Renovating Courts: The Role of Courts in Contemporary Vietnam' in Jiunn-rong Yeh and Wen-Chen Chang (eds), *Asian Courts in Context* (Cambridge, Cambridge University Press, 2015).
——, 'The Death Penalty in SE Asia: Is There a Trend towards Abolition?', *The Conversation* (2015), theconversation.com/the-death-penalty-in-se-asia-is-there-a-trend-towards-abolition-37214.

Nicholson, Pip and Kieu Truong, 'The Modern Propaganda Trial: Drugs Prosecutions in Vietnam' (2008) 34 *Monash Law Review* 430.

Nicholson, Pip with Pitt, Simon, 'Official Discourses and Court-Oriented Legal Reform in Vietnam' in John Gillespie and Pip Nicholson (eds), *Law and Development and the Global Discourses of Legal Transfers* (Cambridge, Cambridge University Press, 2012).

Nigerian Eye, 'Nigerians in Vietnam Prison will be Executed Soon' (20 March 2013).

Nordt, Carlos, and Stohler, Rudolf, 'Incidence of Heroin Use in Zurich, Switzerland: A Treatment Case Register Analysis' (2006) 367 *Lancet* 1830.

Nott, Holly and Paul Osborne, 'Fed: Govt to Plead for Drug Smuggler Facing Firing Squad' *The Australian Associated Press* (10 June 2005) [Copy on file with author].

Nugraha, Panca, 'Many Indonesians on Death Row abroad for Drug Charges' *The Jakarta Post* (10 December 2013).

Ong Teck Hong and Isralowitz, Richard E, *Substance Use in Singapore: Illegal Drugs, Inhalants and Alcohol* (Singapore, Toppan, 1996).

Ong Teck Hong, *Drug Abuse in Singapore: A Psychological Perspective* (Singapore, Hillview Publications, 1989).

Othman, Zul, 'Hair Analysis Used by CNB, Schools to Fight Drug Abuse' *AsiaOne* (13 November 2013).

Ours, Jan C van, 'The Price Elasticity of Hard Drugs: The Case of Opium in the Dutch East Indies, 1923–1938' (1995) 103 *Journal of Political Economy* 261.

Pascoe, Daniel, 'Clemency in Southeast Asian Death Penalty Cases', Centre for Indonesian Law, Islam and Society Policy Paper No 4; Asian Law Centre Briefing Paper No 1 (CILIS and ALC, Melbourne Law School, the University of Melbourne, 2014).

——, 'Explaining Death Penalty Clemency in the Socialist Republic of Vietnam', (2015), [unpublished paper: copy on file with author].

——, 'Jokowi's Dilemma: Amnesty or Clemency for Political Prisoners?' *Indonesia at Melbourne* (20 July 2015).

——, 'Three Coming Legal Challenges to Indonesia's Death Penalty Regime' (2015) 2 Indonesian Journal of International & Comparative Law [forthcoming] 256.

Pereira, EA, 'Exercise of Prosecutorial Discretion in the Administration of Criminal Justice in Singapore' in UNAFEI, Resource Material Series No 22 (Tokyo, UNAFEI, 1982) 148–56.

Perkumpulan Lembaga Bantuan Hukum Masyarakat [Association of Community Legal Aid Foundations] and Open Society Foundations, 'Revealing the Practice of Violations of the Rights of the Accused during the Investigation Stage: Case Study of the Accused of Drug Offense in Jakarta', LBH Masyarakat (2012).

Phạm Hải Sâm, 'Vietnam Court Upholds Death Sentences against 29 Drug Smugglers' *Thanh Nien News* (Vietnam, 20 June 2014).

Phạm Hồng Hải, *Mô hình lý luận Bộ luật Tố tụng Hình sự Việt Nam* [Analytical framework for the Criminal Procedure Code of Vietnam] (Ha Noi, Public Security Publishing House, 2003).

Phạm Ngọc Ánh, 'Băn khoăn chuyện bảo lãnh trong án hình Sự [Concerns about bail in criminal cases]', *Pháp Luật Thành Phố Hồ Chí Minh* [*Ho Chi Minh Law Newspaper*] (Ho Chi Minh), 9 September 2011.

Pompe, Sebastiaan, *The Indonesian Supreme Court: Fifty Years of Judicial Development* (Leiden, Leiden University Press, 1996).

Pragst, Fritz and Balikova, Marie A, 'State of the Art in Hair Analysis for Detection of Drug and Alcohol Abuse' (2006) 370(1–2) *Clinica Chimica Acta* 17.

Primandari, Tika, 'Presiden Minta Disapa "Bapak Jokowi"' [The president asks to be called 'Mr Jokowi'], *Tempo* (7 February 2015).

Prodjohamidjojo, Martiman, *Komentar atas Kitab Undang-Undang Hukum Acara Pidana (KUHAP)* [Commentary on the code of criminal procedure (KUHAP)] (Jakarta, Pradnya Paramita, 1984).

Putra, Fana FS, 'Inmates Accused of Running Meth Ring from Indonesian Prisons' *The Jakarta Globe* (13 June 2014).

Quigley, John, 'Vietnam at the Legal Crossroads Adopts a Penal Code' (1988) 36 *American Journal of Comparative Law* 351.

Radio New Zealand International, 'PNG MP Plays Down Indonesia-PNG Extradition Treaty' (29 May 2015).

Rahman, Fifa and Crofts, Nick (eds), *Drug Law Reform in East and Southeast Asia* (Lanham, Lexington Books, 2013).

Rahtz, Howard, *Drugs, Crime, and Violence: From Trafficking to Treatment* (Lanham, Hamilton Books, 2012).

Rajah, KS, 'Death Penalty: The Unconstitutional Punishment', *The Straits Times* (28 August 2003).

Rappler.com, 'Hukuman Mati Dua Penyelundup Narkoba asal Iran Dibatalkan' [Death sentence of two Iranian drug traffickers cancelled] (20 April 2015).

Raustiala, Kal, 'Law, Liberalisation and International Narcotics Trafficking' (1999) 32 *New York University Journal of International Law and Politics* 89.

Ray, Rajat, 'National Drug Abuse Situation in Vietnam—How Accurate are the Projections?' 103 *Addiction* 544.

Renborg, Bertil Arne, *International Drug Control: A Study of International Administration by and through the League of Nations* (Washington DC, Carnegie Endowment for International Peace, Division of International Law, 1947).

Rikang, Raymundus, 'BNN: Laut Jadi Jalur Baru Peredaran Narkoba' [BNN: Seas new route for narcotics distribution] *Tempo.co* (23 November 2014).

Rikin, Ari Suprianti, 'Kemsos Siap Rehabilitasi Social 10,000 Korban Penyalahgunaan Narkoba' [Social Affairs Ministry prepared to rehabilitate 10,000 victims of drug abuse] *Berita Satu* (30 January 2015).

Roberts, George, 'Bali Nine: Indonesian Court Rejects Andrew Chan, Myuran Sukumaran's Last-Ditch Appeal against Execution' *ABC News* (7 April 2015).

——, 'Bali Nine: Law Expert Says Indonesian Court Has Power to Hear Execution Challenge for Andrew Chan, Myuran Sukumaran' *ABC News* (30 March 2015).

Rogers, Simon and Chalabi, Mona, 'Capital Punishment', Data Blog.

——, 'Death Penalty Statistics, Country by Country', *The Guardian* (13 December 2013).

Rondonuwu, Olivia, 'Asia: Indon Rejects Aust Draft fror Prisoner Exchange' (sic) *Australian Associated Press* (29 December 2006).

Rush, James R 'Opium in Java: A Sinister Friend' (1985) 44 *The Journal of Asian Studies* 549.

——, *Opium to Java: Revenue Farming and Chinese Enterprise in Colonial Indonesia, 1860–1910: Asia, East by South* (Ithaca, Cornell University Press, 1990).

Sabarini, Prodita, 'Coastline Vulnerable to Smuggling' *The Jakarta Post* (6 September 2006).

Salim, Rafiah and Cheong May Fong, *Evidence in Malaysia and Singapore: Cases, Materials, and Commentary*, 3rd edn (Malaysia, LexisNexis, 2013).

Samdin, Nor'ashikin, 'International Co-operation: The Extradition Framework in Singapore—A General Overview', paper delivered at the Sixth Regional Seminar on Good Governance for Southeast Asian Countries: International Co-operation Mutual Legal Assistance And Extradition, Tokyo, 12–14 December 2012 (Tokyo, UNAFEI—United Nations Asia and Far East Institute for the Prevention of Crime and the Treatment of Offenders, 2013).

Saragih, Bagus BT, 'Hadi's Pre-trial Victory a "Disaster" for KPK' *The Jakarta Post* (26 May 2015).
——, 'SBY Approves Clemency for 19 Drug Convicts' *The Jakarta Post* (17 October 2012).
SBS TV 'Condemned to Die', Dateline, television program (17 July 2011).
Scott, David W, 'Alcohol, Opium, and the Methodists in Singapore: The Inculturation of a Moral Crusade' (2012) 29 *Mission Studies* 147.
Shargel, Leon and Kanfer, Isadore (eds), *Generic Drug Product Development: International Regulatory Requirements for Bioequivalence* (New York, Informa Healthcare, 2010).
Shopia, Maharani Siti, 'LPSK: Saksi dan Pelapor Narkotika Wajib Dilindungi' [LPSK: witnesses and informants of drug crime must be protected] *Lembaga Perlindungan Saksi dan Korban*, Press Release (5 July 2012).
Shorthose, Sally (ed), *Guide to EU Pharmaceutical Regulatory Law* (The Hague, Kluwer Law International, 2013).
Sim, Walter, 'Prosecution Not Appealing against Ex-CNB Chief Ng Boon Gay's Acquittal' *The Straits Times* (11 June 2013).
Simanungkalit, Parasian, *Globalisasi Peredaran Narkoba dan Penanggulangannya di Indonesia* [The globalisation of narcotics trafficking and prevention in Indonesia], (Jakarta, Yayasan Wajar Hidup, 2011) 241.
Singapore Prison Service, 'Greater Community Involvement Contributes to Lower Re-Offending Rates: Concerted Focus on Stronger Rehabilitation for Drug Offenders', News Release (30 January 2013).
——, 'Strong Community Efforts Essential in Preventing Re-offending', News Release (23 January 2015).
——, 'Stronger Community and Family Support Help Keep Recividism Rates Low as SPS Maintains Focus on its "Through-Care" Philosophy' (1 February 2012).
Singapore, 'National Report for Singapore's Universal Periodic Review', Human Rights Council, submitted to the Working Group on the Universal Periodic Review, Eleventh session, Geneva, United Nations, 2–13 May 2011, A/HRC/WG.6/11/SGP/1.
Singapore. Attorney-General's Department, 'Annual Report 2010–2011: Appendix 11—Extradition and Mutual Assistance' (2010–11).
Singapore. Bureau of Democracy, Human Rights, and Labor, 'Singapore 2013 Human Rights Report' (27 February 2014).
Singapore. Minister for National Security and Minister for Home Affairs, 'Press Release' (9 July 2012).
Singapore. Ministry of Home Affairs, 'Criminal Law (Temporary Provisions) Act Factsheet' (23 June 2014).
Smith, Harvey et al, *Area Handbook for North Vietnam* (Washington, DC, US Government Printing House, 1967).
Soesilo, Raden, *Kitab Undang-undang Hukum Pidana Serta Komentar-komentarnya Lengkap Pasal Demi Pasal* [The Criminal Code and its complete article by article commentary] (Bogor, Politeia, 1974).
Soo, M, 'The Ups and Downs of Opium in Singapore', *Nanyang Siang Pau* (13–14 January 1977): 1.
Spencer, Bill, 'Drug Certification' (1998) 3(24) *Foreign Policy in Focus*, 1 September.
Sproule, DW and St-Denis, Paul, 'The UN Drug Trafficking Convention: An Ambitious Step' (1989) 27 *Canadian Yearbook of International Law* 263.
Spykerman, Kimberly, 'Trial Run to Prep Lawyers for Changes: From Next Year, Defence Team Will Have Access to More Information', *The Straits Times* (13 October 2010).
Stoicescu, Claudia, 'Forced Rehabilitation of Drug Users in Indonesia not a Solution' *The Conversation* (2 July 2015).

——, 'Indonesia Uses Faulty Stats on "Drug Crisis" to Justify Death Penalty' *The Conversation* (5 February 2015).
Straits Settlements Legislative Council Proceedings (SLCP) (1907) (Singapore, Government Printing Office, 1900–42).
Strang, Robert R, 'More Adversarial, But Not Completely Adversarial: Reformasi of the Indonesian Criminal Procedure Code' (2009) 32 *Fordham International Law Journal* 188.
Sudaryono, Leopold, 'Overcrowding Crisis' (2013) 113 *Inside Indonesia.*
Sugandhi, R, *Kitab Undang-Undang Hukum Pidana Berikut Penjelasannya* [The Criminal Code followed by an explanation] (Surabaya, Usaha Nasional, 1980).
Sukoyo, Yeremia, 'Rise in Criminal Case Witnesses Seeking Protection' *The Jakarta Globe* (30 December 2013).
Sundaryani, Fedina S, 'Govt wants to Rehabilitate 100,000 Drug Addicts in 2015' *The Jakarta Post* (1 February 2015).
Suparman, Fana, 'BNNP dan BNNK Diminta Aktif Ajak Pecandu untuk Direhabilitasi' [BNNP and BNNK asked to actively encourage addicts to join rehabilitation activities] *Berita Satu* (29 April 2014).
Supreme People's Procuracy, 'Kết quả một năm thực hiện thông tư liên tịch số 01 về điều tra bổ sung giữa các cơ quan tiến hành tố tụng [Results of one year implementation of inter-circular no 01 on returning case files for additional investigation among litigation authorised agencies]' (10 January 2012), Viện kiểm sát nhân dân tối cao (Việt Nam) [(Vietnamese) Supreme People's Procuracy].
——, 'Viện kiểm sát nhân dân tối cao: Kiến nghị Bộ Công an về việc quản lý người nước ngoài tại Việt Nam [The supreme people's procuracy: Suggestion to Ministry of Public Security in relation to the management of foreigners in Vietnam]' (2 August 2011), Viện kiểm sát nhân dân tối cao (Việt Nam) [(Vietnamese) Supreme People's Procuracy].
——, Criminal Statistics Bureau, Annual Statistics 2007–2013.
Sydney Morning Herald, 'Australian Faces Firing Squad Over Trafficking' (23 April 2005).
Tâm Lụa, 'Có thể dùng tiền để thoát án tử hình? [Can money be used to escape the death penalty?]' *Tuoi Tre* (Vietnam, 5 April 2015).
——, 'Vụ án oan Nguyễn Thanh Chấn: xuất hiện nhân chứng mới'[Nguyen Thanh Chan case: New witnesses appear]' *Tuoi Tre* (Vietnam, 30 June 2015).
Tejo, Amir, 'Witness Care Body Pushes Change' *The Jakarta Globe* (18 September 2013).
Teo Chee Hean, 'Enhancing Our Drug Control Framework and Review of the Death Penalty, Ministerial Statement by Mr Teo Chee Hean, Deputy Prime Minister, Co-ordinating Minister for National Security and Minister for Home Affairs', Press Release (9 July 2012).
Teo, Michael, 'Singapore's Policy Keeps Drugs at Bay' *The Guardian* (6 June 2010).
Thái Sơn, 'Jury Out as Vietnam Holds Fast to White-collar Noose: Is Vietnam Ready to Abolish the Death Penalty' *Thanh Nien News* (Vietnam, 25 March 2015).
Thanh Nien Daily, 'Australian Drug Dealer Gets Death Penalty in Vietnam' (9 June 2005).
Thanh Nien News, 'Australian Given Death Penalty in Vietnam for Drug Trafficking' (23 April 2005).
——, 'Vietnam Executes First Prisoner with Lethal Injection' (6 August 2013).
——, 'Vietnam's Death Row Inmates Enduring a Wait Worse than Death' (9 July 2013).
Thanh Tùng, 'Có nên cho tòa huyện xử án có yếu tố nước ngoài? [Should district courts be allowed to adjudicate cases involving foreign factors?]', Pháp Luật Thành Phố Hồ Chí Minh [Ho Chi Minh Law Newspaper] (online), 14 January 2011.
The British Empire Series Vol 1, (India, Ceylon, Straits Settlements, British North Borneo, Hong Kong) (London, Kegan Paul, Trench, Trubner & Co Ltd, 1899).
The Jakarta Post, 'Former Makassar Mayor Wins Pre-trial Court Decision' (12 May 2015).
——, 'House Ratifies Extradition Treaty with South Korea' (26 September 2007).

The Straits Times, 'Big Rise in Number of Addicts: Heroin the No.1 Menace' (21 April 1975).
Thu Hằng and Minh Thăng, 'Im lặng thành quyền độc lập khó chống tội phạm? [Recognising the right to silence adversely affects the fight against crimes?]' *Vietnamnet* (17 June 2015).
Tok, Lyn and Turnbull, Hugh, 'Know the Law NOW! 2015' (Singapore, Law Society of Singapore, 2015).
Tra Vinh Public Security, 'Một số điểm mới trong việc triển khai thực hiện Nghị định số 82/2013/NĐ-CP ngày 19/7/2013 của Chính phủ [Some changes in implementing Decree No 82/2013/ND-CP dated 19 July 2013 of the Government]'.
Trace, Mike, 'Drug Policy—Lessons Learnt, and Options for the Future' (2011) Global Commission on Drug Policies Working Paper.
Trần Đình Thanh Lam, 'Death Penalty: Pregnant Woman Escapes Execution in Vietnam' *IPS News* (Ho Chi Minh City, 30 October 2006).
Trần Đức Long, 'Bàn về thẩm quyền giải quyết, xét xử vụ án hình sự có bị cáo là người nước ngoài [Regarding the jurisdiction to process and adjudicate criminal cases with foreign defendants]', Tòa Án Nhân Dân Tối Cao (Việt Nam) [(Vietnamese) Supreme People's Court].
Trần Minh Hưởng, *Bình luận khoa học Bộ luật Hình sự (đã được sửa đổi, bổ sung)* [Comments on Criminal Code (amendment)] (Hong Duc Publishing House, 2011).
——, *Tìm hiểu bộ luật hình sự nước Cộng Hòa Xã Hội Chủ Nghĩa Việt Nam: Bình luận và chú giải* [Studying the criminal code of Vietnam: Comments and annotations] (Hanoi, Public Security Publishing House, 2002).
Trần Văn Luyện, *Trách nhiệm hình sự đối với các tội phạm về ma túy* [Criminal liability for drug-related crimes] (Hanoi, National Politics Publishing House, 1998).
Transparency International, 'Corruption Perceptions Index: 2014' (Berlin, Transparency International, 2014).
Trevaskes, Susan, 'China's Death Penalty, The Supreme People's Court, the Suspended Death Sentence and the Politics of Penal Reform' (2013) 53 *British Journal of Criminology* 482.
——, 'China's Death penalty: The Supreme People's Court, the Suspended Death Sentence and the Politics of Penal Reform' (2013) 53 *British Journal of Criminology* 482.
——, 'Lenient Death Sentencing and the "Cash for Clemency" Debate' (2015) 73 *The China Journal* 38.
——, 'Suspending Death in Chinese Capital Cases: The Road to Reform' in Roger Hood and Surya Deva (eds), *Confronting Capital Punishment in Asia: Human Rights, Politics and Public Opinion* (Oxford, Oxford University Press, 2013) 221–37.
——, 'Suspending Death in Chinese Capital Cases: The Road to Reform' in Roger Hood and Surya Deva (eds), *Confronting Capital Punishment in Asia: Human Rights, Politics and Public Opinion* (Oxford, Oxford University Press, 2013).
Trocki, Carl A, 'The Rise of Singapore's Great Opium Syndicate, 1840–86' (1987) 18(1) *Journal of Southeast Asian Studies* 58.
Tsan Hang Tey, 'Death Penalty Singapore-Style: Clinical and Carefree' (2010) 39 Common Law World Review 315.
Tuoi Tre News, 'Dead Men Walking: Back from the Brink' (4 April 2011).
——, 'Dead Men Walking: Daybreak on Death Row' (25 March 2011).
——, 'In Dead Men Walking: Judgment Day' [no date].
——, 'Locally Made Poison to be Used for Execution' (15 May 2014).
——, 'The End of Firing Squads in Vietnam' [no date].
UK (United Kingdom) Home Office, 'Extradition Requests Received and Made by the UK from January to December 2013' (24 October 2014).
UN (United Nations) Commentary on the United Nations Convention against Illicit Traffic in Narcotic Drugs and Psychotropic Substances Done at Vienna, 20 December 1988, UN Doc E/CN.7/590 (New York, United Nations, 1998).

UN, International Narcotics Control Board, 'Training Material: 1961 Single Convention on Narcotic Drugs: Part I: The International Control System for Narcotic Drugs' (2005).
UNDP (United Nations Development Programme), 'Appointed Counsel in Vietnamese Criminal Law and Practice' (Hanoi, UNDP 2013).
——, 'Right to Counsel in Criminal Law and Practice Vietnam' (Hanoi, UNDP 2012).
——, *Report on the Survey of Needs of District People's Courts Nationwide* (Hanoi, Justice Publishing House, 2007).
——, *Report on the Survey of the Reality of Local Court Governance in Vietnam* (2014).
United Nations, General Assembly, Human Rights Council, 'Report of the Special Rapporteur on torture and other cruel, inhuman or degrading treatment or punishment, Manfred Nowak, Addendum: Mission to Indonesia' A/HRC/7/3/Add.7 (10 March 2008).
United States Attorney's Office, 'Two Extradited from Singapore in Connection with Plot to Illegally Export Military Antennas' (21 December 2012).
United States Department of State, Bureau for International Narcotics and Law Enforcement Affairs, 'International Narcotics Control Strategy Report: Volume I Drug and Chemical Control', US Department of State (March 2010).
——, 'International Narcotics Control Strategy Report: Volume I Drug and Chemical Control', US Department of State (March 2013).
——, 'International Narcotics Control Strategy Report: Volume I Drug and Chemical Control', US Department of State (March 2014).
——, 'International Narcotics Control Strategy Report: Volume II Money Laundering and Financial Crimes', US Department of State (March 2014).
——, 'Money Laundering and Financial Crimes: Country Database' (June 2014).
UNODC (United Nations Office on Drugs and Crime), 'Indonesia: Situation Assessment on Amphetamine-Type Stimulants' (UNODC, February 2013).
——, 'Mekong Region Officials Vow to Counter Drug Threat', 21 May 2015.
——, 'Patterns and Trends of Amphetamine-Type Stimulants and Other Drugs, Asia and the Pacific: Report from the Global SMART Programme' (November 2013).
——, 'The Challenge of New Psychoactive Substances: A Report from the Global SMART Programme' (March 2013).
——, 'The Opium Problem in Singapore' (1958) 4 *Bulletin on Narcotics* 7.
——, 'World Drug Report 2012' (June 2012).
——, 'World Drug Report 2013' (May 2013).
——, 'World Drug Report 2014' (June 2014).
——, Regional Centre for East Asia and the Pacific (2013) 'A Decade of Co-operative Partnership and Progress in the Greater Mekong Subregion through The Memorandum of Understanding (MoU) on Drug Control', http://en.oncb.go.th/document/MOU-2003.pdf.
UNODC, 'A Century of International Drug Control' in UNODC, *World Drug Report 2008* (Vienna, United Nations, 2008), 83.
——, 'Patterns and Trends of Amphetamine-Type Stimulants and Other Drugs: Asia and the Pacific 2012' (November 2013).
——, 'Patterns and Trends of Amphetamine-Type Stimulants and Other Drugs 2013—Challenges for Asia and the Pacific'.
——, 'The Plenipotentiary Conference for the Adoption of a Single Convention on Narcotic Drugs', *Bulletin on Narcotics* (1962) Issue 1, www.unodc.org/unodc/en/data-and-analysis/bulletin/bulletin_1962-01-01_1_page007.html.
——, *World Drug Report 2008* (Vienna, United Nations, 2008).
——, *World Drug Report 2011* (Vienna, United Nations, 2011).
——, *World Drug Report 2014* (Vienna, United Nations, June 2014).
US, *See under* United States.

US Department of State, '2010 Country Reports on Human Rights Practices—Singapore' (8 April 2011).
——, '2013 INCSR: Country Reports –ß Moldova through Singapore' (5 March 2013).
Việt Báo (*Công An TP.HCM* [Ho Chi Minh City Police]) 'Vận chuyển 3 bánh heroin ra nước ngoài, một Việt kiều lĩnh án tử hình [Trafficking in three packages of heroin to overseas, one Vietnamese expatriate receives death penalty]' (26 April 2005).
——, 'Phạt tử hình, tù chung thân những Việt kiều buôn lậu ma túy [Imposing death penalty, life sentence to Vietnamese expatriates trafficking drugs]' (24 March 2005).
Việt Báo (Sài Gòn Giải Phóng [Liberated Saigon]), 'Bắt quả tang 2 Việt kiều vận chuyển 1/2kg heroin [Caught two Vietnamese expatriates carrying 1/2kg heroin]' (7 July 2006).
Viet Nam News, 'Drug Crime Fuelled by Foreigners, Expats' (5 January 2008).
Vietnam. Judicial Training School, 2011 Professional Discussion.
Vietnam. Ministry of Foreign Affairs, 'President of the SRV Tran Duc Luong has Decided to Commute Tran Van Thanh's Death Sentence to Life Imprisonment', Spokesman's Statement (23 August 2005).
Vietnam. Supreme People's Court (SPC), Annual Report of 1999.
——, Annual Report of 2000.
——, Annual Report of 2001.
——, Annual Report of 2006.
——, Annual Report of 2007
——, Annual Report of 2011.
——, Annual Report of 2012.
——, Annual Report of 2013.
——, Annual Report of 2014.
Võ Văn Ái, 'Human Rights and Asian Values in Vietnam' in Jacobsen, Michael and Bruun, Ole (eds) *Human Rights and Asian Values Contesting National Identities and Cultural Representations in Asia*, (London & New York, Routledge Curzon, 2000).
Vũ Mai, 'Những nữ Việt kiều xách thuê heroin lấy tiền đi casino [Vietnamese female expatriates traffic in heroin for gambling]' *Việt Báo (VnExpress.net)* (Vietnam, 25 October 2009).
Vũ Thanh Tùng, 'Vấn đề giám định hàm lượng ma túy và những bất cập cần giải quyết [The evaluation of drug concentration and problems that need to be solved]', Viện Kiểm sát Bắc Giang (Việt Nam) [(Vietnamese) Bac Giang Procuracy].
Vũ Trọng Khánh and Nguyễn Anh Thư, 'Vietnam May Return to Firing Squads amid Shortage of Lethal Chemicals' *The Wall Street Journal* (25 July 2013).
Wagner, Benjamin B. and Jacobs, Leslie Gielow, 'Retooling Law Enforcement to Investigate and Prosecute Entrenched Corruption: Key Criminal Procedure Reforms for Indonesia and Other Nations' (2008) 30 *University of Pennsylvania Journal of International Law* 183.
Wenning, R, 'Potential Problems with the Interpretation of Hair Analysis Results' (2000) 107 *Forensic Science International* 5.
Widhiarto, Hasyim, 'Singapore Refuses to Renegotiate Extradition Treaty with Indonesia' *The Jakarta Post* (29 September 2011).
Wijaya, Indra, 'LPSK Keluhkan Minimnya Anggaran 2014' [LPSK complains about its small 2014 budget] *Tempo.co* (27 December 2013).
Wodak, Alex, 'Demand Reduction and Harm Reduction' (2011) Global Commission on Drug Policies Working Paper prepared for the First Meeting of the Commission, Geneva, 24–25 January 2011.
World Bank, 'Population Total' (World Bank Data [website]).
——, 'World Development Indicators: Singapore' (no date, accessed 8 January 2015).
Wren, Christopher S, 'China Says Vietnam Grows Opium to Earn Funds' *The New York Times*, 26 July 1983.

Xi, Remy Choo Zheng, '2015 Bail Review: Striking the Right Balance' *The Straits Times* (13 January 2015).
Xuân Hoàng, 'Nữ Việt kiều giấu ma túy trong chỗ kín [Overseas Vietnamese secretly hidden drugs]' *Việt Báo (Ngoi Sao)* (Vietnam, 29 October 2009).
Yarock, Saad, 'Drug Trafficking: Ejiogulkechukwu to Die by Lethal Injection', *Youtube* (28 October 2015).
Yeo, Stanley, *Criminal Defences in Mayalsia and Singapore* (Singapore, LexisNexis, 2005).
Yock Lin Tan and Mohan, S Chandra, *Criminal Procedure in Singapore and Malaysia* (Singapore, LexisNexis, 2012).
Zhang, Diane, 'By the Numbers: Indonesia's Executions of Foreigners' *The Drum, ABC* (27 February 2015).

Interviews: Vietnam

Interviewee 3 (23 and 29 May 2012).
Interviewee 4 (25 May 2012).
Interviewee 5 (26 May 2012).
Interviewee 6 (27 May 2012).
Interviewee 7 (5 June 2012).
Interviewee 8 (4 June 2012).
Interviewee 9 (5 June 2012).
Interviewee 10 (25 May 2012).
Interviewee 11 (10 August 2012)
Interviewee 12 (13 August 2012).
Interviewee 13 (14 August 2012).
Interviewee 15 (16 August 2012).
Interviewee 17 (17 August 2012).
Interviewee 18 (20 August 2012).
Interviewee 19 (27 August 2012).
Interviewee 21 (8 April 2011).

Glossary

(I) = Indonesian term (V) = Vietnamese term

foreign word(s)	English definition
abolisi	abolition (I)
adat	traditional customary law (I)
amnesti	amnesty (I)
badan hukum	legal entity (I)
banding	appeal a legal decision (I)
bantuan hukum	legal aid (I)
báo Tuổi Trẻ	Youth newspaper (V)
belum memenuhi rasa keadilan	does not fulfil the sense of justice (I)
berkas-berkas pembinaan	rehabilitation records (I)
bị can	accused (V)
bị cáo	defendant (V)
cải tạo không giam giữ	non-custodial (V)
chất ma túy	narcotic substance (V)
chứng cứ duy nhất để kết tội	sole evidence for conviction (V)
cố ý	intention (V)
đặc xá	amnesty (V)
daluwarsa	limitation/expiration (I)
đầu thú	self-surrender (V)
đẽo gọt	whittle (V)
desa	village (I)
Direktorat Jenderal Pemasyarakatan	Directorate General of Corrections (I)
ditutup demi hukum	closed by law (I)
đổi mới	renovation (V)
đồng thuận	consensus (V)
gây rối	disturbance (V)
giải thích theo chiều hướng có lợi	interpreted to benefit the accused (V)
giám đốc thẩm	cassational review (V)
gián tiếp	indirect (V)
gói	pack (V)
grasi	clemency (I)

foreign word(s)	English definition
habeas corpus	A (common law) legal action to challenge unlawful imprisonment (Latin)
hàm lượng	proportion (V)
hành vi khách quan	ways of being (V)
hình phạt bổ sung	supplementary / additional penalties (V)
hình phạt chính	principal penalties (V)
hình phạt chung	common penalty (V)
hình phạt tử hình	death penalty law or practice (V)
hồ sơ	dossier (V)
họp liên ngành	joint meeting (V)
hukum positif	positive law (I)
ibu rumah tangga	housewife (I)
Idul Fitri	Eid al-Fitr (I)
Jaksa	Prosecutor (I)
Jaksa Agung	Prosecutor General, the Attorney General (I)
kabupaten	district, sometimes called regency (I)
kabur	unclear (I)
kasasi	cassation appeal (I)
kasus cadangan	reserve cases (I)
kejahatan	felony, or crime (I)
kejahatan terorganisir	organised crime (I)
Kejaksaan Agung	Attorney General's Office (I)
kekuatan hukum tetap	binding legal force (I)
Keputusan Presiden	Presidential Decision (I)
kết luận giám định	expert conclusion (V)
ketua	chair, head judge (I)
kota	city/municipality (I)
kurungan	a light form of imprisonment (I)
lebih subsidair	further secondary charge (I)
lệnh bắt giữ	arrest warrant (V)
limatif	limited (I)
lurah	head of a village or neighbourhood (I)
ma túy	narcotics (V)
mafia peradilan	judicial mafia (I)
Mahkamah Agung	Supreme Court (I)
Mahkamah Konstitusi	Constitutional Court (I)

foreign word(s)	English definition
membawa	to carry (I)
memperhatikan pertimbangan	to consider the views of (I)
menguasai	to possess or control (I)
menimbulkan keresahan dalam masyarakat	to cause unrest in the community (I)
menyerahkan	to hand over (I)
menyimpan	to store (I)
narkotika	narcotic (I)
nebis in idem	double jeopardy (latin)
người đang bị truy nã	wanted person (V)
người tham gia tố tụng	person participating in criminal proceedings (for example, defence counsel) (V)
người tiến hành tố tụng	person conducting criminal proceedings (for example, procurators) (V)
niềm tin nội tâm	inner faith (V)
nota kesepahaman	memorandum of understanding (I)
novum	new situation (I)
opium verpakkings bepalingen	opium packaging provisions (Dutch)
Opium-Regie	state monopoly on the import, preparation and distribution of opium in the Dutch East Indies (Dutch)
papaver somniferum	the opium poppy (Latin)
pelaku	perpetrator (I)
pelaku tindak pidana	perpetrator of a crime (I)
pelanggaran	misdemeanour (I)
pembantu pelaku	accessory to a crime (I)
pembinaan	rehabilitation, support (I)
pemeriksaan	trial (I)
pemufakatan jahat	criminal conspiracy (I)
pencucian uang	money laundering (I)
Pengadilan Agama	Religious Court (I)
Pengadilan Militer	Military Court (I)
Pengadilan Negeri or pengadilan umum	State Courts or general courts, the courts of first instance for civil and criminal cases, also 'district courts' (I)
Pengadilan Tata Usaha Negara	Administrative Court (I)
Pengadilan Tinggi	High Court (I)
peninjauan kembali	reconsideration (I)

foreign word(s)	English definition
penjara	prison, prison time (I)
penjelasan	elucidation or explanatory memorandum that routinely accompanies Indonesian statutes and regulations and is read with it (I)
penuntutan	prosecution or indictment (I)
penyalah guna	abuser (I)
penyelidikan	preliminary investigation (I)
penyidikan	primary investigation (I)
peraturan	regulation (I)
Peraturan Menteri	Ministerial Regulation (I)
Peraturan Presiden	Presidential Regulation (I)
perubahan hukuman	sentence amendment (I)
perundang-undangan	legislation (I)
petunjuk	inference (I)
pháp chế	Rule of Law or legality (V)
pidana biasa	regular criminal case (I)
pidana cepat	expedited cases (I)
pidana mati	death penalty (I)
pra-peradilan	pre-trial (I)
prekursor narkotika	narcotics precursors (I)
preman	gangster, thug (I)
primair	primary charge (I)
puskesmas, pusat kesehatan masyarakat	community health centre (I)
putusan	judgment (I)
quyền im lặng	right to silence (V)
quyết định truy nã	wanted decision (in the case of a wanted person) (V)
Reformasi	Reformation or Reform, a term is used to refer to the period of reform following the end of Soeharto's New Order in 1998 (I)
rehabilitasi	rehabilitation (I)
shabu/sabu	crystalline methamphetamine (I)
skenario	scenario (I)
stare decisis	the (common law) legal principle of precedent (latin)
subsidair	subsidiary charge (I)

foreign word(s)	English definition
surat	document (I)
surat edaran	circular (I)
surat perintah penahanan	a detention order (I)
suy đoán vô tội	presumed not guilty (V)
tái thẩm	re-opening procedure (V)
tersangka	suspect (I)
thà bắt nhầm hơn bỏ sót	wrongfully accusing a person is better than missing a criminal (V)
tha tù trước thời hạn có điều kiện	conditional early release of prisoners (V)
tjandoe (candu)	a form of opium containing about 11–13 per cent morphine (I)
Tòa án Cấp cao	Superior or High Court (V)
tội nặng hơn	heavier crime (V)
tội phạm có cấu thành hình thức	formal crimes (V)
tội phạm có cấu thành vật chất	material crimes (V)
tổng hợp	to be augmented (V)
trực tiếp	direct (V)
trục xuất	expulsion (V)
tự thú	confession (V)
tutupan	a form of imprisonment similar to house arrest, generally available for 'respected' prisoners (I)
tuyên truyền	propaganda (V)
undang-undang	Law (statute of the Indonesian national legislature, the DPR)(I)
uy thác	entrust (V)
văn bản xác minh	verification form (V)
verdovende middelen	drugs (Dutch)
yurisprudensi	jurisprudence, decisions of the Indonesian Supreme Court (I)
yurisprudensi tetap	fixed jurisprudence, leading decisions identified as such by the Indonesian Supreme Court (I)

Index